Jane Austen

Jane Austen

HER LIFE

Park Honan

Weidenfeld and Nicolson · London

To Joan and Lawrence Impey
and to
Diana and David Hopkinson

First published in Great Britain by
George Weidenfeld & Nicolson Limited
91 Clapham High Street
London sw4 7TA

ISBN 0 297 79217 2

Printed in Great Britain at The Bath Press, Avon

Contents

CONTENTS

Preface

Jane Austen is the subject of so much attention, each year, that one must be very clear about one's aims in offering a new biography of this length.

The last study based on most of the Austen family manuscripts is the *Life and Letters*, published by W. and R. A. Austen-Leigh in 1913. No biography has taken account of a wealth of Austen family manuscripts that has turned up since; also, new data from research emerges year by year, and not since Elizabeth Jenkins's attractive study in 1938 has anyone seriously tried to assimilate it.

My aim is to show Jane Austen's life as intimately and completely as our new data and the rich, existing manuscript material will allow.

She was so well informed that a narrow focus here would almost be bound to misrepresent her. To the extent that husbands, wives or lovers may be, she was not dominated by or absorbed in the life of any one individual; yet she learned from those near her. The Austens and a few others were so important to her – feeding her imagination, expanding her awareness – that they are intrinsic to her portrait. Hence I have tried to expand the usual viewpoint of the biographer, not mainly for the sake of 'background', but to give an accurate sense of evidence about Jane Austen's mind, outlook and growth as a person and artist.

A familiarity with new and unpublished sources will have helped, I hope, to afford a more thorough examination of her own life and character.

PARK HONAN

Acknowledgements

Jane Austen can have no 'official biographer', and at no time while writing this book did I have that status. But a large amount of manuscript material was made available to me over six years, including Eliza de Feuillide's holographs, Fanny Lefroy's MS 'Family History', transcripts of older Leigh and Austen material, holograph letters by Jane Austen's mother, Austen poems, and other holographs by Jane Austen's brothers James, Edward, Henry, Frank and Charles, along with letters, journals and notes by their descendants. I thank the owners for letting me use the Austen-Leigh collections, with a range of material not fully available to any other biographer since 1913, as well as R. A. Austen-Leigh's 'Annotated Copy' of the *Life*. Gordon Ray let me use his holograph letters by James Austen, Henry Austen and Frances (Palmer) Austen, and letters to and from Charles Austen, including one of the rare letters by Jane Austen's Kentish niece Lizzy in her later life. J. A. P. Lefroy let me use unpublished writings by Anne Lefroy of Ashe (Jane Austen's older friend), as well as material about Mrs Lefroy, and writings by Caroline Austen, Benjamin and Anna Lefroy. I am grateful for access to journals and letters by James Edward Austen(-Leigh). I very warmly thank Joan Austen-Leigh, Helen Lefroy and Henry Rice for their assistance. I thank George Sawtell for Mary Lloyd's affidavit about Cassandra; and, on Admiral Sir Francis Austen's side of the family, I thank the authors for letting me use 'Niece of Miss Austen' and for supplying me with J. H. Hubback's MS notebooks and other items.

I have used some material by Jane Austen that is not in her published letters or works. David Gilson sent me unpublished writing in her autograph, clippings and notes from sale catalogues, and aided my research in other ways. G.P.Hoole sent research notes from Kent. For permission to see (and in some cases to quote from) MS material, I thank Herbert Cahoon and the Pierpont Morgan Library, Betty Kondayan and Goucher College, New York Public Library, India Office at Southwark, National Maritime Museum, the Jane Austen Memorial Trust and Winchester College, besides private owners of holographs and transcripts. Crown Copyright material in the India Office Records is reproduced by permission of the Comptroller of Her Majesty's Stationery Office.

I thank Mary Lascelles for many points of detail, as well as Margaret Weedon, and I am grateful to Diana and David Hopkinson, Deirdre Le Faye and David Lodge for comment on my chapters and other help. Among those in the Jane Austen Society, I thank Sir Hugh Smiley, Joan Impey, Joyce Bown, Violet Hunt, J.Butler-Kearney, Elizabeth Jenkins, B.C.Southam, Philip Vickers, Cicely Beebee, Marilyn Butler and Jean K.Bowden, Curator at Jane Austen's House; I am most grateful to the Jane Austen Memorial Trust for illustrations as well as for access to MSS. I thank staff at the Grolier Club, R.C.Yorke and the Royal College of Arms, Philippa Stevens and the Local Studies Collection, Winchester Library, and Peter D.Partner (Fellows' Librarian) and the Warden and Fellows of Winchester College. I also thank librarians and archivists at: Bath Library, Birmingham University, Bodleian Library, Brasenose College, the British Library, Brotherton Library at Leeds University, Newberry Library, Portsmouth Library, Reading Library, St John's at Oxford, and Southampton Library. For their advice on special matters. I thank Dr P.N.Cowen, E.Duncan-Jones, Dr David London, H.A.D.Miles, Keith Norcross, Barry Pointon and A. G. C. Trollope, Hon. Sec. at Chawton .

For other help I most cordially thank: Ruth apRoberts, Robert Baldock, Julia Birley, J.T.Boulton, Edward and Lillian Bloom, Joan Corder, Joanna Dales, Evelyn Fowle, P.D.Garside, Maria Golescu, Ann Goring, J.Donald Grey, Catherine Hall, Richard Hovey, the Revd William Jarvis, Elaine Jordan, Philip Kelley, Fr Ian Ker, Walton Litz, Phyllis McArdle, Lady Mander, Sally Mapstone, Kim Moreland, Valerie Grosvenor Myer, Constance-Anne Parker, Barbara Rasmussen, Isobel Sanderson, Evelyn Semler, David Spring, G.H.Tucker and Peter Whitlock. I thank Mme Rachel Colin, Mary Blakey, Nicholas and Corinna Inge, Frances Kundert, Natasha and Matthew Honan, and, above all, my wife Jeannette; and I am grateful to Paul Turner as often before, Moira and Gerald Habberjam for advice on genealogy, and Anne Tindall for her typing. Juliet Gardiner, Peter James and Linden Lawson are especially thanked for their comments, and Kathleen Tillotson and the Rt Revd John Moorman and Mary Moorman for other specific help and interest. For grants in aid I thank Leeds and Birmingham Universities and the British Academy.

As I meant to write a fresh, reliable biography I have asked for much help and received it. The errors in this book are mine alone, but on the other hand anything useful in it may well owe to someone else's work. A biography must integrate and I apologize to anyone who feels that a critical debt has been deplorably overlooked: in no case did I mean to steal quietly, and as my intentions were good, I shall hope to be forgiven.

Illustrations

Acknowledgement for the use of illustrations is kindly made to: the Jane Austen Memorial Trust, and J. Butler-Kearney (photos), for numbers 1 through 9, 11–14, 16–18, 21–28 and 31, with thanks to Commander D. P. Willan for permission to use 13 and 14; Constance Hill's *Jane Austen: her homes & her friends* of 1902 and John Lane for 10, 19 and 24; Miss Helen Brown for 15; the British Museum for 20; Mr A. F. H. Austen for 29; the National Portrait Gallery, London, for 30; Linden Lawson for 32 and Steve Mitchell for 33.

Prelude: Frank Austen's ride

His dearest friend, at that improving age,
Was Hounslow Dick, who drove the western stage.
George Crabbe

1

THE ROYAL ACADEMY, PORTSMOUTH, 1787

Frank Austen, only twenty months older than his sister Jane, left a detailed record of his naval training. Frank composed this long before he rose to be Admiral of the Fleet and the significance to us of his alertness at naval school is that he informed Jane Austen of much of what he saw and heard. Their father the Revd George Austen advised him to be 'very minute in what relates to yourself,'[1] and Frank's 'Plan of Mathematical Training' and other sources help us to reconstruct a picture of England outside Steventon in Jane Austen's childhood.

Let us begin at Portsmouth and follow Frank on a ride home.

Frank and other young scholars in training to be midshipmen at the Navy's Royal Academy would row out to an anchored ship, or hulk, in a bottle-shaped harbour at Portsmouth once a week.

Beyond the eelgrass and the black, gold, orange, yellow and silver beakheads of the first- and second-rate warships, the boys would put up their oars. Then after climbing on battens and holding black, greasy ropes at the hulk's side, Frank would come to bright-red bulkheads. Red paint concealed blood. He learned in Gunnery that a ball might send jagged splinters into nineteen boys and men on one deck; badly wounded were thrown overboard and others would go to the Bloody Sail, where a boy could bite into a leather gag as his leg was cut off.

In mornings at sea, deck gratings were hooked upright. You faced the grating with tied wrists as bosun's mates flogged your back into livery pulp. Twenty lashes for minor naval infringements were common: fifty exposed your bones. When three sailors were sentenced to 400, 500 and 600 lashes in this harbour, mates flogged at upright corpses.

Frank had been twelve when an Admiralty letter arrived, citing his full name Francis William Austen, to say he would be trained at Portsmouth. He had left his sisters Cassandra and Jane, then thirteen and ten, and arrived at a rose-coloured building where he studied John Robertson's *Elements of Navigation* as well as French and dancing and the military arts. He made few friends and found aristocrats dangerous: the school was plagued by the wealthy: young Baber and Colepeper had made Mr Dashwood so 'dead drunk' that a surgeon was called. 'Mr. Dashwood', the Admiralty Lords read in horror in London, 'had like to have been destroyed at Sun Tavern', and two admirals later called the school 'a sink of vice and abomination' and a 'nursery of vice and immorality.'[2]

Avoiding the wealthy, Frank kept a very neat 'Plan' of his training with notes, charts and lists of enemy locales or 'Countries' of the recent war:

Louisinia
Maryland
Pensilvania
Jerseys
New England[3]

Though small for his age with brown curly hair and a dimpled chin, he strove for what he called 'regularity' in conduct and later told his family about the proper theoretical training of midshipmen. 'He

2

has a lively and active disposition,' one of his teachers wrote. 'I have never had a complaint [of] F.W.Austen.'[4]

Once a week, he might look across from his ship to coastal Hampshire and see a chalk-flecked hill, the Haslar Hospital which his brother James would visit and the flats stretching down to Sword and Sinah Sands. The masts of laid-up ships showed that the Navy was pressed for funds – and the harbour sight angered naval men. Officers were bitter, too, over the recent war of 1775 to 1783 (coinciding with Jane Austen's first eight years) when American privateers had fired ships at Whitehaven and French frigates had succeeded in sinking formations since they were sleek, fast, better built than the English, and attacked on the leeside. For months the English did not defend their coasts. The Naval Board's lack of energy, privileged officials with 'minds too delicate' for war or lacking the 'stimulus of ambition',[5] had shamed the Navy. A rotting fleet relying on criminals for half its crews might not survive another war. Frank's teachers hardly predicted the full extent of a long war ahead, but a feeble Navy worried them. Young and eager, he would carry home grave reports, and impress his sisters with the need for 'early hardship and discipline' as he himself had a 'consciousness of being born to struggle and endure'.[6] At sea his life would be at risk. Midshipmen were hated by the sailors for reporting on them to the Lieutenant and could be knifed in hammocks – but Frank would have to cheer up those sailors to a lively performance in reefing and furling. His gentle father hardly prepared him for brutality, or even for slavery though the Navy protected the slave-trade. 'Slavery', wrote Frank at last, taking a strong stand on that topic, 'however it is modified is still slavery.' Three years before his sister wrote of Sir Thomas Bertram's Antigua holdings in *Mansfield Park*, Frank denounced that 'harshness and despotism' which is 'justly attributed to the conduct of land-holders or their managers in the West India Islands'.[7]

Gentle as he was, he would live in stench. Men and officers urinated and defecated on deck. He would eat maggoty biscuits tasting like cool calves'-foot jelly and have something to say about stoical endurance. He might even drink a fiery white wine called *mistella* but known to the sailors as Miss Taylor, a name his sister was to use in *Emma*. Some officers felt Miss Taylor only spoiled you.

After reefing exercises the Royal Academy scholars rowed to port, past the anchored ships that had served in the last war. By repute

3

Frank knew of heroes of that war, such as Lord Dorchester, whose dances Cassandra and Jane would attend, or of Lord Moira, who led the British left division at Camden, New Jersey against Washington. But these heroes had not been steadily confined to cramped naval decks. 'I saw blood suddenly fly,' one young sailor wrote of an action such as Frank might soon witness. One boy's 'powder caught fire and burnt the flesh almost off his face. In this pitiable situation, the agonised boy lifted both hands as if imploring relief. ... A man named Aldrich had one of his hands cut off by a shot, and almost at the same moment he received another shot, which tore open his bowels in a terrible manner. As he fell, two men caught up Aldrich and heaved him into the sea.'[8] Sights such as these would make Frank a realist, and his grasp of reality appealed to Jane Austen. At thirteen he longed to be at sea but he was glad enough to have three weeks' leave[9] from the Navy to see his family in pretty Hampshire again.

2

The sea's influence reached up a navigable river to Bucklers Hard where Nelson's many-gunned *Agamemnon* was built and far into Hampshire, one of the most venerable counties in England with boundaries hardly changed since the seventh century; its episcopal seat was Winchester even in 676, and burial grounds for warriors on Portsdown Hill were of a dateless age. In the Austens' time a new age of iron and sail had touched the coast – where the stench of mudflats mingled with that of sailors' taverns. Three hundred prostitutes from inland towns and villages had drowned lately on a naval ship and all along the coast smugglers, sometimes in gangs of 300 and 400, defied revenue officers to bring tea and brandy to the gentry after sailing over from Bordeaux, which Frank called 'a place of great resort for our smuggling vessels'.[10] Crops and pigs for the Navy were raised as far inland as Basingstoke, and three of the county's twenty-six MPs were naval men, representing boroughs.

In the stiff white breeches and tricorn of the Royal Academy, Frank would pass houses which his sister would later describe in *Mansfield Park*. In Portsmouth's High Street there was often a jumble of waggons, sailors, vendors, women. Here were child beggars and pits in which live animals were torn apart. Rows of cook-shops, tailors, drapers, pawnbrokers and trinket-merchants stretched beyond Morgan's sign, 'SAILORS RIGGED COMPLETE FROM STEM TO STERN'; midshipmen waited at Blue Posts to get to Gracechurch Street but for the Winchester route you waited at the Vine for Mr Chartres's advertised post-coach, which could crack your teeth.

An agile boy enjoyed a post-coach. But ladies objected. Since baskets which carried luggage were unsprung a coach might rub to pieces one's neatly packed clothes. Unpaved roads with potholes gave one a thousand miserable jolts every mile, and one stopped at inns where men drank to excess. A banging airless coach often reeked of alcohol. If one escaped the fumes to be an 'outsider', one clung to a handle at the risk of being tossed off.

From on top, a boy might see a naval arsenal at rest. Smells of excrement from streets would be fainter. A loud horn would sound before teamed horses rattled over a drawbridge on the run to Portsdown Hill. Trade and the Navy led to the improvement of main thoroughfares. A Mail Coach system (begun in 1784) and new Turnpike Trusts kept up the chief routes so that in Jane Austen's time the county had healthy arteries bringing goods, gossip and news near Gilbert White's Selborne and the Austens' Steventon – to nourish some of the liveliest and best prose being written in England. (Transport in Hampshire improved more quickly in wartime than anywhere else in the kingdom.)

Trains of waggons moved inland and waterways too were full. At Wickham, Frank was not far from an arrogant James D'Arcy whose name became a scandal when he limited the number of Itchen River barges in the 1790s. From Wickham the coach went on to Winchester, in whose cathedral lay the ashes of Queen Emma, the mother of Edward the Confessor, who had two kings as husbands and two as sons. Emma at last had married King Canute, who fostered trade, but the county's trading wealth was poor in 1787. One might see few 'manufactories' other than kilns of brick-and-tile works that made rosy bricks for barns and estates, and waterwheels of paper mills turning old Navy sails into white paper. The Austens knew the Portals, whose mill had the contract for Bank of England paper.

If some people made sails into bank-notes, Hampshire cottagers in the downlands turned out coarse woollens, and inland market-towns such as Basingstoke and Alton hardly grew in size – whereas even villages in the English North and Midlands were thickening. Manchester mills were turning to steam power in 1787 and Leeds produced everything from books and furniture to wallpaper and the best wigs. Hardware and guns rolled from blackening Birmingham, outside of which for '5 or 6 miles' one might see 'one continued village of nailers'.[11] Leicester worsteds, Nottingham hosiery and Preston yarns came to London with streams of heavier goods from glassworks and foundries and kilns lining the Tyne, from copper and iron works at Cyfarthfa and Amlwch in Wales. Newcastle built more ships in a year than *all* Hampshire – and its coal trade choked even the Thames.

Sucking in the world's wealth London now virtually controlled the trade of Europe, India and China. Frank, as the son of Tory patriots, admired a success that his Navy made possible, and he certainly knew that the ports of Bristol, Hull, Liverpool and London were the age's glory. They drew in the world. They received icy ships from Greenland and Archangel fisheries, East Indiamen with silks and muslins and calicoes, West Indiamen with sugar and coffee and cocoa, Yankee clippers with millions of pounds of raw cotton for the northern mills, Hudson's Bay clippers with fur and skins, wine ships from the Peninsula, topsail schooners from Smyrna and the small ports of Greece. The nation was in a period of unrivalled and progressive expansion of trade with merchant shipping three times greater in tonnage than that of the French. It could absorb enormous losses. When an outward-bound convoy was taken by the enemy in August 1780 marine insurers at Lloyd's Coffee-House at the Royal Exchange had paid out $1\frac{1}{2}$ million pounds in insurance claims with unimpaired credit and prestige. The China and India trade especially had changed English life so that, now, delicate bright colours of rose pink, yellow and turquoise blue in ladies' dresses reflected Eastern fashions. Chinese parasols and furniture made of Indian reed and bamboo were known to Frank's family.

The expanding overseas trade nourished optimism and confidence, and Frank's brothers and sisters typified the nation's cheer and zest. Even the financial worries of their parents stimulated the young Austens – and they were not unlucky to live in a rural village. The dead weight of life in cities was now offset by cultural vigour in some rural centres, and a delicate balance in the attractions of cities and

6

rural towns coincided with immense new vigour in British art and thought.

Holding his hat and peering at Hampshire's chalky downs, an excited homecoming boy would see little to dismay him in the spring – when fields were shining bronze and white-flecked. Swallows, swifts and martins returned at this lovely season. Elms and beeches along the turnpike clung to banked hillside as 'hangers': there would be a line of northerly hangers not far from Basingstoke and Tylney Hall, of Sir James Tylney Long, Bart., for Frank and his sisters to see. If somewhat impoverished, Hampshire was green and safe, sweet and orderly, and indeed even its girl turnip-hoers in the dusk charmed another male traveller at about this time. Those Hampshire girls, as William Cobbett noted, are very 'straight, fair, round-faced' with excellent complexion and 'uncommonly gay'.[12] They would glance up along the hard upland turnpike at the sound of horses' hooves clattering by on the flint.

Frank left his coach at an inn where his sisters often collected the post, and then he passed white cottages. The lane here was overhung with greenery and so narrow that a coachman might complain of having varnish scratched off. In the Navy Frank tried to control his feelings, though his sister Jane never found him dull-hearted: now he might sense those feelings welling up uncontrollably. He would see his father's steepleless church, and beyond a curtain of elms the Digweeds' rented Tudor manor. Then he would come to downhill pasture and he might be running so hard he could barely see. An observer might find him rather absurd, as a small boy in an elaborate uniform running down a flinty land with fists in the air. But Frank had a sense of purpose: he was coming home. He could talk with his father before returning to the red gundecks of King George's Navy, and with the affectionate greeting of a brother he might press his sisters to his heart.

Part One

———◆———

FAMILY IN THE GREEN

1

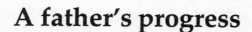

A father's progress

I mind always
That rule which says
Serve that man first who first is.
Mrs George Austen,
in a poem written at Steventon

Frank normally came home to a warm welcome. Several of his older brothers James, George, Edward and Henry, or his younger brother Charles, might be in the rectory to greet him. His sisters Cassandra and Jane mocked his accent and words as when he said 'raly' or laughed over his deliberateness, and Frank's cousin Eliza went a step better by putting him down as 'the little sailor' (perhaps not to his face). In broad daylight, looking from a bedroom window to green meadows that ran up to Church Walk, Frank was far from the Navy.

His mother had disliked Steventon's low, rolling hills and yet Mrs Austen (the former Cassandra Leigh) raised six boys and two little girls while keeping an eye on pigs, cows and her farm's bailiff or overseer. She was aristocratic enough to complain of illness now and then, with her slight body, fine blade of a nose, and memory of her Leigh forbears.

The Revd George Austen was less patrician than his wife – yet his willowy form was elegant. Jane Austen dearly loved him and took pride in his Kentish ancestry, jotting in the margin (some years later) of Richard Warner's *Excursions from Bath* near an allusion to a woollen mill owned by Austens, 'A branch of the Austens – the "Gray Coats of Kent"'.[1] Her father's ancestors had manufactured woollen cloth, and the subtle colour of their cloth – a pearly blue mixed with whitish grey – might have suggested her father's amiable nature. 'As a young man,' George's granddaughter Anna noted of him, 'he was considered extremely handsome, and it was a beauty which stood by him all his life. At the time when I have the most perfect recollection of him' – when he was nearly seventy – 'his hair in its milky whiteness might have belonged to a much older man. It was very beautiful, with short curls about the ears.' A miniature portrait shows George Austen's small mouth with odd little eyes. 'His eyes', says Anna, 'were not large, but of a peculiar and bright hazel.'[2] Among his children, only Henry and Jane Austen inherited that bright, peculiar hazel – a colour which once reminded Dr William Harvey of 'the Eye of a Viper'.

Why had this sensible man left a career at Oxford to find himself in a poor Hampshire village? Jane Austen herself was enthralled by her father's story, and perhaps heard that their name was respectably old in Kentish and Sussex families. In spellings such as 'Astyn' and 'Austyn' it relates in legend to the name of St Augustine. John Austin or Austen in the High Weald of Kent at Horsmonden, seven miles east of Tunbridge Wells, had acquired money and land to go with his old name when he died in 1620. His descendant, another John, spent the money and ran into debt but married with a wary shrewdness (or with a wise sense of female character) that is notable in male Austen descendants. His wife was Elizabeth Weller.

Elizabeth, a great-grandmother of Jane Austen, discovered most of her husband's debts after he died in 1704. She was more valiant than the mother of Elinor and Marianne, although her plight has echoes in the Dashwoods' in *Sense and Sensibility*. She left a detailed record of her struggles. With a daughter and six sons to support, Elizabeth appealed to her father-in-law, who promised her £200 before he died. It turned out that his estate was tied up in favour of his eldest little grandson. Denied even her £200, Elizabeth paid off debts by selling valuables and a leasehold house, and then moved to Sevenoaks to take a roomy old home where she boarded and cleaned for the grammar school's schoolmaster and some of his pupils.

Here she pushed her children through school. 'It seemed to me', wrote Elizabeth, 'as if I cou'd not do a better thing for my Children's good' than getting them through grammar school, 'their education being my great care'. With learning they might get 'better shift' in the world, since they had only 'small fortune'.[3] Her daughter married and her sons did well. Her second son Francis Austen (who was born in the seventeenth century but lived long enough to kiss his great-niece Jane Austen) began as an apprentice to George Tilden, the attorney, and set up as a solicitor 'with eight hundred pounds and a bundle of pens' to become rich at the Red House in Sevenoaks. The Red House still stands on the airy, hilly High Street to remind us of Jane Austen's family. Dr Thomas Fuller had lived in it from 1688 to 1734. William Cranston admired it but sold it in 1743 to Francis Austen, who met his slender twelve-year-old great-niece Jane there in July 1788. Its rows of carved corbels under the roof in front and pillared doorway were the same when the firm became Austen and Claridge in 1832, Austen and Holcroft in 1840, and Holcroft and Knocker in 1864. After three other title-changes the firm began to practise in the twentieth century as Knocker and Foskett, whose name-plate is on the Red House today.

Elizabeth's son Stephen, a stationer, astutely sold medical texts at London's Angel, as well as Bibles in St Paul's Churchyard. Her son Thomas, an apothecary, sired Henry Austen, a Cambridge graduate who held the living of West Wickham until he lost faith in the Holy Trinity and resigned. More respectably, her son William, Jane Austen's grandfather, apprenticed himself to a Woolwich surgeon named William Ellis at a good salary in May 1713 (£115 10s. *per annum*) and married a daughter of the Gloucester physician, Sir George Hampson, named Rebecca. By her first husband Rebecca gave birth to William Hampson Walter in 1721. By her second husband she had three daughters and a son, George, who became Jane Austen's father. He was born on 1 May 1731. His mother soon died. His father remarried but left George as an orphan of six, who, according to a tradition in Austen biography, had a heartless stepmother who failed to mention him in her will. The Austen-Leighs in their *Life* (1913) write that she was 'Susanna Holk, of whom nothing is known except that she died at an advanced age'.[4] As Kent archives confirm, she was Susanna Kelk (a Tonbridge name); and before her marriage to William Austen she had inherited through the will of her aunt Sarah Danvers, dated 23 April 1730, two fields at the edge of Tonbridge known as the Old Hopgarden (of four acres) and School Mead (three acres). We know that William Austen also had owned land since his executors granted a lease of property in Tonbridge called Upper and Lower Barnfield to the blacksmith John Slatter in 1743. By his will William left his widow a life interest from his lands, but on 4 November 1768 his own properties (as well as, by law, her own) began to be sold to purchasers by 'Geo. Austen, son & heir of Wm. Austen', and the proceeds seem to have enabled George Austen to work himself out of debt after he married. It is important that Susanna cared enough for her young stepson George Austen in the 1730s to keep him healthy and well provided for; there is no certain evidence that she was cold or harsh. For one thing, George as a young Oxford man returned to live within two hundred yards of her own house. For another, he shows throughout life the warmest, most sensitive and alert concern for his relatives – a tendency that was to make his daughter Jane Austen alert to the widest connections of her 'family' and proud of them. He had a special reason to value the aid of relatives when his uncle at the Red House paid his way at Tonbridge School, the mere beginning of his Uncle Francis's help. Austen family history now repeated itself. As his grandmother Elizabeth had found *schooling* essential for children without immediate fortune, so George learned that lesson. His care for the education of his daughters (a matter not to be underestimated when we come to Jane Austen) had its origins in his success at school, where he earned a Tonbridge fellowship that took him up to St John's College, Oxford, at sixteen. He repeats the themes of 'money' and advancement so often it is clear he never overcame his early anxieties as an orphan, but this need not be a sign that the former Susanna Kelk had been cold to him.

Habitually neat and handsome in dress and mild and academic in manner, George was inclined for the Church. At college he practised 'disputes' in which he talked on two sides of a question. Testing out his vocation he left the college on a reduced fellowship to be Usher (or assistant master) back at Tonbridge School and also 'Perpetual Curate' of nearby Shipbourne from 1754 to 1757. A relative had asked his cousin, the Revd Henry Austen of Cambridge, to yield the living of Shipbourne to him when Henry took up that of Steventon in Hampshire. George became a deacon in 1754. He took priest's orders the next year at Rochester – but returned to Oxford on 24

14

February 1758 when 'Revenit' next to his name shows that he was safely drinking ruby port again. In 1759 at twenty-eight, this pleasant man was elected (as was William Wright of Merton) as a university proctor, whose most common duty was to fine rowdy students outside his college's gates. Called 'The Handsome Proctor', he was then in line to be a future candidate for the St John's presidency, but a distant relation, Mr Knight, charmingly interfered. When Henry moved to the living of West Wickham, Steventon fell vacant – it was felt that Henry ought to give it up – and so George Austen was instituted Rector of Steventon in Hampshire in December 1761.

And still he resided at Oxford. No opprobrium was attached to his holding a living *in absentia* and Henry had not resided at Steventon, but George at thirty meant to live there. He was not a man to give up a career for the sake of unlettered farmers. He might, however, do more for himself by obeying the *sense* of Mr Knight's desires in serving at Steventon as he had at Shipbourne. He seldom overlooked the wishes of a wealthy relative.

He would need a wife. Not cutting every tie with Oxford, he courted the Master of Balliol's niece, Cassandra Leigh, who was born on 29 September 1739. At twenty-four she was short, fragile, pretty and disinclined to marry. Needing a home for her widowed mother, she changed her mind and George Austen married Cassandra as rationally as his love would permit at Walcot Church, Bath, on 26 August 1764. George was then thirty-three.

His pale wife had 'fine well cut features, large grey eyes, and good eyebrows' and though she lacked a bright complexion she was quick-witted, with 'plenty of sparkle and spirit' her daughter Jane would inherit.[5] Since she had ancestral ties with Oxford, George might in time send academic sons to St John's as 'Founder's Kin' of the Leighs. Unlike any of Jane Austen's heroines Cassandra had a scholarly father, the Revd Thomas Leigh – known as 'Chick Leigh' for his early election as fellow of All Souls – who had been Rector of Harpsden near Henley in Oxfordshire. He was connected with the prosperous Leighs of Adlestrop in Gloucester and with the titled Leighs of Stoneleigh. Both branches were descended from Sir Thomas Leigh, the Lord Mayor of London in Queen Elizabeth's time – and Cassandra herself was named after her great-aunt Cassandra, Duchess of Chandos.

Such an elegant wife might not love a quiet rectory. With her fondness for Westminster Abbey, the Thames and excellent landscape, Cassandra was not keen on Hampshire's chalkhills. George led her to a homely triangle of simple villages at Ashe, Deane and Steventon in a landscape relieved by two or three handsome houses. He did not even install her at Steventon's rectory, not because its curate Thomas Bathurst was slow to get out, but because the house was dilapidated. Even after George's repairs, the house where Jane Austen was born had a cellar that regularly flooded and a patchwork of cracked and exposed rafters.

With four people in tow he moved into Deane parsonage, which in 1764 was empty because the Rector of Deane preferred to live a mile away at Ashe Park. Few clerical marriages at the time began less romantically. The Austens lived with old Mrs Leigh and apparently a boy named George Hastings, a son of the great Warren Hastings of India who was then overseas as a member of the Calcutta Council. Hastings presumably had asked George Austen's sister Mrs Hancock to look after the boy, and she before her return from India with a child of her own ('Bessy' or Eliza) had pleaded with her brother to take charge of Hastings's frail son. Mr Austen welcomed the boy. He sent money to his sister, helped his wife to care for her fragile mother, and soon buried young Hastings and old Mrs Leigh in quiet country graves.

His wife bore several children at Deane. James Austen was baptized there on 13 February 1765; a less healthy little George the next year, and Edward or 'Neddy' on 7 October 1767 (though the year of his birth is usually given incorrectly as 1768). Little George Austen was mentally defective but his parents kept him under their roof for some years before sending him to a home in a nearby parish.

A rutted lane which became a slimy horrid track in the spring ran between Deane and Steventon. Lying in misery, Mrs Austen one day was hoisted on a feather bed which was 'placed upon some soft articles of furniture' and pulled up to Steventon rectory.[6] She was soon carrying her fourth child who was born at the rectory and baptized Henry Thomas Austen on 8 June 1771. By then she knew poverty. She had learned to get along without a new gown for two years, and how to make a red riding-habit do for her day after day.

Yet an indifference to appearances and an amused, ironic view of life helped her to enjoy Steventon's simple, repaired rectory. 'I begin to be very heavy and bundling as usual,' she declares. Her pride was to be heavily pregnant and *also* the mistress of a dairy and overseer of her home. 'I suckled my little girl thro' the first quarter,' Mrs Austen writes after bearing Cassandra Elizabeth Austen on 9 January 1773. 'I want to show you my Henry and my Cassy,' she tells her sister-in-law Mrs Walter, who had a girl named Phylly (or Phila). Cassy 'has been weaned and settled at a good woman's at Deane just eight weeks; she is very healthy and lively, and puts on her short petticoats today. Jemmy and Neddy are very happy in a new play-fellow, Lord Lymington, whom Mr. Austen has lately taken charge of.' 'I have got a nice dairy fitted up, and am now worth a bull and six cows, and you would laugh to see them; for they are not much bigger than Jack-asses – and here I have got jackies and ducks and chickens for Phylly's amusement. In short you must come, and, like Hezekiah, I will shew you all my riches.' George rejoiced in his foresight in marrying a lady who merely needed time to adjust to rural life before she loved it; his wife even became ironic about that 'sad place' London.[7]

What troubled him was the shadow of hard poverty. A study of his accounts at Hoare's Bank shows that he had to borrow a large sum of £865 from his brother-in-law James Leigh Perrot in 1768, and could pay back only £20, partly because his sister needed money. Leigh Perrot must have cancelled the debt in 1772, when George asked for another loan of £300. He perhaps determined to pay that back. But he paid only £12 in 1777, £12 again in each of the years 1780 to 1782, and just before facing fees for his daughters' schooling and Frank's outfitting at naval school, paid off his £300 loan. He received money from Austen estates in Kent, and immediate help from his Uncle Francis, whose gift to him of the living of Deane was announced in the *Gentleman's Magazine* of April 1773 under 'Promotions, Bankrupts, and Stocks':

> Rev. George Austen, to Steventon R. and Dean R.
> Winton diocese.

From 1773 he had permission to hold benefices in two adjoining parishes. But his farm produce sold for little. The nation prospered at a quicker rate than rural Hampshire, and so he began to profit from his extra eggs and pork by taking in pupils. Three or four boys from good families came to live at the rectory for tutoring, and as the house became busier so did his wife. Mrs Austen proved to be a good manager of schoolboys. She was fond of active boys and even of difficult but outspoken girls who revealed what they were, as her love for Anna Lefroy was to show, and she was strict, demanding and good-humouredly fierce. Her pupils lived in good order. She often kept them at bed-making, boot-polishing, cleaning, washing and evening studies, it seems, by chiding them with a laugh or a poem. She was good to F. Stewart and Gilbert East, and attentive to Lord Lymington, Lord Portsmouth's 'backward' little boy, who was polite, and able to take action when Goodenough and Buller said they couldn't sleep under the rectory weathercock. 'Dear Sir,' she wrote on behalf of her husband's pupils,

> we beseech & intreat, a request
> You'd remove a sad nuisance that breaks our night's rest
> That creaking old weathercock over our heads
> Will scarcely permit us to sleep in our beds.
> It whines and it groans & makes such a noise
> That it greatly disturbs two unfortunate boys.[8]

A few agreeable boarding-boys did little to upset her husband's life. She took the sting out of a complaint by burlesquing it, and Mr Austen emerged from his nagging accounts and sermons to be a spirited Latin teacher. If James and Henry and Cassandra resented *enforced* companions, they made up for the pupils by drawing closely together. The Austen children became self-sufficient almost to the point of being clannish: they were amused by outsiders but not in urgent need of friends beyond their doors.

Another more subtle effect of the pupils is that they appealed to Mrs Austen's sense of precedence. The times favoured Dr Johnson's ideal of 'subordination', and she had a good notion of what was due to the more deserving.

Yet some boys protested. One very interesting complaint relates to her favouring little Thomas Craven Fowle, who was later to propose marriage to Jane Austen's sister. A boy named Frank had accused Mrs Austen of 'partiality', and as he implied that her affection was unequally bestowed, she tossed a little spray of verses at him:

1

Ah! Why friend Frank,
    d'ye look so blank?
so wondrous discontented?
    Each lucky hit,
    Each stroke of wit
are by those looks prevented.

2

The cheerful muse
    does here refuse
to lend her kind assistance.
    She cannot bear
    a serious air
So wisely keeps her distance.

3

Yet I must write
    This very night,
Or you will still look graver,
    And I shall be
    Reproached by thee
That rhyming goes by favour.

4

But do dismiss
    a thought like this
which does me such injustice:
    I mind always
    That rule which says
Serve that man first who first is.[9]

Her light wit might have told Frank that she was fair. Her good humour put Mrs Austen in the right. A 'man' who knew himself to be second or third in worth might live pleasantly under her rule *Serve that man first who first is*. Everything depended on how she made up her mind; but she judged a child's behaviour, attitude, social class and other attributes it seems with considerable firmness.

After the rectory's rooms began to fill up she gave birth to Frank Austen on 23 April 1774. Even so, she was very soon 'heavy and bundling' again. 'We are all, I thank God, in good health,' Mrs Austen announced in August 1775 when she was nearly thirty-six. 'I am more nimble and active than I was last time, expect to be confined some time in November. My last boy is very stout. . . . My little girl [Cassy] talks all day long, and in my opinion is a very entertaining companion.'[10] Possibly some room might be found for an infant boy in November – or, with less fuss, for a girl, even if with Mr Austen's concern for 'money' and his wife's decided views of precedence the ways ahead in life for a mere girl would be restricted.

Mr Austen was concerned with advancing his four healthy sons and yet he realized that his wife was no longer young. It pleased him no doubt to find her 'nimble and active' as she awaited the birth of a seventh baby in November.

2

Plaything

> A present plaything for her sister Cassy.
> Mr Austen
> on his baby Jane

But oddly November passed without a birth. At thirty-six, Mrs Austen carried her baby a month past the expected time. Jane Austen was born on Saturday night, 16 December 1775, and next day Mr Austen wrote to his half-sister in Kent: 'You', he apologized to Mrs Walter with good humour,

> have doubtless been for some time in expectation of hearing from Hampshire, and perhaps wondered a little we were in old age grown such bad reckoners but so it was, for Cassey certainly expected to have been brought to bed a month ago: however last night the time came, and without a great deal of warning, everything was soon happily over.

'We have now another girl,' he added, who 'is to be Jenny'. His wife was very well and the wheat was good. Thirty-four of the King's battalions were endangered in the North American colonies where Washington led the militant rebels, and Mr Austen as trustee of one vulnerable Antiguan estate asked Mrs Walter, 'Have you had any fresh news from Jamaica?'[1]

To save her from cold wet weather he postponed Jenny's reception at church until 5 April but baptized her privately at home on 17 December. He saw his son Henry's features in her round hazel eyes and a modest nose. 'She', he wrote, seems 'as if she would be as

21

like Henry as Cassy is to Neddy.' As his wife had suckled Cassy
Austen for three months, so Jane was probably nursed at home before
she was weaned and sent to a cottager's wife. Before weaning, a
girl was usually kept in strong cotton swathing about six inches wide
and ten to twenty feet long. This was wound tightly round her body
from armpits to hips to keep her spine straight and to prevent her
from breaking her legs. After weaning and when living with 'a good
woman at Deane' as Cassy had, Jane would wear loose and light
clothing, and have fresh air and exercise. The more enlightened theories of Locke and Rousseau about letting infants enjoy sunny days
in unrestricting dresses and smocks had taken hold. Jane was trained
to love the out-of-doors, and by April, when ready for a bonnet and
petticoats, she was a fine little person. 'Jane Austen', her father wrote
in the family Bible,

> Born 16 Dec. 1775. Privately baptised 17 Dec. 1775. Rec^d into the Church
> 5 Ap^l. 1776. Sponsors Revd Mr Cooke Rector of Bookham Surry. M^{rs}
> Jane Austen of Sevenoaks Kent, Father's Uncle's Wife. Mrs Musgrave
> of Chinnor Oxon.[2]

Her name paid tribute to her mother's lovely sister Jane and to her
own godmother Jane Austen – wife of her father's wealthy Uncle
Francis. Her second godmother was the wife of James Musgrave,
Vicar of Chinnor in Oxfordshire, whose mother was Mrs Austen's
great-aunt and a rich Perrot. A sister of the Vicar of Chinnor married
a Mr John Knightley. Jane's godfather was Samuel Cooke, Rector
of Cotsford in Oxfordshire and Vicar of the parish of St Nicholas
at Great Bookham in Surrey, where he lived. He had married Mrs
Austen's talented cousin Cassandra Leigh, who in 1799 was to publish, as 'by a Lady of Quality', with the dilatory Cawthorn and Hutt
in London the story *Battleridge, an historical tale founded on facts*. The
Cookes' children George and Mary were early friends of the young
Austens.

Thus connected to clerical and moneyed families at her baptism
in April, Jane was never felt to be insignificant. Her mother would
need a girl's help in sewing boys' shirts, but Mrs Austen did not
welcome her home as a future slave. Rather when – in short petticoats
and surely with pink cheeks and a fresh, healthy look – Jane came
home from a good woman's cottage, she entered a happy, active
and secure world. Her chief role had been discussed when she was

a day old: as Mr Austen had put it, she was 'a present plaything for her sister Cassy and a future companion'.[3]

As well as she could, little Cassy took over her management to keep her from muddying her frock or crawling too close to pigsties. Soon they walked hand in hand, and Mr Austen often thought of them as one. His fine-featured face and neat attire confronted them when he called out, with delight, to 'the girls'. Anna Lefroy later recalled the oddity of his referring to *grown* daughters as 'girls' in such pleasant tones. 'Where are the girls?' he would cry. 'Are the girls gone out?' They dressed alike and lived in unison: 'I remember too their bonnets,' says Anna, 'because though perfectly alike in colour, shape & material, it made it a pleasure to guess, & I believe I always guessed right, which bonnet [and girl belonged] to each other.'[4]

Mr Austen certainly recited from the newspapers and observed a 'public fast and humiliation' for the King's troops in Jane's infancy on 13 December 1776. General Howe had captured New York, as the *Hampshire Chronicle* said, 'and Washington had lost either one hand or one arm', but reports of the war subsided in 1777 when no more was heard of Washington's hand or arm and little of the King's reversals. Jane Austen's talent for comedy and burlesque was to respond to journals, and she perhaps heard her brothers' laughter over newspaper phrases such as 'cloud-capt belles' and 'this age of sensibility' before she knew what the words meant. The Tory *Chronicle* explained a game of 'CHARARDS' which her family played with variations. Somebody would describe the first syllable of a secret, special word in one line of verse, the second syllable in another line, then the whole two-syllabled word in a third one; in the newspaper's examples the ANSWER was also in verse:

Charards

My first, – is *a musical Grace*;
My second, – *a Weapon of War*;
My third, – the *Heart's best commentator*.

ANSWER

I ween that your musical grace is – a *Shake*,
That your weapon of war is – a *Spear*;
Where's the *Briton* whose heart but these two have made ake,
And from *Nature's* own eye forc'd a tear?
SHAKE-SPEAR![5]

23

For a very small child, funny recitals and news reports were strange. Even for adults, the outer world was rather remote. News from the colonies reached Steventon two or three months late, though rumours filtered from naval ports – and travel was so slow in the 1770s that English towns had unique time-systems, with one town four or five minutes behind the next. Yet a visible pattern of life *was* familiar. Servants rose and lit fires, boys clomped downstairs, parents appeared, cows came to the barn, and prayers were said at intervals. For Jane the most vivid features in the pattern besides her parents and Cassandra were her brothers – who towered over her and did nice things and were kind. As her senior by ten years, James was a scholarly, tall, fair-haired boy who loved to ride and strode about in leather. He studied books and wrote enough verses to convince Mrs Austen he was the writer of the family. Less erudite but quick, clever and witty was Henry, whose antics and stories were funny. Jane found Henry confiding, but learned later that his private life was such a rich joke to himself he could happily share it. He is comic in a long letter about his disasters. Ebullient and kind, in touch with publishers, bankers, painters and theatrical people, he was to give Jane Austen a large sense of contemporary society – while remaining a lovable, vexing child until his mind stiffened a little in old age. He said things people wanted to hear, flattered his father as well as great men such as Warren Hastings, and taking his reversals lightly popped up again with a new 'scheme'. Her brother George was probably a deaf-mute, and since Mrs Austen had an 'imbecile brother' in Mr Thomas Leigh, who was placed at nearby Monk Sherborne 'under the care of the Culhams of that parish', George would soon join his uncle. Theophilus Leigh saw George at Steventon in Jane's childhood, when she learned enough finger-language to 'talk' to him. Later when she had 'no cannon at hand' to test a Mr Valentine Fitzhugh's deafness at Southampton, she 'talked to him a little with my fingers', as she had to George, and told her sister she had recommended *him* to read Mme de Staël's *Corinne* – perhaps a joking fib since Madame de Staël had so gravely taken Corinne to Venice, where, when a girl takes her sacred vows, 'a cannon is fired to announce the sacred moment' across the lagoon.[6]

Nobody pitied her brother Edward, a polite, graceful boy with short legs and a good head for sums. He looked presentable and his parents planned to give him away. Before Jane Austen's sixth year, Edward began to visit Godmersham Park in Kent, the estate of Mr Austen's second cousin, Thomas Knight. Knight's father had changed his name from Brodnax to May and Knight to qualify for landed inheritances, and young Knight, after sitting as MP for New Romney and marrying in 1779 a pretty Miss Catherine Knatchbull, a daughter of the prebendary of Durham, withdrew from public life to devote himself to the family estates. As he and Catherine were childless, they yearned for an Austen boy.

Mr Austen was quick to oblige a relative, but he hesitated to give away a son of fifteen or sixteen. He had felt that Edward's Latin lesson would be neglected. 'I think, my dear, you had better oblige your cousins, and let the child go,' Mrs Austen advised.[7] In any case Edward went, and in 1783 the fashionable London artist William Wellings painted a group silhouette to celebrate the occasion – it shows George Austen presenting his son Edward to the Knights and another lady, with the ladies not bothering to rise from an absorbing game at their table to receive him. Jane did not lose him completely. But it is probable that her surprise over losing her brother to the Knights of Kent, in too violent a removal, at first outweighed any idea she had of the good sense of the transfer. 'There is something so shocking in a child's being taken away from his parents and natural home!' she has the foolish Isabella Knightley exclaim in *Emma*. 'I never can comprehend [it]. To give up one's child! I really never could think well of any body who proposed such a thing.'[8] Jane realized in time that the adoption ensured Edward's good fortune in life and that she had hardly lost him at all, but the incident seems to illustrate how she could re-experience and use her earlier, naive feelings. A girl of deep family loyalty might indulge her regret over Edward's transfer and then with good sense become reasonable, with a wry, loving regard for her early dismay. She could draw on that dismay in portraying Isabella, and use her early feeling about the horror of adoptions in making Fanny Price suffer bitterly as an adopted girl in *Mansfield Park*. The lasting, subtle effect of the adoption was to make her more fully aware of how money, land, inheritance and social advantage easily take precedence in modern society over family love in homes less congenial than her own.

Her elder brothers taught and amused her, but as a child she played with the three children nearer her own age. Frank, the future sailor, led Cassy and Jane in outdoor games, and they all looked after little

Charles, who was born on 13 June 1779 when Mrs Austen was nearly forty. Less canny than Frank, Charles was a boy who spoke in a sweet ordinary flowing babble and later a man whose kindness and good sense in the Navy were duplicated in a hundred other officers. He lacked Henry's wit and James's creativity, but he would always be Cassy's and Jane's fat, trim or balding 'particular' little brother – favoured by Cassy, though no less subject to Jane's love and approval.

As in Anna Lefroy's family, small children dined at a separate table, were kept in order and stayed out of adult rooms at certain hours. The foursome of Frank, Cassy, Jane and Charles obeyed rules, but on one occasion Frank opened a forbidden door, poked in a curly head and said in imitation of the servants, 'my be come not to bide'.[9] And Jane toddled all over the rectory. Outside she saw a latticed porch. The three front rooms of the house were the best parlour, common parlour and kitchen. Behind these were Mr Austen's sunny room looking into the garden, the back kitchen and stairs leading up to seven bedrooms and to another flight that led up to three attic dormered rooms where boys slept. The rooms were 'low-pitched but not otherwise bad', as Caroline Austen noted, though cornices were missing and beams for the upper floors 'projected into the rooms below in all their naked simplicity, covered only by a coat of paint or whitewash'.[10] The girls shared a 'smaller' bedroom, but soon acquired the luxury of an adjoining room with a chocolate-figured carpet and a mirror between two windows, as a 'dressing-room' where they kept clothes and books, with Jane's pianoforte.

The rectory had two projecting back wings looking out on an eastern pond and also on the sizeable kitchen-garden with vegetables and flowers, which was flanked by a thatched mud wall and lined by elms. Nearby was a wash-house with an iron pump. The garden sloped up to a terrace of fine, smooth grass beyond which a hedgerow arched over a footpath called Wood Walk or Elm Walk running west across the hill. Another rustic hedgerow covered Church Walk and ran straight up the hill towards the Digweeds' stone manor – which had been rebuilt by Sir Richard Pexall in Elizabeth's time – and on up towards Mr Austen's church.

In the spring, children saw primroses, anemones and bluebells in the footpaths and took as much delight as Catherine Morland would in 'rolling down the green slope'. Their sheltered valley turned into pastel and deep shades of green, and the flowers and trees kept Cassy and Jane outside. They watched Frank ride. At seven he bought a lively chestnut pony called Squirrel – though his elder brothers plagued him by calling it Scug – and after jumping it at everything it could get its nose over, he sold it two years later for £2.12.6 at a profit of one guinea.[11] The pony divided him from Jane since the girls did not ride or hunt, but his riding drew Cassandra and Jane closer. They shared their own private jokes and secrets. The social order dividing boys from girls turned one sex into a critic or entertainer of the other, but it gave sisters some independence, too, and helped them to reach their own verdicts and conclusions about most topics. Naturally of importance to them would be the two solemn, special Sunday walks to church. Morning service of an hour and a half was followed by a shorter 'afternoon' one. At morning service the whole village gathered in varnished, high-backed pews to hear Bible readings in which the '-eds' of participles were pronounced. Squeezed to death beside Cassy, Jane acquired a vivid, hell-fearing awareness of sin before her legs were long enough to let her small wooden clogs, or iron-ringed pattens, click on the floor.

Her father as Rector was a mildly amiable and courteous guide, who, to judge from the clerical practice of later Austens, was less eager to denounce errors than to teach truths. She heard that religion was the basis of civil society. She absorbed a strict Christian and Stoic morality. Talents and achievements are as dust, she learned, and education is nothing if it does not lead to 'self-knowledge', since we are corruptible, easily tempted and likely to err, selfish and self-deluding, responsible for our unhappiness and destruction. Happiness depends not on egotistical feats but on being useful and doing one's duty. Jane's father made these views so ummistakably clear and also rational that she would read sermons with pleasure and find a very compatible teaching in Dr Johnson.

Most of the worshippers were tenant-farmers who lived in thatched white cottages where women spun flax and wool while men did farm work. Her father as Rector and representative of the absent Mr Knight, who owned most of the land, was their spiritual and temporal head. His eminence gave her a sense of *noblesse oblige* and of being bound to visit and help the parish needy, if their numbers were rather small since only thirty-three families lived at Steventon, twenty-four at Deane and fourteen at Ashe by the end of the century.

One day at home, she and Cassy sat with grown-ups. At adult tables, children became polite or heard sharp rebukes. Girls for ages had been told to 'sit up straight, hold your shoulders back, don't lounge, don't cross your legs, don't bite your nails, don't pick your nose, don't blow on your soup'.[12] But Mrs Austen commanded with insinuating good humour, and as Cassy had a fine instinct for good manners and Jane imitated Cassy, few sharp rebukes might be heard. Mrs Austen was not an ogress who withered the wills of the disobedient but a mother who put family first; her girls took up needlework, cleaning, bed-making, cooking, learning by heart and repeating of lessons as naturally as they woke up in the morning; they became dutiful and amiable, ready to oblige, eager to listen, applaud, encourage. In reaction to less disciplined ruffians, Jane later felt that the rod should be used. 'We thought him a very fine boy,' she wrote of her niece's Charles Lefroy, 'but terribly in want of Discipline. I hope he gets a wholesome thump or two whenever it is necessary.'[13]

New evidence shows that Mrs Austen's mother had left much of *her* girls' training to an aunt. All the keener to guide her daughters and perhaps to save them from plebeian rules of Conduct Books (which Jane Austen mocked to the delight of the family), Mrs Austen praised the aristocratic Leighs. Jane probably read Mary Leigh's witty poem of 1777 called 'The Leigh Pedigree', which was filled with sweet names:

> William, Theophilus, James, Thomas and Charles
> All lived to man's estate
> Whilst Emma, Cassandra, Mary and Anne,
> Married each one their favourite mate.[14]

Secure in her home, Jane was free to imagine the pleasant marriages of 'Emma', 'Anne' and other Leighs. One might feel proud to have a Leigh mother. But her own behaviour would have to please Mrs Austen, or involve unthinkable anguish.

3

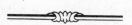

Social class, school class

Here is a line for seeing human nature . . .infinitely superior [to] 'the best education in the world'.

Persuasion

A real, honest, old-fashioned boarding-school.

Emma

Cassandra and Jane derived a fine sense of social class from their mother – and this was one of Mrs Austen's best gifts. The social-class system of the Austens' England was delicately complex, and the boundaries between classes were hazy and obscure – or far less rigidly fixed and plain than those in France. But everyone was conscious of class. It may be said (from our modern viewpoint) that most of the English people from beggars and thieves up to the nobility were snobs. To know just where you were in the class system was as vital for a footpad, a burglar, a chandler or a duke as it was for a young lady, and the comic realism of Jane Austen's novels solidly rests on *her* fine understanding of this system. Let us look into the 'Austens and class' – just before we follow Jane and Cassandra to school.

The Austens were country gentry. This put them well beneath the British aristocracy and a niche below most baronets and squires of the wealthy landed gentry. Mr Austen lacked money and a good estate, but as an Oxford-educated clergyman he hovered at the gentry's lower fringes. His bank accounts at Hoare's Bank reveal from time to time a grave, sometimes a desperate story, and if his income sharply declined he could fall below the ranks of Overton or Basingstoke lawyers, apothecaries and merchants of the 'middling classes'. Socially he was a borderline person. His financial anxieties partly account for his wish to please his relatives, for the transfer of his son Edward to the Knights, and for the Austens' taking the widest possible view of the word 'family'. For Jane Austen that word included more than merely husband, wife and children. Just as she makes Lady Russell in *Persuasion* turn against Mr Elliot for 'declining to be on cordial terms with the head of his family' (Sir Walter Elliot), so she viewed the effective 'family' as a whole collection of second cousins, great-aunts, nephews and ancestors. Her large view of the family was not unique but it was intensely felt. She would view her brothers' children as *her* family, and treat them very specially and confidingly as if Fanny and Anna and several others were her own younger sisters – and furthermore the 'family' touched her pride. Her view of the aristocracy and of local Hampshire society was complicated by her mother's calm, certain belief that the Leigh aristocrats were part of the core family of Austens.

A girl's social class more than any other factor determined her marriage. The higher her class the more likely she was to marry a man with money, prestige, land-holdings and either leisure or a respectable career. Her 'class' was thus related to her chances of happiness and well-being; and as a keen and devoted father Mr Austen was well aware that ladylike accomplishments and good schooling would enhance Cassandra's and Jane's chances in marriage and so he included them both in an Oxford plan.

With deep confidence in Oxford he sent his son James up to St John's College at the age of fourteen in 1779, and he intimated that Henry was to go to St John's later on and take clerical orders, as James would. His idea for Cassy and Jane had rather different features: they were to stay at Oxford with the widow of a former Principal of Brasenose, a Mrs Cawley, who as Ann Cooper was a sister of their uncle Edward Cooper, and meanwhile the rectory would have one extra room while they were away. Usually girls were trained at home and boys were sent away, but he reversed this pattern by training his boys and sending his girls off to a strange city full of towers and quadrangles.

At seven, Jane was a shy country girl with skin 'fine and healthy in hue', large eyes, a small nose and curling hair. She probably wore a new frock, new slippers and stockings and a spencer or extra garment against the weather as she clung to her sister; the girls knew when to curtsey, and Mrs Cawley knew about sums, reading and penmanship – but Jane Austen's phrases such as 'gone unhappy to school' and 'feeling her separation from home' and 'school must be very humiliating' hardly make one feel the teacher had put her at ease.[1]

As a 'stiff-mannered' person Mrs Cawley led them from one loathsome college to the next in sightseeing tours. 'I never, but once, was at Oxford in my life,' Jane wrote at thirteen, 'and I am sure I never wish to go there again – They dragged me through so many dismal chapels, dusty libraries, and greasy halls, that it gave me the vapours for two days afterwards.'[2]

One day Mrs Cawley took them, with their small cousin Jane Cooper, off in a coach to Southampton, where both sisters nearly died. Jane Austen began to vomit and fell ill with 'putrid fever' or typhus, which had been raging as an epidemic at Romsey,[3] and Cassy fell ill too. Mrs Cawley did not write of this news to the Austens, but her niece Jane Cooper did, whereupon Mrs Austen and Mrs Cooper in fright came to take the girls home. Mrs Cooper died of the infection in October 1783, though all three little girls recovered.

Having survived typhus, Jane might have gone next to Miss Dickinson's Basingstoke school. But Mr Austen had a new plan. St John's fellows always sent a 'triennial visitor', or an officially delegated observer, to look over a very excellent boys' grammar school under Dr Valpy at Reading. The founder of St John's College – Sir Thomas White, who was Mrs Austen's ancestor – had left the school two scholarships. Across the green Forbury or walled meadow from Dr Valpy's was its sister academy, Abbey School, whose girls went to 'speeches and play-acting at Dr Valpy's'[4] and joined boys in dances at their own Abbey ballroom.

An odd feature of Abbey School was the lenience of its head, a Miss Sarah Hackett, who – as her employers 'thought it right to introduce her into the school under a foreign name' to teach French – had styled herself 'Mrs Latournelle'.[5] (Jane Austen's biographers have told several myths about her: she was not a widow, nor was she French.) As a Londoner she may have known Francis Latournelle of Kensington Square who in 1761 was minister at Wandsworth's French Chapel. But she seldom spoke French. Her girls believed she knew not a word of it, and at school they loved her for her trusting absences, since she vanished completely after luncheon. At forty-eight she was a heavy woman with a cork leg who brewed tea, hung out washing, darned stockings and cheerfully assigned her girls two-to-a-bed. She also managed three capable teachers and kept the school from any bad scandal.

Mr Austen's banking accounts show that he paid his daughters' half-year school fees as follows:

S. La Tournelle	Aug. 20th, 1785, . . £37 19 0
	Feb. 13th, 1786, . . £36 2 6
	Jan. 2nd, 1787, . . £16 10 0

Jane had a 'passionate anxiety' not to be separated from Cassy, and the low payment in arrears in 1787 is not for one girl but for both daughters for a quarter term. Jane began at Abbey School at age nine and would leave it for good just as she turned eleven (in December 1786).[6]

One day she saw a town of waggon-filled streets, mills and brewing works, and lines of worsteds drying in open spaces. Five-and-a-half minutes behind London and at the busy junction of the Thames and Kennet waterways, Reading was dirty and bustling, with waggons driving through on the main road from London to Bath. But its For-bury was pretty. Here next to the school were ruins of an abbey that had begun as a Cluniac monastery: some of its walls rose thirty feet and had giant oval hollows, like eyes, in masses of flint and pebbly mortar. Outside the school's garden was a massive stone gateway, with skeletal gaping holes above its arch, and this stood before a vast staircase with flaking gilt balustrades. You walked up the steps to enter a wainscoted school parlour hung with embroidery showing 'tombs and weeping willows'.[7] In this Gothic chamber, a fat woman with a peg leg stomped out from behind a cloth screen near a mantelpiece and with sweaty affection and excited chit-chat greeted her new girls.

Mrs Latournelle was so matter-of-fact that shy girls trusted her and found her reassuring. She kept bloody ghosts at bay, including the eyeless corpse of King Henry I (who was buried near the school) Adeliza, the Queen of Henry II, Constantia, daughter of Edmund of Langley, and the pathetic spectres of Isabella and John who were the hapless grandchildren of King John. Abbey girls talked so freely about these ghosts that Jane may have recalled Isabella and John when she wrote *Northanger Abbey*; gruesomely, in her first year one 'perfect skeleton' was unearthed near the Abbey church's walls.[8]

Girls at night told lurid stories; then after tea or cocoa in the mornings they sat 'an hour or two' at lessons in needlework, English and French with some Italian and history. If, as Miss Holt did in 1790, the same lady taught both spelling and sewing, she may have favoured the needle, since Jane's spelling was poor, but Jane heard some perfectly excellent teachers and judged the classes favourably later when she described Mrs Goddard's in *Emma* as a 'real, honest, old-fashioned Boarding-school where a reasonable quantity of accomplishments were sold at a reasonable price, and where girls might be sent to be out of the way, and scramble themselves into a little education, without any danger of coming back prodigies'.

Mrs Latournelle was inclined to whisper at prayers: 'Make haste, make haste.' After luncheon 'no human being ever took the trouble to consider where we spent the rest of the day', as a pupil of 1790 recalls, 'whether we gossiped in one turret or another ...'.[9] A girl might read books in long hours before the 'jovial' supper and Jane already had remarkably got beyond her *Goody Two-Shoes*, *Elegant Extracts* (it seems) and Ann Murry's *Mentoria: or, The Young Ladies Instructor*.[10] There is enough evidence in her own juvenile writing to suggest that in her school years she was at least dipping into Addison, Johnson and the moralists, and scampering through a good many novels from Swift and Defoe to Fanny Burney's *Evelina* and Charlotte Lennox's *Female Quixote*. She didn't get to Arnaud Berquin's *L'ami des enfans* (1782–3) till she received it on her eleventh birthday, probably from her Aunt Hancock, who seems to have written 'pour dear Jane Austen' rather idly in the fifth volume, or to Berquin's *L'ami de l'adolescence* (1784–5) until later; but her French lessons prepared her for Mme de Genlis' vivid, concise stories – which, with Richardson's *Grandison*, were among her major delights – and she may have found at school Walpole's *Castle of Otranto* and a translation of 1779 of Goethe's *Sorrows of Werther* (which she alluded to in a juvenile tale of her own). Zany young Germans had killed themselves lately in blue frockcoats and yellow vests, and the 'Werther Craze' combined with Walpole's influence to produce a taste for high sentiment and the macabre. The shrieking midnight phase of Gothic fiction lay ahead in the 1790s, but when Jane read Mrs Radcliffe and came to overgrown turrets, she had already benefited by living at a Gothic school at Reading.

Ordinary life can be more horrifying than horror fiction and a girls' school consists of other girls. The Austens had no obvious social credentials as the children of a country clergyman. They mingled with daughters of the better gentry, watched them play card-games such as loo or commerce and joined them when they 'lounged about the garden' or took nonchalant walks across the green to Dr Valpy's. No bonneted older girl would be impressed by Jane, but Cassy was acceptable since she knew what to say and her sister seemed an agreeable mouse. Then, and for years later, Jane was shy, mute and uncertain with her peers – she would hardly be more confident with her waspish cousin Phila. At nine and ten she was a timid, imitative observer hovering near a circle of slangy, half-sophisticated girls who talked over her head and laughed at everything. She echoed them as far as possible: 'I could die of laughter at it,' she told Cassy, 'as they used to say at school.'[11]

But at least by not *trying* to conform and by hovering at the edges of fashionable groups, she saved herself from a smooth diminishing of personality. One may be agreeable without trying to be beloved. Just eight years older than Jane Austen, Maria Edgeworth attended a similar school at Mrs Latuffière's at Derby, where she succumbed to what her father called an 'inordinate desire to be beloved'. When Maria found that competitive girls were not liked, she tried to be pleasing, docile and 'feminine'.[12] She suppressed part of herself by learning to disguise her aggression as a pleasant 'improvisatrice' or teller of entertaining stories at the expense of her ability to observe women. She paid a high price for compliance: at Mrs Latuffière's she took small measure of her own needs, desires, impulses. But Jane Austen, however mousy and inconsequential she seemed, did not play false to herself, and her shyness was in some ways an advantage as was the presence of her sister. Abbey School certainly taught her to value Cassandra all the more. The cost of being sheltered and protected by Cassy may have been, initially, that of blunting or diffusing some of her experiences, keeping her from surprises, shocks and the rewards of intimate friendships and 'crushes'. She was amused by girls, and craved to know the world. Hence there

34

is a tendency in young Jane Austen to find the world by racing through bad novels to measure their absurdity against norms of her own close, sanely affectionate family. School affected her less than it does the average girl; she lived behind a human screen. She missed the Austens: they were so much, the rest of the world so little. Only a miracle might have carried a brother to school to see her, and oddly a miracle did. That event was almost too heavenly to bear. Her brother Edward with his cousin Edward Cooper appeared one day to take Cassandra, Jane and Jane Cooper (who had come along to the school after her mother died) out to a Reading inn. The five young people dined in sophisticated style. In July 1784, probably when she was home from Mrs Cawley's, James and Henry already had done something equally magical by staging Sheridan's *The Rivals* in the family barn. Henry Austen then recited James's prologue for Sheridan's play. 'Smile,' said Henry, 'smile but this evening,'

> Our hearts, with genuine grace and beauty caught
> In fervent sighs, shall thank you as they ought.
> You'll see us suppliants at your feet again,
> And they who liked as Boys, shall love as Men.[13]

Who could fail to *love* such brothers? When they put on *The Rivals*, Jane saw for the first time stage-characters such as Mrs Malaprop and Lydia Languish. The incident of Lydia's making curl-papers of Fordyce's sermons in scene two was recalled later, when she made Lydia Bennet interrupt Mr Collins's reading of Fordyce's *Sermons*. Sheridan's sharp management of scenes, his heaped-up wit and the immediacy of his portraits were to stimulate her comic writing. At school she saw girls perform a ballet, skit or play each half-year, but nothing at Reading matched the delicious sight of seeing James and Henry act.

So Edward's taking her to the inn was further proof of her brothers' immense kindness and love, and she 'scrambled' herself into some learning to be worthy of them. At Abbey she became fitter to talk to Henry and James, and so benefited from Mr Austen's plans.

Mr Austen undoubtedly had felt it a good investment to pay for his daughters' schooling. He was a sensible, practical man and within the bounds of reason even mildly optimistic, but as a Tory royalist and the trustee of an Antigua estate, he had with the gravest anxiety heard ominous news, as the war went from bad to worse. What began as a small rebellion became an international conflict: France and Spain helped the Americans, and in 1781 Cornwallis surrendered at Yorktown to rebels who were supported by Rochambeau on land and a French fleet off Virginia.

Two years later at the Peace of Paris the British Crown conceded American independence. This was the nation's gravest colonial loss in the eighteenth century – and yet the war's aftermath was oddly cheerful: by 1785 overseas trade was greater than ever: England seemed to have a sound economy, new buildings and improved estates and even a growing social conscience. Every bishop of Mr Austen's Church declared against slavery in the next fifteen years. People became aware of a new elegance in dress, furnishings and architecture and most importantly of a neoclassical beauty in which ornateness yielded to line and form.

But, as welcome as it was, the new elegance unsettled the young of the gentry and upper classes. Any girl who read the *Lady's Magazine* and came back to Steventon from Abbey School, for example, might find Mr Austen's rectory quaint. She would feel abject pity or horrid shame in a room with a bare floor, stiff old chairs with brocaded seats, a fireplace with crude hobs and a chimney-piece adorned with Old Testament scenes. She might be scandalized by a mother who 'sat darning the family stockings in a parlour into which the front door opened'.[14]

Mrs Austen's darning, however, warned her girls that though fashions and style were changing *the needle* was not obsolete, and the girls soon did embroidery at a tambour-frame, learned the satin-stitch and began to sew clothes. Their mother defied boredom to talk about pigs, and Cassandra, who was charmed by rural economics, wrote later that 'there is so much amusement' in 'attending a Farm in the country'. Jane, in contrast, found the cost of pigs dull and yearned to be 'above vulgar Economy'.[15] But, aping Cassy, she took no line of her own since she was quite fixed by her mother's mild 'sprack' wit and the laws of precedence. A younger sister, no matter how remarkable she seemed or how glorious her needlework might be, could *not* eclipse an older one, and Jane found it perfectly congenial and safe to be devotedly imitative: 'If Cassandra were going to have her head cut off,' Mrs Austen claimed, 'Jane would insist on sharing her fate.'[16] Jane Austen encouraged the idea of Cassandra's superiority to benefit from the shield of Cassy's *savoir-faire*, guidance and normalcy – and the elder Austens found no fault in her meekness. The family 'doctrine' that Jane was less than Cassandra 'in all important' respects was held by Mrs Austen even after Jane died.[17] (It was echoed by two descendants in our own century.)

One might have quarrelled better with a pump handle than with Mrs Austen, and it would have been easier to straighten piglets' tails or make a hen love a fox than to alter her idea of discipline. There was an atmosphere of order in the household – strict, implicit, iron-bound and unchanging. But Jane warmly approved the domestic discipline, quiet strictness and natural order, and took delight in the family's talk, wit and sense of well-being. In a smart waistcoat and powdered hair, Henry was now so resourceful that his father deemed him 'the most talented' young Austen, and James on holidays from Oxford took a share in directing Jane's reading and forming her taste – or at least he gave her books to read.[18] The times favoured clear, bright, yielding talk directed to general observations and seasoned with irony – and the wonderful talk of her brothers became one basis of Jane's early prose style. James despised novels (as his poems and Oxford essays show), but he had 'in the highest degree', as his mother believed, 'Classical Knowledge, Literary Taste and the power of Elegant Composition'.[19]

As Cassy excelled at drawing so Jane did passably well at music. Since she hit many of the right keys a pianoforte, possibly the same one that the family had on loan at Christmas in 1786, was installed upstairs next to the girls' bedroom; Mrs Austen had it put there at a time, it seems, when her husband was filling no more rooms with pupils.[20]

Upstairs in laughing sessions, the girls were in heaven, and many blessings came to Jane from the comfort of the dressing room with its pianoforte and chocolate-figured carpet. Women, as Florence Nightingale wrote later, 'never have an half-hour in all their lives (excepting before or after anybody is up in the house) that they can call their own, without fear of offending someone'[21] and outside only the wealthiest households Englishwomen in the Austens' time were interruptible people. But in a well-disciplined rectory a girl might have daily freedom behind a shut door, and some free space, which itself is a feature of real elegance. Jane's characters would be conscious of the size of rooms – and she would find a room too small even when it was sixteen feet square and could hold two beds. Aloft she could laugh at anything she liked: she could look for morals in Dr Johnson's *Rasselas*, or say outrageous things aloud. Girls in polite society were supposed to avoid jests on poverty, people's looks, infirmity and death (as Mrs Trench remembers), as well as sexual jokes, deliberate mimicry, any discussion of ages or incomes, and all 'superlatives or enthusiasm'.[22] Jane was to violate all of these rules repeatedly in joke playlets and early stories that made her unstraitlaced family laugh – but she gained confidence to do so in privacy.

If her brothers who were plodding at Latin and Greek felt that she was a rapid, light or scatterbrained reader, she cherished all seven volumes of Richardson's *Sir Charles Grandison* (1753–4) and pored over the elegant text so often that Henry was later surprised, and a nephew believed she could recall every detail down to the 'before' and 'after' of a Cedar Parlour kiss. In this gigantic and pleasant novel, she read the story of an orphaned Harriet Byron – all the prettier because she has Jane Austen's red cheeks – who at the age of twenty flies from Northamptonshire bumpkins who treat her 'like a fool' as men do. At her Cousin Reeves's house in London, Harriet tremblingly refutes a stupid Oxford scholar named Mr Walden, who neglects female viewpoints. 'Every scholar, I presume,' she tells him, 'is not, necessarily, a man of sense.' Harriet writes long letters to Lucy Selby to discuss language, the screen of men's talk and the difficulty of discovering human nature. She survives her abduction by Sir Hargrave Pollexfen, who proves pathetically isolated by pride and self-doubt, and falls in love with Sir Charles Grandison, who is really less romantic than virtuous. He is as perfect as a man in fiction can be. Having honourably left Lady Clementina in Italy, he drops on his knees in the Cedar Room – in a tender scene in which the lovers shout in capitals, 'Sir – I CAN – I DO' – and then he rather freely kisses Harriet 'in so fervent a way', before marrying her. *Charles Grandison* – despite the tedium of its Italian episodes – is a psychologically convincing study of a girl learning not to be abashed by her intelligence, as she grows alert to the low status of women in society.

What, asks Harriet of her almost mute friend Lucy, *can* a woman do,

who is addressed by a man of talents inferior to her own? Must she hide her light under a bushel, purely to do credit to the man? She cannot pick and choose, as men can. She has only her negative. . . . [Women] must encourage Men of Sense only. . . . If the taste of the age, among the Men, is not Dress, Equipage, and Foppery? Is the cultivation of the mind any part of their study? The men, in short, are sunk, my dear; and the Women but barely swim.[23]

Jane Austen was at first struck by the consistent power of this novel's portraiture. Then as the book began to free her from James's and Henry's male viewpoints, its tepid feminist viewpoints no doubt impressed her. To be sure, 'feminist' is an anachronism here: the word was not used before about 1850, and no one in Jane Austen's time had anything like an enlightened twentieth-century conception of women's rights, or was clearly conscious of the possibility of taking deliberate political action for women; we may use 'feminist' in this context though to refer to something simpler – the view that since women are just as intelligent as men, every aspect of their status in society is important. Certainly every major writer of the eighteenth century since Addison's *Spectator* in 1711 had contributed to the disputes over woman's social, legal, and economic status.[24] Richardson has little to say of the economic constraints upon women, or of their lack of legal rights which concerned Mary Wollstonecraft; but he is, at least, concerned with the male use of language to keep women subservient, and he makes Harriet complain that women only encourage men to misuse words. Otherwise he hedges his views: Harriet believes that women ought to be eager to please, not very studious, but 'pretty' despite the facial pits of smallpox. Yet what is unique in *Grandison* is its respectful and close attention to the mind of a young lady, a subject not exhausted in a million words.

No other book more completely pictured a young lady's mind and feelings. For this, in 1754, *Grandison* was ahead of its time. Thirty years later it had inspired dozens of novels about the ordeals of young ladies entering genteel society and had set a precedent for stories about the female consciousness. As an enthusiast, Jane at an early age was not likely to read it with dry eyes. If her sister did not understand her feeling for Richardson, Jane had an older female friend who perhaps would.

Mr Austen kept a carriage. He had two beasts with thick shanks and ropy tails to pull it, and one day he drove to Ashe rectory with its arched doorway and pretty casements flanked by a yew hedge. He shook hands with the new Rector of Ashe, Isaac Peter George Lefroy, an Oxford man of worldly, pleasant manners whose parents lived at Leghorn. His elder brother Anthony commanded the 9th Light Dragoons and had a handsome son named Tom Lefroy.

George in 1778 had married an unusual, vivacious woman of twenty-nine in Anne Brydges, who had given birth so far to three children. (Their fourth child, Ben, was born in 1791.) Because of George Lefroy's European connections and his wife's lineage and strange charm, Mrs Lefroy was known in the neighbourhood as 'Madam Lefroy'.

Cassy and Jane, when home from school, were not inclined to avoid a house with worldly occupants. They visited Madam Lefroy. One day in a quiet morning room where casements looked on lovely flower-beds, and solemn folding doors opened into a hall with a polished floor suitable for dances, Madam perhaps caught her breath. She must have considered her young visitor very intently. Twenty-six years older than the visitor, and with a dull husband and three children too small to assuage her loneliness, she was dying a real, emotional death in a small country parish. Mrs Lefroy has been misinterpreted by biographers who have not read her diaries and letters. She was an intelligent and sensitive woman who saw in Jane Austen a kindred spirit, a person of deep and excitable feelings.

Jane became her special friend. What is so interesting is the evidence that Mrs Lefroy was not subtle: she was a dramatic, impassioned woman who had a whirlwind effect on nearly everyone. She gave dances, rode donkeys, flung open her doors to institute a 'daily school of poor children', and after Dr Jenner's vaccine proved effective she inoculated 'upwards of 800' of the poor with her own hand. Her feelings outstripped or pressed at the limits of language: she used phrases such as 'irrepressible pleasure', 'no words can express the delight' and 'inexpressibly thankful'[25] to acknowledge such attentions as she had. Her personality was anchored in religion and her family, but few were likely to respond to her ardent depth of feeling.

Jane as a girl found her wholly equal to the most excessive enthusiasms and exquisite discussions, and managed to assuage this friend's need for talk. Responding to Jane, the Rector's wife became light, gossipy and simply good fun to be with. At moments in her surviving letters, Madam breaks free into interesting trivial reports about Harris Wither, or about advanced news of Mr Appletree's courtship of Miss Shepperdson, and seems not in the least disposed to condemn wild spirits. Jane's fondness for jokes hardly offended her. But it was Mrs Lefroy's responsive sympathy and her very narrow triumph over her own impulsive nature that most impressed a girl who was becoming stifled at Steventon. If Mrs Lefroy felt like shrieking aloud, she neither burned down the parish church nor offended its worshippers – they all paid homage to her after her abrupt, brutal death; she was a living example of sensibility under control. She was the sort of person who could hear ardent remarks, and then reply with good sense but without dampening enthusiasm. She differed from Mrs Austen, who had a managerial interest in ducks and chickens, since with Mrs Lefroy no elegant, imaginative comment went unheard. At Ashe rectory a girl was not brushed aside; she was urged to feel, reflect, probe into human affairs to her heart's desire without fear of being gauche, silly, or puerile. James Edward Austen, who knew her by report, believed that her 'enthusiastic eagerness of disposition'[26] won Jane, but it is clear that Mrs Lefroy also had a quieter, amused and sympathetic responsiveness which put a sensitive young person wholly at ease.

From Ashe one could get home by taking the 'short cut across the meadows and down the avenue and through the little coppice which hung to the side of the hill, and so into the lane almost close to the Rectory gate', if one followed the shortest route.[27] But Jane did not run along this route to and from Ashe *every* day, or pine for her friend as Emma does for Mrs Weston, or think of her 'in place of a parent', as Anne Elliot thinks of Lady Russell. The receptive Mrs Lefroy, hostess and teacher and saint of the poor, does not exist in fiction; but, in later years, Jane's memories of Mrs Lefroy surely helped her to understand Emma's feeling for Miss Taylor and Anne's respect for Lady Russell. Mrs Lefroy, at the moment, did not efface or supplant other relationships but she appealed to a tendency in Jane to seek out dramatic personalities – and prepared her for her own cousin, Eliza. Jane was to be fascinated by Lloyd girls, Bigg girls and others, but it would be long before she took a friend of her own age to heart. (There is no record of any friendship she made at school.) She did what Cassy did, and would have had her head 'chopped off' if Cassy's had to go. After her schooldays, she took up her mother's routine, and waited for a chance to run now and then to Madam Lefroy's. But at this point a most remarkable international lady knocked at the Austens' door.

4

━━━━━◈◈◈━━━━━

Lady from France

I am more in love than ever ... and the provoking creature takes a
thousand sly methods of making me understand he is as much *smitten*
with me, but his *allegiance* will not let him avow of it.

Eliza de Feuillide

What one means one day, you know, one may not mean the next.

Isabella Thorpe
in *Northanger Abbey*

Jane Austen had left the pictured tombs and weeping willows on
Abbey School's parlour walls for the last time, as we know now,
in December 1786, and in fact was home only a short time before
an exotic, fascinating little group reached the rectory. This party
included Mr Austen's elder sister Mrs Hancock and her married
daughter Eliza, Comtesse de Feuillide, as well as Eliza's infant son
Hastings de Feuillide. 'They all look & seem remarkably well, the
little Boy grows very fat, he is very fair & very pretty,' Mrs Austen
informed Miss Walter ten days after they arrived. Eliza as a French
countess 'is grown quite lively', she added; 'when a child we used
to think her too grave. We have borrowed a Piano-Forte, and she
plays to us every day; on Tuesday we are to have a very snug little
dance in our parlour, just our own children, nephews & nieces, (for
the two little Coopers come tomorrow) quite a family party.' Mrs
Austen's nephew and niece Edward and Jane Cooper at sixteen and
fifteen seem to have been cheerful and well mannered, and the Comtesse and her mother had the pleasure of seeing several young Austen

men too. James was then away on the Continent, and Edward also, but Henry Austen at fifteen was being prepared by his father for Oxford, and even Frank was able to get home for a few days from his naval academy. Cassandra at fourteen and Jane Austen at eleven would have been keen for the private dancing, and they must have missed Mrs Hancock and the fascinating Eliza after these ladies left in January.[1]

For Jane, with schooldays over, ensuing months at the rectory were likely to be disappointingly anticlimactic, partly because her elder brothers were being so adventurous. Men had adventures. She herself was too old for school, too young to stay away at the houses of distant relatives – and it was unlikely she could ever do what James and Edward were doing. James had set out to visit Eliza's husband at La Guienne, had become windbound at Jersey on the way to the Brittany coast, but then had reached *terra firma* and was to stay away for nearly a year, journeying in France, Spain and the Netherlands. And as Thomas Knight after leaving Magdalen had made the Grand Tour 'so indispensable for the finished gentleman', so Edward, heir of the Knights of Kent, went to the Continent in lieu of a university education and became part of that 'Neufchâtel set' of young Englishmen abroad who included Sir Henry Campbell and the first Lord Stanley of Alderley. Even Cassandra may have been absent for weeks, in the spring and summer of 1787, since she was considered responsible enough to pay visits to the Cookes of Bookham and the Leigh Perrots at Bath. In any case Jane had ample time to reflect on her recent visitors, to hear what her parents said of them, and also to look ahead to Eliza's promised return for a lively Christmas season of 1787.

Mrs Philadelphia Hancock – Eliza's mother – had said farewell to her brother Mr Austen long before. As an elegant, slender woman with unswept hair, she had, at twenty-one, sailed for India and possible happiness. That voyage took eight months. In less time at Madras she met and married, in 1753, a lonely Fort David surgeon twenty years older than herself, Dr Tysoe Saul Hancock, and then moved with him to Bengal, where in December 1761 she gave birth to her only child, Bessy or Eliza. The child's godfather was Warren Hastings, Governor-General of Bengal.

Possibly Warren Hastings took Mr Austen's sister as his mistress.[2] Hastings was the most brilliant administrator who set foot in India;

his long and celebrated trial for murder, bribery, defiance and misman-agement – which lasted from the time the impeachment vote was given in the House of Commons in April 1787 until he was cleared of all charges in 1795 – exercised Sheridan and Burke and produced a mass of documents. Hastings emerges as a character of rich oppo-sites: he was a lithe, vigorous, balding man of brash temper and deep Christian faith, a restless activist who was a patient Greek and Hindu scholar free of racial prejudice and in love with India's culture, and a kindly, generous, loyal friend who was capable of befriending Dr Hancock's family honourably. Hastings set up a trust fund of £10,000 in his magnificent way later for little Eliza Hancock, who was called Elizabeth after his own stillborn daughter. But after they returned to England in 1765, Dr and Mrs Hancock ran short of ready cash. Mrs Hancock agreed that her husband might best improve their fortunes by returning alone to India, where he quietly died in 1775 without seeing his family again. Meanwhile Eliza and Mrs Hancock lived in smart lodgings in London's West End, visited the Walters in Kent and the Austens in Hampshire, and finally drifted to Ger-many, Flanders and then Paris, since poor Dr Hancock had hoped Eliza would finish her education in Europe.

In the dazzle of Parisian society Eliza glittered. At nineteen she married a well-dressed officer in the *Dragons de la Reine* named Jean Gabriel Capotte, Comte de Feuillide – whose father according to the Feuillide papers in the national archives at Paris was a merchant known as Le Sieur de Feuillide. Eliza herself says that the King had made a remarkable gift 'to Mons. de Feuillide & his heirs for ever, of 5000 Acres of land little distant from his Paternal Estate', the only drawback to this gift being that the land was 'entirely covered with Water'. But her husband was a captain in the Queen's regiment with a plausible title, and she, at nineteen, was truly Madame la Comtesse de Feuillide. It is believed that Jean Capotte confessed before his head was severed that he was a *valet* who had murdered the real Comte de Feuillide – but he had then a good reason to lie. Almost immediately obvious was his bleak poverty. Either Mrs Hancock drew upon Hastings's £10,000 trust fund (as in Eliza's immaturity she had a right to do), or she drew upon new funds from Hastings, because after her marriage Eliza's money kept the Count in style. His estate at Gaboret in Nougeret in the department of Gers supplied him poorly with funds, and though Eliza said later he was 'looked upon as the

Benefactor of a whole Province' because he drained the 5,000 acres of 'stagnant Water', the fact is that he ran up large debts in his own name and in that of his wife. In England Mr Austen at once smelled a rat and grew furious over Eliza's marriage, since he had sent his sister small sums of money and now, as a trustee of Eliza's fund, had to worry over the Count's spendthrift ways. Mrs Hancock already had drawn money unwisely from Francis Austen of Sevenoaks, who had acted as Dr Hancock's agent or attorney in England. Dr Hancock, soon before he died, had warned his wife that the attorney must have 'taken it ill that you should have drawn more money out of his hands at a time than you wanted, especially as I am so largely indebted to him'.[3] George Austen lacked faith in Mrs Hancock's judgement and felt scandalized by Eliza's marriage, but he could do nothing. He perhaps suspected his sister's relations with Warren Hastings, too, the more he thought of this topic.

'Knowing your Heart as I know it,' Mrs Hancock wrote to the Governor-General of Bengal in 1780 (by which time Warren Hastings was at the peak of his power in India), 'and being convinced that in spite of appearances it is not changed for your Friends, I cannot refuse you the satisfaction of knowing my Daughter, the only thing I take Comfort in, is in perfect health.' Actually Eliza enjoyed herself. As a comtesse married to an officer, she acted in theatricals at Versailles, saw the French King and Queen, and wrote letters to her jealous cousin Phila Walter back at Ightham Parsonage near Sevenoaks. ('Poor Eliza,' Phila Walter once told her brother, 'the gay and dissipated life she has long had so plentiful a share of has not ensur'd her friends among the worthy. . . . I always felt concerned and pitied her thoughtlessness. I have frequently looked forwards to the approaching awful period, and regretted the manner of her life, & the mistaken results of my poor aunt's intended, well-meant kindness.'[4] With a curiously trusting, confiding nature Eliza had seen too little of Phila in Kent to understand how venomous she was. Phila was to turn that venom on their mutual cousin, Jane Austen, safely behind Jane's back. But as Phila kept her jealousy of the Comtesse Eliza apparently well hidden, Eliza sent from France the most affectionate, glowing reports about *soirées* in gardens and salons of the Trianon. Eliza had a patient eye for detail that Jane Austen would admire, and a perfect fascination for clothes. Marie-Antoinette appears for example, one night, in shimmering pale green lutestring, covered with transparent silver gauze, with roses and lilacs, and as for the King of France he displays the most refulgent elegance and a minor shower of diamonds. Powder is worn in such quantities by French royalty that their 'heads in general look as if they had been dipped in a meal-tub', but it is not a bore to dance with them. 'It is the custom', Eliza explains, 'to change your partner after every dance, by which means you have [the real] comfort if you are engaged to a person disagreeable to you of knowing it is not for the whole evening, in short it is a fashion attended with so many *agréments*.'[5] By the time Jane went to assemblies, the fashion for changing partners had moved from Paris to the English provinces; it made balls more fun and gave one a chance to meet a range of men.

Eliza was not only a good comic actress but a clever writer and talker, in an age which brought the arts of letter-writing and talk to high levels. Yet she reached perfection as a flirt. Rapid and intuitive, she was a match for the heavy courtiers near Marie-Antoinette. The phlegmatic Louis xvi hardly noticed her. But his ancestor, *le Roi Soleil*, might have. In fact she was qualified for flirtation by quick perception, a fondness for drama, her rational head and an instinct for the main chance. Her husband was pleased: she could entertain the male sex. She fell in love so that gentlemen would fall in love with her, but checked herself: she was petite, innocent, spirited, playful. 'All badinage apart,' she told Phila, 'I don't think either you or I very likely to lose either our gaiety or peace of mind for any male *creature breathing*.'[6] Over in England, she visited spas and seaside resorts with the interest of a young Bengal tiger – observant but not especially hungry – among flocks of bemused long-nosed sheep. She carried pug dogs as little stage-props, juggled many beaux, and quoted as a sensible woman a favourite maxim for nightly action:

> If weak women go astray,
> Their stars are more at fault than they.

With typical generosity, Eliza advised poor Phila Walter – a clergyman's daughter in the arid wastes of Kent – in affairs of the heart and tried to offer that unfortunate cousin the most candid examples of proper feeling and behaviour. Phila regarded her letters as depraved but at least saved them, and a short time ago one could lift them out of a trunk in a Hampshire attic to find traces of the cousin Jane Austen knew and loved. Here are materials that take us closer to the making of *Northanger Abbey*. Here is Eliza talking to 'dear Phillida' about acting and about the nice Austens, about 'your Aunt and *Puggy*' (Eliza's latest dog), about Louisa, Lydia, Captain and Mrs Churchill and a demand to 'let me have a full and particular account of all your *Flirtations*'.[7] 'I want of all things a description of his person,' Eliza asks about Phila's latest suitor, 'is he tall or short, fair or brown, and particularly are his eyes *black* or *blue*?' Why will Phila not be specific about such things? 'I was last night at a Party of about Two Hundred,' Eliza in England later notes helpfully, where there was a certain 'Colonel' as 'captivating as ever – Apropos whom should I see in Hyde Park last Sunday but the charming *Baddy* in his still more charming curricle – How my heart beat! ... To-morrow I dine with a Tunbridge Lady &CC, by the bye I am more *in Love than ever* with this &CC' although his 'allegiance' to another lady it seems crimps that gentleman's style. All in all Phila may not have loved Eliza, but among many reasons why Jane Austen loved her is that Eliza is never boring. She laughs at herself, discusses seriously the charms of a religious life in a nunnery, 'I can believe it *sometimes* is that of Happiness, as some good Nuns who wanted me to increase the Sisterhood once endeavoured to persuade me,' and then tosses off four lines from Pope's *Eloisa to Abelard* to illustrate her point.[8] Very few people whom Jane Austen met expressed themselves with more style, grace and amused intelligence.

When her style was temporarily impaired by a pregnancy, Eliza had crossed over to England and given birth to her son Hastings on 25 June 1786. She lived with her mother and the baby in pleasant lodgings at Orchard Street in London, and did not miss the Comte, who was later to share a house with his mistress in Paris. She met Phila, who told one of her brothers that the visit was enjoyable despite Eliza's 'dissipated' life. Then, after visiting the Austens, she planned to return to their homely, pleasant rectory for theatricals in the Christmas season of 1787 when both James and Henry would be there. Mrs Hancock would join her. 'They go', Phila noted with envy, 'at Xmas to Steventon and mean to act a play *Which is the Man?* and *Bon Ton*. My uncle's barn is fitting up quite like a theatre, & all the young folks are to take their part.'[9] Even before Christmas Eliza was persuaded to scrap *Which is the Man?* and *Bon Ton* and to rehearse with the Austens a saucy play called *The Wonder! A Woman Keeps a Secret* by Mrs Centlivre. Meanwhile she tried very hard to entice Phila to join her at the Austen rectory.

'You know,' she told Phila Walter on 16 November 1787,

> we have long projected *acting* this Christmas in Hampshire. . . . I imme-diately thought of you and am commissioned by my Aunt Austen and her whole Family [to] assure you how very happy you will make them as well as myself. . . . As to any diffidence in regard to succeeding in the Parts, I beg it may be sent to *Coventry*, for I assure you they are neither long nor difficult, and I am certain you will succeed in them. Your accommodations at Steventon are the only thing my Aunt Austen and myself are uneasy about, as the House being very full of Company she says she can only promise you 'a place to hide your Head in' but I think you will not mind this inconvenience. . . . I assure you we shall have a most brilliant party and a great deal of amusement, the House full of company and frequent Balls. You cannot possibly resist so many temptations, especially when I tell you your old Friend James [Austen] is returned from France and is to be of the acting party. I shall be very impatient for your Answer and must take my leave *en attendant* as I really am hurried to Death.[10]

Phila believed it wrong to appear '*in Publick*' with male actors in sexual embraces. 'I assure you,' Eliza replied, in words that were felt to be unfit for print as late as 1942 (and that are published here for the first time),

> if you do justice to my Friendship you cannot suppose I would press You to do any thing in which You could possibly appear either in an improper or disadvantageous light. As to other Persons you men-tion, they are totally out of the question, as I would not have any thing to do with them for the world, for the society of such formal gothic beings by no means suits me; I could not help laughing at your idea of the eldest of the three [sisters] shining in any character; how was it possible My Dear Friend that you should not recollect her Time of Life and Appearance would make her appearing on such a Stage as ours the height of Absurdity?

Phila must hasten to the rectory 'provided however You could bring yourself to act', writes Eliza, 'for my Aunt Austen declares "She has not room enough for any idle young people."'

Then Eliza hits upon an obvious reason for Phila's staying away. It must be that the very prudish Mrs Walter feels that acting is immoral and base. 'Shall I', Eliza demands of Phila, be candid and tell You the Thought which has struck me on the occasion? – the insuperable objection to my proposal is, some scruples of your Mother's about acting – If this is the case I can only say it is a Pity so groundless a prejudice should be harboured in so enlightened [and] enlarged a mind. I believe I have not told you that parts allotted You were so very short that You would [have] no Time for this terrible panic which seems to have *taken possession*.[11]

That was on 23 November. Three weeks later Eliza reached Steventon without Phila. Very talkative and confiding, Eliza possibly repeated her view of Mrs Walter's 'prejudice' against acting to the Austens, since Mrs Austen had been expecting to see Phila. If Eliza at the rectory laughed over Mrs Walter's stupidity then Jane Austen at twelve perhaps joined in. It was silly to find moral objections to acting; but when Eliza began to use rehearsals of *The Wonder* to make love to both James and Henry the Austen girls must have been startled, though they loved her: she was after all affectionate, intimate, petite and stunningly dressed. Her headdress was in style, and indeed she had shopped half a day, at Tunbridge Wells, to find the right green hat with a wreath of pink roses and feathers for Phila. The hair was then crimped or frizzled about the face in a horse-shoe shape topped by a cap or cushion with 'a fabric of wire and tiffany' sprouting flowers or feathers; and a bit of wire threw out a lady's neck-handkerchief like the 'claw of a pigeon'.[12] Under some such arrangement, Eliza's wide-set eyes were sadly appealing.

Since her godfather Warren Hastings was now being attacked by Whigs in the Commons, she could appear as a victim among the Tory Austens. Everyone knew in 1787 that the best speech in the Hastings case had been given by R. B. Sheridan. In his twenties that man had written three bright comedies (and seemed an innocent, merry genius when the Austens staged his *Rivals*) but on entering Parliament he had joined the Whig chorus that was trying to extend parliamentary control of the East India Company while checking the King's power of bribery in domestic politics.[13] Sheridan had maligned the former Governor-General of Bengal in a five-and-a-half-hour speech on 7 February. Then Burke had struck at Hastings's friend and Chief Justice in the East, Sir Elijah Impey, an honourable man who had lived near the Austens at Basingstoke – and whose family was to be allied with the Austen-Leighs in marriage. Seldom, before 1787, had mud been thrown in the Commons by men who spoke more beautifully. The trial's political tones meanwhile were to affect English novel-writing and Jane Austen's art indirectly. Since the keynote of Warren Hastings's accusers was their emphasis on morality, ethics, above-board politics and responsibility, and since his defenders cited his probity and ethics, the spirit of the times favoured the 'ethical search'. People *talked* about ethics. And during the seven years of the trial Jane was encouraged to give more and more 'sense', depth and moral point to her own juvenile joke-writing or *jeux d'esprit*.

But, this Christmas, Eliza surely affected her more. Art may begin with a revised perspective or when we no longer take appearances for granted. 'Literature is born', says Simone de Beauvoir, 'when something in life goes slightly adrift.'[14] Jane had virtually seen her brothers as moral paragons, but when the rectory filled in December with Cookes, Coopers, Portals and other relatives and friends, Eliza went into action. Small Austens might be surprised and gleeful over the stir she caused. James's sophisticated Oxford friends may have laughed at Eliza – or at their amorous wounds – but it is probably true that before the rehearsals of *The Wonder* were over both James and Henry were in love with her. Tall for his age at sixteen and waiting for a chance to go up to Oxford, Henry was restless. His feeling for Eliza might have been predictable, but his behaviour was as unusual as James's neglect of clerical decorum. Jane Austen's attitude to theatricals was not that of Fanny Price in *Mansfield Park*, but she did have a chance to see how rehearsals mix with seduction. Eliza, a world-class flirt, must have been delicious to touch or hug – despite her pins – and her eyes made captains tremble.

This Christmas, the actors learned their lines and *The Wonder* opened in the Austens' cold barn on 28 December. James's 'Prologue' was spoken by the tall, ruddy Henry, gesturing across tallow lights in the expansive, muscular acting style of the day.

In Christmases of old, Henry began in his amusing voice,

> many a trick, and many a gambol neat,
> And many a frolic, helped the time to cheat.
> Nor yet in lov'd Eliza's golden reign
> Did Christmas ever claim its rites in vain.

By turning Queen Elizabeth into 'Eliza', the prologue writer had complimented the Comtesse while making love to her. Whether or not the audience sensed this, Henry struggled on. 'Imported from the

mirthful shores of France,' he said, sexually intimate dancing once
kept Britons happy. If Cromwell's Puritans banished such dancing,
wit and sensuality quickly returned with King Charles:

> But soon alas! these joys were doomed to cease,
> And mirth left Britain's Isle with sense and peace. . . .
> At length with shame each British bosom burned,
> And Charles, & loyalty & wit returned. . . .
> And age almost forgets his pains & cares,
> And whilst their sports his vigour half restore
> He counts the gambols of his youth once more.
> This night, though not with pain, at least with care
> To please our friends a trifle we prepare,
> And if in the attempt we miss our aim
> Indulgence by prescriptive right we claim.
> Then pass upon our faults a censure light,
> And smile upon the gambols of this night.[15]

A sexually overt comedy now unfolded to test everyone's nerves.
Eliza played the seductive Violante, a Lisbon beauty who falls in
love with Don Felix despite her father's plans to make her a nun.
Aiming to take to bed as many Portuguese ladies as he can, Colonel
Britton speaks up for Scottish lust. Before Felix wins his lady and
everyone joins in a country dance, the most shocking lines of the
play are spoken by Donna Isabella to her maid Inis. Here Jane Austen
heard a protest against men in phrases that suggested English Tory
patriotism. Her brother James replied in his Epilogue to Donna Isabella's point that modern women are 'inslaved', while quite missing
the point of Isabella's speech. 'But to be forc'd', Isabella cries out
about typical Portuguese marriages,

> into the Arms of an Idiot . . . who has neither Person to please the
> eye, sense to charm the ear, nor generosity to supply these defects.
> Ah, *Inis*! what pleasant lives women lead in *England*. . . . The custom
> of our country inslaves us from our very cradles, first to our parents,
> next to our husbands; and when Heaven is so kind as to rid us of
> both these, our brothers still usurp authority, and expect a blind
> obedience from us, sothat maids, wives, or widows, we are little better
> than slaves to the Tyrant Man.[16]

'Tyrant Men', James Austen admitted in an epilogue which Eliza
prettily spoke as she stepped forward on a bare stage, once upon
a time:

called themselves Creation's mighty Lords,
But thank our happier stars, those days are o'er;
And woman holds a second place no more. . . .
These men all wise, these Lords of the Creation!
To our superior rule themselves submit,
Slaves to our charms, and vassals to our wit.[17]

By this time in the barn everyone must have been thinking of brandy punch, spiced ale, gingerbread, white whip and plum pudding. Applause, cheers, kisses for the principal actress, and dancing on shining floors were likely to follow an amateur theatrical – whatever its failure or success. The girls went to bed that night perhaps wondering if it was true 'woman holds a second place no more'. But in any case, even if James's epilogue undercut the theme that some women are 'inslaved' by parents, husbands and brothers, Eliza de Feuillide had proved that one or two Austen brothers could be silly flirts. They were weak enough. By showing that the brothers were not paragons, Eliza made them more readily observable to Jane. And Eliza seemed a bold, free spirit herself. As a *comtesse* outside the social ranks, she offered Jane Austen insights into those ranks and also into the theatre itself, which in its rigorous emphasis on characters and relationships became a major inspiration to a young comic writer. As a realist who understood society, Eliza even made it a 'rule' never to buy anything that she was 'not quite sure of being able to pay for directly, never contracting debts of any kind'.[18] She really knew about money and love. What else matters as much?

She loved to act, for the same reason that she flirted. Flirtation 'makes the blood circulate', she said.[19] This dazzling cousin was to supply hints for Jane Austen's portraits of the gauche Isabella Thorpe, the worldly Mary Crawford, and even lazy Lady Bertram (with her pug). Early in 1788 the atmosphere she created at the rectory encouraged Jane to bring downstairs one or two 'jokes' of her own, and in this sense Eliza brought Jane Austen's talent before an audience.

Jane dedicated one of her first burlesque play-scenes, 'The Mystery', to Mr Austen. Along with her missing playlets or 'celebrated Comedies called "The School for Jealousy" and "The travelled Man"',[20] 'The Mystery' was a feature one memorable evening. It unfolds as a piece of nonsense in three tiny scenes, in which nobody explains what he or she is talking about. If this did not restore Mr Austen's peace, it demolished family theatricals in dialogue that mocks *all* stage-talk:

DAPHNE)	My dear Mrs Humbug how d'ye do? Oh! Fanny t'is all over.
FANNY)	Is it indeed!
MRS HUM:)	I'm very sorry to hear it.
FANNY)	Then t'was to no purpose that I . . .
DAPHNE)	None upon Earth.
MRS HUM:)	And what is to become of? . . .
DAPHNE)	Oh! that's all settled. (*whispers* MRS HUMBUG)
FANNY)	And how is it determined?
DAPHNE)	I'll tell you. (*whispers* FANNY)
MRS HUM:)	And is he to? . . .
DAPHNE)	I'll tell you all I know of the matter. (*whispers* MRS HUMBUG & FANNY)
FANNY)	Well! now I know everything about it, I'll go and dress away.
MRS HUM: DAPHNE)	And so will I. *Exeunt* [21]

At nearly the same time Jane Austen handed her mother a joke-novel or 'Tale' in seven tiny letters, no longer than modern telegrams, which end with funny abruptness in three marriages. Here she mocks epistolary romances. Mrs Austen must have enjoyed its wit. It is carefully headed:

AMELIA WEBSTER
an interesting and well written Tale
is dedicated by Permission
to
Mrs Austen
by
Her humble Servant
THE AUTHOR[22]

This too was meant for recital. The main joke, of course, was in *Amelia Webster*'s brevity. Jane's audience settled back to hear what *she* had written for their amusement and her piece was ludicrously over.

If her parents were amused, she also lightened her own spirit in these pieces. She cleared the rectory of heavy theatricals, and kept herself from taking Henry Austen's flirting rehearsals with Eliza too seriously. By writing mock novels and plays, she lifted plays and novels as *things* into the realm of the imagination, so they could be possessed and got over. Her hilarity was a response to the flirtatious excitement and emotional disorder she saw around her but it was a means, too, of digesting a long sober work such as *Sir Charles Grandison* with its troubling themes about the plight of women in a society run by men. The feminism of *Grandison* is not very funny and neither really is that in Susannah Centlivre's *The Wonder*, nor is the patriotic puffing up of the supposedly free Englishwoman in the harem of Bickerstaff's *Sultan* (soon performed by the Austens) entirely hilarious: these comic works have as undercurrents troubling themes and difficult implications for eighteenth-century women. But, by making up what appear to be the lightest, most innocent jokes, Jane Austen sailed over awkward themes. She kept her imagination free. She was to contend with the world in her own good time.

But she was not socially confident. She could not *live* in a world of jokes. Her shyness became evident to others in July 1788, when her family travelled *en masse* to Kent and there met Francis Austen, in his great old age, at the Red House fronting the street in Sevenoaks. The house gave her a good view of Kentish landscape. Possibly Jane Austen was not a total failure on this trip, if we may imagine that her readiness, or hope, or even her embarrassment appealed to a rich and affectionate old man and if Francis Austen really did commission what may be a portrait of her, the fine painting of a 'Jane Austen' of about her age once thought to be by Zoffany. What we do know is that one evening the Walters came over from Seale, with their daughter Phila, a vain girl in her twenties, and that Jane at the age of twelve wilted under Phila's snake-eyed polite stare while Cassandra talked well.

'We dined', Phila Walter wrote critically of the two Austen sisters to her brother. 'I may be allowed to give preference to the Eldest', she decided. 'The youngest (Jane) is very like her brother Henry, not at all pretty and very prim, unlike a girl of twelve.' Next day the Austens visited Seale, where Jane became even more impossible. Did she, at twelve, believe she owned Kent? Phila preferred Cassandra in 'every' respect: 'They all spent the day with us, and the more I see of Cassandra the more I admire – Jane is whimsical and affected.'

'I am sure', Eliza later told Phila Walter soothingly, 'the meeting of our Steventon Friends gave you great pleasure.'[23] As for her own reactions, Jane Austen had a chance to recover from Phila's scorn when her parents stopped at Orchard Street on their return from Kent. Eliza and Mrs Hancock were both outgoing and affectionate, but Eliza in her funny way could joke about almost anything in the world, and make almost anyone laugh at the absurdity of everything.

5

————◈————

Sexual politics: *The Loiterer*

Let the lover be killed in a duel, or lost at sea, or you may make him shoot himself, just as you please; and as for his mistress, she will of course go mad.

> letter in James and Henry Austen's *The Loiterer*,
> by 'Sophia Sentiment'

'I always find', Eliza de Feuillide once candidly told Phila Walter, 'that the most effectual mode of getting rid of temptation is to give way to it.' In Hampshire she had been tempted though she had no reason to believe her husband would approve her flirting with mere *cousins*. Henry Austen was only sixteen, and *she* was married and twenty-six. Yet he had responded well. 'Potent Love will make a Lion of a Lamb,' she knew, and Henry with a mild roar of regret over her departure from the rectory had gone up in the summer of 1788 to St John's College as a Founder's Kin (that is, he would pay no fees at Oxford). Eliza then yearned to see Oxford. It was filled with men hungering for sexual charm, as she felt, and *both* James and Henry were there. 'What can a fair one experience more delightful than *the man of her Heart*? unless indeed it be', as she later told Phila, '*teasing the Men of their Hearts*'?[1]

Oddly enough, Eliza was rather worried when finally she visited James and Henry Austen at Oxford that summer. She was sensitive to politics. Fiscal troubles of the French state had been followed by ugly rioting in Paris. The storming of the Bastille and the start of the most prodigious upheaval in modern history was, in August 1788, only eleven months away. If troubles in France continued, she believed her husband the Comte might be made to shoot at 'his own countrymen' and she felt that a French revolution, all in all, would be unpleasant. But James and Henry met her, and Canterbury Quadrangle with its Flemish grace distracted her from her worries: '[we] were very elegantly entertained by our gallant relations at St. John's, where I was mightily taken with the Garden and longed to be a *Fellow* that I might walk in it every day'. The black gowns and square caps of the men were becoming, and Henry, now six feet tall, looked 'powdered and dressed in a very *tonish* style'.[2] James's style was more muted. Though living at Oxford he had become a curate licensed to Stoke Charity near his home – and despite his saucy prologues he seemed likely to collect parishes like buttercups. (Soon after March 1790, James was to be active as curate of Overton and as Vicar of Sherborne St John in the Steventon area, and later to become absentee Vicar of Cubbington, near Warwick, and his father's curate at Deane and Steventon.)

James meant to quit Oxford for what Eliza felt were silly, clerical duties. The worst silliness about his plans was that he could never hope to be rich. But, before leaving, he aimed with Henry to launch a weekly periodical called *The Loiterer*. The Austens had political aims: James meant to purge St John's College of an old Jacobite taint, satirize the Whigs and give readers a dose of Tory loyalty – and as he was full of his project he may have mentioned his Tory journal to Eliza. She hated the politically liberal and brash Whigs who were denouncing her godfather Warren Hastings. She knew very well that the Austen were good Tory royalists, and that historically the Tories spoke for the hereditary right of the Crown and for loyal Parliaments, whereas Whigs worked for parliamentary power and limiting royal patronage. The most extreme Tories had remained pro-Stuart or Jacobite in sympathy after the Hanoverian George I came to the throne, and it is important that the Austens' St John's College had harboured some of these men. One St John's man for example donated £4,000 to Charles Stuart and tried to enlist support for the overthrow of the English King. Thomas Tooley, a Greek lecturer at the college, even joined a St John's man named Nicholas Amhurst in writing a periodical called *Terrae Filius*, which, striking at the university, called a bishop a 'mitred hog', deans 'courtiers' and Balliol 'Belial', boasted of St John's as having 'Jacobite topers', and claimed that Jesus College smelled of toasted cheese (which was perhaps true).[3] Amhurst went to prison.

But lately the Austens' college with its limes, walnuts, gravel walks and crimson chapel cushions was trying to look very harmless. The Jacobite cause was dead – and most St John's men revered King George III, and looked to him for help against Whig money, vulgarity and irreverence. Supporting the King, the clerical fellows at this college were in effect quietly Tory and outwardly unpolitical – they felt that newspapers, political gossip at the coffee-houses, lounging, loitering and the reading of novels at Oxford all contributed to a lack of esteem for the Crown and helped to focus the minds of students on the cheap, loud hullabaloo of a Whiggish Parliament. '*Clergymen*', wrote President Fry of St John's, '*have no business to concern themselves with Civil affairs.*'[4] The Austens completely agreed. And indeed Jane Austen mainly kept 'Tories' and 'Whigs' and '*Civil affairs*' out of her novels because she was politically astute. Yet the Austens burlesqued 'novel slang' and the absurdities of popular fiction[5] just as they satirized newspapers, partly because they believed that cheap popular writing was Whiggish in tendency. At the heart of every story Jane Austen wrote is a strong political message reinforced with wit, irony and comedy. She herself felt that the Whigs with their emotional rhetoric, misuse of words, casual view of the clergy, moral ignorance, inelegance and simple belief in the individual's liberty are always ludicrously wrong. The Tory who believes in King, country and a responsible and influential clergy is right. 'Nobly said! Spoken like a Tory!' she jotted as a girl in Oliver Goldsmith's *History of England*.[6] She had 'strong political opinions' as a girl, as her nephew James Edward wrote, and her political exuberance was now to be tempered under the influence of James's and Henry's *Loiterer*, so that a sound or creditable Toryism would, in time, give strength to her mature fiction. She would satirize Whiggish materialism and praise the Tory values of reason, dignity and moral responsibility in *Pride and Prejudice*, and show in *Mansfield Park* how an estate is undermined by its owner's neglect of conservative values and saved by a timid girl who feels as a Tory should about loyalty, subordination, clerical duties, the Church and English traditions. (Her Fanny Price looks at life as a Tory, though she is more than a Tory symbol.)

In 1788, James had kept his younger sister and other Austens in a wash of politics at home. In prologues to *The Wonder*, *Tom Thumb* and a Steventon 'Theatrical Exhibition' he had made fun of Cromwellians and Whig squires, while his sisters Cassandra and Jane cheered him on. He was now going to attack the typical Oxford lounger who slumps out of morning chapel to read Whiggish politics in coffee-house newspapers, and he would imply that other forms of time-wasting such as the reading of novels was bad too: *all* loitering encouraged lax talk, political gossip, rowdiness, disloyalty. He advanced his plan at Christmas in 1788, when Eliza was in France. The rectory was then a little forlorn for the girls, since Frank had just shipped out on the *Perseverance* bound for India after finishing his preliminary naval training.

But the new year was unforgettable. Back at Oxford, James Austen's first issue of *The Loiterer* was ready on Saturday, 31 January 1789. It was written mainly in the style of Addison, who was then almost *passé*. Addison's and Steele's *Spectator* had insulted women so often and clumsily that Jane Austen was to respond to that periodical in *Northanger Abbey*, but at the moment the Addisonian irony and wit served James very well. His *Loiterer* ran for sixty issues until 20 March 1790. Most of the numbers were distributed in London by Jane Austen's future publisher, Egerton, and sold for threepence at Birmingham, Bath, Reading and Oxford. Of its sixty essays James Austen wrote twenty-seven, Henry contributed to ten, and the Revd Benjamin Portal and other St John's men wrote the rest.

In the first few numbers James satirizes newspapers, or the fat, oafish 'modern Oxford Man' who keeps a diary:

> Eight to ten, Coffee-house, and lounged in the High Street. .... Jack very pleasant – says the French women have thick legs. .... Went to stable and then looked in at the coffee-house – very few drunken men. .... went back to my room in an ill humour – found a letter from my father, no money, and a great deal of advice. .... Do think fathers are the greatest *Bores* in nature....[7]

The Loiterer neglected some uproar in Paris on 14 July. But a few months later, on 7 November 1789, James printed a story which trumpets the Tory view of France and America by playing on the values of 'prejudice' and 'pride'. A Scottish infantryman fighting against Washington has good, healthy prejudices in favour of monarchy and social rank. But the soldier forgets his monarchical 'prejudices' when he sees happy Americans who lack 'all pride of distinction'. He becomes a democratic fool. With 'shackles of prejudice' gone, he sails back to Scotland to live as a democrat. He loses his beloved Ellen to a nobleman who values the sane, old, decent, social order with its hierarchies and subordination, and, with no sense of value, he marries a rich, vicious, mean-born widow, a symbol of the American ideal of a classless democracy. She brings him only misery. 'I sighed after my old prejudices,' he weeps all too late. 'Sacred prejudices! in tearing you from my bosom what have I substituted?' He should have spurned American ideas, and tried to foster his 'pride rather than renounce it'. Washington's Revolution ruined him.[8]

Cassy and Jane almost certainly read this tale and may have heard James recite it. And the American rebellion indirectly played a part in forming Jane Austen's outlook and methods, since its ideas challenged her family's Tory views of class, a state Church and limited democracy. Her novels were to explore how far liberty is consistent with a responsible Tory view of English society, even as she contributed to a family debate over 'America' in her letters. The Tory tale about America in *The Loiterer* also helped to show how abstractions such as 'pride' and 'prejudice' can give a broad, general meaning to a story's local details, and James applied that same lesson to portraiture. In his own major story, 'Cecilia', taking up two weekly numbers of *The Loiterer*, for example, he illustrated how the 'prejudices' of parents operate against the healthy and good 'sensibility' of children.[9] He told a clever tale, and began to show how moral abstractions such as 'prejudice' and 'sensibility' may help a writer to expose a character's psychological life.

For Jane at thirteen *The Loiterer* was a lively, absorbing school. Its stories slightly improved from issue to issue, and she could anticipate talking about their methods with the authors – mainly her own brothers. Perhaps because the early stories were about men, and lacked female viewpoints, she seems to have sent James a funny letter signed 'Sophia Sentiment', which he printed in No. 9. 'You', Sophia wrote with a cool boast,

> know, Sir, I am a great reader, and not to mention some hundred volumes of Novels and Plays, have, in the two last summers, actually got through all the entertaining papers of our most celebrated periodical writers. . . . My heart beat with joy when I first read your publication.

But having pumped up James's pride, she burst it. 'I am sorry, however,' added Sophia,

> but really, Sir, I think it the stupidest work of the kind I ever saw.
> . . . Only conceive, in eight papers, not one sentimental story about
> love and honour. . . . No love, and no lady.

She explained how Henry's last story would have been saved if the
hero had run off with the French nun. 'You', she told the editor,
'neglect the amusement of our sex, and have taken no more notice
of us, than if you thought, like the Turks, we had no souls.' Unless
James prints stories for ladies awfully soon,

> may your work be condemned to the pastry-cook's shop, and may
> you always continue a bachelor, and be plagued with a maiden sister
> to keep house for you.
>
> Your's, as your behave,
> SOPHIA SENTIMENT[10]

The surest evidence that Jane Austen wrote this letter is that her
brothers soon changed their plan. They wrote less and less about
Oxford, and more and more about love and the blisses and torments
of marriage – which they knew rather little about. Yet in December
1789 with a year of *The Loiterer* behind them, James and Henry Austen
returned in triumph to Steventon where sisterly applause and
laughter might reward them. Jane, at fourteen, was a very pretty
applauder and critic. Mrs Lefroy's brother Egerton Brydges at Ashe,
at about this time, found her 'fair and handsome, slight and elegant,
but with cheeks a little too full'.[11] Henry agreed Jane's blood 'spoke'
in her round cheeks. (In response perhaps to Frank's earlier teasing
Jane was now laughing over 'red cheeks' in a burlesque she was
writing.) Whether or not she played in Sheridan's *School for Scandal*,
Henry and Miss Cooper at any rate learned some witty and amusing
lines for *The Sultan* and *High Life below Stairs*. Eliza was then in France
with the Comte, who was too ill to stop the Revolution by himself.
Bravely (in view of the lack of aristocratic *soirées*) Eliza was cheerful
in revolutionary France, though she wrote to Phila for news of love
affairs in Kent.

Just as bravely, Henry survived Christmas without Eliza. He looked
very handsome and towered over his father now as he strode about
booted and coated. Habitually there were comic recitals of Austen
writings in the parlour, and this season Austens, Coopers and other

guests at least had a chance to discuss *The Loiterer*. 'First impressions', James had maintained in an early issue, 'are seldom affected by subsequent alterations.' Even if nobody challenged *that*, nothing probably was further from the truth since the whole point of *The Loiterer* as a writing exercise was that it corrected 'first impressions' from issue to issue.[12] Slowly improving, its art reached a level of competence that Mr and Mrs Austen and the children could all admire. Jane, it seems, was following James's and Henry's example by writing burlesques and improving her techniques in many very brief experiments. Even later, when she began to select two dozen of her best for little manuscript collections called *Volume the First*, *Volume the Second* and *Volume the Third*, she kept up her earlier habits. Throughout her Steventon years, she seldom worked on one thing for long. Her novels were 'gradual performances', as Henry says.[13] Further, though genius is genius, it is not miraculous. A writer is as good as the people he or she tries to please. Jane Austen at fourteen may have noticed that James and Henry at that time were ahead of her as writers: as *she* dabbled in the funny or absurd, *they* wrote ironic tales concerning major issues with comedy and moral points. For the rest of her life, she saw her first audience of readers as her capable brothers, and though Frank had a special place in her esteem she was especially stimulated by James and Henry. She never wrote at her best simply to please the Lloyd girls (who lacked a formal education) or other young friends. Her family gave her the incentive to polish, repolish, experiment, dare and attain to the finest results.

Lacking experience of women, James and Henry in their *Loiterer* stories had been relying rather heavily on Samuel Richardson. Hardly any theme in James's pieces does not also occur in *Sir Charles Grandison*, a novel discussed by most of the Austens. James's 'Cecilia' illustrates the idea (embodied in Sir Charles's dissolute father) of an interfering older generation, and James also imitates Richardson's treatment of city vanity in opposition to the ideal society of a rural estate. Marriage becomes central in James's *Loiterer*, just as *Grandison* had been concerned with eight different marriages.

The Loiterer, above all, gradually modernizes itself by moving away from Addison's *Spectator* and Johnson's *Idler* to focus on Richardson's values in *Grandison*. And this is why Jane Austen found her brothers' work so useful and inspiring. James and Henry in separate, detached stories were helping to bring the comedy of manners into the era

of political revolutions. They showed that evil may be related to vulgarity in behaviour; and that the root of social evil lies in our insensiti-
vity to other individuals. They avoided 'big scenes' and showed that
in the daily, ordinary encounter between individuals we learn what
we need to act rightly. Even with his political interests, James shows
that moral values depend on character – and that not plot, setting,
action, drama but character day by day is the key thing in any story.
It follows, for both James and Henry as it does for their sister in
her best work, that our behaviour with people close by is the true
field of 'morality', and that happiness and well-being in life depend
on the need for self-observation or clear insight into the self. Jane
Austen climbed aboard *The Loiterer*, and for sixty weeks followed
its experiments straight in the direction of her developing talents,
her passionate concerns and her future novels. Her admiration for
Sir Charles Grandison, her interest in human behaviour as encouraged
by her friendship with Mrs Lefroy, her moral intensity and love of
elegance, jokes, puns, ludicrous situations, ironic remarks and even
her delight in accurate language and in the touching impossibilities
of popular fiction were fed by her brothers' Oxford journal.

Her shyness at times divided her from James and Henry, who
were the centre of attention at Steventon, with Mrs Austen lavishing
praise on James. (Henry, who was exuberant with a 'spirit he could
not repress', was usually in everyone's perfectly good graces.) Her
brothers deserved to be popular. In contrast, she shone in no crowd
and needed the intimacy of 'family' to feel like herself. 'Shyness is
only the effect of a sense of inferiority,' she wrote when she wished
Edward Ferrars in *Sense and Sensibility* to explain his own timidity;
she herself felt rather too strongly to be always at peace with her
moods. Her moods varied more than Cassy's (as Anna Lefroy and
Elizabeth Austen were both to notice). 'What's become of all the
Shyness in the World?' she wrote later after conversing with a 'nice,
natural, openhearted, affectionate girl, with all the ready civility
which one sees in the best Children ... so unlike anything that I
was myself at her age'.[14] But this shyness, at fourteen and fifteen,
helped her to be an enquiring observer. When not with her family
or in a *tête-à-tête* with Mrs Lefroy or upstairs with Cassy, she was
likely to be a 'slight and elegant' onlooker only: but she looked with
sharp eyes. As she gained human insight, James's and Henry's stories
about love and marriage wilted in authority. But since they were

funny, she long remembered these early comic pieces by Henry in *The Loiterer*:

No. 8   Disadvantages arising from misconduct at Oxford, in a letter from *H. Homely*.

No. 20   Study of Heraldry vindicated, in a letter from *Edmund Escutcheon*.

No. 27   Thoughts on *Education* – A new System recommended.

No. 32   Peculiar danger of *Rusticus* from the attacks of a female Cousin.

No. 37   Journey from *London* in company with Sensitive.

No. 47   The indulgence of romantic ideas blamed. – History of *Aurelius*.

No. 48   History of *Aurelius* concluded.

No. 51   The Science of Physiognomy not to be depended on.

No. 57   The danger of a girl who marries a man for whom she has no affection, in a letter from *Clarissa M.*

No. 59   [with Benjamin Portal] Rules for *Prose Composition*.

Still, Henry ridiculed young ladies to make points. The good Tory, it seems, can best find the faults of Oxford gentlemen in mockingly anti-female stories about stupid girls. Henry's contributions are no more charitable than James's, but at least in No. 32, 'Peculiar danger of *Rusticus* from the attacks of a female Cousin', he laughs at himself. It seems that Henry knew about the sexual charms of the 'female cousin' from experience.

In his Rusticus letter, Henry laments that in two months a mere woman has reduced him 'from the happy state of thoughtless content' to a 'tormenting solicitude'. What had happened to Rusticus? As a country squire Rusticus – or Henry simplified – is a bachelor. 'I shot, I fished, I hunted,' he says. 'As to dancing, I know no more of it than the dead.' But one terrible day at his cousin's home when 'Miss Betsy' smiles he slobbers nervously into a cup of tea. That evening Miss Louisa (Betsy's sister) proposes a walk during which she pinches his arm 'black and blue through sheer tenderness' in her passion. He nearly chokes with embarrassment but looks into her eyes and feels his sanity ebbing, when a puff of wind blows away 'two luxuriant tresses from her beautiful chignon' and leaves her half bald. He spills half a glass of lemonade over her train; but, says Rusticus, 'she would not be provoked, for when once a woman is determined to get a husband, I find trifling obstacles will not dampen her hopes'. Sweetly trapped into marriage, he fears his lady as a 'scrophulous complaint'.[15]

Oxford men might roar at this – the scrophulous complaint might bring tears to adolescent boys' eyes – but in his later stories Henry is less juvenile and more humane and controlled; indeed, when he believed in his imagination, he could be sympathetic with characters, so much so that one sees a reason why both Jane Austen and Eliza de Feuillide admired him. Yet his and James's pieces betray a fear of young women as if female sexuality offered a terrible threat to the Oxford male. Though Jane loved her brothers and learned from their journal, this aspect of their work raised a problem, if it was less likely to vex her at fourteen than at twenty. Could a loyal sister deny that her brothers saw life clearly after all? She might be glad they loved her, but how far could she count on their having respect for her? Still, Jane was proud of them and full of merriment as she began her writing career to win their dear applause.

6

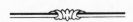

'I could die of laughter'

'No! Never shall it be said that I obliged my Father'. .... It was the Charectarestic [*sic*] of her Mind –. She was all Sensibility and Feeling.
Love and Freindship, dedicated by Jane Austen
at the age of fourteen to her cousin Eliza

Sir, the life of a parson, of a conscientious clergyman, is not easy.
Dr Johnson

Eliza – or Madame la Comtesse de Feuillide – visited Hampshire several times when her cousin Jane Austen at thirteen and fourteen was writing jokes and funny stories. The Austens were very glad to see her. Eliza arrived with her trunks and a pug dog, an infant son, and at least once with an ailing mother, for Mrs Hancock despite her suffering seems to have risked coach-travel. But the Comte was absent. Eliza hardly loved him, since ardent Love was 'not of the number' on her side, although the Comte, despite his mistress, was in a tumult of 'violent' passion for *her*. With other royalists, he was at Turin looking for a 'favourable opportunity' to overthrow the French Revolution.

Could a handful of officers conquer Paris? 'I am no politician,' Eliza admitted, 'but think they will not easily accomplish their purpose.' At Steventon, the girls seemed to her much grown and 'greatly improved' in manner and person. 'They are I think equally sensible,' the Comtesse wrote to Phila, 'and both so to a degree seldom met with, but still my heart gives the preference to Jane, whose kind partiality to me indeed requires a return of the same nature.'[1] They lived in a simple manner and put on horrid clogs with iron-ringed soles for walking in autumn paths and lanes. Outside, one heard the hallooing of hunters: neighbouring squires at Dummer and Deane kept packs of harriers five miles apart, and in the fields mud-spattered Digweeds roamed 'with a few couples of beagles'.[2] Ruddy men in hobnailed boots with poles to help them over the ditches and banks followed the baying hounds – and the men returned at noon simply to drink. In the crude neighbouring villages, as it seemed to Eliza, the Austen girls went to informal parties, but before the age of sixteen Jane had not 'come out' formally and could not go to Basingstoke balls. The autumn might have dragged if the Austen family were not 'disposed to be pleased with one another': indeed, Mrs Austen was witty and alert despite her lost front teeth, and Mr Austen seemed very well. The family's readiness to be amused, it seemed to Eliza, was plain, and she noted 'uncommon abilities' in Jane.

One subtle reason for Jane's bright jokes lay in her father, whom Eliza found congenial and comforting, sympathetic and devoted. Jane was attached to him, and Eliza 'always' tenderly loved him; after poor Mrs Hancock died of breast cancer Eliza simply sat for minutes looking into her uncle's gentle eyes until tears came to hers. 'Often do I sit and trace her Features in his, till my Heart overflows at my Eyes.'[3] Mr Austen, to judge from Eliza's letters, thought about very few topics unconnected with his family. He had broad interests, but children were the focal point, and Eliza might not have been astonished if anyone had called him *successful* as a father. His daughter was to become a classic novelist; two Austen sons became fighting admirals, one rising to the highest rank of all in the naval forces. What was Mr Austen's secret? His attitude was oddly easy and charitable so that he forgave his cousin the Revd Henry Austen of West Wickham for denying the Holy Trinity and abandoning a parish in 1780 to live in idle retirement with his wife Mary Hooker,[4] and in fact Mr Austen let Cassandra and Jane visit this erring cousin Henry at Tonbridge (where Jane met the Childrens, who were keen on theatricals). Guiding his offspring with gentle care, Mr Austen urged them to succeed. Several young Austens were aware of the shrewd, mild advice he gave, for example, when Frank sailed on the *Perseverance* for India. It revealed Mr Austen's very gentlemanly tone, firm insistence and practical sense: 'While you were at the Royal Academy,' he had told Frank in December 1788,

> the opportunities of writing to you were so frequent that I gave you my opinions and advice as the occasion arose. . . . Now you are going from us, [remember that] Prudence extends to a variety of Objects. Never any action of your life in which it will not be your interest to consider what she directs! She will teach you the proper disposal of your time and the careful management of your money, – two very important trusts. . . . Keep an exact account of all the money you receive or spend, lend none but where you are sure of an early repayment, and on no account whatever be persuaded to risk it by gaming.

'Never forget,' he had added,

> you have not upon earth a more disinterested and warm friend than,
> Your truly affectionate father,
> GEO. AUSTEN

Part of Mr Austen's secret as a supremely successful parent lay in the last line of his letter. He was able to listen with pleasure to his children; he was a yielding 'warm friend' who read Gothic novels which Jane handed him, and he might perhaps have smiled when she married herself (as she did) to fictional gentlemen in one of his parish register forms. Possibly whatever 'the girls' did was mainly right – or excusable. The other half of his secret was that he took risks for his children. Whether Eliza knew it or not, Mr Austen had used Warren Hastings's influence for Frank when Hastings was on trial for 'high crimes and misdemeanours' at Westminster Hall and was being pilloried by every Whig newspaper (though Hastings's trial was reported by Tory papers too, including the *Hampshire Chronicle*). It had been dangerous to depend on Hastings when he was on trial, or on his friends. But we may say now, for the first time, that Frank sailed on the *Perseverance* with secret extraordinary directions from Hastings's friends in the East India Company to carry out a mission beyond naval orders. He had to jump his ship at Madras. Frank later petitioned the Company for expenses home.[5] At the risk of his career and if successful to his 'making', since Company directors influenced naval promotions, Frank was to become involved in profitable shipments of silver. One of his tasks later was to carry '93 chests' from China to Madras and to the East India agents, John and Edward Iggulden at Deal; the chests held an estimated 470,000 dollars' worth of silver bullion of no concern to the Navy.[6] In the shady area of collusion and international theft the Navy was blind, or at least admirals winked when their young officers served the Company. Some of the young officers' work was nearly innocent, as when Frank let his crewmen sail the *Perseverance* after the Company had bought it, and some was less so. Frank Austen – who did not become Admiral of the Fleet for nothing – was soon to be mentioned in secret minutes kept by the directorate of the East India Company more often than anyone else of any rank in the Royal Navy. (One of those minutes, as we shall see, mentions a death that embarrassed the Company and directly involved Captain Francis Austen.)[7]

Mr Austen did not stop at seeking Hastings's help with the Company. He used James Austen's wife to secure high leverage in the Admiralty, and boosted Henry's disastrous financial schemes with a barrage of letters to London. After forgiving his cousin for denying the Trinity, Mr Austen (though not in the least evangelical) even solicited admirals of evangelical tendencies who promoted men of similar conviction.

Pressures inside the rectory were now intense. Charles at twelve was being readied for the Navy's Academy where he in turn would conciliate officers while not neglecting (as his father had told Frank) any 'opportunity' to send home extremely detailed reports, or being 'minute in what relates to yourself and your situation'[8] as his father wrote to new patrons. Jane herself wanted her brothers to succeed. She knew Frank worked for the Company and believed him honourable (as in the lax standards of the day he surely was), but she mocked the system of patronage: if dutiful brothers were pushed to captaincies, what would sisters face? Were *they* to seek advantageous marriages, or be made to feel shamed and useless if they didn't marry well? *Pride and Prejudice* arose in part from tensions inside the rectory, and she was to take up patronage explicitly in *Mansfield Park*, where the morally corrupt Henry Crawford schemes with his degenerate uncle (Admiral Crawford) to promote Fanny Price's naval brother William. Sir Thomas Bertram implies that Henry's scheming ought to make Fanny adore him: 'he has been doing *that* for your brother which I should suppose would have been almost sufficient recommendation to you, had there been no other. It is very uncertain when my interest might have got William on' (p. 316). Relations between money, courtship, social advancement and snobbery, of course, are the materials of comedy, and already Mrs Austen's good-humoured snobbery lightened the air in which Jane's 'jokes' were being written. Mrs Austen implied that because her children had Leigh blood in their veins they were superior to their friends, and she mocked the Portals. 'Old Joe Portal', a grandson of a French immigrant, had married Dorothy Hasker, 'whose parents kept a marine store and clothes shop at Portsmouth' – to Mrs Austen's mortification and amusement, she knew how 'very vulgar' merchants are. Yet Mrs Austen was pragmatic. When Joe Portal's eldest daughter by his second wife Miss Drummond married a son of her own Edward Knight, Mrs Austen later greeted a relative with, 'Well my dear, only think of old Joe Portal's daughter marrying my grandson!' She knew what could not be helped.[9]

James, for his part, took such a bold view of fathers who pester boys to keep money-accounts that he must have hoped Mr Austen would smile when he called fathers in his Oxford paper 'the greatest *Bores* in nature'.[10] But Jane Austen, even so, went further in writing jokes that are more than entertainments. She consolidated her family by getting them to laugh at their obsessions and placated them by sending them back to the more moderate Tory good sense of their ways. What distinguished her writing was its lively gaiety, irony and fun; she had an audience on hand to enjoy each twist and turn and joke, and to stimulate her. She was theatrical to please brothers who loved the stage, and they helped her to develop as an artist for without their *Loiterer* stories and eager, ready applause she might have written less in youth. The deepest purpose of her burlesques was always to ensure her freedom within the loving group of Austens, and to reconcile herself to attitudes she did not like without taking positions her family might oppose. Nothing assimilates the world better than humour that makes no case. At thirteen and fourteen she saw herself as a skimming and ignorant reader, hungry for anything funny, bizarre or affecting, quite unable to give up reading sentimental and improbable novels and unwilling to accept her brothers' hard warnings against fiction. Mainly, she cared about comic style, since she needed to impress James and Henry and knew they admired elegance and brevity. None of her burlesques goes on for very long. She also responded to the taste of her times: drawings and political cartoons had become more sophisticated, subtle and self-conscious than formerly. The rawness of Hogarth had yielded to the gentler caricatures of Thomas Rowlandson, James Sayers and the spidery line of Gillray, and sentiment was much in fashion. James Austen for instance admired the emotive scenic descriptions of the Revd William Gilpin and followed his footsteps in a tour down the River Wye. Amused by Gilpin's writings on the 'picturesque', Jane squeezed him into both *Love and Freindship* and 'The History of England'.

She learned from the polished clarity of Mme de Genlis' moral tales in French, and rather more from fashionable monthly journals. Advances in styles of the English sentence were being made not in novels but in political essays, history and short stories. She read popular histories and surely many a periodical which James and Henry brought home. In better journals such as the *Lady's Magazine*, which was read at 'Female Academies', she found the balanced Johnsonian style becoming plastic, sinewy and concise. Journals *had* to be brief – and conciseness was lacking in novelists such as Charlotte Lennox, Charlotte Smith and her beloved Fanny Burney. She found good ideas in journals, too. A serial tale called 'The Novelist' seems to have amused her especially: for example when its Oxford hero Mr Leigh fumes against novels, Miss Watson tells Leigh that he *ought* to admire a well-conducted story 'with the incidents probable, the language correct and elegant, and the characters well pourtrayed, not drawn as monsters of perfection, nor insipid beings, but rational well thinking personages'.[11]

In fact Jane avoided all monsters of perfection with great glee. In one burlesque, 'Jack and Alice', which she dedicated to her brother Frank, she turns herself into a ruddy and charming Alice Johnson who gets 'dead drunk' upon claret and flies into a tantrum when her friend Lady Williams (or Mrs Lefroy) mentions 'red cheeks'.

'But Madam,' says Alice, 'I deny that it is possible for anyone to have too great a proportion of red in their cheeks.'

Lady Williams forgives her: 'Alice', she explains, 'has many rare and charming qualities, but Sobriety is not one of them. The whole Family [of Johnsons or Austens] are indeed a sad drunken set.'

Alice passionately loves Charles Adams or Frank Austen who wears a green coat and looks for a wife who has the minor endowments of Youth, Beauty, Birth, Wit, Merit and Money. Losing him, she becomes quite drunk on claret again. Mr Austen could of course feel better over his paternal advice on gaming and drinking when reading

71

this; the story made him seem in effect all the more calmly sensible.

Or again, in 'Henry and Eliza' Jane gives Henry and the Comtesse a mad, brief fling which puts all flirtation in laughable light: her own Eliza is found as a baby by the Harcourts just as they are punishing their haymakers with a 'cudgel'; later after she steals a bank-note from them and is turned out of doors at eighteen, she sings a song fit for the lips of Eliza de Feuillide:

> Though misfortunes my footsteps may ever attend
> I hope I shall never have need of a Freind
> as an innocent Heart I shall ever preserve
> and will never from Virtue's dear boundaries swerve.

Then after easily seducing Lady Hariet's lover Henry Cecil, Eliza marries him and lives on £18,000 a year in France until, when he expires, she returns gaily to England only to be locked up in a 'Newgate'. She saws through bars, flings down her foreign fluffy clothes and her little boys – who bite off two of her fingers – and is reunited with the Harcourts when at last they recall she *is* their daughter. Finally she destroys the prison to win 'the Applause of her own Heart'.

The moral is that Eliza is nice no matter what she does. Jane dedicated that burlesque on family loyalty to her merry cousin Miss Cooper, who acted in the Austen theatricals.

In other pieces she tested out names she really liked such as Willoughby, Crawford and Dashwood, and used Emma with such affection that her parents might have wondered why they called her Jane. Emma Marlowe becomes a confidante in 'Lesley Castle', and Emma Marlow lives in 'greif' and abject tears because Mr Willmot is away at college in 'Edgar and Emma'. Poor Emma Harley is forgotten by her naval husband until he meets her on a coach in 'The Adventures of Mr. Harley', and Emma Stanhope makes cruel Sir William pay her fourteen shillings after he murders her brother – his rival in love – in 'Sir William Mountague'. Jane Austen laughs at her own brother Charles's slowness and love of horses in 'The Memoirs of Mr. Clifford', in which the hero takes a whole day to ride from Overton to Deane and possesses a fine stud and the most glittering, lovely vehicles anybody might have:

> I can only remember that he had a Coach, a Chariot, a Chaise, a Landeau, a Landeaulet, a Phaeton, a Gig, a Whiskey, an italian Chair, a Buggy, a Curricle & a wheelbarrow.

At fourteen and a half she dedicated a much more elaborate burlesque to 'Madame La Comtesse De Feuillide' as a tribute to Eliza's effervescent humour. Henry, too, lurks behind *Love and Freindship* (which was finished on 13 June, 1790) since it responds to his ironic advice in *The Loiterer* (No. 27): 'Let every Girl who seeks for happiness conquer both her feelings and her passions. Let her avoid love and friendship,' he said. 'No ridiculous principle of Consistency will draw a tear from her when parting with a Parent or a Friend. She will return the blessings of the one and the embrace of the other with a smile, and fly unreluctant to Dissipation and Frivolity.' That was funny and fine – as Henry was funny and very fine – but it mocked young girls, and *Love and Freindship* takes in other degraders of young ladies, too, in the fashionable monthlies, conduct books and stupider novels of the time. Jane Austen's Laura at fifty-five in Scotland tells her life-story in letters to the bemused daughter of her best friend Isabel. Growing up in Wales 'as the natural Daughter of a Scotch peer by an italian Opera-girl', Laura had met the fair Isabel who, like Cassandra, was sophisticated enough to give the worldliest possible advice: 'Beware of the unmeaning Luxuries of Bath & the stinking fish of Southampton.' However, Laura instantly married Edward (two minutes after meeting him) since the 'Charectarestic' of her highly attuned mind is sensibility. Edward is a very wise son. He knows that all fathers ought to be mocked and defied, so, when his father had *approved* his fiancée, he dropped her like a hot brick: 'No! Never shall it be said that I obliged my Father,' Edward had cried in his manly way. Sir Edward oddly wonders where his son picked up his habits and language:

'Where Edward in the name of wonder (said he) did you pick up this unmeaning Gibberish. You have been studying Novels I suspect.' I scorned to answer: it would have been beneath my Dignity.

When Laura's dear and tenderly affecting husband Edward takes her to his friend Augustus' home, she instantly befriends Augustus' wife Sophia forever. And as for the young husbands, Edward and Augustus show the best behaviour in greeting each other:

'My Life! my Soul!' (exclaimed the former) 'My Adorable Angel!' (replied the latter) as they flew into each other's arms. It was too pathetic for the feelings of Sophia and myself – we fainted Alternately on a Sofa.

Yet when the two couples are living together in irresponsible bliss, Laura *has* 'Love and Freindship', and henceforward their story has a curiously appealing emotional content: its characters are movingly zany, as if Faulkner's Benjy and Steinbeck's Lenny had lent them brains and kindness. One believes in married people with the minds of infant angels. When Augustus is gaoled for theft Edward simply desires to weep with him in prison as a child would, and again Laura displays the mind of a believable three- or four-year-old when she pokes her head out of a coach in London to ask people where her husband is:

> No sooner had we entered Holbourn than letting down one of the Front glasses I enquired of every decent-looking person that we passed 'If they had seen my Edward'?

A story so funny would have pleased the Austens, no doubt, even if Laura had not ended sedately in Scotland – as a good Tory should – on £400 a year. *Love and Freindship* is a fine, politically reactionary spoof, but in raising the problem of depicting lifelike emotion it virtually ended Jane's burlesque-writing. It was a lesson to her. Technically the story shows that true comedy (unlike farce) arises from believable illusions and depends on an author's understanding of feeling. *Love and Freindship* ended her childhood; after this she wrote poorer confused portraits which may have amused her family less. Ahead of her lay a future of hard work, self-doubt, failures and probably routine family applause.

Her difficulties in mixing humour, conviction and feeling are evident even in 'The History of England from the reign of Henry the 4th to the death of Charles the 1st', which she finished in November 1791. For this burlesque, Cassandra made twelve funny watercolour medallions of British monarchs. The 'History' mocks popular abridgements of history such as Oliver Goldsmith's *History of England*; in the margins of the family's copy of Goldsmith Jane Austen wrote more than thirty comments – most of them not very ironic, but Catholic, and Tory.

> How much are the Poor to be pitied, & the Rich to be blamed!

> Anne should not have done so – indeed I do not believe she did.

> My dear D^r G—— I have lived long enough in the world to know that it is always so.

Unworthy because he was a Stuart I suppose – Unhappy family.

I cannot express what I feel for you!

When Goldsmith mentioned the last of the reigning Stuarts, Jane Austen wrote:

A family who were always ill used Betrayed or Neglected – whose virtues are seldom allowed while their errors are never forgotten.

('Bravo Aunt Jane,' somebody pencilled later under this, 'just my opinion of the case.')[12]

In her upstairs room with the chocolate-figured carpet she probably wept for Catholic martyrs and the English dead, and at any rate she reserved her best mockery for Protestant historians who treat death lightly, or for writers or those who do not *understand* what it is when a king, queen or saint dies. In her 'History' Jane's Richard II goes to Pomfret Castle 'where he happened to be murdered'. Of King Henry IV she writes' 'Be this as it may, he did not live for ever.' Of Henry V: 'During his reign, Lord Cobham was burnt alive, but I forget what for. ... Inspite of all of this however he died.' Of Joan of Arc: 'They should not have burnt her – but they did.' And humour disappears altogether when she declares herself 'partial to the catholic religion', and attacks Queen Elizabeth and then Queen Elizabeth's advisers for murdering the Roman Catholic Mary Queen of Scots.

Wishing for nothing but death, Mary had remained 'constant in her Religion; & prepared herself', Jane Austen maintains.

And yet could you Reader have beleived it possible that some hardened & zealous Protestants have even abused her for that Steadfastness in the Catholic Religion which reflected on her so much credit? But this is a striking proof of *their* narrow Souls & prejudiced Judgements who accuse her. She was executed in the Great Hall at Fortheringay Castle (sacred Place!) on Wednesday the 8th of February 1586 – to the everlasting Reproach of Elizabeth, her Ministers, and of England in general.[13]

The Protestant Dr Samuel Johnson had apologized for the Catholic Inquisition, and other Tories earlier in the century had venerated Mary Queen of Scots while expressing deep sympathy for the poor.

75

Jane Austen in the rectory found that her own humour was less effective when she thought of Roman Catholic fidelity and the neglected and needy in her own England, and when she did the tone of her writing became uncertain, as in this fragment which she later erased:

> We all know that many are unfortunate in their progress through the world, but we do not know all that are so. To seek them out to study their wants, & to leave them unsupplied is the duty, and ought to be the Business of Man. [And who] amidst those that perspire away their Evenings in crouded assemblies can have leisure to bestow a thought on such as sweat under the fatigue of their daily Labour.[14]

The Austens at any rate were surely touched by her 'History', because its feelings mixed oddly with its jokes. So many earlier books from Swift's *Gulliver's Travels* to Gibbon's *Decline and Fall* had attacked the English Crown by referring to the abuses of arbitrary power that Jane Austen's romantic Toryism and half-mocking sympathy for Catholic royalty could not be taken as objectionable. Her nephew was not the only one impressed by the 'strong political opinions' she had had as a girl.

Feeling and structure alike go askew in her stories of 1792. Her 'Evelyn', 'The Three Sisters' and 'Lesley Castle' all waver between farce and realism. In her best story to date, 'Catharine or The Bower', she introduces a fairly plausible Catharine or Kitty, who is bereft because her intelligent friend Cecilia Wynne has sailed for Bengal and a loveless marriage (rather as Mrs Hancock had). Left alone with her aunt, her bower and her silly friend Camilla Stanley, Kitty shrewdly comments on 'the state of Affairs in the political World' and knows that the most beautiful feature of the novel *Ethelinde* must be Mrs Charlotte Smith's vignette about Grasmere. But Kitty becomes implausible in her gauche behaviour at a ball, and the author breaks off the unfinished story. Jane Austen copied these early pieces with affection, though, into her three manuscript *Volumes*, and later was to add slight corrections as late as her thirties. Also she was to find her early work very useful: the contrast she used in 'Catharine' between a naive younger girl and a silly older one she brought into *Northanger Abbey*, and comic ideas of *Love and Freindship* (such as judging a lover by his books or defying parents with bad results) into novels from 'Elinor and Marianne' to *Mansfield Park*.

In one burlesque novel of five tiny chapters, 'Frederic and Elfrida', she had written in her high hilarious mode a tender love scene in 'Chapter the Fifth' to end all love scenes. Elfrida, with the delicacy of a coal barge under full sail, flies to Frederic in order to splutter out 'in a manner truly heroick' her intention of marrying him the very next day. Frederic rises to the occasion in a very tender reply: 'Damme Elfrida *you* may be married tomorrow but *I* wont.' This answer is too much for the delicate constitution of Elfrida, who falls into such a terrible, ghastly series of fits 'that she had scarcely patience enough to recover from one before she fell into another', and so, as the story ends, Frederic 'on hearing of the dangerous way Elfrida was in' flies back to her '& finding her better than he had been taught to expect, was united to her Forever'.

So beautiful a story *had* to be given to a keen, warm, uncritical laughing friend, and Jane Austen dedicated it to a 'Miss Lloyd' with the following authorial letter:

> My dear Martha
> As a small testimony of the gratitude I feel for your late generosity to me in finishing my muslin Cloak, I beg leave to offer you this little production of your sincere Freind
>
> THE AUTHOR

Martha Lloyd was to be Jane Austen's closest friend, in fact. Martha was baptized at Bishopstone in Wiltshire in November 1765, and her sister Mary in May 1771. It seems surprising that Martha was ten years older than Jane, and that after years of being Jane's household companion she would at the age of sixty-two marry Frank Austen (when Frank was a widower of fifty-four) and that at last 'our humble Martha' would become Lady Austen. Her picture taken in late middle age shows a pleasant-looking woman with wide slanting eyes, full nose and mouth, and a terrier sitting in her lap. Her sister Mary, who distrusted books and read very few of them, was practical, emphatic, kindly, brusque and oddly attracted to the scholarly James Austen. Their mother was a daughter of the Hon. Charles Craven, who was a royal governor of South Carolina. After his death Martha Craven and her sister Jane had escaped from their probably quite insane mother, 'the cruel Mrs Craven', to marry two obscure country parsons, Noyes Lloyd and Thomas Fowle, and to raise four children each. At Enborne in Berkshire an epidemic of smallpox killed Mrs

Lloyd's only son, Charles, 'the apple of his mother's eye', and left Martha and Mary scarred with the pox for the rest of their lives. Fortunately the rectory at Enborne was only three-and-a-half miles from Kintbury where the Fowles lived, and it is probable that when James Austen visited his young friends the Fowles at about the age of fifteen he was introduced to the Lloyd family at Enborne. Soon Mrs Lloyd's daughter Eliza – who seems to have escaped from the smallpox lightly – married her cousin Fulwar Craven Fowle, a brother of Mr Austen's star pupil and of Cassandra Austen's special friend Thomas. By then the Austens were well acquainted with the Enborne and Kintbury area and its two congenial families, and at Mr Lloyd's death in 1789 George Austen in his kind-hearted and practical way offered Mrs Lloyd the lease of Deane parsonage a mile and a half distant from Steventon.

In the next three years Jane Austen thus had good chances to see Martha on many pleasant occasions. But when James married Anne Mathew in 1792 and 'needed a capacious house for his bride', the Lloyds were obliged to give up the parsonage and move fifteen miles away to Ibthorp House on the outskirts of Hurstbourne Tarrant. The very idea of that removal was likely to sadden Jane Austen at sixteen just because Martha Lloyd was as intimate, merry and in tune with her as a friend of her own age might be. She was not going to the world's end and Jane would spend weeks with her, laughing and sharing confidences at Ibthorp House in a room rather removed from that of Mrs Lloyd's garrulous housemate Mrs Stent – and out of doors they would have lovely wooded paths, a clear stream at their feet, walks in a valley under a long line of reassuring hills, and ladies to see or avoid such as 'the endless Debarries' nearby. But for a young person without transport fifteen miles is a long way off, and Martha's receptive, sympathetic presence at Deane would be missed. Martha was so secure in herself, so quick to appreciate a mood or take part in foolery that nothing could replace her.[15]

As the Lloyds' parting approached, Jane gave Martha's sister Mary a housewife with minikin needles and a special poem for the occasion:

> This little bag, I hope, will prove
> To be not vainly made;
> For, if you thread and needles want,
> It will afford you aid.
> And as we are about to part,

'Twill serve another end,
For, when you look upon the bag,
You'll recollect your friend.

Jan. 1792

The verses were inspired by her deepest evident need at sixteen. She wanted to keep and hold those who loved her while being free to think, feel and observe. She lived to reconcile others or to make those she loved feel better about herself, but at the same time she felt it necessary to keep in cheerful, amiable spirits about *them*.

The Lloyds had no formal schooling at all: 'No language beyond their own was thought of,' Caroline Austen recalled. 'I doubt if they could ever have assorted their words by any rules of grammar.'[16] But in contrast, few girls in England had better tutors in their fathers and brothers than Jane Austen, and none conceived of higher demands relating to female intelligence, sensibility and awareness. Few others could have matched the knowledge of Europe she gained through her cousin Eliza and her own brother James, and few other clerical families were more involved with the West and East Indies, national politics and a notorious parliamentary trial of the day than Jane's own. She knew as much literature as any sixteen-year-old then or since. She had joined herself to some of the greatest writers of the century such as Defoe, Richardson, Fielding and Sterne, who instead of imposing older fictional forms on their subjects had looked as she did in burlesques and stories for new ways to let their subjects grow out of the forms they experimented with. She had assimilated much artistic technique and human understanding in her funny 'jokes'.

But her childhood was past. Her brothers were leaving home; Edward and James were married. Jane could go to balls at sixteen, and just for that reason Mary and Martha must have seemed a blessing to her since other young people in Hampshire could resent a girl who seemed too full of Oxford and fancy French ideas. Other girls might see in Jane Austen a rather odd fish.

Part Two

HEAD AND HEART

7

━━━━━◦≫⟨⟨◦━━━━━

After midnight

This is the season of happiness.
                                                    Sense and Sensibility

When the felicities of rapid motion have once been, though slightly,
felt – it must be a very heavy set which does not ask for more.
                                                                    Emma

To enjoy a ball and see and taste all one can it helps to be light,
bright, carefree and superficial for a whole evening. People who
see the surfaces of things see a great deal. Jane Austen had learned
from her cousin Eliza de Feuillide's temperament that good observers
have hard hearts: the Comtesse flirted coolly at Bath or Margate
(where, however, there were too few '*agreeables*') and then carried
back exact and amusing details to Steventon or reported them to
catty Phila Walter. Jane Austen loved Eliza partly for her funny
reports, and the Comtesse defended both Jane and Cassandra when
Phila complained that Jane was 'not at all pretty'. Eliza wrote that
they were 'two of the prettiest girls in England' who, as perfect beauties, were of course gaining 'hearts by dozens'.[1]

It seems that Cassandra, with her natural, pleasing manners and
pretty features, touched a naval heart or two in her aquatic excursions
off Portsmouth, after Charles began at the Academy there in 1791.
Meanwhile with a hungry, eager, hopeful temperament her sister

wanted to know about the Angel Inn at Basingstoke where the patroness at subscription balls introduced girls to grocers' sons. But we hear little of dances until, late in 1792, Jane's social life is active and hectic. She nearly wore out her cousin Eliza, who had to miss one dance because of fever, another because of nerves: 'a Club Ball at Basingstoke', reports Eliza, 'a private one in the neighbourhood, both of which my Cousins say were very agreeable. . . . There is to be another ball the 4th of Novr which I shall go to if I am able.'[2]

There were all sorts of balls. Corpulent guests in satin, the most high-ranking Army and naval officers, landed aristocrats, vain and immaculate 'Barts' and their wives and daughters, and children of Tory clergymen went to the formal balls at Hurstbourne Park – arriving early enough at Lord Portsmouth's home to see the relandscaped view from the south front of 'a large piece of water, which winds through the Park' and a pattern of tall beeches and oaks in the east. Other elegant balls were held by the political Chutes at The Vyne, Lord Bolton at Hackwood or Lord Dorchester at Kempshott Park and Greywell. There were also ample numbers of private balls with the Biggs at Manydown Park, Bramstons at Oakley Hall, Holders at Ashe Park (then owned by Mrs Austen's friend 'Old Joe' Portal), Terrys at Dummer, Lefroys at Ashe rectory, or indeed Austens at Steventon. If one simply wanted to dance, public assemblies in the market-towns gave one a good chance. If one wished to practise turns and the running-step with friends, all one needed was a violin or pianoforte or harpsichord, a convivial supper or tea, and a set of six people on the parlour carpet. Dance was of central importance in eighteenth-century England as it reflected a larger scheme of decorum and rules in polite society, and no student of social manners at the time would have found a public or private ball unprofitable. Henry Austen claimed his sister Jane 'was fond of dancing, and excelled in it', and she did of course make subtle and varying uses of the dance to reveal people and milieux in her fiction. 'There were twenty dances, and I danced them all, without any fatigue,' she once wrote typically. 'I am glad to find myself capable of dancing so much, and with such satisfaction. . . . I could just as well dance for a week together as for half an hour.'[3] In 1792 she might have worn through a dozen pairs of slippers and perhaps did use up four.

Engagements and weddings caused dances. Edward Austen and his wife Elizabeth Bridges entertained at Rowling in Kent, and four months after his brother's wedding James married Anne Mathew and gave parties at the old manor her parents had rented from Joe Portal at Laverstoke (about five miles from Steventon). Then late in this very year, two more weddings of great interest to the Austens were noted in the *Gentleman's Magazine*:

Dec. 3. 1792   Rev. Chas. Blackstone, fellow of Winchester Coll. to Miss Bigg, e. d. Lovelace Bigg Wither, Esq. of Manydown co. Southampton.

Dec. 11. 1792   Thomas Williams Esq., commander of H.M.'s ship Lizard to Miss Cooper, only dau. of late D^r. C. of Sunning, Berks.[4]

The marriage of Jane Austen's lively and happy cousin Jane Cooper, who had taken part so good-naturedly in the theatricals, brought Captain Thomas Williams of the *Lizard* into the family. Charles Austen was to sail with him. The slightly earlier December wedding soon took an elder Bigg girl away from Manydown, but her younger brother Harris (who used the surname Wither) and her sisters Elizabeth, Catherine and Alethea all befriended and continued to invite the Austen girls.

And they in turn dearly loved the Biggs' parties. Many of the houses visited by the Austens lay north of the rectory in a fanlike pattern – with Manydown Park at its righthand fringes. The Biggs' balls, in common with other formal large parties, were held on nights of the full moon since carriage lanterns were feeble, but one could stay over at the house and then drive home in daylight. After a carriage ride through a forested park Cassandra and Jane in their afternoon gowns would come to a brickwalled garden and a large, pleasant, squarish manor near some cedars. Skipping up the front steps of Manydown House, they would probably go at once to Alethea Bigg's room. Alethea at fifteen was an amusing girl with an eye for clothes. 'My dear Alethea,' Jane Austen once kindly told her, 'one circumstance ... I must confess has given me considerable astonishment and some alarm – your having left your best gown at Steventon.' Anyone could feel for her agony: 'I would lay any wager that you have been sorry you left it.'[5] That was in later years; at the moment Alethea was just the sort to run for the lavender water and talk about officers and boulanger dances and hair powder. Powder, at the time, was quite political. If you saw a gentleman *without* it you knew he was more or less a horrid republican, or a Foxite Whig, but men who wore it were patriots: a leftover bill for 'hair powder' in *Northanger Abbey* would show that Elinor Tilney's husband was a good Tory. Anyone who read a magazine knew that the *merveilleuses* in Paris were wearing semi-transparent chemises with pink skin-tights and a girdle under the breasts, but high waists had not yet crossed the Channel and English daughters of the gentry in 1792 wore long, full gowns with muslin or lace flounces and low necklines. If either Austen girl had missed that fashion, Alethea would have set her straight.

Dressing might be exciting. But waiting was usually not. One heard the arrival of coaches and descended carefully into throngs of chaperones, red-coated officers in silvery hair curls, gentlemen stragglers, the portly and stylish, and bewildered knots of eager young ladies. One curtseyed this way and that. There might be a tea or a light supper, along with the horrible fuss and scramble of getting oneself engaged for country dances to come, and finally one might follow the sound of violins into the brilliancy of an ornate and full ballroom. At the top of the room were musicians. Chairs and tables for the elderly and sedate might be at the bottom not far from a blazing hearth, and tiers of candles all round the room would give off a softly diffused light.

To her nervous terror, a girl might be asked to dance the minuet, or to lead and call a later dance. Rules of precedence dictated that age, marriage and social rank entitled a lady to stand up with her partner and 'lead' a set, which meant she would take her position near the violins in the row of ladies facing their gentlemen. But a host or hostess might ask a young unmarried lady to lead and call – Jane was asked to do that, and would have her Fanny Price do so. If one danced in the minuet with its grave movements forwards, backwards, sideways, many eyes watched one. Only the whitest of gloves were worn in this, the most delicately precise and subdued occasion of the evening.

But in country dances such as 'Brighton Camp' and 'Amarillis' and 'My Lady Cullen' and their like, one was a dramatic performer under critical eyes. The onlookers in the room hushed. Violins sweetly began. And then Jane Austen would step out for everybody to see. 'She was pretty – certainly pretty,' Mrs Mozley heard about this young lady who kept the brightness of youth until a few years before she died. She was slender and elegant and firm of step, 'bright' without question, 'and a good deal of colour in her face – like a doll – no, that would not give at all the idea, for she had so much expression – she was like a child, quite a child, very lively and full of humour – most amiable, most beloved'.[6] In dancing, Jane Austen, at least, like Fanny Price, had no handicaps that were not as good as graces. Two or three feet from her partner, with violins on her right at the top, she touched his gloved hand now and again, moved gracefully and lightly and gaily down the set, performed her figures, and touched her partner and spoke to him and moved towards the top again. The country dance was mannered and lively in a gentle, gracious way, with its gaiety toned down to suavity, and in the light running and slipping steps it had vitality with decorum. It was most exquisitely delightful, friendly and kind, an emblem of marriage as it should be. One was obliged to a loyal partner in a dance till the end.

Opportunities for talking were slight, but while one's limbs followed the music, one chatted or tried to do so. If one 'talked to rule' as had been the fashion at Bath assemblies, one said tiresome pleasantries; but if one said nothing a partner could be offended. Jane Austen found the talk of gentlemen at balls frustrating or dull except as it was gossipy, and some partners were perhaps mystified by her. She overcame shyness by flinging out, seeming altogether too eager to dance and perhaps to talk, and then with Tom Lefroy she flouted many conventions. Large crowds irritated her and dust from ballrooms reddened her eyes. She did not object to violins (except in a general way at concerts) but she could be hurt by loud music and paralysed by a clap of thunder outside. She developed the quickest eye for pretensions, hypocrisies, incipient and manifest adulteries, the silliness and emptiness of gentlemen who were available for balls in wartime; and yet dancing, especially in a small and friendly set, was the keenest social delight of her life. Nothing else appealed so to her body, mind and sense of aesthetic decorum and elegance. Dancers and onlookers at a ball were a community: and since everyone enjoyed a 'set', the dance might suggest the necessary and proper functioning of a larger social community. Those who always flouted its rules would show the failure and harm of wilful egotism; a dancer succeeds only when her rhythms and style are in perfect accord with the harmony of the music, and then feels no unpleasant constraint, but rather thrives and creates a share of the community's beauty by attending to the needs of the whole. The dance for Jane Austen suggested the individual's proper relation to society and the artist's functions in that society. And since no other occasion better revealed a person's attitudes to the group and to its needful conventions, the dance was an arena for the display of personality – and a key to it.

The aftermath of a Bigg ball was especially delicious. If the last set ended at 3 a.m. she might talk two hours in bed with Alethea – as she did with Martha Lloyd – till nearly dawn. They could review the ball, and marry officers to clergymen's daughters and make fat dowagers elope to Gretna Green with grooms – using real people for the story's sake – with those 'heightenings of imagination and all the laughs of playfulness which are so essential to the shades of a departed ball'.[7] Or Jane could be very, very exact. Who had danced with whom? Who was vain, ridiculous, pompous, eccentric or mad? Who besides one's bed-mate had been deliciously amiable and shockingly lovely?

With friends of nearly her own age in Catherine and Alethea, she had begun to feel wider sympathies. Her dependency on Cassy was less. 'I once thought', Jane Austen wrote this year, 'that to have what is in general called a Freind (I mean one of my own Sex to whom I might speak with less reserve than to any other person) independant of my Sister would never be an object of my wishes, but how much was I mistaken!'[8]

Yet it would be wrong to say that she valued Cassandra less, or could happily do without her. That sister took in so much at a ball, had such loving sympathy for herself, good sense and sharp eyes, knew a joke and shared what she knew. With amusement the two Austen girls noticed at dances just what most novelists missed: that land and money determined love. The sexual chase of 'matrimonial affairs' depended on wealth: no young lady who was courted at a ball remained ignorant of her suitor's income nor was he of *her* estate. Gentlemen fell in love – partly – with the assets of land. What, then, was love if it depended on whether a girl's father held land in fee simple or fee tail or whether the girl had any estate? With the charm of Cleopatra of the Nile and Helen of Troy a young lady would be less marriageable, most surely, than if she had £10,000 a year from the Navy's 5 per cent bonds.

The girls heard grave news at home in December. Eliza's husband had left Turin for Paris. And there the radical Jacobins talked of a *'révolution en Angleterre'*, while they put the French King on trial for his life.[9] The Austens shared a general sense of horror over developments; patriotic rioters were already in London's streets. Clearly when the French Assembly said it would assist those wishing to overthrow monarchies it had England in view. An old rivalry between the two nations for trade and colonies and the control of Europe was taking – on one side – a terrifyingly aggressive ideological form. On 21 January 1793, Louis XVI was beheaded at Paris, and ten days later France declared war on Britain and Holland.

Few young men in England had deeper feelings about the war than James Austen, who had married the daughter of a very good patriot – General Edward Mathew. The horrors and surprises of the most desperate war in England's history as a modern nation now lay ahead: Jane Austen was seventeen when that war began and would be past her thirty-ninth year when it ended. Still the war was far off.

But the mysteries and surprises of General Edward Mathew's character were rather nearer at hand: Jane Austen met him at Laverstoke and saw him again at Steventon. We may look at the Mathews and also at James's situation closely for the first time in a biography of Jane Austen; the material is important.

Anyone at the time might have concluded that Cassandra's and Jane's eldest brother had done well since leaving Oxford. After putting *The Loiterer* to rest he had taken up pastoral duties at Stoke Charity southwest of Steventon, and starting in March 1790 he had also begun work as curate of Overton, 'this celebrated city' as his sister Jane called it, a village on the road from Basingstoke to Andover. A mile away at Laverstoke James had met Anne Mathew, five or six years his senior. She was oddly small-boned with 'peculiarly dark and handsome eyes', tall and willowy and so extremely thin that her Indian muslin dresses, plain or beautifully sprigged with silver, were the narrowest gowns her grandchild had ever seen.[10] Her mother was the daughter of the Duke of Ancaster, Lady Jane Bertie, who

had married in St George's Chapel at Windsor one of the most promising men in the Coldstream Guards – Captain Edward Mathew. In
an old, truculent line of soldiers, Sir David Mathew, his ancestor,
was murdered by the Imbervilles with whom he had quarrelled at
Neath, and another Mathew, abandoned by his allies and without
food, medical help or other support, in the face of outflanking troops
had formed his wounded into a British square and held out to the
end at the Battle of Almanza in Spain.

If the nation honoured the military Mathews, it did so too late.
Two William Mathews had died at Antigua before they could be
invested with the knighthoods bestowed on them. With no disloyalty
to the Coldstream Guards, however, two daughters of Daniel Mathew
of Essex married into the prominent naval family of Gambier. This
meant that James Austen's wife was related by marriage to Samuel
Gambier, First Commissioner of the Navy, as well as to James Gambier (1756–1833), who in 1793 was getting ready to sail *The Defence*,
74 guns. He ran a 'praying ship' and it was after he cut through
a French line-of-battle and lost his masts that Captain Pakenham
of the *Invincible* shouted at him through a loud hailer, 'I see you
have been knocked about a good deal: never mind, Jimmy, whom
the Lord loveth he chasteneth!' Jimmy became Admiral of the Fleet
– and received so many notes from Mr Austen of Steventon on behalf
of Frank and Charles that he obviously never forgot the name Austen.

James Austen's father-in-law – Edward Mathew – had so excelled
as a Guards captain that he became first equerry to King George
III and then brigadier-general in New York, where he led part of
the infantry attack on Fort Washington. Having fought in Virginia
and New Jersey, he came home to be asked twice by the King to
be Governor of Grenada. Unfortunately, the King forgot to clear his
salary with the Treasury on the second tour of duty. In 1792 the
Mathews were being billed for 'over £11,000'[11] (the total which the
General had drawn in Grenada as legitimate salary from the Royal
Exchequer), and since the King had lost his memory they were later
billed at compound interest for all of £24,000. This they had to pay,
just after Edward Mathew died in 1805.

George III's poor memory and the Treasury demand affected not
only the lives of General and Lady Jane Mathew but those of James
Austen and his wife. James, as a clergyman, was not rich; his and
Anne's *combined* income was '300£ a year', as their daughter Anna

discovered. He had married on the assumption that £7,000 from Lady Jane's estate would be settled on his wife; half of this sum *was* indeed settled on Anne when she married James Austen in March 1792, and the remainder it was thought would be paid when the General died.

But the bill from the Royal Treasury now put James in a bad position: his wife's money would go if the bill were paid. Nine days after his wedding, his kinswoman, the Hon. Mary Leigh of Stoneleigh, had presented him with the living of Cubbington, north-east of Leamington Spa. But its stipend was tiny. (Since he could not leave Hampshire, James Austen hired a curate for Cubbington and did not visit the parish – though he apologized to the Bishop of Lichfield and Coventry.)[12] His finances therefore were precarious when his wife gave birth to her only child, Jane Anna Elizabeth, at Laverstoke on 15 April 1793.

Always called Anna, this girl was a great-niece and god-daughter to the Duke of Ancaster: she was a lively, beautiful child whose birth in 1793 made Jane Austen at the age of seventeen an aunt for the second time. (Edward's wife had already given birth to Fanny Austen in Kent on 23 January.) Whatever her brother James's financial anxieties, Jane Austen merrily inscribed her funny 'Miscellanious Morsels' to Anna when she was only six weeks old. 'To Miss Jane Anna Elizabeth Austen', wrote Jane as a proud and delighted aunt,

> MY DEAR NEICE:
> ... Trusting that you will in time be older, and that through the care of your excellent Parents, You will one day or another be able to read written hand, I dedicate to You the following Miscellanious Morsels. ... Never shall I regret the Days and Nights that have been spent in composing these Treatises for your Benefit. I am my dear Neice
> Your very Affectionate
> Aunt.

Jane dedicated these pieces, including one on 'Effects of Sensibility', very appropriately as it turned out, to the niece who was to have the keenest sense of humour in the next generation of Austens. Jane and Anna were to collaborate on an expert play for children, 'Sir Charles Grandison or The Happy Man', and to invent characters in their talk and exchange serious views on the art of writing novels 'in the two years before my marriage, and in the two or three just

91

after', as Anna wrote later, or in the years between 1812 and 1817.[13] (Anna was to marry the Revd Ben Lefroy on 8 November 1814.)

Trying to be fair as an aunt in the early 1790s, Jane inscribed her burlesque 'Scraps' to her other little niece, Fanny, at Rowling in Kent, who was to quarrel with Anna and insult the memory of Aunts Jane and Cassandra.

As a clergyman of slender means, James of course had expected help from his in-laws with the arrival of a daughter. He could not provide a dowry for little Anna, and knew indeed that his father would be hard put to lay anything aside for Cassandra or Jane. Genteel women, without money, seldom married well and usually dwindled into poorly paid servitude or dependency on relatives if they did not marry at all. Aware of Anna's prospects, the Mathews did save funds for her. But the £100 a year that they allowed was to be lost, and all but £2,000 of the capital that they intended for her was to go, too, to pay the state's cruel claim for General Mathew's salary at compound interest.

'The claim of the government', as Anna's third daughter Fanny wrote in later years, 'was a great anxiety to the Austens.' James's anxiety about money was felt by his parents and sisters especially after he moved with his little family to Deane parsonage in 1793. His dilemma soon entered into Jane Austen's depiction of the Bennets' and Dashwoods' financial circumstances: her novels have no exact parallels in life, but neither *Sense and Sensibility* nor *Pride and Prejudice* would be exactly what they are had it not been for her brother's plight. James believed that his child's future and the fate of his family at Deane were jeopardized by unjust financial circumstances that could not be put right. His father-in-law suffered over the unjust claim for salary payments he had really earned, but could do nothing to stop that claim, and in due course General Mathew – generous and full of honours, kind and crestfallen but with a bitter, stiff, dictatorial presence that frightened Cassandra and Jane in an interview that is on record – would be remembered by the creator of General Tilney. Though her novel characters are unique, family history comprised a magnificent quarry, or a rich mine, used lightly by a deft artist in her mature work.

For her the strangest person at Laverstoke was perhaps Anne's mother, Lady Jane, with her visions, her dark Spanish eyes and her mortal fear of being 'buried alive'. Jane Austen saw this superstitious woman at James's wedding and later at Laverstoke. The mother of Lady Jane's sister-in-law had been Mrs William Blunden of Basingstoke, whose story Lady Jane often told. After her maltster husband left her, Mrs Blunden drank to excess, and one day her nurse gave her a 'narcotic' to bring her out of a stupor but later found her motionless and dead white. Mrs Blunden was interred at the Chapel of the Holy Ghost, and next day some boys were whipped for saying they had heard a groan from the vault – but, at last, a sexton opened it. He was shocked to find the lid moist, and more so because the hands of the abandoned lady were 'bruised and clenched'.[14]

It seems that Mrs Blunden, recovering from a narcotic, had come awake at night in her grave and had beaten on its lid to no avail. Lady Jane took care to relate that the poor woman's bruised, motionless hands were fists.

A story of suffocation – and the sad fists – surely had no relation to Jane Austen's outward life. And yet polite society, as Jane found, was not always so delightful when one became accustomed to it and began to understand it. It was suffocating if one could not say what one felt about it. Public dances were not so pleasing if women were hard, competitive, mean, and the young men only vain or calculating. Oddly, kindness often stopped at the Austens' door and beyond it she was charmed but also disillusioned. Her gaiety of temperament conflicted with a fury and spleen, a rage of protest that she could and did express later in her letters; but as her jokes, irony and fun relieved her she found herself nearly reconciled. Probably between *Love and Freindship* and her eighteenth birthday she took the slight step of deciding to write for profit, to make stories her central effort. All of the Austens – apart from herself – were of real use, as her brothers pursued careers and Cassandra was her mother's trusted shopper, manager, custodian. Jane, however, was likely to earn little, and her wish to write for money set her on a risky course by 1793. Jokes kept her in a happy temper and she meant to be gay, free and spirited, but if she indulged her wit in longer stories and failed to amuse, what then? If she could not reconcile herself to other people in her comedies, what misery awaited her? The inward pressure upon her to write might increase and the habit of hoping for some return, or recognition, might be more complex than it could have seemed to her in 1793. Addicted to her work she would train herself to make whole fictional worlds which, as she grew older, would have to compensate for her edgy, uncomfortable feelings about real people. Cassandra was born with a calm, easy, reliable temper which pleased Edward's wife in Kent. Jane was to struggle to find methods of reconciliation and to learn her craft slowly under tension. In her quiet decision she let herself out over an abyss insofar as her daily well-being was concerned. The smart, witty remarks of her letters do not always conceal her exasperated, growing frustration with the adult world of Hampshire in wartime – or her wish not simply to ignore what she disliked. She would trust in her pen to preserve her equanimity, and her resources included her rational intelligence, her sense of paradox, her quickness to be amused and, at eighteen, a wish to be happy. She did fortify herself against setbacks and was not likely to be daunted by minor outward rebuffs. She would persist. Disappointment would feed into her creative plan, and be useful surely as a goad, but her choice of writing for money set her on another plane from other people. Her letters show an aloof coolness towards many family pieties. The joke – in Jane Austen – mediates between the world and herself, but in taking a chance with her pen as a means of resolving her disillusion or bitterness, she divorced herself from full human comfort. She was living within her family but also outside it while she looked for schemes and structures to make funny and convincing stories, but if her fictive worlds were awkward or did not work out believably her own well-being would be threatened. She fixed on the bright, polished remark in her casual letters to Cassandra, and the manuscripts of her letters show her reworking a phrase for style in the smallest details. So much concern for effect and divorce from spontaneity endangered her resilience, her ability to respond naturally to anything. Nobody on record has risked more than Jane Austen when she sought a 'voice' with which to address the public. She simply had to trust that the Austens would find her agreeable and sisterly *despite* her polished jokes and knowing airs. Yet in 1793 she had her sister's love and no particular concern for gloom in the world. She meant to meet life with all the audacity she had, and was ready to make things boil up or explode at dances, at Madam Lefroy's or the Biggs', with a confidence to meet what challenges Steventon or little friendly Ashe had to offer.

8

Love

What a revolution in her ideas!
Northanger Abbey

Let us put terror on the agenda.
Royer, at the Club des Jacobins
in Paris, on 12 Fructidor (1793)

In 1794 one could hardly sit with friends in a Hampshire parlour
or eat dinner in a rectory without hearing about the French war,
and the war was of deep interest to the maritime county. Naval sons
were being killed. News travelled slowly and the war was remote
– but Mr Austen had two sons at sea. Near the outset of the last
war – when his daughter Jane Austen was a day old – he had asked
for news of 'Jamaica', since in December 1775 British interests in
the West Indies were imperilled. That war had begun with every
hopeful promise. General Sir William Howe's 63rd Foot and 17th
Light Dragoons had suffered at Bunker's Hill but had bayoneted the
last thirty Americans at the hill near Boston and then had nearly
crushed General Washington. The Tory *Hampshire Chronicle* had kept
the county informed, for instance when it had said General Howe
was doing very well in New York where 'the behaviour of both officers
and soldiers, British and Hessians, was highly to their honour. More
determined courage and steadiness in troops have never been experienced.' Mr Austen had not been allowed to forget the American
war since clergymen were obliged by law to observe a fast for the

King's North American troops, and it may well have seemed ominous to him as it did to other Tories that France had waited to seize her chance when Britain had her worst difficulties in the colonies. By 1782 the strain on the Royal Navy had become so unbearable it could no longer protect English coasts. Liverpool harbour was raided with impunity. The kingdom had been in danger of invasion, and who could have stopped the enemy when not one but four wars were being waged against England – by the Americans to gain independence, by France to increase her trade and share of power in Europe, by Spain to recover lost possessions and by the Netherlands to assert trading rights? A fear of being put *again* into a grave strategical position was soon to be voiced in Parliament. The French were bent this time on destroying the British monarchy, and Frank and Charles were part of an often losing effort to defeat France at sea. In the next few years while *Sense and Sensibility, Pride and Prejudice* and *Northanger Abbey* were being drafted, British MPs would speak openly about England's surrender, especially after the nation lost its allies. Every ship of the Royal Navy was soon forced out of the Mediterranean.

The Austens would have been alarmed, even if Eliza's husband had *not* been in Paris. Eliza herself relied on 'private letters' until émigrés brought reports to her, and these conveyed very bad news. Rebellions in La Vendée and Lyon suggested that the Revolution was failing, but mutual jealousies between Britain and her allies and Carnot's renovations of the armed forces stiffened the French will. And, worst of all, Eliza's husband was in Paris when Robespierre's Committee of Public Safety proclaimed a law of suspects that made him liable to arrest. Then the French constitution was suspended: twenty Girondin deputies were beheaded, and Terror became a political word for the first time in Western history as sane, rational men used it as a final solution. Queen Marie-Antoinette, the Duc d'Orléans and 17,000 other men, women and children were guillotined in the fifteen months up to July 1794. The revolutionary assembly closed Paris churches, made Notre-Dame de Paris a Temple of Reason with an opera-girl to impersonate the goddess, cancelled manorial rights and introduced new systems of currency, education and law. A new French calendar unfolded as the Parisian journalist Fabre d'Eglantine renamed the winter months for example Nivôse, Pluviôse and Ventôse (the Snowy and Rainy and Windy), and yet that same journalist argued against female rights. Deputies followed d'Eglantine and

Chaumette in opposing sexual egalitarianism, so that Jacobins of Paris in effect brought to an end an earlier and serious interest of Enlightenment writers in the pathology, sexuality and physiology of women.[1]

The main drift of thought and feeling in England was now set in relation to France. Mary Wollstonecraft and Mary Hays leapt far ahead of the French Jacobins in looking into the real conditions of women. British novelists took sides in a pro-French and anti-French war of ideas fostered by the *Anti Jacobin* journal of 1797–8 and fell back on fictional stereotypes. Charlotte Smith, whom Jane Austen admired, praised the French Revolution in her novel *Desmond* (1792) and attacked it in her *Banished Man* (1794),[2] but even in *Desmond* she depressingly asks her readers to sympathize with a wife who tries to be 'a complete martyr' to a worthless husband. Praising reason, writers denounced feeling as a guide to conduct. Sentiment appeared again in English Gothic horror fiction, but the heyday of sentimentalism in the 1760s and 1770s was past. 'Sensibility' was ridiculed by both radicals and conservatives, though anti-Jacobins in cartoons, songs and stories represented it as a keynote of political radicalism. Jane Austen was to explore sensibility in a complex re-action to her times, and she would use the term 'real sensibility' in a very favourable sense. The French Revolution at least indirectly influenced her understanding of such a term, and helped her to write comic fiction enriched with leading ideas.

Yet her family were shocked by *la Terreur*, which came to Eliza's house in Paris. Her husband was staying there, in the rue de Grenelle, with his black girl Rose Clarisse and mistress 'la citoyenne Grandville', when he did two foolish things. When his friend la Marquise de Marboeuf was arrested for planting grains instead of potatoes on her estate near Meaux, he tried to bribe a man named Morel to release her. Morel worked for the Public Safety Committee; he led the Comte on, and had him arrested on 16th Pluviôse and thrown into a Conciergerie cell. Led out at the Marquise's trial, and then tried himself, Eliza's husband appears to have sworn that he was only a poor, scheming, patriotic valet who had murdered the real Comte de Feuillide – and that was his second mistake. On 4th Ventôse, or 22 February 1794, a falling blade severed his head.

Eliza heard this dreadful news by June. Shocked, bemused and ill, she went up to friends at Durham, and wrote back calmly in September, 'I find myself much the better for the northern air of which I now have made some trial, having been at this place, that is to say on the borders of Northumberland ever since July.'[3] Mr Austen perhaps felt that if the Comte had sworn he was a valet, she might have trouble claiming his estates as a murderer's widow. Had Eliza brought a villain into the Austen family? The gruesome 'valet' story may have been told often enough, as Fanny Lefroy suggests, to give Jane Austen, in any case, the idea of letting Catherine in *Northanger Abbey* imagine General Tilney as a 'murderer'.[4]

Still the Austens loved French culture. Pleading for a good understanding of France, James was now hunting with Stephen Terry, of Dummer, who was proud of his descent from French 'de la Terres'. Jane Austen danced with Stephen, and knowing the devil keeps good tunes she copied out the stirring *Marseillaise*, though she called the enemy's song 'The Marseilles March'. She also copied Stephen Storace's songs about the French Queen, 'Captivity' and 'Lamentation of Marie-Antoinette, Late Queen', and changed the last title to read 'Queen Mary's Lamentation'. If *la Terreur* upset her family, in the sanctum of her room she played what she liked.

She often played for her music teacher, George William Chard, who had an open face with a good deal of chin. It would have been wrong, perhaps, not to fall in love with a kindly teacher who became assistant organist and lay-clerk at Winchester Cathedral, and rode fourteen miles from Winchester to see her. He liked a big chord. 'I am glad', she soon wrote from Rowling in 1796, 'to hear so good an account of Mr. Charde, and only fear that my long absence may occasion his relapse. I practise every day as much as I can – I wish it were more for his sake.'[5] Her practice, at any rate, fed into her writing of fiction and helped her to think of musical 'taste'. Taste, for her, has little to do with preferring one piece to another, or with execution or musical skill. She would make Mary Bennet play demanding concertos in *Pride and Prejudice* without taste, and show Fanny Price in *Mansfield Park* to have taste though Fanny only listens to music. Taste, instead, refers to areas of allowable choice, such as tempo and tone quality,[6] and so it relates to Jane Austen's taking conventional plots for fiction and using 'taste', her concern with variables, to bring them to life. Her regular experience at a keyboard taught her one lesson above all – that the artist must not invent too much. As she favoured the same pieces, gradually changing and perfecting them, so in fiction she worked with given plot-situations and saved her invention for nice variables of character and situation that concerned her. Eliza played the harp and had elegant scores, but most of Jane's scores were theatrical in origin, crass and strong, written for the stage by good professionals such as Shield, Arnold or Dibdin. She spent hours copying them out, since printed music was costly. However, she had two minuets by a 'Mr Handell' and knew of W. A. Mozart, though she called 'Non più andrai' from *The Marriage of Figaro* the 'Duke of York's New March', and she played an air from *The Magic Flute* labelled with Mozart's name spelled correctly. She heard what were called overtures – really symphonies – by both Haydn and Mozart, at Bath concerts, but disliked the concerts because Leigh Perrots and others wanted her half-formed comments on the music, and because most people hardly attended to the music at all. She copied out a Haydn sonata, the one in C, which is Hob. xvi/35 and not one of Haydn's best, and gradually assembled a small repertoire. Soon she was favouring lilting dances such as a cotillion, a gigue, a fandango in triple time, a strathspey or two and some vigorous German waltzes, such as the Waltz Country Dances Mrs Weston enjoys after the Coles' dinner party in *Emma*. But what she especially liked were regimental marches and particularly tender love songs. As her surviving score shows, she took pains with Daniel Steibelt's 'Storm Rondo', from the Concerto in C, which probably roused Mrs Austen's chickens – and it may be the piece Marianne Dashwood plays so that Lucy Steele and Elinor can talk without being overheard. She played a stirring version of Handel's 'Hallelujah Chorus', which in the BBC's rendition of her score is enough to make one's neighbours complain, but love songs were even more important. Playing them, she reached a perfection she did not easily reach in stories that seldom leapt out of her pen in the finished, light form of her early jokes, but seemed wrong and in need of revising, new starts and a skill almost beyond her. Love songs relieved and delighted her, even soppy ones. She believed in love, and used merciless realism against a world that threatened it, though she knew that love is comic itself. In one of her music books nearly all twenty pieces are love songs, mostly about lovers who are apart. We know she played a poignant *Andante con espressione* about the return of a lover's 'bloom', years before *Persuasion*,[7] and copied out (very neatly) 'Whither Love Thy Beauties Bring' with music by Krumpholtz, and also played one of the most beautiful songs about parted lovers ever written, Christoph Willibald von Gluck's 'Che farò senza Euridice'. Having transcribed Dibdin's songs, she changed a line in 'The Soldier's Adieu', with special feeling for a brother back from India. Frank was in the Channel fleet, and she might not see him again:

> A-dieu, Adieu my only life
> My honour calls me from thee
> Sailor's
> Remember thou'rt a ~~Soldier's~~ wife
> Those tears but ill be-come thee.[8]

That would help her to think of Frank.

She had heard much of the language of wartime surely by the time Eliza returned to the spas. Eliza's casual language and self-deprecating apologies, which she seldom meant, such as 'my slovenly scrawl' and 'my brat' and 'I am the worst letter-writer in the world', had a relation to rhetoric of the press; Jane was reading the often impolite Dr Johnson, and when her letters begin in 1796 she is opposed to civil verbiage. She did not deprecate herself or at least not insincerely, though she accused herself of mild vulgarities, and in her novels she would often tinge with disapproval certain words in which rot in our civilized language begins, words such as 'civility', 'courtesy', 'politeness', 'manners' or 'etiquette'. She was becoming even more precise and committed to language. All the Austens knew that Eliza was boastful because her godfather was acquitted at his trial in April, and that now as a free man and a national hero Hastings could help the Comtesse. The trial had cost Warren Hastings all of £70,000, but his Company were awarding him an annuity of £4,000 and an interest-free loan of £50,000. Henry Austen sent him long fawning letters, gave up the Church to be an Oxford militia captain, and then ran after a girl whom Eliza heard was 'pretty wicked' and had 'black eyes that pierced through and through'.[9]

But Eliza seemed too happy to run after young Henry Austen. They had quarrelled before, and Henry had made up to her under the Austens' eyes at Steventon. Feeling free as an unfaded widow of thirty-four, she was flirting with a new passion for turning men into sheep and wives into harridans, though she usually admired the wives and understood a woman's obligation to another woman. Seldom in her letters is she unkind to any female. Yet at Tonbridge, as Phila Walter hears, Eliza de Feuillide has set two wives against each other 'so that M.ʳˢ Gallier & M.ʳˢ Johnstone have quarrelled and don't speak', and skipped away in the nick of time 'to be out of the Fray'. Eliza's 'charming Baddy' and her absurd and beseeching '&CC', with whom she is 'more in *Love than ever*', are crimped in style because they are married, and she doesn't give a faded glove for marriage. No tyrant for her: she has had enough of a French rake of a husband and doesn't care to abase herself to a jealous colonel. Some men are jealous of *her* sexual power. 'My Impulse in favour of Liberty, & disfavour of Lord & Master', she writes like a merry Jacobin, are 'irresistible'. But she knows the value of money: 'I beg you will send Capᵗⁿ Anderson to me with all speed,' she writes with a laugh, 'for his £100,000 will suit me wonderfully well.'[10]

Amused by what *she* heard, Jane drew on Eliza's exploits to write the novelette-in-letters which her nephew later called *Lady Susan*. A master of language and a fine plotter and planner, Lady Susan has Eliza's gaiety and Jane Austen's love of assertion and fondness for making things happen at nineteen and twenty. Here, letters with a witty gusto show off the stupidities of duped men, the frustrations of wives, and the hypocrisies, ruses and fibs of a master liar who has the exuberance of a young artist: indeed Lady Susan arranges scenes as a novelist might, and when things do not work out well retreats into sado-masochistic joy: 'I am doubtful whether I ought not to punish [Reginald] at once after this our reconciliation, or by marrying & teizing him for ever,' she writes delightedly. 'I must punish Frederica, & pretty severely too, for her application to Reginald; I must punish him for receiving it so favourably, & for the rest of his conduct. I must torment my Sister-in-Law for the insolent triumph of her Look.'[11] The letter is one of the few means by which a woman *can* affect society outside ballrooms in the England of the 1790s, and Lady Susan's gaiety, nerve and self-possession make her sympathetic despite her savagery. Her sexually jealous hatred of her own daughter is truthful and compelling, and few other novels are more likely to corrupt young and wholesome readers. This novel seems more subversively anti-social than critics understand, and the fact that Jane Austen never entitled or tried to print it (so far as we know) suggests that she knew how attractive she had made her masterly villainess. Lady Susan is a necessary sketch for the very likeable, assertive Elizabeth Bennet a little later. As 'the most accomplished coquette in England', she enslaves her hostess's husband as well as Miss Manwaring's suitor at Longford, and then as a blonde, soft-spoken and delectable widow in her thirties at Churchill, she tries to seduce Reginald De Courcy and another husband. She has sent Frederica to a harsh school to break her will so that the girl will marry Sir James Martin, a moneyed milksop. After trying to run away, Frederica appears at Churchill, speechless and trembling before her mother, who confines her to her room. No lady should write to an unengaged man, but Frederica shows her mettle: she slips into Reginald's hand her request that he help get Sir James banished from the house, then wins Reginald's love. In defeat Lady Susan has to marry the only man left to *her*, Sir James Martin. The author lets her off easily – with extraordinary sympathy for a female seductress. But contemporary novels have few female villains, and technically this suggests the key to Jane Austen's exercise. She has taken young Frederica's plight as a *donnée* from popular stories (read as early as Abbey School days) about innocent girls sent to hateful schools to force them to marry hateful men. By focusing on a victimizing mother instead of a victimized daughter, she heightens the sheer criminality of a woman who betrays other women, and also heightens ideas about love. 'Artlessness will never do in Love matters,' writes Lady Susan, who reduces love to seductive purpose.[12] Love, in this view, is worthless unless it ensnares with guile and art: Frederica opposes that view in her implicit feeling that love responds to candour, genuineness, artlessness – or to innate qualities.

The oblique way of telling the story has dramatized its ideas about love, and in 'Elinor and Marianne', which she wrote in 1795, Jane Austen may again have heightened her ideas about love in an epistolary frame. Two years later, however, she began to rewrite the work as the third-person narrative we know as *Sense and Sensibility* (1811), and little can be said of the missing draft other than it involved an unromantic dilemma. Elinor and Marianne can review their actions with moral awareness, but how are they to love when their chances are mockingly slight? They have little room to be assertive; they lack Dashwood money. Marianne's assertiveness is punished after her 'sensibility' thrusts her into an affair she helps to create. In 1795 the author, at any rate, has launched a new enquiry into the small scope genteel women have in society, and about the nature of love itself.

Certainly she admired Eliza's energy as a key to happiness, and felt keen to make things 'happen'. There *was* a vicious new pace in 'matrimonial affairs' in Hampshire these days: music, dancing and dress were more competitively used as men became fewer in wartime. Jane Austen believed nothing too trivial to notice (and felt nothing in her writing was too trivial either, so long as it was right). She let herself fall lightly in love with the 'beautiful dark eyes' of Edward Taylor of Bifrons on a visit to Kent, and later laughed at herself for gazing at 'the abode of Him, on whom I once fondly doated'.[13] With more assertion she inspired enough gossip to make Mrs Mitford, at Alresford, call her 'the prettiest, silliest, most affected, husband-hunting butterfly' – a report which could have startled few at Ashe.[14]

She depended on the relief and delight of flirting; and probably love affairs and music helped her to recover after shocking news of Anne Austen on 3 May 1795. Hardly two rooms at Deane parsonage were on the same level, and her brother James stood up in surprise under the low, crooked rafters at tea one evening to find Anne ill. He gave her an 'emetic', sent for a doctor and walked uneasily into his study. Twice he heard 'a loud knocking' and ran to the parsonage door to find nothing, and when help finally arrived Anne was dead. The doctor knew 'there was some internal adhesion of the liver, and he thought it had probably been ruptured and so caused her death'. At the age of two, little Anna was sent up to Steventon rectory to live with her Aunts Cassandra and Jane. Soon after this, Cassandra became engaged to Mr Austen's pupil, the Revd Thomas Fowle, who had a small living at Allington and was going overseas with Lord Craven's regiment.

Jane Austen could feel she was losing her dearest guide, her own sister. She *could not* complain of this. But if she felt the slightest pain about it, perhaps Madam Lefroy at Ashe would understand her grievance.

A gap of twenty-six years dividing her from her friend had lately seemed to shrink; Jane was an adult. And now to cross meadows and come by the coppice and see the yew hedge, so tall that it screened the house, and enter under the brick arch and then to find oneself in Ashe's 'morning-room' with an angelic woman of forty-five, was a delight so great one could hug oneself – and might hug the lady. Anne Lefroy's eloquent power of persuasion kept her short, blue-eyed husband happy, these days and later, and helped her to control her children. 'May God reward you for your duty to your Parents,' Mrs Lefroy tells her stubborn son Edward, 'and the ease and comfort you have given by following or rather yielding to my entreaties.' Or typically a few days later: 'May you go and rejoice in the dutiful resolution you have taken.' Or again, 'May God reward you for your dutiful compliance with our wishes. He will reward you, my beloved child. He whose favour is better than life has promised a peculiar blessing for filial obedience.'[15] Her children found Mrs Lefroy hard to get round, and her son-in-law was to challenge her, but her sense of humour must have prevented outright revolts. When Jane Austen saw her late in 1795 she was in high spirits over her brother Egerton, who absurdly was a militia captain. Egerton was no more likely than Henry Austen to shoot Frenchmen. Jane had seen him at Deane with his wife Elizabeth Brydges, the young niece of Thomas Barrett of Lee Priory. Sir Samuel Egerton Brydges was then – in 1786 and 1787 – a moody, self-regarding poet of twenty-five, who had heard of the Austens' playing of Mrs Centlivre's *The Wonder*, had written an epilogue to rival James's, and had insisted it be spoken at the Austens' one night. Large-eyed and delicate, with a brown lock drooping over a tragically noble forehead, he then returned to London to be near another sister – Anne Lefroy's favourite sister, Mrs Maxwell, who was burned alive. In Harley Street one night she put a poker in a fire, 'and it fell out red hot onto her dress, which being of cotton covered with a very full wide muslin apron was instantly in a blaze'. Her husband 'tore off his coat' to save her, but pretty Mrs Maxwell died of burns and shock.[16] That unsettled Egerton, who now gloomily tried to prove that he and his brother had a claim to the ancient barony of Chandos, the ducal title of which had become extinct. Egerton did show that Brydges were distantly related to the Austens and to the historian Edward Gibbon (who applauded his research from Geneva) but he never proved the Chandos claim, which the Lords Committee of Privileges denied in 1803. Mrs Lefroy's quixotic brother by then had written his novel *Mary de Clifford* (1792) and his even odder *Arthur Fitz-Albini* (1798), in which a romantic Arthur with 'hair combed negligently from the forehead' runs after a simple 'Jane' and rejects an heiress. The *Anti Jacobin* liked his novel, but Jane Austen saw it for what it was: 'We have got "Fitz-Albini,"' she sharply informed Cassandra, presently:

My father has bought it against my private wishes, for it does not quite satisfy my feelings that we should purchase the only one of Egerton's works of which his family are ashamed. ... There are many characters introduced, apparently merely to be delineated. We have not been able to recognise any of them hitherto, except Dr. and Mrs. Hey and Mr. Oxenden [of Kent], who is not very tenderly treated.[17]

Egerton was then living in Kent, where his daughter Jemima married Edward Quillinan of the 3rd Dragoon Guards, who took her to Ivy Cottage in the Lake District. Egerton set up a private press at Lee Priory in Kent, and issued, in due course, some forty books including his own in elegant small editions until it went bankrupt. Then either he or his solicitors set up such a dishonest, greedy land-sale, involving Edward Quillinan, that after Jemima's death Quillinan had to wait for years with a lawsuit hanging over his head before marrying William Wordsworth's only daughter Dora.

Egerton Brydges – though Mrs Lefroy praised him – summed up everything Jane Austen hated in the literary life. He was vain, obsessive, proud, eccentric, with talent for nothing but charming his sister; his novels had heroes who hated society because they were too sensitive to accept it. He was a caution to *her*, but she was not likely to imitate him.

He made a mockery of studying law at the Middle Temple, but, oddly enough, the Lefroys had a nephew who studied *too* seriously. In 1795 this poor young man was coming to recover at Ashe. He was Thomas Langlois Lefroy, whom Madam knew everything about. His grandfather Anthony, who was born in 1703, had gone out to Tuscany and joined the banking-house of Peter Langlois, married his partner's daughter Elizabeth, then seen the Leghorn house prosper with fine contracts for equipping ships of the Royal Navy in the Mediterranean, and as a shrewd, benign, cultivated man had befriended Thomas Hollis – the future benefactor of Harvard University in America. At eleven and nine, Anthony Lefroy's two sons were sent to England for schooling. One of these sons, George, became a parson and settled at Ashe; and the other, or Anthony Peter, went to Reeves' Academy in London to prepare for the Army, and then in 1763 was posted to the 33rd Regiment at Limerick in Ireland. Unfortunately, at twenty-three, when he should have been currying favour with rich uncles, he was secretly married by his regimental chaplain to Ann Gardner, a daughter of an Irish squire. Since old Anthony's bank at Leghorn had by then crashed, the money needed by Ensign Lefroy for the Army could only come from Langlois uncles. Would *they* approve his alliance? Worried to death in 1774, he went through a public marriage ceremony at Limerick Cathedral; happily, his uncles nodded and his wife gave birth on 8 January 1776 to Tom Lefroy – the first child born after her 'honest' wedding.

Now the uncles opened their eyes! As he himself was childless, Great-Uncle Benjamin in London seemed to live for this distant little boy. Tom must take exercise, fence, ride and study the classics. Tom did all of these things. His uncle Benjamin talked of Oxford and promised to buy him a seat in the English Parliament – as a modest aid – but Tom Lefroy went to Trinity College, Dublin. He was a dutiful boy, with such a 'kind disposition and affectionate heart' that his tutor, Dr Burrowes, later Dean of Cork, took him into the Burrowes family circle. He was also shy and reticent. To fight the shyness, he listened to debates in the Irish Parliament and then joined the College Historical Society where he spoke for the Tory and Loyalist interest. His fellows members included Wolfe Tone, Robert Emmet, Tom Moore and Lord Cloncurry, all more or less infected by romantic nationalism and revolutionary France, and, pluckily, Tom won three gold medals and was elected Auditor not long before he took his degree in 1795 – but then, suddenly, his nerves let him down, and his eyes hurt. In alarm, his uncle saw the fault in Tom's tutor, who must have pressed the boy so unbearably that he was sadly denied a fellowship. But on hearing that Tom wished to study law in London and to live with his uncle, Benjamin was pleased. First, he knew, Tom needed a rest. What better place for him than with his Aunt Anne Lefroy at Ashe, a dead-quiet rectory in the chalkhills of poor Hampshire?

Thus one day Anne Lefroy welcomed her bright young nephew. Here he was! She soon introduced him to Jane Austen, perhaps at Ashe or at the Harwoods' ball. Nearly twenty, Jane was then slender and agile and quick, a born dancer, with beautiful sparkling eyes and reddish healthy cheeks which made her less self-conscious, surely, now that she had laughed at her own red-cheeked Alice. She clearly had not been upset by C. Powlett's wish to kiss her lately, or by the antics of John Willing Warren of St John's, or even by Mr Heartley. And she knew more of flirting and finesse than the tired owner of three debating medals who stood before her.

106

You could make of Tom what you wanted and that was his lovely charm. He *seemed* superficially to be a malleable dummy, since he had been dutiful all his life – except in formal debate. He was wearily sore in his eyes, but probably alert enough to know that his 'foreign' Dublin inflections would do him little good in Hampshire; he might best keep his mouth shut. He would be twenty on 8 January; he had the foxy-coloured hair of Lefroy males, with perhaps not enough glint to be called 'Yellow Cockatoo' as a descendant was; but his portrait taken in the new year suggests he wore powder, and shows by then his clear blue, alert, oddly innocent eyes. Not so short as his blue-eyed uncle at Ashe, he was tidy and immaculate, given to well-buttoned light coats, straight and proud in bearing, with a tendency to display a hauteur caused by 'great shyness'.[18] Jane responded to his stupid silences; she admired his conservative air. She had much in common with him in outlook. A political novelist might have put them together. She had decided to fall in love, and she saw little at any time to make her regret that decision.

All the evidence suggests that her Irish lover accepted his assigned role. If 'she did all of the running', as a Lefroy descendant states, she did it only at first. We happen to know Tom came to Steventon once when she did not expect him. At the Harwoods' ball she only had to be there, patently there, in the full gaze of her tolerant and interested friends. There she was, young and fresh, pleasing and attractive and clever, with enough empathy to intuit that he talked only so much and that one did not need to press him to be witty or entertaining. Nobody forces a young man to dance and even a boulanger survives if he sits one out; and Tom chose her, chose her again, and marked her name on his card as she did his on hers, in what Cleone Knox calls 'the excessive light of the candles' with chatter on all sides. Wine at the Harwoods' flowed easily, and the rich, plentiful food with soups, fish, fowls, pies, chickens, jellies, cream, fruit and custards kept everyone else occupied. Red-faced hunters were present on these occasions – hunting something besides almond pie, since a flushed man swollen with drink might grab at a girl in the supper interlude and mutter 'Let's to bed.' There were worse scandals than 'being particular' in country dances, and who cared if people gossiped till they burst?

With Cassandra at Kintbury with the Fowles, Jane lacked her usual social 'guide' and despite herself fell deeply in love, a positive fact reflected in her long obsession with Tom Lefroy, since the trouble with her brave, apparent plan was that it worked; Tom had nothing to lose since he would be in London soon with plenty to occupy him. He had fine powers of application, and as he was capable he rose as high in his profession as any novelist could in hers, but his young friend would have no such distraction, nothing but sewing and cleaning and other housework in years ahead in the same spot where she might, or might not, amuse her family with more 'stories'. After she was 'banished into distance and indistinctness' by Tom Lefroy and became part of the oblivion of his past, she would have him to think about. She did not grip to let go easily. But, at twenty, one knows the future counts for nothing, and so she let herself go and only many years later would reflect that we women 'do not forget you, so soon as you forget us' and that this is 'our fate rather than our merit. We cannot help ourselves. We live at home, quiet, confined, and our feelings prey upon us. ... You have always a profession, pursuits, business of some sort or other, to take you back into the world immediately, and continual occupation and change soon weaken impressions.'[19] That would have been madly irrelevant to her in January 1796, when her felicity in being with him bounded her views. The Lefroys twitted *him*, and her brothers' friend Willing Warren drew *her* a picture of 'Mr. Tom Lefroy'; but she laughed off light, sympathetic mockery. Tom's reticence made him more delicious as she wore away at his reserve. In love, one's sense of society's procedures fades away, and new values fill the void. One becomes quicker to see and yet sees more narrowly. And one becomes less sensible: one holds a prize that common sense does not describe. One longs to advertise one's love, to show off the lover as part of oneself, enriched and changed by devotion, yet unique for what he is. Tom was flattered, and in his literal way he slid down love's slope. A pretty girl put him at ease; he shared with her perhaps no more than a few of his superficial likes and dislikes. On the other hand Jane was living the sweet daydreams of an Emma Woodhouse and certainly investing him with appropriate notions her mind conceived: she was to suffer over the most excessive of her imaginings months after this. Cassandra had sent her one 'scolding' letter before the Manydown ball on Tom's birthday, and she replied early next morning on 9 January 1796 – on Cassy's own birthday. (Tom was three years younger than her sister.) 'In the first place,' Jane begins,

'I hope you will live twenty-three years longer. Mr. Tom Lefroy's birthday was yesterday, so that you are very nearly of an age.' In each witty paragraph she tends to get back to him and to the topic of her slightly scandalous behaviour with him, but her wit has the double function of protecting her pride and keeping Cassandra from being alarmed. At Manydown William Heathcote had begun with Elizabeth Bigg 'and afterwards danced with her again; but *they* do not know how *to be particular*. I flatter myself, however, that they will profit by the three successive lessons which I have given them.'

Jane now stopped, to read Cassandra's latest letter in the morning post, and resumed: 'You scold me so much in the nice long letter which I have at this moment received from you, that I am almost afraid to tell you how my Irish friend and I behaved. Imagine to yourself everything most profligate and shocking in the way of dancing and sitting down together.' *That* would hold for her adviser. Her sister need not worry, need not scold her for being a fool at least. 'I *can* expose myself', Jane adds, 'only *once more*, because he leaves the country soon after next Friday, on which day we *are* to have a dance at Ashe after all.' If Cassandra could only see him! Jane is disappointed that Charles Fowle has not come to last night's ball, 'because he would have given you some description of my friend, and I think you must be impatient to hear something about him.' What is Tom like? Well, 'he is a very gentlemanlike, good-looking, pleasant young man, I assure you. But as to our having met, except at the three last balls, I cannot say much; for he is so excessively laughed at about me at Ashe, that he is ashamed to come to Steventon, and ran away when we called on Mrs. Lefroy a few days ago.'

But Tom Lefroy now calls with his cousin George. He is correct with Mrs Austen, and 'has but *one* fault,' Jane assures Cassy, in that his morning coat is too light. Tom Lefroy admires Fielding's *Tom Jones*, 'and therefore wears the same coloured clothes, I imagine, which *he* did when he was wounded'.[20]

Tom was 'wounded' enough perhaps to be on the brink of declaring himself, and might have blurted out 'I love you' if his aunt had let him; he said in old age that he had been 'in love' with Jane Austen though it was only a boy's love. Suspecting that he loved her this January, Jane sent a cloudy flight of words to Cassandra to assure her that nothing would happen, or that if something happened it wouldn't matter. She might accept Tom, but didn't care for him.

He would propose, but of course he wouldn't, or again 'I rather expect to receive an offer' but 'I shall refuse him', Jane states, 'unless he promises to give away his white coat.' Generously she gives away Mr Heartley, Warren, Powlett and Powlett's kiss to Mary Lloyd since 'I mean to confine myself in future to Mr. Tom Lefroy, for whom I do not care sixpence.'

Then just before the crucial Friday ball: 'I am to flirt my last with Tom Lefroy, and when you receive this it will be over. My tears flow as I write at the melancholy idea.'[21]

In alarm, Mrs Anne Lefroy now made Tom leave Hampshire 'as soon as possible', according to J. A. P. Lefroy. She reasoned correctly that if Uncle Benjamin barely approved the Ensign's marriage, he wouldn't forgive Tom for a less prudent marriage to a nobody. Without Langlois money, Tom's law would be futile. Uncle Benjamin counted on one Lefroy to 'haul up' seventeen other Lefroys, and he had settled on Tom. 'No young man has left our College with a higher character,' as his tutor had written, 'so much respected by all the Fellows. .... I can look with the most assured confidence to his great advancement in life.' And Benjamin agreed that Tom 'in his just ambition' was strong,[22] but if he should take a misstep he would be dropped. Tom was soon writing essays on common law and equity and rising as a barrister in Ireland, acquiring land and declining judgeships and flinging himself into an austere Protestant society. After sitting as MP for eleven years he rose so high that he could not be neglected by the Tory party, and at last, in 1852, when he was seventy-five, Lord Derby's regime made him Lord Chief Justice of Ireland.

Jane was left with her reflections in 1796: she could not see Tom again. Her flirting had been guided by her squeezing of a situation for possibilities never in it. Her pride as well as her friendship for Madam suffered, and that lady finally visited Steventon with news of Tom that was eighteen months old. Jane managed to get 'alone' on a cruel Wednesday in November 1798 with Mrs Lefroy but 'of her nephew she said nothing at all', she told Cassy; 'she did not once mention the name of [Tom] to *me*, and I was too proud to make any enquiries; but on my father's afterwards asking where he was, I learnt that he had gone back to London in his way to Ireland, where he is called to the Bar and means to practise'.[23] Tom returned from Ireland to the capital at Easter Term of 1797, when he gained permis-

110

sion to marry the daughter of Sir Jeffry Paul, Bart, who owned Silver-spring at Co. Wexford, south-west of Dublin. He was very happy with Mary Paul. Called to the Bar in 1797, he was practising law by the time Jane Austen turned twenty-five.

No doubt she wished him well. Her pride had kept her from seeing him as a baffling person with plans uninvolved with her imaginings. She had not known him well enough in candlelight to tell what he might do, or sounded herself accurately, and so two years later she was tense when his aunt spoke of him and 'too proud' to enquire. Pride kept her from self-knowledge. She was resilient enough to recover, but perplexed by her own obstinacy: her imagination leapt ahead with new plans, and a wry sense of her failings probably made her angry. In this new era of war and democracy she learned the price a woman pays for autonomy, and about the real anguish of a Marianne Dashwood. She believed in love, but in 1796 might have found it hard to say why she had behaved so abominably, so selfishly and so wilfully in public that her dearest and kindest friend at Ashe had had to send her young man away.

9

———⊰✦⊱———

Dancing in Kent

M.U.T.I.N.Y. B.R.E.W.I.N.G. A.T. S.P.I.T.H.E.A.D.
Captain Patton's telegraph, relayed from Portsdown on the south coast
to the Admiralty roof in London in twenty minutes on 13 April 1797

Though she admitted to Cassandra that her 'pride' was affected by Mrs Anne Lefroy's nephew, she at first felt that she had miscalculated. The tone of five summer letters in the year he left is light, witty. She had done nothing wrong and could not be to blame. She was far from contrite and happily able to postpone most of her self-accusations. Nobody with energy, glee and physical health beloved by a happy family goes very easily into the deep remorse of sackcloth and ashes, and certainly not in a familiar green landscape among pigs and ducks, near a practical mother and reassuring sights of a pleasant home. Her feelings after Tom Lefroy left for London were concealed behind a screen of light irony and laughter, evident even in tactical words she had sent her sister before Tom left. Of course one could not stand up with the same young man at dances without facing the neighbourhood's gossip, but *that* could not last for long. Jane in her twenties saved her pride by taking a richly amused view of her neighbours: Charles Powlett the simpleton is getting well again, she told her sister, and 'his wife is discovered to be everything that the Neighbourhood could wish her, silly & cross as well as extravagant'.[1] And if she tried to show that Tom had meant nothing to her, her self-esteem and pride soon became driving forces in her own creative work. Ten months after Tom left she began with zeal her Elizabeth Bennet and Darcy story, which she called 'First Impressions', after James had used that phrase prominently in *The Loiterer*. She was gathering social experience to see through her own Elizabeths, Catherines and Mariannes. Her mother's wit impelled her to develop her own wit, and her parents knew how to laugh at what was concise, smart and faithful to the world's absurdity. James Austen at Deane was usually troubled and captious, but his happiness seemed assured when he became engaged to Mary Lloyd at Ibthorp – Martha's sister, who was just practical and simple enough to delight him and look after his motherless little Anna. 'Had the selection been mine, you, my dear Mary, are the person I should have chosen,' Mrs Austen told Mary before the wedding. 'I look forward to you as a real comfort to me in my old age when Cassandra is gone into Shropshire, and Jane – the Lord knows where.'[2]

Cassandra might go to Ryton in Shropshire if Tom Fowle were not killed, but Providence knew if Jane Austen would go to Ireland. After dancing at Southampton in 1793, she had flirted in several of the southern counties and visited the Fowles at Elkstone rectory with its Queen Anne front and Stuart basement, and though her motive in travel was to dance and make things happen she noticed many little links, entwinings or larger and bolder mirror-like reflections that always exist between a house and its occupants. She saw elegant façades in these social travels, and in her novels she would take pains to be exact but brief and implicit too with houses, which would be strictly subordinated to human portraits. Her two abbeys, Donwell and Northanger, were to be distinct and unalike, and her Palladian Mansfield Park, Elizabethan Sotherton or homely old-fashioned Uppercross of William and Mary's reign were to differ again from her Jacobean Pemberley or from Colonel Brandon's Delaford, which Mrs Jennings in *Sense and Sensibility* describes as a typical south-county manor of Wren's period.[3] But the pressure to observe was her amused and robust interest in people. She added to her fun by looking into men's eyes, seeing how the eyes would glow or trying to make them react. Benjamin Portal's eyes were 'as handsome as ever' but no match for Edward Taylor's, and the eyes of Edward Bridges in Kent and of Samuel Blackall at Cambridge seemed to be glazed over with love. The latter, a fellow of Emmanuel College, was a huge, beefy man, a descendant of Offspring Blackall, Queen Anne's Bishop of Exeter, and a friend of Mrs Lefroy. No Cambridge college has wined and dined a man more pleased with himself. Blackall bet money on politics 'and other subjects' while reading theology, owned a pair of bowls, and on near inspection proved to be as grand as Mr Collins of *Pride and Prejudice*, who resembles him in the pontifical mode of address and the unbearable heaviness of his discussion of the lightest matters of everyday life. As a 'tall, overbearing personage', as was remembered, Blackall was once lucky enough to get a valentine from Harriet Stevenson and Jane Thackeray. When these small girls called at his rooms with Harriet's mother and Harriet leaped up to pluck her valentine from his wall, Blackall told the little girl – in a tone that must have made the walls shake – 'that without any Judge or Jury, she had condemned herself'.[4] Then he laughed heavily. If he humiliated two little girls, he lunged in serious pursuit of Miss Jane Austen. He urgently needed a wife. Mrs Lefroy on the very day she came to call after the Tom Lefroy affair 'showed me a letter which she had received from him', Jane noted after his pursuit had begun. Blackall stated in effect 'I am very sorry to hear of Mrs. Austen's illness. It would give me particular pleasure to have an opportunity of improving my acquaintance with that family – with the hope of creating to myself a nearer interest. But at present I cannot indulge any expectation of it.' Now *that* was rational and moderate, with 'less love and more sense in it than sometimes appeared before', she admitted, 'and I am very well satisfied. It will all go on exceedingly well, and decline away in a very reasonable manner.' There was no likelihood of his coming into Hampshire soon fortunately, 'and our indifference will soon be mutal, unless his regard, which appeared to spring from knowing nothing of me at first, is best supported by never seeing me.'[5] On the face of it her experience of such a man is of course absurd, but she put even minor and passing absurdities to use, and it is important that she found in her reading more than enough suggestions to 'flesh out' the egregious Blackall into something funnier, as in Mr Collins's portrait. Blackall's image blended smoothly for example with that of the Revd James Fordyce, whose sermons were to figure in *Pride and Prejudice*. In his *Character and Conduct of the Female Sex* Fordyce at Monkwell Street Chapel had given such a sermon as Blackall might give, for example, in apologizing for the female sex. Jane Austen read it with every possible delight. In honour of 'the softer sex', Fordyce had hailed the intellectual, moral and spiritual intercourse which ought to transcend sex. He asked readers to look at the nation: 'Does it not derive a considerable share of its reputation from its female pens, that eminently adorn it?' he asked. 'Look into the great machine of society as it moves before you: do not you perceive, that women are among its principal springs? Do not their characters and manners deeply affect the passions of men, the interests of education, and those domestic scenes where so much of life is passed'? Yet this was only a prelude to Fordyce's great theme that cities corrupt ladies: 'I have discovered . . . some sensible and deserving women', he wrote as he got to his main point, who 'yet appeared to forget themselves the moment they plunged into the diversions and tumults of the town! Their heads turned round in the whirl of a fashionable life; and their hearts, which went forth to their friends in the quiet of retreat, shrunk and vanished out of sight.' No woman could be safely trusted in London, he most rationally concluded, although as London's lovesick priest he was mocked in a verse satire or two of the day:

> These female sermons are so famous grown,
> That they've the fourth edition undergone;
> Their sale to fair *Londina's* not confin'd,
> Abroad they go to form the female mind.[6]

In the light of his warnings Jane surely wondered if she could keep her virtue for a night in town.

'Here I am once more,' she writes from London in the summer of 1796, 'in this scene of dissipation and vice, and I begin already to find my morals corrupted.' The main preserver of her virtue is Frank, who has shore leave and wants to go to Rowling in Kent. A day or two later with Edward in the coach they rolled past hop-gardens and orchards in Kentish fields. Here they had new reminders of war. The most troublesome mutinies were soon to occur in the Austens' two counties, at Spithead off Portsmouth and at the Nore off Sheerness, and her naval brothers knew that if sailors would not fight the nation was lost. Captain Patton's urgent telegraph 'M.U.T.I.N.Y. B.R.E.W.I.N.G. A.T. S.P.I.T.H.E.A.D.' was to reach the Admiralty roof in London on the semaphore screens twenty minutes after it left the coast, and the war accelerated the transmission of language while it created a new hunger for books of all kinds. As their carriage rolled along, the militia in Kent expected a French invasion. Publicans had so many troops calling for ale that some 'were taking down their signs'. Canterbury, despite the cathedral, had a forlorn and seedy look, 'a melancholy, dirty town, streets all so narrow, and hardly any smart shops', as it seemed at about this time to Mrs Lybbe Powys, whose daughter married a Cooper and made Mrs Austen a godmother,[7] but if one drove over windy fields and down a quaint tree-lined lane one came to a charming and quietly secluded green place. Edward's Rowling House was comfort itself: it had a plain, simple Georgian façade with upright bricks for lintels and a steep roof (and indeed still has today). From an attic window one could see over the farm to a blue bay in clear weather. Stepping from a carriage, one walked into a nook with a Jacobean fireplace, and then into a cosy sitting-room ten feet under generous ceiling-beams. Elizabeth was usually pregnant or getting over a lying-in when Jane Austen arrived, and by no means had yet spoiled her little children Fanny, Edward and 'itty Dordy'. Aided by cooks and a governess and maidservants, she kept her rooms habitable and looked fresh with a wardrobe that preserved her elegance in bed. Her father Sir Brook Bridges III had left his wife a nearby mansion, Goodnestone, as if to repay her for bearing thirteen children. Edward Austen himself was genteel and amiable, a red-faced and polite country squire whose only trouble, as it appears in his surviving letters, was that he was terrified by Bridges ladies and at last by his grown daughter Fanny. Loyal to Jane Austen while she lived, Fanny in time was to write a virulent and priggish attack on her 'Aunts Cassandra and Jane', and we may for the first time be precise about the immediate cause of Fanny's petulance. She certainly was mildly spoiled by her mother's aristocratic airs and then by Edward's literal-minded, nearly helpless dependence on his daughter's whims. But Fanny married a man considerably older than herself, Sir Edward Knatchbull, of Mersham-le-Hatch, who unfortunately had six children by his first wife. In May 1826 Sir Edward's eldest daughter by his first wife – Mary Dorothea – eloped to Gretna Green with none other than Fanny's own younger brother Edward Knight. Jane Austen's brother Edward, though a good manager of accounts, shows in his own writing that he was easily dismayed by women in his family. Anguished over the sudden elopement, he admitted it was 'unseemly' for Fanny's *brother* to marry Fanny's husband's *daughter*

116

for the relationship was nearly incestuous, and most embarrassing if not bizarre. But Sir Edward's and Fanny's mutual anger was not placated. For Fanny to become suddenly, for no fault of her own, sister-in-law *and* stepmother to the same loose young woman, Mary Dorothea! It was unthinkable but it had happened. In an unpublished letter Jane Austen's brother Edward writes of his despair in the tones of Mr Woodhouse in *Emma*: it was 'a sad rash step', Edward advises a relative in 1826, which has 'thrown us all into a sad state of agitation and distress'.[8] To make matters worse the newlyweds returned from Scotland to Steventon and were remarried in the church there, and to crown disaster with irony, Aunt Cassandra and Anna Lefroy both received and sympathized with the lovers – young Edward and Mary Dorothea.[9] To Fanny *that* was unforgivable. Sir Edward would not consent to see a daughter who by marrying his wife's brother had compromised family respectability, and Fanny, who was to become a very proper Victorian, was mortified because Aunt Cassandra of all persons had consoled the elopers. Furious especially because her aunt had thus given pain to her husband, Fanny violently accused *both* Cassandra and Jane of having been ignorant, unrefined and poorly brought up. Rivalry between the cousins and Anna's treachery in the Mary Dorothea affair did not lessen Fanny's bitterness. 'Yes my love,' Fanny assured a younger sister at last, 'it is very true that Aunt Jane from various circumstances was not so *refined* as she ought to have been for her *talent*, & if she had lived fifty years later she would have been in many ways more suitable to *our* refined tastes.' Cassandra and Jane Austen 'were not rich & the people around them with whom they chiefly mixed, were not at all high bred, or in short anything more than *mediocre* & *they* of course tho' superior in mental *powers* & *cultivation* were on the same level as far as *refinement* goes.' It was a wonder the two aunts were not more vulgar. 'But', Fanny continued with venom,

> I think in later life their intercourse with Mrs Knight (who was very fond of & kind to them) improved them both & Aunt Jane was too clever not to put aside all possible signs of 'common-ness' (if such an expression is allowable) & teach herself to be more refined, at least in intercourse with people in general. Both the Aunts (Cassandra & Jane) were brought up in the most complete ignorance of the World & its ways (I mean as to fashion &c) & if it had not been for Papa's marriage which brought them into Kent, & the kindness of Mrs Knight

who used often to have one or the other of the sisters staying with her, they would have been, tho' not less clever and agreeable in themselves, very much below par as to good Society and its ways. If you hate all this I beg yr. pardon, but I felt it at my *pen's end*, & it chose to come along & speak the truth.[10]

Even bitterness may reveal truth in a human situation, and Fanny's words point to one reason why *Pride and Prejudice* and *Sense and Sensibility* were written, for it is clear that Jane Austen met with a certain rudeness in Kent that was more subtle than the bluff, superior manner of Aunt Perrot at Bath, and the satirical bite and fine comic arrogance in her fiction respond to the society she knew most intimately and found at the fringes of her family. Fanny's latent capacity for priggishness, no doubt, had an origin in her mother's attitudes. Jane met with no grossness in Elizabeth Austen, of course, but rather with a smoothly condescending, lazy and well-bred snobbery which could take (in Jane Austen's view and from the evidence of her own letters) a smug, high-handed managerial form when the occasion demanded. But nothing could have been better for a comic artist. In Kent Jane Austen had good chances to observe snobbery, sham, pretence, airs, falsities and other little social monstrosities of attitude and behaviour in her brother's family, and, too, in Elizabeth's friends at Goodnestone and Godmersham Park. She seldom found Elizabeth's children obnoxious by fault of their mother's behaviour. But she kept up a subtle, amused warfare with Elizabeth while loving her for being Edward's elegant wife, and Cassandra never obliterated records of the warfare in her partial destruction of Jane Austen's letters. One may read the surviving letters in their biographical context to see it; and though Anna cannot wholly be trusted she is not unreasonable in recalling that some of Elizabeth's children enjoyed Aunt Jane 'indeed as a playfellow, & as a teller of stories, but they were not really fond of her' (which means no more than that they were not always at ease with her). 'I believe that their mother was not,' says Anna, 'at least that she preferred the elder sister. A little talent went a long way with the Goodnestone Bridges of that period.'[11]

Jane Austen knew all six of Lady Bridges's daughters. Fanny, Sophia and Elizabeth had rushed into early marriages with Lewis Cage, William Deedes and Edward Austen, but the younger and easier Marianne, Louisa and Harriot seemed altogether less narrow, bossy and constrained because they did *not* leap at the altar and had time to flirt and to compare young men. 'Harriot', Jane told her sister, 'goes on now as young ladies of seventeen ought to do, admired and admiring, in a much more rational way than her three elder sisters.'[12] But in September 1796 she found Fanny Cage tolerable: 'Fanny seemed as glad to see me as anybody,' Jane wrote amiably to Cassandra, 'and enquired very much after you, whom she supposed to be making your wedding-clothes. She is as handsome as ever, and somewhat fatter. We had a very pleasant day, and drank some *liqueurs*.' Lady Hales came with her unpleasant daughters, the elder and prettier of whom had kept Edward awake at backgammon. Almost bringing her Elizabeth Bennet story into being by writing terse vignettes of people as exercises, Jane had an understanding with Cassandra that only *parts* of a jokey letter could be read aloud to others, and so could remind her later, 'I read all the scraps I could of Your letter to [Sacree, the nurse]' or 'I read [to Edward] the chief of your Letter.'[13] This very important semi-privacy, depending on sisterly discretion, let her test her wit with nearly perfect freedom or fix for example the two daughters of Lady Hales in two phrases: 'Caroline is not grown coarser than she was, nor Harriet at all more delicate.'

In the mornings she had a pianoforte to practise on, and Frank found a lathe to make little Fanny a small butter-churn. After music Jane joined ladies in their Hepplewhite chairs who stitched Edward's shirts: 'I am proud to say that I am the neatest worker of the party,' she wrote with just pride. Later 'Edward & Fly' or Frank went out 'in a couple of Shooting Jackets, and came home like a couple of Bad shots, for they killed nothing at all'. Hunting was part of the gentlemanly life she disliked but for her brothers' sake *she* offered to shoot a few birds. They flew over windmill-dominated fields and into the farm. 'Delightful Sport!' she notes, 'they are just come home; Edward with his two Brace, Frank with his Two and a half. What amiable Young Men.'[14]

She made no compromise at Rowling with her hunger for books. Mr Austen had just let her add 'Miss J. Austen' to the subscribers' list above such nice names as 'Crawford' and 'Dalrymple' for Fanny Burney's *Camilla*. Even better than Miss Burney's *Evelina* and *Cecilia*, this was a novel about a Hampshire clergyman's second daughter named Camilla Tyrold, with allusions to places Jane knew such as Alton and Alresford and Winchester, and at its best it showed off a prose-style attuned to Camilla's mind, as when the heroine thinks of borrowing £200 to save her brother Lionel:

> To claim two hundred pounds of her uncle, in her own name, was out of all question. She could not, even a moment, dwell upon such a project; but how represent what she herself so little understood as the necessity of Lionel? or how ask for so large a sum, and postpone, as he desired, all explanation? She was incapable of any species of fraud, she detested even the most distant disguise.[15]

Jane Austen at twenty had not written any surviving 'serious' comic narrative of that felicity, and she could regard Fanny Burney as ahead of her, beckoning her on, as when she read the neatly polished sketches of minor characters such as that of Burney's Mrs Mitten, once a milliner's assistant:

> To be useful, she would submit to any drudgery; to become agreeable, devoted herself to any flattery. To please was her incessant desire, and her rage for popularity included every rank and class of society.[16]

That only lacked a natural cadence, or the warmth and wit of the speaking voice of the 'digressions' in Sterne's *Tristram Shandy* (a book she knew intimately and that offered some of the most valuable models of narrative tactics she found). She was to smarten Burney's balanced style much further as in the description of Mrs Bennet in the first chapter of *Pride and Prejudice*, but *Camilla*, published on 12 July and read by Jane Austen before she reached Rowling this summer, seemed enviably good. It gave order to her experiences at Rowling and seemed delicious despite an absurd plot: nothing keeps Edgar Mandlebert from marrying the heroine for five volumes except fussy Dr Marchmont – but Jane killed off *that* character it seems by noting at the end of her own edition of *Camilla*: 'Since this work went to the Press a Circumstance of some Importance to the happiness of Camilla has taken place, namely that Dr. Marchmont has at last. . . .'[17] And nothing could be funnier than Mr Dubster's summer-house when Lionel as a joke removes the ladder by which Camilla, her sister Eugenia and Mr Dubster have climbed up to be marooned at tree-top level.

As Henry Austen was taking her carriage away, Jane was to be marooned too. 'Tomorrow I shall be just like Camilla in Mr. Dubster's summer-house,' she writes home, 'for my Lionel will have taken

120

away the ladder by which I came here, or at least by which I intended to get away, and here I must stay till his return. My situation, however, is somewhat preferable to hers, for I am very happy here, though I should be glad to get home by the end of the month.'

One day Edward drove her to nearby Nackington, where 'we met Lady Sondes' picture over the Mantlepeice ... and the pictures of her three Children in an Antiroom' (there all of the little horrors were, turned into art) as well as 'Mr. Scott, Miss Fletcher, Mr. Toke, Mr. J. Toke, and the Archdeacon Lynch. Miss Fletcher and I were very thick, but I am the thinnest of the two.' Miss Fletcher in her purple muslin gown is a militia-lover, but 'she admires Camilla' and drinks no cream in her tea. Dancing in Kent delighted Jane the most: '*we* were at a Ball on Saturday I assure you', she tells her sister. It had begun with a dinner for the Cages and Austens at high, squarish Goodnestone, where Jane was guest of honour and Lady Bridges's fifth son Edward had asked her to begin the ball. For all his limp toasted-cheese manner Edward Bridges a few years later proposed, or began to propose, and she discouraged him because she couldn't offend Lady Bridges, who behaved decently with Mr Austen's portionless daughter. 'I wish you may be able to accept Lady Bridges's invitation, tho' *I* could not her son Edward's,' Jane urged Cassandra later; 'she is a nice Woman'. Lady Bridges 'could only be kind and amiable, give me good-humoured smiles & make friendly enquiries'.[18] This evening Edward took her gloved hand in his, then genial Lewis Cage stood up with Harriot, Frank danced with Louisa, and Fanny Cage followed with her partner George. Harriot and Louisa so admired Frank in his blue naval uniform, she may have recalled the girls when she wrote of the adolescent Musgroves with Wentworth in *Persuasion*. Elizabeth played a country dance, Lady Bridges another, and Miss Finch did 'the Boulangeries'. It was a friendly set. Out in the Channel sailors were lashed to death for indiscipline, a hard war dragged on, and Jane at Goodnestone was only a modest guest in pretty satin slippers, high-waisted gown and auburn curls with her hair piled up under a cap with a feather. (Later she believed the cap too '*nidgety*' but kept its silver bands when she changed her cocky, black military feather for a coquelicot.) In a dance depending on family goodwill and pleasantness she found an unrushed, polite group sensitive to the past and respecting their heritage, enclosed and safeguarded but giving a temper to Kentish life. Here was a bedrock of value which the enemy denied, though France by now had triumphantly broken the Austrians, brought Spain into the war against England, found in Bonaparte an invincible general proving himself in Italy, and even this year was forcing the Royal Navy into retreat. But if England suffered temporary setbacks her kindly traditions were encouraging; and Frank at any rate did not believe the war was lost. 'We supped,' Jane wrote in high spirits, 'and walked home at night under the shade of two Umbrellas.' The rain that night mingled with her memory of an agreeable, civilized evening. Before they left Frank had orders to report to HMS *Triton*, or had his 'appointment on Board the Capt! John Gore, commanded by the Triton', and would Mr Austen please fetch home his prodigal daughter from London (if someone conveyed her that far) to save her from walking the hospitals, mounting guard at St James's, or falling prey to the arts of a woman who could make her 'drunk with Small Beer'? The hot weather kept 'one in a continual state of Inelegance',[19] and Jane wanted to be home.

Her father fetched her, and almost as soon as she reached home she began 'First Impressions'. In ten months, she wrote out what must have been a clear, straightforward Elizabeth–Darcy story set in counterpoint with an anatomy of kinds of love in Mr Collins and Charlotte Lucas, Bingley and Jane, Mr and Mrs Bennet, Wickham and Lydia. This comic and moral story was *her* war – with no heroism – and the version she wrote between October 1796 and August 1797 probably used Elizabeth Bennet as chief narrator and interpreter. Miss Burney in offering groups of sequential letters such as 'Evelina in continuation' had shown how a heroine's mind may be a glass through which to see a world – and *Pride and ·Prejudice* would be Elizabeth Bennet's world, since even in the final version Darcy filters through her viewpoint. If the draft in some sections was long, loose and anything but sparkling, it was well received at Deane, where it thrilled one small child. The story was read aloud 'in the parsonage at Dean – whilst I was in the room, & not expected to listen', Anna recalled.[20] James probably sensed its literary sources in moral periodical essays, or in the funny piece by Dr Johnson in his 115th *Rambler* essay about the bachelor Hymenaeus who is pursued by love, which begins 'I was known to profess a fortune and want a wife,' and again in James's own 29th *Loiterer* essay about how youth and age comically differ in views of marriage. If 'the great universal purpose' as James said is 'MATRIMONY' then Jane Austen, in accepting that thesis, derived ironic effects from the economic and social plight of five girls and an entailed estate, for their nervous mother is desperate to marry them quickly and a spirited girl resists being traded like a pig. The author gave her own name and Cassandra Elizabeth's second one to the two most alert Bennets, and used her own sensible parents as foils to sketch their opposites, the selfish and irresponsible elder Bennets. Mr Austen's quiet study-room becomes a retreat into which Mr Bennet escapes from his family, and Mrs Austen's amused concern for her ducks and chickens becomes Mrs Bennet's frenetic concern to find wealthy mates for her girls. In its exuberance the story impugns the stilted *Loiterer* as well as the authority of all parents: its heroine is an ideal Cousin Eliza in her self-reliance and delight in fools, who at last goes with Darcy to a Pemberley surrounded by miles of green sward and lets the 'neighbourhood' of Meryton stew in its juice – though she is kind to Kitty and poor Lydia. Elizabeth and Darcy *are* the community that matters, and the elder Bennets fade away.

Untroubled by all this, Mr Austen soon wrote a brief and eloquent letter to the leading publishers, Cadell & Davies, in London:

Sirs

I have in my possession a Manuscript Novel, comprised in three Vols. about the length of Miss Burney's Evelina. As I am well aware of what consequence it is that a work of this sort should make its' first appearance under a respectable name I apply to you. Shall be much obliged therefore if you will inform me whether you chuse to be concerned in it; what will be the expense of publishing at the Author's risk; & what you will advance for the Property of it, if on perusal it is approved of?

Should your answer give me encouragement I will send you the work.

I am, Sirs, Yr. obt. hble Servt:

Geo Austen

Steventon near Overton
Hants
1st Novr. 1797 [21]

Mr Austen had done as much for Frank and Charles. At Cadell & Davies his letter was promptly endorsed in a bold hand,

declined by Return of Post

and that unpleasant news soon reached Jane. Yet she began a new version of 'Elinor and Marianne' this month, at least partly because her will had been stiffened by hard news in the spring.

Cassandra's fiancé Tom Fowle was never, despite minor legends about him, a regimental chaplain to the Buffs or 3rd of Foot, but he had sailed in his kinsman Lord Craven's private yacht to join Sir Ralph Abercromby's military expedition in the West Indies. Yellow fever carried off many troops including Tom, who died at San Domingo in February 1797. As a conscientious young man, he left his fiancée a legacy of £1,000 – as if that might console her – and the Austens were heartsick. 'They are all in great affliction,' Eliza wrote to Phila on 3 May, 'for the death of Mr. Fowle, the gentleman to whom our Cousin Cassandra was engaged. He was expected home this month from St Domingo where he had accompanied Lord Craven, but Alas instead of his arrival news were received of his Death. This is a very severe stroke to the whole family, and particularly to poor Cassandra.' Jane Austen 'says that her Sister behaves with a degree of resolution & Propriety which no common mind could evince in so trying a situation'.[22] But resolution drove Cassandra's grief inwards. After consoling her, Jane contrived some of her anti-Godmersham jokes and death-jokes and childbearing jokes partly to reach her private sorrow, to jog and force Cassandra to happiness with arrogant humour. Her comedy had a mission, it was a sign of defiance. There is no change of tone in her letters more marked than the tone after Tom Fowle's death, and the same Jane Austen who wrote and repeated,

> Have mercy oh gracious Father! upon all that are now suffering from whatsoever cause,

and who implored,

> Have we thought irreverently . . . have we neglected any known duty, or willingly given pain to any human being?

could also use a savage, comic Congrevean muse to get at a locked-in grief. 'Mrs. Hall, of Sherborne', Jane told Cassy with comic ferocity in 1798, 'was brought to bed yesterday of a dead child, some weeks before she expected, owing to a fright. I suppose she happened unawares to look at her husband.'[23]

That was tasteless and cruel, exuberant and healthy. It defied life and laughed at death. Was *she* responsible for Mr Hall's looks or

Mrs Hall's dead infant? Yet Jane Austen's jokes have rather darker implications too and seem to take us beyond (or even beneath) her relations with Cassandra. On the one hand a witty joke could be framed to suggest a necessary self-respect or the importance of honouring one's feelings: *I do not like the Miss Blackstones: indeed, I am always determined not to like them so there is less merit in it.* Or it could be framed even more encouragingly for Cassandra who seems never to have disliked a soul on earth very intensely: *It is you that always disliked Mr. N.Toke so much, not I. – I do not like his wife, & I do not like Mr. Brett, but as for Mr. Toke, there are few people whom I like better.* Or a joke could be used to illustrate the really stupendous ghastliness and continual inadequacy and hypocrisy of the terms of family sentiment: *Charles sends you his best love & Edward his worst. – If you think the distinction improper, you may take the worst yourself.* Or, as justly, a joke could be used to annihilate a young man of the sort who is so smug, blank, empty and unaware that he adds to the unhappiness of the day. Mr Gould was just that sort: *He is a very young Man, just entered of Oxford, wears Spectacles, & has heard that* Evelina *was written by Dr. Johnson.* Or more devastatingly, *Mr. Bendish seems nothing more than a tall young man.*

These and many other examples no doubt entertained Cassandra. Jane Austen was a person of deep moral intensity and commitment who was beginning to construct her comedies on moral foundations, and it is probable that her informal jokes were *meant* to lighten her sister's spirits. A moral meaning hovers over them. Cassandra is not to be broken by Tom Fowle, not to be abject, or to hang her head. As lessons they probably had as much effect as the lessons of brilliant teachers usually have – that is, none whatever. Cassandra remained self-effacing and apologetic but also efficient and cheerful as her letters show. She learned from Jane's comic violence what she knew already – that Jane loved and needed her – and of course she knew her sister's exuberant humour extremely well. In the lightest way it was a jokey black humour which often had the writer herself as its object or which turned upon Jane herself: *I hope I have no reason to hang myself,* wrote merry Jane, *'There! I may now finish my letter and go hang myself;* or *I would spin nothing with it but a rope to hang myself;* or for her nephew James Edward and with exuberant identification with him at College, *Now you may own how miserable you were there; now it will gradually all come out – your Crimes & your*

125

Miseries . . . how often you were on the point of hanging yourself – restrained only, as some illnatured aspersion upon poor old Winton has it, by the want of a Tree within some miles of the City.

These nice, lovely, easy, absurd and trimly set-out jokes were written by a woman fascinated by people. But their effect was to keep nearly everyone she knew at a slight distance, while her humour relieved her exasperation and those fresh shocks of disillusionment that can be sensed in her letters. A certain satisfaction with her own sharp, bitter, angry moods looks rather odd in connection with her prayers and need for close friendships, though she disliked new friendships, even while seeking them. She feared the pressure of human contacts and tried capriciously and lightly to laugh away her reserve: 'I do not want people to be very agreeable, as it saves me the trouble of liking them a great deal.' And one must not press this conclusion too far, since in the densest crowds she still yearned for intimate friends. But she 'gratefully' declined the chance to meet new people, or hoped she would have 'no necessity for having so many dear friends at once again' or complained that people find it 'either their duty or pleasure to call' on her. Beneath these complaints (which she reserved for her sister's eyes) was the darker, more troubling problem of her dislike for the social events that gave her pleasure. Her malignant demon went with her to Hampshire dances where there was 'nobody worth talking to' and she catalogued 'silly' young women and the stiff, dull, dreadful, 'vulgar' or 'noisy' men – and there in the midst of delight she longed for endings and riddance. Politely she could endure being bored by the nauseously proper and affectedly stylish – *I was as civil to them as their bad breath would allow me*. They were fun to watch, delightful to report on . . . though loneliness and dislike tinge her witty accounts of her own impressions. Beneath these feelings were despair, violence and anarchy that would overthrow the complacencies and decencies and politenesses of a society that gave women fixed roles. That anarchy swells up in a phrase, a sentence or two in her letters, a remark given to Anne Elliot or a mood of Elizabeth Bennet's. In her twenties and especially after Tom Fowle's death she kept her equilibrium by means of her jokes, her subordinate place in the family and her means of privacy and retreat in a green and quiet setting. Her jokes helped her to adjust to her deficiencies with a witty frankness – and, by and large, with her family's love, she was proof against threats to

her. Pride could exist in a joke without troubling her Christian conscience: 'Not being overburdened with subject – (having nothing
at all to say)', she later tells her sister gaily, 'I shall have no check
to my Genius from beginning to end.'

Her sister's tragedy had a benign effect in confirming the rightness
of her own comic art. She grieved over Cassandra's loss, as we know
from Eliza's letter, but turned the meaning on all sides. Its Christian
meaning of course was clear. But then, too, if Fowle's death ended
her sister's hopes, the prospect of death did not *belong to* the description of a young woman's struggle with society, economics, suitors
and herself to gain happiness. The comic scene of our choices while
we *have* hope was Jane Austen's subject and the centre of each mature
novel. And now, as if to show that comedy persists, Eliza de Feuillide,
who may earlier have refused James's offer to marry her, gave up
'Baddy' and '&CC' and other forlorn beaux to marry Henry Austen
on 31 December 1797. Most of the Austens were either displeased
or alarmed. Eliza had consented very modestly after Henry as she
said showed 'his Affection for my little Boy' and had agreed to 'the
disposal of my Property in favor of this latter'.[24] The improbable newlyweds meant to become prosperous, and, as it happened, several other
Austens were really becoming so. Jane heard good reports from sea
and land and her mother certainly looked up from her pleasure in
sewing dresses for Anna's dolls. First from the Navy – Charles had
received an award and his bold captain a knighthood, after Thomas
Williams's ship the *Unicorn* pursued the enemy's *La Tribune* for 210
nautical miles and brought her home as a prize without a British
sailor lost or even wounded. That delighted the Austens, and
Edward's fortunes in Kent took an even happier turn. When Mr
Knight died in 1794 rumours had spread to the effect that poor Edward
Austen was his bastard son. (Evil reports were forcibly suppressed
later, but one or two survived.) 'Mr. Austen, who by the will of
Mr. Knight, is to have the reversion of all his estates,' wrote Samuel
Denne to Richard Gough on 6 January 1795, 'is supposed to be an
illegitimate son of the testator, by whom it has not transpired; and
I have understood that he is to take the name of Knight. The two
estates, *viz.* that of Godmersham-park and that of Chawton in Hampshire, are, however, devised to the widow for life, with, it is said,
a nett £4000 a year.'[25] In actual fact Mrs Knight by law had the ownership of Godmersham Park and Chawton for her natural life, but partly

to combat rumours of Edward's illegitimacy, and also to show trust in her adopted son, she vacated Godmersham and signed it over irrevocably to Edward in 1797. She herself lived quietly at White Friars, Canterbury. Thus Edward Austen at twenty-nine became one of the prominent landowners of Kent.

In the following summer Jane Austen's first cousin Lady Williams, formerly Jane Cooper of the Steventon theatricals, was out driving when a dray-horse crashed into her chaise: she was thrown to the ground 'and never spoke again', as Mrs Lybbe Powys writes of her death. That loss compounded Cassandra's troubles, and Mr Austen very mercifully decided in August of 1798 that the time was ripe for a visit to Edward's new domain in Kent.

Whether or not Elizabeth was ready to receive her poor relations, the family were soon on their way from Steventon. Three days later they crossed the Kentish Stour where a bridge bore a legend:

> This bridge was built by the Parish and NOT
> by the County 1698. Thomas Carter and
> Richard Austen SVRVEIGHERS.[26]

They were then eight miles from Canterbury and six from Ashford: Edward's locale included the two-mile-long parish of Godmersham with its southern hamlet of Bilting and its north-eastern part called Eggarton. Two Roman roads ran parallel to the river and a mile to the west along the ridge above the park ran a prehistoric tract known as Pilgrim's Way. The Austens passed under giant trees, saw cottages and a brick-walled garden, and at last halted at a Palladian edifice, where as a queer but pleasant group they climbed out and dusted themselves off. Elizabeth soon eyed them all – Mrs George Austen with her beaked nose and toothlessness, her tall pink husband, a demure Cassandra and a happy, eager Jane.

Probably even before Jane wrote to Frank, she had toured the Palladian house and heard briefly of its special history. When Thomas May had begun to build it in 1732 as Ford Place he had no architect on location, it seems, but had simply bought the plans from a London designer of status, a Flitcroft or a Roger Morris, and had local builders carry them out. The 'south front' of Godmersham Park in consequence bulkily overlooked a good terrace and some acceptable landscape: the scene might have pleased Humphrey Repton, who believed a house should influence the landscape round it, if not 'Capability' Brown, who wanted landscape to have an effect on the house. You could sit on a knoll in one of two small Greek temples and survey a pleasant scene – the good red-brick façade, its sash-barred windows and crudely finished stone dressings. Inside, the local builders had put a staircase in as an afterthought and ruined the effect of the salon, and in the only two fully decorated rooms in the whole building the decorators had spared nothing. One saw amazingly voluptuous Roman friezes, lavish scrolls of wood and plaster, ornate medallions and shields of Roman emperors, stucco fruit and flowers, scallop shells and female masks and acanthus scrolls on ceilings and walls and over the fireplaces of the two main rooms.

But the north front was quite different. One stepped outside to see nothing at all – only grassy parkland, with no other building in view, a lovely upward sweeping tract of land reaching from the River Stour to the heights of Pilgrim's Way. But here on land once known as Godmaer's Ham, belonging to Canterbury Benedictines who had built the simple church of St Lawrence the Martyr, something had happened to builders' chisels. They had worked with uncommon fineness: the northern façade was as lovely as anything the Austens had seen in Oxford or Hampshire. They saw a long, low façade of rose brick and three *oeils-de-boeuf* above the windows, with literally all of the stonework finished in perfection, as well as flanking wings of ten windows each (added by Mr Knight) which gave the masonry a curious grace as if the whole house sat lightly on the earth. Whatever accounted for this harmony the very land of the 'estate' had come down from the monasteries to the Knights, by virtue of Kentish Astyns and Austens. John Austen, who married Elizabeth Weller, had had a sister named Jane Austen who had married Stephen Stringer; their daughter Hannah Stringer married William Monke, and this couple in turn had had a daughter who married Thomas May (formerly Brodnax), who, on succeeding to the estates at Rawmere in Sussex belonging to his mother's cousin, had with his newly acquired wealth built Godmersham Park.

It was possible to take a very personal interest in this house. Had Edward's ancestor Jane Austen never lived, Mrs Knight would have had no estate to give him. The idea of the 'estate' itself, certainly, fascinated Jane. From Edward and Henry she clearly had heard a good deal about inheritance law, or the difference between an estate inherited in fee simple by any heir of the owner, and a fee tail, in which land is descendible to the grantee's lineal issue and frequently only to males. (Lady Catherine in *Pride and Prejudice* inherits in fee simple and is not debarred as an inheritor for want of being a male, whereas the Bennets' Longbourn home is in fee tail, and, for want of a Bennet son, will go to Mr Collins.) The common law courts (such as the King's Bench) and the court of equity (or Chancery) were still separate in Jane Austen's day; and she and her father viewed the law principally through the eyes of the clergy – indeed there would be no lawyer–heroes in her work – although in fact in the late eighteenth century the practice of advocacy was passing from the clergy in an age of increasing specialization to a new class of professional lawyers. However, it was not until 1875 that equity and common law came together under a single Supreme Court of Judicature with its power to administer the two jurisdictions in its three divisions of the Queen's Bench, Chancery and Probate, Divorce and Admiralty, the last with its bizarre jurisdiction over 'wills, wives and wrecks'. So long as equity remained separate, a person entitled to seisin or ownership owned only an abstraction called the 'estate', which is interposed between a person and the land, and indeed different individuals might hold separate 'estates' in the same piece of land.[27] For Tories with a sense of the past the abstract, feudal idea of the 'estate' carried a notion of deeper spiritual inheritance: with a landed estate there might be transmitted also the values that sustained a nation.

All of Godmershan Park, its religious past, the unfinished house, the grounds, and the values of its people of course would 'live' on in Fanny, Edward or Dordy who received them. The expectations of a whole local society might thus depend on the choices and impulses of one frail young person. Godmersham and the structure of inheritance law confirmed Jane Austen in her selection of the *artistic subject* of her novels, the importance of the inner life and moral choices of one young woman.

On a practical level she saw how complex Edward's life was. The house was bursting with retainers, so that even when Edward travelled to Chawton he took along 'the governess and 19 servants', and one could walk from his library into the breakfast-room and up to the partly finished Yellow Room and on to the Chintz Room which Jane 'admired very much', and back through the hall to the kitchen with its barrel churns of polished elm and find many objects to attend to – whole rows and ranks of cooking pots, frying pans, stock pots, stew pans, soup tureens, saucepans, graters, choppers, mills, mincers and moulds in cast-iron or stoneware or procelain with custodians for them all. There were the lower ranks of kitchen and laundry maids whom Edward recruited from his tenants' and labourers' children, then footmen and grooms and stable boys, on up to butler, cooks, ladies' gentlewomen and the house steward and housekeeper. There might perhaps be too little for them all to do, and the task of adjudicating in disputes and deciding their privileges and allowances of food and drink was so complex that the owner of the house might often be drawn in. Edward's life made him practical and literal, and Elizabeth's childbearing and entertaining kept her very frequently occupied. The children were shunted off to retainers who could hardly be expected to look after more than a child's strictly practical needs.

Yet it was a pleasant country-house life, and the two elder Austens entered into it easily. Mr Austen lost his scissors between his bedroom and the garden, and his wife's spectacles vanished – Molly the maid-servant cleverly found both items just where their owners had left them – but Mrs Austen was soon planning a hen-house with Edward and regaling herself on dumplings, oyster sauce and pork. The hen-house plan faltered: 'My mother wants to know whether Edward has ever made the hen-house they planned,' Jane later enquired, and she was more amused by her father's passion for Edward's pigs. 'My father is glad to hear so good an account of Edward's pigs, and desires he may be told', she wrote in the autumn, 'that Lord Bolton is particularly curious in *his* pigs, and has had pigstyes of the most elegant construction built for them, and visits them every morning as soon as he rises.' Starting life as Thomas Orde, Lord Bolton had married the illegitimate daughter of the fifth Duke of Bolton, or Jean Mary Browne Powlett, and inherited through her the fine Bolton estates before being created Baron Bolton in 1797.[28] (The splendour of his pigsties thus owed to the adultery of his wife's mother, and seldom has adultery been better rewarded.)

Yet if adultery brought Lord Bolton *his* pigs, Mr Austen as a Hampshire breeder had an unbiased and happily expansive interest in pork, just as his wife did in hen-houses, and their interests helped to make their daughter an artist of detail. Even pork shows how people behave. In *Emma*, Jane would show her heroine's generosity in having Emma send the Bateses a 'whole hind-quarter' of pork to roast as they liked, and reveal Mr Woodhouse's eccentricity by having him imagine the Bateses wanted fryable pork, 'as our's are fried, without the smallest grease'.[29] She observed many such details in Kent. Above all Godmersham gave her a serene, firm perch from which to judge an odd moment in English social life when the new acquisitive, bourgeois society in England was challenging an old agrarian society depending on inherited titles and family names. The economic and social confusions were abetted by the war, and no other period in social history was really harder to judge, and perhaps no realistic story of the gentry could fail to show England in chaotic transition. At Godmersham Park, Jane may have planned a story about a Susan who later became 'Catherine Morland' of *Northanger Abbey*: as the daughter of a somewhat impoverished clergyman, Susan or Catherine goes with a local landowning family to Bath and there, in that town of social bartering, meets Henry Tilney, whose family have owned their Abbey estates since the dissolution of the monasteries, but it is ironic that Tilney marries the heroine, although Tilney's sister marries on the 'unexpected accession' of her lover to 'title and fortune'.[30] It is remarkable that the author *can* see and judge her people so confidently in a period of social transition and weakening ties with the land. One secret of Jane Austen's success lies in her identification with her brother Edward and his estate – and with his wealth – so that at Godmersham, despite and almost because of Elizabeth's snobbery, she had space to feel and reflect in, with occasional loneliness to consider coolly the social life she knew. She missed the 'Park' when away from it, and wanted to hear of its pleasant or unpleasant visitors, such as the Bridges, the Tokes of Godlington, the Hattons of Eastwell, the Deedes of Sandling, Edward's next-door neighbours, the Wildmans and the Knatchbulls who were his cousins by adoption. They came to call, and she was to require news especially of the romances here: 'Who is Miss Maria Montresor going to marry, and what is become of Miss Mulcaster?' she appeals to her sister. 'Pray mention the name of Maria Montresor's lover when you write next,' and then a little less candidly, 'My Mother wants to know it.' It *was* a wealthy set. 'People get so horridly poor & economical in this part of the World,' she writes when back at home, 'that I

132

have no patience with them. – Kent is the only place for happiness, Everybody is rich there.'[31]

The best visitor was pretty Mrs Knight, her brother's benefactor, who without whimsicality admired Mary Queen of Scots and gave Jane and Cassandra regular gifts of money. She appeared from White Friars and vanished as if the house had conjured her up out of a pumpkin; she was amusing and sensible. Jane felt that *she* would like Elinor Dashwood, but 'Mrs. Knight giving up the Godmersham estate to Edward was no such prodigious act of generosity after all,' she comments, 'for she has reserved herself an income out of it still; this ought to be known, that her conduct may not be overrated. I rather think Edward shows the most magnanimity of the two, in accepting her resignation with such encumbrances.'[32] But late hours of dining took a toll on Mrs Austen, and Edward's oyster sauce and dumplings perhaps a more severe toll. As her mother, on this visit, felt the 'heat' in her face, which foretold loose bowels, the Austens prepared to leave their Kentish paradise.

Cassandra stayed on partly because Elizabeth preferred her ways to Jane's bright, shifting moods – and perhaps sensed she was more malleable and useful with small children.

On the journey home Jane Austen's writing- and dressing-boxes galloped off 'towards Gravesend on their way to the West Indies'. All of her worldly wealth – just £7 – and the writing-box returned after a two- or three-mile-long adventure in the wrong chaise. That night the Austens pulled into the Bull and George at Dartford. It was a good coaching inn, with a plain brick front and galleried court-yard, standing on the pilgrim's route from Canterbury: an earlier inn on the same site was well known to Chaucer himself. As his wife dozed Mr Austen at the fire that night settled into Francis Lathom's *The Midnight Bell*. 'The ghostly hour of midnight had just sounded,' Mr Austen read, '... when a piercing shriek caught his ear.... The girls came running down stairs, with terror painted on their countenances, and the elder of them exclaimed – that her Uncle's bed was all over blood!'[33] Mr Austen's bishop might have been sur-prised that he spent his evenings reading 'horrid novels', which were to be mentioned in *Northanger Abbey*. But, as Jane wrote later of a subscription-library's advent, '*our* family ... are great Novel-readers & not ashamed of being so'.[34] Her father's reading of *Midnight Bell* was, in part, one of many signs of his deep, special affection for her.

Back at home she worked on her novel and in Cassandra's absence gave orders in the kitchen, carried wine keys and dropped out her mother's dose of laudanum. She wrote that Mary Lloyd had given birth to James Edward at Deane on 17 November 1798, but she tried not to seem too eager over parties and dances, partly because her sister did not forget Tom Fowle. There was brighter news: England's favourite sailor Nelson had won a victory at the Nile, and then came the news of Frank's promotion to the rank of commander. 'My dear Cassandra, Frank is made,' Jane began. 'As soon as you have cried a little for Joy, you may go on, & learn farther that the India House have taken *Captn Austen's* petition into consideration.'[35] Now her sister might give way to tears and find good cause to weep.

10

Northanger Abbey and the prospect of Bath

I never saw so many Men weep.
Mrs Leigh Perrot

'Think of me sometimes,' wrote Eliza in her beautiful script to Phila Walter in Kent and then crossed out the word 'sometimes', 'and think of me with some affection, since notwithstanding all my faults I love you sincerely.' Eliza changed this to read *most sincerely*.[1] Taking pains with her letters as she did in flirting, she missed friends and beaux after settling down with Henry Austen, who was ten years her junior and a captain in the Oxfordshire militia. His income was small and he was not the most prudent of men. He had embarrassed his family lately with Mary Pearson, whose father had been commander of HMS *Serapis* when it yielded to an American privateer in the last war, and yet Pearsons did not easily succumb on land. Not very well informed of Miss Pearson's feelings Jane Austen had meant to stay with them on the return from Rowling – though the arrangement had fallen through – but she had noted a difference between Mary Pearson and her picture, which Henry had shown to some of his family: 'Pray be careful not to expect too much Beauty,' Jane had told Cassandra. 'I will not pretend to say that on a *first veiw*, she quite answered the opinion I had formed of her – My Mother I am sure will be disappointed.'[2] Eliza may have heard something similar of that young lady. Mary Pearson at any rate had led Henry a lively chase until he bolted back to Eliza, to whom he had made earlier advances, and then Eliza had yielded – with the result announced in *Gentleman's Magazine* in December 1797 under MAR-RIAGES OF REMARKABLE PERSONS:

[Dec.] 31. At Mary-la Bonne church,
Henry-Tho. Austen, esq. to the
Comtesse de Feuillide.[3]

And as Eliza expected little of any man she was surprised by Henry's tolerance since he allowed her to keep her French maid Manon and 'Pug', who had made a Cheltenham innkeeper so cross when she arrived with Miss Payne and *her* dog: 'You would laugh', wrote Eliza, 'if you were to see the fuss that Manon makes with these black faced beauties, and the notice that is taken of them' and 'laugh too when I tell you that they drink the Waters, being of a *bilious Habit*'. Henry loved her bilious dog and her little boy and herself. 'Unmixed felicity is certainly not the produce of this world,' she wrote among the lovely officers at Ipswich, but 'Henry well knows that I have not been much accustomed to controul & should probably behave rather awkwardly under it, and therefore like a wise man he has no will but mine.'

Her delight in the officers was not affected by Henry's presence and she was tempted to flirt, since at thirty-six she still had her small, elegant form, a child's eyes, and looks that approached Kant's idea of 'free beauty' or the kind that pleases as flowers or birds or designs do and not because it arouses desire. This made her prettiness mag-netic so that she became a source of Jane Austen's success in portray-ing sexuality in the early novels, as in the jumping up, sitting down, fresh and cool Isabella Thorpe of *Northanger Abbey*.[4]

'You would not dislike a flirtation,' Eliza soon told Phila Walter. 'I have of *course entirely* left off *trade*' but 'as to my Colonel Lord Charles Spencer, if I was married to my third husband instead of my second I should still be in love with him. He is a most charming creature, so mild, so well bred, so good, but alas! he is married as well as myself and what is worse he is absent.' She listened to the war-talk of Henry's officers, who were jealous of the Royal Navy, and heard that as the French discounted British good luck at the Nile they would soon invade England in ships and *paddle-wheeled rafts* – about which she had her suspicions. The whole camp was bubbling and stirring. 'We have received orders,' she reports, 'so that I am going to be *drilled*.'[5]

There remained the secret of why she remarried when she hated the word 'husband', but Phila knew the secret. After her mother had died of cancer Eliza's health was uncertain, and if she was less alarmed for herself than for her son, she visited spas at Cheltenham and Bath for cures. She referred to her illness, but in no letter does she beg for pity. She has a 'swelling' which may not be cancerous, though it resists medication, and yet, she says, 'from my Looks no one would suppose any thing ailed me' and indeed she was to entertain many people before her 'long and dreadful Illness' incapacitated her in 1811. Her pluck was not lost on her young cousin, who found her a reminder of the precious value of life. Jane Austen's novels moreover have the gaiety and sanity of having been written in the teeth of death. Eliza had married into the Austens since they felt deeply for her and because she knew Henry depended on her godfather and protector Warren Hastings. As it turned out she judged well of Henry's loyalty to her in illness. She did on several occasions find her own dilemma amusing and could entertain Phila with accounts of her visits to doctors' offices: 'I thought myself materially worse,' Eliza believed in 1796 and so she had sent a pretty note 'addressed to D^r. *Farquhar*, whereas it should have been to *Sir Walter Farquhar Bart.*, but this impropriety he forgave, and appointed a quarter before four that day for our meeting – With a beating heart I repaired to my Rendezvous, and was told that Sir Walter was not yet returned home – The Servant would have shewn me into a Parlour with a good fire in it, but on seeing two smart young Men there, who opened their eyes as wide as Barn Doors to view the Doctor's female Patient, I desired to go into another Apartment.'[6]

Her rustling dress and large hat threw 'two smart young' patients into a stunned panic. Ladies seldom visited a doctor's office unaccompanied, and the men were amazed to see a petite countess in the vestibule. Instead of toying with them she gathered her skirts and went into an empty study where ashes in a grate announced a '*cold reception*', and here she had an odd two hours' wait. A 'Gothic craze' had begun and Eliza knew about midnight castles with bleeding nuns and walking corpses, but as she found nothing horridly sentimental to read she picked up one or two medical books filled with 'shocking cases'. No sounds, no breath of the living, nothing but case-histories filled her senses in the dim light until she noticed two cabinets which might hold 'Skeletons'. Ought she to scream? She *could not* be in her tomb, and she had not known a skeleton that could say a word. But it seemed that she must stare down the ghastly bones. She bent forward and flung open a door. 'I met with nothing but crooked Scissors and other formidable Surgical Instruments, and a few *Embryos*,' she recalled with relief, and, as she put it, the study door opened and in walked the doctor with 'a grave face'.[7]

That story gave Jane Austen a hint for her new novel. Her comic heroine – Susan or Catherine Morland – is to see in her room at General Tilney's abbey a chest which ought to contain Gothic horrors but holds only a white counterpane. Later when shudderingly drawn to a black and yellow Japan cabinet, she opens it to find a 'washing-bill' listing shirts, cravats, stockings and other male garments. The author's skill with fictional sources lay in her lambent running through a store of materials to make fresh, unlikely combinations, and the 'Abbey' chapters draw on recent observations too. General Tilney's character reflects no more of Edward Mathew than the awe Jane and Cassandra had felt when he appeared at the rectory to take Anna 'out to a dinner party' and they 'did not dare to remonstrate'. Family reports show that the General could be 'an autocratic, hot tempered despot', as well as a very soft old veteran with a selfless love for little Anna; 'he carried his money literally and metaphorically *loose* in his pocket'[8] and was never as mean as Tilney – so that what is used of him in *Northanger Abbey* is no more than the effect he has as when calling at the rectory. Again, that Feuillide was a murderer could have provided only a germ of the idea of having Catherine imagine that Tilney had killed his wife. Using initial impressions Jane drew on the emotionally laden, striking effects a personality had had upon her – but James Edward seems right in believing that she never took a whole personality from life.

Yet without Eliza *Northanger Abbey* might be different. Its heroine is amusing partly because of its detached, alert narrator. Eliza with amoral daring and spirit had cut through English society and in her letters had offered a detached, foreign and amused view of the present so that her example helped Jane Austen to take a fresh view of society and an affectionate view of the Gothic craze. No Austen seems to have been appalled by *The Midnight Bell*, *The Mysteries of Udolpho* or other 'horrid' novels they read. The genteel world of Mrs Radcliffe's *Udolpho* contains no social embarrassment, sexual passion or realistic monetary connection, and its heroine is shocking only because she weeps on every other page with unintendedly comic pathos. Jane Austen and Anna were to call the Alton coach 'The Car of Falkenstein' and laugh over Mrs Radcliffe.[9] But *Northanger Abbey* does make serious points about social education and language, and the novel became a running debate with James Austen over the real values of fiction – indeed sentimental and Gothic fiction are only lightly mocked in this work. Catherine is a naive, recalcitrant, modest, sensitive and good-hearted girl who in the country at Fullerton can never learn anything before she is taught it and who at Bath with the Allens misjudges the characters of Isabella and John Thorpe. Her real education begins when she senses the need to judge other people accurately behind the mask of their words. This is a theme of Richardson's *Sir Charles Grandison*, an elementary textbook and a foil, though by now Jane Austen could drop its creaking letter-form: she lets her people interact dramatically but gives us access to Catherine's interior life, and thus counterfeits the real texture and feeling of a young girl's social experiences. Catherine sees Mrs Allen as an open book since that lady's idle, good-natured chatter about dress reveals her as reliable, nice, simple and bemused. But Bath's Rooms are confusing, and here the treatment of Catherine's feelings reaches beyond any insights or hints that could have been picked up from Richardson or other reading – and in fact the narrative anticipates later critics of Western cities, though it is supplied by Jane Austen's memories of Bath. In the 'mob' of the Rooms her heroine sees faces that have 'nothing to interest' and finds bewildering anonymity, expressionless eyes, and alienation with 'crowds of people' at 'every moment passing in and out, up the steps and down; people whom nobody cared about, and nobody wanted to see'.[10] This is nearly the world of Engels or Walter Benjamin. In moving through that mob Catherine Morland leaves behind her schoolroom training, as the narrator implies in an allusion to schoolbook verses that are of no use in the modern mêlée. The author sees through the verses, and yet could believe well enough in 'diligence':

> Quickly lay hold of Time, while in your Pow'r, ...
> Despair of nothing which you would obtain;
> Unweary'd Diligence your Point will gain.[11]

Catherine is diligent chiefly as a discoverer: she meets Henry Tilney who is fluent if a little too arch on the topic of female letter-writing, and as their romantic friendship develops she attends more closely to social language and its relation to character. Mrs Thorpe talks without listening but her daughter Isabella, four years older than Catherine, is friendly and receptive with an easy gaiety of manner and language: 'she could compare the balls of Bath with those of Tunbridge' and even 'point out a quiz through the thickness of a crowd'. Though naively admiring, Catherine becomes wise in one thing. She does not yet know when delicate raillery is properly called for or 'when a confidence should be forced',[12] but she sees that our registers of talk *change*. And her lesson, which is reinforced every time Henry Tilney speaks, is that each mature person may be a dozen different persons so that consistency is no sign of moral integrity. John Thorpe is consistent but a liar; Isabella is charming, but false. The fault of an honest person may be in never learning to penetrate manner or hear 'character' in the talker's talk – and James Morland illustrates that fault. His love for Isabella certainly leads to his crushing disillusionment – but the fault is not mainly that of Isabella, the false, silly, pretty flirt: it is mainly James's.

Bath, then, becomes a place of social talk in which Catherine learns what a girl can never gather from Addison's essays, or from James and Henry Austen's *Loiterer*, the very difficulty of intuiting human character in a society in which men and women shield themselves with words. Ironically her mother searches upstairs at Fullerton for a 'very clever essay' to help her[13] – and one detects in that search a laughing reply to Austen family essayists. At Bath Catherine as a 'sad little shatter-brained creature' has left her mother and all essays rightly out of sight, and at Northanger Abbey, the next stage of her instruction, she has left the maternal Mrs Allen out of sight. When she is invited to General Tilney's abbey, the novel becomes a subtle, alarming and realistic 'Gothic work' itself. Catherine expects to find horrors she has read about in fiction and conceives that General Tilney has murdered his wife, but the saving thing about that comically horrible notion is that it is wholly hers. It leads not to further fantasy, but to truth, or to her accurate understanding of General Tilney's bullying nature. Having mistaken her for an heiress and alarmed that she might marry his son, the General has cruelly ordered her out of his house: we are led to feel in this incident the 'Gothic' reality of a brutal violence lurking beneath a genteel and pleasant surface of English life. Catherine's 'Gothic' discoveries coincide with her increasing understanding of her genteel lover Henry Tilney. She has erred in her supposition about the General, but no girl reaches self-hood without independent judgement and no one becomes free without risk of error. The price of being free is the humiliating one of discovering how wrong we *can* be – and Catherine returns to Fullerton to suffer not as a girl but as a young adult. She has learned at Bath and then at the deceptive abbey the need to pierce through a silky dazzle of appearances to reality; in the absence of parental guides she has erred but with the effect of creating and liberating herself. Thus she is free, sensitive and wise as a woman by the time Henry Tilney presses her to be his bride.

What is weak in *Northanger Abbey* is its freshest and most innovative feature – its narrative voice. That voice was the last feature of her art that Jane Austen developed. A good narrator ought to be craftily unfair in giving access to some minds but not others, in withholding information and in favouring one character's viewpoint over other viewpoints, but here the narrator is a lithe and slithery eel of great energy which is less than fully controlled. The narrator in *Northanger Abbey* often lacks an appropriate tone. It is as though the work had been revised too often between 1799 and 1803, or with too much deference to Austen family opinion, and then at times with a self-conscious flouting of James Austen's advice. It has a curious mixture of narrative tones ranging from heavily ironic and awkward burlesque (in the opening chapters) to intrusions in the almost naive Sophia Sentiment vein, to thoughtful but irrelevant comments and on to acidly witty sentences such as this one on Mrs Allen:

> Mrs. Allen was one of that numerous class of females, whose society can raise no other emotion than surprise at there being any men in the world who could like them well enough to marry them.[14]

Or this drily contrived sentence on men, true as it is fun to read:

> The advantages of natural folly in a beautiful girl have been already set forth by the capital pen of a sister author; and to her treatment of the subject I will only add in justice to men, that though to the larger and more trifling part of the sex, imbecility in females is a great enhancement of their personal charms, there is a portion of them too

reasonable and too well informed themselves to desire anything more in woman than ignorance.[15]

The intelligent narrator's sympathy for the heroine helps us to take Catherine seriously and to feel that her naivety is balanced by a capacity to learn. But that same intelligent narrator is too full of respectful awe for the hazily seen Eleanor Tilney and rather too lenient at first and too harsh later with Isabella, and then over-indulgent with Henry Tilney, in whom Henry Austen perhaps saw himself idealized and graced with as much wit as he ever knew he had, though some passages in Tilney's banter suggest James Austen's lightest manner in *The Loiterer*. The Bath chapters are now and again out of kilter because they focus on Jane Austen's debate with James and Henry on values in fiction and history. The *Spectator* is denounced. The entertaining charm of horrid novels is slyly vouched for and that 'celebrated writer' Richardson is cited on love, named in a footnote and praised only for *Charles Grandison*, which Catherine likes and Isabella believes 'had not been readable'. Catherine on the topic of history, too, is given only the most immature tones of Sophia Sentiment. 'The quarrels of popes and kings,' she informs Eleanor Tilney, 'with wars or pestilence in every page; the men all so good for nothing, and hardly any women at all – it is very tiresome; and yet I often think it odd that it should be so dull, for a great deal of it must be invention.' To which Miss Tilney replies with what may be the weakest apology for historical writing James Austen of St John's College ever felt he had read: 'I am fond of history,' Miss Tilney tells Catherine,

> and am very well contented to take the false with the true. In the principal facts they have sources of intelligence in former histories and records, which may be as much depended on, I conclude, as any thing that does not actually pass under one's own observation; and as for the little embellishments you speak of, they are embellishments, and I like them as such. If a speech be well drawn up, I read it with pleasure, by whomsoever it may be made – and probably with much greater, if the production of Mr. Hume or Mr. Robertson, than if the genuine words of Caractacus, Agricola, or Alfred the Great.[16]

Whatever James Austen thought of *that* after writing about the rationale for historical study in *The Loiterer* he had a good chance to criticize his sister's novel at Deane, though his comments may have been of limited help. Cassandra writes that 'North-hanger Abbey' (and her spelling suggests that the Austen sisters pronounced the first word in a Hampshire way with an aspirate 'h' after 'North') 'was written about the years 98 and 99', and this seems acceptable if we take 1798 and 1799 as the years in which Jane Austen wrote one whole draft, but the author stated in her own short 'Advertisement' that 'This little work was finished in the year 1803, and intended for immediate publication.'[17] She had a good deal of time for revising between 1799 and 1803, and yet never mended the fault of its sharp break in tone, tempo and manner between the Bath and abbey sections, which her heroine's development required but which still seems aesthetically dissatisfying. Yet no amount of fussy complaints about the book are likely to lessen our fondness for her minimally characterized heroine – who seems more real than many well-recorded historical persons. That apparent fact was acknowledged by the British Post Office in 1975 when it issued in an Austen series a 10-penny stamp showing a demure lady in green and violet standing near a Gothic arch over the simple legend 'Catherine Morland'. (One recalls Emma and Mr Woodhouse on the $8\frac{1}{2}$-penny stamp, Darcy on the 11-penny, and Mary Crawford and her adulterous brother on the 13-penny for sending letters to France.) The highest achievement of Jane Austen's talent was not magical but a product of her strongly sympathetic feeling and her powers of close, nearly maliciously funny observations of social stupidity – ringed as her powers were by her psychological defences – in combination with her willingness to try out the rhetoric of presentation. She managed in this and later works to present young female protagonists who are unusually affecting and endearing. We like or love Catherine; we feel with her; and it is her personality that impresses us more deeply than the minor faults of tone and mixed settings, so that the novel remains a flawed masterpiece, or 'only a novel', as the author declares in response to Maria Edgeworth's calling her Belinda in 1801 a moral tale since Miss Edgeworth felt that novels were unseemly – 'only Cecilia, or Camilla, or Belinda', writes Jane Austen with a grand flourish, 'only some work in which the greatest powers of the mind are displayed, in which the most thorough knowledge of human nature, the happiest delineation of its varieties, the liveliest effusions of wit and humour are conveyed to the world in the best chosen language'.[18] There has never been a stronger statement of belief in the novel form. But that sentence is surely only the gist of her reply to Tory brothers who believed modern novels were Whiggish in tendency (though they read them) and to Uncle Perrot's friends the Edgeworths who felt as Dr Johnson did (in the *Rambler*) that a novel has power to corrupt even as it succeeds in social realism. The English novel with few exceptions *was* degenerate in the 1790s because there was no coherent and deeply based theory of fiction to inspire new artistic developments of the genre or to defend it against its moralistic attackers. Jane Austen joined the debate over the moral value of novels not by theorizing, but by showing that what a novel imitates is far less important than its technical 'forms of expression'. Gaiety, persistence and painstaking work with the technical challenges of her story were everything to her. She displayed nothing to the world at this time, but entered the debate of the 1790s all the same and proved to herself that a novelist *can* combine fidelity to detail with a well-considered moral viewpoint.[19] The debate of the 1790s helped her to perfect her narrative voice, her commentator and presenter. By the time she wrote *Mansfield Park* and *Emma*, she would be in absolute control of that narrative voice and highly skilful with tone and tactics. Already she was becoming an 'artist of detail' in a very special sense, usually overlooked by her casual critics. She was rigorously excluding irrelevant detail, so that the carefully selected minutiae that she offers us in *Northanger Abbey* seem totally wrapped up in and relevant to the dramatized personalities. She did borrow freely from the traditions of the eighteenth-century novel. For example she used for Catherine and later for Emma Woodhouse the popular 'Quixotic' formula for satiric novels in which the heroine takes a false view of things from her reading and then has comic experiences exposing the folly of an *idée fixe* – but Catherine is only lightly affected by books and is never made to seem stupidly duped.

If violence lurks beneath the surface of genteel life at the Abbey, that is not so surprising. Jane Austen worked on the Abbey story after *la Terreur* had affected Eliza's life and after the law's cruelty and violence overtook her Aunt Perrot at superficially serene Bath. She could be satisfied with this novel when with her brother Henry's help in the spring of 1803 she sold it, as 'Susan, a Novel in Two volumes', to the London publisher Richard Crosby for just £10. Of her manuscript only a trimmed title-page in her hand survives at the Pierpont Morgan Library today. Yet by 1799 her completed but unpolished draft would have pointed a way ahead for her. She had established a heroine's consciousness as a focal point and limited the reader's vision to correspond with what Susan or Catherine thinks, feels and perceives, and so she had given the illusion of real experience in a sustained work. Also she had found that realism of a heroine's viewpoint depends on an illusion of the narrator's separate integrity. The narrator must not identify with the dramatic character, and in this story does not. At the same time the author may use her own early impressions of Bath, of Henry Austen's bright college talk or of Anne Mathew's cool elegance and of her father the General's illusory harshness, to give an insider's very convincing ring to the heroine's reflections.

'Unwearied diligence' kept her hard at work, though she may have completed a draft when she visited Bath in the spring of 1799. Henry had left the militia. He was pursuing his luck in Dublin while Eliza lived as a 'recluse' at Dorking and merely saw Lady Burrell, Lady Talbot and one or two faded officers. As Edward Austen suffered from the gout, he and Elizabeth had decided to take the healing Bath waters with several Hampshire relations.

Mrs Austen and her younger daughter joined Edward and Elizabeth at No. 13 Queen Square. 'It has rained almost all the way,' Jane Austen wrote back to her sister in May, 'and our first view of Bath has been just as gloomy as it was last November twelvemonth.' At the bottom of Kingsdown Hill they had met a Dr Hall, 'in such very deep mourning that either his mother, his wife, or himself must be dead'.[20] If Dr Hall was a drenched corpse in the rain, other corpses twitched and gossiped in town.

One of the most interesting and lively of these was Jane Austen's 'Aunt Perrot' or Jane Leigh Perrot, whose husband's debilitating gout often caused her to leave her home at Scarlets for a more sociable one at No. 1 Paragon Buildings. At this place her 'dear Perrot' put up with every possible threat to his feet and convenience, since his wife thought little of setting out eight card tables for ninety people. Widely respected if not popular, she was a proudly officious and critical woman with a nasty stinginess in small matters and liberality in large, as well as a habit of finding people stupid as her deafness increased. Even in old age Mrs Leigh Perrot was always right – or could not make an error about anything of the slightest importance – although it annoyed her to read her niece's *Emma* twice to decide on its faults. Only Mr Knightley and Jane Fairfax pleased her: 'Frank Churchill is quite insufferable,' stated Aunt Perrot. 'I believe *I* should not have married him had I been Jane. Emma is a vain meddling woman. I am sick of Miss Bates.'[21] In her fifties she knew that her poor young niece scribbled, but feared that Cassandra and Jane were subject to very bad influences. Their surroundings were ugly and vulgar, not to say depraved. But what *would* become of them at Basingstoke grocers' balls where the women were more forward than the men? 'With your heart', she once advised James Edward Austen, take care not to 'lose your senses by dancing with the Belles of Basingstoke'. The Belles were as distasteful to her as the Navy into which poor Austen had thrown two sons but she admired Mr Austen as a courtly man and perhaps 'could not help loving such a being', as Henry later put it. Mr Austen, whatever his faults, had married the sister of her husband 'Perrot'.[22]

James Leigh Perrot himself had started life as a Leigh. He had become 'Perrot' by the happiest chance after his mother's aunt had begged her brother to alter a will by which he was assigning to her his Northleigh estates and to leave her instead an annuity just sufficient. So generous a command the brother had to obey. Gravely complying in a codicil to his will, he left property to his great-nephew James Leigh on condition that the young man take the surname and arms of Perrot. Thus in 1751 James became James Leigh Perrot of Northleigh, Oxfordshire, and selling his estates to the Duke of Marlborough he thereafter built a smaller house, Scarlets, at Hare Hatch about midway between Maidenhead and Reading. This house had a good, honest square hall connected by broad passageways to its drawing room and dining room and stood on good land, near other gentlemen's residences, so that James could not regret that he had got rid of Northleigh. He lived well enough and married a very pretty girl of seventeen, Jenny or Jane Cholmeley, who was born in Barbados where her father as a friend of the Governor had married a fashionable Willoughby. Jenny fondly remembered Barbados and her last sight of a brother there, but her English schooling refined her colonial accent and outlook. As Mrs Leigh Perrot she soon displayed 'a great idea of the claims of family ties, and a keen sense of justice as between herself and others'.[23] One of her neighbours was Richard Lovell

Edgeworth, the father of Maria Edgeworth the writer. She watched as her husband Perrot helped that neighbour experiment with telegraphing from Hare Hatch to Nettlebed by means of windmills, but she put up with the folly and humoured Perrot and even loved him. Her 'Willoughby' lineage pleased her somewhat, but her husband's name did more. As a childless woman she took keen pleasure in his revered name, 'for the Perrots', as James Austen's children were told, 'are a very ancient race in comparison with whom, Austens and Leighs, Mathews and Lefroys are almost creatures of yesterday'. And Aunt Perrot could support that boast. Descended from 'Havel King of Maw, and Prince of Angelsea' in the year 808, some of her husband's ancestors as she said had gone to Brittany and built a château on the River Perrot 'and from thence took their name' and then their offspring had *returned* with the Conqueror to obtain lands in Wessex where they 'gave their name to a river'. Becoming almost a force of nature the Perrots sired William of Wykeham. Then they combined with royalty. Sir John Perrot's mother was Mary the daughter of Lord Berkeley, and his father was 'that excellent man' King Henry VIII, whom he closely resembled and whose royal blood ran in the veins of the Perrots until it mingled with that of the Revd George Austen's poor children. A relative named Thomas Pope founded Trinity College, and Simon, who was the first Perrot of Northleigh, married Alice White, niece of the founder of St John's College. To be sure it was a pity that the rash, temperamental or possibly crazy sons of Robert Perrot and Alice Gardiner quarrelled over land and began a feud which divided the Perrots of Northleigh. The elder branch or 'the Perrots of the hill' died in a storm of misfortune, but 'our younger branch' survived down to Thomas Perrot, who bequeathed his estate and name, as Aunt Perrot said, to her 'dear Perrot' who had the gout.[24]

This history entertained every Austen before one of Anna Lefroy's daughters wrote it down. Aunt Perrot's pride in being related to rivers and kings seemed comic to Austen children. But her pride had an echo in Mrs Austen's certain belief in the value of aristocratic forbears and in Jane's sense of the Leigh ancestry. One of the forces that drove Austen children to succeed was always Mrs Austen's talk of the Leighs. Jane Austen herself was not vain or foolish on the topic of ancestry, but she was well aware of family. One may feel the smart of being portionless and a financial burden to others, very painfully, in view of one's knowledge of much richer, socially distinguished forbears; and the psychological attitude of the dispossessed can be a prime motive in creative work. To be with Aunt Perrot, in any case, was to be reminded of Mr Austen's small status and income. Aunt Perrot (according to one of James's family) with great dignity pronounced her name as 'PERRət', with a sharp trill: and her manners alone might have proved her husband's ancestry, just as her talk proved her sense of *noblesse oblige*. Usually she was generously condescending to her nieces. ''Tis really very kind of my Aunt to ask us to Bath,' Jane had felt, 'a kindness that deserves better return than to profit by it.' She perhaps gave Jane Austen gowns and handkerchiefs on this visit, while sending her to a 'very cheap shop' near Walcot Church to get gauzes for Cassandra's cloak. 'Very cheap we found it,' Jane Austen wrote amiably, and thought her a good guide.[25] Yet Aunt Perrot in a smart gown with quantities of material to show off her elegance and status at Bath was so imperious that she asked for assent without yielding an inch, and expected her nieces to admire her.

Possibly at Scarlets and Bath as a girl, Jane had found her overbearing and frightening. With Aunt Perrot she perhaps had a foretaste of Elizabeth's experience with Lady Catherine, if not of Fanny Price in a room with Mrs Norris, but the aunt took on gleams and colours the better one knew her. She was 'sad' in disapproving moods, but her 'most thoroughly affectionate words' could be prized. In all she had been a factor in Jane Austen's education in human character and would remain interesting for her eccentricity, self-assurance, sheer nigglingness and courage. At a practical and useful level, she knew arcades, shops, Pump Room and the genteel citizenry so well that one could be grateful to her. But a short visit with her was enough for Jane, who soon formed a tacit alliance with Elizabeth as *that* visitor grew impatient with her own husband and two young children in tow. 'Edward has been pretty well,' Jane Austen reports to her sister on 11 June. 'He is more comfortable here than I thought he would be, and so is Elizabeth, though they will both, I believe, be very glad to get away – the latter especially which one can't wonder at *somehow*,' she adds in imitation of Mrs Piozzi. Martha at home has asked to read 'First Impressions' again, and that is a reminder of an atmosphere for quiet work that Bath dispelled. 'I would not let Martha read "First Impressions" again upon any account,' Jane informs Cassandra, 'and am very glad that I did not leave it in your power. She is very cunning, but I saw through her design; she means to publish it from memory, and one more perusal must enable her to do it.' Jane's eyes had troubled her since early in the year when she began taking drops. 'I find no trouble in doing my eyes,' she tells Cassandra, but the eyes have seen enough of Bath.[26] At twenty-four she was taxing herself with steady enterprise and application needed to write her third lengthy novel, and so far, with no work published and little encouragement from outside, she could well hope to see Cassandra soon. It had been pleasant to raid the shops with Elizabeth and to see fireworks at Sydney Gardens, though a concert there was satisfying because one could 'get pretty well beyond the reach of the sound'. Her aunt's bluffness, too, was tiring. Aunt Perrot ranted about the 'absurd pretensions' of wearing white gowns in town, and Jane jotted seditiously in her manuscript, 'Miss Tilney always wears white.'[27] Late in June 1799 she said goodbye to her aunt at last.

Six weeks after Jane Austen left Bath, her uncle and aunt had an odd experience. There was no luncheon as a regular meal and so, after a rather late breakfast, the middle-aged couple were out walking after 1.00 p.m., on Thursday, 8 August, when Aunt Perrot called at Miss Elizabeth Gregory's millinery shop to ask if some lace from London had arrived. It had not. She bought a card of black lace costing £1 19s, and paid for it with a £5 note. Business was slack in August and the shop was quiet. Miss Gregory made change near a brass rail, hung with veils and handkerchiefs intercepting the view of anyone behind it in the shop, and Aunt Perrot walked out. After strolling under the colonnades to the Cross Bath, she and Perrot were coming back when Miss Gregory ran up and said, 'Pray, ma'am, have you got a card of white lace as well as black?'

Aunt Perrot was taken aback by this. 'No, I have not a bit of white lace about me.'

'See in your pocket, Ma'am.'

Perhaps Aunt Perrot was too deaf to hear. She merely handed over her paper parcel to the milliner, and said, 'If I have your young man must have put it up by mistake.'[28]

Inside the parcel Miss Gregory found a card of white lace beside the black lace, and took the former back to the shop. Events now

149

moved with the quickness of a tragi-comedy. At the abbey church-yard, Miss Gregory's shopman Filby caught up with the couple, and in reply to his demands Mr Leigh Perrot gave his address and said his name was on a plate at his Paragon door. Four days later the Perrots got an anonymous, insinuating letter about 'the piece of Lace stolen from Bath St', and then a constable arrived with a warrant for Mrs Leigh Perrot's appearance before the Mayor of Bath.

Crippled with gout, her husband went with her to the Town Hall where Filby and Miss Gregory had sworn depositions. Mrs Leigh Perrot heard that she would be held in gaol. 'The Mayor and Magistrates, to whom we were well known, lamented their being obliged to commit me,' she wrote but 'to prison I was sent'.[29] As the white lace was valued in excess of 12 pence (or at 20s.), she was accused of a capital crime, which could mean death by hanging, but if found guilty she was more likely to be transported and so could expect to die in exile at Botany Bay.

We do not know how the Austens reacted at first to this news. Comments by Mrs Leigh Perrot, however, show that they were soon less shocked than angry. Here was another instance of the law's cruelty, not less barbaric than the slow attempt of the Whigs to bring Eliza's godfather to disgrace at his impeachment trial. The hardihood that saved Frank and Charles at sea and the aggressive daring that kept Jane Austen at work, are not really consistent with the view that the Austens did little for their aunt. Few clergymen in their ordinary duties worked harder than James, and yet he kept up his aunt's morale, sent her letter after letter, and was preparing to join her at Ilchester when he broke his leg. Though ill, Mrs Austen thought of going to live with Mrs Leigh Perrot in the Ilchester gaoler's house and then proposed to send on Cassandra and Jane. Aunt Perrot had gallantly refused her nieces' cheerful company, and now her seven months' ordeal as a prisoner tested her nerves and those of her husband, who had joined in her gaoler's crude lodgings.

We know that Joseph Jekyll MP, her own Counsel, thought her guilty of stealing the white lace. 'Jekyll considered Mrs. L.P. was a kleptomaniac,' Richard Austen-Leigh later wrote privately, and that she 'did steal the material, and probably meant to'. It seems that wealthy ladies may become more unreliable than other women, as Jekyll blandly supposed: 'Mrs L.P.' was like other rich ladies 'who frequent bazaars and mistake other people's property for their own', he wrote. 'It was the blunder of my client, Mrs. Leigh Perrot.'[30] And if her counsel thought her guilty what would her jurors think? At their own expense the Leigh Perrots were allowed to go to London in the somewhat buttery company of their gaoler Edward Scadding, who thoughtfully found rooms near good supplies of wine and ale at the Angel. 'My dearest Husband is not now my *only Protector*,' commented Aunt Perrot, 'as I have the *Ilchester Jailor* in my suite.' But since a judge of the King's Bench refused her bail, she went back to prison where she was grateful to James Austen, who despite his broken leg is 'a perfect Son to me in Affection, and his firm Friendship all through this trying Business had taught me to look to him and his Wife . . . to have come to us at the Assizes'.[31]

The spring assize opened at last on 27 March 1800 at Taunton, where five prisoners were sentenced to death including a fourteen-year-old burglar. Mrs Leigh Perrot was accused of her capital crime, but Jekyll was not allowed to argue in her defence. Miss Gregory in a circumstantial account said that when the prisoner was met on Bath Street Mrs Leigh Perrot had 'trembled very much, was much frightened, and coloured as red as scarlet', as the white lace on a card 'of a light blue colour' turned up in her packet.

'Yes, it is mine, I'll swear to it,' Miss Gregory vowed to having said to her in the street.

The prisoner had pretended that she was given the white lace by mistake.

''Tis no such thing, 'tis no such thing,' Miss Gregory had cried honestly in the street; 'you stole it, you are guilty.'

But now, when it was pointed out in court that the milliner's shop-clerk Charles Filby had been thrice bankrupted, and had once wrapped up an *extra* veil in the parcel of a customer named Balgrave, the defence revived. Then before some '2,000 persons' the accused was allowed to read a brief statement. In a faltering voice, majestic and vulnerable at once, Mrs Leigh Perrot rose to her finest moment. This was not her most auspicious occasion in society but ranks of benches, leering faces of townspeople, and the abashed looks of friends goaded her to show how a Willoughby who had married into a line associated with kings and watercourses might comport herself. She rather deeply affected the crowds.

My Lord and Gentlemen of the Jury, she began with urgent brevity. *I am told that my Counsel cannot be permitted to address to you any remarks on my Case.* As a woman reduced to defending herself though blessed with a tenderly affectionate husband she would not detain the court, but did they imagine her so depraved as to steal? *Is it possible that at this time of Life,* she asked, *my disposition should so suddenly change and that I should foolishly hazard the well earned reputation of a whole Life of such Conduct, or endanger the Peace of Mind of a Husband for whom I would willingly lay down that Life?*[32]

As Uncle Perrot sat violently weeping, the prisoner faltered. But her husband kept a handkerchief over his face so that she finished her few words. More than a dozen witnesses then spoke for her. Wright the jeweller and Thomas Coward the linen-draper swore she was honest, and the Hayward Winstones of No. 10 Great Bedford Street so outdid themselves that Jane Austen entered a ballroom a year later with her aunt and uncle and gratefully 'linked Miss Winstone on to us'. Maria Edgeworth's father in Ireland announced in a letter which, as he said, was written 'with tears of indignation in my eyes – aye Sir! – with actual, not sentimental tears' that he recalled the Leigh Perrots' decency over thirty-four years,[33] and although that letter was not read in court, Francis Annesley, the MP for Reading, and George Vansittart, the MP for Berkshire, as well as Lord Braybroke were all heard. At last the jurors withdrew. In less than ten minutes they returned with a 'not guilty'.

'I was disappointed in *Jekyll*', Mrs Leigh Perrot declared, but on the other hand her attorney Pell 'showed vast feeling by perfectly sobbing whilst my *Observations* were repeated. Indeed I never saw so many men weep.' In the day following the trial as she put it, 'my whole time has been taken up in *kissing* and Crying'.[34] Still Jekyll remained convinced she was guilty. 'At Stowey met Mr Symes the lawyer,' William Holland the Somerset parson had written of the case. 'He told me that Mrs Parrot had bought off her prosecutor. Alas, alas that money should be able to screen a person from Justice,' he felt. 'She was accused of stealing lace out of a shop in Bath, is a person of considerable fortune & has a poor Jerry Sneak of a husband who adheres to her through all difficulties.' On the other hand it was widely repeated at Bath that Filby in collusion with William Gye the printer, who had launched the *Bath Courant* (in 1773), had frightened Leigh Perrot into buying off Filby, a crucial witness against Aunt Perrot. Filby and Gye at any rate were not tried. Gye's son Frederick carried on his father's printing business so well that by 1807 he was able to buy one of the three successful Bath news-papers.*

It is by no means clear today that Mrs Leigh Perrot was innocent. The letters sent to the Perrots reporting a conspiracy against them have the look of hearsay, gossip and local feuds, and her attorney's belief that she was a kleptomaniac, as well as the Revd William Holland's report that Symes said she had bought off 'her prosecutor', leave the matter of guilt open to question.[35] But the trial gladdened many people in town. Aunt Perrot enjoyed her victory until the age of ninety-two: her ordeal proved the strength of her dignity, and if newspapers advertised her shame what could one expect of Gye and his tribe? She would have been cut 'to the very heart' to see her nieces Cassandra and Jane in the gaoler's house but she was more than ever a heroine to the Austens. (Jane Austen was to visit a prison and had she lived long enough she might have written of one.) We cannot be sure that Mr and Mrs Leigh Perrot visited Steventon just after their ordeal, but it is clear that these events affected Jane Austen's view of the 'littlenesses' of Bath.

Bath was not an especially threatening place and any highway at night was more dangerous, but it seemed to Jane Austen stultifying with its public music, 'white glare' and card-parties where people were too many for intimacy and too few for variety. Mrs. Leigh Perrot's plight had been the vulgar talk because Bath had so little to talk of. The town's anonymity made neighbours into exiles and its concerts and balls did not substitute for natural surroundings which determined the worth of *any* place. 'Oh! when shall I leave you again!' was Jane Austen's attitude to an enforced stay there, and she sympathized with a heroine who 'disliked Bath'.[36] On the other hand as a rural person she was not fonder of any other town. Her social visits to Bath had sent her home amused by the Isabella Thorpes she had seen, but perhaps with renewed eagerness to talk with Cassandra or Martha Lloyd and to hear Mr Austen's evening recitals of Cowper or Johnson. Meanwhile Bath belonged to a strong, deaf aunt who had survived seven months' ridiculous gossip over a card of white lace.

Jane Austen's brother Charles returned from the sea in November. 'We walked down to Deane after dinner,' she reports of a ball in

* The three newspapers, all known to the Austens, were the *Bath Chronicle, Bath Herald* and *Bath Journal*.

which Charles 'danced the whole evening, & today is no more tired than a gentleman ought to be'. There had been as she wrote to Cassandra in Kent, 'only ten dances, of which I danced seven', but then she changed the numbers to *twelve* and *nine* with exactitude. Cassandra expected not only exactness but some account of the evening. Jane deliciously had watched a Mrs Blount who still had 'the same broad face, diamond bandeau, white shoes, pink husband & fat neck', as well as the two Misses Cox, one of whom was the vulgar and broad-featured girl who had danced at Enham, and a pregnant Mrs Warren who 'got rid of some part of her child & danced away with great activity'.

Cassandra must hear matrimonial news too. The widower Sir Thomas Williams was to marry Miss Emma Wapshare, reports an author who loved the name Emma. 'She lives somewhere between Southampton and Winchester, is handsome, accomplished, amiable, & everything but rich.' ('Emma Woodhouse, handsome, clever, and rich,' she was to begin in a novel, 'with a comfortable home and happy disposition, seemed to unite some of the best blessings of existence; and had lived nearly twenty-one years in the world with very little to distress or vex her.') Bath itself and local balls in Hampshire pleased her in being the natural scenes of the beginnings of matrimonial affairs. They were at least the locales of youth and promise, of new starts in the comedy and happiness of life. When *their* resources exhausted themselves and gossip ran threadbare she could invent something to please Cassandra. James Digweed for example has called at the rectory and 'I think he must be in love with you,' she assures Cassandra, 'from his anxiety to have you go to the Faversham Balls, & likewise from his supposing, that the two Elms fell from their greif at your absence. Was not it a gallant idea? – It never occurred to me before, but I dare say it was so. – Hacker has been here today, putting in the fruit trees,' she adds of plantings visible from a window. '– A new plan has been suggested concerning the plantation of the new inclosure on the right hand side of the Elm Walk – the doubt is whether it would be better to make a little orchard of it, by planting apples, pears & cherries, or whether it should be larch, Mountain-ash & acacia. – What is your opinion? – I say nothing, & am ready to agree with anybody.'[37] But her father's feelings are not so happy as the farm has cleared only £300 in the year. His income at best has been as high as £600. The harvests failed in the south but the assessed wartime taxes have trebled in a year – the horse-tax has risen so much the Austens have laid up their carriage. Poor folk pay bitterly this hard winter when old folk are dying for want of fuel. The terrible surplusage of rural poor burdens *every* parish and the Austens are giving away spare clothing. Rich farms grow richer and farmers fewer, and with enclosures of common land more and more people have met with degradation. Mr Austen's poor rates have soared without relieving the parish's tenants. His wife is in weak health, and in his seventieth year he is a hard-pressed man who plants a few cheap fruit trees as an act of faith at an anguishing time. One must read in and between the lines of Jane Austen's letters to find her own sense of the parish's plight: 'At Oakley we bought ten pairs of worsted stockings, & a shift. – The shift is for Betty Dawkins,' she tells her sister. 'She is one of the most grateful of all whom Edward's charity has reached' and she sends him 'a sight of thanks'. Poor Mrs Martin has 'totally failed in her business, & had very lately an execution in her house'. 'Delmar lost so much by the Assemblies last winter that he has protested against opening his rooms.' And at meagre private dances there is after all a boring lack of men, and one sees 'Ladies standing up together', so it e is pleasant after all to sit in idleness over a good fire in a well-proportioned room at Ashe Park in almost complete silence. Funny news to send Cassy is scarce, and yet 'like Mrs Hastings, "I do not despair" '.[38]

Late in November she was glad to visit Martha Lloyd at Ibthorp, where the three Miss Debaries paid a call and not even the endless Debaries were oppressive. 'Martha', Jane writes to her sister, 'has promised to return with me, & our plan is to have a nice black frost for walking to Whitechurch, & there throw ourselves into a post-chaise, one upon the other, our heads hanging out at one door, & our feet at the opposite.' That funny detail rivals anything in her own *Love and Freindship* and arises from a gaiety nourished by Martha, the Bigg girls and Cassandra. When Martha returned with her to Steventon, the hard black frosts of December 1800 had begun. After they came into the rectory from a walk one day, Mrs Austen greeted the two young women with, 'Well, girls, it is all settled. We have decided to leave Steventon in [such a week], and go to Bath.'[39]

At this news Jane Austen fainted, so Anna Lefroy heard. 'All things were done in a hurry by Mr. Austen,' who had decided to move to Bath in the new year and hire his eldest son as a curate.[40] James would live in the rectory. Their father had decided to move to Bath (as Frank Austen says in a little-known autobiographical manuscript) because he felt too 'incapacitated from age and increasing infirmities to discharge his parochial Duties in a manner satisfactory to himself'.[41] His low income and high taxes had steeled his mind, and the social advantages his daughters might have at Bath were not lost on Mrs Austen. Cassandra was absent when the decision was made, and Mary Austen found Jane quite alone and 'greatly distressed' – but a younger daughter's tears were insignificant. Aunt Perrot knew or imagined why Jane was 'distressed'. The family *had* to move, that lady felt, because of a romantic attachment between Jane and a Digweed man. What could one expect? But dear Jane would forget her suitor when she was living at Axford Buildings in Bath, to which there would be no need to bring either Mr Austen's heavy books or Jane's pianoforte. (All of these items were to be sold.)

'We know', Jane wrote dejectedly, 'that Mrs. Perrot will want to get us into Axford Buildings, but we all unite in particular dislike of that part of the Town.'[42] In leaving Steventon she was being uprooted and crushed: she could 'explain' its hillsides to anyone as well as she could tell Charles about landscape between Canterbury and Rowling – and much better. She was being taken from a small community, which she knew well, from people whose words, actions and looks in repose or at work she cherished. There could be no compensation in a jangling crowded town. Her sense of place was part of her confidence, and *that* was being torn from her. One could be sad in leaving a place because connections are cut *too* easily: other people part from one too readily, and friendships are exposed as less significant than one had hoped and perhaps as insignificant as they really are. But the precious intimacy of talk and feeling she had with Martha or Catherine or Mrs Lefroy was rare, and it was cruel to leave. A loss may be a gain, but how does one happily endure without love, friendship, peace and delight? There was no justice or equity here, and she was not even likely to sense the full measure of her loss for months. She meant to be cheerful but until well into January 1801 she found little to allay what Mary called her 'distress' over her father's irrevocable plan and that hard, bitter notion of leaving her home for good.

Part Three

WAR AND THE WILDERNESS

11

———⊰≫⧓⧓⧒≪———

Nelson relaxes

Cease then, nor ORDER Imperfection name:
Our proper bliss depends on what we blame.
Alexander Pope, *An Essay on Man*

'**W**e have at last heard from Frank,' Jane Austen had written when her sister was at Godmersham Park in 1800. 'You must rest satisfied with knowing that on the 8th of July the Peterell with the rest of the Egyptian Squadron was off the Isle of Cyprus.' Frank was so restrained and factual that she and her sister had to 'rest satisfied' with his travel reports and other outward observations. But what were his feelings? His dry, blunt manner led her to comment on his news with exclamations, as when she heard of his six weeks' wait for a new ship and could ironically suppose what he must have felt: 'Poor fellow!' she tells Cassandra, 'to wait from the middle of November to the end of December, & perhaps even longer! it must be sad work! – especially in a place where the ink is so abominably pale. – What a surprise to him it must have been on the 20th of Oct' to be visited, collar'd & thrust out of the Peterell by Capt'' Inglis! – He kindly passes over the poignancy of his feelings in quitting his Ship, his Officers & his Men.' Still she was amused by Frank and could find him consoling. If he endured hardships at sea she might endure some at Bath. Everything neat, compact, efficient and cheerful about him, it seems, told well for the Navy: 'For a time,' she writes in January 1801 about the Bath removal, 'we shall now

159

possess many of the advantages which I have often thought of with Envy in the wives of Sailors or Soldiers.'[1]

Looking for naval news in the papers she noticed Frank's advancement. He had begun in HMS *Perseverance*, and when the East India Company bought it he lent them some of his crew to navigate it. He had left that ship for Cornwallis's *Crown*, and transferred into the 32-gun frigate *Triton* under Gore for eighteen months, then gone from the *Seahorse* into the *London* which was blockading Spaniards at Cadiz. Though France was only three-and-a-half hours from Dover it was a paradox of the war that the Navy sailed far from home: weeks, months had slipped by with no word from Frank. His *London* went as far as Ceuta or Gibraltar, and later he was to tell his sisters some – perhaps not all – of the difficulties he faced aboard that vessel. Six men in his squadron were hanged, and sailors on his own ship were lashed for insolence, mutiny and an 'unnatural crime of Sodomy'.[2] In *Mansfield Park* Jane Austen would have Mary Crawford as niece of the adulterous Admiral Crawford refer in a casual, vulgar way to that crime. The age of elegance was not squeamish, and degradations of the lower decks were common talk in London: 'Certainly,' Mary Crawford tells Edmund Bertram, 'my home at my uncle's brought me acquainted with a circle of admirals. Of *Rears*, and *Vices*, I saw enough. Now, do not be suspecting me of a pun, I entreat.'[3] (Mary makes Edmund imagine *he* had detected a sexual pun.) That apparent allusion in *Mansfield Park* to the 'unnatural crime' is important and indicative enough: Jane Austen did not subscribe to Mary Crawford's vulgarity any more than to Fanny's wilting innocence but insisted on representing what her characters *would* say – and without offence to the reader. Frank, in these years, helped her to know the naval mind in its discussable aspects.

She knew his relief in being sent out of the *London* to command the armed sloop *Peterel* off Egypt. Nelson had reopened the Mediterranean. But Frank's life soon belied any romantic view of the Navy or what would be Mary Crawford's view of its 'heroism, danger, bustle, fashion', since he knew misery. A sloop could become one nauseous stench of bilge and dry rot so that no amount of burning vinegar-and-gunpowder in pans about the decks could get rid of the smell, and those decks could be like wet porous stone with dampness below in every hammock. The hacking coughs of men echoed in every hour of the watch. More men died of tuberculosis than were killed by shot, and other diseases aboard ship were common. But Frank did what a captain should. He tried to keep *Peterel* scrubbed and ventilated, ports open and bilges pumped, tried to make do with scanty provisions and sew up canvas, and asked for stores only when he knew exactly who had them and how he might get them. 'My Lord,' he would write to his commander Viscount Nelson. 'I beg leave to inform your Lordship that I have seen a quantity of Slop Shoes and Cotton Cloth for making Frocks and Trowsers for Seamen in possession of Captain Adair Inspecting, [and] the Crew of His Majesty's Ship under my Command are very much in want of those Articles of Cloathing.' Those Mary Crawfords of the day, who praised the Navy for its dash and fashion, might have been surprised that Frank's men were 'very much in want' when they had to work in freezing rigging in gale-force winds. He endured when his canvas sails were in shreds. Lacking sail he could be dismasted in action, and then his ship would turn broadside-on until timbers were driven in and he and his crew drowned. 'My Lord,' Frank writes in the polite form of the day, 'there are two top Gallant Royals much worn and rendered unfit for use.' 'My Lord,' he writes to Nelson, 'the undermentioned Sails Awnings &ᶜ are much worn, rotten.' 'My Lord,' he appeals again, 'the undermentioned Sails are much worn and rendered unfit,' and above his commander's name he lists his driver sheet, foretopsail, foresail and maintopsail.[4]

He might sail on hope. But the hero of the Nile had begun to notice. Nelson was pleased when Frank took a dispatch about movements of the French fleet to him at Palermo in two days from Minorca, and was impressed to hear from the Admiralty about him. George Austen's notes to patrons had an effect, and evidence suggests that after James's first marriage to Anne Mathew, the relative of Admiral Gambier, the Austens were not overlooked by the Admiralty's 'evangelical' faction. One mentions in passing that Jane Austen's own regard for the evangelical movement, which indirectly helped her brothers, was unsettled. 'I do not like the Evangelicals,' she wrote in 1809 and five years later, 'I am by no means convinced that we ought not all to be Evangelicals.' She disliked the enthusiasm of her cousin Edward Cooper, when he was 'fuller of Regeneration & Conversion than ever – with the addition of his zeal in the cause of the Bible Society', but, on the other hand, she admired the seriousness of evangelical believers when they were not false to the rational believing

161

mind.[5] The religious zeal of Frank's patrons at Whitehall was not necessarily irrational, but we cannot say that she regarded 'Evangelicals' more favourably simply because they helped her brothers.

Still Frank *was* helped. And Nelson was sensitive to appeals of normal patronage: 'You may rely upon all attention in my power to Capt. Austin,' Nelson wrote to Lord Moira, a grandson of the evangelical Countess of Huntingdon and friend of Admiral Gambier. 'A frigate', Nelson writes amiably of Jane Austen's brother, 'would have been better calculated to have given Capt. Austin a fortune out of the Mediterranean, than coming under my command, where nothing is to be got.' But the young man will not be neglected: 'I hope to see him alongside a French gunship.' And the great Admiral adds genially, 'Capt. A. I knew a little before; he is an excellent young man.'[6]

On the topic of Nelson himself Jane Austen was not likely to agree with a brother whose fervour for him was shared by an hysterical public: this sailor conquered hatters and tailors, while influencing everything from the theatre to the cheap souvenir trade. When the Austens moved to Bath his name was mentioned in ballads and on the stage, and his face peered out imperturbably from paper, canvas, pottery, porcelain, metal and muslin. The mameluke cap became fashionable after the Battle of the Nile, and milliners now produced a 'Nelson cap' in coquelicot velvet while dressmakers hung out portraits of the Nile victor and decorated new classical muslins with gold and silver.[7] To live in Jane Austen's wartime England was to be bombarded with images of his face, praise of him, gossip about him, and a wheezy surfeit of Nelsoniana, even if one was not reading every scrap of news for items about two naval brothers. Nobody was more impressed by him of course than his 'Emma' or Lady Hamilton, whose husband Sir William, a minor diplomat in Italy, not only winked at his wife's adultery with her hero but at Naples and Palermo maintained a warm senile friendship with him. The public were not overly concerned with Lady Nelson's feelings, and as 'unpleasant paragraphs' about adultery appeared in the press in 1800 people forgave the Admiral – and looked for more scandal. Some of them saw on display in a print shop in St James's Street Gillray's caricature of the fleet with a ballooning Lady Hamilton called 'Dido in Despair'. The Admiralty for its part believed that Lady Hamilton had gained control of its Mediterranean squadrons.

A spare, nervous, emaciated man of middle height with a large nose and white hair, Nelson in his forties was superficially an adolescent – or sounded like one. 'I tell you what,' he told Lady Minto when she wished he had an imperial army, 'if I had, I would use only one word – *advance*.' One understands why Napoleon kept a bust of him, and why the French believed his mistress was a sea goddess. His vulnerability rather than his talk gave him dignity, and he had read enough in a Norwich parsonage to use the Shakespearian high style with effect: 'My Lord,' he told all of England, 'Almighty God has blessed his Majesty's arms in the late battle.'[8] His patriotism was as genuine as his aggressive, eager love of a fight, or his ability to inspire sailors with blunt and confidential talk. With his theatrical streak and sense of humour and need for female comfort, he had fallen giddily in love with Lady Hamilton before making the mistake of crawling in a carriage with Sir William and the lady across the face of Europe in 1800. At Dresden, in October, he was observed by Mrs St George, whose granddaughter married the eldest son of James Edward Austen, even as Jane Austen's own nephew Dordy was to marry Countess Nelson, a widow of the great Admiral's brother. Unlike the horrified Admiralty, Mrs St George had no fear that England's hero would be assassinated but she was curious about the illicit lovers, and Austen descendants still keep a better record of Nelson's talk at Dresden than has appeared in print. What he really said on hearing that the Dresden Elector would not meet Emma was, 'Sir, if there is any difficulty of that sort, Lady Hamilton will knock the Elector down *and damn-me, I'll knock him down too.*' What he cried out when Lady Hamilton acted was, 'Mrs. *Siddons be damned!*'[9] He melted as Emma performed her 'Attitudes', when she posed in dumbshow to represent classical emotions while Sir William managed lighting effects. In these bizarre performances, of course, one sees not so much 'Emma' and 'Nelson' as an age which elevated theatricality as an antidote to the critical and inhibiting self-consciousness of the times. When Nelson relaxed, he enjoyed 'theatricals' as much as James and Henry had, so that it is almost appropriate that Dordy Austen married Countess Nelson. *Mansfield Park* would not have examined theatricality with such moral intensity and delight but for a social culture which produced Sheridan, family plays, Eliza de Feuillide and James and Henry with their prologues and sexual jokes in a parson's barn at Steventon. Mrs St George's description of Lady Hamilton's acting reflects a bizarre aspect of the Austens' England:

> Lady Hamilton takes possession of [Nelson] and dramatically represents the best statues and paintings extant. She assumes their attitude, expression, and drapery with great facility, swiftness, and accuracy. Several Indian shawls, a chair, some antique vases, a wreath of roses, a tambourine, and a few children are her whole apparatus. She stands at one end of the room with a strong light to her left, and every other window closed. Her hair (which by-the-bye is never clean) is short, dressed like an antique, and her gown a simple calico chemise, very easy, with loose sleeves to the wrist. She disposes the shawls so as to form Grecian, Turkish, and other drapery, as well as a variety of turbans. Her arrangement of the turbans is absolutely sleight-of-hand, she does it so quickly, so easily, and so well .... It is remarkable that, although coarse and ungraceful in common life, she becomes highly graceful, and even beautiful, during this performance.[10]

Public news of Nelson's adultery did not move Frank, whose feeling for him did not waver. As the creator of Wickham and Willoughby and Henry Crawford, Frank's sister herself was intrigued by sexual infidelity. Jane Austen was to be enthralled at Covent Garden by a representation of a Don Juan who was an interesting 'compound of cruelty and lust'.[11] She called 'lust' and 'adultery' by their proper names and already had given one real 'Mary' as well as the moral Mrs Knight illegitimate pregnancies – which was comically fair. At Bath, she represents herself as ready for some adultery in the kitchen. 'We plan', she wrote when newspapers were full of Nelson's dalliance, 'having a steady Cook, & a young giddy Housemaid, with a sedate, middle aged Man, who is to undertake the double office of Husband to the former & sweetheart to the latter.'[12] A married man who *couldn't* fall in love with a giddy housemaid was hopeless, but she also believed that adultery led to real death-in-life or to a dulling of generous sensitive feeling, and so it happened to be sinful. What exasperated her was not an admiral's adultery, it seems, so much as a craze which elevated him for the populace. If young women admire heroes whatever the heroes do, women are belittled. And the female who is cast as admirer, applauder and mindless adorer loses what little initiative there is available to women in society. 'Nelson fever', which had the effect of reducing women, coincided with an equally dubious and debasing journalism of fashion, which helped to keep Jane Austen from describing dress in detail in her novels, and may have prompted her to have silly Mrs Allen in *Northanger Abbey* chatter of nothing but dress. The harmless *Lady's Magazine*'s plates were being replaced by suave, chic weekly hints about how fragile and classic muslins are to cling to the female form to make it a helpless prize. New technical achievements in cotton spinning made it possible to produce fine thread and light gauzes and delicate muslins at a cheap rate. *She* loved those light, cheap fabrics – and who would not? – but even as fashion became a subject for journalism and a popularly obsessive topic as fabrics and styles were influenced by industrial development, the pattern of nineteenth-century social life was changing. Genteel men and women were moving, in effect, farther apart, to be weighed for their inherent value on two separate scales. More and more as Jane Austen turned twenty-five, a woman became a fragile thing to admire, an automaton with no really accredited will, and a prize for the successful naval man or industrialist. Many 'Nelsons' were coming into wealth and fame in the recent naval victories and some were as worthy and undiscerning as Captain Wentworth, with his Musgrove flirts, in *Persuasion*. The worship of the age's hero was amusing but finally tiresome and stupid. 'Southey's Life of Nelson,' Jane Austen wrote at last. 'I am tired of Lives of Nelson,' she told Cassandra after Nelson died, 'being that I have never read any. I will read this however, if Frank is mentioned in it.'[13]

Even in 1801 she separated Frank from his hero. With moral and professional discipline Frank proved himself. Before he left *Peterel* he defeated more than forty enemy ships. In twelve hours, he had met three of the enemy, driven two on the rocks in reach of French shore batteries, killed the captain of *La Ligurienne* and made her strike her tricolour, and filled his ship with prisoners, all with no loss to his crew. For that action of March 1800 he was made post-captain, though she heard news of his advancement before he did.

He deserved his promotion, she felt. And now as she helped to clear Steventon rectory for the removal, she delighted in 'wives of Sailors'. Quick, alert and ready as a sailor's wife she was half eager to go to Bath – and the sea. 'We must all meet at Bath you know before we set out for the Sea,' she reminded Cassandra. 'I get more and more reconciled to the idea of our removal. We have lived long enough in this Neighbourhood, the Basingstoke Balls are certainly on the decline, and there is something interesting in the bustle of going away.' Three areas of Bath with good, cheap houses, as she felt, were the Westgate Buildings where in *Persuasion* her widowed Mrs Smith would live, the streets near Laura Place where Lady Dalrymple would smugly stay, and Charles Street which seemed best for real Austens as it was near greenery. Meanwhile she watched watercolours taken down from walls, helped to itemize chairs and tables and heard a firm decree that the only furniture worth taking would be beds. The risk of breakage was altogether too great, and new furniture could be bought easily in Somerset. 'We have thought at times of removing the side-board, or a pembroke table,' but these were to be sold. Her brother James might buy her father's five hundred volumes, those early companions, at a half guinea each, she felt, if only to bedevil Mary Lloyd.[14]

Her *own* choices were so few that those she had were precious. 'I do not chuse to have Generosity dictated to me,' she announced quietly; 'I shall not resolve on giving my cabinet to Anna till the first thought of it has been my own.' But she had to accept that Cassandra's journey would be delayed and that she and her mother would reach the Perrots first – at the end of the long, frosty, curving terrace of houses in the Paragon – and this made the day of departure from Steventon no easier in May 1801. May 4 dawned lovely and clear. Having known her home for twenty-five years and four months she might feel the cruelty of leaving it under a blue sky. But the route was pleasant; the chaise did not plunge into mud, or stir up hurricanes of dust, and Jane and her mother only found they had no appetite for luncheon near Everley: 'we could not with the utmost exertion consume above the twentieth part of the beef'. A cucumber would be saved as a forlorn, practical gift for someone. The chaise's congenial silence was nearly perfect 'as we did not speak above once in three miles'. When she saw the panorama of Bath the sun had sunk low, 'and the appearance of the place from the top of Kingsdown was all vapour, shadow, smoke, and confusion'.[15]

It was as bad as a naval disaster for Frank might be. She could have seen Bath more distinctly through rain. She would know a lady's feeling of being led to it as a prisoner. Sharp hills protected rows of dwellings lying in a loop of the River Avon, and one could see the edge of a pale-grey or honey-coloured square or crescent. Of course it was one thing to visit here, another to live here forever, but people did admire the Corporation's devices to keep coal waggons out of the parades or Greek columns at the Circus or the traffic pouring through the North Gate, and most people marvelled at fine and convenient paving, stables and warehouses near the Quay, or views, from Beechen Cliff, or the busy activity of cobblers, cordwainers and shoemakers on Avon Street or the elegance of the New or Upper Assembly Rooms. At various times, Jane *had* enjoyed this social hive. It was wealthier and vaster than ever. The hive in 1801 with about 34,000 residents was larger than Nottingham or Leicester or Coventry, half the size of Liverpool or Bristol or Manchester or Birmingham. Walcot parish where her parents were married was the ninth richest in England or in *per capita* terms second in wealth only to St George's, Hanover Square. And Bath's beauty and glitter owed in part to Mrs Austen's own great-uncle, the Duke of Chandos, who, as the Perrots might always have been proud to say, had places named after him in town although it is doubtful they had enquired very closely into the sources of his wealth.

Nobody else before the eighteenth century had robbed England on such a scale as Mrs Austen's great-uncle. At twenty-nine James Brydges was an Admiralty Commissioner before the days of Gambier and Nelson, and at thirty Paymaster-General to the Forces Abroad. Secretly pocketing money on nearly every payment he made to Marlborough's troops, Brydges had exploited the difference between market and official rates of exchange and skimmed the top off £15,374,689 in public funds that were under his control between 1705 and 1711. Supplying inferior equipment to troops who were later defeated in Spain, he made such a fortune that his private turnover with Antwerp and London brokers equalled in a short time one-fiftieth of the national debt, or later what would be one-thirty-seventh of the whole state debt of the kingdom.[16] This great robber had to be hanged or ennobled. Luckily Mrs Austen's great-uncle was created first Duke of Chandos in 1719. A few years later he visited Bath with his second wife Cassandra, who had 'hysteric fits',[17] and saw within its medieval walls a tawdry, forlorn town victimized by gamblers, pickpockets and sedan chairmen; yet it had an abbey in the Perpendicular Gothic style and had had a vogue as a watering place since Roman times, when it had flourished as 'Aquae Sulis', Sul or Sulis being an island counterpart of Minerva, the goddess of wisdom and patron of all the arts. Its waters had enough iron and radium to cure backaches of the legions, and indeed amazing Roman remains were uncovered here twenty years before Jane Austen's birth. Chandos, in the 1720s, found a smelly, tatty Bath; but he sensed a real potential. Investing in development, he hired an architect–surveyor named John Wood in his early twenties, a self-trained mythologist and ambitious vision-ary. Wood aimed to build a new city with designs inspired by lovely precedents of Rome and Greece, by the insights of Vitruvius and the architecture of Palladio, by the myths of Druidical Britain and by the moral force and splendour of the Old Testament. In his own books *The Origin of Building* (1741) and *Order of Columns* (1750) Wood typically sees windows as symbolic Tabernacles, and circles as signs of God's perfection. When the Bath Corporation declined his offer to rebuild 'in a regular manner' he used Chandos's money to redesign St John's Hospital and build Chandos Court, his first works at Bath, and thus the family of Jane Austen's mother provided the first spon-sor of Bath's most influential architect. Wood finished Queen Square, named in honour of Queen Caroline, the wife of George II, and the northward-leading Gay Street in 1734 when he was thirty. He then drew on other patrons and stockjobbers, and when he died in 1754 his son and namesake continued his work. The North and South Parades, the Circus and the Royal Crescent came into being.

Meanwhile an uncrowned king had had a half-century reign. After his ceremonial predecessor Captain Webster was killed in a duel, Richard Nash, a gambler and large, vain, portly man of sartorial splen-dour, became Bath's *arbiter elegantiarum*. No one else more widely influenced English manners or contributed more to form the temper of the world Jane Austen wrote about. His position as a Master of Ceremonies was unpaid, but as he hired musicians with his gambling profits he could dictate when a dance would begin and end in an assembly room, and after getting Thomas Harrison to build a good room for dances and gaming, he negotiated to have John Wood design a second one which opened in 1730 with Dame Lindsey as lessee. (Later John Wood the Younger designed the more elegant New or Upper Assembly Rooms which were built at a cost of £20,000 – the largest investment in any building at Bath – and were opened in September 1771.) 'Beau' Nash did his best to see that people behaved, that the young met each other and civilly enjoyed themselves – and he posted rules of etiquette in the Pump Room for all to see.[18] Refined visitors streaming into the city may have overlooked God's grandeur in Wood's columns, but they found tasteful buildings, safety and pleasure, well-behaved sedan chairmen and above all social sanity and quiet retreats; and no English city perhaps ever attracted a higher proportion of the gifted. Alexander Pope came to see Bath. So did Henry Fielding and Sarah Fielding, Dr Johnson, Horace Walpole, Smollett, Goldsmith, and later Wordsworth and Scott. Addison and Defoe and Boswell visited the city, and so did Gay, Arbuthnot, Prior, Parnell, Young, Richardson, Byrom, Collins and Shenstone as well as Edward Gibbon, and the Burneys, and Sterne and Cowper, and the men of the Enlightenment such as Newton, Locke, Shaftesbury, Berkeley and Hume. So did Colley Cibber and Chesterfield, Lord Clive and Gainsborough, Garrick and Mrs Linley and Mrs Siddons and Mary Wollstonecraft and Lawrence and Hoare. Nelson as a young captain lived in Pierrepont Street, and the future Lady Hamilton worked at Pierrepont Place. Burke and Goldsmith resided in the North Parade, Johnson's friend Mrs Thrale in the South Parade. Josiah Wedgwood the potter lived in Gay Street, and Samuel Wilberforce the abolisher of slavery in Great Pulteney Street. Sheridan the play-wright lived at the Royal Crescent, and Herschel was living in King Street when he discovered the planet Uranus.[19] If the list of distinguished eighteenth-century visitors and residents is nearly endless, so it attracted every social class and drew in aristocrats by the score – twenty-four earls and seventy-seven countesses and viscount-esses and baronesses in one season (autumn 1765) – as well of course as quacks, sharpsters, prostitutes and the gouty, sick and dying. But upstarts, hucksters, usurers, petty brokers and jobbers of every kind did not set its prevalent tone. By 1801 it had forty thousand visitors a year with a twenty-week social season that was important. Some £3 million had been invested in its buildings or a sum equal to the total investment in the cotton textile industry in Great Britain, and the city was comfortable with lodging houses and places of enter-tainment and recuperation. Fifty-four Improvement Commissioners had adopted a scheme to widen the streets and refurbish the centre as early as March 1788 (the same month in which the first stone was laid in Laura Place when Jane Austen was twelve), but banks failed in the financial crash of 1793 and after that the crescents failed to attract *quite* such exclusive company as formerly.

Yet Bath still glittered. Merchants did well in season, and ever since the town's charter in 1189 had granted the same privileges as

Winchester to its merchant guild, the burgesses by and large had made money. Many had become evangelical after the onset of Methodism in the 1730s, and in time John Wesley paid eighty visits to the city. Even more successful with the merchants had been 'Doctor Squintum', or George Whitefield the Calvinistic Methodist, one of whose blue eyes was marred by a cast. His strenuous friend and ally the Countess of Huntingdon lived in Bath when she was setting up her national 'Connexion' of sponsored evangelists. Hannah More's play *The Inflexible Captive* was produced by Garrick here at the Bath Theatre Royal in the year of Jane Austen's birth, and twelve years later Hannah More was supporting Thomas Clarkson, one of Jane Austen's favourite authors, in his dangerous job of gathering evidence from ships' crews to support the anti-slavery campaign. Hannah More met Wilberforce at Bath in 1787 and soon afterwards moved to the city, where as a good Tory evangelical propagandist she lived with her sisters and turned out her *Cheap Repository Tracts* for the moral, religious and educational improvement of the poor. That sensible evangelist – whom Cobbett described as 'the old bishop in petticoats'[20] – was active at Bath in 1801, and though Wesley and Lady Huntingdon were then ten years dead and Whitefield too was gone, the evangelical creed of self-surrender appealed to the same Bath bourgeois who hailed Nelson's victories. Evangelical admirals knew Bath too, and most of them were perhaps saner than Admiral Sir John Duckworth who at sea chose Christmas Day of this year (1801) to hang a sailor with a knot under the man's chin to prolong his agony, and saved Boxing Day to expose every bone in a sailor's back with 500 lashes.

Bath nevertheless had a staid autumnal gaiety, with its retired clergymen and lawyers. Many of the fashionable had drifted off to Cheltenham or Brighton, and the well-to-do here often avoided public balls. (Jane Austen included those dances in *Northanger Abbey*, but she would not do so in *Persuasion*.) The city was mellow but reserved, though still growing with new houses on the southern slope of Lansdown as a counter to the growth of Bathwick. But the Improvement Commissioners were timorous, buildings remained unfinished and Mr Pulteney's bridge over the Avon showed cracks. The squares and crescents were too stuffy and remote and exclusive to fulfil the elder Wood's belief that squares are for public assembly. Jane Austen came to a town that was socially brittle and fragmented by class privilege and money and snobbery. Here the intercourse of the social classes was more difficult and improbable than at Steventon, and one had a vaguer responsibility for the poor, no chance to become conversant with people at every level of the community. The assemblies had given way to private parties, and the well-to-do lived out of touch with the town's vital life. Indeed, Jane Austen's works more nearly resemble the city of Nash and Wood than the place she came to live in, since her novels are as concerned in the idea of community as Wood or Nash were. She, too, created limited 'places of assembly' in the sense that her characters and settings are genteel, but restricted herself only to comment broadly on life just as painters and philosophers who had come to Wood's Bath commented gloriously on the human condition.

Her aunt and uncle were busy with tea when Jane Austen and her mother reached the Paragon just after 7.30 p.m. on 4 May. Frank the servant's black head waited in a hall window and then her aunt led the way into the dining room with a 'violent cough'. They had not been there two minutes before her benign, talkative, modest uncle praised the Navy and asked of his relatives. 'I did my best to give information,' Jane Austen noted. She learned she might see Green Park Buildings next day with her uncle, who believed 'all the houses in New King Street' were too small. Mrs Austen seemed content to stay at the Perrots indefinitely, a notion alarming to Jane. Then she was led up two flights to her *own* room' where with a hot and suffocating feeling she went to bed – to the bliss of unconsciousness – and woke up with a start before five: 'I fancy I had too many clothes over me,' she complained. 'I thought I *should* by the feel of them before I went to bed, but I had not courage to alter them.' She could imagine other oppressions ahead. 'Bath is still Bath,' she wrote later, and when she heard that Janet Dundas sensibly had left the city she told Cassandra, 'Instead of Bath the Deans Dundases have taken a house at Clifton' and were as glad of the change as 'you and I should be, or almost'.[21]

Uncle Perrot was a slow-moving valetudinarian. On her first day he led her with a clumping stick to the Pump Room for his second glass of water, but as the stick was the only reminder of his lameness she optimistically planned a long walk with him to the 'Cassoon', which was Robert Weldon's Caisson Lock at Combe Hay on the

171

Somersetshire Coal Canal. It was just such a sight to please an uncle who experimented in windmills with Maria Edgeworth's father, a lock with a vertical rise of forty-six feet, but it had already been abandoned in favour of Benjamin Outram's inclined plane – itself to be replaced in 1805 by a system of twenty-two locks. Jane Austen took an amused interest in the canal mania that gripped the nation and later congratulated Edward when she read that the Weald of Kent Canal Bill, that 'villainous bill', had been postponed. She prepared now for social assaults. Evelyns, Chamberlaynes, Mrs Lillingstone and Mrs Busby left their cards, and a dance at the Upper Rooms was advertised. Though critical of those who cared for nothing but dress she was concerned to look her best – and wanted Cassandra to *see* how she looked. 'Mrs. Mussell has my gown,' she soon wrote with faith in a hairdresser's wife, 'a round gown, with a jacket and a frock front, to open at the side.' Cassandra would see how minute and accurate her particulars of a gown could be and visualize it to her heart's desire: 'the jacket is all in one with the body', Jane Austen continues with joy,

> and comes as far as the pocket-holes – about half a quarter of a yard deep, I suppose, all the way round, cut off straight at the corners with a broad hem. No fulness appears either in the body or the flap; the back is quite plain in this form $\overline{\text{Y}}$, and the sides equally so. The front is sloped round to the bosom and drawn in, and there is to be a frill of the same to put on occasionally when all one's handkerchiefs are dirty – which frill *must* fall back.

Her design is conservative and as for the sleeves there is to be nothing frilled, fancy or innovative at all – 'they are to be plain, with a fulness of the same falling down and gathered up underneath, just like some of Martha's, or perhaps a little longer. Low in the back behind, with a belt of the same. I can think of nothing more, though I am afraid of not being particular enough.'

Mrs Austen prepared for the terrors of cribbage and tea. 'My mother', her daughter adds, 'has ordered a new bonnet, and so have I; both white strip, trimmed with white ribbon. I find my straw bonnet looking very much like other people's, and quite as smart. Bonnets of cambric muslin on the plan of Lady Bridges' are a good deal worn, and some of them are very pretty; but I shall defer one of that sort till your arrival.' Cassandra was her *arbiter elegantiarum*, but Jane played the same role for her sister in turn.

Her new white bonnet and a sense of being 'in good looks' saved her from stupefaction at Mrs Lillingstone's party where she met nobody new.[22] She heard that the *last* ball of the season was to be at the Upper Rooms on Monday, 11 May 1801. (Beau Nash might have had it so and drawn up with his cream-coloured hat, outriders, footmen and French horns to see that it *was* the last, but another dance at the Rooms was held on 18 May.) On the 11th the activity in the long shining room under the candelabra was slight when at nine she entered with her aunt and uncle. Nothing at all happened, or rather a dismal tea was followed by one lugubrious dance: 'Think of four couple, surrounded by about an hundred people, dancing in the upper Rooms at Bath!' Her boredom was relieved after tea when a breaking up of private parties sent others to the ball – but the number dancing was inhumanly small, and but for the fact that she picked out an 'Adultress' in the crowd her evening would have been lost.

She would have been amused to find adultery in the kitchen and she was only a little surprised to find it in her blood relative, Mary Cassandra Twisleton. Mary's sister Julia a few years earlier had married James Henry Leigh, a descendant of the Leighs of Adlestrop, and so the 'Adultress' was related to Jane Austen by matrimony and descent.[23] 'She is not so pretty as I expected,' Jane decided. 'Her face has the same defect of baldness as her sister's [Julia Leigh's], & her features not so handsome; – she was highly rouged, & looked rather quietly & contentedly silly than anything else.'[24]

Miss Twisleton's party was not dull because it included a wild Mrs Badcock, who, now and then, detached herself from her young ladies to chase her drunken husband round and round the Upper Rooms.

As for the man who might be involved in Miss Twisleton's sexual delight every bit of gossip and suspicion focused on old Mr Evelyn, who usually spoke of nothing but horses. Jane believed him to be Edward's friend and had observed him on her last visit – when nothing about him had seemed dangerous or contagious. She measured him now against the boredom of Mrs Busby's friends, and found him rather delightful. She had not created Mr Wickham and Mr Willoughby out of thin air, and Mr Evelyn seemed quite as substantial as most men who made fools of women. If in the absence of his wife he had a liaison with Mary Cassandra – the sister of James Leigh's wife – Jane Austen made no attempt to avoid him, and a few days after the ball accepted his companionship. He lived at St Clere in Kent and in season at No. 10 Queen's Parade very decently, an older married man polite with his friends and in possession of a phaeton-and-four. She would not condemn him for adultery though Aunt Perrot obviously turned white to hear of him. 'I met him this morning for only the 4th time,' Jane wrote to play on Cassandra's usual alarm. '– There is now something like an engagement between us & the Phaeton, which to confess to my frailty I have a great desire to go out in; – whether it will come to anything must remain with him.' That teasing sentence is half-intended to make her sister see the ravishment of Miss Jane Austen's honour on the brink of Beechen Cliff, but 'I really believe he is very harmless; people do not seem afraid of him here, and he gets Groundsel for his birds and all that.' Aunt Perrot became very apprehensive over her going with him and 'she ought to be particularly scrupulous in such matters & she says so herself – but nevertheless ...'. Jane came back refreshed from her ride: 'just returned from my airing in the very bewitching Phaeton and four', she admits on the 27th. 'We went to the top of Kingsdown & had a very pleasant drive.'[25]

The Evelyn incident would not be worth observing, perhaps, if it did not show how her quiet independence allowed her to enjoy the company of an interesting man whose adultery was his concern, not hers, just as it was no obstacle in the way of discourse: he was far worthier than silly Miss Twisleton.

What she missed – very understandably – was a chance to form a female friendship in her sister's absence. As a married woman with a daughter on hand Mrs Chamberlayne at first seemed a poor candidate for friendship, for reasons other than her horrid beaver hat. When she called at the Perrots Mrs Austen noted her oddity, but at another 'stupid party' where there was nothing but one card table and six people to talk nonsense she seemed more human. 'I cannot anyhow continue to find people agreable,' Jane Austen felt and 'I respect Mrs. Chamberlayne for doing her hair well, but cannot feel a more tender sentiment.' But after a walk to Westdown was planned and others dropped out she found herself striding along by Mrs Chamberlayne's side. The day was hot. She knew the feel of her friend's hand by now. 'It would have amused you to see our progress;

– we went up by Sion Hill, & returned across the fields; – in climbing a hill Mrs. Chamberlayne is very capital; I could with difficulty keep pace with her – yet would not flinch for the world.' And so they posted away, '*She* without any parasol or any shade to her hat, stopping for nothing, & crossing the Church Yard at Weston with as much expedition as if we were afraid of being buried alive.' To touch Mrs Chamberlayne was to know her more frankly and 'I cannot help feeling a regard for her,' Jane decided, but her friend after all was only blandly and predictably 'like other people'. Mrs Chamberlayne was too indifferent and reserved and half-hearted and slow to intuit anyone else's feelings, and this incident points to one of Jane Austen's insistent complaints with the city. It allowed neither time nor proper encouragement for acquaintances that were as close and valuable as those she had with the Biggs or Martha to develop at all. On a second stroll with her friend she outwalked Mrs Chamberlayne on the way to nearby Lyncombe and Widcombe: 'for many, many yards together on a raised narrow footpath I led the way', Jane wrote. 'The walk was very beautiful as my companion agreed, whenever I made the observation – And so ends our friendship, for the Chamberlaynes leave Bath in a day or two,' and the transient artificial nature of the watering place would close in over the little emotional gap. In the country, in contrast, she had talked with Martha, dined with her, slept with her, walked and joked, and found her available to renew civil intimacies. And one insight she seems to have derived from present superficialities was that in a rational society our parties must be earned: 'Another stupid party last night' was her repeated comment on Bath's delights since the party-goers had nothing to do in intervals between parties, no outlet for thoughts or energies, and as one who believed that 'there is nothing which energy will not bring one to' she had to deny that mere energy could either make herself agreeable or cause her to find others so.[26] If elegant manners encourage nothing more than a disposition to be polite, elegance may not be worth much.

She was vexed and lonely in the days between 4 May and about 1 June as any young person would be when divided from real friends and from daily and welcome pursuits, and sent to live in a house with older people who were full of complaints, cautions and timidities. Her interest in Mr Evelyn was partly a response to living at No. 1 the Paragon with her mother, aunt and uncle. When she listened to young women at teas and found the teas stupid she compared the talk with what she knew of female intelligence from the implicit confederacy of female novelists. In the hands of writers who influenced Jane Austen – Fanny Burney and Charlotte Smith, Mrs Inchbald and Clara Reeve – the novel really did report on emotional and intellectual lives of women, and it was not possible to accept that intelligence and sensitivity in the female sex were common enough to be depicted in popular novels without feeling exasperated with 'stupid parties' in which everyone was blank. Women were more important, had more depth and a more interesting complexity than those she saw in May 1801. Exasperated by bores, she longed for news of her family and in particular of her father and Cassandra and Frank, whom she might expect to see, as they were coming to Bath in roundabout fashion. She would not forever be trotting alone on raised pavements or walking with her slow uncle into one damp unrentable house after another. Frank had touched port, but he meant to go first to Kent. When Jane's great-uncle Francis Austen died at ninety-two in 1791 his son Francis Motley Austen came into possession of the Red House at Sevenoaks, Kent, then disposed of it five years later and bought a grander Kippington House, which had been rebuilt in 1780. Motley was a wealthy, hospitable man, but at last Frank's visit had to be put off: 'you know from Elizabeth I dare say', Jane wrote to her sister on 12 May, 'that my father & Frank, deferring their visit to Kippington on account of Mr. M. Austen's absence are to be at Godmersham today.'[27] Mr Austen went on to the Fowles at Kintbury to bring Cassandra directly to Bath, but Frank had other plans.

Would he ever arrive? As a Royal Navy man he might not be expected to have complex financial dealings, but he certainly worked for the East India Company. He was to be in London on 27 May for a 'money' negotiation after visiting Lewis and Fanny Cage, at Milgate. Meanwhile the sister-in-law and niece of James Holder, the tenant of Ashe Park near Steventon, were calling on Jane and her mother. 'I cannot utterly abhor them,' Jane felt, 'especially as Miss Holder owns that she has no taste for Music.' *That* simple and unique star-burst of candour endeared Margaret Holder to Jane Austen; moreover the two Holder ladies civilly wore white gowns and had the further and extremely good recommendation of being unpopular at Bath: 'It is the fashion to think them both very detestable,' Jane

Austen wrote as her sister's arrival drew a day nearer. Bath would be tolerably funny if Cassandra did not procrastinate. When her young acquaintance Marianne Mapleton died Jane took it upon herself to visit the bereaved sisters Jane and Christiana, who were pale, shattered, polite and reasonable in praise of Marianne. 'Many a girl on early death', she wrote to Cassandra as another comment on Bath's insincerity, 'has been praised into an Angel I believe, on slighter pretensions to Beauty, Sense & Merit than Marianne.'[28]

Miss Twisleton by now had faded away. On 27 May as Jane returned from her drive with Mr Evelyn (whose manners were extremely mild and agreeable) she found two letters on the Perrots' table. One was from Cassandra and the other from Charles, who had had a unique view this year of scandal in the royal family: 'Charles spent three pleasant days in Lisbon,' she had noted in February. '– They were very well satisfied with their Royal Passenger, whom they found fat, jolly & affable, who talks of L^y Augusta as his wife & seems much attached to her.' Charles's guest on the *Endymion* had been the sixth son of George III or Augustus Frederick, the Duke of Sussex, whose asthma had led him to seek a milder climate in Portugal. The Prince's marriage to Lady Augusta Murray, whom he called 'my amiable Goosey', had been declared void by King George, but the Prince continued to live with his Goosey, who gave him a son and a daughter. Yet the *Endymion* had more serious business, too, and Charles had seen naval combat and received a little prize money. At the end of May Jane Austen was touched and embarrassed by his news: 'He has received 30£ for his share of the privateer & expects 10£ more,' she wrote of the reward her brother had got for risking his life. But why had Charles thought of his sisters? 'But of what avail is it', she asked with the lightest admonishment, 'to take prizes if he lays out the produce in presents to his sisters. He has been buying gold chains & Topaze crosses for us; – he must be well scolded.' She could not conceal her pleasure and would remember the gift when she wrote of Fanny Price's delight in her brother William's present of an amber cross in *Mansfield Park*. 'We shall be unbearably fine,' she commented. Sexual scandal was now in fashion at Bath, in the Navy, and everywhere else, and so it was funny that she and Cassandra might go to the fireworks on 4 June with scandalous Mr Evelyn, or do so if Mrs Austen and Mrs Leigh Perrot decided not to come along. Pope said that our bliss depends on what we blame. Far from blaming anyone Jane Austen looked forward to the comfort of being with Cassandra and to getting along in the city of yellow–golden houses as well as they might, for together they could be happy, modest and elegant, the most agreeable ladies at Bath. Mrs Mussell by now had made up her dark gown beautifully and had made mistakes with the white one – nothing could be perfect. 'My white one I was obliged to alter a good deal. Unless anything particular occurs I shall not write again,' she advises her sister.[29] Cassandra would be coming to the city from Kintbury rectory which her fiancé Tom Fowle had known before he sailed to his death overseas, and the tone of Jane Austen's last letter to her in May is appropriately mild and cheerful, full of implicit affection and need.

12

————⟶⟡⟵————

Harris Wither's proposal

the sisters returned to the Rectory as the guests of their brother James and his wife, and from thence they went to stay with their friends the Miss Biggs who were living with their Father Mʳ Bigg Wither at Manydown Park, They had been near neighbours for some years and the families were intimate. There were three of the sisters, one the Mother of the late Sir William Heathcote, the other married an elderly clergyman a Mʳ Hill Uncle of Robert Southey, and the third remained single and with her the friendship was kept up as long as she lived. Cassandra and Jane came intending a long visit of a week or two but it was suddenly cut short by their Brother Mʳ Wither proposing to Jane .... he would take her from the Bath she disliked and restore her to the country she loved

     Fanny C. Lefroy's unpublished 'M.S. Family History'

Despite the boredom of teas and the dreariness of being without Cassandra, Jane Austen had seen much in May while looking for a house. Though not sent ahead just to scout she took an active part in a search. To go about honey-coloured streets looking over railings into grey and empty area-ways, following an uncle's clumping stick to yet another terrace and then to wonder about the sizes of rooms, about furniture and about where one might sleep, dine and converse can be for a while a pleasing pursuit. A house-hunter sees details of architecture and setting that are usually taken for granted and notices at Bath little degrees between the fashionableness of this neighbourhood and that. The problem of finding a house had become urgent when Mrs Austen tired of staying at the Paragon. *Something* had to be found. Jane's uncle had broached the topic when he said 'all the houses in New King Street' were too small and proposed Seymour Street. He had not helped Maria Edgeworth's father for nothing and his gout relented when he had something decisive to do. After his second glass of water at the Pump Room he had led his niece on a little raid to Green Park Buildings, where one of the rentable houses had a pleasing upstairs apartment divided in two with a 'very nice-sized dressing-room, which upon occasion might admit a bed'. Here one might duplicate rooms at the rectory: 'The only doubt', she felt, 'is about the dampness of the offices' of which there were symptoms.

Then dampness seemed a plague of Bath, and she might have rebuked the Avon for its influence on 'these putrifying Houses'. The more putrifying they were, the more quickly landlords praised them. Even No. 12 had seemed ideal until they went into the kitchen. The proprietor pledged to dry it out and raise the kitchen floor 'but all this I fear is useless', Jane wrote to Cassandra with a practised eye, 'tho' the water may be kept out of sight, it cannot be sent away, nor the ill effects of its nearness be excluded'.[1]

Her uncle's slowness and the wetness of rooms began to irk her. 'I have nothing more to say on the subject of houses,' she wrote at last.[2] Pride in her own efficiency made her less willing to do things at someone else's pace. She was not especially patient – even as a novelist she dropped one manuscript to work on another, though she was persistent despite her self-doubt and the hard work of revising her 'gradual performances'. At Bath her uncle's doggedness was a trial, but when her father and sister joined the hunt she might have written a fair guide to neighbourhoods. She had seen the town with primed imagination, she had exhausted the hints of the Perrots, and certainly she had let her mind wander from an elegant façade to speculations about who lived behind it. Probably her experiences helped her to place her own comic people here, and she would continue to locate them with an accurate felicity, a niceness and appropriateness bred of many a walk with her aunt and slow, fussy uncle. For instance, the merry Musgroves would live at the White Hart Inn in Small Street when they came to Bath. This was a leading hotel near the Pump Room. It might be enough to send Mrs Rushworth – after that confident lady hands over Sotherton to her son in *Mansfield Park* – to live with propriety at an unfixed Bath address, but rude General Tilney would live at wide, rich Milsom Street designed by the elder John Wood, where he might have legions of shoppers under dictatorial surveillance – 'Milsom Street – you know', says complacent Mrs Allen. The Dowager Viscountess Dalrymple and Lady Carteret would live at Laura Place in the best part of New Town across the Avon, but Sir Walter and his eldest daughter would go to the long, shallow crescent of Camden Place which was *very* new and ever so slightly vulgar (though the *nouveaux riches* of course were happy to live there). Their friend Lady Russell would put up in Rivers Street, which was at least moderately fine, whereas Sir Walter's tenants Admiral and Mrs Croft would have to be happy in Gay Street with its sliding scale of rentals and fashionableness. Colonel Wallis in *Persuasion* would find modest style and comfort at Marlborough Buildings, at the far end of the Royal Crescent. And where would a heroine live? With the Allens in *Northanger Abbey* Catherine Morland stays just comfortably if not finely in Pulteney Street (not too far from Laura Place) and the Thorpes are a little farther down the social ladder at Edgar's Buildings, which were close to the borderline of easy vulgarity and showed a commonness in the ugly façade and deprived view. Of course some locales were too faded for the respectable and Sir Walter Elliot would turn up his nose at Mrs Smith's Westgate Buildings beyond the Hot Baths, though the author was not indisposed towards those buildings in the town's lower end, as they were in a broad, comely and civilized street. John Wood's Queen Square had lost so much glamour that Musgrove girls would cry out pathetically, 'Remember, Papa, if we do go it must be to a good situation – none of your Queen Squares for us!' The Austens had stayed at No. 13 in the summer of 1799 and eighteen months later Mrs Austen still pined for it: 'My Mother hankers after the Square dreadfully,' Jane had noted.[3]

She amused herself with speculations about houses, occupants and newlyweds. She had married off Cassandra to James Digweed and sent them to live at low-ceilinged rooms and funnily uneven floors in Deane parsonage. She could easily picture denizens of houses that disappointed her when a blooming kitchen-maid or faceless estate-agent met her at a baize door. Oddly one early circumstance had given hope before all of her mother's preferences were defeated. When Chapel Row proved impossible the Austens followed a bright

181

lead – whether or not they read about it at first in the *Bath Chronicle*:

> The lease of No. 4 Sydney Place, 3 years and a quarter of which are unexpired at Midsummer. The situation is desirable, the Rent very low, and the Landlord is bound by Contract to paint the two first floors this summer. A Premium will thereafter be expected. Apply Messrs. Watson and Foreman. Cornwall Buildings, Bath.[4]

In June or at latest July, they must have heard more from Messrs. Watson and Foreman about No. 4 Sydney Place. This was a row of terraced houses, four storeys tall, across the river at Bathwick estate looking east; No. 4 was elegant, though smaller than houses in adjoining Pulteney Street, and from it they might walk three hundred yards on broad pavements across Mr Pulteney's bridge and on into the centre of town with its abbey, Pump Room, markets and shops all to hand. Convenient, too, would be Laura Chapel, a proprietary chapel opened in 1792. Though stolidly urban with rising tiers of three front windows, Sydney Place was at the edge of open country. Mr Austen negotiated for the lease and here they were to live for three years. Mrs Austen with normal alacrity accepted the inevitable, and felt so relieved to get over an illness here that she was to celebrate her escape in a poem which does credit to her daughters. 'Says Death,' she wrote,

> I've been trying these three week or more
> To seize an old Madam here at Number Four,
> Yet I still try in vain, tho' she's turned of three score;
> To what is my ill-success owing?

> I'll tell you, old Fellow, if you cannot guess,
> To what you're indebted for your ill success –
> To the prayers of my husband, whose love I possess,
> To the care of my daughters, whom Heaven will bless,
> To the skill and attention of Bowen.[5]

Nothing better shows off the happiness of the Austens – and in a city of invalids Jane gladly nursed her mother. Bath was the locale of her parents' marriage and contentment. They soon had their likenesses taken in profile by Mrs Collins, a lady who once assisted the profilist Sarah Harrington of Bath and London. Two silhouettes painted on card in shades of black and grey show them in old age: swathed up to her chin, Mrs Austen peers from under a flowered cap, and her husband with a large collar and a wisp of curl at his neck looks fragile. William Bowen the apothecary attended them well and at forty also looked after Aunt Perrot's pills: 'I have got Mr. Bowen's Recipe for you,' Jane told Cassandra later, 'it came in my aunt's letter.'[6]

Her parents were so much the centre of her life that she had hardly needed her father's interest in 'First Impressions' to know that he took pride in her, nor did she need to be reminded that her mother's wit and gossip were blessings. As James Edward implied later of Jane Austen, her family were enormously more important to her than the world. The 'stupid' parties of May might have been bearable had all four Austens sat at them – but much was lacking, and much, much was wrong no matter how well she loved her parents. They did not transform Bath any more than grass beyond Sydney Place compensated her for Steventon. She might have met women whose books she most admired and talked with female writers who would easily have offset the tea-party crowd: Uncle Perrot could have put her in touch with Maria Edgeworth, and her relatives the Cookes might introduce her to Fanny Burney. The Revd Samuel Cooke, whose wife was Mrs Austen's first cousin, remained at Great Bookham, and it is certain that Fanny Burney or Mme d'Arblay when living there had befriended the Cookes. 'Mr. Cooke, our vicar,' the author of *Camilla* had written to her father Dr Burney, the celebrated authority on music, is 'a very worthy man & a goodish – though by no means marvellously *rapid* Preacher.' 'Mr. Cooke', as Fanny further reports to her father, 'tells me he longs for nothing so much as a Conversation with Dr. Burney upon the subject of Parish Psalm singing. – He complains that the Methodists run away with the regular Congregations, from their superiority in Vocal devotion.' It was humiliating to be outdone by Methodists: music helped to attract churchgoers. Dr Burney stood ready to advise Mr Cooke on how he might hold a congregation and just as surely as his daughter, who writes of Mrs Cooke that she is 'very sensible' and 'excessively kind to me', might have advised and encouraged her friends' young relative Miss Jane Austen, who had been an original subscriber to *Camilla*.[7] Nor would kindly help have stopped there. Overshadowed only by Miss Burney in Jane Austen's opinion was Charlotte Smith, author of *Emmeline* and *Ethelinde*. Separated from her husband, Mrs Smith had applied lately to Dr Burney while Fanny was a neighbour of the Cookes for advice on how her second daughter Anna Augusta, who had married an émigré, might find a priest willing to perform a second ceremony to make Augusta's marriage 'binding according to the laws of France'. That matter put families of two novelists in touch, and so if Jane Austen *had* wished to meet Miss Burney she might also have met Mrs Smith.[8]

Yet she clung to her family. If she thought of it, the kindness of novelists would have seemed as merited as an audience with the King whom Miss Burney befriended. The high patronage needed by her brothers had no parallel in her requirements: she could not *be* Frank, or offend James with pretensions, and she was properly less than Cassandra. If someone did press her to meet Miss Burney she made little of the meeting if it ever occurred. (There is no sign of it in any family tradition or in all of the collections of holograph letters and other papers of the Austens.) She would have escaped such a meeting had she been able as surely as she later avoided a chance to meet Mme de Staël, whose *Corinne* she liked. It is implicit but clear in many of her letters that she viewed herself as a person dependent on her family's approval not of her stories but of herself, and of no consequence without them, and so if her modesty told her that ladies out of her sphere were unnecessary it is very likely that a wish to meet the famous never crossed her mind as consistent with decency. There were deeper reasons for Jane Austen's modesty too. She did not resent her family's solidarity but approved and abetted it, not merely because it amounted to her best protection but because an independence separating her from their love would have been ashes in her mouth. She excelled as an entertainer and relied on those who had loved her since birth. There was a disparity too between the gay and comforting feeling she had with people who knew her well, and a reserve, an affrontedness that could chill her to silence among strangers, as sociable as she normally was. She met a roomful of Kentish or Bath people best as an observer. She was a very private person, and her strong psychological defences and her need for Cassandra, her delight in a few unambitious female friends, as well as her fondness for stillness in nature and quiet places and simple and sane routines all depended on her having easy relations with the Austens. She lived before we had created a *mythos* of the artist as isolated, agonized, lonely and hopelessly at odds with society. And what inwardness for creativity is possible if one lacks the love of a cloistered community, a dear companion or a family? She never made the mistake of confusing personal freedom with separateness; she was contented with her family – but not with their city: what she needed was some passing relief from Bath, and this she had mentioned even before coming to her uncle's house.

She had put a 'Dawlish scheme' in the centre of their summer plans, so when her father's former pupil Richard Buller urged the family 'to come and see him', Jane approved. Buller would not oppress a flea with stupid self-congratulations or seem too nauseously happy in his marriage to Anne Marshall. He was Vicar of Colyton near Exeter, not far from the Channel towns of Dawlish, Teignmouth and Sidmouth. In the summer of 1801, it seems before they were installed at Sydney Place, the Austens accordingly made their head-quarters at Sidmouth. 'Sidmouth is now talked of as our summer abode,' Jane had told her sister earlier and had urged her to find out about it from Mrs Charles Cage.[9] Sheltered by hills it was a nook where families had medicinal benefits of sea-bathing and salt breezes and a harbour walk. Here or at Teignmouth, she really did her best to oblige parents who came to Bath partly for her social advantages – she fell in love boldly, or at least met a clergyman whom her sister compared with the 'very pleasing and very good looking' Mr Edridge of the Engineers.[10] She knew him for a few weeks; he wished on parting to know when he might see her again and convinced Cassandra, thoroughly, that he had 'fallen in love'. What is certain is that Sidmouth on the coast is disgraced if its young ladies fail to strike love in clerical hearts. On holiday it is bizarre not to fall in love with bright eyes and a pretty figure, and an unattached gentleman failing to do so is derelict and irrational. Why should he not love? Even if her lover spoke like Dr Johnson, however, she was not quite a straw in the wind, for she had known Tom Lefroy and Edward Bridges, and had contended with young men who were rational and irrational in most of the southern counties. Love was a central topic of her analysis of human behaviour, as well as the object of many witty jokes. Emotionally conservative and jealous of her loyalties she walked on a promenade with Cassandra on one arm and a tall gentle-man on another – there can hardly be a doubt of that – and much can occur in such a situation. She seems to have agreed that her gentleman gave promise of being an acceptable suitor – and he did earn Cassandra's approval – and so there is nothing particularly un-likely in the simple account of this episode written by Louisa Lefroy, who became Mrs Bellas. 'In the summer of 1801,' Louisa recalls, the

Austens had been visiting at 'Teignmouth, Starcross, Sidmouth etc. *I* believe it was at the last named place that they made acquaintance with a young clergyman when visiting his brother, who was one of the young doctors of the town. He and Jane fell in love with each other, and when the Austens left he asked to be allowed to join them again further on in their tour, and the permission was given. But instead of his arriving as expected, they received a letter announcing his death. In Aunt Cassandra's memory he lived as one of the most charming persons she had known, worthy even in her eyes of Aunt Jane.'[11] This is the most detailed account of Jane's summer affair, though all accounts derive from Cassandra, who on another occasion said she was able to meet the brother of the deceased clergyman. She later told the tale in so many versions that what mainly emerges from reports written by Fanny and Louisa Lefroy, Caroline Austen and James Edward Austen-Leigh is her own gratified concern with the tragic lover, who showed the best taste by loving very briefly.

His death appealed to Cassandra, who never forgot the tragic loss of Tom Fowle, but we have no reason to believe that the romance left Jane Austen mentally paralysed and totally distraught, unable to feel or think or climb into a carriage. Fanny Lefroy, as the most industrious family recorder, says rather logically that the gentleman's death deepened Jane Austen's strong bond with her sister. 'The similarity of their fates', wrote Fanny, 'endeared the two sisters to each other and made other sympathy unnecessary to each. No one was equal to Jane in Cassandra's eyes. And Jane looked up to Cassandra as one far wiser and better than herself. They were as their mother said "wedded to each other".'[12] The fates were less equal than Fanny allows inasmuch as Cassandra knew Tom from childhood and was engaged to him, whereas Jane had seen her reputed lover only a few times. At summer's end the two sisters visited Steventon and saw Mrs Lefroy, who was bound to be sympathetic. 'The Miss Austens spent the day here,' Madam wrote simply at Ashe on 29 September. 'Next week they mean to return to Bath & after that I suppose it will be long before they again visit Steventon.'[13] She dined with them at James's rectory on Saturday, 3 October, and two days later they returned to Bath, where they heard of the death of Eliza's young son, Hastings de Feuillide, though Eliza was as selfish and plucky as ever. This winter they thought of Wales and in the summer the Austens visited Tenby in South Wales, with Charles happily to swell their group, and made their way up to Barmouth. '*She*', Anna wrote with pride of Aunt Jane, 'was once I think at Tenby, and once they went as far north as Barmouth – I would give a good deal, that is as much as I could afford, for a sketch which Aunt Cassandra made of her in one of their expeditions – sitting down out of doors, on a hot day with her bonnet strings untied.'[14]

Meanwhile the war had taken a curious turn: Napoleon sued for peace, and Cornwallis and Talleyrand with clerks and portfolios met at Amiens to restore the *status quo ante bellum*. Mr Austen had no reason to trust France – and with two captains in the Navy other Austens perhaps did not rejoice. France would leave Naples and the papal states, while England agreed to vacate Malta and other conquests except for Ceylon and Trinidad. The illusory peace began on 1 October 1801 when articles were signed, and lasted until 17 May 1803, when Napoleon was ready for renewed hostilities.

The French benefited enormously. Ready to crush the British, their troops were resupplied and reorganized whereas England had no very potent army. As for the Austens the peace cheated Frank and Charles of sea-prizes but gave Eliza the hope of recovering Feuillide's property in France: very rashly Henry and Eliza set sail in the second year of the truce, as if Jane's story 'Henry and Eliza' were proving true. They found that as the Comte had died a confessed murderer and thief they could not get back his holdings, and also that they might be interned at Verdun as British subjects. As acute as that dilemma was, it was not beyond Eliza to get out of it when she decided they might masquerade as a French couple. 'Eliza took charge,' as John Hubback records. 'They agreed that Henry should be relegated to an invalid role in the corner of their travelling carriage. No one at the posting stations could detect her nationality; her perfect command of French, spoken as it would be at Napoleon's court, disarmed all suspicion.' Eliza sneered at the tricolours which had replaced the familiar fleur-de-lis, but she got Henry on a boat and safely back to England.[15]

For Jane the peace was at best a slight relaxation, an interval when sailors and soldiers drifted home to establishments unlikely to re-employ them. She wrote her best work during the war, and the determination of Frank and Charles in the Navy with the sense her family had that the nation was fighting a just cause against French pretensions and viciousness did not lessen the rigour of her thinking. She portrayed the war from a woman's viewpoint, but she was conscious of the male view. James and her brothers were dedicated patriots. And now with the peace an era seemed to have passed; time was going by. She went in the late summer of 1802 to visit Godmersham, where Elizabeth was pregnant as usual; between 19 April and 15 May beforehand James, Mary and Anna had visited at Bath, and then the Austen sisters had stayed with them at Steventon rectory that summer before reaching Edward and Elizabeth on 3 September. Elizabeth's free spaces in between pregnancies had become shorter – so that in Kent she can hardly have been the most welcoming of hosts. By 28 October when back at Steventon, Jane Austen surely looked foward to a reviving, carefree visit with her sister at Manydown Park with the Biggs, partly because the house was linked to the delightful days of her girlhood. Biggs had the stability of the Edward Austens in *their* pleasantest days, with the inestimable joy and peace of living in Hampshire.

Also there might be a bracing effect in a visit here. The green park with cedars and beeches, the long vistas and squarish old mansion were in the heart of England. Lovelace Bigg Wither was a genial widower – even his jowls and squat, stubby nose under a bulbous brow fringed with downy white hair gave him an aristocratic look – as though, his tenants might have said, a horse had sat upon a very fine face. Widowed at Chilton Folliat in 1784, he had come to Manydown Park with two sons and seven daughters in 1789. He was a cousin to the grandest lawyer of the century, Sir William Blackstone, and in Hampshire he proved to be an able magistrate himself. As Deputy Lieutenant for the county in 1793 he had founded an association to help the labouring poor in the neighbourhood of Basingstoke, and then a poorhouse for the Wooton district. 'His life is so useful,' Jane Austen thought of him, 'his character so respectable and worthy,' and she never met a more generous country squire.[16]

Lovelace's ancestral uncle had married Mary Hunt, who gave birth to Hampshire's greatest poet. Sent to prison twice for the wit and boldness of his satires, the poet was George Wither, who wrote one of the loveliest lyrics in English:

> Shall I, wasting in despair,
> Die because a woman's fair?
> Or make pale my cheeks with care
> 'Cause another's rosy are?

Be she fairer than the day,
Or the flow'ry meads in May,
  If she be not so to me,
  What care I how fair she be?

I will ne'er the more despair;
If she love me, this believe,
  I will die ere she shall grieve.[17]

Much ardour, talent, and distinguished work had kept the family in the public eye, and their name had come down unchanged since the Domesday Book. Under their motto 'I grow and wither both together' and a coat of arms of a field argent surmounted by a hare with three wheat ears in its mouth, Withers had looked after Manydown. Thomas, John and Richard held it for a hundred years before Queen Elizabeth's accession, and after 1679 it had only three owners. William Wither IV owned Manydown for fifty-four years, and William Wither V for fifty-six. When Lovelace Bigg took possession in 1789 and met the nearby Austens, he livened up the mansion with children between the ages of nine and twenty-one, though marriage and death soon broke into the family circle.[18] Dorothy Bigg-Wither and her fourteen-year-old brother Lovelace died early in the 1790s. Elizabeth, now a widow, had married a son of Sir William Heathcote of Hursley Park and had been living at Manydown since March 1802 with her young son William. The other Bigg-Withers at the manor were Harris, who at twenty-one still wished to be called 'Harris Wither', and his lively sisters Catherine and Alethea who took the name 'Bigg'.

When on Thursday 25 November Jane and Cassandra walked up stone steps into the fine hall of Manydown they were, very naturally, greeted by affectionate friends whom they had missed in a city of 'white glare'. They were in the warmth and dignity of the country, where talk was luxurious because it was unaffected, and here they had a sense of continuity because their friends were interested in all that had happened to them, in Mrs Austen's health and in Mr Austen's modest book-collecting and in recent reports from Edward and Elizabeth about their children. In the drawing room over the large dining room designed by Lovelace when he added a new front, Jane Austen could be as simple as she usually was with Alethea. 'We have just had a few days' visit from Edward,' she might report typically. Alethea could listen to what was said to her: 'He grows still,' Jane Austen would rattle on merrily, 'and still improves in appearance, at least in the estimation of his aunts, who love him better and better, as they see the sweet temper and warm affection of the boy confirmed in the young man.' In accents such as these she gave her news to Catherine and Alethea, heard theirs, and by the time Lovelace and his son led her downstairs to the dining room she surely felt at home. 'We spend our time here quietly as usual,' she had noted at Manydown: 'One long morning visit is what generally occurs.'[19] As likely as not Mrs Penelope Lutley Sclater came bustling over from Tangier Park. (Lovelace had been trying to buy her adjacent estate for several years. Tangier Park with its bowling green and 'wilderness' of eight acres bordered by laurels and intersected by grass walks, once belonged to the Withers but had passed by purchase to the Hookes and to Henry Limbrey, and then by marriage to the Sclaters, and was only bought back by Harris Wither's son after Jane Austen's time.) Its inheritor Mrs Sclater was a nerve-wracking pest, but Jane was fond of this chatty soul with marriage on the brain who decried *Mansfield Park* but liked *Emma* just because so many weddings came cleverly in the last volume. 'Kill poor Mrs Sclater if you like it when you are at Manydown,' Jane once told Cassandra. On this visit wine from Seville oranges and the normal jollity of the Bigg girls were enough to put anyone at ease. Catherine had a long, thin, humorous face rather like Marianne Bridges', and Alethea was so 'pleasant, cheerful, and interested in everything about her' that at a later date Jane was on the point of calling her similar friend Harriot 'Alethea'. The Biggs were disarming. 'Among so many friends it will be well if I do not get into a scrape,' Jane believed, but there could be no mishap in November.[20]

About the young master of the house she almost had to be curious, since it was odd that a nice, composed-looking girl like Catherine did not have a settled or composed brother. Harris was confused first by his stutter and secondly by being overgrown. His awkward body had been ill, and he was just the sort to lounge about in the new black Hessian boots which came to a few inches of the knee with tassels, and to wear pale-yellow breeches while contributing little to gentle conversation. Even after his adolescence he was so tactless as to be insulting. He was 'very plain in person – awkward, & even uncouth in manner', Caroline Austen reports, 'nothing but his size to recommend him – he was a fine big man'.[21] After the death of his fourteen-year-old elder brother, however, he became heir to Manydown.

'Owing to his stuttering he was a man of few words,' says Reginald Bigg-Wither of Harris. He 'rather avoided society', and although quick-tempered and rude he could be just barely hospitable. One evening later on when he had ordered the butler to make a punch of ill-assorted wines, and dinner-guests had tasted the brew with wry faces, he rose to make a speech. 'Gentlemen,' Harris said to his guests, 'my punch is like you. In your individual capacity you are all very good fellows, but in your corporate capacity you are very disagreeable.'[22] With that he sat down. At twenty-one, he was very probably a silent admirer. Jane, who was six years older than Harris, at least half-pitied him as she was much more alert, worldly, sensible and controlled – and perhaps as amused as she would have been by a large puppy. A week after her arrival, it seems, Harris to her amazement asked her to marry him.

Jane certainly at once sought her sister's quiet and tactful advice, but others were soon to know what was up and James's wife Mary was to be quite vociferous. 'I can give', writes her daughter Caroline, 'the *exact* date of Mr Wither's proposal to my Aunt' from pocket-book entries 'which make *no* allusion to anything of the sort – but some peculiar comings & goings coinciding exactly with what my Mother more than once told me of *that* affair, leave me in no doubt that the offer was made, & accepted at Manydown on Thursday the 2d of Dec – 1802.'[23] The realities of the proposal were not complex. If Harris was 'uncouth' he might become polished, gentle and responsive and though he had been an idle boy with a stammer, he was now intent on Jane. Her kindness to him had been enough. Cassandra approved, it seems, and Jane accepted his offer before she retired that evening.

She could not have visited Manydown had he revealed his intentions in advance. (And we have no evidence to suggest that.) If he made up his mind in adolescent haste, he had a future as Manydown's heir. From the time that an earlier Lovelace Bigg (1661–1724) had married Dorothy, the fourth daughter of William Wither, late in the seventeenth century two great families had been allied, so it was fitting that Harris's father as heir general to the Wither estates did assume by royal licence the arms and surname of Wither. Born at Chilton Folliat in Wiltshire on 18 May 1781 and baptized Harris Bigg,

Harris rightly had taken the name of prior owners. But a novelist might have put him in a very realistic romance, since there was nothing light or tentative or engaging about him: he never spoke in taffeta phrases or 'silken terms precise', let alone in hyperboles or fanciful images, as he was not a Biron of *Love's Labour's Lost* or even addicted to subtlety. His father, who attended Winchester and Queen's College before he became a New College fellow and worked hard at French and Italian, had been so worried about Harris's stutter that he had sent him to Mr Wallington. From that private tutor Harris went along to Worcester College, Oxford, and returned as a half-formed man to find at Manydown dusty piles of books. 'Ladies', Jane Austen decided, 'who read those enormous great stupid thick quarto volumes which one always sees in the breakfast parlour' at Manydown 'must be acquainted with everything in the world', and her complaint may suggest that Harris had beaten about the bush, if his terrible stammer combined with erudition to make him a little pedantic. 'At Manydown,' she believed, 'they will not understand a man who condenses his thoughts into an octavo.' But Jane perhaps also had despaired over the heavy legalistic talk of Lovelace Bigg-Wither. Captain Pasley's succinct book on military policy was, she felt, 'too good for their Society'.[24] And yet for six days with Catherine and Alethea she had known the delights of old wainscoted chambers, and of a beautiful historical setting. Timber in Manydown Park had been used to make the roof and nave of Winchester Cathedral. The house was built round a square Cheyney Court, off which was the old room where Withers over four hundred years had held their Court Leet and Customary Leet when affairs of their tenants were settled, and the lands beyond were as green as those she pictured in *Pride and Prejudice* round Darcy's mansion. Few lands had been lost over the years, though Withers had sold off Bighton which they had bought from Shakespeare's patron Henry Wriothesley, the third Earl of Southampton, as well as Chilton Folliat, which Lovelace sold when he succeeded to Manydown. But he had used the income to extend Manydown Park, and indeed had added a thousand new acres in 1791 with his arable farms at Monk and West Sherborne and Basing and Wortley, Bramley, Pamber and Up Nately with almost five hundred acres more at Wymering and Widley – near Portsmouth and Fareham. The master and mistress of Manydown would thus in any case possess a great deal of county land. Other people here became so poor that Jane comically had lost patience with them, and her own future did not look well. When Mr Austen died their income would be so reduced that she, her mother and Cassandra might face penury. Marriage is the greatest felicity on earth, as her mother believed, and to have said no to Harris Wither would have been patently foolish and very nearly selfish.

Yet as the future Mrs Wither she hardly found the night of 2 December her shortest or most restful. She was not in love and none of her family believed she was, but she could not dismiss sentiments of approbation 'inferior to love'. Undefined tracts of feeling exist between esteem, fondness, finding a person amiable and truly loving anyone, and the plain Harris, with his gift of silence, was amiable enough at least to be loved by his sisters. He might improve. He was still young. An engagement between man and woman formed for the advantage of each was just what she had implied marriage ought to be, and so she was not inconsistent, false or grasping at Manydown. Nor could she feel remiss if her sister Cassandra approved her reply. Her not 'loving' Harris was too irrelevant to have taken first place in her thoughts for long. Romantic love among the gentry was more preached than practised. Mere love might have distracted a young romance heroine, but hardly a realist in a practical matter between herself and Harris. A *desirable* match was a thoughtful one engineered by persons unswayed by feeling and whatever 'sacrifice' of her hopes she might make in marrying this young man, it would be a small and frail one. The inheritor of Manydown offered her a chance of wedlock as against becoming a socially outcast and burdensome spinster, an appalling handicap to her brothers and worry for Cassandra and their mother. She was nearly twenty-seven: 'It is something for a woman to be assured, in her eight-and-twentieth year, that she has not lost one charm of earlier youth' and the value of such assurances as she had received was increased by her knowledge that Harris had so much to give the person he desired. Marriage in her own eyes was the most social of acts, properly leading a young woman to break her family ties for a fulfilment more desirable than home can guarantee. But home in this case was Bath, a rootless place of temporary sojourn for many others, and a fixity for herself. She had been torn away from her own dear roots and indeed from all of the converse of Hampshire families she knew well, her father's excellent library, her own pianoforte and all of those scenes and sounds and smells of the country that reassured her. Bath was epito-mized for her in such a line as 'There was a monstrous deal of stupid quizzing and commonplace nonsense talked and scarcely any wit.' But then, what new obliteration of herself, what new degree of gratui-tous and unnecessary disarrangement of her life was she being asked to countenance? A grown daughter who suffers the loss of home for the sake of her parents need not welcome *new* bitterness if she can help it. A wedding with Harris Wither, whom she most certainly did not care for, would divide her spiritually and emotionally from the chief human source of happiness she had left, her family. And what else was he to *her*? She was not so taken as to lie awake as a young Catherine might, asking herself what Harris was doing 'now' and 'now' and 'now', and nothing obviously had induced her to view him as a lover before he spoke. Initial attraction, flirtation and a deep, particular concern develop within a social world subject to intense social scrutiny, but neither she nor Cassandra nor anyone else could have seen that happening in her relations with poor Harris. The luck of one member of a family may be luck to all, and a good marriage may diffuse its benefits, but she had been 'bewitched' by the prospect of finding a home through Harris, and so she had said her 'yes'. 'It was necessary to sit up half the Night & lie awake the remainder to comprehend,' she wrote later of her Anne Elliot, and pay 'by Headake and Fatigue'. She owed him her gratitude and com-passion and kindness. Her acquaintance with him had been flattering, and now it was terribly painful. With her reflection came 'such a revulsion of feeling', in the words of Fanny Lefroy who heard of this night from Anna Lefroy whose mother actually talked to Jane Austen some twelve hours after Harris Wither's proposal. There was in this 'revulsion' very much matter to regret. She had not rationally balanced her attitudes in Harris's presence, it seems, inasmuch as the prospect of what he offered was so tangibly present in the great house at Manydown. The night therefore became as long as Caroline Austen heard it was. Harris's 'advantages' and her long friendship with his family had lulled her defences, but having consented 'she found herself miserable', as Caroline later reported.

Jane's relatives, Catherine Hubback, Caroline Austen and Fanny Lefroy all knew 'letters' about this episode and its aftermath – and their comments are not in accord with those in the *Portrait* of Jane Austen by Lord David Cecil or those in the popular biography of

Jane Austen by Elizabeth Jenkins. (Miss Jenkins calls Harris Wither 'Harrison', though he was named after his father's mother Jane Harris, and invents a fictive character for him that has no relation to documentary evidence about him given by Reginald Bigg-Wither as well as by James's daughter Caroline.) And again it is difficult to dismiss the words of Catherine, Caroline and Fanny since they seem to have been told the gist of what Jane Austen said to Mary Lloyd directly after the proposal. Jane was tempted *not* to reverse her decision since Harris's sisters 'were already her friends, he would take her from the Bath she disliked and restore her to the country she loved', as Fanny Lefroy states, and after listening to what her own mother reported Fanny borrowed a phrase to say that the offer had affected Jane Austen because it was 'aided by all the horrible eligibilities and the proprieties of the match, and the pleasure it would give all her family and his'. One gathers that personal happiness was not the only factor and that the night became longer, nothing resolved. This odd episode became a major one from which Jane Austen could learn, and it was more painful because engagements were not easily broken. If she retracted, she might anger legalistic Lovelace Bigg-Wither and a family that had given England one of the gravest judges in the nation's history, Mr Justice Blackstone of the *Commentaries*. *Whatever* she might do the next day was wrong. 'She should not have said yes – over night – but I have always respected her for the courage', Caroline wrote, with what has proved to be a good memory of her mother's reports of Jane Austen. 'All worldly advantages would have been to her – & she was of an age to know *this* quite well' at nearly twenty-seven. 'My Aunts had very small fortunes & on their Father's death they & their Mother would be, they were aware, but poorly off – I beleive most young women so circumstanced would have taken Mr W. & trust to love after marriage.'[25]

But Fanny and Caroline suggest something else about an aunt's 'courage'. What *was* her courage as it could have appeared to her on this night? Had she not been presumptuous, selfish and blind to propriety and every regard of decency by hastening to consent? A beggar in rags might not sell his soul for copper, but she had said her 'yes' because the grand estates would be lost to her if she said 'no', and the worst of it was that she had played with other people's lives. In her own eyes she was in error. She was hideously wrong. No dreamer or imaginist could have interfered more naively in the lives of others, for indeed she had intimated that Martha Lloyd must marry Frank, and at just this time had been planning a little society of women to include Martha, Cassandra and herself. Only the latter plan in its innocence survived. Her parents if she married would reside at Manydown and presumably the sacrifice of learning to care for Harris would be paid for by their felicity. No Austen was a stranger at Manydown. But this surely was to disregard what Frank's, Martha's or Harris's feelings *might* be, and to neglect what would happen if plans did not work out as she had imagined. Was there evidence that Frank admired Martha Lloyd? or, for that matter, that she herself could be an acceptable wife to Harris to compensate him for his trust? He had been a boy of nine or ten when she first danced at Manydown and later, it seems, his cruel stutter, shyness and moodiness became the despair of his father; Harris either before or after he insulted guests with his 'wine' speech was to react to the authority of his parent by moving from his father's home, where there was ample room for him, to Wymering two miles from Portchester near the north shore of Portsmouth Harbour.[26] Lovelace's brilliant, nervous, active temperament did not harmonize with the awkward, tactless, bulky presence of his son. Whether or not Catherine and her chatty sister spoke frankly about him to the Austens it was plain that he was in a hurry to marry. He was much her junior and in haste to establish himself elsewhere, and so the question surely arose in her mind whether *he* cared for *her*, or whether she happened to be perhaps a convenient object in his marital search.

If we perceive that our conduct is wrong we may release a flood of reasons for it, all more or less tinged with vexation and self-accusation or self-apology. It may be impossible to hold back the flood. By dawn Jane Austen had enough evidence, bitter about herself at any rate, to reach a decision, and thus in the morning of Friday, 3 December, she met her fiancé and told him she had retracted her consent and perhaps that she was ashamed. She felt that she could not have him, and never would. She had made a major mistake. She was to blame, to blame.

A marital engagement was a contract between families. No matter how bizarre or mute the scene at Manydown's entrance-hall was it involved more than a few people. Servants certainly rushed to and fro with belongings, people appeared and vanished, a carriage rolled up and was not occupied. Eyes tried to speak, trembling embraces were repeated. And suddenly two young ladies were moving under a blur of trees.

Nothing else Jane Austen ever did, it seems, upset so many people as her retraction of her word. The damage to her peace of mind was considerable. It was imperative that she reach James as quickly as she could and, when the carriage stopped at Steventon and she ran out, Mary Lloyd was on hand. That practical countrywoman could hardly believe her ears: Harris had proposed? And Jane Austen had accepted and *then denied him*? Mary 'thought the match a most desirable one', and Jane had refused it much to Mary's 'sorrow'. But the Withers might not feel hopelessly beaten, and the ghost of Blackstone might not allow them to be humiliated for nothing. Catherine Hubback, Frank's daughter, later read the now missing letters Cassandra had shown her about this event and concluded that 'it was in a momentary fit of self-delusion that Aunt Jane accepted Mr. Wither's proposal' and that it was assuredly not settled at once but 'eventually'.[27] People at the Park had *not* taken her negative as final. On 3 December James faced his sermon-writing for Sunday, but the sisters made him convey them to Bath and out of Harris Wither's reach. Here in the blank streets Jane Austen had a chance to review her first reply to Harris's offer. What had led her to this error among affectionate friends? In a moment of carelessness she had struck through Harris at Alethea and Catherine, who could hardly fail to be deeply upset. She had much to pay for and could not quickly set things right whatever Harris and his father said; it might easily have been felt at Manydown that she had repaid hospitality with adventurousness. She was grieved and vexed and embarrassed. Very, very little that she could tell the Bigg girls could quickly absolve her of the guilt of misleading them, of imagining and playing with notions of what would be best for Harris, herself, her parents, Martha and Cassandra. She did *not* order her life well; and as the comments by Anna, Caroline and Catherine in this instance suggest it was only in the aftermath of reflection that she plumbed the depths of what constituted 'sense'. One of her sources in novel-writing was clearly the reconstruction of moods, feelings and perceptions after she had seen the folly of them, and it is unmistakably true that she had more than a few blunders to draw upon. Madam had sent Tom Lefroy off to London in a hurry because Jane Austen had played at love-making with him and so she had been left with bitter–sweet reflections of her own lack of sense. Her behaviour at Manydown surely helped her to understand the pride, conceit and puerile attitude of an Emma Woodhouse, a notable imaginist who with Frank Churchill's advances but not his character or feelings in focus would sit 'drawing or working, forming a thousand schemes for the progress and close of their attachment, fancying interesting dialogues, and inventing elegant letters' and foreseeing 'the conclusion of every imaginary declaration' on his side. This is not to deny her painstaking artistry or to underestimate changes that heightening gave to raw materials of her art – but it is to say that Jane Austen is in her comic heroines. In her social mistakes she had good evidence of the habits, feelings and psychological attitudes that would lead an apparently rational person into error, and nothing helped her to know herself better than acute vexation. When Catherine read the letters that Jane Austen wrote about Manydown she concluded that 'the affair vexed her a good deal' and that Jane was 'much relieved' when Harris and his father did finally relent. Harris, for his part, was not discouraged to have won her consent and sent her away in tears. Only twenty-three months after the proposal he married Anne Howe Frith, a daughter of Beddington Bramley Frith of Carisbrooke who was a lieutenant-colonel in the North Hants Militia. 'Harris Wither and his wife are still at Quidhampton and seem very happy,' Mrs Lefroy lightly remarked late in 1804. 'I am to meet them at the Prices tomorrow. Everyone in the neighbourhood seems pleased with the bride.' Harris and his wife soon settled at Wymering where seven of their ten children were born. He was to return to the Justice Room at Manydown House in 1813, and lease it eventually to Sir Richard Rycroft, Bart, while living in Tangier Park House. When Harris at last died of apoplexy in his fifty-second year on 25 March 1833, he was succeeded by his eldest son Lovelace. Four of Harris's five sons took holy orders and the youngest of his five unmarried daughters, Marianne Bigg-Wither, survived until the twentieth century. Alethea and Catherine without the slightest hesitation kept Manydown open to Jane Austen and urged her to visit them, as she was to do.

Her conscience was *not* of the kind that adjusts quickly to error. Blank days advanced. Grieved, vexed, we finally tire of our own wretchedness. Jane, in any case, exerted herself. And she was soon helped by *one* stroke of luck when Henry Austen secured for her through his man of business, Mr Seymour in London, a not wholly bad arrangement with Richard Crosby & Co. to publish *Susan, a Novel in Two volumes*. Ten pounds for the copyright was not a derisory amount, since it was equal to what would be a fair advance for an untried writer in later times, and it swelled her personal dress allowance of £20 enough to suggest a new measure of freedom, almost success: it was a happy event. It further ensured that she would keep on writing, even as *Susan* sank into a pit of oblivion.

She still had her plan to have Martha live with her, and she wanted to see Frank. War had resumed. It was feared the French would invade from maritime provinces, and that if they landed enough troops in Kent they would soon be in London. As a student of Pasley's work on military policy Jane Austen was to read demonstrations showing how numbers favoured a Napoleonic victory – and she would discuss foreign affairs, though women of the gentry were not meant to heed *public news*. 'The last current report as to public news, and the general opinion of the day must be understood,' as she wrote ironically in *The Watsons*, 'before Robert could let his attention be yeilded to the less national & important demands of the Women.'[28] Frank did not condescend with her, as Robert Watson does with his sister Emma, and she now understood that his new position was one of the two or three most vital and responsible in the whole coastal defence strategy. Frank had charge of a long strip from the North Foreland on the easterly promontory of Kent over to Sandown, with Pegwell Bay in the heart of his district – an ideal place for French landings – and he had to raise a corps of fishermen and others known as the 'Sea Fencibles', who were exercised and kept in readiness for the invasion. Nevertheless he was quartered at Ramsgate, where the Austens visited him and where he fell in love.

At that seaside town, Frank had met a Miss Mary Gibson who lived with her father and seemed a shade common by Mrs Austen's standards. Jane, when she reached Ramsgate, was coming to a better understanding of her own illusions, but it took her time to adjust to Frank's infatuation. The world it seemed existed to prove her wrong about people, and she confessed at last that 'nobody ever feels or acts, suffers or enjoys as one expects'.[29] Whether or not she met Miss Gibson at Ramsgate in 1803, she disliked the town thoroughly in its hot, crowded ordinariness. Its baths and bazaars and promenade seemed vulgar. She was seen by Sir Egerton Brydges, just the sort to love the town, and later she became ironic when she heard that Edward's relatives the Bridges drove there of their own free will: 'They have been all the summer at Ramsgate for *her* health,' she wrote about Harriet Foote, who had married Edward Bridges. 'She is a poor Honey – the sort of woman who gives me the idea of being determined never to be well – & who likes her spasms & nervousness & the consequence they give her, better than anything else.' Ramsgate suited those fond of indulging such nervousness. 'He talks of fixing at Ramsgate. – Bad taste!' she wrote of poor Mr Hussy, who had been a trembling leaf at Godmersham.[30] Irritated by Mary Gibson, she thought of Ramsgate in light of persons she associated with it, and did rather little justice to the town or its vicinity.

Not wholly refreshed by September, she saw another seaside town this year. A coach probably took the Austens south by way of Shepton Mallet, Somerton and Crewkerne and onwards to the junction of the Lyme Road at Hunter's Lodge inn, and then they rolled through cheerful Up Lyme to a long descending road and into the still steeper street of a curious town. Its oddity was that it seemed to rush headlong into the sea. It may not have belonged on the Dorset coast near Devon at all, but even if it was not an outpost of heaven, Lyme became the real place that she most adored outside Hampshire. It was beautiful and funny and sweet and fascinating, even if it was no dearer to her than her county's villages. It was also provincial. When in the Lyme Assembly Room she was stared at by an unabashed Irishman she told Cassandra he was related to 'bold queer-looking people, just fit to be quality at Lyme'.[31] Yet queer as the quality was she made excuses for what she saw *here*, and faults of Ramsgate became rare blessings when reflected in any way at Lyme. Thomas Hardy was not more ingenious in praising Dorset, and the novelist John Fowles has not lavished a more subtle affection on it – but Jane Austen was the first writer to love it for explicit and excellent reasons. First 'the retirement of Lyme in the winter' meant it could rejuvenate itself in a huddled isolation between invasions of summer visitors, and then to be at Lyme was to think of nature forcibly and continually, and to see the truth that place is defined by its surroundings. Beyond the town, a country of cliffs with long views of earth and sea gave one a sense of the beauty unequalled.

The Austens were here probably on 5 November 1803 when there was a fierce fire. 'The Flames', Jane Austen wrote with remembered fear about a later fire at Southampton, 'were considerable, they seemed about as near to us as those at Lyme.'[32] As the fire consumed central dwellings she may have been staying that November at the Royal Lion or at the Three Cups, an inn which after another fire was rebuilt higher up and on the other side of Broad Street. In her own time it stood at the bottom of the main street and turned slightly away from it.

They liked the town well enough to return in 1804, after summer rambles with Henry and Eliza. And indeed by September, Jane and Cassandra had danced several times at the Assembly Room near Bell Cliff and Cobb Gate. It has since been torn down to make way for a parking lot, but it had been built in 1775 in a simple, enduring style. Three glass chandeliers hung from an arched ceiling, and visitors by daylight felt almost afloat, since nothing but blue sea and sky were visible from the windows. An orchestra of three or four instruments played on nights of the regular ball, and one Thursday evening Jane and Cassandra typically reached the dance at 8 p.m. Mr Austen quietly left at 9.30 and walked home accompanied by their new servant, who held a 'lanthorn' which did not need to be lit since the moon was up. Mrs Austen meanwhile played cards, and Jane danced with a Mr Crawford. Then a few days after her sister had left with Henry and Eliza to see Weymouth, Jane wrote to her about one of their admirers known as *le Chevalier*, and also with a novelist's instinct worked up her prose style with her usual series of jokes. Her paper is tinted with tiny close-space brown horizontal lines and her hand vigorously corrects her style. 'It was absolutely necessary', Jane writes at Lyme,

> that I should have a little fever & indisposition as I had; – it has been all the fashion this week at Lyme.

She paused to improve her style with a 'the' and a 'which' for cadence and grammar,

> that I should have *the* little fever & indisposition, *which* I had – it has been all the fashion this week at Lyme.[33]

Lyme, as she believed, might be useful, and in this letter she revealed her delight with it while sketching the Austen ménage. 'I detect dirt in the water-decanter as fast as I can,' she writes of their home life at Lyme, '& give the Cook physic, which she throws off

201

her stomach.' The new servant is so good he reminds her of Uncle Toby's one hundred and twenty pounds a year plus half-pay in *Tristram Shandy* as he is 'quite an uncle Toby's annuity to us' and has more than mere cardinal virtues. What are the cardinal virtues after all? 'The cardinal virtues', she instructs her sister deliciously, 'in themselves have been so often possessed that they are no longer worth having.'[34] That joke might amuse Cassandra, and the truth at its core was liberating and fortifying. Her spirit was as anarchical, immoral and in love with comedy and calamity as it could be in a light letter from this pretty town. What oppressed her was the tiresomeness of platitudes that she heard even here.

Her new friend Miss Armstrong, of Lyme, was one of her better discoveries. It is true that Miss Armstrong lacked wit, was almost complacent, filled with second-rate notions and some sense, but she was pleasing in long walks on the Cobb. For centuries Lyme had had its Cobb, which had become a necessary object for all visitors to try above the sea. It is a massive stone semi-circular pier jutting out on the farther side of the harbour with two causeways on different levels which form the Upper and Lower Cobb. Even today it reveals the often repaired masonry of the Austens' time. We 'walked together for an hour on the Cobb', Jane reports. In the sparkling light they repassed a precipitous, rough flight of steps connecting the two levels, and known today as Granny's Teeth. These steps protrude precariously over empty space, and remind one of the danger of a fall to the stone below and certainly of what formidable obstacles the steps were to ladies in long dresses. Possibly Jane did not walk on the Upper Cobb if a Lyme historian is right in believing that before 1817 a stroll along the 'parapet from the gin shop, a niche so called, to the outer pier, was too rough for a promenade'.[35] But the rough steps *could* be climbed by a lady, and it is likely that Granny's Teeth helped to inspire the idea of Louisa Musgrove's fall from the Cobb in *Persuasion*, the most famous event in the history and legends of Lyme. When Tennyson later saw the town and his friends spoke of the reputed landing place of the Duke of Monmouth he became very indignant: 'Don't talk to me', cried the poet, 'of the Duke of Monmouth. Show me the exact spot where Louisa Musgrove fell.'[36]

From the Lower Cobb could be seen one of the loveliest, most spacious views along the south coast. A stretch of sand formed a highway for waggons taking freight into town, and horses stood up to their flanks in flowing tide as boats were unloaded. Beyond were neat cottages where captains of the Royal Navy might live in cramped but adequate comfort. To the east was a beautiful line of hills near Charmouth, to the west a fine line of grey and blue. Cliffs pushed into the sea, and even now people were collecting fossils. One day Jane Austen had taken a certain broken lid to be valued in town 'by Anning': his daughter Mary Anning, who was born in 1799, soon advanced science by discovering between Lyme and Charmouth in 1811 the fossil of an ichthyosaurus. If the world's past and its delightful present came together here, Jane lived some of her happiest days possibly at the cottage of Wings overlooking the Cobb. When Captain Boteler arrived to command the Coastguard Service in 1827 he was emphatically told she had stayed there.[37]

Lyme in any case stimulated her enterprise. In 1804, as Anna's daughter Fanny says, she was working on a new story. 'Somewhere in 1804 she began "The Watsons",' says Fanny, 'and it was never finished.'[38] Anna Lefroy and others have tried to write completions of the intriguing story. Jane Austen's manuscript shows that she began boldly, turning her first sheet length-wise and writing so swiftly that she was surprised perhaps by the number of corrections she had to make. The dialogue came more easily and a story-line was quickly established. The Watsons are a needy, ill-assorted family in Surrey when Emma Watson, who has been raised in another county by an aunt who has remarried and left for Ireland, returns home to be counselled in hard advice by her elder sister Elizabeth. 'You know we must marry,' Elizabeth tells Emma. 'I could do very well single for my part – a little company and a pleasant ball now and then would be enough for me, if one could be young for ever, but my Father cannot provide for us, and it is very bad to grow old and be poor and laughed at.'[39] Warned against the facile charms of Tom Musgrave, Emma Watson goes to a winter ball at the fashionable Edwardses where to oblige a widow she dances with ten-year-old Charles Blake, as Jane Austen may once have danced with young Harris Wither. Mr Howard, the clergyman of the parish, as well as the fine young Lord Osborne with his air of coldness, carelessness and awkwardness, are attracted to her in the ballroom. However, a day or two later, when Musgrave and Osborne call at the Watsons, Emma and Elizabeth are vexed by their own shabby poverty. Their brother Robert, 'an Attorney at Croydon, in a good way of Business', is just such a patronizing man of the law as the author disliked, and he resents sisters too poor to bring him business. He has married a lady with six thousand pounds and a similarly hard, obtuse and dismissive nature. Refusing to visit at Croydon, Emma is glad to get away to her father's room where she finds relief 'from the immediate endurance of Hard-hearted prosperity, low-minded Conceit, & wrong-headed folly, engrafted on a untoward Disposition' – and the story breaks off before we know whether any suitor is worthy of her. The well-etched character portraits, the black comedy of the *nouveaux riches* Robert Watsons and the care shown in the author's revisions all suggest that for months the story was meant to be finished. We even have hints of what was to happen. As James Edward said when Cassandra showed the manuscript of this work to some of her nieces, she also told them something of the intended story 'for with this dear sister – though, I believe, with no one else – Jane seems to have talked freely of any work that she might have in hand. Mr. Watson was soon to die; and Emma to become dependent for a home on her narrow-minded sister-in-law and brother. She was to decline an offer of marriage from Lord Osborne, and much of the interest of the tale was to arise from Lady Osborne's love for Mr. Howard, and his counter affection for Emma, whom he was finally to marry.'[40]

Its title *The Watsons* was given when James Edward at last published the manuscript in his 1871 *Memoir* of his aunt. The reasons why Jane Austen never finished it may be found not entirely in outward events, as she could have resumed it at Chawton, but in deeper and more ambiguous considerations. The darkest, oddest fact about Emma Watson is that she is flawless. She lacks the psychological interest of a Marianne, the good luck of a Catherine or the healthy egotism of an Elizabeth Bennet, and because economic odds against her are heavy the atmosphere of the story is oppressive and uniform. Emma Watson is a victim – cruelly disadvantaged as a stranger in her home and too genteel for her life in Surrey. Her sister Elizabeth is a poor housekeeper but otherwise is like Cassandra in being frank and sociable, good-humoured, rational and fearful by turns and not unpleasantly 'shrinking under a general sense of inferiority'. The two are affectionate but unable to help each other, hence the energy of the story pours into the depiction of their economic plight and the horridly complacent people set against them, so that one feels

Elizabeth is right to say, 'It is very bad to grow old and be poor and laughed at.' That sentiment of fear in the presence of poverty and increasing age was felt by Jane Austen, though expressed in light remarks, even after her removal to new lodgings in the Green Park Buildings. It touched on one of the deepest reasons why Jane so unguardedly had accepted Harris. She had feared poverty and degradation for herself and Cassandra, and despite her resources of spirit she was not so confident as to think she might become old and poor with good grace. Marriage can be a cure for economic insecurity. For herself marriage was not essential, but she had considered it, hoped for it, planned it without a partner in view, and for one night had gambled on it as a fitting choice. Her 'vexing' humiliation told her she had been wrong and thus she faced the Austens' narrow circumstances again. Her heroine illustrates resources of courage, but the autobiographical topic was not easy to quicken with comedy.

Yet she had written several chapters lately. She had found Lyme delicious to revisit, and could know that her family were as loyal as ever as she approached her twenty-ninth birthday at No. 27 Green Park Buildings in the late autumn of 1804.

A family of new occupants, the Coles, had moved into the Austens' former house at Sydney Place. 'The Coles have got their infamous plate upon our door,' Jane Austen announced.[41] The Coles only mattered as a joke, but perhaps were another sign of her exile at Bath where a joke counted. To laugh one needs an audience, and she could rely on those female friends who laughed with her – on Cassandra, the Biggs, Martha Lloyd, and Madam Lefroy. Even so she was in a narrower avenue of life than ever, and the buildings of Green Park implied a constraint that she had never known at Steventon. Her old inspirations were far off and new friendships were unlikely, she had lost her chance to help her family by marrying to advantage and in that sense had failed them. She was still in a city from which she could expect no release. If she became a burden on her brothers their regard for her would be affected by her dependency, to the extent that she could lose their love as she had known it. There is an element of rage in her jokes – as if, sometimes, wit had to endure without comedy, or any hope. But in any fury, privately and quietly, as her cheerfulness was crushed and her father's health failed, she could be pleased with her quick little joke on the Coles.

13

———❦———

Trafalgar

Seas roll to waft me, suns to light me rise,
My footstool the earth, my canopy the skies.

Pope

Jane Austen was quick to see the ludicrous in exclusive conversations of men about public events, partly because her brothers confided in her. Good St John's College Tories *talked* discreetly about
politics (without as a rule either writing directly of public affairs or
taking part in any phase of the Whiggish hubbub), and Henry found
it natural to discuss imperial policy with his sister. Every war is political; every action of Frank's for the East India Company could be
of interest to the beaten Whig opponents of Warren Hastings; and
especially while George Austen lived it is virtually certain that his
children were discouraged from prying into Frank's Far Eastern work.
But Frank's normal duties in the Navy were another matter. Jane
Austen found Pasley's *Essay on the Military Policy* 'delightfully written
and highly entertaining' and one of her favourite books (partly
because her own delight in it surely surprised Cassandra); and then
its charm was not less because such a book took her closer to Frank.
She soon overcame any real reserve she had felt over Frank's engagement to Mary Gibson. Her attitude to a new situation was to make
fun of it, to see the irony of it, and so reconcile herself as far as
possible to what she *had* to accept. If Frank had disconcerted her
at Ramsgate by consorting with very ordinary Gibsons Jane Austen

was soon to share a house with Mary Gibson: that lady was accepted by all the Austens once Frank[2] made his intentions plain. Meanwhile it was hardly possible to neglect the war because it affected Frank and Charles, and with rumours that the enemy were at last ready to invade Kent with 'a corps of guide-interpreters, ready to take up their duties directly the force landed', naval families were uneasy. The nation was vulnerable. Nelson's fleet was being pulled to pieces by demands of convoys for his frigates. Invasion might or might not be likely, and girls in boarding-houses near the sea who kept under their beds 'Napoleon blankets', with tapes attached, to be worn in case of midnight alarm, were only a picturesque instance of the real state of matters: if swift, well-built ships of France intercepted an India-bound convoy now – and destroyed it – the East India Company could, after all, be bankrupted. The British answer to a double threat of invasion and convoy interception was a 'close blockade' of enemy ports, and hence Jane's brother, as one of Nelson's favoured captains, was appointed in May 1804 to the *Leopard*, flagship of Rear-Admiral Louis who commanded the squadron off Boulogne.

The Austens were fascinated by Frank's sea life, and Mr Austen's curiosity had been so great that in August 1802 he and his wife had boarded the *Neptune* at Portsmouth – even as Dr Johnson at that port once stepped on to the *Ramilies*, a '74, and complained of the Lieutenant's habit of swearing. ('I beseech him', Dr Johnson implored, 'not to use one oath more than is absolutely required for the service of his Majesty.')[1] If the adventurous Austens heard few oaths, they saw the long, dismal gangways emptied of gear and running from end to end with the 32-pounders in position. It was not easy to picture these decks when *Neptune* was in action, but a genteel family came away better informed, and their talk increased Jane Austen's confidence in portraying naval men in *Mansfield Park* and *Persuasion*. She took an informed interest in Frank – and again he was at sea after his service in the *London* off Cadiz during which he had seen the penalties of blockade duty. He said of himself that he was a good nautical 'Observer' but did not presume to be essential to the Navy. He served, as he claimed, for 'pecuniary advantage as well as the professional credit',[2] an honest statement which accorded pretty well with his outlook. Since childhood Frank had been aggressively busy and practical yet almost too aware of his responsibilities as a 'young gentleman' from his Academy days on. He was exceptional in his respect for the cloth; at Ramsgate he was *the* officer who knelt in church, and he was so unassailably correct in daily life that for Jane he had become a figure of fun. But her respect gave her licence to find him amusing. Eliza found his halting, factual talk and small stature hilarious, too, but failed to see the moral sense that so appealed to Jane.

In earning 'professional credit' he was crawling higher up a crowded ladder since the change in his fortunes which had occurred when he was 'made post', and that, as the Austens knew, was a crucial point in a naval officer's career. A 'post ship' was large enough to have a master in charge of navigation while the captain directed the fighting and commanded the ship's crew. Another step up the ladder was to get a flagship, and hence by the spring of 1804 Frank was on his way to new advancement – if he did not blunder and he stayed alive. Aboard the *Leopard* he lived at the quarterdeck's after end with the Admiral's cabin below his and the ward-room of the lieutenants and Royal Marine officers below the Admiral's, and he had only to open a door to be beside the ship's wheel and compass binnacle. In gales and heavy seas Frank's chances of survival were reduced as his ship pitched and rolled, wallowed and shuddered with its ropes creaking and the hull groaning, the lower deck damp and dark and miserable, the heavy guns dangerously straining and the enemy close by on a fortified coast. *Leopard* stood off Boulogne in all weather, heeling on its lee side where chain-tackles for its guns were strongest, 'with the town bearing from s.s.e. to e.s.e., distant about four miles', as he put it, the ship in sixteen to twenty fathoms of water over 'coarse sandy bottom, with large shells and stones, which would probably injure the cables materially, but that from the depth of water and strength of the tides little of them can ever drag on the bottom'.[3] Standing that close unnerved sailors more experienced than Frank and tested even Admiral Collingwood, who found a similar station off Brest needing 'constant care and look out, so that I have often been a week without taking my clothes off, and sometimes up on deck the whole night'.[4]

For companionable cheer Frank had on board an 'old Crocodile', in his early forties, one of the grimmest of men, Thomas Louis, who was made rear-admiral just before Frank joined the *Leopard*. Louis was known for sailing broken wrecks. A veteran of Ushant and Cape St Vincent, he had placed his ship ahead of Nelson's at the Nile to draw the severe dual fire of *L'Aquilon* and *Le Spartiate*, the latter of which he dismasted while killing most of its gun-crews. 'Your support', Lord Nelson wrote to him, 'prevented me from being obliged to haul out of the line.' Louis was to die on the *Canopus* – Frank's next ship – and his presence off Boulogne was a sign that Frank in action might be in the van under heavy hire. The Crocodile was Nelson's shield: he would not hang back. But as the flotilla did not emerge, it was vital that Frank do what he could to keep *Leopard*'s crew busy. He demanded of the Naval Board an extra allowance of paint and waged war with the Board, while alluding to Louis to strengthen his case: 'With respect to "no colour other than white being allowed for boats",' wrote Frank, 'I would only ask you, as knowing something of the King's naval service, how long one of our six-oared cutters would look decent painted all white, and whether a darker colour would not be both more durable and creditable? If, however, such be the regulation of the Board (from which I know there is no appeal), I have only to request, when you receive any order to supply the paint, that you will give an additional quantity of white in lieu of black.' The old Crocodile thought *black* proper and wanted plenty of paint, it seems: 'Nor is it more than sufficient', Frank adds of his ship, 'to make her decent and fit for an Admiral to hoist his flag in.'[5] He soon got into a new, horrid contention over ballast.

His main relief was that in a flagship he called often at Dungeness or Spithead for a bundle of post including letters from home, and so he heard of Jane Austen's tragedies in late 1804 and early 1805.

She had seemed the merriest of young women with a power of drollery exercised at his expense, but there was also in Frank's view of his sister a recognition that her sensitive nature was vulnerable to appeals from those she cared for and at variance with a reticence she displayed with others: she 'was cheerful and not easily irritated', he wrote later of Jane, 'and tho' rather reserved with strangers so as to have been accused by some of haughtiness of manner, yet in the company of those she loved the native benevolence of her heart and kindliness of her disposition were forcibly displayed'.[6] As he knew of her friendship for Madam Lefroy he might appreciate the effect of hard recent news.

Mrs Lefroy, in her pleasant house at Ashe, had been lonely after the Austens' removal to Bath and her children had left home. She dramatized that emptiness of heart and used her feelings to impress those who loved her: 'I have just had my solitary breakfast,' she had written to a son at the Isle of Wight, 'and tho I try to keep up my spirits I cannot always succeed when I look back to the happy days when in your father's absence I was surrounded by my children. The contrast is too much for my feelings and I feel forlorn and wretched beyond description.' Yet she wrote gaily of Harris Wither's recent marriage to Anne Frith and busied herself in charitable projects, compensating herself for a not unkindly but bland, dull, unresponsive husband.[7] She was not always forlorn, and Mrs Lefroy's daily riding improved her morale. 'Between 3 and four o'clock' in the afternoon of 15 December, however, she was thrown from her horse. Charles Lyford of Basingstoke attended her, but with a 'violent concussion' she lingered twelve hours and died at 3.00 a.m. on 16 December 1804, Jane Austen's twenty-ninth birthday. Lyford cushioned the news to her son by writing to Richard Clarke at Newport who told him of his mother's death, but very little cushioned the effect at Bath. Jane had known few grievous losses, and in Tom Fowle's or Lady Williams's death the worst grief had been felt by a survivor so much closer to the person who had died that she could not have felt singled out – and there was nothing extenuating about this loss to modify its cruelty. The effect was likely to be worse than her shock over the loss of a 'seaside lover' she had known for a fortnight. Praise in obituaries for those we have loved is seldom excessive, and she could see, as doubtless she did, the press tributes to that unusual lady who at fifty-six had left a 'chasm in society which there is no second to fill'. One paper wrote in accents suggesting the death of Johnson. 'The splendour of her talent, her powerful and energetic language, the beaming and eager benevolence of her countenance' and her ministrations to the poor had made her a 'good angel'.[8] One *might* grieve with a good conscience, but for Jane Austen this was a unique, anguishing personal calamity with a tinge of accusation since, after all, she had been forced to follow her family to Bath when Mrs Lefroy had needed her loving, kind, happy presence. Four years later she wrote her stanzas 'To the Memory of Mrs Lefroy', and although the poem reflects the language of the newspaper obituaries it suggests a depth and complexity in a more acute grief:

The day returns again, my natal day;

What mix'd emotions to my mind arise!
Beloved Friend; four years have passed away
　　Since thou wert snatched for ever from our eyes.

The day commemorative of my birth,
　　Bestowing life, and light, and hope to me,
Brings back the hour which was thy last on earth.
　　O! bitter pang of torturing memory!

The best elegies are written by those not too entangled with memories, but as a poem for the Austens and a reminder of her own feelings, 'To the Memory of Mrs Lefroy' is tenderly moving. Even its mistake is interesting. In one of two manuscripts believed to be in Jane Austen's hand there is a reference to Edmund Burke, one of the Whigs who had led the long, cruel attack on Eliza's godfather.

At Johnson's death by Burke t'was finely said,[9]

Jane Austen wrote, and then perhaps after a glance at Boswell's *Life of Johnson*, in which she would have found William Gerard Hamilton mentioned as the real author of the remark she wished to allude to, she changed her words to read,

At Johnson's death, by Hamilton 'twas said,
　　'Seek we a substitute – Ah! vain the plan,
No second best remains to Johnson dead –
　　None can remind us even of the Man.'

So we of thee – unequalled in thy race,
　　Unequall'd thou, as he the first of Men.
Vainly we search around thy vacant place,
　　We ne'er may look upon the like again.[10]

She had not refused to credit Burke for the fine remark 'at Johnson's death', any more than she hesitated to play the Marseilles March at her keyboard, and indeed her Oxford brothers had prepared her to absorb *aperçus*, styles and leading ideas of writers inimical to the Austens' political thinking. She lived at home in an open, amused, easy intellectual atmosphere gaily raiding the enemy as she wished and plundering what she would, so that it is not surprising to find echoes of Mary Wollstonecraft and William Godwin later in *Persuasion*. After reading the radical Godwin's novels *Caleb Williams* (1794) and *St Leon, A Tale of the Sixteenth Century* (1799) she told Cassandra lightly about the fashionable Pickfords of Bath: '*She* is the most elegant

211

looking Woman I have seen since I left Martha – *He* is as raffish in his appearance as I would wish every Disciple of Godwin to be.'[11] She was no disciple of conservative Whiggery *or* Radicalism, but it is important that she was quite sophisticated enough to read Whigs and Radicals without fret, to learn from them, to extract brightly what she wished. At a deep level her poem on Mrs Lefroy indicates an attitude that she shared especially with Frank, as it is the work of a Christian activist, a doer who is not abashed or even very modest in her view of herself and is grateful to that 'Angelic woman', the kind and witty hostess of Ashe who composed poetry and furthered her brother Egerton's literary career for having stimulated Miss Jane Austen's being and nourished her piety and early energy and talent. 'Her partial favour from my earliest years', writes Jane, 'consummates all,' yet not even Fancy with the iciest Reason explains why the lady died on the author's natal day. Her optimism was modified by this event, and not eight weeks later she suffered a graver loss.

Her father had been ailing for weeks and after the holidays his forgetfulness, fever and tremulousness returned. Green Park Buildings were damp, and Bath's wintry desolation was at its worst when William Bowen and then Dr Gibbs came to look after their frail patient. On 20 January he joined his daughters at breakfast, walked about gamely with his stick, peered at the weather and said he felt no 'symptom'. But his fever returned that afternoon. Bowen found his state 'most alarming' when he called at ten that night, and twelve hours later, or at about 10.20 a.m., George Austen died.

'Heavy as is the blow,' Jane wrote that day to Frank, 'we can already feel that a thousand comforts remain to us to soften it. Next to that of the consciousness of his worth & constant preparation for another World, is the remembrance of his having suffered, comparatively speaking, nothing. Being quite insensible of his own state, he was spared all the pain of separation, & he went off almost in his Sleep.' Her stoicism enhanced her piety, and under duress guaranteed a practical composure and permitted her to be rational, to look to the better side of things and be thankful that an anguishing event had not been drawn out. She was consoled by those who meant to comfort, encouraged by the alerted Perrots. 'My Uncle and Aunt have been with us, & shew us every imaginable kindness,' she continues in her first letter to Frank. 'And tomorrow we shall I dare say have the comfort of James's presence, as an express has been sent to him.'

212

(Above) 'The Handsome Proctor', Jane Austen's father, the Revd George Austen
(1731–1805), in a miniature made in 1801 and in a silhouette.
(Below left) Jane Austen's mother, the former Cassandra Leigh (1739–1827),
of aristocratic descent. (Below right) Jane Austen's devoted sister,
Cassandra Elizabeth Austen (1773–1845).

The Rectory at Steventon, Hampshire, where Jane Austen was born in 1775.
It is believed that her niece Anna made both sketches in the year she was
married, 1814. The front (top) shows a gate leading into a small sweep before
the front door with its lattice frame or 'porch'. At the back (below) are two
projecting wings, on either side of George Austen's ground-floor study.
His daughters' bedroom was up one flight. Here Jane Austen drafted her first
three novels, and left with regret in May 1801 to reside with her family in Bath.

Back Front of Steventon Rectory. 1814

Jane Austen's two Oxford brothers. The oval miniatures show her eldest
brother, James Austen (1765–1819), above left, and on the right her happier,
scheming, funnier brother Henry Thomas Austen (1771–1850). Both stimulated
Jane's intellect and artistry. At St John's College, Oxford they launched their
satirical weekly *The Loiterer*. James later attacked novel-writing, and wrote
poems as a country clergyman. Henry joined the militia, flirted to the
embarrassment of his family, risked Austen funds, married his worldly cousin
Eliza de Feuillide, survived the crash of his bank, and to Jane Austen's
amusement at last settled down into clerical respectability.

(Above) from William Wellings' silhouette in 1783: the Revd George Austen presenting his son Edward to Mr and Mrs Thomas Knight of Kent. (Below) from George Romney's painting of Edward's benefactor Mrs Thomas Knight, *née* Catherine Knatchbull (1753–1812). Deeply fond of her, Jane Austen wrote of her before *Sense and Sensibility* was published: 'I think she will like my Elinor, but cannot build on any thing else.'

(Right) Edward Austen of Kent (1767–1852), Jane Austen's third brother, painted when he was on the Grand Tour at twenty-one and becoming a part of the 'Neufchatel set'. (Below) Elizabeth Bridges (1771–1808), whom he married. Not long before she died in 1808 as a result of bearing his eleventh child, Elizabeth signed her name in a work by the radical London feminist Mary Hays.

Jane Austen's two naval brothers. (Opposite page) Captain Francis William Austen (1774–1865) with a picture of HMS *Canopus*, aboard which he carried Nelson's second-in-command in 1805 at the time of the Trafalgar action. (This page) Captain Charles John Austen (1779–1852) with a picture of his HMS *Winchester*.

Admiral Sir Francis William Austen in a valuable daguerreotype in which his features suggest those in Cassandra's sketch of Jane Austen; he was the brother closest to her in age. Hints of his personality appear in her captains in *Persuasion*. Jane Austen shared two of his houses at Southampton, and listed his opinions of *Mansfield Park* and *Emma* above everyone else's. He never retired from the naval list. After marrying Martha Lloyd, 'Frank' rose to be Admiral of the Red, and then at eighty-nine Admiral of the Fleet.

Martha Lloyd (1765–1843), Jane Austen's close friend and companion at Southampton and then at Chawton during the composition of *Mansfield Park, Emma, Persuasion,* and *Sanditon.* She 'preferred' *Mansfield Park* to the other novels before it, and even to *Emma.* Jane Austen joked with her, confided in her, discussed public events with her, sent her a letter touching on imperial foreign policy, and valued her good judgement. In 1828 Martha married Frank, and became Lady Austen at Portsdown Hill.

(Top) a winter sketch of the manor at Manydown Park, Hampshire, with its squarish front. Here on 2 December 1802 Jane Austen accepted the marital proposal of Harris Bigg-Wither, then twenty-one. She precipitated an embarrassing crisis that was not quickly resolved to anyone's satisfaction, and one that involved the family of Sir William Blackstone of the *Commentaries on the Law*.
(Above) placid Lyme Regis on the Dorset coast which she first saw a few months later.

Early, important friends. From miniatures of the Revd Isaac Peter George Lefroy of Ashe, born in 1745, and of his wife Anne, born in 1749. Anne Lefroy's 'inexpressible' pleasure was to know and encourage her young friend Jane Austen of Steventon. Alarmed by Jane Austen's flirtation with her husband's nephew Tom Lefroy, Anne sent the young man off in a hurry.

(Top left) George Austen's sister Philadelphia (1730–93), who in India married
Tysoe Saul Hancock, twenty years her senior, and then was rumoured to have
'abandoned herself to Mr Hastings'. (Above right) her daughter Eliza de
Feuillide (1761–1813), beneficiary of Warren Hastings' £10,000 trust fund.
Eliza flirted at the English spas before and after her husband was guillotined,
and brought her talents to the Austen family theatricals. Witty, comic remarks
and incidents in her letters are reflected in *Lady Susan* and *Northanger Abbey*.
'Still my heart gives the preference to Jane', she wrote of her Steventon visits.
She married Henry Austen in 1797.

Jane Austen's two favourite nieces. She compared Anna (top right), 1793–1872
with Niagara Falls because of Anna's ardent, tempestuous nature. As James
Austen's elder daughter, Anna brought peace to her family by marrying Ben
Lefroy in 1814, and after her husband's early death wrote children's stories.
(Above left) Jane Austen's elegant niece of Kent, Fanny Austen (1793–1882),
who wrote tirelessly in her diary and married the widower Sir Edward Knatchbull.

(Top left) Jane Austen's uncle James Leigh Perrot, with whom she searched for rentable houses at Bath. (Above right) his strong-minded wife 'Aunt Perrot' or the former Jane Cholmeley (1744–1836). Thought by her own counsel to be guilty of stealing a card of lace, she silenced a courtroom and saved herself at her trial. Her formidable personality and knowledge of Bath were helpful to Jane Austen. Yet Mrs Leigh Perrot upset relatives and caused quarrels until the age of ninety-two.

The only two authenticated portraits of Jane Austen, both by Cassandra. The watercolour back view was made around 1802, when she was 'sitting down out of doors on a hot day with her bonnet strings untied'. The accuracy of the front view, made around June 1811 on a card of 4½ by 3⅛ inches, tends to be confirmed by details in a letter by Mrs Beckford that came to light in 1985: 'I remember her as a tall thin *spare* person, with very high cheek bones, great colour – sparkling Eyes not large but joyous & intelligent' and with a 'face by no means so broad & plump as represented' in the round-cheeked, prettified Victorian adaptation of Jane Austen's portrait (made by Lizars) that was first printed in the 1870 *Memoir*.

Jane Austen's house at
Chawton – (above) before the
pond at the crossroads was
drained, and (right) the
house as it is today. (Below)
the house in College Street,
Winchester, where Jane
Austen died in 1817.

But having written in care of the *Leopard* at Dungeness and finding news in the post that Frank's ship would be at Portsmouth, she sent another letter to him on Tuesday evening, 22 January, thirty-six hours later. She only means to catch him as soon as possible but her mood has changed, and her grief is no longer controlled. Her practical Anne Elliot, giving cool orders after Louisa's fall from the Cobb, represents no more than the author's initial reaction to a crisis. Her father's death had consequences for her art, for her outlook on the future, also for her morale and courage; she had depended on his sympathy, learned to trust in it, and her adjustment was never to be perfect – her great loss enhanced her capacity for sympathy and even the subtlety of her understanding of the psychology of feeling. Her early work sparkles in confidence and humour but it is not especially strong in testing comedy's darker side, or in exploring heroines who are not so lucky, cheerful and adaptable as Elizabeth Bennet and Catherine Morland – whereas the stories she began at Chawton are grave as well as comic, more probing, widely alert in their humanity, and display heroines such as Fanny Price and Anne Elliot who do not necessarily adapt with agility to anything in their lives. She learned from her deep initial despair: 'My dearest Frank,' she writes in grief, 'Everything I trust & beleive was done for him that was possible! – It has been very sudden!' She could not take in the sudden, terrible change in her father's being from the sight and sound of his gentle, reassuring valour, to the sight of his still form – 'within twenty-four hours of his death he was walking with only the help of his stick, was even reading! . . . To have seen him languishing long, struggling for Hours would have been dreadful! & thank God! we were all spared. . . . – The Serenity of the Corpse is most delightful!' she tells Frank, '– it preserves the sweet, benevolent smile which always distinguished him.'[12]

Grief can be shared. James came quickly from Steventon and Henry from Kent, and besides attending Mr Austen's funeral at Walcot Church they offered their mother assurances. Her income would fall to around £210 with the ending of clerical stipends, and that sum, including interest from Tom Fowle's legacy to Cassandra, was too small to support three ladies. Henry was witty and talkative, but, with concern for 'our dear trio', he heard James pledge them £50 a year. 'James behaves like a man of feeling and a true son,' Henry wrote to Frank. Henry offered his mother £50 a year, too, and thought

Edward would be good for about £100 more. Frank, a captain on blockade, need not give a penny – but 'when you have taken a Galleon', Henry gaily told him, 'you shall keep a carriage for my Mother if you choose'.

Frank replied from Spithead that he offered £100 a year and wished it kept a secret, but Henry blurted that to Mrs Austen: 'With the proudest exultations of maternal tenderness the Excellent Parent has exclaimed', he wrote, 'that never were Children as good as hers – She feels the magnificence of your offer, and accepts of half. I shall therefore honour her demands for £50 pounds annually on your account.'

Besides what Edward might give, the ladies would thus have £450 *per annum* – such a fine sum that Henry's optimism soared before he left Bath. 'I really think', he wrote to Frank, 'that my Mother & sisters will be to the full as rich as ever. They will not only suffer no personal deprivation, but will be able to pay occasional visits of health and pleasure to their friends.'[13] This optimism was logical but it overlooked a subtle, psychological change involved in the dear trio's new finances, as the Austen ladies must now rely on voluntary contributions from three or four brothers – all with commitments of their own – instead of on a head of a household, and it would be hard for them ever to own a house. Prices rose in wartime. Mrs Austen would keep only one servant in her rooms till Lady Day and then take 'furnished lodgings' at No. 25 Gay Street, where they would observe strict economies.

Thinking this over, James was satisfied. 'I believed her summers will be spent in the country amongst her Relations & chiefly I trust among her children,' he wrote with the complacency of clergymen who saw dozens of impoverished families in far worse straits, '– the winters she will pass in comfortable lodgings in Bath.' He was not parsimonious but he seemed to think genteel ladies needed no more than bread in their mouths and cloth on their backs, and as the practical country economies of Mary Austen guided him, he applauded his own generosity. 'It is just satisfaction', he reassured Frank about their mother, 'to know that her Circumstances will be easy, & that she will enjoy all those comforts which her declining years & precarious health call for.'[14] James does not say how his sisters might feel about moving dependently among relatives in the summers and living in rented Bath lodgings in the winters, and one feels that kindly as he was Jane had no reason to feel indebted to him for finesse. To the extent that James and Frank epitomized for her the professions of the clergy and the Navy, she did not draw from them an impartially balanced impression of two callings, and it must be noticed that in her novels she is a good deal less inclined to find the open, generous, imaginative heart in gentlemen of the cloth. She leans to the Navy, and yet the reader returning to *Persuasion* for the fifth or sixth time may be more convinced of the good-heartedness of her captains than of their perspicacity, sense or subtlety. She had cause, however, to be grateful to Frank for offering twice as much as he needed to do, and for his tact in wishing to keep his first offer a secret. Her brothers' letters do not indicate what they may have said, but judging from the facts we have Frank is tactful and thoughtful in the January crisis, Henry is too convinced by superficial reasoning, and James is too preoccupied with himself. Jane could be irritated by her brothers – indeed, those with the most power to irritate are those we truly love. Frank rose in her estimation because he was absent, and his letters in courtesy and tact appeared in the best light. Her attachment to him was being justified by events nevertheless, and it is not coincidental that the Austen ladies were to share his house. (They declined an offer to live with or near Edward.) Despite his limitations – literalness and lack of humour – he seldom offended an associate. In his dogged, risky work he lived in hardship just as Jane lived in another kind of adversity, and she now had to endure Bath without her father.

Grief contributed to her stopping work on *The Watsons*, and it is likely that the only time in her creative life when she was not writing or revising her manuscripts occurred in the months after George Austen died in 1805. Even so, she soon wrote out a fair copy of *Lady Susan*, as we know from the watermarks on her paper. There is a difference between starting creative work and revising what one has done, but there is no evidence that she went through years of inactivity – or had any totally barren or inactive months in her career save for this time. We have seen that aspects of *The Watsons'* story failed to release a certain gaiety of feeling her comedies called for, and we may find a modern critic's comment apt: she had felt 'deep affection for her father and had now to face', says Mr Hopkinson, 'all that must follow from the disruption of their family life. Would anyone', he asks, 'have chosen to go on with such a story at such a moment?'[15] She was not so fretful at Bath that she could not write or revise, but she lacked the well-being to pursue the story of a heroine who has too many worldly circumstances against her. When she recovered, she had picked up *Lady Susan* and livelier manuscripts.

Her faith reconciled her to mortality. But her letters register time's passing and amidst streets and near bow-windowed shops where her father walked in the daily, busy and genteel stir at Bath she can value 'that sort of quiet composedness of mind which always seems sufficient to itself'. A signal division between time past and present is the event of January. If she looks back it is through new eyes. She moves altogether in a different 'set' from the one of seven years back, 'but seven years I suppose are enough to change every pore of one's skin, & every feeling of one's mind'. What is loyalty if time changes the very pores of one's skin? There are dances, concerts, teas, old friends and comically predatory young ladies at Bath, so that days shrink and combine almost pleasantly. One day 'it is March & April together, the glare of the one & the warmth of the other'. She jokingly adjusts to the fact that it will be possible to be a vagrant. 'Our Tea and Sugar will last a great while,' she tells Cassandra. '–I think we are just the kind of people & party to be treated about among our relations; – we cannot be supposed to be very rich.'

In caring for her mother she is well occupied. She had been too busy to send poor Frank more than a line or two about a bequest: their mother has found Mr Austen's 'Compass & Sun-Dial' in a black shagreen case, a round metal object made by Adams of London calibrated with roman numerals and perched on three little projecting feet with flat metal coin-like tops. 'Would you have it sent to you now, & with what direction?' she asked Frank. 'There is also a pair of Scissars for you.' Although these objects may have been held for him, a letter about them went all the way to the Mediterranean, where Frank this year had a fine chance as the new captain of the *Canopus* – a bristling 80-gun ship named originally after Benjamin Franklin, who had written about 'the united states of America' in a piece the *Hampshire Chronicle* printed without comment during the American war. In 1798 Nelson captured *Le Franklin* at the Nile, and it was formidable. This spring Frank and his admiral in the *Canopus* joined the southern fleet and met Nelson in the 100-gun *Victory*.

'We are all very happy to hear of his health & safety,' Jane wrote presently about Frank, '–he wants nothing but a good Prize to be a perfect Character.'[16] She was confident about him as he was not bent on self-mortification and had given very striking proof of his skill at sea. He might have illustrated Cowper's lines in *The Task*:

> I would express him simple, grave, sincere;
> In doctrine uncorrupt; in language plain,
> And plain in manner; decent, solemn, chaste,
> And natural in gesture.[17]

The chances of his death might demand a consideration of probabilities but she recognized the Navy as risky, and knew that a meritorious sailor needed action. Nelson might bring him to it. 'May Health, Success, & Honour attend you,' James wrote to him when his command of *Canopus* was known. 'May you have a speedy return & reap the reward which your Principles & Exertions deserve in the enjoyment of Domestic Comforts & in the Society of Her who can best make your Home comfortable for you.'[18] But others wrote to Frank more simply and Jane was concerned to reach him at all. She craved news and went out of the way to hear praise as she did when she visited Lord and Lady Leven at Bath who were full of Charles for his kindness to their son. The trouble was, in Frank's case, that the enemy intercepted couriers and left the southern fleet out of touch for months at a time. 'The *Ambuscade*', Jane notes, 'reached Gibraltar on the 9th of March and found all well.' So said the papers. But how was Frank managing in a weatherbeaten fleet? Henry said he had dispatched a letter of Mary's to Frank by favour of General Tilson waiting at Spithead. 'Would it be possible for us to do something like it,' she asked Cassandra, 'through Mr Turner's means?' She later honoured Mr William Turner of No. 85 High Street in Portsmouth when she had Mr Price tell his son William in *Mansfield Park*, 'I have been to Turner's about your mess,' and she also celebrated the *Canopus* by having young William cry out happily at Portsmouth, 'Whereabouts does the Thrush lay at Spithead! Near the Canopus?' She felt Frank would have to be told of *her* plans no matter how far away he was, and so when she decided to reveal the idea of having Martha Lloyd live with them she told Cassandra, 'I have sent word of it to the Mediterranean in a letter to Frank,' and when she received one of his notes about Mary Gibson she remarked lightly, 'he is in a great hurry to be married, & I have encouraged him in it'.[19]

But Frank had more than matrimony to think about. Nelson did not believe *he* could physically endure another winter on blockade, and although Frank met the Admiral on the canvas white-and-black squares of *Victory*'s stateroom he submitted formal complaints in May and June about his ship. Lacking repairs and on the move, a vessel became torn, battered and 'crazy' to handle, and *Canopus* (as we have seen) sometimes lacked an adequate foretopsail, maintopsail, driver and boatsails. There was a chronic shortage of oak for replacements, but what Collingwood called the horrific spectacles of the lash and yard-arm were no longer necessary. The morale of Frank's crew was high and their discipline was good in view of the fact that sailors were cooped up with few amenities. In what she heard from him Jane Austen had reminders of those advantages of hardship and discipline she praised in *Mansfield Park*. Nelson's luck had run out: his attack on an enemy port had resulted in British casualties while heartening the enemy's Admiral Pierre de Villeneuve, and Villeneuve's luck at the Nile held. When he slipped Toulon with eighteen sail to stand for Martinique where he could do harm to British islands, Nelson was out of touch twelve days without a report of him. Finally the Admiral, with Frank Austen in his squadron, followed the enemy out of the Mediterranean, and Frank took part in the longest chase of the war when he pursued Villeneuve for 3,459 nautical miles across the Atlantic Ocean and then 3,227 miles back. When the *Royal Sovereign* – so slow it was known as 'The West Country Waggon', to the despair of Plymouth – dropped out ignominiously, Rear-Admiral Louis in Frank's *Canopus* became Vice-Admiral Nelson's second in command. The ships groaned and heaved over the Atlantic, with Austen recording, '*Victory* north one mile', and Captain Keats's unseaworthy ship holding everyone else back. Nelson made a bad error in turning south in the West Indies, and Villeneuve overtook fourteen sugar ships escorted by a schooner. The schooner escaped to report the enemy's course and strength, but, even so, the long chase back did not endear the Vice-Admiral to their Lordships and Frank and the Crocodile recrossed the sea with nothing to show for their pains. Nelson was welcomed in London by loyal crowds, but his reception at the Admiralty was muted. He had let Villeneuve escape. Their braided Lordships were edgy, and Pitt, the prime minister, did not allay the fears of mercantile interests by telling them that the Royal Navy would sooner or later skewer the enemy, not after Vice-Admiral Sir Robert Calder's action. In a deep mist he had met the enemy's combined squadron on 22 July but captured only two sluggish Spaniards before standing off. He requested his own court-martial: 'Trial of Admiral Sir Robert Calder, held on board his Majesty's ship Prince of Wales', *The Times* was to proclaim. With fifteen sail of the line, armed and fully manned, the King's ships had not even laid 'their heads to the enemy'.[20] That reflected no discredit on Nelson but did not look well even before the trial.

Having led the lee line to the West Indies despite his poor sails, Frank took up his station off Cadiz where in the ship *London* he had seen men hanged for nearly every crime possible at sea. Supplies from England were inadequate and *Canopus* began to run short of food and water. The public meanwhile praised the fleet for its dull inconclusive work, but the *Naval Chronicle* turned on Calder and began to attack the Vice-Admiral of the White: 'We greatly lament', wrote the *Chronicle*, 'that ill-judged and over-weening popularity which tends to make another demigod of Lord Nelson at the expense of all other officers in the service, many of whom possess equal merit and equal abilities and equal gallantry with the noble Admiral.'[21] Nelson knew what Pitt wanted, and certainly needed no reminder from that or any other innuendo: what was wanted, Nelson wrote, was 'annihilation'. Meanwhile Frank was ordered to stand in close to Cadiz, so close that one of his escort ran aground and had to be towed off.

'We stood in till all the enemy's fleet were open of the town, and had an opportunity of distinctly counting them,' wrote Frank on 16 September. 'Their whole force consisted of thirty-three sail of the line and five frigates, all apparently quite ready for sea, with the exception of two ships of the line.'[22] If this armada engaged the small force of blockading ships, *Canopus* would be among the first to be raked. The Crocodile would see to that. Frank's sorrow, however, was that he lacked a swift frigate to take prizes: *Canopus* had been well designed by its French makers, but it was slow and in much need of the coppering and repairs which the *Royal Sovereign* had recently had. On 28 September, Frank's 'Right Honourable Lord Nelson KB' arrived off Cadiz without a welcoming salute and in his concern for supplies ordered the Crocodile aboard. Water and stores could be had only at Tetuan and Gibraltar and hence *Canopus*, with an escort, must go to the Rock. The Crocodile was puzzled, dismayed.

'You are sending me away, my Lord,' Louis told Nelson. 'The enemy will come out, and we shall have no share in the battle.'

'My dear Louis,' Nelson replied cordially. 'I have no other means of keeping the fleet in provisions and water but by sending them in detachments to Gibraltar. The enemy will come out, and we shall fight them, but there will be time for you to get back first. I look upon *Canopus* as my right hand, and I send you first to ensure your being there to help beat them.'

In October Frank set sail but he shared Louis's misgivings, and as his chances of being killed faded his real frustrations increased. '*Canopus* AT SEA, OFF GIBRALTAR,' he wrote back to Mary Gibson. 'We sailed again last night to return to the fleet, having got on board in the course of two days, with our boats alone, 300 tons of water.' At Gibraltar he and Louis had seen a production of *Othello* by brother officers, with less delight even than Washington's when he watched a stage play at Valley Forge. The Crocodile got up in a huff after the first act. The theatre was very close and hot, the enemy might be out of Cadiz. 'Having borne our share in a tedious chace and anxious blockade,' wrote Frank, 'it would be mortifying indeed to find ourselves at last thrown out of any credit or emolument which would result from an action. Such, I hope, will not be our lot.'[23]

Nelson was weakened by *Canopus*'s absence. News of an absent squadron reached Villeneuve and Gravina by 18 October. On the 19th five allied quadrons left Cadiz. Nelson followed in varying winds which suggested to old salts that an attack, carried out at a walking pace, would be costly. Light weather persisted, and in gaps in the sea-mists, on 21 October, lookouts saw distant hills on a cape the Moors had called Tarif-al-Ghar, the hills of Trafalgar. On that morning, to help any amputating surgeon get at his legs, Collingwood very thoughtfully wore silk stockings and low shoes. Nelson came on deck with the four stars of his orders on his breast, and when reminded that he would be a good target, said it was too late to remove his coat. Light winds and the slow pace of the ships were unfortunate. *Victory*'s range was found, and when a man was nearly cut in two he was heaved overboard. Sailors tied handkerchiefs tightly about their ears, the marines on *Victory*'s upper deck were spattered with blood and entrails as a shot swept through them, and in a fine and beautiful curve six miles long the enemy's fleet of thirty-three ships appeared on the sea's breast. The Captain of the French *Redout-*

able, a 74, had trained his crew in 'every sort of drill' and had canvas pouches to hold grenades distributed in gun-crews as well as a hundred carbines fitted with long bayonets, and men who climbed half-way up shrouds to open musketry fire. The enemy's shot hissed 'like the tearing of sails', and when it hit a British ship there were ear-splitting crashes like the smashing of doors on a city street simultaneously with crow bars. Blocks, spars, heavy ropes came down with a clatter, and when the *Victory* closed the whole ship was involved in slaughter, fire, acrid black smoke, and uproar, with sixteen guns in a row firing and recoiling, an upper battery of carronades roaring at each shot, marines firing muskets and topmen their swivels, guns bursting or thudding out of their carriages, and wounded men appealing as they were maimed by their guns or disembowelled with chunks of oak. Even so British gunners beheaded files of troops with single gun-volleys, firing through the rear windows of French and Spanish vessels so that as many as 490 men on the *Redoutable* were killed. There were 480 casualties on *Achille*, 546 on the *Fougueux*, and the entire crew of the *Berwick* drowned. A storm carried off prizes, but on 21 October the enemy's sea forces were crippled as none of the ships that escaped saw action again. Nearly everyone on Collingwood's quarterdeck was hit and among the wounded were blinded and burnt common sailors and boys, but the action ensured England's dominion of the sea in the nineteenth century.

Frank overtook a ship which signalled that it had heard firing off Trafalgar for 'five hours'. He heard of the death of Nelson, who of course had recently praised Frank while saying he could not 'be better placed than in the *Canopus*'. Frank gave way to his feelings. 'A melancholy situation', he wrote. 'Great and important as must be the victory, it is alas! dearly purchased at the price paid for it.' As for Nelson, Frank wrote an entry in his log that suggests none of the proper restraint expected of a captain: 'His Memory will long be embalmed in the hearts of a grateful Nation; – May those he left behind in the service strive to imitate so bright an example!!!' Still in disappointment he wrote to his fiancée, 'Alas! my dearest Mary, all my fears are but too fully justified.' He had missed the finest naval action and every chance, 'but', he told Mary, 'as I cannot write upon that subject without complaining, I will drop it for the present, till time and reflection reconcile me a little more to what I know is now inevitable'.[24]

Readers of *The Times* heard the news in November. By the time Jane knew Frank was safe it was claimed that a dead admiral had saved England from invasion. Napoleon had called off his invasion plans before the battle, though Jane Austen – who later proposed a 'History of Buonaparté' to swell *Pride and Prejudice* – might have been amused by his final boast. 'Pitt did not laugh,' Napoleon later told the Count de Las Cases, 'in four days I should have been in London ... not as a conqueror, but as a liberator. I should have been another William III; but I would have acted with greater generosity and disinterestedness. The discipline of my army was perfect. My troops would have behaved in London just as they would in Paris. No sacrifices, not even contributions, would have been exacted from the English. We would have presented ourselves to them, not as conquerors, but as brothers, who came to restore them to their rights and liberties. I would have assembled the citizens, and directed them to labour in the task of their regeneration because the English had already preceded us in political legislation...'[25] In 1805 he had lost nothing but the sea, and could point to impressive land victories. Even six years later Jane Austen was to read in Charles Pasley's 'delightfully written' *Essay on the Military Policy* that:

> the British nation is placed in a situation of danger, to which its past history affords no parallel – menaced with destruction by a much superior force, which is directed by the energy of one of the greatest warriors that has appeared. ... Nothing but our naval superiority has saved us from being at this moment a province of France.[26]

She followed news closely, and might have written a most comic, enlightening and entrancing History of Bonaparte had she wished.

James once remarked on the exasperating tedium of hearing accounts of Bunker's Hill and its bayonet charge (in which nearly everyone in Hampshire's militia must have taken part, to judge from his petulance). The Austens could not minimize naval valour but they heard more than enough of Trafalgar, as the word entered British culture. The humblest lady at her needle was beset by the Admiral's formations. James's wife Mary laughed over 'the Trafalgar stitch' and newspapers praised Nelson for his romantic and adulterous love – had he not thought of Lady Hamilton when dying? Jane of course was bored by lives of Nelson without reading any, but she noticed that 'Trafalgar' was a commercial commodity. Well after Frank proved himself in a 'tickling' which he gave the enemy at St Domingo, she promoted Wentworth in *Persuasion* to commander, for *his* heroism at St Domingo, and let Croft be a veteran of 'the Trafalgar action'. But her best reaction to Trafalgar is in *Sanditon* when Mr Parker, busy developing his property, celebrates names dear to a patriot's heart: 'One other hill', he tells his visitors, 'brings us to Sanditon. ... You will not think I have made a bad exchange, when we reach Trafalgar House – which by the bye, I almost wish I had not named Trafalgar – for Waterloo is more the thing now. However, Waterloo is in reserve.' What is in a name? 'The name joined to the form of the Building, which always takes,' says Mr Parker, 'will give us command of Lodgers.'[27] 'Trafalgar' is frozen in time, in the few hours of 21 October when on green swells off the Spanish mainland over 4,000 lives were lost and 3,000 more men lay wounded, but its living meaning is in our designing, ordinary lives. If Nelson is a deity, Mr Parker is his worshipper and the new Englishman of a commercial age. Even the Navy is vulnerable, comic and exploitable, and if Admiral Croft's goodness and charming naivety typify the best of its officers the Louisa Musgroves of the day lie in wait for its marriageable captains: 'Louisa had the fine naval fervour to begin with.' Yet there is no cynicism in Jane Austen's response to the Navy or Trafalgar: she valued Frank's and Charles's perseverance, self-discipline and courage and above all their loyalty to *her* and to the ladies they married. They may have winced over her fine tribute at the end of *Persuasion* to their naval profession, 'which is,' she wrote, 'if possible, more distinguished in its domestic virtues than in its national importance'.[28] That summarizes her viewpoint, and much of her intention as a novelist in showing what things are like for young women in England during the Revolutionary and Napoleonic Wars. It replies to a fervour which vulgarized Trafalgar just as the Winchester Theatre did in December, when it invited people to see a 'superb transparency' showing 'the great Nelson expiring in the Arms of Victory with Britannia pointing out his name and Deeds, – borne by the Wings of Time and the trumpet of Fame to Immortality; with a view of His Majesty's ship Victory, which bears Nelson's Flag, pouring irresistible thunder on the Enemy's Fleet which appears sinking, burning, and striking under the superiority of the British Fleet'.[29]

Jane Austen's own use of language responds often enough to emotional falsities engendered by the commercial instinct which exploits heroism. Furthermore at nearly every point in her career as she worked on her stories between the 1790s and 1815, her interest in her brothers Frank and Charles and the naval war helped to save her as a novelist from the unreality of her novel form – its psychologically restricting emphasis on a few sets of characters in a near-vacuum. We perhaps think we ought to find, and we never do really find, a certain 'hot-house' atmosphere in Jane Austen's stories about a heroine who rather single-mindedly is concerned with one or two gentlemen in the comic vicissitudes of courtship or 'matrimonial affairs' on the way to the altar. Instead we laugh at scenes that seem fresh and realistic partly because distant events and forces implicitly or overtly affect her people. So the militia in *Pride and Prejudice* (and a general atmosphere of England in wartime) or news from Antigua in *Mansfield Park* or the naval fortunes in *Persuasion* or national matters that concern General Tilney and Henry in *Northanger Abbey* for instance play a part. She was indebted in this sense even to the bizarre public appreciations of Trafalgar.

She was restless at Bath, and the city seemed no better after Frank's touching reports from afar. Again she seems to have drawn a strict line between her brother's honest feelings and the ever mounting Nelson craze with its sentimental sanctifying of the hero in death, so that she could not have endured the ordinary, daily falsities of her milieu at Bath a day longer than she felt she had to. Luckily Mrs Austen proposed an entire change in 1806, and on 2 July she and her two daughters with Martha packed their things. If Mrs Austen was tired of Bath, Jane and Cassandra were heartily sick of it. They left with Martha, visited Clifton and went on to Adlestrop, in Gloucester, where Mrs Austen's first cousin, the Revd Thomas Leigh, had startling news, that on 2 July the Hon. Mary Leigh had died after being life tenant of Stoneleigh Abbey for twenty years. As other Leighs in her branch had died out, Thomas Leigh seemed to be legal owner of Stoneleigh. Advised to take possession quickly, he persuaded the Austens to accompany him into Warwickshire.

Mrs Austen was keen to go since it seemed likely that her brother Mr Leigh Perrot would, under Lord Leigh's ambiguous will, at least have a life interest in the estates. Jane and Cassandra had never seen anything as grand – and, perhaps, very little else in Shakespeare's county would have rivalled what they saw from their coach one day near Kenilworth. A mansion of warm sandstone with impressive, large, plain gables rose in a declivity against woods on the far side of a hill, and a battalion might have lived behind its façade, which protected the cloister of a twelfth-century Cistercian abbey. The great saloon, originally meant as an entrance hall, engulfed any mere human visitor who gazed at its richly moulded plasterwork telling the story of Hercules on the walls and ceiling near columns and half-columns in yellow scagliola. In inner rooms were ancestors in their ornate frames against dark panelling. Here was Sir Thomas Leigh, who received Charles I at Stoneleigh Abbey when Coventry's citizens refused him, and Elizabeth, the Queen of Bohemia and sister of Charles I, who was brought up at nearby Coombe Abbey. In the velvet drawing room was again the Leigh who was Queen Elizabeth's Lord Mayor of London, and in the silk drawing room the first Duke of Chandos who robbed the nation as Paymaster of the Forces, the Hon. Mary Leigh and even the insane Edward, third Lord Leigh, not far from a memento in the hall of Lady Audrey Leigh, who was exhumed from her grave after 1640 to surprise everyone as a pretty and lovable corpse, 'her flesh quite plump as if she were alive, her face very beautiful, her hands exceedingly small and not wasted. She appeared as if asleep, being dressed in fine linen profusely trimmed with point lace, and seemed not more than sixteen or seventeen,' it was said. Leighs breathed in this dark, enormous, intricate, spooky, and almost impossibly grand house, and even Mrs Austen was awed.[30]

But in her sixty-eighth year Mrs Austen soon looked at the house as if it were a novel's setting; she counted forty-five windows in front, measured the garden and noted strong-beer casks in a hoary cellar. 'Behind the smaller drawing Room', she observes, 'is the state Bed Chamber, with a high dark crimson Velvet Bed: an *alarming* apartment just fit for a heroine; the old Gallery opens into it.' None was livelier than she, and after a visit to Kenilworth she planned to take Jane to Warwick Castle. When Leigh said he couldn't find his way about, Mrs Austen proposed setting up *'directing Posts'* in Stoneleigh's hallways – at the 'angles'.

Enjoying themselves, Cassandra and Jane were entertained by their relative Lady Saye and Sele. Her late husband, the father of Miss Twisleton the 'Adultress', had tried to drown himself in cold water at Kensington gravel-pits and then had cut his throat with a razor, while stabbing himself with a sword. These events were reported in the *Hampshire Chronicle* and the Austens would not have alluded to them, but Lady Saye and Sele expanded upon them.

Her talk at dinner concerned death and food. Cassandra was to repeat to Anna 'amusing particulars' of it. One evening Lady Saye and Sele was asked if she would take 'some boiled chicken'. 'No,' said the lady. 'I cannot.' After her lord 'destroyed himself', she explained, she had eaten nicely boiled chicken every day for a fort-night in her chamber as she was an epicure, and hadn't 'been able to touch it since'. On another evening she broke decorum and fiercely accosted the Clerk of the Kitchen, who was supposed to stand rigidly in silence behind her chair. Could he say in the plainest terms 'if the macaroni was made with Parmesan'? There was a bad moment. 'Yes, my lady,' came the gravest answer.[31] The Austens tried not to laugh, but at last the lady proved tiresome. 'Poor Lady Saye & Sele to be sure is rather tormenting,' Mrs Austen wrote on 13 August, 'though sometimes amusing, and affords Jane many a good laugh – but she fatigues me sadly on the whole.' Yet of course the grand house was rather more than a mausoleum in which the talk was of macaroni and gravel-pits, and Jane watched quiet servants in a hardly varying routine, and noticed that her mother patterned the days of their visit: 'At nine in the morning we meet and say our prayers in the handsome Chapel,' Mrs Austen carefully noted, 'now hung with Black. Then follows breakfast consisting of Chocolate, Coffee and tea, Plumb Cake, Pound Cake, Hot Rolls Cold Rolls, Bread and Butter, and *dry toast for me*. The House-Steward (a fine large respectable looking Man) orders all these matters.' Then Joseph Hill, who was Mr Leigh's agent and a correspondent of the poet Cowper, would take his master off to some remote unsignposted inner office near the cloister, and the Austens would go for a walk in cool, deep, leafy woods that kept out the August sun. When they returned Mrs Austen went out to sit among blackbirds and thrushes in the extensive kitchen gardens – 'four acres and a half' – and Jane and her sister noted the quiet ponds and the park, the dairy, the stout baker who did nothing all day but 'Brew and Bake',[32] the breakfast room in which it was pleasant to sit for the view, and nearby cavernous, hushed rooms, sepulchral in their apparent timelessness, lined with brown wainscot and having old dark furniture with crimson uphol-stery. Her mother's wish to see *'directing posts'* here was amusing and doubtless significant too for the massive, nearly unexplorable house had an oddly comforting grandeur. An observant visitor would not forget the traditions of its chapel and servants' routines or the way in which the place tied centuries together – and these things were not lost on Jane Austen when she wrote of Mansfield Park and Sotherton. Stoneleigh appealed to deeper levels of her moral conservatism as well as to her sense of history and continuance: it was the only house on the grandest English scale that she could feel connected with, and along with Godmersham Park it was a main source for her ample fictional mansions. Its west range in ashlar stone which is all of fifteen bays long and three-and-a-half storeys high is itself 'a monumental ensemble in the tradition of Chatsworth', and its effect on her lasted. When she left she had had a rare experience – her equivalent of Frank's awe in the Navy.

Few of our unhappy trials last as long as we imagine they may, and now her months in a city of white glare had ended. In 1806 the Austens had lived at temporary lodgings in Gay Street and Trim Street but they would not return to live at Bath. From Stoneleigh, they went to Hamstall Ridware, in Staffordshire, where Jane's cousin, the Revd Edward Cooper, had the living which the Hon. Mary Leigh had presented him seven years before. Jane spent five weeks at Hamstall in the Midlands and may have visited nearby Lichfield, as well as Cheadle – where Mrs Inchbald's play *Lovers' Vows* was performed. Later she could look ahead to a visit at Steventon and then to sharing a house with Martha, Frank and his bride; it was expedient that the Austen ladies stay on at Southampton, and the harbour might be pleasant. They would see much of Mary Gibson and Frank while entertaining James Austen and his family. But it is not so certain that a dependency on charity, even that of loving brothers, ensures a satisfying degree of freedom or well-being. It may cause us to take renewed interest in those on whom we depend and Jane Austen was not a little interested in James and his wife Mary Lloyd. Her eldest brother had been quick to feel satisfaction over the fixed, meagre financial arrangements he made for her mother and she was to observe his elusive character with her sharp and appreciative eyes.

14

A house with Martha and Frank

Abuse everybody but me.
Jane Austen

Looking back Jane Austen later used the word 'escape' to suggest how she had felt in 1806. She might have been a person landing on her feet after jumping from a gaoler's wall, or a girl leaving a horrid seminary for the very last time. She was a prisoner of sculpted white squares and crescents no more – and Bath might sleep in a river valley or reach out and cling to its hillsides without her. Its carriages in their genteel clatter had reached her ears too often; she would no longer see smug ladies in gauze and taffeta at card-tables. It was not that she had had her fill of *all* polite social discomfort, and indeed she would sample it eagerly at Southampton. Her life had found a centre in the act of observing normal behaviour, in finding what was ridiculous and touching in that ordinariness, and at thirty-one she observed all the better by not drawing attention to herself in company. She was a slender, active woman still with her high colouring and expressive eyes and her auburn ringlets tucked up under a cap or a plain bonnet; in a social group she seemed unpretentious and dutiful and rather quiet or given to mildly comic remarks – her mother's 'sprack wit' was legendary among Austens, whereas Jane was felt to be merely clever. No one in her family had a high idea of her novel-writing. She would have stared to be named with Fanny Burney or Maria Edgeworth, and others would have stared as hard. She developed outside any public limelight, and within limits of what her family felt to be normal behaviour, and yet not since Shakespeare had anyone else watched people so well while evolving a manner with language that was sensitive and flexible enough to describe character while giving confident hints of psychological depths within. Her experience had given her frames for observing what was comic and useful to her, and so had her 'strong political opinions'. James and Henry had helped to guide her talent at a vital time and, in their reactions to war and politics, to Whiggery and to the American Revolution for example, the writers of *The Loiterer* had given her good examples of moral satire in her girlhood. Their stories had appeared as she left off jokes to try serious comedy, and as she began the task of trying to hold a character in focus by means of a narrative voice the politics of the Austens had helped her. She had begun with a consistent view of society, a frame for exploring comic behaviour and the mind of a heroine; and her modified Toryism helped her to draw convincing pictures of social pretension and striving among the gentry.

Her family recognized her wit, humour and sense of style but there is no hint that in these years they saw her as an 'artist'. (No one else in the family could be deemed equal to her brother James, the poet.) It was felt widely at her time, too, that fiction was not an 'art'. A novelist needed no apprenticeship: Miss Burney for example had written *Evelina* in youth and won every recognition. Mrs Mary Brunton was almost more typical as a modern novelist. Born in the Orkneys and favouring 'the quiet and privacy of a Scotch parsonage' Mrs Brunton in her provincial home wrote out her stories *Self-Control* and *Discipline*. Her titles suggest a fine moral intent – and the second novel has appealing good sense, as when at a ball the heroine Ellen hears:

> dialogues, consisting of dull questions and unmeaning answers, thinly bestrown with constrained witticisms, and puns half a century old. The easy flow of conversation, which makes even trifles pass agreeably, was destroyed by the necessity of being smart; and the eloquence of the human eye, of the human smile, was wanting to add interest to what was vapid, and kindliness to what was witty.[1]

That is only too well etched, or the sort of writing that made Jane Austen seriously fear later on that the style of *Pride and Prejudice* lacked ease and relief. *Self-Control* is a romantic and dramatic novel. But 'till I began Self-Control', as Mary Brunton said, 'I had never in my life written anything but a letter or a recipe, except a few hundred vile rhymes'. She had worked without a plan in between doing her husband's washing and darning (or while he was studying oriental languages for his later ascent to Edinburgh's academic chair) and had only meant 'to show the power of religious principle in bestowing self-command'. The result, however, was good enough to make Jane Austen edgy. 'Tried to get *Self-controul*,' Jane soon told Cassandra, but 'am always half afraid of finding a clever novel *too clever* – & of finding my own story and my own people all forestalled.' But then noticing the heroine's ride down a wild American river she was relieved to find Mrs Brunton not so clever. 'I am', writes Jane, 'looking over *Self-Control* again, & my opinion is confirmed of its being an excellently-meant, excellently-written Work, without anything of Nature or Probability in it. I declare I do not know whether Laura's passage down the American River, is not the most natural, possible, everyday thing she ever does.'[2]

As her own subject was the natural and possible she might find materials in a seaport town with Frank. But how long *could* she bear a town? Sharing Mrs Brunton's rural preferences she became facetious about her own dislike of cities. To prefer rural life is a 'venial fault', as Jane put it when Henry's servant William quit London for a country place. William never enjoyed the full tide of life at Charing Cross and had 'more of Cowper than of Johnson' in him and loved tame hares and blank verse, but she shared his venial fault. At Bath with her family she had had almost no status, no real way of showing her worth naturally and no wish to win over and impress people. Yet she believed the venial fault forgivable and that a person who prefers sun-time and a few friends, simple routine duties and dirt's inconvenience and the hope of a ball rather than a regime of parties – and who may fret over the inelegance in all that – is not lost. In repeating the ordinary, one stays in touch with one's inward sense of the world and oneself, and prepares for creative work and social intercourse. She loved dancing as well as ever though at thirty-one she was out of touch with the fast social sets of wartime. But, at Southampton, there *would* be one benefit, one rare blessing in living with Martha Lloyd, ten years her senior; if Eliza found her 'neither rich nor handsome', Jane found her slim, elegant and natural. Once she had suffered in a broken romance, and recovered slowly: 'I hear Martha', Jane had told her sister, 'is in better looks and spirits than she has enjoyed for a long time, & I flatter myself she will now be able to jest openly about Mr. W.' But, it seems, Mr W. had left a mark and Martha had become more receptive and self-effacing. Her one fault lay in her goodness or in a slavish running off to those in need, such as to Mrs Dundas, her invalid friend, at Barton Court in Kintbury: 'You have obliged me to eat humble-pie,' Jane told her, or 'you are made for doing good'. Still Martha was womanly enough later to suit Frank's notion of a wife, and not so angelic as to fail to love gossip and jokes. She took cues in humour from Jane while meeting Mrs Austen's standards, so seemed an ideal companion. 'With Martha Lloyd,' Jane once wrote, 'who will be so happy as we?'[3]

Twice earlier in the year Jane had visited Steventon, once happily with Martha, and for a week before they left for Southampton the Austen ladies again saw James and his wife Mary. The rectory was 'almost a pretty place' as Eliza had felt after James's painting and varnishing: jars of milk on a table, dripping meadows and the noises of a farm were refreshing, even if Mary Lloyd ruled with swishing skirts and brusque talk. She could be shrill with her children James Edward and Caroline and waspish with her stepdaughter Anna, who at thirteen saved up complaints to regale Aunt Jane in secret. Anna portrayed herself as a victim, a Cinderella whose father James left her alone for *whole afternoons* or urged poor little Caroline to canter up and down a meadow with only a groom to watch. And no sooner had James left the house than Mary Lloyd revealed her nature, as Anna said: Mary was 'abrupt & sharp, & she had a tartness of temper' that made Anna hate her. She 'did not love her step daughter, & she slighted her, she made of her no estimation, & the last & least in her father's house.' It never entered Mary Lloyd's 'imagination', Anna felt, that by rights she ought to 'make no difference' between her stepchild and her own children. But James Edward was so gentle that he and Anna were inseparable, and after that boy left for school Anna suffered under Mary's 'snobbery and faultfinding' and found life 'unbearable'.

Anna, at thirteen, talked with sparkling eyes, and no Cinderella looked better fed. Jane Austen had recorded stories Anna 'invented for herself' even before Anna could write and had told her other tales of 'endless adventure and fun which were carried on from day to day or from visit to visit'.[4] Anna's confidences had brought her in key with her aunt's imagination. Listening to her, one day, Jane may have found the germ of Fanny Price's dilemma with her selfish Aunt Norris for *Mansfield Park* and a suggestion of Edmund Bertram in Anna's touching friendship with James Edward, but the novel owes more to Anna's embellishments than to fact. James's wife was not a mean Aunt Norris, and it is amusing that Mary Lloyd was later 'very much pleased' with *Mansfield Park* and 'enjoyed M[rs] Norris particularly'.[5] (It is hard to believe that Mrs Norris enjoyed Mrs Norris's portrait.) Anna admitted in later years that her stepmother was 'a clever cheerful hospitable woman, generous where money was concerned though a careful and excellent manager'.[6]

Yet Anna, just at present, *did* need reassurance. What kept James from asking his wife to treat her more kindly? James did suffer Mary's jealousy, as when she fretted over his absences or when she rebuffed Eliza's attention to Anna in resentment over James's early feeling for the Countess. But Mary's jealousy could be offset by her generous impulses. Jane Austen was more vexed by James, and in her clerical brother there were troubles in a shy, creative personality that casts light on her own.

We know more about her brother James today than appears in any printed source. In 1806 he felt vexed and outmanoeuvred because a new wartime Whiggish Ministry of All the Talents, including R. B. Sheridan as Treasurer of the Navy, had demanded that General Mathew's debts be paid at last to the Royal Exchequer: this was not the last straw for James, though he was no longer the happy scholar who had staged Sheridan's *Rivals*. He hated Whigs who had squeezed him, hated them with reason, but what were Whigs in London born to do if not grab at landed fortunes in the provinces? Mathew was dead, and the King who forgot to authorize his salary was old, subject to fits of delirium or insanity, and James was hardly likely to blame *them*. It was ironic that after leading the Coldstream Guards so well and obeying a royal command to go to the West Indies poor Mathew had been dunned until he died, pressed to pay back unauthorized salary at compound interest. But James could not reverse the past. Mathew's estate was punished and crippled, the sum paid out was very large, and James lost money that belonged to him as Anne Mathew's widower. Mary was not likely to hang herself as she had heard more than enough of the Mathews, and her husband's income lately had risen to a good sum (soon to be around £1,100), but she felt otherwise about money in June when James was offered the clerical living of Hampstead Marshall in Berkshire. Would James accept it? Gratified but not tempted, he came to a decision in a scene that might have been staged by Mr Bennet in *Pride and Prejudice*. The evidence of Anna's daughter's memoir is that he used his clever daughter Anna to make a fool of his unliterary wife Mary. With all her heart Mary Lloyd had urged him to accept Hampstead Marshall since they were not wealthy enough to refuse a good benefice, and she could hardly bear James's hesitating. But he dithered. James 'doubted whether a promise to give up the living did not go against the clerical statement' he had to sign to accept it. Then, it seems one evening, he prepared a little scene: he called Anna to his side in Mary Lloyd's presence and asked the girl to recite his clerical statement of acceptance.

'Now,' said James to his daughter, 'tell me what you understand by that passage.'

Anna, at thirteen, would have done much to please him. She was not slow to put Mary Lloyd in a bad light and so she commented pleasingly on the hard theological words.

'And now', James announced to his wife, 'you see how she interprets them.'

'What does it signify,' Mary Lloyd said, 'what a child like that thinks of the meaning? What is the sake of asking her?'

'Because', James said in triumph, 'being a child, it is only the most obvious and natural sense of the words which she will see, which is the sense we must suppose in which they were meant to be taken.'[7]

So he refused Hampstead Marshall and stirred up trouble; and the meaning of his scene, which Anna recalled, illuminates not only his marriage but primary sources for such a novel as *Pride and Prejudice*. Jane Austen knew her elder brother as well as any man. It is not that she turned him into Mr Bennet – who is more cynical and perverse – but that she found the tension between James and his second wife interesting, touching and in a way comic. He made up for his unhappiness by keeping Mary in thrall to his scholarly wit and understanding, and mildly tortured a wife who otherwise dictated to him. Jane perhaps extracted enough from that to help her create two of the funniest, most convincing parents in her novels.

James and Mary might as well have supplied material for tragedy, but they represented an amusing *status quo*, and did not seem so perverse as to be outside a normal tenor in married life. For his part James did not crave new livings but bitterly missed Oxford. In youth he had written a sonnet to pretty Lady Catherine, a daughter of the sixth Duke of Bolton of Hackwood Park, and then had poured creative energies into play prologues and epilogues, and later with public ambition into his Oxford *Loiterer* of which he now spoke 'very slightingly'.[8] He was apologetic, distant and bemused. In his forties, in the gentle tradition of Hampshire writers from George Wither and Anne Finch to Gilbert White and James's favourite William Gilpin, and now and then with Thomson's *Seasons* or Cowper in view, he wrote of nature in long poems. He produced comic verse too for his son, some of it savage in tone, but did his best in the moral poem.

> Oh! then as now, may no remorse
> Increase affliction's native force,

James Austen wrote for his son,

> No vain regrets for joys abused,
> Neglected friends and time misused,
> Imprint a sorrow on your breast,
> More hard to bear than all the rest,
> May the light woes of early youth,
> Teach you this salutary truth,
> That every sorrow will be light,
> When all within the breast is right.[9]

When is all right in the breast? He recalled his St John's days when he had hunted more than he had studied, and with old Oxford prejudices he kept up a rather zealous little warfare against novels. If 'rich and high born neighbours', wrote James,

> Where duty called for mental labours
> Shrink from the duties of their state
> [And] neglect their minds to cultivate –
> If Dogs and Horses, Lines and Hooks,
> (Save Novels) leave no room for books,
> They too will feel, and sore lament
> The many hours of youth misspent,
> And of all poverty, will find
> The worst is Poverty of Mind.

He attacked novels in his poem 'Morning – to Edward' as late as 1814. James possessed his mother's dearest love as well as the kindest affection of each of his brothers and sisters. His declarations against 'novels' ensured that Jane Austen's trifling performances, if amusing, would not be held for more than what they *were* by others in the family. That was as things should be. He did not feel it becoming to forbid novel-reading in his parlour, but trained his son well in the classics. He shared his sister Jane's interest in history, yet, at times, he could feel himself forlornly mixed in the processes of history and torn from hope. 'Can sorrow', he wrote,

> entrance find midst scenes like these?
> Can nature's beauty ever cease to please?
> Less softly blows the breeze, or flows the stream
> That when entranced in youth's delightful dream
> I mused along its banks.[10]

He had Wordsworthian moments and explained his melancholy as part of the universal sorrow. Still he was restless – and his poems point to a troubling area beneath any of his named complaints. He had the odd embarrassment of a literary man and a heartsick, nagging condition of mind in which he felt he could only *be* himself by being arrogant with his brothers and humble with his children. The immense concern of the Revd George Austen for his sons' success helped James much less than it did Frank, or Charles, or Edward, or even Henry. James was an example to his sister Jane. Every word that she wrote responds in a certain way to the spectacle of James, who was the pride of her mother's heart. Jane Austen would not let herself succumb to *his* moods, but softened and changed her worst impulses by an effort of conscience and will, and kept on terms with the world and herself by making up alternative fictional worlds, 'outlaw polities', which were persuasive and deliciously funny. She could be far more delicate and humble and tender than James while being true to herself, and with comic invention and good grace she kept uppermost in her own nature a certain civility.

James felt best riding over the fields, not sitting in a parlour with a wife who had never been to school but on whom he relied. 'We travel', he quoted Gilpin, 'for various purposes.' He travelled for almost any purpose and once in the very greatest hope that 'the woods and heaths of the New Forest would brace relaxed nerves, and the motion of a postchaise rectify a disordered stomach'.[11] His daughter Caroline wondered at his passion for riding, but a fondness for rain in his face perhaps kept him in humour with Mary Lloyd. He was not ill in these years but proud of his endurance and goodwill and glad enough to profit in the Stoneleigh business. His uncle Leigh Perrot had relinquished rights to Stoneleigh Abbey for a personal bond of £20,000 and a yearly income of £2,000 to continue if Aunt Perrot survived him, and James for refusing Hampstead Marshall was awarded by his aunt and uncle £100 a year. (They remembered certainly his offer to go to gaol with them just before he broke his leg.) Yearning for the past, he invested his love in his children and became gentle and meek with them: 'My dear Edward,' he tells his son typically, 'it is now high time that I answer your welcome and affectionate letter – which gave me such pleasure; and which I expected your Mother to thank you for immediately only because I had a sermon to write, which I was behind hand with; and you know how soon my hand and a pen grow tired of each other.' And he is not so very learned, as he tells Caroline. He dislikes female classics, such as Mme de Sévigné's letters, which his sister Jane read and alluded to, and has not even got hold of those elegant French letters, 'but I believe they are thought patterns for a Familiar and Affectionate Epistolary Style, which I suppose is their chief recommendation; for if I have not formed a wrong idea of them, they contain little beyond the Gossip & Tittle Tatter of *their* French Court, which cannot be very interesting to the present Generation – We have enough to do to talk of the follies of our *own* great people.'[12] He enjoyed Jane Austen's comic poems and improved one of them wittily; she, in turn, was surprised when his opinion of a book differed widely from hers, and was glad to read his verses. 'I wish', Jane once wrote to Cassandra from London, 'I had James's verses, but they are at Chawton.' His nostalgic mood added little to her joy, though, and *her* comic prose did not suit his view of novels – although he read her manuscripts and seems to have criticized *Northanger Abbey*. But on visits he hid behind Mary Lloyd's opinions stupidly and infuriatingly: 'I am sorry and angry', Jane Austen wrote later of him at Southampton, 'that his Visits should not give one more pleasure; the company of so good & so clever a Man ought to be gratifying in itself; – but his Chat seems all forced, his Opinions on many points too much copied from his Wife's, & his time here is spent I think in walking about the House & banging the doors, or ringing the bell for a glass of water.' 'He cut up the turkey last night with great perseverance,' she had mocked him.[13] If James pined for Oxford men *she* found most of them conceited or buttery, taking refuge behind their spectacles with a calm hauteur that might have appalled Richardson's Harriet Byron but she was forbearing when James did not seem under Mary's thumb. He was the most creative of her brothers, elegiac and yearning for university life but adjusting to the present by yielding to Mary Lloyd, while taunting her in private and keeping Anna as his ally. His relations with his wife were instructive, and his loyalty to Jane was unequestionable. He had a large fund of Christian kindness and his shyness, intelligence, resignation to duty and the sharp point of his impatience were similar to aspects of her nature – so she could be angry, it seems, in part because she hoped for more of his stimulus than he was able to give.

After visiting him at Steventon, Mrs Austen and her daughters with Martha Lloyd on 10 October had finally reached Southampton, where they rented a house with Frank and his bride Mary Gibson, whom he had married in July. (Mary Gibson, who was then pregnant, knew no more about babies than Cassandra, Jane or Martha did.) Frank found the town convenient to Portsmouth as he awaited a new command, and Mrs Austen hardly expected to be in a seaport long. As it was, Jane Austen's home was to be at Southampton for two-and-a-half years, from 10 October 1806 to early in April 1809.

She found the town much as it had been when she had danced there in 1793. It was not yet a large harbour despite the wool it sent to Jersey and Guernsey and its trade with Portugal and the Baltic, but it was a pretty town of 8,000 souls and only twenty-three miles from Steventon. Summer crowds loved its wheeled bathing-machines. The Itchen and Test flowed into the sea on either side of the harbour and from the South Gate for half a mile ran a delightful tree-planted 'Beach' walk from which one had a view of Southampton Water and the merchant ships and men-of-war. Inside the town was a High Street lined with brick-built shops running north and south from the Bargate to the quay – off Winkle Street was Gods House Gate and at places along the walls were stone towers known as Catchcold, Arundel, Bugle and Polymond. Small houses huddled in the area of Back-of-the-Walls and the Canal and a ring of pleasant villas lay beyond, while the Long Room or assembly room for dancing (with Mr Martin's new chamber) overlooked the sea on one side and a green vista on the other.

Frank's house was not uniquely odd in wartime but it included five women devoted to one man. He was now the quiet, modest centre of an adoring circle including Martha Lloyd, who was later to marry him, his two devoted sisters and their mother and his sweet and unliterary wife Mary. He painted and carpentered, mended and stitched: 'Frank', Jane wrote, 'has got a very bad cough for an Austen; – but it does not disable him from making a very nice fringe for the Drawingroom-Curtains.'[14] He measured out love as fairly as the breakfast coffee, yet his restraint was famous even in the Navy: he was a man who once said calmly to an officer who went for a swim in the tropics, 'Mr. Pakenham you are in danger of a shark – a shark of the blue species.' The man in the water had thought Frank was joking. 'I am not given to joking,' Frank replied very slowly. 'If you do not immediately return, soon the shark will eat you.'[15] Jane Austen at all events soon had insights in Frank's ménage into the limits of brotherly love: it seemed to her that the conjugal tie was less important than the fraternal one and that children of the same blood have 'some means of enjoyment in their power' denied to others, but still, as she wrote in *Mansfield Park*, 'Fraternal love, sometimes almost every thing, is at others worse than nothing.'[16] Her anger over James is partly a reply to Frank's inattention, calmness and lack of intuition into the feelings of women – and his decency was unvarying (as one may judge from his autobiography and over five hundred of his naval letters). It does not follow that she respected him less or would have had cause to find fault with him, or to be bitter about him. Her criticism of the naval sensibility in *Persuasion* is offset by respect for the naval profession, and Frank's judgement she honoured. In her new freedom at Chawton she was to send him lovingly comic verses. But her tensions at Southampton appear in her letters, and the old processes by which the energy of her feelings and her comic maliciousness were released came into play. In letter after letter at the best of times she had found something intolerable in the placid decorum she loved, and now if James's banging of doors irritated her Frank's calm and fairness oppressed her. *He* was nearly perfect, it appears, but there was no Lucy Steele, Aunt Norris or Mrs Elton in the perfection of his household to hate. 'Pictures of perfection as you know make me sick,' as she wrote, and she had often found vent in the clipped, stylish, innocent malice of her remarks to Cassandra.[17] In the claustrophobic ménage at Southampton there was no outlet for a person in need of privacy, no place to retreat to, nothing apparently upstairs or downstairs to call one's own, no recourse other than to be sisterly and polite. Her dilemma was worse because the conventions did not ever allow her to say more than 'I am sorry and angry', and also because she might have been the first to say that every sisterly effort was required of her. To find fault with Frank would be to quarrel with decency: she held him in as high esteem as any man. *He* did not complain uselessly of moods; he earned his living and when on half-pay made himself continually useful in his quiet, incessantly practical and good-natured way. Jane was to register his 'opinions' of both *Emma* and *Mansfield Park* first above those of all other names on her lists of critical readers she happened to know. Yet his very fairness, his equanimity and the close quarters of the household made 'fraternal love' worse than nothing, and she seems to have found herself without much joy. The more dutiful she tried to be the more her resentment grew, and her sense of release at Chawton appears partly to derive from these years. Her resources were gathering for her comic writing, which offered a resolution for her conflicts and the surest way in which she ever set herself right.

She could be happier when the household *was* in rather gross tension, as when Mary Lloyd came down from the country with her scorn for books and city ways. The ladies read aloud one night from Charlotte Lennox's *Female Quixote* which Frank's ignorant wife 'enjoys as one could wish; the other Mary, I believe, has little pleasure from that or any other book'.[18] But the other Mary – or Mary Lloyd – was probably soothed on another occasion by a recital of a dialogue on 'the business of mothering', a simple and anonymous work. It is found in the Austen papers in a hand not Jane's own, and its modern editor believes it may have been written by Mary Lloyd herself, possibly with some tactful help from Jane. We know that Jane had sent to Kent for advice on baby-care, and again it is possible that the worry and fright of young Mary Gibson (who would soon be in trouble and pain in a hard childbirth) were lessened by practical reassurances on feeding. Perhaps in a close room lit by firelight and candles Mrs Austen, Mary Lloyd and Jane recited the parts one evening. In any case Mrs Denbigh is a silly, spoiled young mother with an ignorant Nurse, and Mrs Enfield is just such a wise country-woman as Mary Lloyd herself, who knows what is good for any child:

Mrs Denbigh. I am so fearful that I would sooner depend on any one than myself & as to experience, this is my first child, so I could not have much.

A Nurse then dandles a squalling baby, who will not eat or suck:

Mrs Denbigh. You are very troublesome nurse, try him with a bit of plumb cake & go dress him.

Mrs Enfield. [But] if you please Mrs Denbigh, I would not recommend the plumb cake, which will only cloy his stomach, & make him have no appetite for plain wholesome food.

Mrs Denbigh. Surely if he eats one piece, I will give him more my little precious shall have plumb cake so long as I have any & it will melt so sweet in his mouth.

Mrs Enfield. Perhaps you forget that such a quantity as his stomach ought to require would certainly make him sick, but if you only give him plain food, he will relish it & will not take it except he wants it.[19]

The dialogue makes Mary Lloyd's views sound wise – and Jane often managed to be a reconciler. 'Our acquaintances increase too fast,' she noted in January. With her elder brother's door-slamming, Mary Lloyd's brusqueness, Cassandra's absence in Kent, Mary's nausea and Mrs Austen's gastric complaint it was not easy to greet the world in a sitting room. Frank's household had the three servants Jenny, Molly and Phoebe, but Jenny was detained by her relatives at Itchingswell for the whole of James Austen's visit in the holidays – and dinners suffered 'not a little by having only Molly's head and Molly's hands to conduct them'. Admiral Bertie had recognized Frank and come to call with his daughter Caroline. Captain Foote of the Navy, who disliked underdone mutton, came to dine on a broiled leg that was undercooked even for James but was so merry Jane did not mind starving him. The Lances not only called but offered to introduce them to other friends, 'which we gratefully declined'.

'Prepare', Jane wrote to her sister in Kent, 'for my ringing the Changes of the Glads and Sorrys for the rest of the page. – Unluckily however I see nothing to be glad of, unless I make it a matter of

Joy that Mrs. Wylmot has another son, & that Lord Lucan has taken a Mistress, both of which Events are of course joyful to the Actors.' The best aspect of the house was that they might leave it soon. Possibly through a Mr Husket, who let them make a dressing-room table out of a kitchen table of his employer's, Frank had heard of a fine house and garden at Castle Square. Mr Husket was Lord Lansdowne's domestic painter and Jane imagined that whenever my Lord's walls were done, he was 'employed about my Lady's face'.[20] Their future landlord himself was a talented and eccentric aristocrat whom the King had called 'the best-bred man' he knew. Living across the Itchen in 1804 he had been on poor terms with his father, the first Marquess of Lansdowne. Disliking his father's Bowood he had bought Castle Square in Southampton, where in the north-east corner of town a Norman keep had stood, and here he built a whimsical castellated mansion. This fairy castle seemed to have no door and to lack space outside as it was blocked on nearly all sides by houses with cracked chimney pots, but it pleased the new Lord Lansdowne. He lived in it with his recent bride, an overdressed widow who was in Lady Bessborough's opinion 'a vulgar Irish woman near fifty and larger than Mrs. Fitzherbert'.[21]

Frank rented from him the most spacious house in the square, and after the family moved in around 9 March 1807, they entertained visitors comfortably. James Edward was amazed to peer from Mrs Austen's window and see below Lady Lansdowne's little phaeton drawn by six or eight ponies 'each pair decreasing in size, and becoming lighter in colour, through all the grades of dark brown, light brown, bay and chestnut, as it was placed further away from the carriage. The two leading pairs were managed by two boyish postillions.' It was a delight to see this 'fairy equipage' put together, he recalled, and in looking at the fairy castle his aunt had a ready-made setting for impromptu jokes and stories. Outside the commodious house was a garden bounded by city wall wide enough to make a walk and 'easily accessible to ladies by steps'. Shrubs and borders along the terrace appealed to Jane, who was nearer the rural setting she desired. Frank's man cleared the border to receive currants and gooseberry bushes, 'and a spot is found very proper for raspberries', she noted. 'At my own particular desire he procures us some Syringas. I could not do without a Syringa, for the sake of Cowper's line.' Indeed she knew Cowper's *The Task* well enough to love:

Laburnum, rich
In streaming gold; syringa, iv'ry pure.

'There,' she presently told Cassandra in Kent, 'I flatter myself I have constructed you a smartish Letter, considering my want of Materials. But like my dear Dr. Johnson I beleive I have dealt more in Notions than Facts.' At least she had fresh 'notions' about novels, as family readings resumed: she had listened wryly to a recital of de Genlis' *Alphonsine*, which bothered her for its indelicacies – she preferred sexuality in real life – and found Sarah Burney's *Clarentine* worse to hear than to reread: 'I remember liking it much less on a 2^d reading than at the 1st & it does not bear a 3^d at all. It is full of unnatural conduct & forced difficulties without any striking merit of any kind.' Anne Grant's *Letters from the Mountains* and her *Memoirs of an American Lady* on the other hand had a breath of reality: 'The American lady improved as we went on' she told Cassandra, before letting Mrs Digweed borrow the two volumes.[22]

But she lost Frank. Two weeks after moving into Castle Square he became captain of HMS *St Albans* with special orders. The East India Company was now involved with opium-trading in Canton, although there is no good reason to believe that he consciously supported its blacker dealings. The books of the Company show that it had obliged the Royal Navy by shipping masts to the Indian fleet, so that the Navy in turn helped the Company on long voyages – and kept its profits safe from interception. After Frank convoyed his ninety-three chests with 470,000 dollars' worth of silver bullion from China to Deal, the Company in secret enquired into his connection with a death: but then it received a letter from 'Cap^n F.W. Austen, dated the 17th Inst.' that stated 'in reply to the Secretary's Letter of the preceding day's date, the result of the investigation made into the circumstances connected with the death of a native of China'. The death of a Chinese native linked with Captain Austen would not have figured in their minutes had it not embarrassed the Court of Directors. But to judge from the minutes Frank's reply satisfied them, and it is probable, all in all, that the death or murder of 'a native of China' did not for long upset or detain Sweny Toone, Chicheley Plowden or Campbell Marjoribanks, who were men of considerable wealth in an East India Company directorate which amply paid Frank. After he had lent them some of his naval crew to manoeuvre one of their ships and risked weakening the *St Albans*'s fighting capacity, his crew were rewarded. And Frank continued to prosper and to merit the loyalty of crews. 'The undermentioned Letters were read,' noted the East India Company's minutes, 'two to the Secret Committee.' 'RESOLVED That a Warrant be made out for £525 to Francis William Austen Esqr Captain of His Majesty's Ship St Albans who is appointed to Convoy the Outward Bound Ships to China', and 'RESOLV'D That Lieut. Hore of H:M:S St Albans be complimented with the sum of one hundred guineas', and again 'RESOLVED', as the minutes read, 'the sum [to] Capt Austen of H.M.S. St Albans on account of Treasure, brought by him from China to England, be encreased to £1500' – but these entries must be read in light of his long hours in sailing in hard seas while watching his men and craft vigilantly and doing his best in the line of duty as he understood it. Profiting from running bullion nevertheless, he pleased 'the Select Committee of Supra Cargoes' at Canton, China, and seemed discreet in his deliveries to 'Mr Iggulden at Deal', so much so that he impressed his employers as a model captain.[23] Just how well his moral books balance may be another matter, and Jane Austen's deep uneasiness over patronage is on record. Again one considers her interest in books such as those by Buchanan and Pasley, which were partly about distant fringes of the British Empire, or evidence that she knew Frank was employed by a Company which had dealings in China. One finds at Greenwich not only a great many of Frank's letters, but Charles Austen's naval letter-books, and one concludes that Jane was reasonably well informed of their activities. Readers who find her heroine's moral severity in *Mansfield Park* extreme or priggish might note that the book condemns not only patronage but the moral ambiguity of a family's distant overseas wealth.

But Jane judged Frank for his behaviour at home. His chances of success in the Navy, as she knew, had been helped by her father, who had used Hastings to advantage and drawn on James Austen's marital connection with the Gambiers of the Admiralty. One gathers that she limited her concerns to what she knew at first hand and did not take fanciful, irrelevant, unsisterly views of what Frank did for special or occasional employers. Her policy with herself was to be strictly accurate about what she observed, yet her knowledge of Frank's employment by the Company encouraged her to keep the war more at a distance. When news trickled in of the Peninsular campaign and she heard of General Sir John Moore's death and of the losses of troops at Corunna, she coolly expressed what she felt. The General had a mother in Scotland. 'I am sorry', Jane told her sister, 'that Sir J. Moore has a mother living, but tho' a very Heroick son he might not be a very necessary one to her happiness,' and 'I wish Sir John had united something of the Christian with the Hero in his death. – Thank Heaven! we have no one to care for particularly among the Troops.'[24] By then Frank on the *St Albans* was evacuating some of Moore's troops.

In Frank's absence, Mary gave birth to a little girl, Mary Jane, on 27 April – and Jane wrote this way and that to announce the birth, but few ever saved her letters. She spent a good deal on postage or all of £3–17–6½ for 'Letters & Parcels' in 1807, and today one goes to the Pierpont Morgan Library in New York to find that Jane Austen bought a pocket diary for 1s 4d this year. Only two fascinating pages survive – but they show that she itemized her expenses very carefully for the year 1807:

	£	S	D
Washing	8	14	5
Letters & Parcels	3	17	6½
	12	11	11½
Servants &c		13	9
Charity	3	10	3½
Presents	6	4	4
Journey	1	2	10
Waterparties & Plays		17	9
Sittings in Church		11	—
Hire Piano Forté	2	13	6
	15	13	5½
	12	11	11½
	28	5	5
Cloathes & Pocket	13	19	3
	42	4	8

DECEMBER	£ s D	£ s D		£ s D
	50 15 –	43 16 6		
Washing ——		11 – 6½		
Pocket book –		1 – 4		50 15 –
Medecine ——		1 – 1½		44 10 6
		44 10 6		6 4 6

Her income, with about £20 from Mrs Austen as well as Mrs Knight's and Edward's gifts, came to £50–15–0 in 1807, or about enough to support a lean curate. It is interesting that she spent about 18 shillings on 'Waterparties & Plays', £14 on clothes and pocket expenses, and a quarter of her whole income on charity and presents and 'Sittings in Church'. Jane Austen had also spent £2–13–6 to hire a pianoforte.[25] When the rectory's instrument was sold she had rented one at Bath and would have another at Chawton, 'as good a one as can be bought for thirty guineas'. She needed her daily music and other harmonies, such as her recitals of Cowper and Crabbe or of the prose of Lennox and Burney. Music and recitals were an antidote to silent reading, which, in a good deal of later English prose, breeds rapidity without warmth or accent, and causes too many modern poets to be embarrassed by rhyme and unable to assimilate tonal effects; one of the greatest qualities of Jane Austen's prose is its 'ear' – she is one of the best authors to read aloud. Recitals, good talk and music had helped to train her ear, and *Pride and Prejudice* was to have a lyric texture as heightened above ordinary prose as Racine's *Phèdre* is above ordinary French alexandrines. Her prose rhythms are the result not simply of 'genius' but of long listening and much writing.

Edward, so far, had hinted that he *might* offer Mrs Austen a house, and, providentially, she and her daughters visited him at Chawton Manor near Alton late in 1807, and kept themselves from freezing in that large, stuccoed, tapestried, chilly old Jacobean home of the Knights. It was near the village church. Beyond were fields with ash and elm plantations. A mile away near a pond was a pretty redbrick cottage – their future home. Jane went on to see the Biggs at Manydown and the Fowles at Kintbury, but waited for the spring to fulfil her pledge to see Henry and Eliza at Brompton.

Eliza was living not in London but in a low-lying village built on damp ground and known jocularly as Flounder's Fields. Brompton was then well outside the city. She and Henry were in a terraced house at No. 16 Michael's Place, the only exotic glamour of which was that it was designed by Michael Novosielski, who, as the son of an émigré Polish count, had also rebuilt the Opera House in the Haymarket. ('I hope you will see everything worthy,' Jane had told her sister, 'from the Opera House to Henry's office in Cleveland Court.') Age and illness took more light out of Eliza's eyes, perhaps, than out of her spirit, and her usually apologetic, loving, embracing, talkative ways were pleasant. She had surrounded herself with theatrical people. Nearby at No. 17 lived Miss Pope the actress, who was praised by the great Garrick. At No. 15 lived 'the most celebrated singer of her time', Mrs Billington, and at No. 21 lived the comedian John Liston, whom Jane later saw in London: 'We had Mathews, Liston & Emery; of course some amusement.' As for Henry, he probably deserved to be treated by his sister with her usual warmth. As a financial acrobat he had become a banker with offices in town wonderfully enough, but without a net under him if he should fall. 'Oh what a Henry!' was Jane's comment on him. She was pleased when James and Mary and their younger children arrived at the hotel assigned to them to join forces for a visit to Kent. 'Henry saw us into our own carriage, and we drove away from the Bath Hotel,' Jane wrote, 'very dirty, very noisy, and very ill-provided.' She put up with a hot carriage and with the complaints of Mary Lloyd, who fidgeted over a restless Caroline, and then they 'drove, drove, drove' to reach Godmersham Park in its quiet evening setting at about six, where two of her brothers were out on the grass before the house and Fanny and Lizzy kissed her before she could catch her breath. Then Jane was shown to the Yellow Room, after Elizabeth for 'a minute' gave the required welcome, though it is probable that Elizabeth was friendlier than Anna remembers. 'I feel rather languid and solitary,' Jane wrote soon after her arrival, but if her visit was uncomfortable the fault was perhaps on both sides since her own suppressed vigour was clearly too much for a sister-in-law who resented a youthful-looking relation who seemed to have no cares. Jane at the moment tried to fathom a new chilliness: 'I cannot discover even through Fanny', she noted, 'that her mother is fatigued by her attendance on the children.' However, she refused to dwell on Elizabeth's manner and sent back bright chit-chat to Castle Square.[26]

A day or two later she rode in a coach to Canterbury with Mary Lloyd. That sister-in-law was upset because Cassandra had taken tea with a sibling of James's first wife, and also because the Revd George Moore, a sleek timeserver, it seems, had married Elizabeth's sister Harriot. No love was lost between Mary Lloyd and the Bridges of Kent, as Jane knew, but Mary could not harbour a grudge and fortunately their first stop was at White Friars to see Mrs Knight. That lady, Edward's benefactor, was mild, gracious and intelligent – Jane owed her gratitude for a 'usual fee' of spending money and also for Catherine Knight's habit of not expecting others to echo her opinions. But they had not been at Mrs Knight's a half hour before the sleek, horrid George Moore called: she had agreed to hate him before seeing him or did not mean 'ever to like him', but she was curious. His oily manner betrayed that he was a son of an Archbishop of Canterbury and grandson of a butcher. Harriot had married him and borne him a child, but Jane was not bound to admire him for Harriot's sake. What was Moore really like? At Godmersham she was used to conceit – but now she withheld a verdict: 'Well! – & what do I think of Mr. Moore?' she quickly wrote to Cassandra. 'I will not pretend in one meeting to *dislike* him, whatever Mary may say, but I can honestly assure her that I saw nothing in him to admire. – His manners, as you have always said, are gentlemanlike, but by no means winning.'

She met him again at White Friars, where in the manner of Fanny Price she sat sewing till 10 p.m., 'when he ordered his wife away, & we adjourned to the Dressing Room to eat our Tart & Jelly'. He was less oily but tense, impatient and not disposed to find anything in his world quite to his liking: 'nothing seemed to go right with him', but 'he is a sensible Man, & tells a story well'.[27]

By then she was fascinated. At a subsequent dinner with the James Austens Mr Moore was disturbingly reserved, but she was told she had not seen him 'at all as he is in general; – our being strangers made him so much more silent & quiet'. Mary Lloyd and James reacted to the two married Moores with a comical difference: 'Mary was disappointed in *her* beauty, & thought *him* very disagreeable; James admires *her*, & finds *him* conversible and pleasant.' Still later she happened to meet Mr Moore on a London street, or rather he made the mistake of trying to rush past Jane Austen: 'I beleive he would have passed me, if I had not made him stop – but we were delighted to meet.' She would not let him go and *made* him talk. Finally in Kent she was glad to see him one day in a tiff with his coachman: 'Mr. Moore was very angry, which I was rather glad of. I wanted to see him angry; and, though he spoke to his servant in a very loud voice and with a good deal of heat, I was happy to perceive that he did not scold Harriot at all.' He was too angry to feign his behaviour at that point, and one sees in Jane Austen's reports about him her own aggression, cunning and patience in finding him out. She characteristically had indulged her fancies and feelings even before meeting him. She trusted in her feelings and prejudices while respecting the authority of what her reason told her about Mr Moore, and so in her final estimate retained some truth about him that she had seen by indulging her emotions in the first place. She did not shake the Revd George Moore by the shoulders but had not 'let him go' on the street and later had watched till he exposed his temper under pressure. What she most delightedly noticed was the comic disparity between what *ought to be the case* about him and what *the case really was*, or Mary's and Cassandra's judgements of the Archbishop's son and the real 'Mr Moore' who revealed his nature at dinner or in story-telling, with or without his wife at White Friars or at Godmersham, then in a city street, and finally in a pet of anger over his coachman. She knew that character is elusive and that to observe anyone, however closely, is to be misled, but that we may never learn until we *are* misled; she had refined and added to her opinions of Mr Moore while keeping something from her 'first impressions'. And finally she felt that Harriot had chosen well. Moore was not forthcoming but civil and gentle with his wife and if his father the Archbishop had left a butcher's shop to marry the daughter of Sir Robert Eden, the son was probably only as defensive and cautious as anyone from a family of sudden prominence ought to be.[28]

Her stay in Kent unaccountably had lengthened. 'It will be two years tomorrow', she wrote at the Park on Friday, 1 July 1808, 'since we left Bath for Clifton.' That reminiscence of escape suggests she felt that with the better weather it was time to leave Kent, but meanwhile as she told her sister 'I shall eat Ice & drink French wine, & be above vulgar Economy.' The price would be to endure Elizabeth a little longer and the reward at home would be 'luckily the pleasures of Friendship, of unreserved Conversation, of Similarity of Taste & Opinions'. Not that that was a cruel remark in an intimate letter. Her sister-in-law seemed to be well despite her pregnancy and unusually active for her 'situation and size'.[29] To her airs, managerial ways and unfeeling comments Jane perhaps had been too sensitive: but she stored up materials and perspectives here that would give an edge to her social criticism in *Sense and Sensibility*, the first novel to be revised at Chawton.

Back at Castle Square this summer, a delightful visit by Catherine and Alethea Bigg gave her freer pleasures than she had enjoyed in Kent. At the age of thirty-five Catherine Bigg was engaged to marry Herbert Hill, a clergyman who was twenty-four years her senior and uncle to the poet Robert Southey. With the most complete love for Catherine and very gentlest irony about her prospects, Jane handed her a cambric handkerchief along with an original poem – 'Cambrick! with grateful blessings would I pay / The pleasure given me in sweet employ,' she wrote after some hours at her needle,

> Long may'st thou serve my Friend without decay,
> And have no tears to wipe, but tears of joy!
> J. A.   Aug:st 26. – 1808.[30]

Tragic news arrived in Catherine's wedding-month: a few days after giving birth to her eleventh child, Brook John, Elizabeth Austen fell ill at Godmersham Park and died on 10 October. In her condolences Jane said very little about her ('We need not enter into a Panegyric on the Departed') and of course aimed to console Cassandra, who was then in Kent, as well as Edward and his bereft children. 'I suppose you see the corpse? How does it appear?' she wrote to her sister, although her attention focused on the child of Edward's she knew best: 'My dear, dear Fanny! – I am so thankful that she has you with her!' Jane wrote. At fifteen Fanny would have to regard herself as her father's dearest comfort and friend 'who is gradually to supply to him, to the extent that is possible, what he has lost. This consideration will elevate and cheer her.' Fanny's interest in her Aunt Jane and Aunt Jane's writing were decidedly to grow stronger. Edward's boys Edward and George were now ordered home from Winchester College and at first sent to Steventon, but 'I should have loved to have them with me,' Jane wrote rashly, and on Saturday, 22 October, they actually arrived on the seven o'clock coach at Castle Square, somewhat comforted by Mr Wise the coachman's greatcoat.

'*They behave extremely* well,' she wrote of the boys, who were then thirteen and fourteen. Her test of their worth was whether they were

249

feeling, whether, for example, they wept as they should over their father's letter. Satisfied of that, Jane became a cheerful player who led them in a round of games including cards, ships, riddles, bilbo-quet or 'bilbocatch' at which she excelled in catching a tossed ball in a cup or on the point, and spillikins or pick-up-sticks, in which the idea was to flick a chip or small rod from a pile without disturbing the rest. After seeing to their mourning clothes she took the boys across the ferry to Northam to a 74-gun ship, patrolled the river on foot, watched them shoot at paper boats with horse-chestnuts, and at last encouraged them as they sat twisting in chairs over their reading. Before they left happily distracted and ready for school again, she had heard that her brother Edward could offer the Austen ladies either a home at Godmersham or a cottage at Chawton near Alton. There could be no doubt in *her* choice and clearly her mother, she knew, would view the Chawton Plan 'with more and more pleasure'.

'There are six Bedchambers at Chawton,' Jane informed her sister on 20 November. 'Henry wrote to my Mother the other day, & luckily mentioned the number – which is just what we wanted to be assured of. He speaks also of Garrets for store-places, one of which she imme-diately planned fitting up for Edward's Manservant – & now perhaps it must be for our own – for she is already quite reconciled to our keeping one.' Moreover she felt pleasure in thinking about this man-servant: 'his name shall be Robert, if you please'. From then on her life was changed, since the more she considered the Chawton Plan the more she lived imaginatively in the cottage even with 'Robert'. Martha would remain with them. To have the house was a dream to end a fictional romance, and it put Southampton in a new light. But advantages had to be seized: 'Martha ought to see the inside of the Theatre once while she lives in Southampton, & I think she will hardly wish to take a second view.'[31] Martha's ignorance could be remedied, although that very self-effacing friend took little interest in any phase of life in which she could not serve or be useful. Frank admired her passive virtues: 'Joined', he wrote of her, 'to the posses-sion of much good sense,' Martha had those valued blessings of 'sweet temper, amiable disposition and what is of far greater impor-tance, a mind deeply impressed with the truth of Christianity'.[32] It was not a disadvantage to him or anyone else that Martha's gentle temper had the asset of letting people near her live their own lives, by allowing silence and self-possession in a household. Jane Austen enjoyed watching Martha's elegant form and movements and did not praise her gracefulness to Cassandra idly, so that there was no more than a slight trace of guilt in her joy over Martha's person: later she would give Emma Woodhouse nearly the same joy as Emma sits 'so busy in admiring those soft blue eyes' of Harriet Smith and 'in talking and listening'.[33] Observers from a harder age might see lesbianism in Jane Austen's delight in her friend, but it seems too fierce to attach labels to the mass of persons who can find both sexes attractive. (Twentieth-century sexual categories are too crude to be of much use in understanding male or female friendships in Jane Austen's day – and perhaps in our day, too.) Her regard for Martha, it must be said, was deeper and more considered than Emma's for Harriet. Not the least joy of Chawton decidedly would be Martha, whose absences so far had left Jane for weeks and months in Frank's two houses without a friend of her own tastes and background. Cassandra, too, who was often away, lingered this autumn in Kent – and it was at least partly the lack of a stable, reliable audience that had kept a novelist from beginning new work. Another vexation was that she had been at the beck and call of anyone who arrived and it is important that her charity and patience had been under strain, and had begun to break down. News of relatives arrived unceasingly, and she was supposed to be gladdened by nearly anything except penury, illness and fatality. Charles at his distant naval station had married a daughter of Bermuda's Attorney-General named Frances Fitzwilliam Palmer who gave birth to a little Cassy on 22 December. Mary Gibson's fatuous American cousin, Miss Curling, meanwhile was at Portsmouth: 'I wish her no worse however than a long & happy abode there,' Jane Austen wrote testily. 'Here, she w^d probably be dull, & I am sure she w^d be troublesome.'

In a cottage they might exclude every living horror. At an exasperated point Jane Austen's attitude to bores was quite simply *Kill Mrs. Sclater if you wish*.[34]

Her boredom with Southampton was becoming almost sublime, and yet, it seems, Martha Lloyd at least set examples of busy, resourceful and distracting work in the kitchen for anyone in love with pots and pans. While Cassandra consoled Edward in Kent, Martha's cooking did much to keep everyone content at Frank's table. Martha's recipes were well known in the family, and Jane had tasted her apple

251

snow and quire-of-paper pancakes, hog's pudding and 'harrico' of mutton, and of course the veal cake favoured by Mrs Dundas. Martha jotted these recipes in a leatherbound book for which she made a neat index and then added notes on perfumery, home remedies and household tips with an occasional cheering word for the reader: 'Good luck to your jamming,' wrote Martha Lloyd for all to see.[35]

By Christmastime, Jane had decided to make the most of her last weeks in a seaport: she would squeeze the town in her own way, attend those assemblies she could, and observe them for what they were worth: 'Yes,' she wrote to Cassandra, 'I mean to go to as many balls as possible.' For Mrs Knight's sake she decided to marry (before he could say yes or no) the lucky bachelor Rector of Chawton, John Rawston Papillon, whose niece eventually (in 1820) was to marry Henry Austen. 'I *will* marry Mr. Papillon,' vowed Jane, 'whatever may be his reluctance or my own.' She might become a bigamist by marrying the poet Crabbe too.

As for winter dances she met and danced with a foreigner who couldn't give his name (his romantic black eyes were his best feature), and saw forlorn or ecstatic ladies with ugly shoulders exposed by the new gowns. By then she was watching people without much reflection on any of them, though she knew that her sister might expect smartish reports: 'Miss Hook is a well-behaved, genteelish woman,' she wrote after a dull evening at Mrs Kelly's; 'Mrs. Drew was well-behaved, without being at all genteel. Mr. Wynne seems a chatty and rather familiar young man. Miss Murden was quite a different creature this last evening. . . .' But she commented more fully on Cassandra's report about an old friend at Nackington in Kent: twenty-three years after her *first* wedding Lady Sondes was marrying for love the elderly General Montresor. 'I like his rank very much,' Jane decided, and 'I consider everybody as having a right to marry *once* in their lives for love, if they can, and provided she will now leave off having bad headaches and being pathetic, I can allow her, I can *wish* her, to be happy.'[36]

She believed in having as many holds on happiness as possible and only felt that Lady Sondes's attitude was poor. The world, Jane Austen felt, neither conspires to make us happy nor asks us to punish others, and the worst we can do is to be complaining or 'pathetic'. In her novels the words 'happy' and 'happiness' show that she often associated 'to be happy' with sexual fulfilment, so that when Elinor

Dashwood enquires about when Edward Ferrars 'will be at liberty to be happy' sexual union seems almost explicit. Yet the controlling concept of happiness in her stories is not quite the same in meaning as her often repeated word, and her idea of 'happiness' is more complicated than Jefferson's in the Declaration of Independence or even than Dr Johnson's. Debates on the East India Company took up the idea of 'happiness' in connection with the Indian government, but Jane Austen takes a rather more inward view. To be 'happy' is to seek one's potential character and a state of being in which one is accurately aware of others' feelings, with real sensibility, and can behave well in adversity. Her narrators are important in showing, for example, that not simply outward events or money or good luck in meeting Tilney and Darcy are so basic to Catherine's or Elizabeth's 'happiness' as the growth of awareness is. Still, happiness is a spiritual pursuit with rewards, for Jane Austen, who never denied the world's charms or the worth of having them, though she showed the comedy of our attempts to obtain them. Her concern with being 'happy' – and her subtle probing of that idea – reveal her as a true child of the bright eighteenth century. Because people in her time honoured the idea of happiness her novels in this sense respond to an almost sacrosanct faith in that very word; thus, when she was less than a year old, delegates from the Thirteen Colonies at Philadelphia quickly approved Jefferson's 'self-evident' idea that happiness is a human right (if the world had not accepted it as self-evident the syllogistic logic of the Declaration would have collapsed for rational readers), but spent two-and-a-half days pruning his intemperate remarks on King George.[37]

The first day the Austens had fixed for leaving Southampton was Easter Monday, 3 April 1809. Jane Austen was to sleep over at Alton and go on to the Cookes at Bookham and to Godmersham briefly before settling in at Chawton. But the most precise plans go awry – and in the fuss of a delayed removal she thought of her dilatory publisher. Still at Southampton on 5 April, she posted a letter to Messrs Crosby & Co., who so far had done nothing with *Susan* or *Northanger Abbey*. She may have been anxious because she had begun to revise another 'child', her 'Elinor and Marianne' story, but then *Susan* had been kept by Crosby since 1803. She was very angry and signed herself M.A.D. – for Mrs Ashton Dennis. 'Six years have since passed,' wrote M.A.D.,

> & this work of which I am myself the Authoress, has never to the best of my knowledge, appeared in print, tho' an early publication was stipulated for at the time of sale. I can only account for such an extraordinary circumstance by supposing the MS. by some carelessness to have been lost.

She offered to send a fresh manuscript and pressed for a reply. Crosby replied three days later to say, yes, he had the work and would stop anyone *else* from printing her novel, which he was not bound to publish, but that she could have it back for £10.

She let that matter rest. There was much to attend to when she reached Chawton on 9 July and soon she heard that Frank's wife Mary had given birth to a boy. Now she could twit Frank. She sent him a poem that is so bland, simple and charming that one nearly overlooks a grand phrase in it that pertains to her mood, outlook and energized attitude to the manuscripts she had carried with her. She praised just that vital and joyous 'insolence of spirit' that she remembered in Frank as a child.

'Chawton', she wrote brightly. 'July 26. – 1809 –':

> My dearest Frank, I wish you joy,
> Of Mary's safety with a Boy,
> Whose birth has given little pain
> Compared with that of Mary Jane. – . . .
>
> Thy infant days may he inherit,
> Thy warmth, nay insolence of spirit; –
> We would not with one fault dispense
> To weaken the resemblance.
>
>   As for ourselves, we're very well;
> As unaffected prose will tell. –
> Cassandra's pen will paint our state,
> The many comforts that await
> Our Chawton home, how much we find
> Already in it, to our mind;
> And how convinced, that when complete
> It will all other Houses beat
> That ever have been made or mended,
> With rooms concise, or rooms distended.[38]

In these rooms she produced the most delightful comedy in our language since Shakespeare. She had not reached Chawton without suffering, but she felt grateful to a Providence that put her there. She was in the cottage for her salvation. It had not been only attending church twice a day that kept her from writing far more often, 'I begin to hate myself' or 'I am so ashamed', but an unceasing effort of conscience. And yet her impatience as she thought of a 'Miss Curling' or dozens of other irritating people did not sit easily with the idea of a Christian's meekness. There is no greater contrast in Jane Austen's writings than that between her sharp, comically malicious letters and the Christian prayers she composed. She did not *act* uncharitably or cruelly, but behaved well partly because she insulted others brutally in quiet jokes. Yet was not her aggression still there? Was she any more Christian in her own eyes because her maliciousness had style and wit? Her prayers suggest that as a rational woman of deep feeling she felt abject and solemnly and terribly accountable, by no means pleased with herself. The effort of reconciling her faith with her fury was enough to try her, and as happy as she was in green country at Chawton she was to make amends in part through her fictional comedies in which no living being is attacked, but life itself is recreated and appraised for every reader.[39] 'Father of Heaven!' she wrote, 'whose goodness has brought us in safety to the close of this day, dispose our hearts in fervent prayer. Another day is now gone, and added to those, for which we were before accountable. Teach us almighty father, to consider this solemn truth, as we should do, that we may feel the importance of every day, and every hour as it passes, and earnestly strive to make a better use of what thy goodness may yet bestow on us, than we have done of the time past.' 'Incline us oh God!' she implored, 'to consider our fellow creatures with kindness.'

Part Four

THE CHAWTON PLAN

15

Two nieces and
Sense and Sensibility

Here the gray smooth trunks
Of ash, or lime, or beech, distinctly shine. . . .
Oh, friendly to the best pursuits . . .
Friendly to thought, to virtue, and to peace,
Domestic life in rural leisure pass'd!
William Cowper

Within easy walking distance of Alton, Chawton lies in Hampshire's north-east corner near open downs in more sweeping
and undulating country than one sees round Steventon. Winchester
is off to the west. A visitor might suppose that Mrs Austen and her
ladies had buried themselves far from any town – and even a new
national passion for improvements in farming was slow to take hold
here. Looking at the chalky fields, kitchen gardens and countryside
one might never imagine Hampshire rushing into an industrial revolution. King George III had earned his nickname as Farmer George
by encouraging farming, and almost everyone knew one or two anec-
dotes about the good, red-faced King walking over furrows and talking to men about the wheat or the weather at Windsor in nearby
Berkshire; he perhaps wrote or authorized two pieces himself in the
1790s for the *Annals of Agriculture* under the pseudonym of Ralph
Robinson (the name of one of his shepherds) and a nation had followed the King's lead. New threshing machines soon appeared. In
wartime their efficiency was welcome. They could be set up within
two hours of arriving at a barn and worked by horses and be used

very handily, too, for cutting straw and grinding and crushing. There were more of the new threshers elsewhere than here – though Chawton parish *was* modern in one way.

All of its land had been enclosed in the eighteenth century. Wealthier landowners felt that this of course was truly progress! Families at the lower fringes of the yeomanry, though, suffered cruelly when they lost the right to graze a cow or a few sheep on common land. The medieval common lands had vanished: all was fenced in. Poor farmers gradually had been pushed down into the ranks of wage labourers; ironically they would have to buy their food, instead of raise it, and at prices that climbed steadily until 1813. In *Mansfield Park* and *Emma* a deep feeling about land and the community is a response to what Jane Austen saw and heard in her Chawton years. Oddly there had been food shortages here, when London began in wartime to draw in its grain not only from the Home Counties and East Anglia, its usual sources of supply, but from Hampshire as well. The Mayor of Winchester had cried out that his neighbourhood was being deprived of grain, and a need for horses and tax revenues hurt farmers who were surviving.

The war seemed hungry for young men, too. One in every six adult males was now at war by land or sea, and the toll of the dead, maimed and crippled had been alarming lately on the Peninsula. Books, newspapers and sermons allude to the strain on manpower, and in Berkshire there were petticoat harvests when women brought in grain.

But, to the eye of anyone who loved the country, Hampshire was still charming, and nature in the area around Chawton touched on every part of a community's life. A few miles to the south lay the village of the county's naturalist Gilbert White: White's *Natural History of Selborne* had appeared in 1789, and it was already a classic; he was gone, but a member of his family was to invite Anna Austen to the King's birthday fête. His Selborne consisted of its quaint straggling street under a hanging wood – and round about were sheep downs, green and brown hills, large tracts of heath and pretty streams that went this way and that. As a branch of the River Wey, Selborne's tumbling stream met Blackdown's at Hedleigh and then the Farnham-and-Alton stream at Tilford Bridge where it swelled into a considerable river – and then nearly everywhere one travelled in this region one might see groves of beech, that loveliest of all of Hampshire's trees. Yet the paradox was that the world of commerce, quick transport and industry was not really remote: Chawton *also* lay at a vital junction of the Winchester, London and Gosport roads only fifty miles south-west of the capital. One did not have to walk far to see much evidence of the new commercial spirit. Alton, only a mile to the north of Chawton, had what John White calls with disappointment only a 'small market' (so that he had to go elsewhere to buy coal) but it had many good shops. Jane Austen was to walk to Alton several times a week in all weather, and to know by sight some of its 288 houses and 2,000 inhabitants, many of whom were employed in making corded stuffs, black bombazines or other good cloth material. A hundred workers in Alton's poorhouse or 'house of industry' sat at their calico-weaving looms, and fine light worsteds for the overseas market went from another factory here all the way to Philadelphia, to be worn – says a gazetteer of the time – 'in the summer by the town and country gentlemen'.[1] Alton was commercial enough to get a branch of Henry Austen's London bank, and lively enough to have a good assembly room (where Mrs Austen's spies, as usual, watched the local belles before reporting back to her). A good daily coach, though it was known to overturn, left the town to drive up a turnpike through Farnham, Leatherhead and Epsom and soon into London. (This was the privately famous Car of Falkenstein.)

Chawton itself was almost a racecourse for teams going north to the capital, west to Winchester or south to the naval ports. The Austens lived next to the junction of these routes and dangerously close to the London road since only a small space with a fence protected their house 'from danger of collision with any runaway vehicle', as a nephew writes.[2] Again one notices how the geography of her county, lines of transport and commerce, and the strategic importance of Hampshire in relation to the capital and the ports all place Jane Austen near a great current of outward motion – and how it is that she thrives as a writer living not in rural solitude but at the edge of pulsing activity. The waggon wheels and carriage wheels just outside her windows were more than appropriate for her – they were continual reminders of the commercial and social world of her England. The sophisticated culture and elegance of the capital, the suave talk of her brother Henry and his friends, and the current of ideas and news running south from the capital modified her experience of cows, sheep and talk of the weather. And yet she needed to be at a remove from the thronging, noisy, distracting centre of England, and the coaches that raced past her house only guaranteed that the remove would not be too great. It was with no sense of meek resignation to solitude that she had come to Chawton.

The careering coaches near Mrs Austen's windows are well lost in time today, of course, when one visits her cottage to find it lovingly restored by the Jane Austen Society. It has become a fascinating museum, with the world's lively and curious sightseers on display. One observes at one's feet the recent punctures of stiletto heels in fine, old eighteenth-century floorboards, and one stares into glass cases at the Topaz Crosses or at a lock of the novelist's hair, lately dyed an improbably bright and brazen auburn. (The same commercial company that dyed the novelist's hair, not long ago, has microphotographs showing bits of Jane Austen's skin clinging to its roots). One meets visitors and cameras of every nation, and now and then overhears a charming comment. *Oh I just think this house is so darling! Why it's so – British!* Still one senses the quiet of time here and imagines that all of the objects on display, the manuscripts, the daguerreotype of Frank Austen showing duty and kindness in his face, or even the lock that Cassandra took from her sister's head are less pertinent to the novelist than her many living visitors – who read her and represent her.

Her cottage* stands at the very end of its quiet street as an ample-two-storeyed house of good, rosy Hampshire bricks, a high-pitched roof and two attic dormers, all looking rather larger than it is because of an 'L'-shape. A long arm of the 'L' lies parallel to the road and meets the shorter arm to form two main downstairs chambers. Mrs Austen's drawing room is at the left as one faces the road, and her dining room to the right of the front door. James Edward reports that 'a good-sized entrance and two sitting-rooms formed the length of the house', and also notes that his Uncle Edward had kindly bricked up a front window and cut another into the wall facing the garden. From its position at the end of the village, its outbuildings and its many small rooms one gathers that he was probably right in believing that the house in former times was an inn.

One enters a garden door to find oneself in the drawing room with a cosy dining room beyond, both looking out on the London

---

* Now called Jane Austen's House.

road. Then one climbs six steps to a cheerful landing, eight steps more, and sees at the left a bedroom which Cassandra and Jane probably shared, ten feet wide and barely more than thirteen deep. A fireplace is at one end, and near a window looking on the garden hangs a patchwork counterpane made by Mrs Austen. Outside one tries to imagine that lady in her coarse green work-apron or Cassandra in her China crape, or Jane Austen in 'my kerseymore Spencer' running to a bakehouse where implements still wait – a round clothes-tub lacking a drain, a brick oven and a heavy bacon roller, and a low-wheeled donkey-trap.

Perhaps because of the hush of visitors it is harder to imagine a cadence of hooves on packed pebbles and a loud, staccato banging and rattling of a mail coach as it passes near Mrs Austen's table. A wooden fence and hornbeam hedge shut out some of the noise, and trees within the enclosure protected a shrubbery walk giving space for exercise. 'There was a pleasant irregular mixture of hedgerow, and gravel walk, and orchard, and long grass for mowing, arising from two or three little enclosures having been thrown together,' and Caroline herself noticed '*some* bedrooms very small – *none* very large' and found Mrs Austen delighted to watch the road. One might nearly regulate a clock by the morning coach from Winchester drawn by six horses or the evening one drawn by four, or by Portsmouth's passing at midday, and Mrs Austen opened her eyes as Collyer's six horses clattered past. 'Most delightful was it to a child', Caroline recalls, 'to have the awful stillness of night so frequently broken by the noise of passing carriages, which seemed sometimes, even to shake the bed.'[3]

Jane Austen could wake up in a green setting to see tilled fields, a pond and groves of ash and elm from a front window. When it rained, her mother kept curtains open so that Mrs Knight observed on 26 October this year, 'I heard of the Chawton party looking very comfortable at breakfast from a gentleman who was travelling by their door in a post-chaise about ten days ago.' Jane was not fond of rain, and in a recently found manuscript she writes of *sad* weather and of a nephew's ride from Chawton that 'could only be tolerable by its taking him home'. In winter her fields turned to water: 'We have a great many ponds,' she wrote once, 'and a fine running stream through the meadow on the other side of the road.'[4]

But her joy in Chawton would have survived floods. She claimed that the weather was better *here* than at Steventon. '"A very sloppy lane" last friday!' she quoted Cassandra when that sister was visiting James. 'I cannot at all understand it! It was just greasy here on friday, in consequence of the little snow,' she adds merrily. 'I cannot imagine what sort of a place Steventon can be!' The cottage is so good and beautiful, so snug and precious beyond praise it sets a model for everywhere else, just as her local book society set a model for the Miss Sibleys of West Meon. Book societies were quite in fashion. You collected a dozen or so members who paid an annual fee out of which a book was bought, read by all and offered for sale to members, and then if nobody wished to own it the proposer had to buy it back at half-price. 'The Miss Sibleys want to establish a Book society,' she advised Cassandra, 'like ours. What can be a stronger proof of that superiority in ours over the Steventon & Many-down Society, which I have always foreseen and felt? No emulation of the kind was ever inspired by *their* proceedings; no such wish of the Miss Sibleys was ever heard, in the course of the many years of that Society's existence; – And what are their Biglands & their Barrows, their Macartneys & Mackenzies . . .?'[5]

In her underlying mood at Chawton were glee, energy and a re-siliently light and healthy feeling for combat and rivalry. In a house which would all others beat she meant to *do* a good deal. She had a useful routine with mild people who depended on her and loved her – and here at first she had no one she *had* to please but her mother, Cassandra and Martha, all good and busy workers. At seventy Mrs Austen let herself be superseded by her daughters and ceased to sit at the head of the table, but she was not idle and her devotion to work was an incentive to those who had to live with her. That good lady 'found plenty of occupation for herself in garden-ing and needlework', as a relative heard. 'The former was, with her, no idle pastime, no mere cutting of roses and tying up of flowers. She dug up her own potatoes [and] planted them, for the kitchen garden was as much her delight as the flower borders.'[6] Cassandra and Martha, as they were three and ten years older than Jane, could afford to indulge the youngest in the cottage, and Jane Austen had the lightest duties of these three. She rose early so as not to disturb others when they came downstairs and practised before breakfast 'when she could have the room to herself' with her pianoforte, and she practised daily. At nine o'clock she made breakfast for her ladies, 'and *that*', as Caroline emphasizes with admiration and envy, 'was *her* part of the household work – the tea and sugar stores, were under her charge – *and* the wine – Aunt Cassandra did all the rest'. She had no method of parcelling out her day, though mornings were of a pattern, and she spent them in the drawing room with her manuscripts and then when visitors were present would sit in that same drawing room and emulate her mother in sewing. Fond of her needle, she would show off her overcast or satin stitch to her young visitors and take pride in her neatness. Sewing in Jane Austen's day helped to forge an important female bond, and as Rozsika Parker has said it 'allowed women to sit together without feeling they were neglecting their families' or wasting time. For Jane embroidery had been a means of proving her initiative, skill and ability to finish work with smart quickness. As it *was* distinctly work that women did and one of the few ways in which their creativity might flourish without being questioned or considered too aggressive, forward or unladylike, she respected it. There is no hint in her letters that she objected to it, and at Chawton it linked her with her own creative childhood. 'After luncheon, my Aunts generally walked out – sometimes they went to Alton for shopping,' Caroline recalls, or they walked to Chawton House and strolled under the pretty beeches. Caroline adds interestingly that Jane Austen only 'rarely' called on a neighbour, but the fact that she herself was then staying at the cottage may have affected her aunt's normal routine. And here one ought to judge Caroline's childhood memories more delicately than biographers so far have and see them in the light of what James Edward says, and in the perspective of Fanny Lefroy's unpublished words and of the Beckford letters with their recollections of Jane at Chawton that surfaced only in the 1980s. Caroline *is* right in saying that her aunts 'were upon *friendly* but rather *distant* terms with all', and that since they had no carriage their visitings could not extend far. But we know, now, that Jane Austen was often with the Middletons at her brother Edward's nearby house, and that she not only talked with virtually everyone in the village and knew their concerns and heard a great deal of gossip in these years, but, in private with Cassandra, was censorious and critical about them and turned a number of them 'into ridicule', despite what Caroline implies about her aunt's innocent and good-natured remarks on the neighbours.[7]

The evidence suggests that she held herself aloof, and did not closely befriend any new Martha or Alethea or Catherine. But she made exceptions of people who were not in the little local, working, money-getting society, or who were outside the normal stream of adult life, and so she took an interest in one or two bemused, ineffectual old ladies, also now and then in an amusing and pretty young woman, as well as in the children of her brothers and Mr Middleton. She had no wish to make herself popular or to become confidential with anyone simply on the basis of prior acquaintanceship. With amusement she had written the surname 'Digweed', as her manuscript letters show, with a long, exulting and backward-swooping line for the 'D', but the numerous family of the Digweeds seemed born to follow her, and at Chawton she was cautious. A branch was nearby. Mrs Harry Digweed was at Alton: she 'looks forward with great satisfaction to our being her neighbours', Jane remarked. 'I would have her enjoy the idea to the utmost, as I suspect there will be not much in the reality.' Though fearing the Digweeds, she was in principle less alarmed by Digweed's bailiff and his wife since *they* would not presume on intimacy and encroach on her: she was easier with people than she had been in earlier years – but the nearby Digweeds were persistent. Hugh and Ruth Digweed, who were tenants of Steventon Manor when she was born, had had five sons, of whom she knew three very well: James had married into the Basingstoke Lyfords, William stayed at his manor and Harry at thirty-seven had married his silly Jane Terry, of Dummer, and had moved to Alton. Yet when dining with the Alton couple Jane was touched by Mrs Digweed's pleasure in charades and her fondness for a ball, and by her local phrases such as 'it was beyond everything!' The very language of London seemed 'flat' beside hers – 'it wants her phrase'. Still Jane Austen took her in small doses: 'Dear Mrs. Digweed!' she later exclaimed, 'I cannot bear that she should not be foolishly happy after a ball.'

Some neighbours were likely to be curious about her novel-writing. William Prowting nearby was a justice of the peace who, in time, sold his house to the Knights and built another across the road called Denmead.[8] 'Mr. Prowting', Jane told Cassandra, 'has opened a gravel pit, very conveniently for my mother, just at the mouth of the approach to his house; but it looks a little as if he meant to catch all his company. Tolerable gravel.' He was unlikely to catch *her* in any sense, but she had reason to be on guard with the Clements.

When Ann Mary Prowting, the JP's daughter, married Captain Clement, Jane noticed that they were 'reduced to read' and had a novel by Miss Edgeworth. Despite her Book Society she was wary of the bookish and was to be troubled by those who found herself and Cassandra and then Anna in her heroines. More harmless was Miss Harriot Webb, a bent woman who could not say her r's and read aloud Hannah More's *Practical Piety*. Jane was relieved when the Webbs left – having already invited them in for an evening with Captain and Mrs Clement, Miss Benn and Mrs Digweed – 'But why not Mrs. Digweed?' she told Martha lightly. The most *unavoidable* neighbour was poor, garrulous Miss Benn, who wore a ragged 'long fur tippet'. When Martha wished to buy her something Jane suggested a shawl – 'but it must not be very handsome or she would not use it'. Like Mrs Stent of Ibthorp, Miss Benn chattered of almost nothing – of her mignonette seeds or her brother's insipid children – but as she fixed on trivia that nobody else noticed, her talk was fresh and unique. Jane Austen did not reserve charity for loud, capable people but listened to boring, finicky souls such as Miss Benn and Mrs Stent, and found herself in them. 'Poor Mrs Stent!' as she had written after that woman exclaimed about the chickens for the hundredth time, 'it has been her lot to be always in the way; but we must be merciful, for perhaps in time we may come to be Mrs Stents ourselves, unequal to anything and unwelcome to everybody.' There was a difference between the bright, young arrogant Jane Austen who ridiculed a rural neighbourhood in 1796 and the person she had become, and her new charity was compatible with her gaiety and necessary insolence. She found in Miss Benn and Mrs Stent wisdom most of us are too quick and self-satisfied to acquire. Her portrait of Miss Bates in *Emma* is enriched because she knew these women. And her social feelings had a chance to develop at Chawton, partly because when we are miserable we are defensive, cautious and less able to see who needs help – but happiness opens our eyes, and in green lanes at Chawton and Alton she took the poor and needy into account with a grace that is not so evident in her earlier remarks on the poor. One proof of this is in a new social conscience evident in her Chawton novels. She noticed more aspects of a place in its *entirety* here, too, than she could have at Bath or Southampton, and rural politics concerned her. When she knew she was moving to Chawton she had brightened over the news that Thomas

Thistlethwaite the MP was smarting under the payment of 'late election-eering costs' and wouldn't oppose Thomas Heathcote's standing for Parliament. (Heathcote was a brother-in-law of Elizabeth Bigg.) Then she was amused when Alethea electioneered, boldly, and asked for Jane's political interest: Alethea 'hopes for *my interest*, which I conclude means Edward's – & I take this opportunity therefore of requesting that he will bring in Mr. Heathcote,' she had said in a letter to Kent. She had joked about local politics before as when she had entered a drawing room to find two self-assured, boring men standing there and had mocked them to Cassandra as 'Heathcote & Chute forever' – making fun of an inane election cry. When politics became part of her confidence, she could feel that no aspect of this community's life was beyond her grasp. Her understanding of its connections was one basis of her ability to portray communities with an easy, self-assured pen.[9]

In Eleanor Papillon, a niece of the Rector, she found a pretty woman who joined her in visits to the poor. They might have been two amateur sociologists, before anyone ever heard of sociology. Though she was no Elizabeth Bennet Miss Papillon had no horror of walking into Alton or getting dirt on her petticoat: 'Yesterday', Jane told Cassandra a little later, 'Miss Papillon & I' walked together to call on Dame Garnet. '*I* had a very agreeable walk, & if *she* had not, more shame for her, for I was quite as entertaining as she was.' They found Dame Garnet surrounded by well-behaved and large-eyed children: 'I took her an old Shift & promised her a set of our Linen,' and Eleanor gave her some money or 'left some of her Bank Stock with her'.[10] Jane came to know rather well, too, the yeomanry and some of the poorer tenants or their survivors. She knew Dame Libscombe 'with her deaffy child, as she calls it', and Mary Doe in her '*Pondy house*' and old John Philmore who in his sixties had lost his wife Rachel and scraped along. To Triggs the gamekeeper at the great house, she was to send her love through Cassandra. And so she earned a right to speak of how 'all Chawton would feel' as she came to know this village virtually in its entirety.

One day not long after moving to Chawton, she had visited its great house and met a family staying there. Her brother Edward had leased Chawton Manor in 1808 for a term of five years to a widower named John Charles Middleton, who, rather like Lovelace Bigg-Wither, had arrived at a large estate with dependants. He had six children between five and sixteen, and a sister-in-law in Miss Maria Beckford to help manage them. Maria, who served as his hostess, shared a sense of humour with her cousin William Beckford, who wrote *Vathek* and comic satires. In response to a funny anecdote, Jane soon celebrated Maria's visit to Dr Newnham and his calomel bottle at Alton:

> I've a pain in my head
>   Said the suffering Beckford,
> To her Doctor so dread.
>   Oh! What shall I take for't?
>
> Said this Doctor so dread
>   Whose name it was Newnham
> For this pain in your head
>   Ah! what can you do Ma'am?
>
> Said Miss Beckford, suppose
>   If you think there's no risk,
> I take a good Dose
>   Of calomel brisk.
>
> What a praiseworthy notion
>   Replied Mr. Newnham.
> You shall have such a potion
>   And so will I too Ma'am.[11]

By the time she wrote that in 1810 or early in 1811, she was familiar with merry Miss Beckford and also with her younger niece Charlotte-Maria, and would have seen them in church. At the foot of the great house was the parish church of St Nicholas, with its square belfry and a cross and a weather-cock on the roof. It had been associated with the Knights since 1578, and it silently bore testimony to the delightful power of a Knight woman: Mrs Elizabeth Knight's coffin lay under its chancel with the coffins of her two husbands, William Woodward and Bulstrode Peachey, both of whom had been MPs who had changed their names to Knight when they married her.

From the church one walked up a pretty, sheltered path near elms and oaks to the great house, a fine old Jacobean mansion with gables and elegant windows. Its thick, imposing three-foot walls of flintwork and stone had been stuccoed over early in the century, so the house seemed less appealing then than it does today in its pearly grey appearance. It was large and chilly. One saw squarish wooden pilasters near dark tapestried walls, and a heavy principal staircase dating from 1655 (a date carved in the wainscot of one door). Even the buttery was over twenty feet long. But a troop of young Middletons scampered in one wing 'modernized for comfort', and here Jane became a child herself.

It is very important that we should have an accurate picture of her at just this time and luckily we do, since Cassandra sketched her and Charlotte-Maria wrote two descriptions of her that help to confirm the accuracy of Cassandra's sketch. The descriptions came to light as recently as 1985. Charlotte-Maria Middleton, who later married her cousin Charles Beckford, was in old age not at all pleased by the round-faced, sweet-looking picture of Jane that illustrates the 1870 *Memoir* about the novelist. 'Jane's likeness is hardly what I remember,' Charlotte-Maria writes of that Victorian picture (it is the one engraved by Lizars from an idealized drawing worked up by a Mr Andrews of Maidenhead). No, Jane Austen was rather different: 'There *is* a look, & that is all – I remember her as a tall thin *spare* person, with very high cheek bones, great colour – sparkling Eyes not large but joyous & intelligent, the face by *no means so broad &* plump as represented; perhaps it was taken when very young, but the *Cap looks womanly* – her keen sense of humour I quite remember, it oozed out very much in Mr. Bennett's Style – Altogether I remember we liked her greatly as children from her entering into all Games &c.' And again 'We saw her often,' Charlotte-Maria remembered. 'She was a most kind & enjoyable person *to Children* but somewhat stiff & cold to strangers. She used to sit at Table at Dinner parties without uttering much, probably collecting matter for her charming novels which in those days we knew nothing about – her Sister Cassandra was very lady-like but *very prim*, but my remembrance of Jane is that of her entering into all Children's Games & liking her extremely. – We were often asked to meet her young nephews & nieces [who] were *at Chawton with them.*'[12]

In recalling her childhood, Caroline wrote of her two aunts in a similar vein: 'Of the two,' Caroline says, 'Aunt Jane was by far my favourite – I did not *dislike* Aunt Cassandra – but if my visit had at any time chanced to fall out during *her* absence, I don't think I should have missed her – whereas, *not* to have found Aunt Jane at Chawton, *would* have been a blank indeed.'[13] At just the period of her greatest creativity, Jane Austen was happiest and most fully herself among children. The two nieces who meant most to her were, as formerly, James's daughter Anna, who came on long visits from Steventon, and Edward's eldest daughter Fanny, whom she had last seen in 1809 in Kent and who would stay at Chawton's great house. Both were turning eighteen. They were as funnily different in temper as two young ladies could be, with traits as dramatically opposed as Jane and Elizabeth Bennet's or as Elinor and Marianne Dashwood's.

'Anna has been a most agreeable inmate & I shall miss her very much,' Mrs Austen wrote in a chatty letter of June 1811.[14] Anna was very affectionate, but also outrageous and unpredictable and in Jane's own opinion could be counted on to 'be doing too little or too much'. She cut off her long hair to get attention at a ball, or made a mishmash of romantic affairs, or of course denounced Mary Lloyd at every chance. 'She is quite an Anna with variations,' as Jane told Cassandra, '— but she cannot have reached her last, for that is always the most flourishing and shewy — she is at about the 3rd or 4th which are generally simple and pretty.' To have her at the house was like having a version of Niagara Falls between the kitchen and the garden. Mrs Austen loved the wild exuberance of Anna, who was naive and witty by turns, and Jane herself compared her to Lake Ontario and, happily, to the whole Canadian and American watercourse:

> Her wit descends on foes and friends
> Like famed Niagara's Fall;
> And travellers gaze in wild amaze,
> And listen, one and all.

To define Anna's odd mind, as Jane Austen wrote, is an exercise that all 'America exhausts'.[15] Her judgement is just as thick, black and profound as those dank, dark savannahs of Georgia. Such cheerful and loving exaggerations show that Anna's frankness, energy and confessional talk at Chawton time and again brought the bloom of girlhood into the cottage.

Fanny, in early life, was also confessional, but *her* confessions were precise and cool, and for years they did not have anything even in the faintest degree innocently scandalous about them. We know a good deal about Fanny today partly as a result of the rediscovery of her diaries in the Kent Archives Office: the diaries were used by Lord Brabourne in 1884 in his *Letters of Jane Austen* but 'were never seen by any subsequent biographer'. They point to several interesting facts about Fanny. She was less inventive and clever but more active as a daily writer than her cousin Anna – and the writing chiefly concerns herself. Though let in on the secret of her aunt's authorship she hardly refers to Jane Austen's novels apart from a remark on *Sense and Sensibility* on 28 September 1811 (its publication is unrecorded by Fanny) and some praise of *Pride and Prejudice* at the end of January 1813. Fanny does not mention *Mansfield Park* or *Emma* at all. On the other hand she often refers to Aunt Jane in relation to herself: 'Aunt Jane and I had a delicious morning together,' wrote Fanny. 'Spent the evening with Aunt Jane' or 'Had leeches on for headache. Aunt Jane came and sat with me.' And tirelessly from 1803, when she was ten, until 1857, Fanny wrote to her ex-governess, Miss Dorothy Chapman, and from the age of eleven onwards for the next sixty-eight years she kept up her diaries. From one viewpoint Fanny may be said to have been wrapped up in her own self-importance, her dignity, her calm sense of obligation to her father and to his estate until she married, and wrapped up increasingly after that in her notion of her social position. But from another viewpoint – and this is to see her as nearly as we can through her aunt Jane Austen's eyes – she was a dutiful, observant person who played her role with courage and undeviating loyalty to her father Edward. There was a poignancy about the motherless Fanny, passing from adolescence to maturity as mistress of her widowed father's Godmersham Park. And up to a point she was frank with Aunt Jane and even imaginative, wilful, playful and capricious, putting herself into romantic dilemmas that were not dilemmas because she had not committed her feelings, or opening her heart theoretically so often that she seemed to expose every corner of it, and in the most convincing way braving fate and the future while all the while saving herself for an impeccably proper husband. No doubt she deserved the widower she married after her aunt's death. It is true Fanny later betrayed Jane Austen. But there are betrayals and betrayals. The letter of Fanny's which we have quoted earlier, beginning 'Yes my love it is very true that Aunt Jane from various circumstances was not so *refined* as she ought to have been ...' was a private one, sent to her unmarried younger sister Marianne Knight on 23 August 1869, and it is perhaps a pity that Fanny's words in old age have become famous. While Jane Austen lived, a 'deep affection existed' between herself and her aunt partly because Aunt Jane was eager to love and to admire, and to do her credit Fanny clearly loved as far as she could: she became a student, an acolyte of Jane Austen, a pretty and loyal chameleon. It may be slander to say of a pretty chameleon that it changes colour with amazing facility, since it may in fact cling to one green, strong branch with charming consistency. Cassandra with her level-headed, practical view of the world later told Fanny what Fanny perhaps wished to hear and merited when she said that Jane Austen 'I believe was better known to you than to any human being besides myself'. Cassandra paid just tribute to Fanny's adaptable nature, too, five days after Jane Austen's funeral when in grief she told her, 'There are certainly many points of strong resemblance in your characters; in your intimate acquaintance with each other, and your strong mutual affection, you were counterparts.' Fanny and Aunt Jane were counterparts in being persons of reserve, of extreme privacy, at their best on paper where the private person can create a consistent self, and one is not surprised that, for example, Jane wrote to Fanny over thirty times between 1814 and 1816. (Jane's surviving letters do not suggest the real frequency of her correspondence with her brothers' children.) Furthermore there was a larger matter here – Jane was grateful to Fanny's father for giving Cassandra and Mrs Austen the first home in the country they had had since Steventon. And it would be wrong to imagine Fanny was conscious of falsity in any of the sweet things she said or wrote – or that Jane Austen was in the slightest way duped by an 'insincere' niece. A discerning adult knows that a young person may define and discover herself through her loyalties, and that we all assume roles and act a little. Fanny at eighteen and nineteen was in no easy position in Kent, and her regard for Jane Austen, a strong, optimistic, creative woman, was a rich blessing for her. As for herself, Jane held both of her loving nieces at a slight distance, as all of her existing letters to them show. 'I am greatly pleased with your account of Fanny,' she had told Cassandra in October 1808. 'I found her in the summer just what you describe, almost another Sister, – & could not have supposed that a neice would ever have been so much to me. She is quite after one's own heart; give her my best Love, & tell her that I always think of her with pleasure.' Yet when she noticed how closely and self-consciously her own letters were commented on by Fanny, she was more cautious: 'While she gives happiness to those about her, she is pretty sure of her own,' wrote Jane carefully. 'I am gratified by her having pleasure in what I write – but I wish the knowledge of being exposed to her discerning Criticism, may not hurt my stile, by inducing too great a solicitude. I begin already to weigh my words and sentences more than I did, and am looking about for a sentiment, an illustration or a metaphor in every corner of the room.' She might use a joke to adorn a letter to Kent but there is no evidence that she accepted any of Fanny's 'criticism' of her formal work. That niece heard of a novel in MS only a little before Anna did. At eighteen, Fanny merrily made up a language with her aunt in which the letter p is to be used as funnily as possible, so that a song title was written by Jane as 'Poike pe Parp pin praise pof Prapela'.*[16] But Fanny's request for a letter in the style of Miss Darcy in *Pride and Prejudice* was to be firmly resisted: it made Jane laugh, 'but I cannot pretend to answer it,' she had to say. 'Even had I more time, I should not feel at all sure of the sort of Letter that Miss D would write.' She would not let her talent be trivialized, and while believing in her niece's taste she was reluctant to advise her in love – though charmed by Fanny's delectable little scrawl on the table: 'You are worth your weight in Gold, or even in the new Silver Coinage.' That queer heart seemed at once cold, bizarre and delightful and also so very rational and well controlled that Jane at one point had to tell her never 'to speak ill of your Sense'. But there were contradictions in the sweet little mistress of Godmersham Park that troubled Jane Austen until the final year of her life: 'The most astonishing part of your Character', she told Fanny at last, is 'that with so much Imagination, so much flight of Mind, such unbounded Fancies, you should have such excellent Judgement in what you do!' And very respectfully she adds, 'Religious Principle I fancy must explain it.'[17]

She most surely had not discerned Fanny's cold streak in 1809 and 1810 when *Sense and Sensibility* was readied for the press, and one must not assume that a certain smug, frigid aspect of Fanny after she became Lady Knatchbull was apparent in the young woman. Jane probably did not find Elizabeth's faults in this child, and Fanny's 'Sense' in contrast with Anna's 'madness' and impulsive rash independence offered at least reminders of opposed traits of her own

* 'Strike the Harp in Praise of Bragela.'

Elinor and Marianne. Just as she later felt that 'Religious Principle' accounted for Fanny's judgement, so religion is the basis of Elinor Dashwood's good sense.

Sense and Sensibility leaves some foundations of her artistry exposed, as if we could see ledges of underlying stonework above the grass level round a fine house – and critics have noticed minor faults in the house. The author never revised out of the story traces of her 'Elinor and Marianne' tale, even though her art had matured since the 1790s. We also find hints of the old periodical essays she had read, as in the improbable revelations about the two Elizas by Colonel Brandon, or in Brandon's wooden and undeveloped character, or traces of burlesque and parody of the sentimental school in Marianne Dashwood's speeches and, possibly worst of all, an odd didactic content in the novel's psychologically unconvincing ending. We may wonder that Jane Austen revised the work so long after it was rewritten in 1797 and 1798, but she did not find it easy to expunge faults of her original epistolary story. She *might* not have printed the novel in 1811 but for Henry's enthusiasm – and may not have been satisfied with it then. Yet her novel reveals a strength of her art in her religion: a stoical Christian faith underlies all of Jane Austen's comedies and gives them their moral confidence, a severity and certainty, which in turn allow her comic talent to flourish lightly. C.S.Lewis has written well of this feature of her art, and her contemporaries were well aware of it: 'Miss Austin has the merit', Richard Whately said in January 1821, 'of being evidently a Christian writer: a merit which is much enhanced, both on the score of good taste, and of practical utility, by her religion being not at all obtrusive.'[18] In the Dashwoods' story it is Elinor's religious outlook that Marianne awakens to after her illness. She has had 'the torture of penitence' while entertaining, at last, some 'serious reflection' – and that phrase has religious overtones. 'I wonder', Marianne Dashwood remarks, 'that the very eagerness of my desire to live, to have time for atonement to my God and to you all, did not kill me at once,' and the narrator speaks of her regeneration in religion. Faith is not discussed in Jane Austen's novels because the author felt it too important: it was not to be mixed with jokes, but implicit. Hence her comic work rests on religion without arguing for it.

But this novel does brightly respond to an interesting religious and ethical debate over the philosophy of sentiment. That debate had had its origins in late seventeenth-century latitudinarian preaching, or in such a work as the third Earl of Shaftesbury's *Characteristics of Men, Manners, Opinions, Times* (1711), in which happiness was said to be possible for those who heed promptings of virtue and act on their instinctive benevolence. Morality, in this view, depends on 'heart' and not on 'head', and though Shaftesbury does not deny our rational access to truth he encourages partisans of 'heart'. Indeed, the eighteenth century bred a good many moral sentimentalists. Ethical rationalism was discouraged even by David Hume when he wrote that morality is 'more properly felt than judged of', and when this stress on *feeling* was aided by Adam Smith's theory of sympathy and by Rousseau's later influence as a philosopher of man's natural goodness, the rational access to truth was often denied. Rational moralists opposed the tendency, and a debate was in full swing by the 1790s when novel after novel took up the twin themes of prudence and benevolence, reason and passion, head and heart, or sense and sensibility.[19]

That debate is fun to see – and one might think that many authors were writing Jane Austen's novel before she did. An essay called 'Sense and Sensibility' of the 1790s in the *Lady's Monthly Magazine*, for example, taking an allegorical form beloved by the Mrs Cawleys and Miss Hacketts of the day (or at any rate favoured by magazines read in girls' schools) shows a lady named Sensibility, who trusts in every profession of friendship, 'and every fancied distress of those she thought she loved gave torture to her heart'. Her 'cunning adorer' plays on her susceptibilities and reduces her from a gay, innocent cheerfulness to 'passionate fits of weeping' and a decline of health, before Sense guides her back to reason and happiness. Or again, Mrs Jane West's *A Gossip's Story* (1796) concerns two daughters, the younger of whom, Marianne, shows all the dangers of a very ill-regulated sensibility. Marianne behaves foolishly with her young neighbour Mr Clermont, who rescues her from a runaway horse, before her elder sister guides her back to prudence and self-restraint. Mrs West's *The Advantages of Education* (1793) shows another sensibility heroine in Maria Williams, who believes in her man of feeling, Sir William Milton, until she learns that he has seduced and deserted another young girl. The idea that a feeling heart if not regulated by 'sense' will be taken in by unworthy objects is also shown in Maria Edgeworth's story 'Mademoiselle Panache' (1795), with its calm rational Emma and her warm-hearted, impulsive, sensibility-governed sister Helen who at last sees a need for sense and circumspection in human relationships. Moreover Mrs Inchbald's *Art and Nature* and Fanny Burney's *Camilla* had both created versions of the typical heroine of 1796.[20]

Even before then, Jane had mocked the sensibility debate in *Love and Freindship*. But now in revising her 'Elinor and Marianne' story she accepted that debate's terms. She wrote *Sense and Sensibility* at last musically, with interest in symmetries in her composition and variations on accepted patterns of a very popular story. By not trying to improvise too much she could concentrate on telling a sensibility story through Elinor's consciousness – in which Sense registers Sensibility's ordeal – and so, in showing Elinor's inward struggle, she gave her story an emotional intensity which *Northanger Abbey* lacks. Her second innovation was to give her work strong social implications, starting with social attitudes implicit in the subtle terms of her novel's title. Elinor and Marianne have *varying degrees* of sense and sensibility – and the terms as the author uses them depend on perception and are related in a kind of continuum. To have 'sense' at its best means being able to control one's emotions through observation, reason and moral understanding. To have 'sensibility' means having an accurate perception of other people and their feelings, in social situations, so as to behave appropriately. Yet even Lucy Steele has sense, and Anne Steele sensibility of a kind. Robert Ferrars has 'his own sensibility', and when he marries Lucy, the horrid Fanny Dashwood suffers whole 'agonies of sensibility' (how we feel for her!). Marianne Dashwood really has an 'excess' of sensibility, which is shown to be a mode of self-appreciation that keeps her from understanding anyone. Clearly the meaning of sense or sensibility is determined by its quality, and in the novels she revised at Chawton Jane Austen explores and develops the negative and positive aspects of *sense, sensibility, pride* and *prejudice* through the whole range of her novel structures and the pattern of her characterizations. Despite and partly because of her 'excess' of sensibility, Marianne thoroughly wins the reader – and she is meant to be winning. After all, she and her sister are intelligent young women of feeling and culture who live in a world that is mean, dull, grasping and calculating, hypocritical and indifferent to most innate qualities. This is a young author's view of the modern world – but also it is comically the world

277

of *King Lear* with its vicious or obtuse Gonerils, Regans and Glouces-
ters transformed and made funny by an admirer of Shakespeare burlesques. The *Rejected Addresses* by James and Horatio Smith (the two
'Smiths of the City' with whom Jane Austen was 'much in love')
came too late to affect her story, but its comic verses illustrate a trend
of the Regency in reducing high tragedy to merriment. (We would
not be likely to see these lines in a present-day issue of *Punch*, for
example.) Thus a comic, absurd Lear sings for Jane Austen's 'two
Mr Smiths of the city':

> Dance, Regan, dance with Cordelia and Goneril,
> Down the middle, up again, pousette, and cross . . .
> They tweak my nose, and round it goes, I fear they'll break the ridge
>   of it,
> Or leave it all just like Vauxhall, with only half the bridge of it.[21]

Her own novel opens with a funny version of Goneril's and Regan's
bidding to strip their father of his knights, when Fanny and John
Dashwood face the dilemma of giving any inherited money to poor
Dashwood ladies: '*Let* something be done for them,' says Fanny,
'but *that* something need not be three thousand pounds.' 'Perhaps,
then, it would be better for all parties if the sum were diminished
one half,' says her husband, but Fanny cringes at sparing a hundred
or even fifty pounds for an annuity. 'I believe you are right my love;
it will be better that there should be no annuity,' agrees John Dashwood. 'A present of fifty pounds now and then' will do. 'To be sure
it will,' says Fanny. 'Indeed, to say the truth, I am convinced within
myself that your father had no idea of your giving them any money
at all.'[22]

Sense and Sensibility itself is a bookish novel. Marianne reads books
with such naive passion that she imitates them. She has her author's
family loyalty and enough high-spirited honesty, pluck and moral
edge to defend Elinor against dragons beleaguering them – and is
never slow to take up her lance, as when Mrs Ferrars ignores Elinor's
painted screens, in Harley Street, and fatuously praises the absent
Miss Morton. Marianne is splendid as she says with warmth:

> 'This is admiration of a very particular kind! – what is Miss Morton
> to us? – who knows, or who cares, for her? – it is Elinor of whom
> *we* think and speak.'
> And so saying, she took the screens out of her sister-in-law's hands,

to admire them herself as they ought to be admired.

Mrs. Ferrars looked exceedingly angry, and drawing herself up more stiffly than ever, pronounced in retort this bitter phillippic: 'Miss Morton is Lord Morton's daughter.'[23]

We do not feel as we read that Marianne is wholly selfish with Willoughby, or that she puts the happiness of Mrs Dashwood or Elinor in jeopardy. Exiled from Norland to Barton Cottage and at the mercy of self-contented people – Sir John and Lady Middleton – or confronting those who are purely vicious, Marianne, we feel, has a right to create her happiness if that means flouting social convention, religion, custom, decorum or anything else, and risking herself. Why should she not? The author colludes with her and against Elinor's common sense, and Marianne is not a Jacobin of Paris but a very believable, winning English girl of seventeen. She has 'a life, a spirit, an eagerness which could hardly be seen without delight'. She is further endearing because of the sincerity of her enthusiasms, her genuine fondness for books (she seems to have read more of Mrs Radcliffe than of Cowper), and in her love of music and drawing and her disappointment in Edward Ferrars because he 'has no real taste'. She has her author's dislike of Gilpinesque jargon and indeed of 'jargon of every kind' and perhaps, at seventeen, with such a view of language, might be forgiven for speaking now and then in clichés. 'Sometimes', Marianne tells Edward Ferrars, 'I have kept my feelings to myself, because I could find no language to describe them in but what was worn and hackneyed out of all sense and meaning.'[24] We do not admire her less because she is tactlessly truthful, nor do we feel that Elinor's ability to lie (to save the feelings of vicious people) is a great deal better than Marianne's rash candour. Marianne is one of the most interesting and appealing characters in English fiction. She is also naive and funny. Jane Austen in creating her clearly drew on her own early highspeed reading of books, on memories of her own intelligent impressionability and mistaken judgements of people, when her book-knowledge and enthusiasm must have come into collision with stringencies, disappointments and discoveries in her social and competitive Hampshire. Looking back, laughing at herself and reviewing herself, she found clues for such a portrait: she could not write a 'serious romance', as she later told J.S.Clarke, 'and if it were indispensable for me to keep it up and never relax into laughing at myself or other people, I am sure I should be hung before I had finished the first chapter'.[25] Her letters do not suggest that the process involved in *laughing at myself* was simple, nor is it perhaps ever in life: we do not laugh at and cancel out former selves easily if we have self-respect, or admit that our intendedly honourable conduct has been wrong because it does not work, or does not succeed. The follies of others are most amusing when we understand our own. But it may be very painful to understand our own – and we may regret the circumstances that made them seem follies. There is a poignancy about Marianne that is deep enough to criticize not only society but all adulthood. No young person in fiction, perhaps, has reached maturity less easily. Marianne emerges from books to collide with experience and to be bitterly modified by events, rather as her author was modified by inner isolation, loss, economics, exile and wartime. In terms of the 'heart' debate Marianne is a Shaftesburian who sees no authority higher than the feelings. She would be rude rather than insincere, or would show that virtue is a matter of high-spirited honesty and determination and generosity and daring and a warm heart.

But what if rational affection, self-control and low expectations make for happiness? If the comic spirit 'is always for reason against romantic enthusiasm' Marianne pays a high cost for her independence, egregious neglect of social convention, and determination not to let economic circumstances of Dashwoods interfere with her idea of love. After Willoughby carries her into Barton Cottage on the day of their meeting, she begins to create him. He follows her lead, adopts her tastes, proposes nothing she would not advocate herself. When he leaves Barton she helps to increase her own suffering – and after Elinor and Marianne travel to London with Mrs Jennings, Marianne's agony of impatience and emotional pain are more intensely shown than anything else in Jane Austen. When at the ball she goes to Willoughby and asks, 'Will you not shake hands with me?' society seems condemned, and when she hands over to her sister Willoughby's heartless letter, and 'covering her face with a handkerchief almost screamed in agony', she reduces the rational Elinor to tears. The narrator sympathizes with her immature passion and her temperament, and finally lets her off easily – rather too easily and too quickly since one is far from convinced that Brandon will ever be a satisfying husband for her: 'Marianne could never love by halves; and her whole heart became, in time, as much devoted to her husband as to Willoughby.' What her story deeply illustrates is how society preys on the inexperienced, naive, feeling heart of a genuine person who is physically as well as mentally vulnerable, and very palpably of flesh. She is tall and pretty, 'brown' and 'brilliant', puts her arm round her sister's neck and one cheek close to hers, speaks in a low eager voice, becomes 'dreadfully white', faint and giddy from lack of rest and proper food with her 'aching head, a weakened stomach, and a general nervous faintness', or becomes delirious and falls into a heavy stupor: her almost fatal illness is of body and mind. Her agony has 'affected every feature', and in London has made her sister 'screen her from observation of others' and caused a callous John Dashwood to notice her ruined looks.

Elinor in contrast has an 'exertion' that is nearly martial: she would have been a good Coldstream captain. She is reserved, circumspect, bristling, tactful but also tactical, a creature of will, quiet ferocity, deep feeling and controlled hatred. Her dialogue is priggish at Barton, but incisive in the social mêlée in London. She fends off an encroachment with: 'Did you?' She is fastidiously reflective, always thinking or 'wondering at her own situation' and taking steps to combat a hostile world and save her sister, and it is just this that gives the novel a subtle detective-story aspect as she seeks the truth about Willoughby: 'Elinor was resolved not only upon gaining every new light as to his character which her own observation or the intelligence of others could give her, but likewise upon watching his behaviour to her sister with such zealous attention, as to ascertain what he was and what he meant.'

Through Elinor we feel that Marianne is important: she analyses her sister with Colonel Brandon, or with Edward Ferrars in Marianne's presence. The sisters are symbiotic; as Elinor looks after Marianne, so Marianne gives her something to be moral and sensible about: they make up for deficiencies in each other, and now and again we are surprised to view them nearly as one through the eyes of such a genial observer as Mrs Jennings. Thus to atone for Marianne's rudeness in the coach on the way to London 'Elinor took immediate possession of the post of civility which she had assigned herself, behaved with the greatest attention to Mrs. Jennings, talked with her, laughed with her, and listened to her whenever she could; and Mrs. Jennings on her side treated them both with all possible kindness.'[26] The sisters seem to coalesce in the last clause as they are seen with the utmost good humour by a gross, warm-hearted and loyal friend.

Most of the subordinate characters are deliciously funny because they are seen within value-frames that the narrator establishes for the Dashwood sisters. Feeling, talent, taste and the educated mind are ludicrously lacking in Lady Middleton, who becomes funnier when her very blandness offers Elinor moments of relief. Sir John's good heart and sincerity spring from an amiable, cheery mindlessness. So he can believe for example that 'to be unaffected was all that a pretty girl could want to make her mind as attractive as the person'. Other horrors come in pairs. As Mrs Palmer lacks sense so Mr Palmer lacks all sensibility. Fanny Dashwood finds Lady Middleton one of the 'most charming women' and furthermore 'there was a kind of cold hearted selfishness on both sides, which mutually attracted them; and they sympathised with each other in an insipid propriety of demeanour, and a general want of understanding'. The Miss Steeles, themselves, are foils for the heroines, with the 'vulgar freedom and folly of the eldest' (Anne) and the 'shrewd look' of her calculating, artful and illiterate sister (Lucy). Music, the tones of human talk, noise and silence are so prominent that the novel is nearly a discourse on sound. Marianne plays at a pianoforte to which no one listens, a loud concerto drowns out sound so that Elinor and Lucy can talk, and little Annamaria – scratched by Lady Middleton's pin – screams as loudly as only a girl with so many vowels in her name could. Inarticulateness is the result of society's vapid, corrupt clatter. 'John Dashwood had not much to say for himself that was worth hearing, and his wife had still less' and Mrs Ferrars 'was not a woman of many words; for, unlike people in general, she proportioned them to the number of her ideas'. There can be no light, urbane Henry Tilney here. Hardly anyone except Colonel Brandon talks fluently, and *he* is unexciting and remote – as if he were submitting his statements in writing. Edward Ferrars is often silent and usually dull, or we learn that 'poor Edward muttered something, but what it was, nobody knew, not even himself'. Moreover the atmosphere is closed in, and here news does not penetrate from a larger world (except in one implicit reference to the French Revolution when we learn that the needle books Fanny gives to the Miss Steeles were 'made by some emigrant'). London is claustrophobic, and after incessant bad weather at Barton there is 'heavy and settled rain' and 'continued rain' at Cleveland.

In focus, then, is the extreme narrowness of a young woman's chances in a closed-in society ruled by money, social climbing, hypocrisy and (as the narrator says of Robert Ferrars) 'sterling insignificance' in faces. This novel in 1811 suggests that recent evangelical notions of 'heart' and of the equality of souls have duped us into forgetting the depravity, stupidity, meanness and selfishness of the idle and the wealthy and socially aspiring. Hence this is the darkest of Jane Austen's comedies. The tone of the writing is Elinor's own and the narrator's cynicism is well assimilated in her reflections, as when she considers that Marianne lacks reason and candour 'like half the rest of the world'. Or again when Elinor admits that the vile Lucy Steele is 'a woman superior in person and understanding to half her sex' (hardly a tribute to one quarter of the human race). Or when she takes leave of London as any of us might do, if the Devil were excusing us from the fires of Hell: 'She left no creature behind, from whom it would give her a moment's regret to be divided for ever.' Yet Elinor is not cynical. She offers against social depravity her message of girding up, cunning, observation, right action, sense and integrity. It is no punishment that she in honour has had to conceal the fact that Lucy Steele has been engaged to her own friend Edward Ferrars for four years, since at Barton 'she was stronger alone', as the narrator declares, and she epitomizes the novel's deepest theme: the survival of right feeling through sense's protection. Elinor cannily opposes sentimentalism with a thoroughly Stoic rationalism that reminds us of Dr Johnson or Epictetus. She holds that our impressions delude, that we have no control over others' behaviour and that the main part of our moral duty is to refrain from imprudence and accept cheerfully any loss.

'So calm! so cheerful! – how have you been supported?' Marianne asks her naively on learning of Edward's foolish engagement to Lucy Steele. 'By feeling that I was doing my duty,' replies Elinor. 'I owed it to my family and friends. . . . I am not conscious of having provoked the disappointment by any imprudence of my own, and I have borne it as much as possible without spreading it farther. I acquit Edward of all essential misconduct. I wish him very happy.'[27]

Hence the loss of her lover is not unbearable, and Elinor shows convincingly that she will endure very well if Edward is to marry the artful, ignorant and pretty Lucy. Happiness does not depend on any particular person. That speech shows how close she is to an enlightened female view current in her time: she does not pander to stupid, lazy or rash men, or cringe under circumstances too hard to bear for a portionless woman. Elinor's doctrine of exertion condemns not only the gross Willoughby (though he charms her at their final interview) but the almost equally gross laxity and laziness of her lover Edward. And yet Edward sees the truth of *her* outlook. He explains at last with the philosophic dignity of twenty-four that he had been 'completely idle' in earlier youth: 'I had not even the nominal employment, which belonging to the university would have given me, for I was not entered at Oxford till I was nineteen. I had therefore nothing in the world to do, but to fancy myself in love' with Lucy.[28] James Austen of Oxford's *Loiterer* might have heard the note of his university stories in *that* Oxford man's confession, and the now reformed Edward might well have stepped out of the didactic pages of the Austen brothers' Oxford paper. In every way the severe good sense of Elinor triumphs over laziness, irresponsibility, thoughtlessness in love and the rather confused mind of a decent and good-hearted Oxford graduate. As Marianne began to create Willoughby, so Elinor has perfected Edward.

Yet, powerful as it is, the novel does not make Elinor's good sense very appealing. Her stoicism all along seems duller than Marianne's audacity or Willoughby's rakishness, and few readers are pleased to see Marianne manipulated quickly into Brandon's arms. Still the novel's portraits are intense and darkly funny. The beauty of the writing – even the neat, marshalled symmetries and antitheses of themes and characters – make it just as elegant as a Haydn or Mozart quartet and a delicious pleasure to reread.

It was a good novel to test the public with, and it *had* to appear before the 'heart and head' debate was forgotten. Jane Austen was hopeful for it, even if Henry is right in saying that her 'friends' (meaning her family) had trouble getting her to publish it. In the spring of 1811 she went to London to correct the printed sheets and stayed with Henry at Sloane Street. She had a new bonnet made by a Miss Burton, went with her cousin Mary Cooke to see the Liverpool Museum and Bullock's Natural History Museum at Piccadilly and joined Henry and Eliza at a play.

She also heard of the birth of Mary Gibson's new baby Henry:

'I give you joy of our new nephew,' she wrote to her sister in April, 'and hope if he ever comes to be hanged, it will not be till we are too old to care about it.'

But what of her manuscript? Is she too embroiled with London's shops for *that*?, her sister asked. 'No indeed,' Jane replies, 'I am never too busy to think of *Sense and Sensibility*. I can no more forget it, than a mother can forget her sucking child; & am much obliged to you for your enquiries.'

Her sucking child is at Egerton's printer, but Henry Austen sees to it:

> I have had two sheets to correct, but the last only brings us to W[il-loughby]'s first appearance. Mʳˢ K[night] regrets in the most flattering manner that she must wait *till* May, but I have scarcely a hope of its being out in June. – Henry does not neglect it; he *has* hurried the Printer, & says he will see him again today. – It will not stand still during his absence, it will be sent to Eliza.[29]

'The *Incomes* remain as they were, but I will get them altered if I can,' she added, inasmuch as she had opened her story with an inheritance crime similar to the one her ancestor Elizabeth Weller of Kent had faced: having overlooked his wife and daughters in order to leave his wealth to his son and his four-year-old grandson, Mr Dashwood in his will has not provided for those who were 'most dear to him, and who most needed a provision, by any *division of the estate*, or by any sale of its valuable woods'. Henry Austen may well have told her that she could not open her novel with a 'division of the estate'. One cannot provide for modern daughters by *dividing* an estate (as Lear divides up England) and she later changed the incomes sentence to read: 'by any *charge of the estate*, or any sale of its valuable woods'.[30]

Henry was reasonably astute with her publisher Thomas Egerton of the Military Library, Whitehall, and understood the main options available to an author wishing to publish fiction. A novel, as she learned, could be brought out in several ways. A publisher might buy the copyright outright if he were confident of your success. She used that method when she sold the copyright of *Susan* for too little to Crosby. If a publisher were less confident of your success he might offer to pay all of your costs and share the receipts, and you as author might then receive from a third to two-thirds of the profits – a method that had worked well for Edward Gibbon, who received two-thirds of the takings from his *Decline and Fall of the Roman Empire*. A third method was left when the publisher had reason to doubt your book's success. He might then offer to publish 'on commission', which meant that the author paid all publishing costs, took receipts and paid the publisher a commission for handling the book – and this is how *Sense and Sensibility* was published. Jane Austen happily kept her copyright. Under the Act of 1709 it would last for fourteen years and be renewable for another fourteen if she were still alive. (The Act of 1814 amended this arrangement, so that the author kept the copyright for twenty-eight years or for life, whichever was the longer.)

Since it cost between one and two hundred pounds to produce a fair-sized edition of a two- or three-volume novel, it is likely that Henry advanced her the money to publish. She was 'so persuaded', he said, that the sale would never repay the publication cost that she 'actually made a reserve from her very moderate income to meet the expected loss'. But, says Henry, 'she could scarcely believe what she termed her great good fortune when "Sense and Sensibility" produced a clear profit'.[31] In fact the edition netted her £140, which perhaps made the canny, businesslike Egerton offer her £110 for her next novel, *Pride and Prejudice*. She had hoped for £150 for that, but sold the copyright of *Pride and Prejudice* for just £110, probably to save Henry more trouble. (It may seem an understatement to say Egerton made a good bargain, but then Fanny Burney had got only £30 for *Evelina*, and Goldsmith £60 for *The Vicar of Wakefield*.) Royalty agreements were then unknown and the wholesale booktrade was only beginning in Jane Austen's time. 'Publishing was still in a state of flux, with large and prosperous firms like Constable, Longman and Murray gradually developing out of the combined publisher–booksellers of the eighteenth century,' as J. A. Hodge points out.[32] Perhaps Henry should not have let the *Pride and Prejudice* copyright go for £110, but then a publisher who paid such a price for a copyright might not, after all, clear his expenses until a third or fourth edition, and so he tended to spend money on advertising and publicity, and *that* was in the interest of the author. *Pride and Prejudice*, which Egerton bought outright, was the only one of Jane Austen's books to go into a third edition. Egerton was not a large and prosperous publisher, and it is likely he could not afford more than the minimal formal advertising for *Sense and Sensibility* or *Pride and Prejudice*, but he may have found other ways of 'puffing' her second novel.

She was right in thinking her sucking child would be delayed. It was advertised in the *Star* on 30 October 1811, and then the same newspaper repeated its advertisement on 7 and 27 November. It was also advertised in the *Morning Chronicle* on 31 October and then on 7, 9 and 28 November, the work being described as a 'New Novel', 'Extraordinary Novel!' or 'Interesting Novel', the word 'interesting' having a specialized meaning indicating a love story. The author was identified variously as 'a Lady' and 'Lady —' and finally as 'Lady A—' but of course never as Jane Austen. 'Letter from At. Cass.', Fanny scribbled in this hectic season, 'to beg we would not mention that Aunt Jane wrote Sense and Sensibility.' Just what her novel really looked like when Jane Austen unwrapped her first three volumes may be hard to say, because there were variant bindings. But we must imagine that *Sense and Sensibility* looked cheap and pretty, with cream or grey–green paper spines, little blue–grey paper boards and either pink or white paper labels.

This was the most important moment of the author's life. She was making her first claim on the public's attention and was sure that everyone would notice first that Chapter 22 was wrongly numbered xx.

Yet the world maintained silence. Book prices had been rising in the last century, and in wartime they went up again so that in 1811 they were relatively higher than ever before or since, and at 5 shillings per volume (15 shillings therefore for the three volumes of *Sense and Sensibility*) circulating libraries had to be the main buyers of the 750 or 1,000 copies. Already, in any case, the precious secret of her authorship began to leak. 'Some persons who knew the family slightly', wrote James Edward, 'surmised that the two elder Miss Dashwoods were intended by the author for her sister and herself.' Then at last the *Critical Review* spoke early in the new year to say, with truth, that the majority of novels were trash but that this one had probable incidents and living characters, with the whole 'just long enough to interest without fatiguing'. In Willoughby there were indeed to be seen 'manly beauty, uncommon gracefulness, superior gallantry, and fascinating manners. In short, Marianne and Willoughby are strikingly alike,' it said. In the only other review, the *British Critic* gave the following two paragraphs of praise and liked everything except an 'overcharged' portrait of Sir John Middleton and a confusion it saw in 'the genealogy of the first chapter'. This is what Jane Austen read in its entirety – and in its masculine kindness, boredom and routine condescending praise the *British Critic*'s review of *Sense and Sensibility* in May 1812 gives us a suggestion of what she could expect from her critics:

> We think so favourably of this performance that it is with some reluctance we decline inserting it among our principal articles, but the productions of the press are so continually multiplied, that it requires all our exertions to keep tolerable pace with them.
>
> The object of the work is to represent the effects on the conduct of life, of discreet quiet good sense on the one hand, and an overrefined and excessive susceptibility on the other. The characters are happily delineated and admirably sustained. Two sisters are placed before the reader, similarly circumstanced in point of education and accomplishments, exposed to similar trials, but the one by a sober exertion of prudence and judgement sustains with fortitude, and overcomes with success, what plunges the other into an abyss of vexation, sorrow, and disappointment. An intimate knowledge of life and of the female character is exemplified in the various personages and incidents which are introduced, and nothing can be more happily pourtrayed than the picture of the elder brother, who required by his dying father, to assist his mother and sisters, first, resolves to give the sisters a thousand pounds a-piece, but after a certain deliberation with himself, and dialogue with his *amiable* wife, persuades himself that a little fish and game occasionally sent, will fulfil the real intentions of his father, and satisfy every obligation of duty. Not less excellent is the picture of the young lady of over exquisite sensibility, who falls immediately and violently in love with a male coquet, without listening to the judicious expostulations of her sensible sister, and believing it impossible for man to be fickle, false, and treacherous. We will, however, detain our female friends no longer than to assure them, that they may peruse these volumes not only with satisfaction but with real benefits, for they may learn from them, if they please, many sober and salutary maxims for the conduct of life, exemplified in a very pleasing and entertaining narrative. There is a little perplexity in the genealogy of the first chapter, and the reader is somewhat bewildered among half-sisters, cousins, and so forth; perhaps, too, the good-humoured Baronet, who is never happy but with his house full of people, is rather overcharged, but for these trifling defects there is ample compensation.[33]

Sense and Sensibility was translated into French later, in the year of Waterloo, as *Raison et Sensibilité, ou les deux manières d'aimer, traduit librement de l'anglais, par Mme Isabelle de Montolieu*. And indeed Mrs Henry Austen (or Eliza) had she lived might have been pleased by early French recognition of her cousin. Serialized extracts in French of *Pride and Prejudice* and *Mansfield Park* were to appear in the Swiss periodical *Bibliothèque britannique* in 1813 and 1815, and though none of the Austens earned a penny from these foreign printings all six novels were to appear in French adaptation or translation between 1815 and 1824. In the twentieth century *Sense and Sensibility* has appeared in many tongues, though it has been favoured in Italy. The author might have found the Bologna version *Sensibile Amore* and the third Portuguese one *Razões de Coração* meaning 'Reasons of the Heart' charming, but the greater accuracy of the Finnish translation, at least in its title, *Järki ja tunteet* (which means literally 'sense and sensibility') surely pays her the highest tribute.

Though advertisements seldom got it straight, on her title-page she had announced that the novel was 'By A Lady'. A later reviewer assumed the author was a man, but a female pseudonym or a 'by Jane Austen' would not have asserted female authorship more plainly since men, especially in satirical works, often wrote under female pseudonyms. The word 'author' and not 'authoress' appears at the bottom of her title-page: 'London: PRINTED FOR THE AUTHOR, By C.Roworth, Bell-yard, Temple-bar, AND PUBLISHED BY T. EGERTON, WHITEHALL. 1811'. So she burst on the world.

Those who most liked *Sense and Sensibility* were young or aristocratic – or both. Anna liked it best of her aunt's works, despite her feeling for *Pride and Prejudice* and felt it ranked as 'a composition' only with *Emma*. Lady Bessborough wrote that her friends were 'full of it at Althorp', and Princess Charlotte read it after she had heard that Lady Augusta Paget wrote it. 'I have heard much of "Sence and Sencibility" and shall certainly read that as well as Ld Charlemont's life, with *peculiar interest*,' wrote the Princess on 1 January 1812, just turning fifteen. 'I can only say with respect to the novel that I saw it advertised as being written by Lady A.P[age]t, and that the Duke of York, who was praising it, told me it was written by her.' And three weeks later, '"Sence and Sencibility" I have *just finished* reading; it certainly is interesting, & you feel quite one of the company. I think Maryanne & me are very like in *disposition*, that certainly I am not so good, the same imprudence, &c, however remain very like. I must say it interested me much.'[34]

Mrs Augusta Bramston, however, with a candour so refreshing in a true 'freind' told Jane later that 'she thought S & S. – and P. & P. downright nonsense'; but, as Jane recorded, she 'expected to like M.P. better, & having finished the 1st vol. – flattered herself she had got through the worst'.[35] Like Mrs Bramston some of the public and most reviewers were sick of novels. There was a surfeit of hackwork. 'We are indeed so sickened with this worn out species of composition that we have lost all relish for it,' a critic had written.[36] Looking back one might see plainly that a literary form had culminated in Richardson and Fielding and that novels now were degenerate. Maria Edgeworth and Fanny Burney had hesitated to call their fictions 'novels', and the subtitle of Jane Austen's work, 'A NOVEL', perhaps only tempted fate. Yet a public appetite for realism was increasing and Miss Burney after getting £250 from Payne and Cadell for her *Cecilia* had published *Camilla* by subscription to make all of £3,000. Something was changing. The truth is that in the forty years between *Humphrey Clinker* (1771) and *Sense and Sensibility* the novel *had* been in the doldrums but there was a promise in the air. It took twenty months to dispose of Jane Austen's small edition, but on 3 July 1813 she could at last tell Frank, 'You will be glad to hear that every Copy of S. & S. is sold.'[37]

And indeed two factors – the kindness of two reviews, and a steady little sale of her first novel – filled her with a glee that surfaces now and then in her letters. Her life was being justified, and all of her main effort, her hard work to improve her art, even perhaps her very evident and odd loneliness and sense of isolation in the pleasantest company were being changed or put into perspective by a seeming miracle. People wanted her. They bought her novel and read it. She had *Pride and Prejudice* at hand and *Mansfield Park* underway, very appropriately, it seems, by the time Cassandra at last sketched her as she was. Cassandra had a steady and rational outlook, and her amateur drawing was said to be good. In Wales she had made her rather demure back-view watercolour of Jane Austen, who sits in blue and white with her face hidden by a poke bonnet as if the watercolourist had wished to reveal very little. That picture and her new, facing portrait of her sister, a good portrait on a card of about $4\frac{1}{2}$ by $3\frac{3}{8}$ inches once owned in our century by F.R.Levering, and now in the National Portrait Gallery, are the only likenesses of Jane Austen that can be authenticated. Among other possible pictures of Jane is that painting of a girl of about twelve in a high-waisted gown with 'very poppy eyes and a small mean mouth', once thought to be by Zoffany, which her great-uncle Francis may have asked Ozias Humphry to paint when Jane was in Kent.

Jane is believed to have sat for Cassandra about 1810 or 1811, and around June 1811 there was evidently talk of portraits in her home. In days before daguerreotypes and photos the test of a good likeness was its accuracy, when you had your picture 'taken' by a profilist, an itinerant artist or willing friend or relative. James's wife had just had *her* portrait taken and shown to the Chawtonians: 'My dear Mary,' Mrs Austen begins in June. 'Thank you for the sight of your picture, tho' I cannot say it has afforded me pleasure. The upper part of the face is I think like you & so is the mouth, but the *nose* the feature that always strikes me, is so unlike that it spoils the whole, & moreover he has made you look very cross & sour.'[38] Cassandra in drawing may have risen to a challenge this June. Her sketch, at any rate, shows the woman of about thirty-five whom Charlotte-Maria recalls, a 'tall thin *spare* person' with high cheekbones and good colour and 'sparkling Eyes not large but joyous & intelligent', and a face not plump or rounded.

Jane's auburn curls appear under her cap and her arms are folded. 'Her hair, a darkish brown, curled naturally,' Caroline recalled, '– it was in short curls about her face (for *then* ringlets were *not*). She always wore a cap – Such was the custom with ladies who were not quite young – at least of a morning I never saw her without one.' Living with older women Jane made less of her youth by wearing a cap and could be neat and presentable as soon as she was up. She looks to the left with a defiant, slightly aloof expression, matched by a tone in her letters, in an attitude she had with some neighbours, and if curls dance on her forehead there is a hint of suffering under her eyes and thin brows. A small, turned-down mouth calls attention to her cheek lines and a puffiness under her pupils, which nevertheless look calmly and with a certain sparkle at an upward angle at the world, and far off, high and sharp in their irises, which have the viper's hazel colour.

16

———❦———

The Regency and
Pride and Prejudice

It is all very fine, but not *too* fine.
Jane Austen in 1811

'But I intreat you, dear Lizzy, not to pain me by thinking *that person* to blame, and saying your opinion of him is sunk. . . . Women fancy admiration means more than it does.'
     'And men take care that they should.'
Jane and Elizabeth Bennet in *Pride and Prejudice*

'Heaven and earth! – of what are you thinking? Are the shades of Pemberley to be thus polluted?'
Lady Catherine in *Pride and Prejudice*

The first year of the Regency of HRH the Prince of Wales, 1811.
     Drums! Cymbals! – a military cadence. Crowds wait at the edges of cobblestones or they stand back on raised flagstones of pavements to see. 'Milk-women', as a traveller in London notes, 'with their pails perfectly suspended at the two extremities of a yoke' shaped to fit the shoulders and surrounded with small tin measures of cream, make tinkling noises as they hurry up the crowded side pavements. But most shops are just opening as people gather.
     The Grenadier Guards . . . the Guards, the Guards! . . . They appear in rain or mist in full dress with slanting bayonets and red coats and smart black Africans in the lead, and the pace is brisk and efficient. Drumbeats and clashes fill the air – and the first morning stir in London 'is the drum and military music of the Guards, marching from their barracks to Hyde Park, having at their head three or four negro

giants, striking high, gracefully, and strong, the resounding cymbal'.[1]

They are observed by an enemy of the realm, the Frenchman Louis Simond who travels for reasons of his own in Jane Austen's England. He is not a spy but a canny social observer pleased to watch. London's air, he notices, is filled not only with music but with a heavy disgusting soot. 'You just feel something on your nose, or your cheek, – the finger is applied mechanically, and it fixes into a black patch!'

In 1811 the whole city stretches out horizontally under a cloud of soot north of the Thames with its long fine principal avenues Piccadilly and the Strand, Oxford Street and Holborn uniting near St Paul's and separating into two other large avenues, still east and west, Cornhill and Bishopsgate Street. St Paul's has a naked interior – 'naval trophies hang down from the inside of the dome', as he notices with a Gallic wistfulness. Do the English worship naval gunners? or only Nelson?

Porters, carters and market-women answer civilly if he asks a direction. These English people do not pull off their hats as Parisians would but make a polite motion with a hand or incline the head in parting, and though he has not avoided night-time lanes – or failed to see urban misery – he is impressed by orderliness, decency, civility. Like William Cobbett, Louis Simond is also struck by a certain neatness in Regency England and by the skill and care of the nation's craftsmen. He observes in town the sensible elevated pavements covered with smooth flagstones 'out of reach of carriages, passing swiftly in two lanes, each taking to the left'. Yet London is deeply infected by social distinctions – how elaborate these seem to him to be! – and the mud and waggons and crowds thicken as he walks from a fashionable West End with its green, pretty, contiguous public parks 'like formal wildernesses' towards grimy warehouses of the east, or down to the East India and West India and city docks. How odd that the compass reflects class! – at least in London. A social line of demarcation runs through Soho Square so that 'every minute of longitude *east*', he believes, 'is equal to as many degrees of gentility *minus*, or towards west, *plus*'. Money rules British society – little else does – and yet London is a social engine 'which rivals in utility, in vastness of operation, as well as wisdom of details, the phenomena of nature herself!'[2]

He is puzzled again by a thirst for humour and satire in Britain. 'My countrymen', he notes in despair over the tinted or painted caricatures he sees in print-shops, 'never fail to be represented as diminutive, starved beings.' England wages war on France by cartoon. 'It must be owned, however, that the English do not spare themselves' in their satire. Even their churchmen 'are thus exhibited and hung up to ridicule, often with cleverness and humour and a coarse sort of practical wit'.[3]

That coarse wit and irreverent satire were typical of the London that Jane Austen knew. At a house-party when she was in town to attend to her *Sense and Sensibility* proofsheets she had her fill of loud talk, laughter, coarse wit and some refined music after Eliza had invited eighty people to Sloane Street and sixty-six turned up, with musicians arriving at 7.30 followed by 'lordly company'. To avoid a hot drawing room Jane stayed in a cool connecting passage with her cousins the Cookes where she could hear the music – Wieppart playing his harp, or Miss Davis in blue singing glees. To her surprise, Captain Simpson, who was 'certainly in liquor', told her that Charles was due home on the *Cleopatra*. Later she heard that Wyndham Knatchbull had called her a 'pleasant looking young woman'.

'That', she told Cassandra, 'must do; – one cannot pretend to anything better now – thankful to have it continued a few years longer!' At thirty-five she was pleased to seem 'young' to Mr Knatchbull and grateful for the brevity of his reported remark, too. Kindness need not cost much.

She was glad to have avoided Theophilus Cooke, a man of 'nothing-meaning, harmless, heartless Civility' as she felt.[4] Svelte and harmless, he typified another aspect of new Regency manners – not coarse wit or drunken laughter, which she could pardon, but a cold politeness, a stylish rudeness that did not conceal indifference and had the effect of an icy insult. The rudeness of Darcy was to be so much in fashion that reviewers hardly stressed it, but found him a man of 'easy unconcern and fashionable indifference' or 'family pride'.[5] (Later readers discovered he was no Chesterfieldian gentleman.)

If she was lucky to have *him* in fashion, she knew social manners could easily seem dated, and she might well fear for a novel drafted in the 1790s. What was her new world like – and why was it changing?

The war was being won although her brother Henry worried when the Americans jeopardized the struggle by declaring war on Britain on 18 June 1812, and 'Mr Madison's War' alarmed her. '*His* view,' she wrote to Martha after listening to Henry's gloom, 'and the veiw of those he mixes with, of Politics, is not chearful.' The Americans cannot be conquered, she told Martha. 'We are to make them good Sailors and Soldiers, and gain nothing ourselves. – If we *are* to be ruined it cannot be helped – but I place my hope of better things on a claim to the protection of Heaven, as a Religious Nation, a Nation in spite of much Evil improving in religion, which I cannot believe the Americans to possess.'[6] Her remark on the Americans and religion is political, and, one may note, it is a sign of her good opinion of Martha Lloyd's intelligent interest in public affairs. By overturning the idea that the Church should have a role in a national polity, Jane Austen implies, the Americans after their Revolution had created a secular state which left the individual spiritually unguided. Her Oxford brothers shared this view. In terms of the story about the Scottish infantryman who fought against General Washington and lost his good, Tory principles in America, in James Austen's *Loiterer*, the American ideal of a classless democracy helped few people to honour with *prejudice* and *pride* those social and religious institutions which help and protect the vitality of each person's inward life. That story, we recall, was published in 1789, and indeed the words 'pride' and 'prejudice' had been reiterated in James's paper as signs of a Tory's respect for needful traditions. Even so, *Pride and Prejudice*, rather like the American ideas of the 1780s, was to be concerned with the problem of the individual's freedom within needful traditions and restrictions of society.

As for the war of 1812, which America declared because of the harsh treatment of her ships in pursuance of the blockade of Napoleon's ports and the impressment of sailors, it turned out to be a small irritant for Britain. It gave Frank, for example, new chances. In command of HMS *Elephant* he was sent to cruise off the Azores where he captured the privateer *Swordfish*: and Charles's friend Captain Broke of the *Shannon*, surely, had better luck, though he was wounded, when he killed the Captain of the *Chesapeake* and brought that shattered prize in with fingers of its crew sticking in its timbers. (The timbers, some over thirty feet long and eighteen inches square, were used to rebuild the 'Chesapeake Mill' at Wickham.) When the fleet redeployed part of its strength to the North Atlantic, the enemy's shipping barely moved, and one land raid was hardly opposed. Peace was to settle none of the issues that caused the war, but it ushered in a lasting amity, so that Frank years later was to be entertained at Saratoga in New York, where he complained of the too-bold manners of American women. (Perhaps anyone raised with Jane was unlikely to find the feminine ideal in upstate New York.)

But pride and confidence were only indirect products of naval and military success: the nation could feel proud of its industry. At Birmingham one factory manned by only 300 men was producing 10,000 heavy gun barrels each month, with great steam-powered hammers crushing red-hot iron bars. At Leeds one looked over rows of windows in factories along the River Aire, and saw in the Armley Mills a factory beautiful enough to delight Humphrey Repton. From her naval brothers Jane Austen heard reports of an exotic world – from Scandinavia to North Africa to China – but from Henry, who travelled as far north as Scotland, she gleaned much about her own nation. She took in many details when travelling in the Home Counties, and noted what Henry's business acquaintances talked about. Changes caused by improved farming, better roads, faster communications and the factory revolution were common topics of conversation. England was not becoming one giant factory, but the nation seemed more intently commercial – and the commercial spirit with its tendency to swallow up other human concerns would be one comic theme of *Sanditon*. Jobs, habits of work were changing. Workmen were nearly obsolete at Barclay's Breweries in London – a 'must' for every foreign visitor in Jane Austen's day – where, in one building, 'rakes with chains moved by an invisible power stir to the very bottom an immense mass in boilers 12 feet deep' and 'elevators which nobody touches, carry up to the summit of the building 2500 bushels of malt each day, thence distributed through wooden channels to the different places where the process is carried on'.[7] A machine-filled cask here holds 3,000 barrels equal to a ship of 375 tonnes. Naturally the City worried over England's national debt, up from £136 million in 1776 to almost £1 billion in 1810, and nobody was likely now to amass a sum equal to a large fraction of the nation's gross debt as Mrs Austen's relative Lord Chandos had. But Henry's banking firm had been thriving in the inflationary wartime economy, and not everyone suffered in Hampshire, where the rural population actually fell as men found work in naval dockyards. By August 1812 the price of wheat rose to an all-time high of 155 shillings a quarter. But in January (when *Pride and Prejudice* was published) wheat was unsteady and by the end of 1813 it had plummeted to 75s 10d a quarter – with further price falls ahead – as the prospect of peace and hence of cheap imports of grain from the Continent embittered many farmers and soon created new hardships in Hampshire. It is no coincidence that *Mansfield Park* takes a graver, more worried and conservative view of the land and society than Jane Austen's earlier novels do.

But the industrial revolution, inflation, the war and confidence among entrepreneurs, investors and land-improvers – a swelling band – so far had ruined very little of England's outward appearance.

Nature may be the only check on society's inherent greed, ambition and tastelessness. In Regency England nature was respected by improvers and architects, visible in the neat squares of London with their trees and shrubs enclosed by iron railings and gates, for which each neighbour who paid for the upkeep of the square was issued a key; or again visible in the sedulous attention to landscaped lawns rolled in the spring and mowed once a week with long, sharp scythes with wide blades set obliquely on the handle, 'to lie very flat on the sod'. From the centre of London one could walk easily into the country. Nature everywhere was tended, coddled, criticized, revered and kept in sight. It was sentimentalized no doubt in the popular craze William Gilpin had inspired for the *picturesque* (often gently satirized by Jane Austen) and indeed in his series of essays on picturesque beauty, on the beauties of the River Wye, on the West, on Scotland, or on the *Coasts of Hampshire, Sussex, and Kent* (1804), all with their delicate aquatint illustrations. ('It added, I think,' wrote Gilpin, 'to the beauty of a sketch to stain the paper slightly with reddish, or yellowish tinge.')[8] When Jane Austen had laughed over William Combe's brisk satire of Gilpin in the *Tour of Dr. Syntax in Search of the Picturesque* with Rowlandson's funny drawings, she told Cassandra, 'I have seen nobody in London yet with such a long chin as Dr. Syntax.'[9] And Humphrey Repton and 'Capability' Brown in their ardent, lucrative devotion to landscape improvement were popularly satirized, too, but still a respect for nature often guided the hand of the civic planner, architect or engineer.

Regency style had as its norm a neoclassicism in which decorative elements submitted to line and form. In this respect the over-elaborate symmetry of *Sense and Sensibility* and the simpler, elegant structure of *Pride and Prejudice* are both 'Regency'. In this mode the whole form is prominent, graceful and stylish. Clothes usually followed that principle. Men's tight breeches outlined the human form. Dresses were high-waisted and in pale colours with long straight skirts based on a classical design which did not either distort or over-emphasize the figure. Breasts *had* been forced up – but 'I learnt from

Mrs. Tickars's young lady, to my high amusement,' Jane Austen noted in town, 'that the stays are not made to force the bosom up at all; *that* was a very unbecoming, unnatural fashion.' White was so much in vogue that she was nearly apprehensive over a colour she had once preferred: Miss Hare was to make her a pretty cap of '*white* satin instead of blue', as Jane informed Cassandra. 'It will be white satin and lace, and a little white flower perking out of the left ear, like Harriot Byron's feather' to conjure up *Sir Charles Grandison*. 'My gown is to be trimmed everywhere with white ribbon plaited on somehow or other. She says it will look well. I am not sanguine. They trim with white very much.'[10]

But this normal elegance, this purity of colour and form were not the whole of the Regency mode, and in speaking of dress or any of the arts, fine or practical, one might more accurately refer to 'styles' – and architecture in this light was symptomatic of a tendency in *Pride and Prejudice*. Formerly British architects had often built in a prevailing style of the day, but by 1811 or 1812 their options were almost too many – they might choose either of the staple styles, 'Grecian' or 'Gothic', or even Turkish, Indian, Egyptian, Swiss or Rustic as a model, and patrons might not be content with purity. In one Regency building or its interior many diversities crowded together. Regency Gothic in its domestic form was a pastiche based on a mixture of ecclesiastical kinds, and even the widespread feeling for the picturesque helped to produce irregularity in building plans, informal furnishings and eclecticism in style. Jane Austen's remark about interlarding a variety of things in *Pride and Prejudice* (such as an essay on writing, 'a critique on Walter Scott', a history of Napoleon, or a chapter of specious nonsense) seems a nice little joke on Regency eclectic. And with so many 'styles' jostling together the landed classes seemed to have large sums of money to add to building chaos. So did the Crown, as when Thomas Nash carried from Jane Austen's Bath, or the Bath of the two John Woods, ideas that took shape in plans for a 'Regent's Park' and a 'Regent Street' in town. Nash was able to go ahead because of the reversion in January 1811 of a lease of 552 acres in Marylebone from the Duke of Portland to the Crown and in effect he brought town planning to London. He built terraced houses round the edge of Regent's Park and planned Regent Street along picturesque (not formal) lines 'with deliberate breaks' in its silhouette.[11]

Their classical training saved architects from mistakes or at least made their Turkish and Egyptian mistakes charming – and pluralities of style were in effect publicly legitimized in the Britain of Jane Austen's day. *Pride and Prejudice* with its smart, rather Sheridan-like and dangerously undeveloped early scenes of dialogue and epigram among the Bennets, and its much more subtle later discursive prose for Elizabeth's psychological development, does itself resemble a work of Regency architecture. The artist lived when choice and variety were sanctioned by what one could see, and the fracturedness of a 'made thing' was in tension with a concern for seamless organic form. Not that all was genuine *or* unified that met the eye, and nothing seems more typical of Regency England than its fondness for illusion (not only on the stage or in 'panorama' exhibits but in its very building materials). Was a mauve Turkish minaret prettier because it seemed a fake fake? or did William Atkinson patent his method of forming false ashlar stone from bricks and cement because he enjoyed the obvious falsity of fake stone? Jane Austen dedicated herself to telling lies, and the pleasantness of much in English life depended on the nation's delight in transparent deceit. 'No work of art can be great, but as it deceives,' said Edmund Burke, and transparent lies can be very attractive. Regency things show off a merry, specious integrity, a lovely exuberance, and imply a fine, hungry daring that often seized on the fake, exotic or unlikely to make it glorious, restrained and after all full of fun.[12]

Still the pretty form and smart finish of a thing recommended it, and a classical norm was felt. The face of England was steadily becoming more Greek. If 1806 was the *annus mirabilis* when William Wilkins was building at Cambridge and George Dance brought Greek taste to London with his Ionic porticos, by the time Jane Austen was lopping and cropping *Pride and Prejudice* many country houses, churches, town halls, hospitals, law courts and museums resembled rather staid Greek temples. But at least the typical and favoured building materials of the Regency – stucco and cast-iron (which was moulded and factory-produced) – could be used to adorn with harmony what was Greek and to make it conform further to nature, to the sense of place, and very interestingly to painterly values. Painting may be the age's key art, one feels, just because no other art seems free of its influence – and one is not surprised that Jane Austen learned from pictures. Long before Cassandra painted the watercolour medallions for 'The History of England', amateur works had adorned the walls at Steventon, several of the earliest books Jane read had engravings – even

Goody Two-shoes did – and in these years Henry took her to oil and watercolour showings in London. Scenic paintings by Claude and Poussin had influenced landscape designers and builders, and now pictorial values guided the historical novelist – as in Scott's depiction of his Highlanders, or the panorama of the battle of Preston, in *Waverley* – and helped to guide in a more subtle way Jane Austen's imagination. She uses painterly frames of composition in her novels, privately associates Elizabeth and Jane Bennet with colours and finds Mrs Bingley on a wall at the Spring Gardens exhibit (as we shall see). Her treatment of the Sotherton garden sequence in *Mansfield Park* for example is clearly influenced by contemporary garden engravings.

Watercolours – by 1810 or 1811 – were a province of female artists, though not exclusively so, and two watercolour exhibits were superior to anything in oil that Louis Simond could see in London. 'And to anything, I believe', adds that traveller, 'of the sort in Europe'. It seemed strange to him that native watercolourists 'should choose a mode of painting which has great disadvantages, inferior capabilities, and is less lasting' than oil. 'But this is a female mode of painting', he says; 'the only practical amateurs of the art here are women, therefore artists are to look for encouragement from them'. Watercolours remind one of a fondness for mildness in Regency decoration, for subdued tones and shades and everything smartly unemphatic such as 'rooms of pearl colour', as the magazine *Le Beau Monde* had advised, 'shaded with dark and light lines', or architraves of light satin wood or walls papered in pastel colours 'to imitate cloth'.

Calmness, itself, was an ideal of the age's art, and might be felt in Benjamin West's picture of the death of Nelson – exhibited at Somerset House in 1811 – or in the oval outlines and regular features of watercolour portraits, and 'this calmness extends to the composition of English pictures', says Simond, 'and forms a great contrast with the show and bustle of the French school, called here *flutter*'.[13]

Calmness or an absence of *l'impatiente ardeur* points to something deeper in Regency art too, for this was an age of summation and retrospection in which people were not backward-looking in a morbid sense, but conscious of a heritage of style, wisdom and political moderation under Hanoverian kings. The age did not need to boast or proclaim itself so much as it needed to recollect, combine, explore and further construct. Its politicians were sleepy or inept Tories, but its best writers were calmly assimilating romantic ideas about the individual and his or her possibilities in society. Calmness charmed Jane Austen. She searched for it in a practical way at Chawton – where nieces, nephews, returning naval brothers and their wives or other casual visitors found her out. London seemed to her too busy and rich, though her complaints are not obsessive: 'I must have reached Grafton House by ½ past 11 – , but ... the whole Counter was thronged, & we waited *full* half an hour before we c^d be attended to', she wrote to Cassandra. Or 'I am very snug with the front drawing-room all to myself, & would not say "Thank you" for any companion but you. The quietness of it does me good,' she reports from Henry's house in Sloane Street. 'For *her* sake I was glad to hear of her going', she writes later about Martha Lloyd, 'as I suppose she must have been growing anxious & wanting to be again in scenes of agitation & exertion.'[14] Scenes of agitation she dearly wished to avoid, and allusions in her letters often show her pressing for quietness, oppressed by Anna's noisiness, or finding her home too small, cramped and tiresome or unnerving when full. She could mildly envy Frank when he was sent out of a bustling England to a quieter northern country full of rich historical associations, which were *douceurs* for the mind or for anyone with a mind as alert as Frank's. She had wondered what he would do before he was commissioned to the *Elephant*, and then she heard of his lucky naval mission to Sweden: 'It must be a real enjoyment to you, since you are obliged to leave England,' she wrote when he was in the Baltic. 'You must have great pleasure in it ... – Your Profession has it's douceurs to recompense for some of it's Privations; – to an enquiring and observing Mind like yours, such douceurs must be considerable. – Gustavus-Vasa, & Charles 12th, & Christina, & Linneus – do their Ghosts rise up before you?'[15]

If spectres could arise in the northern sea, Mrs George Austen at Chawton was unlikely to be bemused by any ghost. Her letters show her preoccupied with her spectacles, health and money, and indeed she slyly had to tell Mary Lloyd in June 1811 that she had not yet bought *lamb* in the year for 'tis too dear for me to buy', which encouraged James and Mary to send her a lamb. (Relatives kept the Chawton larder supplied with occasional gifts of meat and fish or a welcome consignment of wine, port or brandy.) But she was fond of the 'poor

King', a living ghost, whose health was so alarming that his nausea, paroxysms, colic and constipation as noticed in the press may have made her wonder when *she* 'would get a better inside', to quote her phrase. King George III was fading. 'The most serious consequences were apprehended,' as the *London Chronicle* noted. 'An inflammation of the bowels, it was supposed, had taken place suddenly. His Majesty continued through the principal part of the night in extreme pain. . . .'[16]

When would he die? Mrs Austen, who knew something about bowels, resolved to buy some black funereal bombazine, a dress material of silk or wool with a twilled or matt surface worn for mourning because of its dull texture, and wear it whether he died or not. It would be 'cheaper now', she told Mary Lloyd, 'than when the poor King is actually dead. If I outlive him, it will answer my purpose & if I do not somebody may mourn for me in it. It will be wanted for one or the other I dare say before the moths have eaten it up.'[17]

Mrs Austen wore her black bombazine for months. She surely had good wear out of it when sewing gloves for Anna or gossiping with Miss Benn, or when tying roses in her garden – because the King lived on, playing his flute or his harpsichord and singing to himself. He had alarmed the Austens before, and their feeling for him helps to explain their attitude to the Prince Regent, and a shift in tone and theme between *Pride and Prejudice* and *Mansfield Park*. Jane Austen was not a weathervane affected by every breeze from Whitehall and we must not suppose that her novels very simply respond to public influences – but the 'Regency' represented an important, continuing shift in the politics and social climate of the nation, and we may notice a healthy retrospective tendency in the public mood when *Pride and Prejudice* was being revised for Egerton. 'The "Regency" seems to have been heard about only here,' she wrote at Southampton as early as January 1809; 'my most political correspondents make no mention of it.'[18] Her 'correspondents' included her brother Henry, who kept abreast of national and international politics, and in these years she was visiting London and reading political satires, Buchanan on India, war treatises and the newspapers. Lately the nation had been in a joyful, grateful mood when it twice celebrated the jubilee of its monarch, and hardly before had the public been made more conscious of the past. The King had taken his throne on 25 October 1760 (when the mother of Cassandra and Jane was a girl of twenty-one), and his fêtes began on the Grand National Jubilee day of 26

October 1809 when sermons lauding his reign were preached, a medal was struck, skyrockets were launched and he was toasted in every hamlet. Claudius Buchanan, whom Jane Austen read, had his laudatory jubilee discourse printed and oxen and sheep were roasted whole at Windsor, to give feasters meat charred to a cinder or other pieces that were nearly raw, and the Guardian Genius of England was sung:

> (Tune – 'God Save the King')
> King George's Fiftieth Year
> Of sceptred greatness cheer,
>   Each loyal heart.
> May the stain'd sword be sheath'd;
> Amity once more breath'd;
> Commerce, with Plenty wreath'd,
>   Sweet Joy impart.[19]

Rejoicings were as fervent at the end of his fiftieth year of reign in October 1810, and for months afterwards anxiety for his health held the public. It was a good time for an author to revise her manuscript of *Pride and Prejudice*, to put herself into moods of her own youth, while being true to the spirit of a work that was readied for the press in the middle 1790s. Jane Austen's novel retains its charm – and aesthetic appeal – because its sophisticated author in 1811 and 1812 perfected what its naive, enthusiastic author had penned at twenty. As England looked back, so Jane Austen saved and revised a work of her past. And anyone with a memory as long as Mrs Austen's could recall the reign's past. The King – whose life was no mystery to the press – had seldom disappointed country Tories.

Yet the Crown's influence was at low ebb when he first met his Privy Council at Carlton House, his mother's residence, after acceding in wartime – then in 1760 a tall, florid and winning man of twenty-two who in his ignorance of politics had wished to create a reign of virtue. Having married by choice (and not for political reasons) a Princess of Mecklenberg-Strelitz who at seventeen spoke no English, he had confronted a wild, changing nightmare of ministries, unlikely coalitions, rancour and cabals and, within seven years, five first ministers whom he hated. Falling ill, he proposed a Regency Bill himself to prevent family 'factions' or to keep the Duke of York out of the succession. But his affability won over diehards, and in Jane Austen's early years he had a good following – and in Lord North a minister whom he trusted.

If the City of London opposed him in war, the King learned from Lord North that the secret of making war is to keep the confidence of those paying for it. He recruited troops, kept public confidence and dispatched to America the largest field army ever sent from Great Britain (and hoped to win the war even after Cornwallis surrendered the bulk of the army at Yorktown). Since he viewed the seat of the war of the American Revolution as the West Indies he took steps to save those islands. Mr Austen, while he lived, as 'principal trustee' of an Antigua plantation perhaps never had lost faith with a government which tried to save West Indian islands from the French – and the King, of course, had had good reason to do so, since in the 1770s Antigua and the other islands had sent thousands of tons of cotton and tobacco and some 100,000 hogsheads of sugar and 11,000 puncheons of rum annually to England, at a value of £4½ million compared with East India imports of £1½ million. A part of the Austens' pleasure in King George III was that he was an economic realist. But he was never a political realist and after the Peace of Paris he had faced new nightmare ministries and the laughter of Charles James Fox who called him 'Satan' and a 'blockhead' and undermined him by striking up an alliance with the debt-ridden Prince of Wales. But the King's personal authority was then increasing in a widespread change of opinion that made his final years a triumph. People heard of him as a pious, stout, ruddy man in a silver wig down to his ear-lobes, rising at six, writing letters in his own hand without a secretary or standing on his feet four or five days a week at St James's from 11 a.m. to 4 or 5 p.m., talking with each person as he moved down a long circular line at his levées. He wearily tried to abdicate. He had little artistic taste and less subtlety of manner – but he perhaps did not forget 'the glory and happiness of these kingdoms' when he gave his own funds to art, literature, music and science, or when he founded the Royal Academy for artists, or entertained and held his own with Dr Johnson, or when he revised in MS some of Dr Burney's judgements of Handel, or when he commissioned the telescope which led Herschel to a theory of galaxies.[20] The Austens at least – in common with many others – would not have said that he ever neglected the poor, who were an inconvenience to their rulers and not a menace. The first duty of government in Jane Austen's England was to preserve order. But the King used constraint and collusion in dealing with London riots, and he seemed truly fond of his yeoman subjects. He issued proclamations on behalf of the poor during food shortages and in his last thirty years became as popular as any monarch since Elizabeth I. If politics depends on theatricality the ruling classes made what was impressive in themselves most visible, and in his case his baffling illnesses and the moral abominations of his children only added to his stature. 'The mass of people look up to his good moral character, and to his age, and to comparison with his sons,' as Lord Bulkeley said in 1809,[21] and nobody would have said that his virtues descended to the sons. The Prince of Wales had committed vicious follies, and after crying by the hour over Mrs Fitzherbert had run up £550,000 in personal debts. Frederick, Duke of York gambled into debt, and William, Duke of Clarence left the Navy to settle at Richmond with his mistress Mrs Jordan, just as Edward, Duke of Kent lived in debt with his mistress Mlle St Laurent. The King had one legitimate grandson after forty years on the throne. Hardly neglecting these faults, the press reported and exaggerated them, as did caricaturists of the day. The Queen, who was ridiculed as a shrew, said that every remark she made on Weymouth's esplanade or Windsor's terrace got into the press and that ladies listened to her only to tattle to the newspapers.

The King's health itself puzzled the public. (His inherited disease of porphyria, then unidentified and unknown, was caused by his body's over-manufacture of its porphyrins or cell pigments so that delirium resulted in the acute stages.) The Cookes, whom Jane Austen saw in London, may have heard intimately of his illness from Miss Burney. In his first relapse the King had struck his page savagely and on another day he took a pillow in bed with him and talked to it as if it were his dead four-year-old son, Octavius, 'who He said was to be new born this day'. He recovered, however, from two more relapses and even in his sixty-eighth year wrote out his official and private correspondence until he became blind. He was seen at last in his light-grey farmer-like Windsor uniform on his terrace, where four people helped him to walk and a band played.

He wore a hat to shade his eyes, and 'a cockade and a gold button and a loop'. Two attendants helped as he felt his way down the steps, and then he linked arms with two royal daughters, and made his way along. 'On passing the band, before ascending the steps on his return to his apartment, his invariable custom was to raise his hat, saying audibly – "Good night! gentlemen; I thank you." '[22]

Then he retreated into a fantasy world, and the Queen stopped seeing him. The Act which made his son Prince Regent on 6 February 1811 was welcomed by some Whigs and Tories alike. Whigs said that the King always had been wholly unfit for the throne, and Tories felt that the quarrels of Whigs had broken his mind. 'For want of terms,' wrote one of his doctors that autumn, 'His Majesty's present state might be call'd Insanity.' The King was 'engaged in imaginary scenery all day' and amused himself 'by arranging offices and appointments for a large company whom His Majesty conceived were standing about him'. For the remainder of Jane Austen's life he was still monarch – but without any royal power, sleeping on a camp-bed and seldom visited by any of his family. 'He imagines', wrote his doctor, 'that he can call from the dead whomsoever he pleases & make them of any age ... and he actually describes the dress, the conduct, and the conversation of different persons.' Except for a gap between delusion and creative brilliance, the blind old man had come to live in a world that has an eerie relationship to the novelist's own.[23]

He had, however, united his kingdom in war, and set lasting examples of morality and good taste. 'The King's Library struck me,' wrote the American minister John Adams in a comment that might apply to the King himself, or to the character he displayed throughout Jane Austen's first thirty-five years. 'In every apartment of the whole house, the same taste, the same judgement, the same elegance, the same simplicity, without the smallest affectation, ostentation, profusion or meanness.'[24] In 1811 the impoverished still died in city streets and women had not only the law but an ethos against them, so that Mary Wollstonecraft might never have lived, but parish registers of the Austens' own county show that much *had* changed in the reign. 'Now buried James White, who was sent from Fulham near London to this Parish, in the height of the small pox', one reads in a parish entry made at Newtown, Hampshire in 1757, – 'he died the next day. This is inserted that it may stand upon record as a monument of inhumanity to future ages.'[25] The sick were less often than before trundled from one parish to die in the rain and be buried at the expense of another in 1811, and if viciousness had become a little more refined or polite, and 'Human Justice' was only what it would be in Charlotte Brontë's *Villette*, or a red-faced, smug woman smoking her black pipe by the fire and seizing 'the poker or hearthbrush' to strike at the weak or throwing out sugar-plums to the strong when necessary, still people *talked* of social justice. Count Rumford, after inventing his stove, devoted himself to the Royal Institution 'with a view to improving the living conditions of daily life'. The evangelicals increased the public's social awareness, and Methodism affected the upper classes. The nation's conscience was evident not only in movements to abolish slavery and the slave-trade but in factory Acts, penal reform, educating the poor and modernizing government. There were of course the profligate rich and their gambling, drinking sons, Regency 'bucks' and others of relaxed morals and easy ways, as well as a great many dull, diligent, frugal people who were saving money and providing most of the nation's capital and beliefs.

Pride and Prejudice is a smart celebration of the reign, and a tribute to Jane Austen's happy security in her family and under a moral, just and exemplary King George III. She had done much to revise it since writing it at twenty and twenty-one as 'First Impressions', but had kept in it her laughter over imbeciles. The imbecilic letters of Mr William Collins point to her early burlesques, and she may even have seen the name 'William Collins' in Steventon's parish register, though she was probably familiar with Arthur Collins's fawning, dedicatory prose in his *Peerage of England* and could have taken her clergyman's name from that source. She kept 'First Impressions' as her title as late as June 1799, or up to a year before Mrs Holford published a four-volume novel under the same title with Minerva Press.

Her new, alliterative title-phrase 'pride and prejudice' had had a lively history ever since Jeremy Taylor had used it in *Liberty of Prophesying* (1647) and again in his *Holy Living* (1650), a book that was perhaps owned by the Revd George Austen and almost certainly known to him.[26] Richardson's collection of *Sentiments* from his novels had indexed 'Pride' and 'Prejudice' with amusing remarks on both, and Gibbon had endorsed 'pride and prejudice' very early in his *Decline and Fall* in 1776. Fanny Burney's use of the same phrase in the fifth volume of *Cecilia* surely caught the public eye, and then in the Austen circle the words 'pride' and 'prejudice' were played on for their Tory values in the story of the Scottish infantryman in James's and Henry's *Loiterer*. Since Oxford undergraduates wrote disputes on two sides of the same question or term, James, Henry and their friends would have been attracted to the ambiguities of such moral terms – and one notes that 'pride' and 'prejudiced' occur in the same smart paragraph of Jane's own *Lady Susan*.

So far the Bennet story had entertained Anna and charmed Martha. Further analysis may reveal dates of Jane Austen's main revisions, but at present we think she reworked her story in 1799 and rewrote it substantially, perhaps, in 1802, and yet she left something to be done in the months before she sold it to Egerton in November 1812. She cut out a quarter of her prose (if her early version was the length of *Evelina*) and perhaps modified her novel-burlesque and attended to her heroine's important psychological development – but she emphasizes the cutting she has done: 'I have lopt & cropt so successfully, however,' she told Cassandra when she saw the novel in print, 'that I imagine it must be rather shorter than S &. S. altogether.' It was about the same length as *Sense and Sensibility* after all, and differed in having a form that was at once elegant and useful and unmarked by excessive antitheses and symmetries. 'I am quite vain enough & well satisfied enough' with *Pride and Prejudice*, she told her sister, though whimsically she felt that her prose style wanted shade or needed to be 'stretched out here & and there' since 'the work is rather too light & bright & sparkling'.[27] These are not faults likely to dishearten any novelist. She had used a simple Cinderella tale very expertly to interpret social confusions and strivings of young women in the reign. Reality may be baffling and elusive and full of ambiguities, but it submits to comedy's order – and comedy here spiritedly arises from a confident, happy young woman's assault on her future. Conduct books and education manuals had advised daughters to heed their mothers, fathers or guardians, but Elizabeth's parents are useless – Mrs Bennet is as puerile as her husband is cynically detached, wry, bitter and only affectionate when it suits his mood or his convenience. Jane Bennet perceives only what is benign, and younger Bennets are ignorant. Thus Elizabeth is her own teacher – and after a static opening, the novel becomes modern, questing and exploratory in showing her own errors and development. Yet she is obliged to develop within a fixed milieu. A conflict between impulse and obligation may be in every psyche, and a young woman's freedom to develop is in any case limited because other people turn out not to be what she believes them to be: Wickhams and Darcys are always conundrums and, scorn or admire them as one will, one must observe, test, understand and reform oneself in order truly to know anyone else. ('Getting to know a man' in this sense may not be much easier for a young woman today than in the

Regency – Lydia is no wiser about herself or her man after sleeping with Wickham.) *Pride and Prejudice* is rooted not so much in the social conventions of its time as it is in the human problem, and what gives it its special edge of meaning is the way in which it heightens social forces, the individual's gaiety and struggle, and the need for self-understanding by making Elizabeth Bennet the heroine of a comedy of manners.

But in the final version this is a much pruned comedy, smacking of the stage. Elizabeth seems to have had no childhood. Nature is nearly excluded – and few novels of country life have had so little rural scenery. Places at first are reduced to names, people, occasions. The prevailing note of comic irony is charged with high glee, as though the novel had been written with panache by an undergraduate and edited by a worldly moralist – and one thinks of Jane Austen listening to play prologues written by young Oxford men, attending Mrs Cawley's at Oxford and going on to a school associated with Oxford, only to come home to listen to Oxford brothers, have her reading prescribed by a fellow of St John's College, and then imitating comic moral satires by Oxford undergraduates and others. The undergraduate panache of *Pride and Prejudice* keeps the movement swift, the narrator's devices realistic but witty. 'Sense' is put in the mouth of Mrs Bennet – the only person fully aware of the bitter dilemma of a family of five unmarried daughters with its modest wealth entailed to a Collins. The law of entail appealed to novelists who needed a portionless heroine – Scott in *Waverley* makes the Baron of Bradwardine uphold the law of entail despite its injury to his daughter and he makes the main plot turn on an entail in *Guy Mannering*. Jane Austen, whose interest in inheritance law we have noticed, did learn as much of the law as she needed to know, but her entail is not entirely clear though her story turns on it: Mr Collins has, it seems, 'an illiterate and miserly father' (Chapter 15) who had quarrelled with Mr Bennet, and Longbourn-house in default of male heirs was settled on young Mr Collins, who, as Mr Bennet tells his daughters, 'when I am dead may turn you all out of this house as soon as he pleases' (Chapter 13). But the Bennets had planned to have a son, who, when of age, could bar the Longbourn entail and make the freehold free of it. It is less clear, though probable, that the original entail document had required use of the surname 'Bennet' (and this, perhaps, is why Mr Bennet and his wife so often mention their surnames and why Lady Catherine with justice can call this family 'upstart'). Born Collins (a paternal relative of Collins senior), Mr Bennet had taken the name Bennet then without scruple – and so in Jane Austen's history the Knights had changed names to qualify for landed inheritances.

Bennet's ill-luck was to have five daughters, and his dilemma is exaggerated in wartime when men are scarce and daughters burdensome, or when his wife's urgent laments have the most point. But the narrator loads everything against his wife for she lacks a sensitive awareness of the rules of human association – *that* makes her obsessive, ridiculous and very funny – and, among the Bennets, it is only Elizabeth who finds that in the delicate encounter of individuals we learn what we need to act rightly. This motif or theme has antecedents in stories James and Henry Austen had published at St John's College, stories clumsier by far in their execution than in their intention. Every movement of Jane Austen's novel is made to occur on a plane where social manners count most – from the stir caused by Mr Bingley's coming to Netherfield Park as an eligible bachelor from the North of England, to Bingley and his sisters appearing at the ball with Darcy, whose rudeness Elizabeth will respond to, and so on through the story. A convenient illness keeps Jane at Netherfield so that Elizabeth can come to her with muddy petticoats to exchange wit with Fitzwilliam Darcy while disliking him enough to fall in love. His first name is less darkly romantic than suggestive of vulnerable traits befitting a comedy of manners – wounded dignity, defensiveness, pride. The author as a girl had married herself to a 'Fitzwilliam' in any case – funnily if not romantically – by jotting in a specimen page of Steventon's Marriage Register (here in italics),

The Banns of Marriage between *Henry Frederick Howard Fitzwilliam* of *London* and *Jane Austen* of *Steventon*,

and married herself to *Arthur William Mortimer* of *Liverpool* too as an afterthought.[28] Her larking about in the register itself suggests that she had, even at twenty, portrayed some perceived aspects of herself in Elizabeth. Both took less kindly than exuberantly to fools, both were inoffensively smug, jokey and high-spirited as well as prejudiced and comforted by the appearance of good sense and worldly realism in their illusions as young women.

'You are too good,' says Elizabeth to her sister as the author might once have told 'the beautifull Cassandra'.

310

There are few people whom I really love, and still fewer of whom I think well. The more I see of the world, the more am I dissatisfied with it; and every day confirms my belief of the inconsistency of all human characters, and of the little dependence that can be placed on the appearance of either merit or sense.[29]

Only a slight overbalance in the last clause betrays a young woman who does not know herself or anyone else, and who will be deceived by Wickham's own appearance of 'merit' and 'sense'. Elizabeth is proud of her robust wit and defiance, and of her judgement as for example that Charlotte Lucas betrays herself in giving her hand to that 'conceited, pompous, narrow-minded, silly man' Mr Collins.

And she is nearly right. The comedy of manners enlarges in importance the tone of even the most trivial acts of social intercourse, linking vulgarity of rudeness with evil, so that in Elizabeth's eyes Wickham is admirable, and Darcy crass, proud, spoiled. Yet the movement of the episodes is always towards character illumination – and this makes the novel riveting. Manners within a social group offer deceptive comfort, exclude or disconcert the outsider and make insiders prone to the errors of their prejudices. Visiting Charlotte and Mr Collins later at Hunsford Parsonage, Elizabeth finds the newlyweds strangely at ease, settled and contented, and then in her chamber feels obliged 'to meditate upon Charlotte's degree of contentment, to understand her address in guiding, and composure in bearing with her husband, and to acknowledge that it was all done very well'.[30]

But Elizabeth is in many ways helped by her own pride and prejudice, as they reinforce her self-respect and boldness and guarantee her continuing development, as when at Rosings she is 'quite equal to the scene' and will not be bullied or overwhelmed by Lady Catherine. The novel is written in Elizabeth's tone, and normal scenic descriptions of fiction may be sacrificed. 'Scenery' is often presented through her own awareness of what it tells her of the fools around her, and hence we see Mr Collins or Lady Catherine partly in and through objects, so that even the scenery at Rosings becomes funny and psychological:

As the weather was fine, they had a pleasant walk of about half a mile across the park. – Every park has its beauty and its prospects; and Elizabeth saw much to be pleased with, though she could not be in such raptures as Mr. Collins expected the scene to inspire, and was but slightly affected by his enumeration of the windows in front

of the house, and his relation of what the glazing altogether had originally cost Sir Lewis De Bourgh. . . .

From the entrance hall, of which Mr. Collins pointed out, with a
rapturous air, the fine proportion and finished ornaments, they followed the servants through an anti-chamber, to the room where Lady
Catherine, her daughter, and Mrs. Jenkinson were sitting. – Her Ladyship, with great condescension, rose to receive them.[31]

Intensely, then, the novel is Elizabeth's, and if prejudice and pride
cause her fall, she falls with their saving graces – perhaps not far
enough since she is protected by the light militia of her wit, good
humour, mild vulgarity and effrontery. She knows neither the pain
nor the humiliation of an Emma. Saved from evil despite her mis-
judgement of Wickham, helped by the Gardiners, quick and accurate
in seeing Darcy's pride, she has been all along more nearly right
than wrong. She *is* surrounded by fools, and by a village of gullible
nonentities, and as fools make for fun and the world is more foolish
than novelists had shown it, she is the reader's flattering representative in a story which of course highlights its own very realistic
romance. Through her relations with Darcy she matures, and a day-
dream-story of a Cinderella making a good match and of the middle
class allying itself with prestige, wealth, ancestry and culture satisfies.

Darcy's visible disgust with a Meryton society lacking in grace,
culture and variety has deeply allied him with her at first. 'Nay,
gentle Romeo, we must have you dance,' Mercutio had said in *Romeo
and Juliet*. Mr Bingley's first words to Darcy echo the Shakespearian
scene: '"Come, Darcy," said he, "I must have you dance. I hate
to see you standing about by yourself in this stupid manner. You
had much better dance."'[32] If Darcy, like Romeo, is a self-obsessed
spectator, and Bingley is like Mercutio the reveller, the author's early
role as a self-conscious Steventon spectator led into the freedom of
the dance is suggested. Courtship and dance are linked in this novel
not only at the outset ('To be fond of dancing was a certain step
towards falling in love') but by remarks and events of the central
romance, and even the structure of country dancing has a bearing
on the story's smart form. Yet dancing flourishes in *Pride and Prejudice*
in a desert, where men are much of the problem, and the main activity
is not dancing but waiting. Women wait in a dull mercenary milieu
which (but for Mr Bennet's cynicism) is full of the cant of truisms
and the blind rationalism of fools. Miss Bingley is no fool – she and

Mrs Hurst talk wittily and observantly with Elizabeth – but the ladies become fools as soon as a man joins them. Thus when the Bingley sisters squeeze out Elizabeth in the narrow shrubbery path at Nether-field, and Darcy politely suggests that they walk in a wider avenue, Elizabeth cries out to all three walkers, 'No, no; stay as you are. – You are charmingly groupd, and appear to uncommon advantage. The picturesque would be spoilt by admitting a fourth. Good bye.' Comically Miss Bingley and Mrs Hurst with Darcy are reduced to *cattle* since Elizabeth alludes to Gilpin's notion of grouping – he had advised that one should unite three cows in a print for the picturesque effect and remove the fourth. The joke is fine – and serious – since it implies that a man's presence reduces women, as rivals, and it is not only Charlotte Lucas who does not 'think highly of either men or matrimony'. When Jane Bennet remarks in privacy that women fancy admiration means more than it does, Elizabeth replies, 'And men take care that they should.' Her exasperation at twenty is just grave enough to cut through the normal cant about men that she hears: 'I am sick of them all,' Elizabeth appeals later to her Aunt Gardiner. 'Stupid men are the only ones worth knowing, after all.'

Elizabeth's own energy and defiance of character respond to Rous-seau's and the popular notion of the pliant, submissive female, but she and her sister, when alone together, discuss only Bingley and Darcy, nothing else, so that the novel seems to sketch a society in which the hegemony of men has deprived most women of thought. Just for this reason Elizabeth in love is especially refreshing. Her dialogues with Darcy are intelligent sexual combats, full of challenge, thrust and hurt. She never countenances resignation – a term favoured by Mr Collins ('Resignation to inevitable evils is the duty of us all') – but insists on movement, encounter, laughter, observation and renewed assault. She attacks so as not to be intimidated, and if she has the impatience of Jane Austen, one must say the vulgarity in her playful assaults is not the author's but is in keeping with Mery-ton's milieu: 'There is a fine old saying,' says Elizabeth, ' "keep your breath to cool your porridge." ' She thinks privately rather than aloud, often talks to herself, and is given much time for her reflections, first in her bristling regard for Darcy, then after she compounds errors of self-assurance in responding to Wickham, Mr Collins, Lady Catherine and Colonel Fitzwilliam and to Darcy's first proposal and letter, and later in her humiliation over her family and her visit to Pemberley.

She is like a novelist in supposing what Darcy 'would probably feel' or how Lady Catherine would react if she, simple Elizabeth of Long-bourn and Meryton, appeared before her as her 'niece': 'What would she have said? – how would she have behaved?' Darcy in contrast is dismissive and abrupt, gravely, philosophically poised, inhibited in talk if not in letter-writing and at times almost a Gothic demon as he filters to us from a distance with his 'most forbidding, disagree-able countenance', £10,000 a year and gnomic talk. He is less of a gentleman than Mr Gardiner, who is in trade but whom he socially accepts despite Gardiner's residence in London's Gracechurch Street near the warehouses of Cheapside. The social class of the moderately genteel Gardiners is an Austen family joke since the proud Leigh Perrots were related to 'Gardiners' and the Kentish Knatchbulls, of fine lineage, had a branch in the city at Gracechurch Street. Both Darcy and his aunt Lady Catherine come alive, however, in their snobbery, but Darcy reaches out of a dark privacy to question the values of his social world as Elizabeth does of hers.

Pemberley is a symbol of what hope, gaiety, persistence and self-knowledge are worth to Elizabeth, and the novel autobiographically becomes a brisk parable about the female and artist in confronting society's overbearing claims, preserving her feeling and sensitivity, and making way in an environment of often dangerous fools. Mery-ton and provincial society are at last lightly damned; Lydia's running off with Wickham is condemned implicitly by the author because neither lover is a person of feeling – neither cares – and when Lydia and Wickham marry (by grace of Darcy) 'all the spiteful old ladies in Meryton lost but little of their spirit' because Lydia's 'misery was considered certain'. Mrs Bennet's relief is fully merited when on hear-ing of Elizabeth's engagement she exclaims, 'Ten thousand a year, and very likely more! 'Tis as good as a Lord! And a special licence. You must and shall be married by a special licence.' But surely the notes on that remark in modern editions of Pride and Prejudice are as inaccurate as Mrs Bennet is since special licences, requiring no banns, could be granted only to peers, peeresses and certain others of title or office and could be issued only by the Archbishop of Canter-bury (not by the bishop) and through Doctors' Commons.[33] Still Mrs Bennet in wishing to thrust her daughter into an exclusive circle has become a fitting, delicious chorus: 'Good gracious! Lord bless me! only think! dear me! ... Three daughters married! Oh, Lord! What

314

will become of me. I shall go distracted.' And she will have further good news: 'We learned', wrote the author's nephew James Edward Austen-Leigh in recalling what his aunt had told him,

> that Kitty Bennet was satisfactorily married to a clergyman near Pemberley, while Mary obtained nothing higher than one of her uncle Philips' clerks, and was content to be considered a star in the society of Meryton.[34]

None of her novels delighted Jane Austen more than *Pride and Prejudice*. Her lopping and cropping reduced some chapters to theatre and epigram, but she had developed her heroine's interior life with great care. She had shown how a person of strong feeling is to survive – and it is this that links *Pride and Prejudice* with her later novels. She had given a rare example of fiction as a highly intelligent form, and though building on precedents of Miss Burney's *Evelina* and *Cecilia* she had used a simplified, believable version of a Burney plot in the service of realism. Her comedy was likely further to please her brother James, who had addressed 'pride' seventeen months before she sold her novel to Egerton. He was anxious about his children. 'Fear', wrote James with grave point – and with his daughter Caroline in mind,

> will sometimes my mind assail,
> Lest the bright bloom of early youth,
> Failing, in generousness & truth,
> Should shrink & vanish from the sight,
> Withered by fashion's chilling blight,
> And we should grieve to see our child,
> By pride misled, by flattery spoiled,
> Selfish, & vain, & full of art,
> A modern Miss, without a heart.[35]

Jane Austen never denied *that* family vision, with its implicit comment on education, and yet she perhaps played upon her brother's humourless poem in having Mr Bennet warn his daughter not to be '*Missish*'. We ought not to be too confident about her sources, but just as there are parallels between James and Mary Austen on the one hand and Mr and Mrs Bennet on the other – not so close, surely, that James and Mary could not laugh over the Bennets – so, perhaps, Mrs Leigh Perrot's voice may be heard in some of her ladyship's phrases such as 'a young woman of inferior birth, of no importance in the world' or 'I am most seriously displeased' or even

'But do not deceive yourself into a belief that I will ever recede.' Whatever she thought of Lady Catherine de Bourgh, however, Jane's Aunt Perrot frankly loved this novel.

Egerton granted five free sets of her three-volumed *Pride and Prejudice*, which was published with the decent anonymity of its predecessor as 'by the Author of "Sense and Sensibility"' in January 1813 and advertised late in the month. She was provoked because Henry in London had sent off two of the first three sets to Edward and Charles, whereas she had wanted them to go to James and Mary at Steventon and to Frank at Portsmouth. Egerton probably did not follow her own divisions of the work into 'volumes' and in any case the second volume looked short. But she was very pleased: 'I want to tell you', she wrote to Cassandra on 29 January, 'that I have got my own darling Child from London.' Evening recitals of the novel at Chawton with a toothless Mrs Austen, who usually fought with her spectacles, reading out Darcy's and Elizabeth's lines in a rapid drone in the presence of Miss Benn who was not told who had written the book and who hardly knew what was going on or why she was being entertained, were not very satisfying – but Miss Benn 'was amused, poor soul! *that* she c.^d not help you know, with two such people to lead the way', Jane wrote to her sister. 'But she really does seem to admire Elizabeth. I must confess that *I* think her as delightful a creature as ever appeared in print, & how I shall be able to tolerate those who do not like *her* at least, I do not know.' Her comments illustrate her high regard for her readers and lack of condescension, and remind one of the strong personal element in her writing and of the warmth and accent and intimacy of her most epigrammatic prose. Readers would have to accept here the typographical errors and abrupt dialogues, lacking a 'said he' or a 'said she', as she advises her sister with an allusion to Scott's *Marmion*, since:

> 'I do not write for such dull Elves
> As have not a great deal of Ingenuity themselves.'[36]

Three critics soon welcomed *Pride and Prejudice* with very pleased yawns of approval, for although bored by novels they could be stirred by talent. Still uncertain of her sex, the *British Critic* in February 1813 thought the work 'very far superior' to most publications of the sort. 'It has a very unexceptionable tendency, the story is well told, the characters remarkably well drawn and supported, and written with great spirit as well as vigour,' it said. 'The story has no great variety,' it admitted before summarizing the plot in ten sentences. The *New Review* also rehearsed her plot.

The *Critical Review*, quite overlooking her jibe at male attitudes in Mr Collins's use of 'my fair cousins', kindly addressed the novelist as 'the fair author' and her public 'our fair readers' – as if Mr Collins graciously had condescended to write this review. The theme of the reviewer is that the author, while writing a lucid, agreeable tale and dotting her i's and crossing her t's, has offered only very suitable moral instruction: 'An excellent lesson may be learned from the elope-ment of Lydia: – the work also shows the folly of letting young girls have their own way, and the danger which they incur in associating with the officers, who may be quartered in or near their residence.' Indeed 'the sentiments, which are dispersed over the work, do great credit to the *sense* and *sensibility* of the authoress. The line she draws between the prudent and the mercenary in matrimonial concerns, may be useful to our fair readers,' concludes the critic. 'Nor is there one character which appears flat, or obtrudes itself upon the notice of the reader with troublesome impertinence.'[37]

The odd fact that most of her reviewers sound like Mr Collins points to a deep, general malaise affecting them. Their lack of wit or relish seems one sign among others in 1813 that the talk, reading, interests and hopes of genteel women are separated from those of men, and also that women are felt to be of less importance intrinsically than often in the eighteenth century. 'Women', notes Louis Simond, 'do not speak much in numerous and mixed company' – since they must not be forward, or seem to share male interests. A man in talk-ing observes a 'restraint necessary before women', and *Pride and Preju-dice* was reviewed with as much restraint as that. It was noticed with few exceptions in the next hundred years as an innocent love story in praise of the *status quo*, despite its heroine's shame over the society that reared her; but it was read even in the author's day. Egerton's first edition of about 1,500 copies was sold out by July, a second edi-tion was published in late October or November, and a third in 1817.

Jane Austen was fearful of notoriety, for again her trusted spies and relations just failed to keep her authorship secret. 'I should like to see Miss Burdett very well,' she admits in London with no special desire to become a literary lion, 'but that I am rather frightened by hearing that she wishes to be introduced to *me*. – If I *am* a wild

Beast, I cannot help it. It is not my own fault.' Warren Hastings sent a letter of praise, and then in Scotland Henry blabbed to wealthy friends. 'The truth is that the Secret has spread so far as to be scarcely the Shadow of a secret now,' she told Frank later. '– People shall pay for their knowledge if I can make them. – Henry heard P. & P. warmly praised in Scotland, by Lady Rob[t] Kerr & another Lady; – & what does he do with the warmth of his Brotherly vanity & Love, but immediately tell them who wrote it! A Thing once set going in that way – one knows how it spreads! – and he, dear Creature, has set it going so much more than once.'[38] More important than Henry's loose tongue was the warmth of his brotherly pride, she felt, but she thanked Frank and Mary for '*superior* kindness' in keeping the secret of her authorship. (Some of Henry's damage was undone later when rumour had it that the clever Lady Boringdon was the author of *Sense and Sensibility* and *Pride and Prejudice*.)

At the risk of multiplying our examples, it is worth looking at the gossip about *Pride and Prejudice* in the months just after it appeared. First it is interesting that the novel appealed to writers who began to sense its luminosity and delight: 'Buy it immediately,' Richard Brinsley Sheridan told a surprised Miss Shirreff at a dinner party, for it 'was one of the cleverest things' that playwright had ever read. The novelist Maria Edgeworth as early as 14 April 1813 heard about it from her friend Pierre Etienne Louis Dumont, the Swiss scholar, who was then in London: '*Pride and Prejudice*', he told her in his rather genial way, '– *j'ai lu celui-ci et il m'a amusé, il y a quelque valeur d'observation dans les caractères et l'idée de rapprocher deux personnes qui avoient une antipathie réciproque étoit un noeud assez ingénieux et qui m'a paru nouveau. La rupture est une scène excellente,*' he advised her. Intrigued perhaps by that report, Miss Edgeworth read it in the next two weeks: 'I am desired not to give any opinion of *Pride and Prejudice*,' she then wrote to her brother Charles on 1 May, 'but to beg you all to get it directly and read it and tell us what [your opinion] is.' On the same day Anne Isabella Milbanke (the future Lady Byron) enthused over the novel, having heard early in the London social season that *Pride and Prejudice* was 'written by a sister of Charlotte Smith's and contains more strength of character than other productions of this kind'; she noted that it had become 'at present the fashionable novel'. Miss Milbanke was not disappointed, although by 1 May she had begun to doubt that the sister of the novelist

Charlotte Smith had written this new work. 'I have finished the Novel called Pride and Prejudice, which I think a very superior work,' Miss Milbanke told her mother that day. 'I really think it is the *most probable* fiction I have ever read' and 'I wish much to know who is the author or *ess* as I am told.' Nine days later the novelist Susan Ferrier was alerted to a work that everybody seemed to be talking about. 'I should like amazingly to see that same "Pride and Prejudice" which everybody dins my ears with,' Miss Ferrier wrote on 10 May – and later showed how impressed she was by using the phrase 'pride and prejudice' three times in her own novel *The Inheritance*. Lady Davy, the wife of the chemist Sir Humphry Davy, could not easily deny what seemed an elegant literary fashion, but, it seems, hoped it might pass: '"Pride and Prejudice" I do not very much like,' she told her friend Sarah Ponsonby on 14 May in a tone of unaffected candour suited to the social set at Llangollen. 'Want of interest is the fault I can least excuse in works of mere amusement, and however natural the picture of vulgar minds and manners is there given, it is unrelieved by the agreeable contrast of more dignified and refined characters occasionally captivating attention. Some power of new character is, however, ably displayed, and Mr. Bennett's indifference is in truth not exaggeration.' And with this judgement Mme de Staël, who in London in 1813 borrowed a copy of *Pride and Prejudice* from her friend Henry Colburn, might have agreed, for she later said that she found one of Jane Austen's works *'vulgaire'*. It may have been fortunate that Jane refused to meet that brilliant woman whose *Corinne* she liked well enough to recommend to poor, deaf Mr Fitzhugh. But the family of Henry Mackenzie, author of the sentimental novel *The Man of Feeling*, really applauded. A comment by his daughter Margaret Mackenzie suggests that *Pride and Prejudice* could be well received by political liberals of the Mackenzie sort: 'Do you ever read novels?' Margaret asked her brother Hugh. 'Because we have been much pleased with one lately – *Pride and Prejudice*. It is published anonymously, but it is said to be by Mrs. Dorset, the renowned authoress of *The Peacock at Home*.' Mary Russell Mitford, who knew who the author was, in writing to Sir William Elford on 31 October 1814 declared Jane's novel 'extremely good', and elaborated her verdict in a letter to Sir William on 20 December. Finally, Henry Austen says that soon after *Pride and Prejudice* appeared a gentleman 'celebrated for his literary attainments' casually asked a friend of the authoress to read it, and added, 'I should like to know who is the author, for it is much too clever to have been written by a woman.'[39]

These valuable contemporary reports at least show that three solemn reviews of *Pride and Prejudice* do not tell the *whole* story of its reception. For a few months it became fashionable and talked about, avidly read by novelists and their families and a topic of gossip and debate that crossed lines of social class and of political feeling. Yet Regency England treated it uneasily as if *'probable* fiction' about a self-reliant woman of intelligence and gaiety who laughs at her betters – and makes the reader laugh at Lady Catherine – was suspect. Still, as its author's most successful work *Pride and Prejudice* was steadily read in its second (1813) and third (1817) editions. Its copyright, expiring in 1841, was retained by Egerton until its purchase by Richard Bentley for his series of Standard Novels in 1832. Bentley's offer of £250 in that year for the copyrights of her five other published works was accepted by Henry Austen on behalf of his sister and himself. Bentley played a shrewd game, however, since on 20 September 1832 he paid Henry and Cassandra only £210, after deducting £40 that he had to pay to Thomas Egerton's heirs for the remainder of the copyright of *Pride and Prejudice*.

This remains her most popular and widely translated novel. Its deepest subject is happiness, and it seems to portray the truth about worldly felicity, as if it were carrying the hope of the eighteenth century with psychological validity into the future. It treats life with a light grace in the nonchalance of a witty, lyric style well attuned to Elizabeth's mind, and it has multiple appeals – one reads it as a convincing love story and finds several of the funniest characters in fiction. It reminds us of society's economic basis (most of us worry not about love, but about money) and just as it attracts philosophers and economists so it appeals to critics in an era of feminism and semiotic theories, post-structuralism and Derrida's deconstruction. Newspapers borrow its phrases, and many people know its opening sentence (or recognize it as the most famous in English fiction). The habit of calling a thank-you letter after a visit a 'Collins' – William Collins writes one with a 'solemnity of gratitude' – began in the nineteenth century. Among myths about the novel Jane Austen is said to have written it at the Rutwell Arms in Derbyshire, and to have modelled Pemberley on Chatsworth three miles away, but there is no evidence that she ever went to Derbyshire, and even Fitzwilliam

Darcy's reputed £10,000 a year could barely have kept up the palace of Chatsworth amidst its 32,000 acres. Possibly Collins's Hunsford and Lady Catherine's Rosings were suggested to her by the estate at Chevening in Kent, which she may have seen, but any inspiration she may have had there remains unknown.

She was in a retrospective mood a few days after her work was published: 'It seemed', she wrote of a walk to Alton on 4 February, 'like an old February come back again.'[40] She had very remarkably saved a novel of her youth by revising it over the years. This spring in London she gaily searched for two of her characters. With an appetite for painting Henry took her to see the ninth exhibition of the Society of Painters in Oil and Water Colours, where she found herself in the Great Room at Spring Gardens, looking at 250 pictures on display. The *cognoscenti* at these times bought their catalogues, talked in whispers, bent their often elegant necks or stood back in monumental poses on polished floors, or opened their fans to show how pained they were to look at such dreadful pictures as they had come to see, and Jane Austen usually felt that viewers were more amusing than pictures. This, as she put it, 'is not thought a good collection'. There were Clennell's *Going to Church*, for the sentimental viewers, and whole rows of Oxford colleges and Welsh scenery by Varley and Pugin, MacKenzie and Cox. Also some Swiss and Scottish views and a farmyard by Hills, ruins and bridges, ploughmen, wrecked ships and moonlit abbeys. Mrs Mulready and Mrs White and Mrs Gouldsmith displayed cottages and landscapes in conventional styles. For eight years the society had stuck to watercolours, but now oils climbed up its walls. Suddenly she was pleased to see 'a small portrait of Mrs. Bingley' – her own Jane Bingley! This work was possibly a miniature by Hüet Villiers who had five of his sweet, mild female portraits on display, but so far it has not been located. Mrs Bingley's portrait 'is excessively like herself', Jane wrote with delight to Cassandra, 'size, shaped face, features and sweetness; there never was a greater likeness. She is dressed in a white gown, with green ornaments, which convinces me of what I had always supposed, that green was a favourite colour with her. I dare say Mrs D. will be in Yellow.'[41]

She had no chance of seeing Mrs Darcy in any painting by Sir Joshua Reynolds, whose work she disliked. She preferred the mildness and literalness of Benjamin West, the King's favourite painter, and felt that West's girlish, vulnerable Christ in the painting of *Christ Rejected by the Elders* was the best portrait of the Saviour. It may be true that she was not a good critic of painting and that she was unduly influenced by the vogue of 'calmness', but she looked for a power of composure that appealed to her imagination. She was not likely to respond to an Ingres or a Reynolds who put so much detail into a face that the painting forced its interpretation on the viewer, and somewhat like Blake with his watercolour of the 'Tyger' she had no patience for overstatement. Mrs Darcy might be in 'Yellow', but her quieter, deep-feeling Jane Bingley she associated with 'green', that psychologically calmer, fresher and cooler colour of the natural world which renews itself. 'I hope Cassy will take care that it is a green one,' she joked later about a carriage that might be sent for her. And when she noticed in July that Samuel Blackall was married at last to a Miss Lewis, she told Cassandra, 'I would wish Miss Lewis to be of a silent turn & rather ignorant, but naturally intelligent & wishing to learn; – fond of cold veal pies, green tea in the afternoon, & a green window blind at night.'[42] Miss Lewis might need coolness to live with that noisy piece of perfection, Jane Austen's early suitor.

Already working on *Mansfield Park* she had lost two women who were dear to her, and such losses usually stiffened her mood and her resolve. When Edward's gracious benefactor Mrs Knight died in October 1812 Edward and his children were obliged to assume the surname Knight. 'I must learn', Jane told Martha, 'to make a better K.' Mrs Knight had been sensible and amusing enough to admire Mary Queen of Scots, a monarch who had only four defenders in the modern world, as Jane Austen once had put it, 'Mr Whitaker, Mrs Lefroy, Mrs Knight & myself' – and the Revd John Whitaker of *Mary Queen of Scots Vindicated* had died in 1805.[43] Queen Mary, it seems, had one living defender left. With a joke or two for Martha or Cassandra, she concealed her grief for Mrs Knight, but Henry Austen seemed to have little grief for his own wife to conceal. His wife Eliza de Feuillide died on 25 April 1813. Eliza was buried in Hampstead under a headstone that lied about her age. 'Henry talks of a drive to Hampstead,' Jane noted. 'His Mind is not a Mind for affliction. He is too Busy, too active, too sanguine.' He had foreseen the event and so it had come as a relief, but more than two months later she noted quietly of the bright, funny Eliza, 'our mourning for her is not over'.

322

17

Godmersham revisited

No banners, cousin, to be 'blown by the night wind of Heaven'. No signs that a 'Scottish monarch sleeps below'.

Fanny Price in *Mansfield Park*

Who shall inherit England?

L. Trilling

In the spring and summer of 1813 a colourful noisy horde of visitors reached Chawton. They did not appear all at once but by carriage or on horseback they came – large, lazy, witty boys with red faces who laughed over the stupidities of Winchester College and demure young ladies who were half-ashamed of their brothers. The boys were dressed very well. They must have looked handsome in tailed riding-coats, double-breasted, with light muslin stocks of mauve or white or yellow wound about the throat and tied in a bulky bow. The visitors probably shouted 'Aunt Jane!' and hugged Mrs Austen nearly to death, if they did not damage her bonnet-strings too. Later they stomped round the pond at the junction and carried fishing tackle to the streams in a cold wet July, or lifted skirts to get past the mud. Miss Beckford and the Middletons had left, and Edward Knight, with his children, came to stay at the great house till mid-September. 'The pleasure to us of having them here is so great,' remarked Jane, 'that if we were not the best creatures in the World we should not deserve it!'[1]

She craved to see the lively Knights. Up at the great house under the elms or under its high ceilings, they made up for the Middletons. She had last seen all the Knights when revising earlier work, and now in the first part of their stay she finished *Mansfield Park*, if her sister's notes are correct. Cassandra wrote one memo on a little card as if to ensure its permanency:

> Mansfield Park
> Begun somewhere
> about Feb^{ry} 1811
> Finished soon
> after June 1813
>
> Persuasion
> Begun Augt 8th 1815
> Finished Augt 6th 1816
>
> Emma
> Begun Jany 21 1814
> Finished March 29
> 1815

That memo was once thought to be in Jane's own hand[2] but the handwriting is the same as in a second, later note – which is initialled 'C.E.A.' and is the most important record of Jane Austen's novel-writing that we have:

> First Impressions begun in Oct. 1796
> Finished in Augt 1797. Published
> afterwards, with alterations & contractions
> under the Title of Pride & Prejudice.
> Sense & Sensibility begun Nov. 1797
> I am sure that something of the
> same story & characters had been
> written earlier & called Elinor & Marianne
> Mansfield Park, begun somewhere
> about Feby 1811 – Finished soon after
> June 1813
> Emma – begun Jany 21st 1814, finished
> March 29th 1815
> Persuasion begun Augt 8th 1815
> finished Augt 6th 1816

on the verso
North-hanger Abbey was written
about the years 98 & 99
C.E.A.[3]

This summer, then, *Mansfield Park* was finished, but Jane did not show it to Henry until March 1814 – or until she perhaps carried the MS into Kent to revise it and read from it aloud for the entertainment of the two elder Knight girls, Fanny and Lizzy. Envy is a good preserver of memory and Marianne recalled that when Aunt Jane came to Kent 'she used to bring the MS of whatever novel she was writing with her, and would shut herself up with my elder sisters in one of the bedrooms to read them aloud. I and the younger ones used to hear peals of laughter through the door, and thought it very hard that we should be shut out.'[4] She was exclusive in recitals at Chawton, too, since Fanny at twenty deserved to be favoured and Lizzy at thirteen took precedence over Marianne at eleven. As for the Knight boys, who were less interested in her writing, Edward had begun at Oxford and her itty Dordy or George had left Winchester and would now join him at St John's. 'Edward, George & Charles are collected already,' she wrote on 3 July, 'and another week brings Henry & William. – It is the custom at Winchester for Georges to come away [early] for fear they should overstudy themselves just at last, I suppose.' She needed her nieces' friendship now that she was being praised for *Pride and Prejudice*: Cassandra was calling it 'brilliant', the Leigh Perrots felt its lovers had 'spoilt them' for anything else and Mrs Austen could not get over her joy in Mr Collins and Lady Catherine. Jane had felt vain and satisfied enough. Believing as Clara Reeve and Fanny Burney did in glory, in excellence, in fiction's possible 'perfection' as a form, she knew and admitted her satisfaction; she had carried her portrayal of the Bennets far towards a high, artful perfection, and her letters suggest it was no easier, now, to reconcile her talent with the notion of being a humble, simple woman, or to be a humble sister and believe a novel displays 'the greatest powers of the mind'. This is one reason why she prized her niece Fanny, shared her bed at Henrietta Street, kept her close, loved and protected her at the theatre and the dentist, for Fanny was constant: Jane was threatened with more than being made into a wild exceptional 'Beast' for the public. What was endangered was her ordinariness in her family, or her status as an obedient daughter and sister: her vanity was not under siege – but Fame would be harsh if it made her into a 'wild Beast' in her brothers' eyes and affected their love as she knew it. She viewed her novels as honest work in return for money, and hoped to be paid very well indeed, and in detesting the notion of personal fame, she avoided being beguiled into slackness or repetition. Each novel she began at Chawton would be fresh, risky, experimental. Her heroines Fanny and Emma would be rather less conventionally pleasing than Catherine or Elizabeth, and would exist in fine, bold innovative structures, and in courting failure and eschewing romance conventions, she could feel she was not giving in to being 'vain and satisfied enough'. The cost she paid for excellence was high since there was a tension between her integrity, and her evident wish not to be separated, isolated, or raised too high by her relatives. Even in Emma, the happiest of her late heroines, there is a quality of *esseulement* or dividedness from easy comradeship and the ready understanding of others, and the late novels have an elegiac strain despite their comedy. Her awareness of her own estranging uniqueness quickened her love for her nieces. She mocked fame this summer in an old joke when she heard that Frank had got a fine pilot for his ship: 'Why are you like Queen Elizabeth?' Jane wrote to him. 'Because you know how to chuse wise Ministers,' she explained, and added lightly: 'Does not this prove you as great a Captain as she was a Queen?'[5]

Edward's grumbling remarks on his garden, near the great house, were a pleasing sign that he might soon revisit Chawton, and meanwhile he had invited her to Kent. In September she and Edward and the three elder girls set out to town. Henry, after his wife's death, was living above his bank at No. 10 Henrietta Street near the fruit and vegetable market at Covent Garden. He had a tall narrow house with a view from a second-floor room where Jane and Fanny shared 'poor Eliza's bed', and as an acrobat with money he had become Receiver General for Taxes in Oxfordshire – while Mme Bigeon and Mme Perigord kept him from starving. No sooner were Jane and the girls greeted on their arrival than they sat down to 'soup, fish, bouillée, partridges, and an apple tart', all Mme Bigeon's doing.

Henry planned to amuse them for two nights in town. On the first night he took them to a friend's box near the stage in the middle of Samuel Beazley's *Five Hours at Brighton*, a play none the worse

326

for their missing Act One, though as *The Boarding House* it later charmed Charles Dickens. 'Rather less flat and trumpery', Jane said of musical skits that followed. She was a good judge of theatre. When bored by Eliza O'Neill in Garrick's version of *Isabella*, she had to admit that Miss O'Neill 'hugs Mr Younge delightfully' and of course she enjoyed a Don Juan for his 'cruelty and lust' as much as anything. A tradition of theatricals in her family had prepared her well, and Mrs Austen's cousin Cassandra Leigh at twenty-two had thought nothing of going unchaperoned with a friend to see *The Jealous Wife* and *Farce of the Honest Yorkshireman*. But sex and bawdy are not *always* dramatic, and the theatre was 'in low ebb' as Jane said – though it was showy and noisy and plentiful. Scenery consisted of flats wheeled in or dropped from the ceiling, lighting was provided by feebly flickering candles and oil lamps, the costumes were bizarre, and an actor's or actress's size or debility made no difference. Mrs Jordan wore tight breeches for young parts when 'fat and forty' and Mrs Pritchard's spirit lived on. Over fifty, at rehearsal, when she read through the part of a young heroine, Mrs Pritchard had refused to have her heroine's age raised from sixteen to twenty-three. She beamed through her spectacles and said, 'I think you will find it all right in the theatre,' and sixteen her age remained on stage.[6]

Also, the few good plays were quickly sold out. Jane had to wait till winter to see Edmund Kean in *The Merchant of Venice* with Fanny, and felt lucky then: 'Shylock, a good play for Fanny – she cannot be too much affected, I think.' As the best living tragedian Kean lately had taken the town by storm, and Jane Austen judged him well: 'It appeared to me', she reported, 'as if there were no fault in him anywhere; and in his scene with Tubal there was exquisite acting.' One evening in that same period of theatre-going she met and sat near a grand, dignified Major-General Chowne, who had changed his name from Tilson. He was a brother of Henry's banking partner, and had conveyed one of Mary Gibson's letters to Frank. Jane was amused because she had seen him earlier in an amateur showing of Mrs Inchbald's *Lovers' Vows*, when he played a youthful Frederick. 'He has not much remains of Frederick,' she told Cassandra, but 'I was ready to laugh at the remembrance.' By then she had already used Mrs Inchbald's play in *Mansfield Park*. She could hardly see a play without thinking of the players, and a performance made her think reflexively and self-consciously. Indeed she caught herself in a self-conscious joke this season while reporting on her playgoing to Cassandra: 'I am going to write nothing but short sentences. There shall be two full stops in every line,' she writes at Henry's house. 'This house looks very nice. ... I talked to Henry at the play last night.'[7] She gave up short sentences, but one finds in her self-consciousness a source of her power in writing about a play's effects on its actors in *Mansfield Park*.

Lizzy and Marianne had *one* bad hour. Since their teeth worried Edward, they went bravely with Jane to the dentist where Mr Spence did his worst with file and pliers, filling Lizzy's teeth and pulling two of Marianne's. It was *too* much when he found something wrong with Fanny's 'pretty teeth' – but next morning Jane and her nieces were with relief on the road to Kent.

She had not seen Edward's house in four years. There would be improvements at Godmersham, and much unchanged too in the pretty houses in their valley between steep hills, with the church of St Lawrence the Martyr in the village. Crossing the Stour, they rolled under tall trees near a lovely green expanse rising up to the Pilgrim's Way. Usually at Godmersham she was shown from room to room, and now the younger Knights had come on from Chawton and she could take delight, too, in Anne Sharp the governess: 'Oh! I have had more of such sweet flattery from Miss Sharp!' Later about *Mansfield Park*, Miss Sharp would be charming: 'I think it excellent,' she brightly told Jane, 'and of its good sense and moral tendency there can be no doubt. Your characters are drawn to the Life – so *very, very* natural & just – but as you beg me to be perfectly honest, I must confess I prefer P & P.' So warm a friend deserved a good husband, and a candidate eventually turned up in Sir William Pilkington: 'I do so want him to marry her,' Jane admitted later. 'Oh, Sir Wm.! Sir Wm.! how I will love you if you will love Miss Sharp!'[8]

'Let me shake off vulgar cares,' she wrote a week after her arrival, 'and conform to the happy indifference of East Kent wealth.' Elizabeth while she lived had shown style in her south drawing room, and Jane sat near ladderback chairs and mahogany pieces and counted 'five Tables, Eight & twenty chairs & two fires'. Johncock the butler solemnly brought her meals, and failed to twitch when she laughed aloud. The hall chamber and its adjoining yellow room were comfortable and in the library where she and Fanny spent evenings she might read or sew: 'Aunt Jane would sit quietly working,' Marianne recalls, 'saying nothing for a good while, and then would suddenly burst out laughing, jump up and run across the room to a table where pens and paper were lying, write something down, and then come back to the fire and go on quietly working as before.'[9] Luckily a billiard room drew the men. One evening Jane and Fanny recited from a book on Modern Europe, and got through twenty-five pages.

Elizabeth had her books here. She had put her name in *Wareham Priory*, a sentimental romance 'by the Widow of an Officer' to which Deedes and Cages subscribed.[10] She had also acquired a six-volume work called *Female Biography* by the radical Mary Hays, whose novel *The Memoirs of Emma Courtney* was denounced for approving sexual licence for women. Three years before she died, Elizabeth interestingly had signed the work of a London radical and the date 'Decbr 27th 1805'.[11]

No one would have accused *her* of being provincial, and Edward had turned into a gentle widower. He disliked hunting, but would ride out visiting his estates 'with a little roll' behind his saddle to stay simply over-night. As a magistrate and High Sheriff, he took Jane one day to a gaol in Canterbury where she felt its sadness: 'I was gratified – & went through all the feelings which People must go through – I think in visiting such a Building.' She could not doubt Edward's kindness. A timid man, he passed along his horror of politics to his sons and one of them said later that Knights showed their teeth 'without being prepared to bite'. Yet Edward Knight, with his fleshy chin, vulnerable look and egg-shaped head and mild eyes, readily gave in to his sons' whims after Elizabeth's death, as Jane felt, and her sister agreed. Cassandra explained the problem at Godmersham Park in a letter of 1812 to Phila Walter, who had married a gouty Mr Whitaker in Kent: 'I hope those young people will not have so much happiness in their youth as to unfit them for the rubs,' Cassandra told Phila. 'But with so indulgent a Father and so liberal a stile of living I am aware there must be some danger of it.'[12]

Young Edward and George enjoyed every luxury, and Jane was annoyed by their father and remarked on his 'nerves'. His sons at home were spoiled: 'I wrote of my nephews with a little bitterness,' she noted at Godmersham this October. George and Edward took the sacrament in chapel – but now 'these two Boys who are out with the Foxhounds will come home & disgust me again by some habit of Luxury'. The boys' visitors seemed crass, casual, conceited

– and she hated a place where sympathy had no time to form: 'there is a constant succession of small events, somebody is always going or coming'. The harmless Knatchbulls, for example, left behind one evening their Wadham of nineteen 'in our arms', as she wrote to Chawton. 'I wish you had seen Fanny and me running backwards and forwards with his Breeches' after he got into the wrong room. But he proved a nullity with nothing to like or dislike in him, since he shot with others in the morning fields and wouldn't talk. John Plumtre, who liked Fanny, was hardly better, and as for the Tyldens one evening at Milsted, they had backgammon for Fanny and 'engravings of the Colleges at Cambridge for me'.

These elegant banalities once had charmed her. The difference since Elizabeth's death, she felt, was that Knights were deteriorated. She had seen the results of indulgence in 1809 – well before beginning to write her darkly comic *Mansfield Park* – and believed her own flesh and blood, Dordy and Edward, were very clearly in danger. They had little moral education despite Winchester and Oxford, and the very idea of giving a simple feast for *friends* dismayed them. Their mother had irked her, but then Elizabeth had been accommodating, polite and amenable by training – and now a gap of social class had widened between Hampshire and Kent. Nettled by titled visitors Jane was dry and caustic because Frank's simple wife Mary, at Deal, had not been invited to the Park: 'I should like to have Mrs. F.A. & her children here for a week – but not a syllable of that nature is ever breathed,' she told Cassandra. After meeting Lady Fagg and her five daughters 'I never saw so plain a family, five sisters so very plain!' wrote Jane. 'It was stupidish; Fanny did her part very well, but there was a lack of Talk altogether.'[13]

What had been concerning her was that Godmersham Park had to depend on talk and manners for the happiness and continuance of Edward's family. 'Manners are of more importance than laws,' said Edmund Burke, and she would deeply have agreed: 'manners are what vex or soothe, corrupt or purify, exalt or debase, barbarise or refine us,' and the ruling class's concern for grace and charm perhaps had not been frivolous. The structure of society depended on that class's amenity and sensitivity, but in the Regency period when she wrote *Mansfield Park* a great deal had been changing as new wealth, casualness and city morals struck at privacy and civilized intimacy, which she felt were the only means of our ever learning enough to be kind, just, amenable and happy. To be in Godmersham's Pagoda for an hour with Fanny was to be safe from what she abhorred, but she could not avoid the shallow, stupid, mute heartlessness of the Lady Faggs she met. 'It is the habits of wealth that I fear,' she has her future clergyman Edmund say in *Mansfield Park*. In a Protestant attention to conscience and inwardness, however, she found some medicine for an 'indulgent' Edward Knight. Jane liked the new local clergyman, Mr Sherer, who preached 'from the heart'.

When Charles, her naval brother, arrived in October she felt better. Living on his guardship *Namur* at the Nore (where Sir Thomas Williams was now commander-in-chief) he had brought his family earlier to Chawton where his four-year-old Cassy had misbehaved. His wife Fanny Palmer had admitted the girl was 'riotous and unmanageable' but Charles indulged her and so did Aunt Cassandra. Jane had not been won. Now Charles and his family arrived at 7 p.m. in the middle of dessert, and Jane and Fanny Knight ran into the large, solemn hall for a storm of kisses – though little Cassy delayed her wet kiss until the library. Next day Jane sat at breakfast watching them – Fanny Palmer 'looking as neat & white this morning as possible, & dear Charles all affectionate, placid, chearful good humour'. Charles's blonde wife was a daughter of John Palmer, Bermuda's Attorney-General, who had enforced an unconstitutional law against the Methodists and gaoled people for carrying prayer-books: he was a truculent man at Bermuda who had once claimed that the Methodists caused 'the rebellion in America, the revolution in France, and the disturbances in Ireland'. But his harshness – or nearly insane fanaticism – had not descended to his pink, modest, cheerful daughter Fanny. Jane drew on some aspects of her for Mrs Croft in *Persuasion*, and admired her unfussiness and gallant good sense: 'You well know the uncertainty of Naval people,' Fanny wrote a little later, '& that their private arrangements must yield to public duty; indeed I find there is little use in planning. . . .' She had only a few months more to live (before dying in childbirth in September 1814), and had never known a warship designed for health or comfort. Yet Fanny had made her quarters snug. She raised three children aboard ship and took what joy she could in making 'tidy little Spencers', feeding pigeons and reading in the ship's library and – to her special pleasure – going to a theatre aboard the *Namur*. She loved acting. '[We waited] for *the play* last night,' she wrote aboard ship to her sister Harriet at Keppel Street in November 1813, 'however we were all disappointed for *the Theatre* was not finished, & consequently they were obliged to postpone acting'.[14] In the next month, a young 'mid' named Douglas Jerrold was assigned to Charles's ship. He recalled that he owed his start to Captain Austen, 'a relative of the novelist', when he became well known as a humorist, playwright and contributor to *Punch*.

'I think I have just done a good deed,' Jane wrote during her naval brother's visit, '– extracted Charles from his wife and children upstairs, and made him get ready to go out shooting, and not keep Mr. Moore waiting any longer.' Charles was under his wife's thumb, but he was good-hearted and sweet, even if he sometimes addressed ladies as if he were saluting the captain of a flagship. Jane's portraits of William Price in *Mansfield Park* and of her captains in *Persuasion* are original but her sensitivity to Charles enriched them. 'My dear Mary,' Charles could write in his simple, hearty way to Mary Lloyd, 'though we are not violent correspondents . . . I shall never fail of communicating any event of consequence that occurs,' or just as kindly and bluntly, 'I shall be happy if circumstances will admit of my getting a peek at you.' He had a relaxing effect at Godmersham Park, and after he arrived she decided she could fall safely in love with Stephen Lushington, the young MP from Canterbury: 'I am rather in love with him,' Jane wrote home. 'I dare say he is ambitious & Insincere.' He had 'very good teeth',[15] and after Lushington left of course she meant to fall wildly in love again.

She heard some news of real, genuine lovers. A funny, explosive situation had developed when her niece Anna in Hampshire became engaged to Mrs Lefroy's youngest son Ben. Moody and defiant, Ben Lefroy had come back from Merton College at Oxford to court Anna and face Mary Lloyd's wrath. Ben was religious and well connected, but he strongly disliked company and Anna was fond of it, and with 'queerness of temper on his side & much unsteadiness on hers', love was unpromising. Lately the news was worse. Unemployed, Ben had alarmed James by refusing a curacy, and Mary Lloyd had banished Anna to live at Chawton beyond Ben's reach. Mrs Austen thus had Anna, who vowed 'to get home again as soon as possible'. Niagara Falls was in the garden again.

'This will be an excellent time for Ben to pay his visit,' Jane wrote to her sister, 'now that we, the formidables, are absent.' She knew that the front door would yield to Ben since no door keeps lovers apart, but as she said in a letter about Ben, 'Whatever is, is best.' Pope had written '– is right' but in misquoting him Jane touched on the observer's duty. She felt that whatever reality gives is best – best to understand, best for the artist to show too with ironic detachment. Her *Mansfield Park* is a gorgeous comedy in which all the characters are seen ironically, and though its themes deeply concerned her she could take a cool, artistic view of them. She was detached usually from her own petulance at Godmersham: 'How do you like your flounce?' she asks Cassandra and then after commenting on Kentish fashion, 'in short, I do not know and I do not care'. But she did care, this season, about her chance to meet Mrs Anne Lefroy's sister and young Ben's aunt, Mrs Harrison, towards the end of her stay. What could she say to her about Anna and Ben? 'My dear Mrs. Harrison,' she tells Cassandra, 'I shall say, I am afraid the young Man has some of your Family Madness – & though there often appears to be something of Madness in Anna too, I think she inherits more of it from the Mother's family than from ours.'

That meeting went well, since Mrs Harrison was a sociable woman and Jane almost felt she was talking to 'Madam' of Ashe. After *that* interlude, however, next morning the vapid, lifeless daughter of the Earl of Mansfield walked into the high square hall with her daughter. Jane intensely disliked her: 'Yes, they called,' she noted in Kent. 'They came & they sat & they went.'[16]

Mansfield's daughter, Lady Elizabeth Finch-Hatton, had mildly annoyed Jane Austen before. She had seemed limp, with astonishingly little to say for herself even in 1805. She had not changed. Once Jane had the choices in Kent of sitting with the Mansfield grandsons at cards or going to Lady Yates's ball – yet was there anything to choose? Lady Elizabeth's daughter 'says as little as ever, but holds up her head and smiles', she wrote, and one of Mansfield's grandsons seemed no more than a species of stuffing and fabric known as a gentleman: 'I saw him,' Jane wrote with exasperation, 'saw him for ten minutes; sat in the same room with him, heard him talk, saw him bow.'[17] He had to be alive and that was all. But Mansfield, on the other hand, was a name famous for high, honourable courage. As Lord Chief Justice the first Earl of Mansfield had struck at the roots of the African slave-trade when he gave his famous decision that the black man James Somerset could not lawfully be confined in irons aboard a ship in the Thames. Jane herself read a book by Thomas Clarkson on African slavery in which the most villainous figure was named Norris, and in her *Mansfield Park* she would allude to slavery. Also she knew this: the second Earl of Mansfield's daughter in marrying a Finch-Hatton had allied herself to another great Tory family, the family that produced in Anne Finch the Countess of Winchilsea, a leading female poet, and carried talents in diplomacy to Sweden and Russia; it provided one great First Lord of the Admiralty and Queen Anne's Secretary of State. In the name Mansfield and its associations, in short, one might see traditional strengths of the nation's old Tory families – evidence of high and selfless achievement, gaiety and courage, a devotion to moral and intellectual training, and excellence in law, diplomacy, politics, the arts. By 1805 what Jane Austen had seen of *this* family at Godmersham Park was only the smug stupidity of Lady Elizabeth and her offspring.

And still, she did not satirize the names Mansfield or Yates in her novel, although she often chose names that had a relation to her characters and themes. She transferred no one she knew into *Mansfield Park*, but she meant to reflect the failure in Tory families to train their children as responsible inheritors. She saw what had happened when a good, self-disciplined king was succeeded by a fat, fair-haired Prince Regent – and indeed she had read a pathetic letter the Princess of Wales published in the *Morning Chronicle* when her husband accused her of adultery. Lately the first lady in England, after defending herself, was reduced to saying *this*:

> If these ought to be the feelings of every woman in England who is conscious that she deserves no reproach, your Royal Highness has too sound a judgement, and too nice a sense of Honour, not to perceive how much more justly they belong to the Mother of your Daughter – the Mother of her, who is destined, I trust at a very distant period, to reign over the British Empire.[18]

The daughter who might reign over the Empire was Princess Charlotte, the same child who found 'Maryanne & me are very like'. She had read Jane Austen's first novel when cruelly and meanly forbidden to see her mother more than once a week. Jane did not know that the Regent's child was one of her admirers, but she commented on the mother's published letter: 'I suppose all the World is sitting in

Judgement upon the Princess of Wales's letter,' Jane had written. 'Poor woman, I shall support her as long as I can, because she *is* a Woman, & because I hate her Husband.'[19] She hardly had had a better opinion of the Regent in 1811, and adultery in high places is generally reflected in the Crawford–Rushworth affair in her novel. When writing she also had in view the 'indulgence' in Edward's family. But a family dilemma could be comic, and she really uses vital, important themes not to reform society, but chiefly to make something delightful, readable and fun. This is why *Mansfield Park*, though modish, is not ephemeral; she was concerned to write a spirited, convincing, polished and subtle comedy – and her care focused on character, psychology and style. John Henry Newman was reported to have said he 'read through *Mansfield Park*' regularly 'to perfect and preserve' his own style, and in this novel Jane Austen's prose, though not as lyrical as in *Pride and Prejudice*, has its best 'ear'. The narrative voice in its continual, subtle and unobtrusive changes in tone and diction adapts itself to the temper of each character in turn. Fanny Price's viewpoint predominates, and she is rendered not only through *what* is said of her but through tone, rhythm and sound patterns as they influence the sense of a passage:

> She had not supposed before, that any thing could ever suit her like the old grey poney; but her delight in Edmund's mare was far beyond any former pleasure of the sort; and the addition it was ever receiving in the consideration of that kindness from which her pleasure sprung, was beyond all her words to express.[20]

Jane Austen had begun this novel while revisions of previous work were in progress. She had put *Mansfield Park* aside, and resumed it with evident zeal and affection for her heroine. Fanny Price would be an exiled, adopted child at a beautiful estate in Northamptonshire in good hunting country, rather far from the Prices' poor home at Portsmouth. Austens and others were asked for help with details, since she needed to be right about facts. 'I learn from Sir J. Carr that there is no Government House at Gibraltar,' she had told her sister on 24 January 1813, in an allusion to Chapter 24, and also referred then to 'the round table at Mrs Grant's' in Chapter 25. Five days later when reporting on *Pride and Prejudice*, she abruptly switched the topic of a letter to Cassandra – a letter so badly printed in our own time that critics sometimes suppose she meant to say ordination was the subject of her novel. Using a text that changes her capitals and adds an '&' she never wrote, the modern editor of her letter has reported her words this way:

> Now I will try to write of something else, & it shall be a complete change of subject – ordination – I am glad to find your enquiries have ended so well. If you could discover whether Northamptonshire is a country of Hedgerows I should be glad again.[21]

Jane Austen's holograph letter survives, and what she wrote was this:

> Now I will try to write of something else; – it shall be a complete change of subject – Ordination. I am glad to find your enquiries have ended so well. – If you c^d discover whether Northamptonshire is a Country of Hedgerows, I sh^d be glad again.[22]

Her punctuation and capitals make a difference. She only meant to tell her sister that after discussing her last novel she was changing her letter's subject to thank Cassandra for enquiring about clerical ordination at James's rectory; she of course never had said 'ordination' was the subject of *Mansfield Park*. This matter shows, too, that Cassandra was not the only lady at the cottage to help her. 'I am obliged to you,' she tells Martha in February, 'for your enquiries about Northamptonshire, but do not wish you to renew them, as I am sure of getting the intelligence I want from Henry, to whom I can apply at some convenient moment "sans peur et sans reproche".' Her brother Henry was so light, mobile, talkative and engaging, she described Henry Crawford in phrases that are close to those she applies to Henry after Eliza's death. Henry's unpublished letters show his sense of locale. He may have described for her his friend Sir James Langham's Cottesbrook, which resembles Mansfield Park, and she may have taken further hints from Robert Andrew's Harlestone, an estate Humphrey Repton had 'improved' with the help of a storm that had blown down its elms. But all the while the confidence of her work depended on her knowledge of a vivid, verifiable and well-understood milieu at Godmersham Park. In William Price and Admiral Crawford, the Navy also came into her novel. 'I have something', she at last had told Frank on 3 July, 'which I hope on the credit of P. & P. will sell well, tho' not half so entertaining. And by the bye – shall you object to my mentioning the Elephant in it, & two or three other of your old Ships? I *have* done it, but it shall not stay, to make you angry.' HMS *Elephant* had been

Nelson's flagship at Copenhagen, but Frank allowed it to float in her novel with his other ships, and sent her a 'kind hint'.[23]

She could be pleased with *Mansfield Park*. Once she had been content to put family jokes in fiction – but now she had worked in a bright range of comic allusions to England's culture. Readers might grasp or miss the joke of Fanny Price's having the poet Crabbe's *Tales* among her books since the joke depends on our knowing that Fanny Price is the name of Crabbe's own 'meekly firm' heroine in *The Parish Register*. Jane smothered Crabbe in jokes. She pretended to look for him at the theatre when she saw boxes in the crimson velvet of coffins he describes in *Burials*, and she still laughingly wanted to marry him. Her poetry-loving Fanny Price is a tribute to his vivid, etched realism. Crabbe – while showing how the gentry are ever more unsure of their function, how shallow prudery rules England's great houses and how 'improvements' in the countryside only separate the social classes – also uses language to depict states of mind that novelists were neglecting, and so he *earned* Jane's jokes and love. Fanny also adores William Gilpin on the picturesque as she gazes at a transparency of 'Tintern Abbey' on her cold attic window, though she is not a Wordsworthian. Other jokes point to Laurence Sterne, as when Jane has Maria Bertram echo the passage in *A Sentimental Journey* when Sterne's Yorick as a passportless man in wartime France complains, '"I can't get out – I can't get out," said the starling.' Maria says to her willing seducer, Henry Crawford, in the park at Sotherton, 'But unluckily that iron gate, that ha-ha, give me the feeling of restraint and hardship. I cannot get out, as the starling said.' That joke attacks Sterne's Whiggery, but all of *Mansfield Park* on the other hand relies on the precedents of Sterne and other sentimental novelists in using language in new ways to imitate feelings rather than thoughts. Jane Austen replies to Mme de Genlis' tales, too, and makes an amusing point of echoing Mme Cottin's novel, *Amélie Mansfield*, partly because of its title and because in its English translation as *Amelia Mansfield* (1803) it had had a popular vogue in London for about six years.[24]

She lightly mocked Mme Cottin but took special pains to allude to serious female writing. Fanny Price embodies the lesson in Hannah More's *Strictures on the Modern System of Female Education* (1799), for example, that a woman needs studies which avoid display but which

337

'will lead her to think' and will give her courage and judgement 'to reject what is dazzling' and 'to prefer, not what is striking, or bright, or new, but what is just'. With the evangelical movement at its height, Fanny duplicates precepts of other evangelical writers, too, but Hannah More is at the centre of *Mansfield Park*. Jane Austen admired that skilful and vigorous woman who wanted to train the female intellect, though Miss More's popularity made her uneasy: 'I shall be delighted, when I read it, like other people,' she had said of Hannah More's novel *Coelebs in Search of a Wife*, 'but till I do I dislike it.' That novel itself is echoed in *Mansfield Park*: 'I call education, not that which smothers a woman with accomplishments, but that which tends to consolidate,' says Miss More's Charles Coelebs as he sets out on his 'search' for a wife, 'not that which is made up of shreds and patches of useless arts, but that which inculcates principles, polishes taste, regulates temper, cultivates reason . . . habituates to reflection,' and attaches one to God.[25]

Fanny Price in effect subscribes to such an outlook. Yet Jane Austen's rather modish allusions to right-conduct works and especially to Miss More's are among the many devices used to distance Fanny from the narrator – and author. For the subject of *Mansfield Park* is education, or the discipline and training of the feelings; and Fanny is not intended to seem worldly, sparkling, clever, or even forgiving, mature and understanding – her talk is minimal and usually gauche; but in her deep feeling and disciplined conduct and simple gentleness she is a measure of the failure of the training the young Bertrams and Crawfords have had. Limited as Fanny is, she lights up or exposes what is wrong at Mansfield Park. In volume one she is hardly more than a timid, trembling mouse. Never a favourite with Mrs Price at Portsmouth, she is at ten adopted by her wealthy uncle Sir Thomas Bertram in a superficially well-ordered house in Northamptonshire sixty or eighty miles north-west of the capital. She is shuddering, aggrieved and passive after her cousin Edmund consolingly helps her to write to her naval brother William. Very believable monsters peer at her. There is, first of all, Sir Thomas, so coldly reserved with three of his children, Tom, Maria and Julia, that he has never encouraged them to be open, and since he does not understand their feelings he has totally failed to train their moral natures. Maria and Julia are polite, smug and pretty versions of Goneril and Regan and of the elder sisters in the Cinderella story. Mrs Norris – the shrewdest of the three former Ward girls, who include Mrs Price and Lady Bertram – is a sharp-eyed and stingy witch, a grasping flatterer of Sir Thomas and spoiler of his children, and so an encourager of ruin. But just as the overall structure of the novel is ironic, and Fanny as the most passive of heroines becomes a potent, deeply effective redeemer of Mansfield, so dramatic ironies support the main structural irony. Minor characters express aspects of the spiritual truth at the Park: 'You are everything that is just and considerate,' Mrs Norris tells Sir Thomas Bertram, whose fault is that he is absolutely nothing more than that. 'What', Mrs Norris remarks sharply of Fanny Price, 'would she have been if we had not taken her by the hand?' The implied answer (that Fanny, then, would have been forlorn, miserable, a nobody, without the help and opposition of people at Mansfield) challenges the reader to refute it, and indeed if Fanny's home at Portsmouth is a place of suffocation, it is just as important in the story that Mansfield saves Fanny as that Fanny saves Mansfield. A hundred Lady Elizabeths or wives of the Tory elite up and down the nation seem caught up in Lady Bertram, who is perfectly insipid and indolent as she lies on her sofa with Pug. 'I tell you what, Fanny,' she says with glorious irrelevance, 'the next time pug has a litter you shall have a puppy.' (Lady Bertram has forgotten the dog's sex.) She is also the novel's Grecian urn, speaking truth with no more sense of her meaning than a dumb artefact lasting from age to age would have: 'Humph – We certainly are a handsome family.' Or as she says limply of Fanny, 'it is a comfort to think that we shall always have *her.*' The author's special interest in passivity is dramatized here. That interest is artistic – passive minor characteristics allow for irony, indirection and double meaning beyond what may be granted by a robust Mr Collins or Lady Catherine once set in motion – and temperamental too. We recall Jane Austen at art exhibitions: what is bland, meek, mild is attuned, open: Benjamin West receives the viewer, whereas Sir Joshua is less inviting.

Freezing in her cold attic room where Aunt Norris prohibits a fire, Fanny has her travel books, her Scott and her Crabbe, and becomes a useful house-slave. To Edmund she is far less interesting than the charming Londoners, Henry and Mary Crawford, who visit from the home of their adulterous uncle, the Admiral. Like Eliza de Feuillide, Mary is small, well formed, pretty and neurasthenic; she talks compulsively, soothes herself with a harp and lightly sets her eye on Edmund. In Mary, Jane Austen draws on her own playfulness, anarchy and callousness (as she felt it to be), her delight in making things happen: 'She does not *think* evil,' Edmund remarks of Mary as the author might have said of herself, 'but she speaks it – speaks it in playfulness – and though I know it to be playfulness it grieves me to the soul.' Mary is a Lizzy Bennet of gaiety and charm but with no inward life, and for a long while remains an index of Edmund's dull impercipience. She and Henry take on major interest and complexity when Fanny Price is under stress and test. Yet when the young people visit Mr Rushworth's fine old Elizabethan Sotherton in volume one, Fanny Price's viewpoint in its naive aspect is more impressive than Mary's. Fanny is romantic and gauche as they walk into Sotherton's old, bare, disused chapel: 'there is nothing awful here, nothing melancholy, nothing grand', she tells Edmund in a low voice. 'No banners, cousin, to be "blown by the night wind of Heaven". No signs that a "Scottish monarch sleeps below".' Fanny has not read Walter Scott for nothing, and she becomes a vehicle for subordinate themes about history, Tudors and Georgians, the play and pulpit. Of what use is a chapel in modern England? She expresses the author's own early immature Tory romanticism and the sense that before King Henry VIII's dissolution of the monasteries the pulpit had a more vital role in country life. But times have changed. Mary Crawford laughingly implies that the servants in Sotherton's chapel, or the Mrs Bridgets of old, only thought of sex anyway, and alludes to Gray's stylish poem 'A Long Story', in which hooded ghosts mockingly exclaim,

> 'Jesu-Maria! Madame Bridget,
> 'Why, what can the Viscountess mean? . . .
> 'The times are altered quite and clean!'[26]

Gray has made the point well, and two playwrights are summoned to give frameworks for much of the action and discussion about times in modern England which have been altered so 'quite and clean'. What is deeply impressive is the swift, light and amused manner of the author's integration of her sources in Shakespeare and Mrs Inchbald, and again the manner in which she plucks something from Austen family history for a touch of authenticity which in turn will be used to colour a theme. African slavery becomes a large, distant emblem of Sir Thomas's blindness and even of his half-conscious and craven opportunism. (Jane Austen surely never treated a character with more subtle irony.) Mr Austen, we recall, was principal trustee of the Haddon or Weekes Antigua plantation, owned by James Langford Nibbs of St John's College. The Antigua planters were threatened in the war in Jane Austen's childhood when the Navy was hard-pressed and the survival of the kingdom was imperilled, and the Tory severity of this work is rooted in something older than Jane Austen's superficial 'hatred' of a silly, cultured Regent, that is in her family's feeling for Great Britain as a sea kingdom and for threats to the polity from within and without. Nibbs had felt dangers well enough. He once took his spendthrift son on a voyage to Antigua to detach him from 'undesirable connections', and later, in fury, disinherited his son. Sir Thomas Bertram takes his own son Tom on a dangerous wartime voyage to Antigua to detach *him* from spendthrift ways. Tom returns home before Sir Thomas, and with the moral guide and father of the Bertrams away, the young people at Mansfield reveal themselves. So smart and crass that he mocks a recent bereavement, the Hon. John Yates proposes that the young people rehearse *Lovers' Vows*. At Mansfield the amateur dramatics are welcomed. *Lovers' Vows* gives Henry a chance to be hugged by a very willing Maria Bertram, who is already engaged to the stupid, wealthy Mr Rushworth of Sotherton.

Jane Austen uses the play to precipitate the moral crisis of Henry's adultery with Maria. The moral fault of her young people is that they do *not* act but express real feelings – and so use an indirect means of indulging desires they will not take responsibility for. But the author is aware that Mrs Inchbald's play itself oozes with good intentions. Kotzebue had aimed his politically liberal *Das Kind der Liebe* ('The Love Child') at stiff, inhumane mores of German society, before it was translated by the former London actress Mrs Inchbald as *Lovers' Vows* in 1798. Its praise of feeling as against tradition aroused the *Anti Jacobin*, but the *Lady's Magazine* admired the play for heartfelt correctness. It went into twelve editions by 1799, and had six productions at Bath while the Austens lived there. Jane perhaps saw Tilson play the young part of Frederick several years before 1805, when Tilson as a brigadier-general left to reinforce the Gibraltar garrisons, and possibly as early as 1798–9 when he was a handsome captain.[27] In the novel, she assigns her characters roles in *Lovers' Vows* that amusingly predict several of their fates. Yates, as the false head or 'manager' at Mansfield, plays Baron Wildenhaim, who has failed to marry the peasant girl Agatha whom he seduced. As the action opens their illegitimate son Frederick, played by Henry Crawford, comes home to find his mother starving. There is a fine maudlin scene in which the mother Agatha hugs and fondles her son. (Henry and Maria rehearse it often.) When Frederick tries to rob for his mother and is overcome he at last morally persuades the Baron to marry her. Meanwhile the Baron's legitimate child Amelia, played by Mary Crawford, refuses her wealthy and stupid suitor Count Cassel (suitably acted by Mr Rushworth) and wins her clerical tutor Anhalt, whom she boldly loves. Edmund Bertram plays Anhalt, and Fanny Price despite much coaxing just escapes from having to play the Cottager's Wife and becomes a 'prompter'.

Though she clearly admired Mrs Inchbald's novels, what Jane Austen found laughable were the 'Remarks' in which the translator claimed *Lovers' Vows* struck a blow at the crime of seduction. These 'Remarks' had offered an implicit comparison between the moral efficacy of the theatre and pulpit. 'And surely', Mrs Inchbald had claimed in a defence of *Lovers' Vows*, prefacing her 1808 edition of the play, 'as the pulpit has not had eloquence to eradicate the crime of seduction, the stage may be allowed an humble endeavour to prevent its most fatal effects.'[28] Mrs Inchbald also said that harsh criticism of a parent is wrong, since if a child should strongly condemn a father 'all respect is lost, both for the one and the other'. And she defended the woman's right of the heroine Amelia to love first before Anhalt returned her love.

Mansfield Park approves the last point, but tactfully and firmly condemns the father Sir Thomas Bertram. As for Mrs Inchbald's moral idea that the stage is more potent than the pulpit, or that plays eradicate the vice of seduction as the Church of England dithers, Jane Austen treats it as a serious joke. She shows that her evangelical heroine Fanny with her regard for 'memory' and religious England is a far more potent force for good at Mansfield than the charming, stage-loving Londoners Henry and Mary Crawford. Henry speaks of the pulpit simply as a stage, while Edmund takes its right measure. *Lovers' Vows* hardly prevents seduction, but is shown comically to assist it. Yet in avoiding literalness and in a use of irony to suggest two sides to a question *Mansfield Park* has its real thematic strengths. In volumes two and three, Fanny is under severe trial. 'I cannot be satisfied without Fanny Price, without making a small hole in Fanny Price's heart,' boasts Henry. Restlessly he sets out to get her to love him and brings 'all that talent, manner, attention and flattery can do' to the purpose. Fanny 'felt his powers', and so, it seems, did Cassandra Austen, who argued with Jane to let Henry Crawford at last marry Fanny. Louisa Knight later recalled a dispute: 'Cassandra tried to persuade Miss Austen to alter' the story 'and let Mr. Crawford marry Fanny Price', and Louisa remembers her aunts 'arguing the matter but Miss Austen stood firmly and would not allow a change'. Of course Henry Crawford could not be allowed to wed Fanny after ruining Maria Rushworth. Jane was tolerant of rakes, fascinated by them, and not put off by the charming flatterer she rode with at Bath. Yet she bristled because adultery and divorce struck at women, and so when her niece Fanny enthused over Lady Caroline Paget's engagement in the Marquess of Anglesey's family, in which there was divorce, she wrote back, 'What can be expected from a Paget, born & brought up in the centre of conjugal Infidelity & Divorces? – I will *not* be interested in Lady Caroline. I abhor all the race of Pagets.'[29] In the same vein, she hated the Prince Regent for humiliating his wife with a false charge of adultery, and she kept her animus against betrayers of women and women who let themselves be used.

Yet her treatment of Fanny Price and Henry Crawford has the realism of life. Far from being diabolic, Henry is merely idle. His culture is required at Mansfield. When he reads from *Henry VIII* and puts himself so well into the parts of the King, Queen, Buckingham and Wolsey, both Fanny and Edmund are delighted. 'His acting first taught Fanny what pleasure a play might give, and his reading brought all his acting before her again' as he animates King Henry VIII. 'Henry the 8th,' Jane Austen once wrote as a child,' . . . why should a Man who has no Religion himself be at so much trouble to abolish one which had for Ages been established in the Kingdom.'[30] Her point in *Mansfield Park* is that the King's modern living namesake and civilized representative, Henry Crawford, brings Henry VIII into the present in an important way. The brutal King has been lifted into art by Shakespeare, whose own nearly perfect art is now central in modern English culture. 'I once saw Henry the 8th acted,' says Henry Crawford modestly and amiably to Edmund, who agrees that 'we all talk Shakespeare, use his similes, and describe with his descriptions' but maintains that Henry has performed a singular feat in giving the playwright's exact 'sense' at Mansfield. That comment is double-edged. Henry Crawford is at once a callous misuser of women, as Henry VIII more brutally was, and also a cultivated and talented man whose feeling for the stage is needed. But of what point is Crawford's eloquent culture without the moral training that must precede it?

At a deeper level the allusions to Henry Crawford's eloquence re-inforce a broader meaning of the novel. Modern social life seems to force role-playing, compromise and duplicity upon all of us, so that we have an ever smaller chance of being true to ourselves. This is why the theatricals and play-readings of *Mansfield Park* seem pecu-liarly haunting, and perhaps why, in this very subtle and profound novel, Fanny Price in the intensity of her uncompromising religious nature is oddly disturbing – at once naive, puerile, perceiving and burning with feeling. She withers when Sir Thomas upbraids her for not accepting Henry's proposal of marriage. She is too struck with love for her naval brother William to perceive his ordinariness, and too mute and unworldly to console a sufferer – though Fanny is humanized by her developing jealousy of Mary Crawford: 'You don't speak, Fanny,' Mary cries wildly over her loss of Edmund, '– Miss Price – you don't speak.' Fanny's melting gratitude is under-standable when Edmund gives her a golden chain to wear with Wil-liam's amber cross as her solitary ornament: 'My dear Fanny, you feel these things a great deal too much,' says Edmund to her with love and wonder. But when Sir Thomas Bertram banishes her to Portsmouth, she seems prudish and undutifully severe even with her own parents. Typically, on hearing of Henry's adultery with Maria Rushworth, Fanny wishes nothing better for Maria's whole family than 'instant annihilation'. (On *that* principle some of the author's friends would have caused mayhem in their families.) Gently mocked as she is by the author, Fanny is redeemed neverthe-less by her loyalty to Mansfield and her sensitivity to locale. It is not so much her slatternly mother or coarse father that she cannot bear at Portsmouth as it is noise, tumult, disorder, mean sights. Fanny needs Mansfield for her religious life, and so that place is part of her. Locale affects *the inward life* of every person, and this lesson Jane Austen brings from her years at Bath and Southampton. Mary Crawford has no keen sense of place, no inward life and no support, but sees life as a foray in a glittering jungle in which nothing is of much worth and conquest and amusement are the only aims: 'very few young ladies', she says, 'have any affections worth caring for'. It is in opposing that cynicism with her naive enthusiasm and faith in Mansfield that Fanny makes a modest claim on our affections. A dubious claim some readers have felt it to be. One may be offended by her, but artistically her portrait is a complete, profound and delicate success. She and Edmund in marriage represent *no* ideal of cultural sufficiency, but they will be wise parents of Mansfield Park's inheritors. Sir Thomas, for his part, sees belatedly, through his delight in Fanny and the amelioration at Mansfield (after his daughter Julia's elopement with the finally reformed Yates), 'a repeated reason to rejoice' and to 'acknowledge the advantages of early hardship and discipline, and a consciousness of being born to struggle and endure'.[31]

Long before her visit to Kent, Jane Austen had been fascinated by itty Dordy, who had sobbed openly at Southampton after Elizabeth's death. In November 1813 he and his brother Edward were at last at Oxford. A day or two later George wrote back to say he had been to a lecture and Oxford was too expensive: 'I am afraid I shall soon be poor,' he moaned. 'I am glad he thinks about it so soon,' Jane told Cassandra. Her worry over George had helped her to write her modish evangelical comedy. Later Henry Austen sadly found itty Dordy at twenty-seven still drifting – some years before he redeemed himself by bringing Countess Nelson's glittering name into the family. 'George', wrote Henry in a pessimistic mood about the young men who were raised at Godmersham Park, 'is not in such good looks – he is quite a shade – I fear the youths of that family will be old before they are mature – An indifferent constitution worse managed. – He is really going into orders at Lady Day if he *can get* in.'[32] Jane earlier had collected varying opinions of her novel, and she neatly recorded Dordy's. 'George', she wrote of her nephew, is 'interested by nobody but Mary Crawford'.[33]

On 13 November she left Kent with her brother Edward Knight, who had a legal problem on his mind. He was concerned that he might lose his Chawton estates. James Baverstock of Alton, an heir-at-law of Mrs Knight, had filed a suit to assert his claim to the Chawton properties. 'Perhaps you have not heard', Jane presently told her sister, 'that Edward has a good chance of escaping his Lawsuit. His opponent knocks under.' But Edward was later to be served with a writ of ejectment from his Chawton holdings in October 1814. Distressed and fearing that he would lose two-thirds of his annual income, he filed a countersuit. The case dragged on until he at last paid out £15,000 to the plaintiff and nearly denuded Chawton Park Wood by selling his trees to pay that large sum. However, at the moment, he did not know the worst, and after two days with the Moores at Wrotham, Edward took Jane to London in time for her to dine with Henry, who in turn conveyed her to Chawton.

Jane Austen's prospects were then very cheerful. Every copy of *Sense and Sensibility* had been sold, bringing her £140, and with £110 for the copyright fee from her Bennet story she had earned £250, 'which only makes me long for more'. Her two published novels went into second editions this November. She had dined on goose at Michaelmas Day, 11 October, to bring more money, for:

> Who eats Goose on Michael's Day,
> Shan't money lack, his Debts to pay.

Eager and happy, she began a fresh pursuit of fortune at home on 21 January 1814 and called her new work *Emma*. Later Henry arrived in deep snow to take her to town for the *Mansfield Park* proofsheets, and as the horses skidded through Bentley Green near Cobham he began to read about Fanny Price for the first time. He got up to Maria's wedding, early in volume two, where the service is read by Dr Grant, who later dies of three institutional dinners. 'He has only married Mrs. Rushworth,' Jane noted next day in London, and 'gone through the most entertaining part'. But later, 'he admires H. Crawford', she noted with relief, 'I mean properly, as a clever pleasant man'. Henry's agent meanwhile told her that peace was expected in Europe. Now it was a race as to whether Egerton's printers or the Duke of Wellington in France would bring a victory first. While her novel languished in March 1814, a weary British regiment under grimy banners entered Napoleon's Paris at last.

'Henrietta Street', she wrote of her own campaign on 21 March. 'Perhaps before the end of April, *Mansfield Park* by the author of S. & S. – P. & P. may be in the world. – Keep the *name* to yourself. I sh[d] not like to have it known beforehand'.[34] Egerton had his 1,250 copies ready by Monday, 9 May 1814, when the *Star* advertised her work as 'this day ... published', and two days later a purchaser

346

signed a copy of the novel '11th May 1814'. For 18 shillings, readers at last were buying *Mansfield Park: A Novel. In Three Volumes. By the Author of "Sense and Sensibility," and "Pride and Prejudice."*

Chawton stirred with pleasure. Miss Dusautoy, in the spring, claimed that she was Fanny Price – 'she and her youngest sister together, who is named Fanny', Jane noted. Sending their own praise, the Cookes looked forward to seeing Jane herself in June: 'Mr. Cooke', she recorded, 'says "it is the most sensible novel he ever read."' But later at Great Bookham Jane found that Fanny Price's initiative in love was *not* so well liked, although in having Fanny love Edmund before Edmund returned her love, she had mocked Samuel Richardson and agreed in effect with Mrs Inchbald that a woman has as much right to love first as a man does. The Cookes' daughter Mary was shocked.

Her book enjoyed a mild vogue. 'Not much of a novel,' the Dowager Lady Vernon told a friend, 'more the history of a family party in the country, very natural' – as if Lady Vernon's parties mostly featured adultery. 'I have only just begun it,' wrote the Earl of Dudley after noticing that the author composed with deep feeling and 'never plagues you with any chemistry, mechanics, or political economy'. 'It has been pretty generally admired here,' Lady Anne Romilly warned her novel-writing friend Miss Edgeworth, just as the last copies were being sold in November, and then Maria Edgeworth privately admitted that 'we have been much entertained with Mansfield Park'.[35]

But the journals were silent. After all her work over twenty-eight months and her boldness in giving the public an intensely moving and intelligent comedy about modern England, the reviews said nothing. Jane Austen read not a word in a journal. Egerton's squibs in the *Star* and the *Morning Chronicle* were followed by nothing. But Jane copied down comments her family sent her. Her brother Frank headed her list with the words, 'Fanny is a delightful Character!' and she was grateful. 'You need not fear the publication being discreditable to the talents of it's Author,' he told her. Lady Robert Kerr moreover wrote to say the novel was 'universally admired in Edinburgh, by all the *wise ones*', and Lady Gordon indirectly sent her some praise. At home Mrs Austen found 'Fanny insipid', but her comment was typical of those who expected Niagara Falls in the garden. Anna couldn't bear Fanny Price, and Fanny Knight sweetly was delighted with her. The clergy understood Jane Austen's work perhaps: her brother James admired *Mansfield Park*, and Ben Lefroy was highly pleased by Fanny. Perhaps unexpectedly, John Plumtre from Kent told her that Sir Thomas 'proves admirably the defects of the modern system of education'. Nearly every verdict on *Mansfield Park*, for or against, was a strong one, as if her novel had said that the question of what training we give to the young cannot be dismissed with a shrug. Oddly the narrator's firmness had given the work its open, challenging nature. To this day, Fanny Price scandalizes some readers, while being the most inward and sensible of her creations. Jane Austen had hardly expected reviewers in her day to welcome Fanny, but though in November every copy was sold Egerton refused to print a second edition, and that was a setback. In the novel her young people at Mansfield lounge over their 'Quarterly Reviews'. But as she told John Murray later she was very sorry that his own reviewer in his *Quarterly Review* should consider her novel as 'unworthy of being noticed' at all.

18

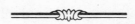

A progress to Carlton House

A bride, you know, my dear, is always the first in company, let the others be who they may.

Mr Woodhouse in Emma

As lively as Jane Austen's niece Anna might be she was upsetting. If she was popular at Chawton she was certainly *not* at Steventon, and her stepmother found her ungrateful and wild – but Anna's mood changed. For anyone who loved Mme de Sévigné's letters and compared Ben's aunt with 'la Mère Beauté', the event that changed Anna was just as odd as the engagement of Gaston d'Orléans' daughter, for this was the most unheard of thing, the most peculiar, the greatest, smallest and commonest – perhaps the worst – that was likely to happen in James Austen's old church: on 8 November, the girl was married to Ben Lefroy, *who had no curacy*.

Mary, even then, could not forgive Anna. Complaining that James dressed her in rags, Anna said she had been thought of as 'the prettiest and worst drest girl' at Steventon and that she had overthrown Michael Terry of Dummer because he was a 'Mr Collins' (so Fanny Lefroy heard) – though her father had to end *that* engagement.[1] Her affair with Ben so upset Mary that Jane Austen feared for her own mother's nerves: 'How can Mrs J. Austen be so provokingly ill-judging?' Jane had noted. 'I should have expected better from her professed if not her real regard for my Mother. Now my Mother will be unwell again. Every fault in Ben's blood does harm to hers, &

every dinner-invitation he refuses will give her an indigestion.' Jane rose to defend the young, but took pains not to bristle at those whom the young upset, and by seeing such an opposer as Mary Lloyd comically she kept on terms with her.

The wedding was as simple as Emma Woodhouse's would be. All the gentlemen walked on a dull cloudy day, and the flinty lane leading up to Mr Austen's former church, the narrow windows with 'no stain to give warmth' and icy, high-backed pews with 'no flowers to give colour or brightness, no friends, high or low, to offer their good wishes' created a puritan effect. Caroline walked dreamily with a smaller bridesmaid, a Lefroy, and the little girls had ribbons in their straw hats. Anna with her bright brown hair and hazel eyes wore white muslin, a shawl shot with primrose, and a cap trimmed with yellow lace. At home at the wedding-breakfast James Edward as the bride's half-brother offered a poem, because he was very proud:

> My Anna's marriage rites to view,
> To see her former joys resign,
> And bid us all a long Adieu.[2]

Anna's prospects were good. After Brownlow Mathew paid the Exchequer's claim of £24,000 on General Edward Mathew's money there were *still* several thousand pounds left for her, and so Ben would not need a curacy at once. Jane had felt happiness for this pair to be improbable (and there may be a parallel between her earlier comments on Anna, and Emma Woodhouse's failing to see that Harriet Smith would find *her* happiness as Mrs Robert Martin) and yet the simple, unpretentious wedding might have been a sign of the bride's good sense and moral reform. Mrs Austen feared highway robbers would attack the girl, but Ben carried her up to his brother's at Hendon, from where Anna for the first time visited London. Anna's money made Ben so conscientious that he next took her back down to Wyards not far from Chawton in August 1815. It was 'a large farm belonging to an Alton shopkeeper, one end of which was occupied by a sort of bailiff', says Anna's daughter; here they were close to Anna's grandmother and aunts and also to the Knights who stayed at the great house.[3] Ben took a curacy as his wife's money ran out, and gave Anna seven babies so that she became a 'poor animal' in her aunt's eyes – though he minded the babies too. When Anna travelled Ben wrote of one fat baby, 'he sat quiet the whole time

350

in my lap and sang By Bye to his dolly. I asked him where you were and he pointed to your chair and looked about for you.'[4]

Before the wedding she had begun a novel, as if to signal Ben's love in a merry triumph over Mary Lloyd. She felt ready for fun in writing 'Which is the Heroine?' and so she sent parts of this work to Chawton, where Jane Austen enlisted her sister's and mother's help in appreciating it. 'I read it to your Aunt Cassandra,' Jane wrote of a packet, 'in our room at night, while we undressed – and with great pleasure. We like the first chapter extremely.' She had helped Anna with stories and with their play 'Sir Charles Grandison', which Fanny Lefroy says that Anna herself dictated, but now to have Anna launching a whole novel imposed a new responsibility. Then when James Edward, Caroline and other nieces began stories, too, Jane had to be very impartial. While writing her own *Emma* she lived in a glow of amateur enterprise, and when the authors came to call they were likely to be curious about *her* writing. Still if her smaller and naive nieces quizzed an Oracle, she was only the person they already knew, so amusing and ordinary that they did not think her very 'clever': she was only a pretty aunt who knew funny stories. 'She had large dark eyes and a brilliant complexion,' Louisa recalled with awe, 'and long, long black hair down to her knees.'[5] With more curiosity, Caroline though noted that Aunt Jane's lap-sized mahogany writing desk 'lived in the drawing room' and that she wrote on it to brothers 'when they were at sea' and 'I believe she wrote much of her Novels in the same way – sitting with her family, when they were quite alone' but 'I never saw any manuscript of *that* sort, in progress'.

Fascinated by Jane Austen's writing habits after *they* began to compose, Caroline and James Edward do illuminate her creative situation by the time of *Emma*. They help to explain why she was able to spend 'much time in writing' – if they did not see her working on a novel. Routines at the cottage were settled. Mrs Austen and the three younger women were busy in a disciplined, efficient ménage in which idleness in daylight hours was unusual. When Mrs Austen could not work in the garden she sat with her patchworks or prided herself on sewing them when bedridden. Jane, with her light household duties, was not only shielded and favoured by Cassandra and Martha but actively helped by their critical opinions and at least by Cassandra's willingness to argue over details in a story. The fact that Jane's novels had begun to win public admiration could only have confirmed in the eyes of her companions the rightness and worth of her labours; and if the cottage attracted too many family visitors, it was otherwise a good place for uninterrupted work. In an atmosphere in which others kept at their duties one did not have to apologize for being busy with a manuscript, and with indulgent companions one had a sense of being valued with a respectful toler-ance. Here Jane Austen's mild peculiarities – her private laughter, absence of mind, obsessive enquiries into factual details, or her wish to conceal her novel-writing as much as she could from all outsiders – were well understood. A visitor would be kept away from the draw-ing room where she wrote, or, upon entering, would find her in a cap and work-smock as if jotting a shopping list. She could write 'when sitting with her family', and when alone she had a special protection. She 'wrote upon small sheets of paper, which could easily be put away, or covered with a piece of blotting paper. There was, between the front door and the offices, a swing door which creaked when it was opened', her nephew recorded later, 'but she objected to having this little inconvenience remedied, because it gave her notice when anyone was coming.'[6] If the door was vital, it was the vigilance of older women that left her secure so that her imagination and recollections were free to interact. For composing she prepared with elaborate care, folding ordinary sheets of writing paper in half until she had a number of them to make fascicles of perhaps thirty-two, forty-eight, or eighty pages, to judge from her *Sanditon* MS. These were, at some point, stitched to form small booklets, so that she had a sense of her novel coming physically into being; and the tidy home-stitching of folded pages seems to have been her very early practice. She thus had a neat arena for her pen – before or after the stitching. Her corrections altered her rhythms or attended to fine details of diction and phrasing, and though the space she allowed herself was narrow or cramped it helped her to focus upon phrasing and cadence. With a mature sense of the challenge and craftsmanship entailed she relished her art – and valued her com-panions who ensured that she had 'much time' for it. The practical world was always at hand, but its demands were largely met by her housemates.

The price of her success, as she well knew, was her anonymity. To have become known as 'Jane Austen, novelist' would be to be left open to those who would accuse her of autobiography, of writing from experience, or of having lived through the ordeals of her characters. That would have inhibited her freedom as an artist. Further, her notoriety could damage the Austen family; it might be assumed that their circumstances had obliged her to try to support herself by earning money. By temperament too she needed her concealment to help her in the modest roles she had as a daughter, sister and aunt.

Yet her larger 'family' were finding her out. On first learning that *she* was the author of works he had read, her nephew James Edward had sent her a poem with a gross, boyish insult. He was amazed, he said,

> When I heard for the very first time in my life
> That I had the honour to have a relation
> Whose works were dispersed through the whole of the nation.

Leading up to his insult, he was surprised by Aunt Jane's 'witty brain':

> And that you (not young Ferrars) found out that a ball
> May be given in cottages never so small.
> And though Mr. Collins so grateful for all
> Will Lady de Bourgh his dear patroness call,
> 'Tis to your ingenuity really he owed
> His living, his wife, and his humble abode.
> Now if you will take your poor nephew's advice,
> Your works to Sir William pray send in a trice;
> If he'll undertake to some grandee to show it,
> By whose means at last the Prince Regent might know it,
> For I'm sure if he did, in reward of your tale,
> He'd make you a countess at least without fail,
> And indeed, if the princess should lose her dear life,
> You might have a good chance of becoming his wife.[7]

Well! *She* might be the Regent's *new* wife, indeed! – to plead her innocence in a newspaper and swear she was not an adultress, as the Princess of Wales had done. Whether or not her nephew knew that she detested the Prince Regent, James Edward's joke was in keeping with their banter. When that same nephew began a novel, Jane said he might throw up his scholarship if he went ahead with his story since 'that will be the honourable Exhibition which no V. Chancellor can rob'. Then when he lost two-and-a-half chapters she was glad she hadn't seen him lately to be accused of stealing them, but 'what should I do with your strong, manly, spirited Sketches, full of Variety and Glow?' she asked James Edward, elevating him to a Walter Scott and reducing herself to a weak Chinese miniaturist in a parody of what her reviewers were saying – 'How could I possibly join them on to the little bit (two Inches wide) of Ivory on which I work with so fine a Brush, as produces little effect after much labour?'[8] Yet she kept her nephew from thinking her exceptional. When he arrived to show how sleek, subtle and clever he was at eighteen he was bent on finding her out, and wanted to know if she modelled her characters on her friends. He thought *that* likely. But she did not invade the 'social proprieties', as he could well understand. In a novelist, she said, it is unfair to record 'peculiarities and weaknesses' of real people, and her aim was 'to create and not to reproduce' comic characters. 'Besides,' Jane Austen said, 'I am too proud of my gentlemen to admit that they were only Mr. A. or Colonel B.' Friends wrongly found the Dusautoys, Anna, Cassandra or herself carried straight over into her fiction, but even so her imaginary people were not of a 'higher' order than are in nature. Speaking of two of her favourites, Edmund Bertram and Mr Knightley, she later said, 'They are very far from being what I know English gentlemen often are.'[9]

Her nephew was impressed at the cottage by her fun and charm – but of others she was wary. When a sister-in-law of Edward's legal opponent called, Jane met her in stiff silence, and a report by that lady duly reached Mary Russell Mitford. Possibly the day had been horrid in the Chawton hills – or at least Jane's stare transformed the day and filled the lady with deliciously amazed, scandalized horror. What poor, poor countrywoman could be found behind wet red bricks here? She says, Miss Mitford wrote with zest, that Miss Jane Austen 'has stiffened into the most perpendicular, precise, taciturn piece of "single blessedness" that ever existed, and that, till *Pride and Prejudice* showed what a precious gem was hidden in that unbending case, she was no more regarded in society than a poker or a fire-screen, or any other thin, upright piece of wood or iron that fills the corner in peace and quietness.' Cassandra's drawing gives a hint of how Jane with eyes fixed may have made her visitor squirm. 'She is still a poker – but a poker of whom every one is afraid,' adds Miss Mitford. 'But a wit, a delineator of character, who does not talk, is terrific indeed!' – and then in justice, 'I do not know that I can quite vouch for this account, though the friend from whom I received it is truth itself; but her family connexions must render her disagreeable to Miss Austen.'[10]

Writers report evil of each other when they can, and the poker and firescreen may very well be Miss Mitford's additions. A visitor looking for what she could see and chatting with the tact of a gross, silly Mrs Elton was likely to find 'Miss Jane Austen' fierce. Yet Miss Mitford's report has echoes in Anna's saying that her aunt's play could abruptly stop and that 'when grave she was *very* grave',[11] and Anna's implication that Jane was less equably cheerful than Cassandra in these years has causes. Jane Austen's energy was flagging, even as her reports of physical ills increased: her three trips to London in a year to see Henry, the disappointment of Egerton's refusal to reissue *Mansfield Park* and new ground she was breaking in *Emma* added to her strain. Partly to keep up her gaiety, her half-concealed literary jokes were important to her, as were light poems full of word-play. What she stresses for Anna is that the spirit of writing – its zest and élan – counts most, and while writing out a sermon of James's she underlined a word or kept James's emphasis: 'It is difficult to conceive how they can pray with the *Spirit*,' Jane Austen copied down, '– how they can keep up a *Spirit* of devotion in their Minds & prevent their thoughts from wandering.'[12] She borrowed a religious term to suggest that art's devices are less important than an attitude, and one of her best tributes to Anna's novel is that 'the Spirit does not droop at all'.

A story *may* skip spiritedly from setting to setting, and here, in advising Anna, she is less strict than Cassandra: 'I allow more Latitude than she does,' Jane admits, 'and think Nature and Spirit cover many sins of a wandering story.' Even a story's title bears on spirited-ness. She favoured an abstract title which her characters might comically illustrate, and so she doubted Anna's stage-comedy title for her novel was best. 'I like "Which is the Heroine?" very well,' she told her eager niece, 'but "Enthusiasm" was something so very superior that every common title must appear to disadvantage.' Anna, by grouping everyone in her story under the half-dangerous, half-attractive idea of 'Enthusiasm', might achieve fun and unity.[13]

Just at this time, Jane Austen was playing on an abstract idea herself, in the very word 'Emma'. In a novel full of conundrums, riddles, and wordplay she has Mr Weston in *Emma*'s important Box Hill epi-sode comment rather oddly on the heroine's name: 'I am making a conundrum,' announces Mr Weston to Emma Woodhouse mystify-ingly, 'What two letters of the alphabet are there, that express perfec-tion?'

'What two letters! – express perfection! I am sure I do not know.'

'Ah you will never guess,' says Weston. 'You (to Emma), I am certain, will never guess. – I will tell you. – M. and A. – Em–ma. Do you understand?' To which Mr Knightley, who is affronted just then by Emma's selfish antics, replies that *'perfection* should not have come quite so soon'. Mr Weston's joking allusion is to the eighteenth-century philosopher of happiness Francis Hutcheson, who in his *Beauty and Virtue* had worked out a small, bizarre formula with M and A as its keys: 'Since then *Benevolence*, or *Virtue* in any *Agent'*, he had written with some mathematics to help him,

is as $\dfrac{M}{A}$, or $\dfrac{M+1}{A}$, and no *Being* can act above his *natural Ability*; that must be the Perfection of Virtue where M = A, or when the *Being* acts to the utmost of his power for the *publick Good*.[14]

Comically her novel *Emma* would have a mathematical allusion in its title, and the joke would be half-serious and partly played on the reader. A reader of *Emma* becomes an enquirer into Emma Wood-house's 'perfection' and has to decide to what extent she truly has benevolence and virtue. Jane Austen's fourth novel has a profundity similar to that of *Pride and Prejudice* or *Sense and Sensibility*, only more elusive since Emma's character is far more subtle than Elizabeth's or Marianne's. We locate 'pride' in Darcy or Elizabeth more easily than we can decide on Emma's faults or virtues, with shifting clues to character and conduct – and the clues will be extremely minute and sometimes half-buried in the rattle of Miss Bates's monologues or concealed in conundrums within conundrums. *Emma* seems to leave us with much to discover after each new reading. Feeding into its richness was a fondness for wordplay that was shared by many in the Austen family. Not to multiply examples – though all are amus-ing – Jane lately had written on the back of an advertisement for A.F.Holstein's absurd Gothic novel *Love, Mystery and Misery* a simple, clever lyric playing on the letters e and i in a recent marriage:

Of Eastbourn M.ʳ Gell
From being perfectly well
Became dreadfully ill
For the Love of Miss Gill.

So he said with some sighs
I'm the slave of your i.s
Ah! restore if you please
By accepting my e.s.[15]

Her sister herself wrote a conundrum on the letter o with a better hint of Jane's outlook on life than of her own. 'Tho I never was married,' Cassandra declared,

I'm always in Love
& still am in hopes – how fallacious they prove,
I'm of great use in Oxford that fountain of knowledge
And a place is found for me in every College.
Tho' with knowledge & learning I'm very ill stored
Without my assistance you can't write a word.

It was not any shimmering dazzle in these conundrums that appealed to Jane but rather their homely suggestion of good-natured wit. Thus at Kent once her family had joined in a contest to find rhymes with 'rose', and Mrs Austen began spontaneously:

This morning I woke from a quiet repose,
I first rubbed my eyes, and I next blew my nose . . .
I employed myself next in repairing my hose,

Cassandra more sedately offered verses that begin,

And when the heart has full repose,
'Tis mutual love the gift bestows,

while Jane in Edward's earthly paradise hailed a workman 'in his Sunday clothes' who 'envies not the gayest London beaux', although he prefers:

the prayers whose meaning least he knows,
Lists to the sermon in a softening doze,
And rouses joyous at the welcome close.

The Austen's wordplay reinforced affection and a family bond, or lightly turned impatience into amusement, as Jane did when a Mr Best meanly failed to take Martha to Harrogate after promising to do so:

> Oh! M<u>r</u> Best, you're very bad
> And all the world shall know it;
> Your base behaviour shall be sung
> By me, a tuneful Poet. –

'Arise ennobled – as Escort,' Jane demands of the worst Best, 'of Martha Lloyd stand forth',

> But if you still refuse to go
> I'll never let you rest,
> But haunt you with reproachful song
> Oh! wicked M<u>r</u> Best![16]

In these mild, simple exercises she kept alive a spirit of play rooted in the word, and not only her half-concealed jokes but her complex verbal tapestry of embedded clues and disguised and subtle allusions in *Emma* developed out of them.

In her remarks on Anna's work she appropriately stresses gaiety: Anna must not let any character go slack since a dullard after all can be *made* to interest. 'What can you do with Egerton,' Jane asks about her niece's developing novel, which was now arriving in earnest packets. 'If you could invent something spirited' all would *work* for him. 'I wish you could contrive something, some family occurrence' to draw him out 'or something to take him mysteriously away, & then heard of at York or Edinburgh – in an old great coat.' Anna's novel seems at times much too timid, as if she were only imitating other writers, but rival novelists are dangerous and her aunt hopes to avoid them: 'I am quite determined however not to be pleased with Mrs. West's *Alicia de Lacy*,' she advises, 'should I ever meet with it, which I hope I may not.' The *Gentleman's Magazine*'s letters had praised the novelist Mrs Jane West because she 'pays the greatest care and attention to her farm, manages her dairy, and even carries her butter to market' or else because she supervises her cheese-making while knitting stockings for her husband and sons – and that efficiency is *unfair*, though Jane Austen found in Mrs West's *Letters to a Young Lady* a dance with an 'antiquated *caro sposo*' that was surely useful. 'I have made up my mind to like no Novels really, but Miss Edgeworth's, Yours & my own,' she decides, while implying that if fiction must seldom mimic fiction, it should be more natural than life. It is wrong for Anna's Sir Thomas to go to a stable with a broken arm – though James Austen did so after *his* arm was set. Since social customs cannot be avoided, one must not have a surgeon introduced to a baronet – and 'when Mr. Portman is first brought in, he would not be introduced as the *Honble*'. One has to inspire a reader's faith and do much to keep it, and again it is lost if one is irrelevant. 'You describe a sweet place,' she tells Anna, 'but your descriptions are often more minute than will be liked.' Much, however, may be pardoned if one's people are well assembled and amusing; 'You are now collecting your people delightfully,' she reports encouragingly, 'getting them exactly into such a spot as is the delight of my life: – 3 or 4 Families in a Country Village is the very thing to work on – & I hope you will write a great deal more & make full use of them while they are so very favourably arranged.' But large effects depend on details, and Anna must avoid the horrid phrase 'vortex of dissipation', used by Mrs Holford in her *First Impressions*. 'I do not object to the thing,' Jane adds, but 'I dare say Adam met with it in the first novel he opened.' In a practical spirit she implies that her niece must think of what the public wants and credit a deep, incessant, normal desire of ordinary readers for fun. 'You are *now* coming to the heart and beauty,' she concedes. 'Till the heroine grows up, the fun must be imperfect – but I expect a great deal of entertainment from the next 3 or 4 books.'

Burlesque featured in her own early fiction. She and Anna now read together a Gothic novel printed in four volumes in 1806, and elaborately rebound in eight, it seems, at Alton: this was *Lady Maclairn, the Victim of Villainy* by Mrs Hunter of Norwich. The heroine Rachel Cowley is sent to gloomy Tarefield Hall, where she meets Maclairns, Flints, Flamalls and Howards who in turn tell pitiable life-stories while tears wash the pages as perjury, bigamy, bastardy, lunacy and suicide become everyday events. 'Miss Jane Austen begs her best Thanks may be conveyed,' Jane writes in keeping with the maudlin tone, and 'Miss J.A.'s tears have flowed over each sweet sketch in such a way as would do Mrs Hunter's heart good to see, & if Mrs H. could understand all Miss Austen's interest in the subject she would certainly have the kindness to publish at least four volumes more about the Flint family'. Mrs H. *en route* to her publisher may find better locomotion than Alton's coach or the Car of Falkenstein, which has recently overturned, and her novel will remind Anna that Gothic beings are bizarre but not dull: a realist finds neutral portraits difficult because nothing can be 'very *broad*' there. But Mrs Hunter's very gross fault is prolixity: 'I hope when you have written a great deal more you will be equal to scratching out some of the past,' Jane reminds her niece. 'The scene with Mrs. Mellish I should condemn,' for it is prosy whereas the prose of a novel needs poetry, intensity. 'The more you can find it in your heart to curtail,' she warns, 'the better.' Anna *can* wonderfully rise to wit and paradox, and the name 'Newton Priors is really a Nonpareil,' Jane says admiringly. 'Milton would have given his eyes to have thought of it.'

After her retreat to Hendon, Anna wrote improbably of St Julian's love affair. 'Very well told,' Jane admits, 'and his having been in love with the Aunt, gives Cecilia an additional Interest.' Almost any young man on earth is mad about an aunt. 'I daresay Ben was in love with me once, & would never have thought of *you* if he had not supposed me dead of a scarlet fever.'[17]

Her own novel was advancing. Her nieces amused her, and though not dependent on them she found them reassuring. She was touched by Anna's novel-writing and her romance with Ben, and by her confidences, which were a check on what could be intuited, a licence to invent and suppose and one more sign of how young love evolved. She was more relaxed, assured and trusting in the full mastery of her artistic power now. Her nieces helped her to relax: she revealed her happiness about them, and their creative strivings reminded her of her own hopes and trials. *Emma* looks into her own life and at least echoes dozens of minor observations about herself: Emma has the effrontery of a child and the freedom of an artist, as she starts projects without finishing them, and yet she trusts beyond reason in her own rightness and power. By deciding who should marry whom to fulfil her imperial will she is godlike – and rather like a novelist she knows how the future will *turn out*, and has a father to support her illusions: 'Ah! my dear, I wish you would not make matches and foretel things,' says Mr Woodhouse to her, 'for whatever you say always comes to pass.' She is quick, adept and decided, with an alacrity surprising in a person aiming to do everything well and luxuriating in 'real good-will of a mind delighted with its own ideas'. Emma Woodhouse appropriates neither money nor land, but the fate of human beings, and abhors practical, literate farmers of the yeoman class, though the poor class below that has her full tolerance. Given a blue-eyed and pretty Harriet Smith of uncertain parentage, she invents to fill out the character before her: 'There can be no doubt of your being a gentleman's daughter,' Emma tells Harriet, 'and you must support your claim to that station.' But in spite of her masterful and aggressive verve she retains the capacity to correct herself and recover, keeps her initiative, and obtains the prize of an inward life. 'I am going to take a heroine whom no one but myself will much like,'[18] Jane Austen had said and had meant the novel's overall design to be that of the quixotic girl kept from self-knowledge by pride, gaiety and well-being. The story's realism would grow partly from its sources and yet stands in mocking opposition to them. One of the sources was Kotzebue's play *Die Versöhnung*, which Jane Austen had seen at Bath on 22 June 1799 in Thomas Dibdin's version as *The Birthday*, a play glamorizing filial love by showing a faultless Emma Bertram whose almost slavish devotion to her invalid father has kept her from marrying.[19] In *Emma* the valetudinarian Mr Woodhouse keeps his own Emma from growing up. From Mme de Genlis, Jane Austen borrows the technique of the concise, seemingly full opening description of a heroine's traits and by failing to complete the list and not mentioning Emma's failure in self-knowledge she makes the reader into a moral searcher.

Her narrator would be subtle, confiding, hinting, not wholly reliable. The reader is to share in Emma's illusions and repeat the author's process of getting to know others, and be misled, to come at last to sympathetic but still incomplete understandings. The method is affective as well as mimetic, ironic in impetus, and avoids 'very important, very recordable events' to show many of the nearly unrecordable. Frank Churchill's repair of a tiny rivet in a pair of spectacles involves duplicity, illusion, passion and the fate of Jane Fairfax as well as a heroine's self-love. This artistry in detail is not only potent and funny but as elaborate as any novelist has ever achieved in a work of *Emma*'s length. In general the three volumes broadly suggest three movements blending ordinary events in Highbury with the funny motif of Emma's match-making and mistakes. Volume one shows her off at twenty in her glory and full of mastery as Highbury's queen, indulged by her former governess as well as by her father and by a gentlemanly Mr Knightley, who at thirty-six believes wives should be subordinate and fails to understand himself. Carrying a child's imagination into adulthood, Emma disturbs and magnetizes nearly everyone. Unread books and unfinished drawings mutely accuse her of a fussily debilitating self-regard, but as an 'imaginist'

361

she fulfils herself by creating the future. Although her friend Harriet loves Robert Martin of Abbey Farm, Emma 'matches' her with a smiling, spruce, black-coated Mr Elton, who loses clerical decorum by making violent love to Emma herself after the Westons' Christmas Eve party. Volume two is richer with hidden problems and elusive characters, so that her mistakes multiply. She finds Jane Fairfax only cool, and far from sensing that Frank Churchill is attached to Jane, she imagines a dark alliance between the latter and Mr Dixon of Balycraig. Missing clues at the Coles', she thinks that Jane's pianoforte was sent by the married Dixon. She feels she loves Frank, dismisses that thought only to imagine Frank loves *her*, then that Knightley loves Jane Fairfax, who is favoured by the vicar's brassy new bride Mrs Elton. In volume three she compounds her errors by imagining that Frank is truly suited to Harriet, and also by impulsively assuring Mr Knightley that there is nothing between Frank and Jane she makes Knightley bitterly jealous of Frank – Emma's own possible suitor. The characters are neatly collected at Emma's tea, at the Donwell strawberry party and then on the climactic trip to Box Hill, where Emma wantonly insults Jane Fairfax's aunt Miss Bates, whose monologues have clues in them which Emma is too self-obsessed to attend to. Hearing at last that Frank has been secretly engaged to Jane Fairfax all along, she is sorry for Harriet but still bemused. Only in feeling she has lost Knightley's love does she recognize that she has meddled all along, overlooked facts and made a puppet of an illegitimate Harriet. Knightley's proposal rewards her recognitions, but even in the last chapter she is surprised that Harriet has accepted a faithful and suitable Robert Martin – 'unaccountable as it was!' Kindly as ever, Emma delays her own wedding until the robbery of a hen-house persuades Mr Woodhouse to welcome a son-in-law in his house. She then marries her patient, loving, almost brotherly Knightley, just as Harriet weds Martin and Jane Fairfax will soon have Frank. 'We learned', wrote the author's nephew later, 'that Mr. Woodhouse survived his daughter's marriage and kept her and Mr. Knightley from settling at Donwell about two years and that the letters placed by Frank Churchill before Jane Fairfax, which she swept away unread, contained the word "pardon".'[20] The portraits of Miss Hetty Bates and Mr Henry Woodhouse are two of the best minor ones in fiction. As a believable saint, Miss Bates talks nonsense which becomes the most lucid sense. Self-centred but not selfish, and roundedly living even in his cadences, Mr Woodhouse is called 'the kind-hearted, polite old man' and he is as funny as Miss Bates is compelling. Even his coachman James or Hannah and the Hartfield horses live in his plaintive tones: 'The carriage!' he exclaims. 'But James will not like to put the horses to for such a little way; – and where are the poor horses to be while we are paying our visit?' A half-inch snowfall brings two pages of consternation. 'My dear, did you change your stockings?' he calmly asks Jane Fairfax when she is half-insane with anxiety. 'Ah! my poor dear child,' Mr Woodhouse tells his daughter Isabella, who lives sixteen miles away in Brunswick Square, 'the truth is, that in London it is always a sickly season. Nobody is healthy in London, nobody could be. It is a dreadful thing to have you forced to live there! – so far off!' Or – very gently in a society that adores dancing – 'The sooner every party breaks up the better.'

Miss Bates and Mr Woodhouse are rural beings, not observable in cities, and the comic audacity and verve and disguised power of their portraits show the author's need for rural life, a need so acute and basic that when it was unfulfilled she was a soul in a desert without water. But they also are extreme Tory portraits, deny- ing the forward motion of Highbury's life and hinting of old truths nearly lost in a vicious, fractious era. Highbury is a hermetic micro- cosm in which social concerns become intense themes: the author plays on a national ethic to exalt things 'English' but shows that Jane Fairfax's poverty may lead to slavery in the 'governess' trade, and that Mr Elton's smugness is a sign of rot in a Church losing touch with its yeomanry. Mrs Elton praises her *nouveaux riches* Suckling relatives and disdains dirty industrial Birmingham (which she might pronounce 'Brummagem') as a divide opens up between polite and plebeian cultures. The church no longer gathers villagers in by setting its mark on festivals, sports or other outings as in the eighteenth century, and Emma's Box Hill party is secular, savage, split and uneasy. Though by no means a snob who cultivates those of rank, Emma strikes against Highbury's safety and its last vestiges of cohesiveness in denying that the farmer Martin (who reads *Agricul- tural Reports* and *Elegant Extracts* as well as Goldsmith's *Vicar of Wake- field*) is fit for Harriet. Martin is to *be* a gentleman – and the nation has been saved from violent turmoil partly by ease of access to its social classes. (One sign that Highbury is authentic is that we might imagine here the rick-burnings and riots that lay just ahead for rural villages.) Emma separates the classes, colluding with Mrs Elton in destroying real accessibility, and this is her worst crime: as in *Mansfield Park* the author highlights attitudes that destroy social tolerance and harmony. Knightley's telling insult of Frank indirectly points to the recent French spectre of *la Terreur*, in that he 'can be amiable only in French not in English' because he lacks English social sensitivity. In showing fractures, tensions and deficiencies the author convinces us her setting is real, and that her village is worthy of an intelligent woman with a soul, an interior life. *Emma* in its autobiographical aspect reaches back to an early gaiety at Steventon, but also to Jane Austen's disillusionment, aloneness and animosity at pretty balls where the selfish, vicious and calculating revealed themselves, and more deeply into regions of anarchy and defensiveness surfacing now and then in her letters: her strongly mixed feelings gave her the objectivity to portray Highbury. She is indebted to Maria Edgeworth, who in *Belinda* involves the reader in an ethical search, and to E.S.Barrett, who in *The Heroine* mocks fiction's conventions – but her self-knowledge, her love of detail and her ambiguous attitude to rural people were more essential in helping her to create a proud, self-willed, self-guided, vexing and outrageous Emma and her greatest novel.

Jane Austen had not modelled a fictional place on any locale but had taken hints from places she knew and data available to her, and Cobham, sixteen miles from London, and Leatherhead with its neighbouring Box Hill were both known to her. Highbury is pretty and snug and consoling, and she could delight in Emma's laurels and the bench round Hartfield's tree or the bow-window of a shop, without feeling that she had idealized a setting. Journeying between Chawton and London she might very well envy Emma's staying in a simple village. She finished her novel on 29 March 1815, and after some planning began *Persuasion* on 8 August, just as Ben and Anna were settling nearby at Wyards farmhouse. In the summer Edward's children came to Chawton's great house, and after seeing Fanny again, Jane Austen braced herself for a trip to Henry's house at Hans Place. Since *Emma* would need a more committed publisher than half-hearted Egerton, she had applied to John Murray, the friend of Scott and Byron, at Henry's urging. 'Mr. Murray's letter is come,' she wrote from London on 17 October; 'he is a rogue of course, but a civil one. He offers £450 but wants to have the copyright of M.P. & S. & S. included. It will end in my publishing for myself,' she felt. 'It is an amusing letter. You shall see it.' Henry seemed languid and bilious, so she dined *tête-à-tête* one evening with his romantically inclined man Mr Seymour, and next day noted poor Henry worse.[21]

For Cowper the town was a 'crowded coop' – and for Jane it could sometimes be a trying necessity with its stucco and warm red brick blackening over under the effects of smoke, no prettier when.she had to visit her brother Charles's children, who had lost their mother and were looked after by Frances's sister Harriet Palmer at Keppel Street. Charles, when home from the Navy, lived with his dead wife's sister respectably at her parents' house; but gossip focused on his behaviour with Harriet, to judge from his friends' defensive congratulations when he decently married her. Mrs Austen railed at Harriet's temper in one letter, but Jane understood that Miss Palmer was devoted to Charles's children. She noted that her brother Henry, after Eliza's death, had a lady-friend. The speed, tumult and moral ambiguities of London might have been symbolized in Pall Mall's dazzling gas lamps – which had replaced feeble whale-oil lamps – even as a dreary blankness lay over Henry's neighbourhood. 'I cannot flourish in this East Wind', she had noted, and then on a typical Sunday there seemed to be 'plenty of Mortar and nothing to do', but on such a day she could read Thomas Sherlock's sermons. Once Bishop of London, Sherlock opposed evangelicals and valued dignity and self-assertion: in a famous sermon he had said, 'the very Desire to be better than we are, and to render ourselves more acceptable to God, makes us think ourselves worse than we are, and quite out of his Favour'.[22] For Jane Austen religion was an aid to good conscience, to rational assertiveness, and she told Anna that 'I am very fond of Sherlock's Sermons, prefer them to almost any'. It was not to be tepid, cautious or captious that she lived since she was formed on an active ethic of her father's household. She still meant to test the world, to take on as many social meetings and outings as she could contrive in London – so long as she could also retreat. She sought society here as in Kent, while falling (facetiously, quickly and imaginatively) in and out of love well enough. For all her awareness and good sense her *habitual* attitude was that of an 'imaginist' Emma and so she was particularly cautious in advising Fanny Knight in love – though ready to 'imagine' and love lightly herself. An instance occurred when Henry, who was failing on tea and barley-water, required two physicians. Jane was so alarmed she sent for James, who took his wife to Chawton to look after Mrs Austen (since Martha was in Berkshire), and then came straight up to London.

'For several days they thought him dying,' as Caroline heard, and Jane found herself – not so oddly – drawn to a physician. He was Charles Thomas Haden, surgeon at Chelsea and Brompton Dispensary; a sketch shows fine, swept-back Greek hair and a big, knifey, Apollonian nose, as if he spread silvery wings to fly to the sun for remedies on his way back to a low-roofed dispensary. He hated nurses, honoured his own sublime wisdom and believed 'when a new view of things opens to anyone, the prospect is sufficiently boundless if the eyes only take the right direction'.[23]

His eyes took *her* direction: 'Mr. Haden', she had told her sister, is 'a young man, said to be clever, & he is certainly very attentive' – as he was to Henry, but he had a way of turning up to see her. 'Tomorrow Mr. Haden is to dine with us,' she writes. 'There's Happiness! – We really grow so fond of Mr. Haden that I do not know what to expect.' Amused by his svelte air of being someone who pooh-poohed the fact that he saved lives and helped Henry, she waited for him. 'And what is to be fancied next? – Why that Mr. Haden dines here again tomorrow,' she boasts. By the time he was 'reading Mansfield Park for the first time', she was appropriating him, as if, in her imagination, he was comically but totally perfect. 'He is a Haden, nothing but a Haden,' she writes with overt fun and love, 'a sort of wonderful nondescript Creature on two legs, something between a Man & an Angel – but without the least spice of an Apothecary,' let Cassandra think what she may. He is very funny. He bustles over with cures for Henry, charm for her and talks solemnly of music but 'he has never sung to us,' Jane admits, 'he will not sing without a P. Forté accompaniment', though he might have sung all night. She is so amused that when the weather turns balmier – as if her Apollo ordered it – she lets it caress her. '*I* enjoy it,' she says, 'all over me, from top to toe, from right to left, Longitudinally, Perpendicularly, Diagonally.'

'I am rather in love with him' – as she said of another man – is a phrase very chiefly framed for her sister's benefit. 'You will get acquainted with my friend Mr. Philips,' she had advised Cassandra, 'and hear him talk from books.' But 'be sure to have something odd happen to you, see somebody that you do not expect, meet with some surprise or other, and find some old friend sitting with Henry when you come into the room. Do something clever in that way.'[24] Life is to be wrung, squeezed fully; if events yield little, imagination must work them up. She was prepared for much to happen to *her* – as modest as she was with Haden. When, it seems, his fellow physician, who had intimate access to the Prince Regent, told her that the fat, cultivated Regent enjoyed her novels and 'often read them, and had a set in each of his residences', she was not helpless with awe; nor was she, perhaps, very flustered to hear that his Royal Highness had been told 'Miss Austen was now in London' or to know that 'by the Prince's desire, Mr. Clarke, the Librarian of Carlton House, would speedily wait upon her'.[25]

Mr Clarke came to Hans Place. He invited her to visit the Prince's ornate Carlton House, once the home of a royal mother and now the Prince's glittering wonderland. Her dilemma was then comic. The Revd James Stanier Clarke, author of a work on Nelson and more learned tomes, was unctuous, ceremonious, obtuse, kind and absurd. He felt about the Prince rather as Mr Collins does about his titled lady, and treated Jane with ceremony as a fellow author. There is an irony in her acquaintance with an author so unaware of his pedantry and turgid writing that he might have stepped out of a comic novel or a satire. Clarke's books were formidable. He began his enormous, beautifully illustrated work *The Progress of Maritime Discovery* of 1803 with a grandiloquent three-page apostrophe to the Prince, a stupendous preface and an introduction of 230 pages before writing 'Chapter 1'. In some of his moods, he was the sort of man who cannot tell you the time of day, height of a room, or whether it is raining outside in less than ten sentences. His explanations paralyse the mind. But in his letters, there is an almost touching modesty too, an absence of hectoring and posturing. Unlike Sir Egerton Brydges he had a redeeming innocence, and it seems not the slightest trace of self-righteousness or self-importance. In any case, Jane Austen was to write to him with more than the formal courtesy that his position called for, and to treat him as a well-meaning friend.

As comic as his unctuousness was, she gladly accepted his invitation to see Carlton House. Almost forty, she became a Cinderella on 13 November 1815, riding in a coach over smooth cobblestones south of Piccadilly. With his gold-fetish the Prince Regent had not wholly rebuilt Carlton House, but had turned its remodelling at vast expense over to Henry Holland, who had used a French foreman, French furniture-makers and French decorative painters to give it a Louis Seize grandeur – and a semblance of interior taste. Her coach must have stopped at the north portico near a Corinthian screen and then – perhaps on Mr Clarke's black arm – she went up wide marble steps. Inside was a forest of silver and gold, a dazzle of chariot-back chairs, decorative marbling, effigies of Venus with leaves and fruits in giltwork and stone. A fan-vaulted conservatory here might have silenced almost anyone, but she seems to have seen much more, such as the round Second Drawing Room and ante-chambers and dining hall before she was led into a magnificent forty-foot library by her host. She knew Stoneleigh but not such richness, and Clarke's flow of words in a bizarre setting sent her away at last confused. At Henry's two days later, she wrote to ask if Mr Clarke had meant that it was incumbent on her to dedicate her *Emma* to the Prince.

'It is certainly not *incumbent* on you,' Mr Clarke replied, adding she might if she wished, and that he hoped she would take an English clergyman for her *next* hero, a man like himself, 'no man's Enemy but his own'. Would she think of it?

Though reluctant to do so, she felt in honour bound to dedicate *Emma* to the Regent. Meanwhile Murray was slow to seal her contract, and his printers were slower, but when she asked Murray if her dedicating *Emma* to the Regent would speed up printers, she got a compliment from the publisher and a deluge of proofsheets. 'A *sheet* came in this moment,' she reports to Chawton. 'I am sure you will like Particulars. – We are not to have the trouble of returning the sheets to Mr. Murray any longer, the Printer's boys bring & carry.' Martha Lloyd might think her wholly mercenary, but she was enjoying these days, luxuriating in affection and stir and delighted to have Fanny in London to flirt with Mr Haden, who was clearly losing his mind. 'I have been listening to dreadful Insanity,' Jane writes of that talkative man. 'It is Mr. Haden's firm beleif that a person *not* musical is fit for every sort of Wickedness.' She debated with her Apollo after he cured Henry Austen, who in stiff white 'strengthening Plaister' for his torso was now going off in Chelsea coaches to sign bonds and keep his bank from collapsing. The war was quite over, and after the Emperor's escape from Elba and the

One Hundred Days, poor Henry's financial world was in a turmoil. Charles's children called to claim her time, and little Caroline sent along manuscripts. 'I wish I could finish stories as fast as you can,' she told that niece. As for the father of Caroline's heroine she hoped he would hang himself, or take the surname Bone for a penance, or undergo a direful ordeal.

For a while she put off her 'very sincere friend' Clarke, who seemed to be writing her next novel for her. After a month she informed him that she could never depict his educated clergyman since she was the most unlearned, uninformed female who ever dared write. He wanted to her to show the clergyman 'burying his own mother – as I did', offered to let her stay with him at Golden Square, and, since he was to be English secretary to visiting royalty, also suggested she might write a romance 'illustrative of the history of the august House of Cobourg'. (Better *that*, perhaps, than a wet-eyed clergyman who was no man's enemy.)

But taking up Clarke's hints – and a few others – she wrote her funny 'Plan of a Novel' to help her to compose a perfect work. Her heroine's father would be an enthusiast, 'nobody's Enemy but his own', and her heroine would be as pure as her cousin Mary Cooke wished. They would flee to Russia,

> into Kamschatka where the poor Father, quite worn down, finding his end approaching, throws himself on the Ground, & after 4 or 5 hours of tender advice & parental Admonition to his miserable Child, expires in a fine burst of Literary Enthusiasm, intermingled with Invectives against Holder's of Tythes.[26]

That would suit everyone!

She was serious enough about *Emma*. She told Mr Clarke almost what she told Frank, that she was anxious that her fourth novel should not disgrace what was good in the others and that she felt it might be inferior in wit to *Pride and Prejudice*, and in good sense to *Mansfield Park*. She was subject to worries once a novel was ready, and Henry testifies to her lack of faith, of self-confidence, once she had done her best. She fretted herself over what was brilliantly finished and became vulnerable, with little confidence in her art. Yet her brothers reassured her, and Henry particularly exerted himself for her at a crucial time. She faced Lord Byron's publisher now, and John Murray had been cagey, trying to buy her cheaply and using guile in offering her £450 for the combined copyrights of *Emma*,

Mansfield Park and *Sense and Sensibility*. Henry had duelled with the publisher from a sickbed, and in modest and obsequious phrases had made strong points. He made good use of the pitiable fact that he seemed to be dying: 'Severe illness has confined me to my bed ever since I received yours,' Henry had begun,

> I cannot yet hold a pen, and employ an amanuensis. The politeness and perspicuity of your letter equally claim my earliest exertion. Your official opinion of the merits of *Emma* is very valuable and satisfactory.

Murray by then had his reader William Gifford's opinion of *Emma*'s 'plainly written' MS, which had a few expressions Mr Gifford, as a literate man, might set right. 'Though', Henry had said on his sickbed,

> I venture to differ occasionally from your critique, yet I assure you the quantum of your commendation rather exceeds than falls short of the author's expectations and my own. The terms you offer are so very inferior to what we had expected that I am apprehensive of having made some great error in my arithmetical calculation. On the subject of the expence and profit of publishing you must be much better informed than I am, but documents in my possession appear to prove that the sum offered by you for the copyright of *Sense and Sensibility*, *Mansfield Park* and *Emma* is not equal to the money which my sister has actually cleared by one very moderate edition of *Mansfield Park*; – (you yourself expressed astonishment that so small an edition of such a work should have been sent into the world) – and a still smaller one of *Sense and Sensibility*.[27]

Then, as Henry lay ill, negotiations had hung until Murray agreed to publish *Emma* at the author's expense with profits to her after she had paid a 10 per cent commission. When he proposed a reissuing of *Mansfield Park* on the same basis, Jane dispatched a marked copy of her first edition on 11 December, 'as ready for a 2^d edit: I believe, as I can make it'. (Including new naval details for her Portsmouth scenes, she made other minor changes, some not recorded in the notes to the modern Oxford edition of *Mansfield Park*.) *This* venture was disastrous. *Pride and Prejudice* had prepared readers for more sparkling Eliza Bennets and no public had ever been created for *Mansfield Park*. Murray pushed the second edition, but his ledgers tell a sad story. The trade baulked. At 12s 6d for an 18-shilling work, wholesale firms took thirty-six copies in advance, then after the second edition of *Mansfield Park* appeared on 19 February 1816, wholesalers took only ninety-four more at a reduced rate of 11s 6d. The book died so far as Murray could see, for in December 1817 he had 588 sets left and so he remaindered *Mansfield Park* with the last 498 copies cleared at 2s 6d each. Still, his sales plans for her *Emma* began while she was in town – and she was hopeful for this new child. It was announced in the *Morning Post* on 2 and 6 December 1815, and on Sunday 10 December the *Observer* frankly promised it 'on Saturday next'. Seeing that advertisement, Jane settled a few last points with Murray and warned she would be at Hans Place till the 16th, but after that at Chawton. When *would* her novel appear? The 16th passed with nothing to show. On the 21st the *Morning Chronicle* began with a promise of 'Saturday next' and then on 23 December 1815 it announced her book as 'PUBLISHED THIS DAY'. For £1 1s, readers could buy for Christmas EMMA: *A Novel. In three Volumes. by the Author of "Pride and Prejudice," &c. &c.* Murray had used Egerton's tidy little format – in which no more than 180 words are printed on a page, sometimes only four or five words in a line to make for easy reading – and used a whole page for her grand royal dedication, while adding this at the end of volume three in each copy:

Lately were Published,

BY

THE AUTHOR OF EMMA:

1. SENSE AND SENSIBILITY: a Novel. Second Edition. 3 Vols. 12mo. 18s.

2. PRIDE AND PREJUDICE: a Novel. Second Edition. 3 Vols. 12mo. 18s.

3. MANSFIELD PARK: a Novel. 3 Vols. 12mo. 18s.

Anonymity did not protect her when her whole career was on test. She had feared *Emma* would be thought slight, but brief notices in 1816 and 1817 piled up in the *Champion, Augustan Review, British Critic, Monthly Review, British Lady's Magazine and Monthly Miscellany, Gentleman's Magazine* and *Literary Panorama* – and her book was honestly praised for its 'inoffensive and well principled' story or 'harmless amusement'. 'We are not less inclined to speak well of this tale', offered the *British Critic*, 'because it does not dabble in religion; of fanatical novels and fanatical authoresses we are already sick.' Her fame leaped far beyond the Channel so that at Moscow in June *Vestnik Evropï* praised her pretty picture of domestic life, and at Jena and Tübingen she was called a happy painter. '*Sie ist*', wrote a German reviewer as if he were Mr Collins's cousin, '*eine glückliche Beobachterin der stillen häuslichen Familienlebens.*' But the grandest notice was engineered by John Murray, whose *Quarterly* so far had ignored her. 'Have you any fancy to dash off an article on "Emma"?' he had asked Sir Walter Scott on Christmas Day in 1815. 'It wants incident and romance, does it not? None of the author's novels have been noticed and surely "Pride and Prejudice" merits high commendation.' Walter Scott sent in his review on 19 January to say he did not need proofs 'as Mr. Gifford will correct all obvious errors, and abridge it where necessary', and anonymously his notice appeared in the March issue of the great *Quarterly Review*.[28]

Two years earlier Scott had surprised the public with his lifelike *Waverley*, a book 'which has afforded me more entertainment', Mrs Austen told Anna, 'than any modern production (Aunt Jane's excepted) of the novel kind that I have read for a great while'.[29] Indeed he seemed too good: 'It is not fair,' Jane Austen seriously joked. Walter Scott has no business to write novels because 'he has Fame and Profit enough as a Poet, and should not be taking the bread out of other people's mouths. – I do not like him, & do not mean to like *Waverley*.' She perhaps saw his hand in the *Emma* review, by far the most intelligent critique of her fiction she read. Glancing at her early work, Scott slashes his tail and shakes his mane amiably in coming to 'this before us, proclaiming knowledge of the heart'. Her realism, as he notices, turns every reader into a critic because everyone 'can criticize that which is presented as the portrait of a friend, or neighbour'. On this plane she stands 'almost alone'. He likes Frank Churchill and Emma, finds enough here for bloodshed and broken hearts (if *he* were treating them) and yet concedes she is absolutely true to her mode. Not to praise her too highly, he warns against mean, selfish motives which her fiction may encourage 'in the youth of this realm'. Yet he finds her exceptional and sees that her psychology and skill are fine. A third reading of *Pride and Prejudice* much later tells him he can do 'the Big Bow-wow strain' but that her subtlety is denied him. 'Quite above everybody else',[30] he says of her scene endings, and her slow rise in his esteem does suggest that her novels – to an unusual degree – will depend on her critics. Emma may seem a silly, meddling snob until we know her well, but readers cannot know her until a climate is created for *Emma's* text.

Emma – though more elusive than James Joyce's *Ulysses* – is like *Ulysses* a novelist's novel, repaying slow reading or giving intense rewards to anyone who will take two months for it. But since only a handful of writers read it and nobody challenged the reviews it had little appeal in London in 1816. 'So much one wishes to forget,' as Lady Anne Romilly felt, but one other lady was more encouraging. That same Lady Boringdon who was said to have written Jane Austen's novels was born Frances Talbot, a daughter of a Norfolk surgeon, and in 1809 she married John Parker, who as the second Lord Boringdon kept up his estate at Saltram near Plymouth. Her name was to change again. On 29 November 1815 her husband was elevated to the earldom of Morley, and Jane Austen, who met her through Henry's help, it seems, thereafter had an intelligent if not wholly candid admirer in Lady Morley. Receiving but not yet having read far in her copy of *Emma*, Lady Morley said she *could* give the Woodhouses no higher praise than that they were equal to 'all their admirable predecessors'.[31] With this friendship Jane was not overawed, but touched and consoled, as something had come round in her life; aristocrats – for whom she had no love as a social class – had been among the first to praise her, and in the long traditions of the realm they had sponsored art as a duty. She replied to Lady Morley that her praise led her to 'believe that I have not yet – as almost every Writer of Fancy does sooner or later – overwritten myself'. She also drew up a list of opinions of *Emma* for her own sake. She was eager for that of Anna, who was then a young mother: 'As I wish very much to see *your* Jemima, I am sure you will like to see *my* Emma,' she told her niece.[32] Anna's novel soon faltered, but she was to add to her aunt's story 'Evelyn' and to write a funny continuation of *Sanditon* while printing stories for children such as *The winter's tale*, *Springtide* and *Mary Hamilton*, all anonymously.

Leading her list of 'opinions' Jane put down Frank's name. He buoyed her up the most and reassured her by finding her latest novel her best. Her list grew as if nourishing *Emma*, and in adding Anna's verdict she was relieved to have that niece nearby at Wyards, although her own walk to the farmhouse became oppressive. A country walker may stride over fields and down lanes one day, but next day pretty fields swim in a grey and green blur as if fences a few yards away are at the universe's end. Jane Austen became very ill, as if she had foolishly carried back Henry's cloud and had no Mr Haden to make it vanish. She was to be puzzled, as we know, by black onslaughts of 'discharge' when her body was wrong. There may be nothing honourable in suffering, and we may be spared the indignity of severe pain – to become more impatient with ourselves, embarrassed to cause others trouble, and mystifying to a good apothecary who calls with his pills and bottles – or we may decide to keep pills, bottles and doctors from our door. If fate really meant to break her, she had the satisfaction of knowing that *Emma* was recognized and commented on. In the spring she was equal again to Anna's babble and her nephew's wit. The reviews were kindly. The French issued her book as *La Nouvelle Emma*, and Americans pirated the English edition whether she knew it or not. She had in her hands a letter from Mr Clarke to say that the Regent was pleased, too. Famous as she was in odd corners, Jane Austen was not neglected in golden rooms south of busy Piccadilly where the First Gentleman of Europe knew her name.

19

═══━◆◇◆━═══

Henry's fate and
Persuasion and *Sanditon*

If there is any thing disagreeable going on, men are always sure
to get out of it.

Mary Musgrove in *Persuasion*

In his own illness her brother Henry had seemed 'ready to swallow anything' as an ideal patient – mute and uncomplaining – and now happily his tall, lithe form seemed likely to flourish. His bank was in trouble but if anyone could face normal worries easily, he could. He did not have a mind for affliction, as Jane felt, and she believed him shrewd and lucky. He had joined the militia when funds were pouring into recruiting and had got out when the nation, then forced off gold, was short of cash to pay troops. With Henry Maunde and James Tilson, both militia officers, he had set up a banking firm of Austen, Maunde and Tilson in town and acted as its link with country branches at Petersfield, Hythe and Alton.

Here, perhaps, his fate played a trick. Henry Austen's linked banks were risky, as if he had a ship which would sink if punctured anywhere. Still the breezes were fair. Once paper money had been rare, but after 1798, when few gold and silver coins were struck, banks issued much paper. Everyone accepted tradesmen's tokens and Spanish dollars over-stamped with the English King's head and became used to hearing of forgeries, credit, money. At Chawton Park James Tilson talked of little else: 'Mr. Tilson admired the trees,' Jane wrote, 'and greived that they should not be turned into money.'[1] She

375

laughed over Henry's talk, too, but his actions as Receiver-General for Taxes in Oxfordshire were so questionable that she perhaps heard of them. The land and assessed taxes were collected by such medieval methods that the bankers, among sixty receivers-general, could delay in returning monies to the Tax Office in order to use public funds for private profit. Though not quite illegal this practice upset Parliament when a committee reported that banker–receivers 'commonly retain in their hands the whole of each quarterly collection for about six weeks'.[2] By 1815 Henry's bank in a flush of success had riskily issued many bank-notes in small denominations and had relied, for its solvency, on merchants taken in as partners. Henry also risked much by putting his brothers and servants in jeopardy, banking their funds. To meet a suretyship of £30,000 he had got £10,000 from his Uncle Perrot and £20,000 from his brother Edward Knight, who was now fighting to save his Chawton holdings. If Henry should bring down Edward, Mrs Austen and her daughters could be turned out of their house. The crisis came with a sharp, sudden deflation and a cutback in government orders for foodstuffs, cloth and other stores in southern counties; when Gray the grocer–partner wavered he brought down Austen, Gray and Vincent at Alton, and a panic began. This affected Austen, Blunt and Louch at Petersfield. A great many bank-notes were not redeemed by gold, silver or anything else. Over-extended, Henry's London bank fell like a house of cards and a docket of bankruptcy was struck against Austen, Maunde and Tilson early in 1816. 'A bad year', Caroline recorded. Henry's bankruptcy on 6 March was 'an entire surprise at our house and as little foreseen I believe by the rest of the family', and Jane wrote to Murray in April in deep anxiety over 'the late sad Event in Henrietta S^t'.[3]

Henry was to be the one partner disgraced not only in London but at three provincial towns – one of them a mile from Chawton – and would face an ordeal of gazetting, commissions and being bled financially to death or 'sued out' of existence. Mr Leigh Perrot's £10,000 and Edward's £20,000 would disappear and Henry's servants would suffer with savings gone. Charles Austen lost 'hundreds' in the bank's failure. This was a heavy calamity, but, in the crisis, Jane Austen felt for Henry, yearned for him, and did not lose faith in him. With no belief in static virtues, his or her own or anyone else's, she viewed life as a struggle never won, and felt that even a conquest of the self was meaningful only for a moment. People revealed themselves to her as they advanced and fought against their contraries. She could be glad that Henry saw the town as hostile and that he was not dashed, snivelling or playing a martyr to his failure. In repose nobody was anything, she felt, and she might have accepted Cowper's truth,

By ceaseless action all that is subsists.

She was most relieved that Edward survived the bank failure, and that Charles was not flattened. Henry aimed to pay back some of his debts by taking clerical orders, and indeed he took orders with ease to be Papillon's assistant at Chawton from December 1816. Six years later at Farnham after briefly holding Steventon parish, he still owed money, but, as he told Charles, 'in the midst of all my struggles, doubts & difficulties, my heart beats as warmly towards you as in days of Sunshine – of sunshine never to return as far as regards my worldly circumstances'. He could only 'mourn to see so little chance of my being able to heal those wounds by me inflicted on the property of others. ... I had hoped by this time to have paid off Mad^e Perigord entirely, & thereby to be on the threshold of repayment to you – but I still owe her One hundred pounds. The cheif cause of my error in calculation was that I was obliged to reduce the tithes of Steventon Seventy pounds a year for two years. – Do not think that I am in any present distress. Not at all – We are up to this moment before hand with the world.'[4] Just as typically, Henry, when briefly attached to the embassy in Berlin, gave his *Lectures upon some important passages in the Book of Genesis*, and on the title-page grandly described himself as chaplain to HRH the Duke of Cumberland and the Rt Hon. the Earl of Morley. (It is very doubtful that Henry really served formally or for long in Lord Morley's household.) After marrying Eleanor Jackson, a niece of the Revd J.R.Papillon, he was to become in 1824 curate of Bentley where, with some of his own money, he at last secured 'the erection of a cage for the drunk and disorderly that replaced the time-honoured stocks and whipping-posts'. But Henry's good deeds were ahead of him when Jane saw him as Mr Papillon's cocky assistant at Chawton. 'Our new clergyman is expected here very soon,' she told Alethea Bigg. 'It will be a nervous hour for our pew, though we hear that he acquits himself with as much ease and collectedness, as if he had been used to it all his life.'

All in all, she was amused. 'Uncle Henry writes very superior Sermons,' she told James Edward. 'You and I must try to get hold of one or two, & put them into our Novels; – it would be a fine help to a volume; & we could make our Heroine read it aloud of a Sunday Evening.'[5]

As Henry preached his way to solvency, other Austens pursued their vocations. Charles had had a disaster in the *Phoenix* when she was lost in a gale near Chisme in Asia Minor, though his crew survived. Acquitted of blame by a court-martial, he gave Jane a notion of the real 'Admiral Crofts' of her day. He knew old veterans such as Admiral Broke, whose wounds racked him after the *Chesapeake* slaughter but who recalled him from youth: 'My dear Austen,' Broke told Charles, 'you was such a good temperd sociable little fellow in our *evening tea party* at the Academy – that I always recollect you with pleasure.'[6] Jane did not see that letter, but she could imagine such an unaffected, simple flag officer retired at Bath. As for Edward, who was almost winning his legal battle, he came to her one day in elation. He had found an error in *Emma*. 'Jane,' he began, 'I wish you would tell me where you get those apple-trees of yours that come into bloom in July.'

This July had brought so little to bloom in soggy fields that the year 1816 was to be the one 'without a harvest'. It rained as if some tragedy were afoot, as if Mary Lloyd's sudden, severe illness were typical news, or as if Frank's poor pregnant wife at Alton would not survive. 'Little Embryo is troublesome I suppose,' wrote Jane. Frank on his half-pay had stayed at the great house before Edward took it and of course had not modified his habits after being made Companion of the Most Honourable Order of the Bath on 4 June, 1815, and now at Alton was as busily domestic as Harville would be in *Persuasion*. Later he did not see himself in Wentworth's character 'but I think parts of Capt. Harville's were drawn from myself', he said of his sister's novel, 'at least some of his domestic habits, tastes and occupations bear a strong resemblance to mine'. He was at least partly right. Writing *Persuasion*, Jane drew lightly on Frank for a *few* hints for all three of her captains, taking Harville's trim habits at Lyme, Wentworth's fine competence, and Benwick's 'soft sort of manner' possibly from what she knew of his character.[7]

But the rains were grey and incessant. Jane had rheumatic back pains and felt how silly they were. On 9 July she set off in a donkey carriage with Frank's girl Mary Jane to see Mr Woolls' great farming improvements. 'But we were obliged to turn back,' she wrote, and 'not soon enough to avoid a Pelter all the way home. We met Mr. Woolls,' she told her nephew. 'I talked of it's being bad weather for the Hay – & he returned me the comfort of it's being much worse for the Wheat.' Her own vexing malady returned, but it did not keep her from getting ahead as she could with Anne Elliot's story. She was conjuring up that heroine's quietly observing mind, and meanwhile accepting Mary Jane at nine as a very good companion – if only because Frank and Mary had not in the least spoiled her. Frank had taught this child a lesson or two in suffering and death, it seems, by asking her to think about animals: 'I had the misfortune', Frank had written from his ship, 'to lose that pretty little kid.' Mary Jane had seen the goat running, playing and leaping on deck but 'one cold evening wishing I suppose to keep itself warm, it got into the Oven, and not knowing it was there somebody shut the door of the Oven so that', Frank instructed his daughter, 'it could not get out, and so was burned to death: Poor thing! I fear it must have suffered much pain before it died.'[8]

Jane took counsel with herself about her illness, and had *two* attitudes; by now, it seemed so stupid, so baffling and elusive she knew it might be incurable, yet she felt she must not alarm others and if only she could fathom the trouble she *might* be well. Already she and her sister had tried Cheltenham spa for a cure, and at Kintbury one person, perhaps, sensed her deeper attitude: 'Mary Jane Fowle', Caroline wrote, said 'Aunt Jane went over the old places and recalled old recollections associated with them in a very particular manner' as if 'she never expected to see them again'. On the way back they found everyone almost happy at Steventon. Caroline had been bribed by a shilling to find her missing gloves and shoes and was likely to be in a perfect mood. On 11 June they had drunk tea at the Harwoods and later dined with the Stiles and Ben and Anna, and at last had a sumptuous tea with the W. Digweeds. 'The Miss Austens and Cassy left us,' wrote Mary Lloyd on 15 June[9] – when Cassy joined them in the carriage – and on that same day Jane returned home to her *Persuasion* MS.

With this she had made very good progress. From the start – on 8 August, 1815 – she had been amusing her nieces with fanciful, impromptu joke-stories and freeing herself from the tighter, restricting frames of realism; her own works are nearer the 'suppose' of children's stories and folklore than at first they seem. In the folktale one person is central and all depends on the dynamics of action, while time is strange, and a lack of correspondence with reality offers a special delight. People are in grotesque contrasts, so that if one is a 'beauty' another is 'ugly'. In Cinderella's tale and in *Persuasion* there are three sisters, and the worthiest is in exile in her own home, unable to free herself, to find a listener or impress anyone. Anne Elliot is a good, faded little person at twenty-seven of sweet manners and an elegant mind – 'you may *perhaps*' like her, Jane told Fanny, 'as she is almost too good for me'. We like her because of the intense elegiac and comic portrayal of her plight, and we note a difficulty that still vexes critics of this novel, since although Anne is portrayed with psychological realism the characters around her are sketched in varying registers. Jane Austen gives us a comic portrait, a deliberate stereotype, a myth figure and sometimes little more than a black smudge of paint. Sir Walter Elliot resembles a 'humour' in Molière or Ben Jonson: he is not unpleasant, but only a narcissist who steadily reads the Baronetage and thinks of appearances and is proud of the orange cuffs of his livery. His daughter Elizabeth is given as a smudge, so that his daughters Mary Musgrove and Anne Elliot may be teased into contrasting fullness. The narrative is mixed in time as the human mind is, visual and retrospective with 'tawny leaves and withered hedges' or 'the influence so sweet and sad of autumnal months in the country' and remarks such as 'one does not have to love a place less because one has suffered in it'. The elegiac tone is Anne's own, but she also has an intelligent passion, a fury for those of lucky status who victimize or ignore others, even a fury directed at a society which favours men and reduces unmarried females to silence.

Wonders happen in folktales. Appealing to her decency, Lady Russell had persuaded Anne eight years before to release her poor naval suitor Wentworth, and Anne gave him up not to hobble him. This is as if Madam Lefroy, instead of boldly rescuing her nephew from a flirt, had worked on Miss Jane Austen's conscience to get her to give up Tom Lefroy. (Anne in 1817 is still 'almost too good for me'.) In the story, time has intervened. Wentworth returns from the sea as a creature rich and strange – with naval prize money – to find Anne Elliot unmarried and mute and faded: she is worthy, but every fact is against her. When Sir Walter leases Kellynch Hall to the Crofts and takes Elizabeth and Mrs Clay to Bath, Anne goes to stay with her whining and spoiled sister Mary – one of Jane Austen's funniest people. She again meets Wentworth since he is Mrs Croft's brother, but he is only formally polite at the Musgroves' great house where young Henrietta and Louisa set their caps at him.

Time and change, false feeling and modernity confront her. Like Jane Austen she is an acute, estranged observer. 'She had given him up to oblige others,' Anne feels about her lover. 'It had been the effects of over-persuasion. It had been weakness and timidity.' She has her author's Tory sense of 'duty' and a view that to be happy means having real sensibility, or an awareness of others' feelings and the generosity to behave well in adversity. Happiness is inward and spiritual, but, so valued, it permits us – as it permitted Dr Johnson – at least to suffer and struggle.

Anne's torture is that Wentworth, so naive and fine and naval, plays at love. Why should he not? Wentworth rides on a crest with sea-wealth, good looks, mental and physical well-being and loyal comrades: he has the best prize society can give a young *male*: the privilege of being confused without penalty. He yearns for a lady of 'strong mind, with sweetness of manner', but courts two silly Musgrove fribbles at once: 'Anybody between fifteen and thirty can have me for the asking. A little beauty, and a few smiles, and a few compliments to the navy, and I am a lost man,' he says. And so he laughs with Louisa and talks amiably and well, while Anne in tears plays for the company at Uppercross. Others are foils for Anne. Mrs Musgrove's 'large fat sighings' for an unfeeling naval son Dick – whose death never fazed her – put Anne's pain in clearer light. Benwick is only sentimental in grief, and the Crofts and Harvilles have Anne's kindness without her sensitivity. 'I wish', says Croft about the Captain's Musgrove flirts, that 'Frederick would spread a little more canvas, and bring us home one of these ladies to Kellynch'. Versed in the Navy's terms and ways the author easily enters into its grievances in days of jobbery and can have a fling at the Admiralty – which sends men to sea in foul ships, among 'thousands that may just as well go to the bottom as not'. Here Jane Austen is not Tory but Radical, and her grasp of a war profession gives her story an edge as she treats the Navy 'at this present time, (the summer of 1814)'. Sir Walter's agent knows that 'this peace will be turning all our rich Navy Officers ashore', a situation of fine comedy since naval men may know comparatively little of polite society, of finesse, subtlety, courtship, manners. The naval officer with his idiosyncratic romanticism was being treated as less than a gentleman by the landed gentry, as Jane Austen knew. Yet Wentworth has £25,000, and *Persuasion* becomes the story of how a woman of 'maturity of mind' and 'consciousness of right' truly implants these things in a well-to-do officer who is her social and intellectual inferior.[10]

As an emotionally complex novel, *Persuasion* also brings tragic feeling to bear on comedy. Anne is like Cordelia and Ophelia, holding her tongue and not knowing the mind of the man she loves. The atmosphere before Louisa's fall is full of buzz, empty words or 'cobweb dialogue' (in the phrase of a recent reader). Little Charles's broken collarbone and the arrival of Mr Robinson the apothecary foreshadow a major calamity – which turns out to be illusory in its damage and ironic in effect: a flirting Louisa jumps from Lyme's Cobb into Wentworth's arms and falls senseless to the stone: and few symbols of sexual mishap have so entertained others. When Louisa's sister faints, boatmen gather round 'to enjoy the sight of a dead young lady, nay, two dead young ladies for it proved to be twice as fine as the first report'.

Some of the Austens' acquaintances at Bath had held off from the social mêlée: 'Friends were very angry,' Mrs Lybbe Powys had written, but 'we begged to be excused so many dinners and parties, as Mr. Powys riding, and I constantly walking all the mornings, we were so old-fashioned a couple as to enjoy ourselves (by ourselves)'.[11] Admiral and Mrs Croft have the Lybbe Powys' sanity, and Anne benefits. At Bath, too, time itself stops to reveal time's depredations. Visiting her schoolfriend Mrs Smith, now crippled, Anne admires her pluck and will-power, only to find in her a dark mirror-image of herself. Having married imprudently she gives Anne a glimpse of an alternative fate – of what *could* have happened if mere romance had led Anne to marry Wentworth – and like a good oracle in a fairy-story Mrs Smith withholds her knowledge of evil, and then reveals it to equip Anne to understand Mr Elliot's depravity and the hazards of yielding to advice. She tests Anne. Mr Elliot with his scorn for the baronetcy is as vicious as any *nouveau riche* Whig whose cry is for 'money, money' alone. (He is the type of Whig who had impugned Eliza's godfather, insulted a beloved King, or deprived James Austen of rightful Mathew money.) Beside him Sir

Walter is benign. Anne has misjudged her slick cousin Mr Elliot. She is no paragon of intuition, and allusions to Matthew Prior's poem 'Henry and Emma' and to Burney's *Cecilia* highlight by contrast Anne's lifelike normalcy, with her anxiety, aching need for love, raw nerves, dislike of noises and nearly shattered self-respect.

She waits – as if in a purgatory made by men – until Wentworth opens his eyes to see he has been a fool. In the story's *first* ending, he makes love to her in a clumsy scene at Admiral Croft's, at Bath, hopping his chair across the room to claim her 'with an expression which had something more than penetration in it, something softer; – Her Countenance did not discourage. – It was silent, but a very powerful Dialogue; – on his side, Supplication, on her's acceptance. – Still, a little nearer – and a hand taken and pressed – and "Anne, my own dear Anne!" – bursting forth in the fullness of exquisite feeling. . . . They were re-united.'[12] That might have satisfied many a novelist, but it displeased its author, who had penned her last two chapters (10 and 11 for volume two) in a mere eight days and had jotted 'Finis' and 'July 16 1816' on her manuscript. Erasing those words and adding a new paragraph, she jotted 'Finis July 18. 1816' and still went to bed one night 'in very low spirits' over her work, as her nephew heard. By 6 August, though, she had redone her Chapter 10, keeping only a fraction of the original, and had written a wholly new Chapter 11. (Hence the old Chapter 11 became number 12 in her final version.) In her new writing she collects the Musgroves at Bath and brings her lovers together with an understanding of the past, but her rejected 'Chapter 10' survives to show how Jane Austen at first could write with an eye to outward action rather than with delicate care for psychology. She gets gaiety and edge, too, with new depth in Chapter 11, especialy in Anne Elliot's debate with poor gentle Captain Harville, who has claimed that all the world's histories and songs only show that woman is fickle. 'But perhaps you will say, these were all written by men,' Harville adds. 'Perhaps I shall,' replies Anne Elliot. Feminist critics illuminate this scene, and nothing they have said in the twentieth century perhaps would have offended the author. However, Anne Elliot appears chiefly as a reconciler, and without exalting either males or females *Persuasion* has a strong moral theme, for *both* sexes, countering the philosophy of Shaftesbury and matching the tough eighteenth-century rationalism of Joseph Butler in his *Fifteen Sermons* and *Analogy of Religion*. The Earl of Shaftesbury had judged a moral action partly by its effects, but Butler held that the consequences of any action have nothing to do with its basic *rightness*.[13] And so in the novel Anne had been right to refuse her lover (even though Lady Russell's advice to give him up was mistaken) and right to be persuadable, right to save at one time a penniless Wentworth's future and herself. To be persuadable of duty means being conscious of what we rightly owe others in our behaviour. Jane Austen's outlook is paradoxical, but deeply stoical, and the narrator reprimands Lady Russell for her rash, blind, prejudiced advice but treats that lady fondly and with respect for her steadily good and loving intentions.

Henry Austen, sued and gazetted, had helped his sister to recover another work. Jane had got back from Crosby her copyright of *Susan*. Still profoundly irked over his neglect of her Northanger Abbey tale, she now wrote, with a view to publication, an 'Advertisement' to say in part that in 1803 *Susan* was 'even advertised, and why the business proceeded no farther, the author has never been able to learn'. New evidence points to a fascinating buried story behind *Susan*. Back in 1803 Crosby & Co. had touted it in their *Flowers of Literature* as 'In the Press, SUSAN; a novel, in 2 vols.' just as by coincidence they were defending modern fiction against moral attackers. With German shockers then under fire, they had quoted from William Barrow's *Essay on Education* for example to show that 'the novels of Fielding, of Richardson, and of Radcliffe' can all be read without harm. The last name in that short list is interesting, since Crosby & Co. had a financial interest in Mrs Radcliffe and included 'Mysteries of Udolpho, by Ann Radcliffe, 4 vols.' as among the 'MOST APPROVED MODERN NOVELS' they sold. *Susan*, if it resembled *Northanger Abbey* in having a flippant attitude to parental advice, might have subverted their campaign to publish morally approved novels. But *Susan* surely had run counter to Crosby's interests in seeming to be a lightsome, laughing attack on a pillar of English fiction, Crosby's own Radcliffe. Richard Crosby was not about to cut his own throat, and we cannot assume that he later regretted his refusal to publish Jane Austen, who, for years after *Mansfield Park* was remaindered, did not do exceptionally well for any publisher at home or pirate publisher of her works abroad.[14]

Changing *Susan*'s name to *Catherine*, Jane found her story hard to revise. 'Miss Catherine is put upon the Shelve,' she told Fanny in the new year, 'and I do not know that she will ever come out.' 'But', she wrote about *Persuasion*, 'I have something ready for publication, which may perhaps appear about a twelvemonth hence.' That may suggest she felt *Persuasion* would need tidying up, but not necessarily that she thought it unfinished or in need of any major improvement. Her art, though never perfect, is of such a high order that we may too easily become confident about what she may have found wrong in it. Even the objection that we are not well prepared for Mr Elliot's taking Mrs Clay as his mistress at the last in *Persuasion* does not surely hold. In a flash of mischief the author has put two rogues of like aptitude together. Satisfied enough with her work, Henry later offered the novel to Murray, who brought out four volumes of *Northanger Abbey* and *Persuasion* together at the end of 1817 with Henry's memorial notice of his sister. Murray's edition of 1,750 copies sold, but not briskly enough to be reprinted. 'Pray send us Miss Austen's novels the moment you can,' Lady Abercorn had told the publisher, 'Lord Abercorn thinks them next to W. Scott's (if they are by W. Scott)' and 'it is a great pity that we shall have no more'.[15] After polite reviews, *Persuasion* was translated into French and German by 1822, and in the twentieth century it has been felt to be her most emotionally powerful work and perhaps the most difficult to judge. 'Of all Jane Austen's works,' a critic claims, '*Persuasion* suffers the most from easy generalizations, and requires the most minute discriminations.' By 1980 three translated versions of it existed in Portuguese, seven in Spanish, two each in Czech and Serbo-Croat, but none in Tamil, Telugu or Thai or even in Hindi, Marathi, Sinhalese or Gujarati, though Elizabeth in translation speaks to Darcy of course in all of those tongues and in many others, too.

Late in 1816, her fickle illness tired her. Since her mother preferred the only downstairs sofa, Jane rested on three hard chairs. 'I think she had a pillow, but it never looked comfortable,' wrote Caroline, who heard that she avoided the sofa for fear her mother would not use it. When able, Jane Austen crossed the garden to see the Prowtings, and inspired a neighbour to say later, 'We called her the poor young lady.'[16]

She walked slowly, but treated her debility lightly and (to amuse a niece) called herself 'JA', the old Jackass. 'Not so stout as the old Jackass', she wrote about the two Mrs Hulberts of Speen Hill, and joked that all the baronets were dying. 'Sir Tho: Miller is dead,' she had told Cassandra. 'I treat you with a dead Baronet in almost every letter.' As news of her illness spread among friends and relatives, she used her wit as a defence against pity she did not want, and against humiliation worse for her perhaps than diarrhoea and pain. She was now under siege. She gave others comic illnesses. She was afraid James Edward was detained 'by severe illness', she told him, 'confined to your Bed & quite unable to hold a pen, & only dating your letter from Steventon in order, with a mistaken sort of Tenderness, to deceive me'. Her nephew must go to the sea, perhaps to watch the waves at Sandown Cottage which Mrs Lybbe Powys liked. 'Your Physicians', said Jane, 'I hope will order you to the Sea, or to a house by the side of a very considerable Pond,' she slyly added. She was then planning her novel about a comic Sanditon, an invalids' resort near the sea.

She was not always stoical with Cassandra. When her sister was at Cheltenham in September, Jane admitted that her back pains were less severe, but that the cottage was wearisomely hectic: 'I wanted a few days quiet, & exemption from the Thought & contrivances which any sort of company gives,' she wrote. 'Composition seems to me Impossible, with a head full of Joints of Mutton & doses of rhubarb.'[17] Cassandra returned quickly and seldom left her alone again. Then, as visitors dwindled, she could feel the absurd egotism of an invalid and how illness may allow for a new angle of insight, a funny assessment of people. Jane Austen learned as she died. She had noted that the sick are seldom heroic, and in *Persuasion* had had Mrs Smith say, 'Here and there human nature may be great in times of trial, but generally speaking it is its weakness and not its strength that appears in a sick chamber.' And now when her niece Anna called, the topic changed from Jane's trouble to the comic absurdity of people obsessed with illness.

She meant to write until she died. But with backaches, nausea and many days when she *could* do nothing, she needed help beyond Martha's or her sister's power. It may be one thing to say I shall do such-and-such until the end, and another to realize that a slow death is messy, unpleasant and isolating. She needed gaiety and trust – just as the seriously ill hardly ever need our pity so much as they perhaps crave friendship and confederacy.

But her two nieces helped her, and Anna and Fanny were resolute. Much may be said against them since Anna's vanity at last was almost as bad as Fanny's spite, but they cheered her: and Anna helped her to turn illness into comedy, even if she was later to take too much credit for the inception of *Sanditon*. Mrs Austen and others they knew were gentle hypochondriacs, who complained while keeping fit through hard work that nearly belied their ills. Mrs Austen chatted of bile, it seems, as others do of the weather. Anna and Jane thought of funny sufferers, so that Anna could write later of the comic hypochondriacs in her aunt's *Sanditon* that 'members of the Parker family (except of course Sidney) were certainly suggested by conversations which passed between Aunt Jane & me during the time that she was writing this story. – Their vagaries do by no means exceed the facts from which they were taken.'[18] Jane had begun *Sanditon* on 27 January 1817, and taking stock of her career she branched out in a new way. In childhood she seems to have known *Elegant Extracts* and probably Dr William Enfield's *The Speaker* with its excerpts from journals, its poems by Cowper and quotations from most of the works that become Catherine Morland's readings in *Northanger Abbey*.[19] Such compendiums and her later reading habits had given her a broad, useful overview of English society, and she had packed society into her early novels by giving a representative quality to her Morlands or Bennets. She had written three formal comedies in which a heroine comes to maturity after mistakes, where the emphasis is on the outcome; and alternating with these, three stories which stress a heroine's suffering and enduring rather than the ending. *Sense and Sensibility*, *Mansfield Park* and *Persuasion* are her darker stories – each more inwardly searching than the last – but they do not allow for a very wide canvas, or satire on a whole community; she had evolved her art towards psychological complexity and usually avoided social satire as an end. Her power depended on her devotion to the novel form, or on a refusal to use the novel to prove anything: actions spring from her characters, not from a seeming desire to correct abuses or reform society. This purity of belief in the novel was the best effect of her defiant light comic glee, undergraduate and free as it is in *Pride and Prejudice*; she had an attitude well nourished by Oxford brothers who after all in *The Loiterer* had meant to show off, to be funny. She detached herself from all causes to assimilate her materials, as well as her moral feelings, and this had not made her indifferent but more of an artist, as the pressure of her private feeling was subjugated to a story's needs. Finally she had learned in *Emma* not to show her hand, a practice which gives its modern critics an added difficulty. In writing *Sanditon* she turned back to a sense of place, to a wide overview of locales as she had begun to use in Bath scenes in her Northanger Abbey story. Anna interestingly was to compare these two stories; 'The Heywoods', as she later told James Edward, 'stand in place of the Morlands. In the last named family the Wife is the more prominent character – the *talker* in short: in Sanditon it is the Husband, & I think Mr. Heywood talks as much to the purpose as Mrs. Morland. Perhaps we were to have seen very little more of the Heywoods; in which case they were made enough of – on the other hand, in Northhanger Abbey Mrs. Allen stands out. ...'[20] Anna has authority, we must feel, because she had talked with her aunt in January and February 1817 while *Sanditon* was in process, but Jane may not have wished to *replace* her Morland tale or even counter its defects. She felt it might never appear, but she may have had it in mind as an aid for experiment. She had good precedents for a fetish over locale, too. Seaside resorts in 1817 were touted absurdly as they competed for clients, and Mrs Lybbe Powys had praised seaviews at the Isle of Wight (Sandown there was near the home of Charles's commander) no more lyrically than others praised Bognor, or the benefits of Eastbourne, then one-and-a-half miles from the sea but extending itself to the coast.

Nearly confined to bed and seeing fewer people, Jane let her imagination work in opposition to her circumstances so that *Sanditon* is full of open views – and she nourished herself on Fanny's letters. Today we may find it hard to imagine Fanny's demure accent, but we do have hints of her personality in her diary, and we begin to see what sustained Jane. 'Oh! the miserable events of this day! My mother, my beloved mother torn from us!' Fanny had told herself when Elizabeth died. 'After eating a hearty dinner, she was taken *violently* ill and *expired* (my God have mercy upon us) in $\frac{1}{2}$ an hour!!!!' And then more trivially about names, 'Robert is too hideous to be born except by my two Aunts, Cassandra & Jane, who are very fond of both *Robert* & *Susan*!! did you ever hear of such a depraved taste? however it is not my fault.' Romantic events naturally held her, and so she had informed her diary about Anna's early suitor, whom she met and liked: 'Heard from Anna, she is actually wishing to break off her engagement!!!! What a girl!!!! Wrote to her', and then, 'Heard from Anna, and *all* is *over*, she has no longer anything to do with Mr. Michael Terry. Heavens! What will she do next!' Having called her own friend George Hatton 'Jupiter' or 'the Planet' or the 'brilliant object' and lovingly praised him, she had got a lecture from Aunt Cassandra 'on *Astronomy*' at which George faded in her firmament. (Cassandra had been popular enough in Kent to make her views felt for Fanny.) As for her father's abjectly changing his name to Knight, Fanny was truly mortified: 'Papa changed his name,' she wrote, 'in compliance with the will of the late Mr. Knight and we are therefore all *Knights* instead of dear old *Austens* How I hate it!!!!!!' She called the Dowager Lady Bridges her 'dearest Grand Mamma' but did not use such an endearment for Mrs Austen of Chawton.[21] Aloof and lonely, Fanny by January 1817 was losing her suitor John Plumtre, who courted another lady. Mr Wildman of Chilham Castle was warm, but was she on the shelf at twenty-four, and had she made a mistake in refusing Plumtre instead of marrying him? She put these doubts to Jane Austen in a letter sent on 27 January, the very day *Sanditon* was begun.

Jane was vastly amused: 'You are the Paragon of all that is Silly & Sensible, common-place & eccentric, Sad & Lively, Provoking and Interesting,' she replied to her niece dramatically. 'Who can keep pace with the fluctuations of your Fancy, the Capprizios of your Taste, the Contradictions of your Feelings? – You are so odd!' Though advising her well about Mr Wildman, Jane pumped her up into almost more than she was. Fanny had few capriccios of taste and her heart was normal, but Jane's gaiety did the girl little harm and showed its cause later on in her own letter: 'I am almost entirely cured of my rheumatism,' Jane told her niece, 'just a little pain in my knee now and then, to make me remember what it was, & keep on flannel.' Fanny's letters did dispel the heavy air of a sickroom. Jane was glad to have Fanny's brothers William and Henry visit at this time, even though Henry was bound for France. 'He is come back from France,' she had said of Edward Lefroy, 'thinking of the French as one could wish, disappointed in everything.' It was as though a long war with France had meant nothing. But she might have smiled to know that their Emperor was now learning English and saying about novels, in his island prison, 'See the effects of imagination!' and 'Imagination rules the world!'[22]

Her novel advanced well in February. Illness affected her muscles and bodily functions, not her intellect, acuity and style, and *Sanditon* is very remarkably vigorous. To judge from her MS., when her hand trembled she wrote in pencil and later went over in pen. Trimly and funnily Jane Austen had begun with Mr Parker's quest for a surgeon to adorn his health resort: after his coach upsets on the wrong Sussex road and he is cured of a sprained ankle by the Heywoods, he takes young Charlotte Heywood on to Sanditon as a guest. Here, one-and-three-quarter miles from the sea, Charlotte meets grotesque or romantic oddities, all of them livelier than Parker's silly wife. His two brothers and two sisters, at least, echo the Austens of Hampshire. Sidney is as dashing as Henry Austen was before bankruptcy, and Diana, Susan and Arthur Parker might be Cassandra, Jane and James as hypochondriacs. Jane meant to call her novel *The Brothers* after Crabbe's tale, according to a family tradition, and the Parkers have her own brothers' delight in each other: 'the manners of the Parkers were always pleasant among themselves' as Charlotte notes.

Picking up a copy of *Camilla* in Sanditon's library, and dropping it when she thinks of the heroine's debts, Charlotte becomes the reader's amused guide. She sizes up Diana and Susan well: they have the 'enjoyments of Invalidism'. Susan talks with salts in hand or takes drops near a hot fire in mid-July, and Diana dashes about to do useless good deeds or forgets her own weakness, her spasmodic bile, to rub a coachman's foot for six hours. The sisters outwit life and death, exaggerating and then ignoring their frailties to laugh at the mortal coil. And yet Diana is chiefly a busybody, and her brother Arthur is mainly a slow, sodden oaf, wolfing butter in secret and talking of the horrors of gunpowder tea – as well he might since the Prussian Blue colouring in green tea (used to colour or face the leaf) had paralytic effects.

Every resort needs a seducer, a poet. The local version of Sir Egerton Brydges is the fatuous young Sir Edward Denham. Dependent on his stingy aunt Lady Denham, he is lightly reminiscent of Anne Lefroy's brother but he uses books only to seduce, so that the author at this point reverses her Morland tale to show how *men* ruin themselves (and try to ruin others) as readers of poetry and novels. Sir Edward is very satisfied to be in 'the line' of Richardson's Lovelace: 'Pathos to madden one!' he tells Charlotte about Robert Burns's lyrics. 'If ever there was a Man who *felt* it was Burns,' but 'Wordsworth has the true soul' of poetry. Unimpressed by Romantic poetry Jane Austen had mocked it in *Persuasion*, and in a letter to her sister about a Byron poem: 'I have read the Corsair, mended my petticoat, & have nothing else to do.' But her mockery is reserved here for the lesser literary man, the critic with jargon, or the type such as Mrs Lefroy's brother Egerton who had forced the Austens to recite his poetry at their theatricals and later tried to behave as a long-locked, proud hero.

Locales are so suggestive that our brief glimpse of a sickly, rich West Indian visitor Miss Lambe is compelling. 'Half Mulatto, chilly and tender', the author describes her with an allusion to Shakespeare's clown Lavatch, who in *All's Well That Ends Well* knows 'the many will be too chill and tender' for the narrow gate and will go to the great house.[23] Miss Lambe, it seems, will be ruined by wealth.

Very ill in March, Jane Austen at last began to write her Chapter 12. Here she takes Charlotte on a pleasant walk between green fields and past poor Clara Brereton, who sits outdoors near a seducer. Charlotte enters Lady Denham's house, and there on the walls in an empty room she finds two dead husbands glaring at each other, one in a miniature and the other in a great picture near the fire. 'Poor Mr Hollis', Jane Austen wrote of the smaller husband. 'It was impossible not to feel him hardly used; to be obliged to stand back in his own House, & see the best place by the fire constantly occupied by Sir H. D.' or Sir Harry Denham.

It was a good joke, and her last in a novel. She had made her Charlotte likeable, close to us, a companion who makes us believe in Sanditon's grotesques. Jane Austen's success moreover, here and elsewhere, is partly in a quality of intimacy: no other novelist seems to believe as deeply and happily in readers, and a close, enlivening companionship, or Charlotte Heywood quality, keeps her novels read. (Charlotte's very slight degree of primness only adds to *her* charm.)

She left off her story on 18 March, but managed a letter to Fanny five days later: 'I have had a good deal of fever at times & indifferent nights,' Jane admitted, 'but am considerably better now, & recovering my Looks a little, which have been bad enough, black & white & every wrong colour.' This suggests that she had developed either hyperpigmentation of the skin or vitiligo (sharply demarcated patches of depigmented skin in areas of increased pigmentation). Increased pigmentation is a feature of Addison's disease which results from destruction of the adrenal glands. The adrenals are cup-like structures which sit on the kidneys. Destruction is usually by tuberculosis or infiltration by tumour, both having spread from primary sites in other organs. Typically the tuberculosis would have started in the lungs or bowels and may have involved the spine as well. This would account for her abdominal and back pain – and the spread of tuberculosis to the adrenals would account for the hyperpigmentation. On the other hand, though modern pathologists state it is less likely, cancer of the stomach or bowels is known to spread to the adrenal glands, destroying them and, again, causing Addison's disease and hyperpigmentation. The primary cancer would be responsible for abdominal discomfort or pain, nausea, vomiting and diarrhoea. In any case the Addison's disease would also cause muscle weakness and fatigue, but these may not have been specific symptoms, only the result of general disability from any disease.

Complicating the story is the possibility of idiopathic Addison's disease where the body produces antibodies to its own adrenal (and other) glands, thus destroying them. In this condition, vitiligo, as distinct from hyperpigmentation alone, is well recorded in modern cases.

In 1964 Sir Zachary Cope diagnosed Jane Austen's illness as Addison's disease, but he has been challenged by a specialist who, rightly, notes that if the changes in skin colour were ignored, the other complaints could be attributed to cancer or tuberculosis *per se* without incriminating adrenal damage and consequent Addison's disease.[24]

Modern pathology at least is cautioning. It is surely inaccurate to say, as a careless writer does, that she had Addison's syndrome beyond doubt when it is only *likely* that she did. Sir Zachary had called his finding a 'surmise'. Jane was reticent – not prudish – in describing her illness for fear of alarming others: but in March 1817 she suffered from muscle weakness, fatigue, epigastric or upper abdominal discomfort or pain, bouts of nausea, vomiting, diarrhoea, and it seems from alarming vitiligo.

Her looks were then slowly being destroyed. She gave up brushing her hair. In January she had played at the pianoforte and told Caroline, 'the Piano Forté often talks of you; – in various keys, tunes

& expressions I allow'. But in March when she had shut her instrument perhaps for the last time, she simply wrote, 'The Piano Forte's Duty, & will be happy to see you whenever you can come'.

As she lost her vitality, she hoped air and rides with a new saddle would help. 'I was languid & dull & very bad company,' she wrote after conceding that her looks were poor. 'I am better now – to my own feelings at least' and 'air & exercise is what I want'. Her sister and nephew then walked beside her donkey: 'I took my 1st ride yesterday & liked it very much,' she claimed. 'I went up Mounters Lane, & round by where the new Cottages are to be, & found the exercise & everything very pleasant.'[25]

After Egerton sent her a last payment for *Sense and Sensibility*, she drew up a memo on her earnings:

Profits of my Novels, over & above the £600 in
the Navy Fives.

	£
Residue from the 1st Edit: of Mansfield Park, remaining in Henrietta S^t – March, 1816	13 . . 7 ——
Rec^d from Egerton, on 2^d Edit: of Sense & S— March 1816	— 12 . . 15 —
Feb^r 21. 1817 } From Profits of Emma ——— —————	38 . . 18 —
March 7. 1817 } From Egerton – 2^d Edit: S & S. - - - —	19 . . 13 —

With £140 from her Dashwood story, then thirty pounds as first payment on its second edition, as well as £110 from selling her *Pride and Prejudice* copyright and perhaps all of £320 from *Mansfield Park*, she had invested £600 in the Navy 5 per cents. She may have lost £13 7s. in Henry's bankruptcy but she had earned about £684 13s. in her lifetime as an author.[26]

Any joy she had in that, certainly, was overshadowed after her uncle James Leigh Perrot died at Scarlets on 28 March. He had faded slowly enough to revive old memories of Mrs Austen's. 'The expectation of bad news from Scarlets keeps us in worry, your Grandmamma especially,' Jane had informed a niece; 'she sits brooding over Evils which cannot be remedied.' Perrot's main evil was that he obsessively had consoled his wife for every affront while neglecting the Austens' urgent needs. 'My dearest Wife,' he had penned for instance when he gave Mrs Leigh Perrot some lovely seed pearls,

> With thee no Days can Winter seem,
>   Nor Frost, nor Blast can chill;
> Thou the soft Breeze, the cheering beam,
>   That keeps it Summer still.
>
>   yours Faithfully
>   January 4th   lovingly & Wholly
>   1800   James Leigh Perrot[27]

Wishing to keep the Austens under an obligation to her, he virtually left her everything. Unchanged since March 1811, his will simply put his Scarlets and Bath properties at her disposal, left funds subject to her own life interest to James and £1,000 apiece to each of Mrs Austen's children who survived his wife. With one brother on half-pay and another bankrupt and Edward Knight, too, embarrassed for funds, Jane was deeply cut. 'The shock of my uncle's will brought on a relapse,' she wrote to her brother Charles on 6 April; 'and I was so ill on friday & thought myself so likely to be worse that I could not but press for Cassandra's returning.' Her sister did not linger long at the Scarlets funeral. 'I am the only one of the Legatees who has been so silly,' Jane admitted, but she had her uncle's will in mind when she made out her own will on 27 April. She did not forget Henry or his elder servant, but left her small fortune to Cassandra,

> subject to the payment of my Funeral Expenses, & to a Legacy of £50. to my Brother Henry, & £50. to M^{de} Bijion – which I request may be paid as soon as convenient. And I appoint my said dear Sister the Executrix of this my last will & Testament.[28]

Hearing soon after the Perrot will that Aunt Jane was 'too ill to have me in the house' Caroline went to stay with her sister at Wyards, but next day walked over with Anna. They found their aunt upstairs in a dressing-gown seated like an invalid in an armchair, but Jane rose and 'pointing to seats which had been arranged for us by the fire, she said, "There's a chair for the married lady, and a little stool for you, Caroline"'. The visitors were soon ushered out and Caroline remembered her pallor, but warmer weather helped. '*Now*, I am getting well again, & indeed have been gradually tho' slowly recovering my strength for the last three weeks,' Jane wrote on 22 May. She had been in bed since April and Mr Curtis had failed to stop her diarrhoea, until a consultant arrived, but it was felt Jane ought to be under expert care. 'Our nearest *very good*, is at Winchester,' she wrote to Miss Sharp, 'where there is a Hospital & capital Surgeons.' At Winchester with her sister she would be under the care of Giles King Lyford, a surgeon at the county hospital, and Mrs Heathcote had taken lodgings for them near the cathedral.

Enslaving others as nurses, Jane now praised the ladies of her cottage and wrote that 'if I live to be an old woman, I must expect to wish I had died now'. Yet her letter of 22 May betrays guilt over worrying her family, and above all a wish to be gone from a gloomy fuss. She had acted the invalid too long when playfulness was her best aid. Sickness hardly kept her from being bored or from thinking of Alethea's luck in 'being frisked off like half of England, into Switzerland'.[29]

One last fuss was made before she was bundled into a carriage on Saturday, 24 May. It rained as she was riding westward with her brother Henry and William Knight, who accompanied her on horseback. Winchester was not far off, though it upset her to see two men she loved 'riding in rain almost all the way'. But, before nightfall, she arrived at the Davids' home with its bow window in College Street, not far from the long old solemnly grey and lovely shape of a cathedral she knew well.

20

—————————⬥⬥⬥—————————

Winchester

The Lord is my Shepherd; I shall not want.
Psalm 23

A change of scene refreshed her: the journey had caused 'very
little fatigue', and at College Street she felt better in late May.
Above all she wished not to seem pitiable. Though weak and thin,
Jane Austen was ready to exert herself, unlikely to be beguiled by
doctors, not frightened by the humiliations and alarms of her illness;
James found her 'well aware of her condition' – not appalled by it.
In *Persuasion* she had given invalid Mrs Smith a calm spirit with an
urge to be *of use*, and one of her boasts was now of usefulness; but
she had to rely upon Cassandra and this was an unequal point,
mocking her self-reliance. A nurse was hired for pay at Winchester
only to be dismissed by Cassandra and replaced by Mary Lloyd.
Meanwhile she tried to combat the effects of dependency: she was
unworthy, and as for her chief nurse, 'my dearest sister, my tender,
watchful indefatigable nurse, has not been made ill by her exertions.
As to what I owe her, and to the anxious affection of all my beloved
family on this occasion, I can only cry over it.' So she kept on terms
with her conscience in May.

'I continue to get better,' she wrote on her third day at the Davids'.
Her looks and handwriting were poor, but she was 'very fast' recovering: 'I am *now* out of bed from 9 in the morn^g to 10 at night – upon
the sopha t'is true,' she informed James Edward, 'but I eat my meals

with aunt Cass: in a rational way, & can employ myself, and walk from one room to another.'[1]

She had a view of the headmaster Dr Gabell's garden from upstairs rooms, and she knew responsible landlords. Matthew David, at fifty-three, was an overseer of the poor in the parish of Little St Swithun; he lately had married Mary Miller, a widow in her sixtieth year who was to be famous as great-aunt to the college's pastry cook. David's small rooms and low ceilings had satisfied Mrs Heathcote, but he was not well-to-do; his payments of poor rates were bracketed with larger ones of a Miss Gauntlett, a relative of local wine merchants, and Arabella Gauntlett was perhaps aware of the Austens upstairs.

Elizabeth Heathcote, with Alethea, paid a call each day. Elizabeth's son William was to recall that in 1808 or 1809 he was 'at a Twelfth day party where Jane Austen drew the character of Mrs. Candour, and assumed the part with great spirit'.[2] With lively friends now, it was surely impossible to play the part of a poor invalid, especially as Giles King Lyford found her better. 'You will be happy to know that our accounts from Winchester are very good,' Mrs Austen told Anna after reading a report from Cassandra that said: 'Jane has had a better night than she has had for many weeks. . . . Mr. Lyford says he thinks better of her than he has ever done, though he must still consider her in a precarious state.'[3] Her last weeks were to include surprising rallies, and at these times she felt alert and creative. Lyford, who was one of the best doctors in Parchment Street, with more than a local reputation, seems to have believed that she had *a wasting disease*, usually meaning cancer or TB; he must have known remissions were possible, but he found her 'precarious' before he timed her racing pulse.

Still she was better: 'Mr. Lyford says he will cure me,' she joked, '& if he fails I shall draw up a Memorial and lay it before the Dean & Chapter, & have no doubt of redress from that Pious, Learned, and Disinterested Body.'

If he failed she must complain from the grave. Opposite the Davids were outgardens, stables and neat houses with prebendal occupants who lived in or near Dome Alley for a part of each year. The Dean and his Chapter were responsible for Winchester Cathedral and not subject to the see's bishop in their jurisdiction over burials. Burials in the nave were not just then in excellent repute: Charles Ball in his *Winchester Walks* (1818) found 'a general comparative want of interest' in its graves, but to be buried under that fretted roof was a rare honour. Dean Rennell it seems had known Mr Austen, and Prebendary Nott, a slim, crippled, eager scholar, had been up at All Souls College in 1788 just when James Austen as a fellow of St John's was printing his weekly Tory journal. Nott and James Austen had opposed Whiggery and supported King and Church in the colleges. Their views were in harmony. Possibly James was to write the inscription for his sister's grave, and we know that he came to Winchester just after his sister died but *not* to attend her funeral; if he spoke of his sister's merits to Rennell and Nott, both men listened with sympathy. Both accepted a comic novelist for burial in Walkelyn's cathedral, though as she was read by the Regent she had her recommendations.

Yet late in May her rally held: 'I live chiefly on the sofa, but am allowed to walk from one room to the other,' she reports; 'I have been out once in a sedan-chair, and am to repeat it, and be promoted to a wheel-chair as the weather serves.' She sent a note to Caroline to say 'that if I would take her advice I should cease writing till I was 16, and that she herself often wished she had *read* more, and written *less* in the corresponding years of her own life'.[4] She hoped James Edward would prosper – and indeed he inherited most of the Perrot money. In 1820 Mrs Leigh Perrot was to settle £300 a year on him, though he irked her by becoming an Anglican priest; she increased that sum after he married Emma Smith, and then, when he named a child Cholmeley after her own maiden name she exalted him; he took the name Austen-Leigh, and inherited Scarlets when at ninety-two Mrs Leigh Perrot died – to the accompaniment of a windstorm. Her memorial tablet survived a fire that burned down her church, and her seed pearls danced on an inheritor's slim neck as late as 1987. Perhaps 'Aunt Perrot' had earned the sympathy of windstorms and fires – but she was grim while she lived. Favouring some Austens with money, denying others and changing her mind, in old age she had stirred up trouble, as when she neglected Frank Austen, then tried to bribe him while offering lures to James's family. James's daughter Anna became suspicious of Frank Austen's daughter Catherine Hubback: *Sanditon*'s MS is 'at the mercy of Mrs Hubback', Anna later wrote, 'and she will be pretty sure to make use of it as soon as she thinks she safely may'.[5] James Edward compared the Knights unfavourably with 'Lloyds & other such loving people', while cooling towards them,[6] and Fanny turned against Anna. Though not wholly to blame for minor family misunderstandings, Mrs Leigh Perrot in her unequal dealings had soothed no one in her later years.

But she never divided Jane Austen's brothers, and *their* mutual affection held: James was uneasy, edgy or morose, but his final letter displays a simple trust in family. 'Dear Charles', he dictated to Anna ten days before he died at Steventon in 1819, 'If you have not bought the books do not give yourself any more trouble about them [and as for the shirts] I shall return them by my Brother Edward, & get them changed, & then the books & shirts can all come down together – I shall write to you by him, in the mean time accept my thanks & my love – I am much as I have been for some time past. Y^{rs} affect^{ly} J. AUSTEN.'[7]

Jane Austen's other brothers knew a longer happiness. Edward Knight – who watched all of his children reach maturity – in 1817 took Fanny and Lizzy to Paris, where Lizzy at seventeen met her future husband Edward Royd Rice, by whom she would have fifteen children. Some Knights were long-lived, and the eldest daughter of Jane's agreeable nephew William – Elizabeth Caroline – was to reach her hundredth birthday as late as 1926. Marriage and the Navy in turn did well for Frank and Charles Austen. To the particularly scandalized horror of Mrs Leigh Perrot, who disliked the Lloyds, Frank as a widower in one year gave away Mary Jane's hand and married his capable and self-effacing Martha Lloyd, or 'in the year '28 he married first his elder daughter and then himself', as Cassandra put it. 'He chose for his 2nd wife a very old friend of mine, who makes an excellent mother to his younger children.' When Frank was knighted Cassandra marked that event by giving Jane Austen's copy of *Camilla* to the new Lady Austen, and visited them on Portsdown Hill, where it seems the ladies 'often read the novels aloud'. Frank knew fifteen years with his lady; he went to sea again on the *Vindictive*, before he became Admiral of the Fleet at eighty-nine. Almost as enduring, Charles at seventy-three served in action and died of cholera off the coast of Burma on HMS *Pluto* to be buried at Sober Island.

Jane Austen's brothers had been not unlike Mr Austen in being religious, self-disciplined, keen on details that would help them. Frank was splendidly unemotional, cool, and modest. Jane knew the defects of his fairness perhaps, but her family's love was based on mutual respect and generous behaviour. James's strong affection for her survived his dislike of novels, Edward gave her money when facing ruin, and Henry despite illness had dealt with Murray and worked hard for her. She felt their deep kindness, and at Winchester she knew their loving, urgent concern.

In June her condition worsened. Every bit of ground was lost – and Mr Lyford felt he could not save her. Charles hurried to her bedside, where he found her 'very ill'. On the 19th Charles saw her 'in the evening for the last time in the world, as I greatly fear, her doctor having no hopes'. James for his part made her doctor tell the worst. 'Mr Lyford has candidly told us that her case was desperate,' he wrote to his son; 'Lyford said he saw no signs of immediate dissolution but added that with such a pulse – 120 – it was impossible for any person to last long.'[8]

Yet 'Jane began to get better,' Mary Lloyd noted, and the crisis oddly passed. In pernicious anaemia and Addison's disease severe gastro-intestinal disturbances may for a time abate, then the patient may feel 'much better and be hopeful of recovery'. Late in June the invalid lived on, and the wry or black comedy of the desperately ill was perhaps not lost on her; she had sent mourners home early and was still to read Fanny's letters, talk sensibly and write a poem.

Winchester had amused her before. Its weekly Tory paper had begun to advertise that at Jacob's shop one could buy instalments of Rowlandson's comic designs 'THE DANCE OF LIFE' – and Winchester was in a new dance, cleaning itself up after its years as an Army barracks and appealing to the tourist trade. A bust of Charles II's mistress had been removed lately from Water Lane, and the county gaol in Gaol Street, soon to revert to its more respectable name Jewry Street, had a glittering new front. Debtors could now peer out from windows in a white-brick façade 'enriched with rusticated coins' (Mr Moneypenny's happy idea). To make way for commerce and the population, the fine old historic churches of St Boniface, St Nicholas, Allhallows and St Mary Odes were all gone without trace – and dances occurred in a hospital which St Brinstan once idly dedicated to Christ's herald. At Westgate the old keep was a billiard room. Perhaps Mr Powlett's golden jutting clock in the High Street told the time very well for a secular age.

On Monday, 14 July, the *Hampshire Chronicle* advertised the 'WIN-CHESTER RACES' for horses, mares and geldings and also happened to announce that Jane Austen's former music teacher Mr Chard was soon to play 'the piano forté' at St John's Hall.[9]

The next day, Tuesday, 15 July, was St Swithun's day. Jane Austen by then had rallied remarkably, and felt so well that Charles recorded in his diary forty-eight hours later, 'a letter from Cassandra raising hopes of dear Jane's recovery'. In the poem she now composed, she imagines lords and ladies who have set their races without getting gentle St Swithun's leave to hold them. Why should the town care for its soul? Hearing of the races, Winchester's or Venta's saint jumps from his shrine to curse a people who have neglected *him*:

Oh! subjects rebellious! Oh Venta depraved!
When once we are buried you think we are dead
But behold me immortal! By vice you're enslaved
You have sinned & must suffer. Then farther he said

These races and revels and dissolute measures
With which you're debasing a neighbouring Plain
Let them stand – You shall meet with your curse in your pleasures
Set off for your course, I'll pursue with *my* rain.

Ye cannot but know my command o'er July
Henceforward I'll triumph in shewing my powers
Shift your race as you will it shall never be dry
The curse upon Venta is July in showers –

J.A.

St Swithun's rain is mainly unkind to ladies' hats. Cassandra, it seems, underlined the words, *When once we are buried you think we are dead But behold me immortal!*, and at the bottom of a badly written, misspelled manuscript (as if the poem had been dictated to Mary Lloyd) one finds the clear words: 'written July 15th: 1817: by Jane Austen who died early in the morning ($\frac{1}{2}$ past 4) of July 18th. 1817 aged 41 y^{rs}'.[10]

In the evening of 15 July when 'her complaint returnd' she rested as if she had no more to do. 'She slept more & much more comfortably,' Cassandra noted, 'indeed during the last eight & forty hours she was more asleep than awake. Her looks altered & she fell away, but I perceived no material diminution of strength & tho' I was then hopeless of a recovery I had no suspicion how rapidly my loss was approaching.' She later wrote that Jane Austen had been 'a treasure, such a Sister, such a friend as never can have been surpassed, – she was the sun of my life, the gilder of every pleasure, the soother of every sorrow', and in the last forty-eight hours, on 16 and 17 July, she watched with attentive devotion and spoke when Jane was feebly awake.

Jane deliberately had used and flattered her, learned from her and pried into her mind and nearly monopolized her heart so that Cassandra later admitted to her niece Fanny, 'I am conscious that my affection for her made me sometimes unjust to & negligent of others.'[11] But in a hierarchy of loyalties Jane had held her first, jokingly to the detriment of witty Oxford brothers and their stories as when Jane told her, 'You are indeed the finest comic writer of the age.' As for Edward's new Kentish wealth, 'I am as glad as I can be at anybody's being rich except you and me.' Such jokes had reinforced an alliance deep, fierce, protective and implicitly advertised to others: 'She would frequently say to me,' Caroline recalled, 'that Aunt Cassandra could teach everything better than *she* could – Aunt Cass. *knew* more – Aunt Cass. could tell me better whatever I wanted to know.'[12] She had made Cassandra into an audience, an applauder who could love a joke as a joke, and so Jane's play of wit and clarity had flourished in the family. It perhaps had been no bad thing to have a mother who disliked 'blind fondness' and was not shrivelled up with gratitude, not silly or self-indulgent but at her patchworks and gardening all the week. Jane had remarked with mock weariness, 'my mother will like me to write to her. I shall try at least,' or referred to friends 'all of whom my Mother was glad to see & I was very glad to escape'. But her mother had been a prod, a gossip, a fellow spy, and with security at home she had been free to be ruthless and acerbic, candid and hilarious in her stories, free to avoid what was tame, bland, expected, false, ladylike. Her mother's hard, unsentimental clarity and Cassandra's common sense had lighted her way. She had not defied *them*, but gathered them in, 'thankful for praise, open to remark, and submissive to criticism'. And if she was ever quite so 'submissive' as Henry thought, she had learned this from her dependency – that no one is self-sufficient, and so our behaviour with those close to us and the influence a woman may exert in her relationships is a prime field for realistic fiction. The influence of women in every aspect of society is implicit in Jane Austen's focus on a small arena in her domestic comedies of manners; she had been artful, for example, in showing how a woman may lead a man from ill-conceived, false or mistaken behaviour into better judgement and a more sensitive relationship. As much as Aphra Behn or Mary Astell or gifted writers of her time such as Hannah More and Mary Hays, Jane Austen was a woman's advocate – and yet unlike others she had presented the real thing, real men as viewed by believable women and views of real female consciousnesses. We feel that she tells the truth, not that she belabours a thesis. Her portrayals are so accurate and clear that her works have become tests of truth in Western culture, refreshing and clarifying us as deeply as Dante, Cervantes or Shakespeare may. She had not stinted in what she knew as 'the labour of the novelist'. She had pursued technical mastery, intensity, lightness. Flexibility had become her keynote. She unravelled emotions in narrative, while working for a balance and a blending in her descriptions of feeling, analyses, interior views of character and the overtness of dramatic collision and talk and event; her mark was in a seeming casualness with a maximum of pressure, a vibrant intensity of effect. To convey the 'liveliest effusions of wit' she had attended to rhythm and had polished and pruned to Cassandra's usual satisfaction. That nearly unimpressionable and deep-feeling sister had been a judge and opponent, a supplier of wisdom and detail, a co-conspirator and censor not easy to please even with *Mansfield Park*, and Cassandra's absences were painful and her letters urgently needed. She was Jane's buffer. 'I am sure nobody can desire your letters as much as I do,' Jane had told her truly and not to put herself down added, 'and I don't think anybody deserves them so well.' She saved Cassandra's letters, as her sister in turn devotedly saved *hers* only to face the problem later as to which of Jane Austen's letters she ought in good conscience to destroy.[13]

For so much unfailing devotion Cassandra was to inherit £561.2.0 from her sister's estate. The details may be trivial to us, but they would have interested Jane, who had meant to provide what little money she had for Cassandra's well-being: only that modest sum from her estate was to remain after debts (£25) and a probate fee (£21.1.0) and funeral expenses (£92) and legacies were paid, and her sister would still have to pay 3 per cent of the principal or £16.16.8 as a death duty. Cassandra's main legacy was in an ardent memory, surprising because when she talked of Jane there was 'an accent of *living'* love in her voice. 'She looked to me quite different from anyone I had ever seen,' a relative wrote of Cassandra's later years, 'a pale, dark-eyed old lady, with a high arched nose and a kind smile, dressed in a long cloak and a large drawn bonnet, both made of black satin.' But James Edward's fashionable wife could not understand the silly fuss over her husband's poor relative, and felt that Aunt Cassandra was no more than 'a very nice delicate looking thin elderly woman with a good deal of conversation', perhaps boring, in a kindly way, but ladylike in 'manner'.[14]

Lyford had warned Mary Lloyd that his patient would die in pain. Her worst hours were ahead, and he 'feared suffering'. Mary had returned to Jane Austen's bedside in July to find Cassandra then barely managing, relieved after eight weeks' vigil by one maidservant. Hoping to be of use – in the acute and alarming distress near the hour of death – she made herself busy at College Street and heard the invalid say, 'You have always been a kind sister to me, Mary.'

In the little act of dying Jane Austen was now most kindly watched: Lyford noted she was critically thin and weak. But on Thursday, 17 July, she sent her sister out on an errand she 'was anxious about' and Cassandra returned at about 4.45 p.m. to find her getting over faintness and oppression; by six Jane was talking quietly. What can one say on one's deathbed occasion? In *Pilgrim's Progress* when the hero at last sees that 'Mr Civility' is only a cheat who may rob him of salvation, the author writes, *Now Christian looked for nothing but death*. When Jane's pain returned on this summer evening and her sister asked if she wanted anything, she replied aptly, 'Nothing but death.'

Lyford had been sent for. Cassandra bent very close to her. Jane said she had little 'fixed pain' but could not describe what she felt. She called out in a small voice, 'God grant me patience, Pray for me, oh Pray for me.' Lyford then arrived to give her a drug such as laudanum for her 'ease', and she was unconscious for nine-and-a-half hours: 'a slight motion of the head with every breath remaind till almost the last'. Her sister sat six hours with a pillow in her lap to support Jane's head 'which was almost off the bed', and in fatigue yielded to Mary Lloyd, only to take up the vigil again. 'Given the choice, I should like to have died in my nurse's arms,' Mme de Sévigné once had said, and in one quiet, final dark hour before dawn

Cassandra was a nurse, and then at about 4.30 a.m., on 18 July 1817, she was able to shut her sister's eyes.

Lyford supposed 'a large blood vessel had given way', and this helped to console her family. Woman did not attend funerals, and doctors often assured women that the deceased had felt no pain. The Austens were deeply shocked and saddened, but relieved to know Jane Austen's sufferings were over. She 'went off without a struggle', Frank wrote. Anna volunteered to come to her grandmother but Mrs Austen declined that offer: 'I had a letter from Cassandra this morning', Mrs Austen replied to Anna. 'She is in great affliction but bears it like a Christian. Dear Jane is to be buried in the Cathedral, I believe on Thursday. In which case Cassandra will come home as soon as it is over. Miss Lloyd does not go. – Your father, Mr. Knight who is now here, your Uncle Henry (who is now at Winchester giving the necessary directions) and your Uncle Frank will attend.'

Mrs Austen, nearly seventy-eight, was struck and grieved. On the other hand, there is no sign in her letters that she mourned more than she would have done over the loss of any one of her children. Her practicality, stoicism and curiosity about her living family saved her from being morose. Jane had been her daughter, but Anna was her joy. 'As to my health it is much as usual, sometimes bad sometimes tolerable', she told Anna in 1820. And a little later she wrote to her son Charles, 'I am much broken since you were here. I never now quit the house except to creep about the gardens but my spirits are good and I am able to enjoy the society of my relations and real friends, and my eyes are in general well enough to permit me to employ some part of every day at my patchwork. . . . T'is a miserable scrawl, but I can't perform better. I can manage a needle better than a pen or your quilt would not be worth acceptance.'[15] Looked after by Cassandra and Martha, she kept at her sewing for months after she became bedridden and until shortly before her death in January 1827 at the age of eighty-seven. At the moment, in the crisis of Jane's death, she was watched at Steventon by the attentive Martha.

Despite Henry's help at Winchester, a burden of work fell on Cassandra as mourners arrived and nieces needed comfort. She wrote to Fanny very fully about Jane Austen's last days and hours; 'even now in her coffin', as Cassandra added on Sunday 20 July, 'there is such a sweet serene air over her countenance as is quite pleasant to contemplate'. She kept one lock of Jane's hair to give later to Harriet Palmer, sent another lock along to Fanny, and yet another as a memento to Miss Sharp with a pair of Jane's clasps and a small bodkin.

The *Hampshire Chronicle* ran a short, stark notice under a Saturday report about Jane Austen's death. A fuller obituary, actually written out in one version beneath a fair copy of Jane's last poem, was sent along to the *Courier*, which edited it for its issue of 22 July. Here importantly a few days after her death, she was identified for the first time as 'Authoress of Emma, Mansfield Park, Pride and Prejudice, and Sense and Sensibility', and that notice was reprinted in the *Salisbury and Winchester Journal* on 28 July. Obituaries ran in the *Star*, *London Chronicle* and *Gentleman's Magazine* in August and in the next month's *Monthly Magazine* and *New Monthly Magazine* – and Henry easily did more for his sister's reputation in his edition of her two last novels in December by saying that Winchester Cathedral 'in the whole catalogue of its mighty dead does not contain the ashes of a brighter genius or a sincerer Christian'.

James and his son wrote elegies; James's 'Venta' is a conscience-ridden, troubled work, arguing that Jane Austen was lovable despite her fiction:

> But to her family alone
> Her real, genuine worth was known,

as James put it.

> They saw her ready still to share
> The labours of domestic care,
> As if *their* prejudice to shame
> Who, jealous of fair female fame,
> Maintain that literary taste
> In womans mind is much misplaced,
> Inflames their vanity & pride,
> And draws from useful works aside.
> Such wert thou Sister![16]

If 'womans mind' is inflamed by literary pride his sister was a rare exception. Having attacked novel-writing often, James certainly approved (if he did not write) the memorial text which does not mention her fiction at all. An allusion to her novel-writing, on her grave, might have implied she had *had* to write for profit and that her brothers had failed to support her. Still with her works out of print in the 1820s, people were to wonder why she was in the cathedral. Others for years were to walk over her bones without knowing who she was, or why she was there.

Stories, true and untrue, about her partial obscurity might have amused her very much. 'Will you put up a notice board outside my shop to say that Jane Austen died there?' asked Octo La Croix of a college master's wife when he was a pastry cook at No. 8 College Street. 'Americans come in and want to know if she died there; they never buy anything and they waste my time.' But later he wanted to take the notice board down. 'Why, Octo?' asked his patron. And Octo replied, 'Because English people come in to know who Jane Austen was.' Or there was a visitor who wanted the polite verger to say where her grave was. 'I'm often asked,' said the verger wonderingly. 'Can you tell me if there was anything special about that lady?'[17] With profits from the *Memoir* of his aunt, James Edward was to pay for a brass tablet on the cathedral wall near her grave, alluding to the work of her life.

James Edward had been her youngest mourner. If Cassandra had wished to attend, she would not have been allowed to go to the funeral, or to walk behind her sister's coffin. On Thursday, 24 July 1817, there had been a busy, early stir at College Street. Jane's service had to be at 8 a.m., so that the burial office could be read and mourners dispersed before the canons' Morning Prayer at ten. When a hearse reached the Davids', and a coffin was handed down narrow steps in the house and put in position, Edward Knight with James's only son, Henry, Frank and Charles Austen began to follow the horses on foot, slowly walking west near the wall of the close towards St Swithun-upon-Kingsgate. With so much to prepare, Cassandra felt she had had no time for 'additional misery', but as she meant to see the last, she stood at her window: 'I watched the little mournful procession the length of the street & when it turnd from my sight & I had lost her for ever – even then I was not overpowered.' The service was taken by the Revd Thomas Watkins, Precentor, who read the burial office and saw the coffin laid to rest in the north aisle of the nave.

Cassandra usually thought of herself last. The funeral day was 'not so dreadful' she felt, but she was drained, empty and good for little, and as she admitted, 'I certainly have had considerable fatigue of body as well as anguish of mind for months back.'[18]

In July she started for home, leaving her sister 'for ever' in an historic town in the lovely valley of the Itchen. She would recall her sister's comic ferocity, tough good sense and love for the country: 'It is a Vile World, we are all for Self & I expected no better from any of us', her sister had written this very year. '–But though *Better* is not to be expected, *Butter* may, at least from Mrs Clement's Cow.' Travelling east to her home, Cassandra went back along a chalk road. In Hampshire in July the lark sings day and night, and in towns the fern-owl begins chattering after dusk. Farmers cut their hedges and spread the hay. The bloom of the lime hangs in long yellow tassels, and young swallows dart and sparkle in fields. Roses and irises and honeysuckles all make a show. Cassandra was perhaps consoled by the country and surely by her duties at home, but 'of course', as she wrote in her firm, clear hand, 'those employments suit me best which leave me most at leisure to think of her I have lost, and I do think of her in every variety of circumstance. In our happy hours' and also 'in her sick room, on her death-bed, and (as I hope) an inhabitant of heaven. Oh, if I may one day be re-united to her there!'

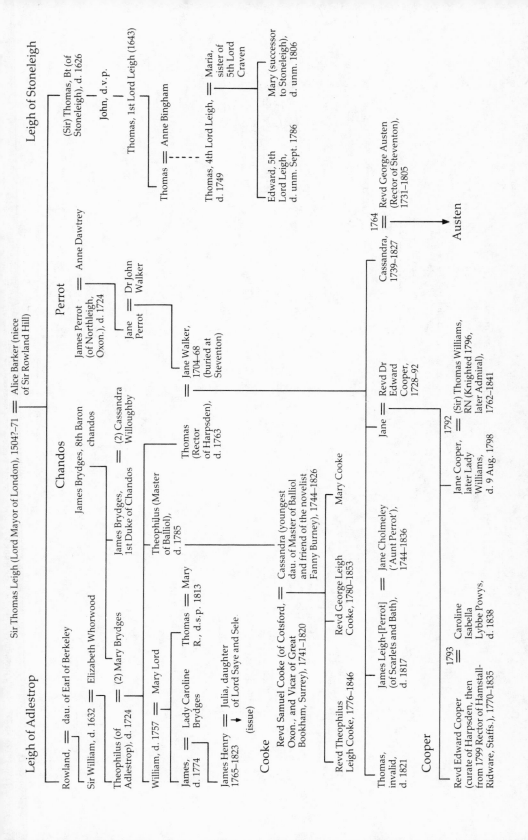

Leigh of Adlestrop

Sir Thomas Leigh (Lord Mayor of London), 1504?–71 == Alice Barker (niece of Sir Rowland Hill)

Leigh of Stoneleigh

Rowland, == dau. of Earl of Berkeley

(Sir) Thomas, Bt (of Stoneleigh), d. 1626

John, d.v.p.

Sir William, d. 1632 == Elizabeth Whorwood

Thomas, 1st Lord Leigh (1643)

Theophilus (of Adlestrop), d. 1724 == (2) Mary Brydges

Chandos

James Brydges, 8th Baron Chandos == (2) Cassandra Willoughby

Thomas == Anne Bingham

William, d. 1757 == Mary Lord

James Brydges, 1st Duke of Chandos

Thomas, 4th Lord Leigh, d. 1749 == Maria, sister of 5th Lord Craven

James, d. 1774 == Lady Caroline Brydges

Thomas == Mary R., d.s.p. 1813

Theophilus (Master of Balliol), d. 1785

Thomas (Rector of Harpsden), d. 1763

Edward, 5th Lord Leigh, d. unm. Sept. 1786

Mary (successor to Stoneleigh), d. unm. 1806

James Henry 1765–1823 → Julia, daughter of Lord Saye and Sele.

(issue)

Perrot

James Perrot (of Northleigh, Oxon.), d. 1724 == Anne Dawtrey

Jane == Dr John Perrot Walker

Jane Walker, 1704–68 (buried at Steventon)

Cooke

Revd Samuel Cooke (of Cotsford, Oxon., and Vicar of Great Bookham, Surrey), 1741–1820 == Cassandra (youngest dau. of Master of Balliol and friend of the novelist Fanny Burney), 1744–1826

Revd Theophilus Leigh Cooke, 1776–1846

Revd George Leigh Cooke, 1780–1853

Mary Cooke

Thomas, invalid, d. 1821

James Leigh-[Perrot] (of Scarlets and Bath), d. 1817 == Jane Cholmeley ('Aunt Perrot'), 1744–1836

Cassandra, 1739–1827

1764 == Revd George Austen (Rector of Steventon), 1731–1805 → Austen

Jane == Revd Dr Edward Cooper, 1728–92

1792

Jane Cooper, later Lady Williams, d. 9 Aug. 1798 == (Sir) Thomas Williams, RN (Knighted 1796, later Admiral), 1762–1841

Cooper

Revd Edward Cooper (curate of Harpsden, then from 1799 Rector of Hamstall-Ridware, Staffs.), 1770–1835

1793 == Caroline Isabella Lybbe Powys, d. 1838

2. Descendants of John Austen of Horsmonden, Kent

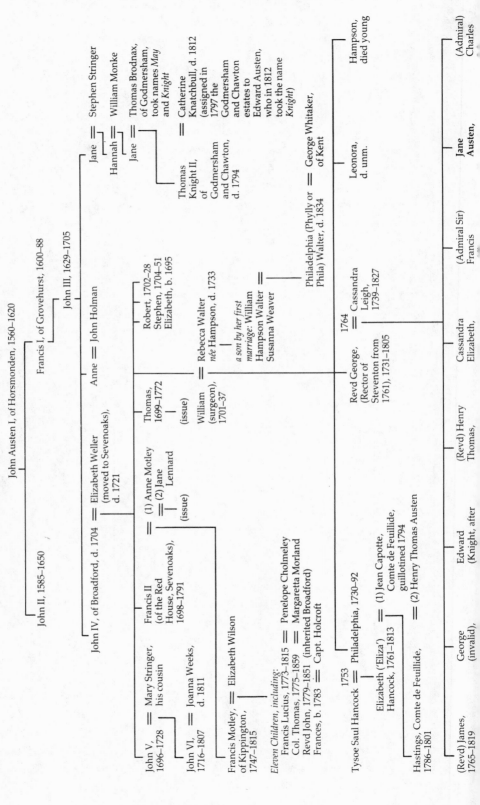

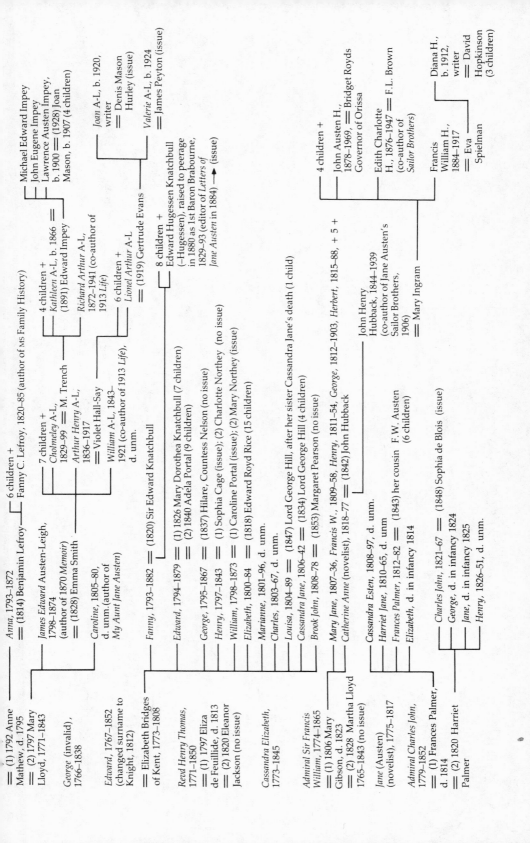

= (1) 1792 Anne Mathew, d. 1795
= (2) 1797 Mary Lloyd, 1771–1843

Anna, 1793–1872
= (1814) Benjamin Lefroy

6 children +
Fanny C. Lefroy, 1820–85 (author of MS Family History)

James Edward Austen-Leigh, 1798–1874 (author of 1870 Memoir)
= (1828) Emma Smith

George (invalid), 1766–1838

7 children +
Cholmeley A-L, 1829–99 = M. Trench

4 children +
Kathleen A-L, b. 1866 (1891) Edward Impey

Arthur Henry A-L, 1836–1917
= Violet Hall-Say

Richard Arthur A-L, 1872–1941 (co-author of 1913 Life)

Michael Edward Impey
John Eugene Impey
Lawrence Austen Impey, b. 1900 = (1928) Joan Mason, b. 1907 (4 children)

Joan A-L, b. 1920, writer
= Denis Mason Hurley (issue)

Valerie A-L, b. 1924
= James Peyton (issue)

Caroline, 1805–80, d. unm. (author of My Aunt Jane Austen)

Edward, 1767–1852 (changed surname to Knight, 1812)
= Elizabeth Bridges of Kent, 1773–1808

William A-L, 1843–1921 (co-author of 1913 Life), d. unm.

6 children +
Lionel Arthur A-L
(1919) Gertrude Evans

Fanny, 1793–1882 = (1820) Sir Edward Knatchbull

8 children +
Edward Hugessen Knatchbull (–Hugessen), raised to peerage in 1880 as 1st Baron Brabourne, 1829–93 (editor of Letters of Jane Austen in 1884) → (issue)

Sir Edward Knatchbull

Edward, 1794–1879
= (1) 1826 Mary Dorothea Knatchbull (7 children)
= (2) 1840 Adela Portal (9 children)

George, 1795–1867
= (1837) Hilare, Countess Nelson (no issue)

Henry, 1797–1843
= (1) Sophia Cage (issue); (2) Charlotte Northey (no issue)

William, 1798–1873
= (1) Caroline Portal (issue); (2) Mary Northey (issue)

Elizabeth, 1800–84
= (1818) Edward Royd Rice (15 children)

Marianne, 1801–96, d. unm.

Charles, 1803–67, d. unm.

Louisa, 1804–89 = (1847) Lord George Hill, after her sister Cassandra Jane's death (1 child)

Cassandra Jane, 1806–42 = (1834) Lord George Hill (4 children)

Brook John, 1808–78 = (1853) Margaret Pearson (no issue)

Rev'd Henry Thomas, 1771–1850
= (1) 1797 Eliza de Feuillide, d. 1813
= (2) 1820 Eleanor Jackson (no issue)

Cassandra Elizabeth, 1773–1845

Admiral Sir Francis William, 1774–1865
= (1) 1806 Mary Gibson, d. 1823
= (2) 1828 Martha Lloyd 1765–1843 (no issue)

Mary Jane, 1807–36, Francis W. 1809–58, Henry, 1811–54, George, 1812–1903, Herbert, 1815–88, + 5 +

Catherine Anne (novelist), 1818–77 = (1842) John Hubback

John Henry Hubback, 1844–1939 (co-author of Jane Austen's Sailor Brothers, 1906)

4 children +
John Austen H., 1878–1969, Governor of Orissa = Bridget Royds

Edith Charlotte H., 1876–1947 = F.L. Brown (co-author of Sailor Brothers)

= Mary Ingram

Francis William H., 1884–1917 = Eva Spielman

Diana H., b. 1912, writer = David Hopkinson (3 children)

Jane (Austen) (novelist), 1775–1817

Admiral Charles John, 1779–1852
= (1) Frances Palmer, d. 1814
= (2) 1820 Harriet Palmer

Cassandra Esten, 1808–97, d. unm.

Harriet Jane, 1810–65, d. unm

Frances Palmer, 1812–82 = (1843) her cousin F. W. Austen (6 children)

Elizabeth, d. in infancy 1814

Charles John, 1821–67 = (1848) Sophia de Blois (issue)

George, d. in infancy 1824

Jane, d. in infancy 1825

Henry, 1826–51, d. unm.

4. Bigg-Wither and Heathcote family relationships

(Though unrelated to her, these families included friends mentioned in over forty of Jane Austen's letters.)

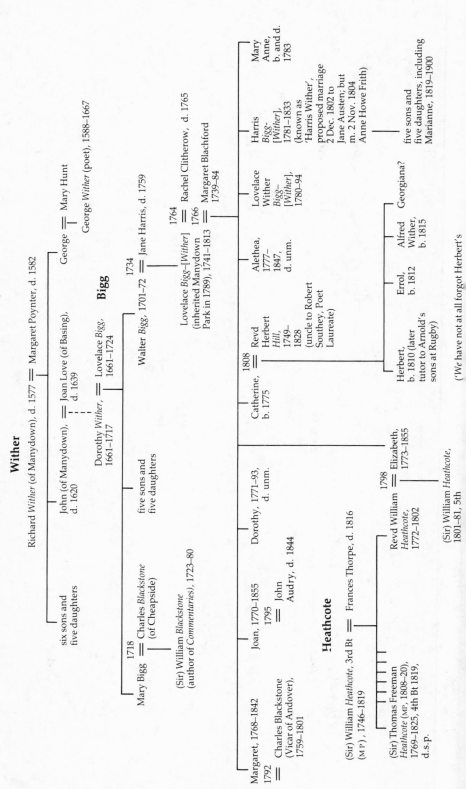

Appendix: A selection of studies relating to Jane Austen

Bibliographical works. Sir Geoffrey Keynes's guide in 1929 has been replaced by David Gilson's *A Bibliography of Jane Austen* (Oxford, 1982), with its 'publishing histories' for each novel among other features. An exacting bibliographer, Gilson has published a list of minor 'Corrections' (Locks', Brisbane, 1983) for his now standard work. Studies of Jane Austen from 1952 to 1972 with brief notes are listed in B. Roth and J. Weinsheimer's *Annotated Bibliography* (Charlottesville, Va., 1973); and brief comments on those of 1973–83 may be found in B. Roth's second *Annotated Bibliography* (Charlottesville, 1985), which is often amusing: in the Soviet Union, as M. V. Chechetko writes at Moscow, Jane Austen's ironies are well liked but Russian study so far has centred chiefly on 'S and S and P and P' and is 'only beginning'.

Biographical studies. Of most value are works by those who often saw and spoke with Jane Austen: the most informative are Caroline Austen's *My Aunt Jane Austen* of 1867 (London and Colchester, 1952) and James Edward Austen-Leigh's *Memoir* (London, 1870, 1871, often reprinted) to which Caroline contributed. Written in his seventy-first year by the Vicar of Bray in Berkshire, the latter is a classic of memory, style, urbanity, family piety and discernment, mentioning what the author had heard of his aunt's early life (including word of her 'strong political opinions') and recalling her from his Southampton and Chawton visits. Henry Austen's 'Biographical Notice' (London, 1818, 1832, the first version prefacing several modern edns of *NA* and of *NA & P*) is suggestive on his sister's authorship, reading and homelife despite its obituary tone. John H. Hubback (who as a boy knew Admiral Sir Francis Austen) collaborated with E. C. Hubback to publish *Jane Austen's Sailor Brothers* (London and New York, 1906); it is rather slight on the Austen wives, though Frances Palmer's letters exist.

In 1913 James Edward's son William, with the latter's nephew Richard Arthur Austen-Leigh, produced the standard, factual *Jane Austen: Her Life and Letters: A Family Record* (London and New York), one of the few studies of the novelist's life based on many MS sources; it neglects nearly every reference to family tensions, such as those between Jane Austen and Elizabeth, Anna and Mary Lloyd, Anna and Fanny, Mrs Austen and Harriet Palmer, in the MSS then available, and offers a benign Austen-Leigh family version of Jane Austen's character. Much is kept at a distance, such as Eliza de Feuillide's character: the second biographer later made silent verbal changes in the texts of Eliza's holograph letters when editing them for his *Austen Papers* (London, 1942). But the *Life* is responsible with evidence it treats, moderate and skilful in assimilating a selection of the facts known in 1913. It has only served badly when mistakenly accepted as a balanced or objective account of the MSS upon which it is based, since it omits much on the basis of propriety. Later R.A.A.-L. kept an 'Annotated Copy' of the *Life* in which he added notes and minor corrections in pen and ink for over thirty years. Popular biographies derive from the *Memoir* and *Life*, and the best of these with its charming sketches of Regency manners, artefacts and many aspects of Jane Austen's milieu is Elizabeth Jenkins's *Jane Austen* (London, 1938, New York, 1949); it is supplemented by Lord David Cecil's affectionate, urbane *Portrait of Jane Austen* (London, 1978). In other popular biographies Hampshire is unvaryingly green and smiling, and Jane Austen is a person in no need of self-control (or thought) because she is light, gifted and untroubled; she 'runs' (when the evidence says she 'walked'). Partly in reply, D.W.Harding's 'Regulated Hatred' (*Scrutiny*, 1940) and Marvin Mudrick's *Jane Austen: irony as defense and discovery* (Princeton and London, 1952) find her consistently hostile to society. Between 1938 and 1952 we thus constructed two extreme images in this century of Jane Austen, with a young lady of 'tearing high spirits' and a 'temper that needed no control' at one side and the absolutely dark and angry figure suggested by Harding and Mudrick at the other.

These two views of Jane Austen have at least encouraged debate and interest, and moderation has had a voice, too: Mary Lascelles's *Jane Austen and her Art* (Oxford, 1939) corrects the popular image while delicately observing oppositions in Jane Austen's temperament and the subtleties of her art. Brian Southam (in *Jane Austen's Literary Manuscripts*, London, 1964) in effect offers a close study of the novelist's mental development, a topic neglected by biographers, and depending mainly on cautious comments on surviving MSS of her works. Austen homes and locales are illuminated by Constance Hill's *Jane Austen: her homes & her friends* (London and New York, 1902), and in shorter works such as W.Watson's *Jane Austen in London* (Alton, 1960) or J.Freeman's *Jane Austen in Bath* (Alton, 1969) and in Anne-Marie Edwards's able, detailed *In the Steps of Jane Austen* (London, 1979). Marghanita Laski's *Jane Austen and Her World* (London and New York, 1969) has insightful, intelligent commentary, and B.Wilks's study (London, 1978) is well illustrated. Jane Aiken Hodge's *The Double Life of Jane Austen* (London, 1972; issued in New York, 1972, as *Only a novel: the double life of Jane Austen*) is based on the premise that the novelist in her dutiful, obedient outward behaviour was more conventional than she was as a professional writer, and Hodge is particularly helpful on her relations with her publishers, and offers new data. In contrast, John Halperin's *Life of Jane Austen* (Brighton and Baltimore, 1984) shows little fresh research and is very inaccurate; but Halperin has commissioned useful papers for *Bicentenary Essays* (Cambridge, 1975). Supplementing the fine work of Laski and Hodge is G.H.Tucker's excellent *A Goodly Heritage: a history of Jane Austen's family* (Manchester, 1983), which has new data to inform its treatment of the Steventon Austens, and moderate and sensible comments on Jane Austen herself.

In no other decade since the *Life* (1913) has more new and pertinent Austen and Lefroy family MS material come to light than in the 1980s. Our understanding of many aspects of Jane Austen's character and life is being modified in the direction of accuracy. This is clear not only in Tucker's, Gilson's and the late Patrick Lefroy's works but in the exacting publications based on the new material which Deirdre Le Faye, of the British Library, has so far printed in the *Times Literary Supplement*, *Notes & Queries*, the *Book Collector*, the annual Jane Austen Society *Reports*, and elsewhere. Since holographs of Eliza de Feuillide's letters and many of Jane Austen's are available, we need not repeat the errors fostered by bad transcripts in *Austen Papers* (London, 1942) or in some important texts in *Jane Austen's Letters* (Oxford, 1932, 1952, repr. 1979) such as its misleading, editorially changed text of her letter of 29 January 1813 about 'Ordination' and *Mansfield Park*. (R.W.Chapman had been obliged to print in his Oxford University Press edition versions of some letters that were available in 1932 only in faulty transcripts.) Accurate texts of some of Jane Austen's letters appear in *Five Letters* (Brisbane, 1981).

Critical approaches, 1815–1950. Essayists of the nineteenth century often tell us more about themselves than about Jane Austen's works but modern readers have found of special interest the comments of Walter Scott (1816), Julia Kavanagh (1862), Margaret Oliphant (1870) and Richard Simpson (1870). Richard Whately (1821) notices a religious basis in Jane Austen's art, and the informal remarks by Newman and by C.Brontë have pith; vide *Critical Heritage*, ed. B.C.Southam (London and New York, 1968). C.Brontë's complaints about Jane Austen's novels certainly have more depth and urgency than Emerson's or Henry James's remarks. In a fine essay (in *Quarterly Review*, 1917) Reginald Farrer set a note for twentieth-century critics in arguing that Jane Austen is a 'conscious' artist concerned with technical problems and 'technical mastery'. Virginia Woolf, in her various comments, is refreshingly concerned with a technical mastery inseparable from Jane Austen's quality of mind and a woman's outlook and advocacy; a continuity runs from *The Common Reader* (London and New York, 1925) through Trilling's essays to later intelligent feminist criticism. R.W.Chapman in his edition of the *Letters*, now clearly in need of redoing, and again in his *Jane Austen: facts and problems* (Oxford, 1948), which was so persuasive that it discouraged further research for a while, has made a strong contribution. There is much of value in his papers and his unpublished letters to Mary Lascelles. The latter, in her own *Jane Austen and her Art* shows, above all, that Jane Austen's works call for the utmost critical flexibility and delicacy. Margaret Kennedy, whose skill as a popular novelist impressed Thomas Hardy, is vivid, brief and shrewd on some of the novels' aspects in *Jane Austen* (London, 1950).

Criticism, 1950–1986. Some of the best work will be found in issues of *Nineteenth-century Fiction, University of Toronto Quarterly, ELH,* and the Jane Austen Society *Reports – R* hereafter. Excellent criticism has come from Oxford (especially St Hugh's College). It may seem unfair to men that British critics such as Margaret Lane, Rachel Trickett, Marilyn Butler, Barbara Hardy, Margaret Kirkham, Elsie Duncan-Jones among others have been so discerning. The prime focus has been on the novels in their social context. R. Trickett explores satire, irony and attention to manners in 'Jane Austen's Imagination' (*R*, 1970) and in pieces on 'Comedy' (*Critical Essays*, ed. B. C. Southam, London and New York, 1968) and 'Manners and Society' in J. D. Grey (ed.), *Jane Austen Handbook/Companion* (London/New York, 1986). M. Lane on the fictional settings (*R*, 1962), E. Jenkins on the Regency (*R*, 1963) and R. Wade on the writer's attitudes (*R*, 1972) are usefully detailed. Before her 'Disregarded Designs' on volume format (*R*, 1978), M. Butler in a major work, *Jane Austen and the War of Ideas* (Oxford, 1975), offered an approach to the context of sentimentalist, Jacobin and anti-Jacobin ideas of the 1790s, with fresh criticism of the six novels. Alistair M. Duckworth's *The Improvement of the Estate* (London and Baltimore, 1971) importantly relates the novels to the sense–sensibility debate and the Austens' Tory sense of the inherited estate. Earlier, A. W. Litz in his work on this novelist's *Artistic Development* (London and New York, 1965) had drawn attention to debate on the novel in Jane Austen's time, and, in an article in *Review of English Studies* (1961, 251–61), to implications in the Austen brothers' Oxford *Loiterer* essays. Frank Bradbrook's *Jane Austen and her Predecessors* (Cambridge, 1966) and K. L. Moler's close work in *Jane Austen's Art of Allusion* (Lincoln, Neb., 1968) remain valuable.

Thoughtful (if unexciting) critical readings of the novels are in W. A. Craik's *The Six Novels* (London and New York, 1965) and Y. Gooneratne's *Jane Austen* (Cambridge, 1970). Fresher, more specialized approaches are given in H. S. Babb's *Fabric of Dialogue* (Columbus, Ohio, 1962), A. H. Wright's *Study in Structure* (London and New York, 1953), J. Wiesenfarth's *Errand of Form* (New York, 1967) and B. J. Paris's *Character and Conflict* (Detroit, 1978). Lloyd W. Brown's *Bits of Ivory* (Baton Rouge, La., 1973) has insights into narrative technique, a complex enough topic which Joseph Kestner further addresses in *Spatial Structure* (Salzburg, 1974) and in his later pieces on rhythm in Jane Austen's narratives.

Ideas and concepts in the novels are treated in Jane Nardin's *Elegant Decorums* on propriety (Albany, NY, 1973) and C. C. Barfoot's *Thread of Connection* on choice and fate (Amsterdam, 1982). Susan Morgan's *In the Meantime* (Chicago, 1980) studies the novelist's characters in relation to perceiving and receptiveness. Yet Jane Austen's ideas and techniques depend in part on her contemporaries and forbears. Margaret Anne Doody in 'G. Eliot and the 18th-c. Novel' (*NCF*, 1980) makes a bold case for an ur-novel form which may have influenced Jane Austen, and has good comments in her study of Samuel Richardson (Oxford, 1974); Jocelyn Harris's edition of Richardson's *Grandison* (conveniently in Oxford's World's Classics) is informative. David Cottom in *The Civilized Imagination* (Cambridge, 1985) compares Austen with Radcliffe and Scott; and interesting pieces on Jane Austen and romanticism by Kroeber, McGann and Langbaum are in *The Wordsworth Circle* (vol. 10, 1979).

A fine response to feeling and 'story' in the novels may be found in B. Hardy's *A Reading* (London, 1975); and Derek Brewer, with background in V. Propp's *Morphology of the Folktale*, opens a new approach to Jane Austen's work in *Symbolic Stories* (Cambridge and Totowa, NJ, 1980). J. Odmark offers a structuralist reading in *An Understanding* (Oxford and Totowa, 1981). V. G. Myer's study (London, 1980) and the essays collected by David Monaghan in *Jane Austen in a Social Context* (London and Totowa, 1981) are typical of this period. Tony Tanner's *Jane Austen* (London, 1986), which includes material from his separate introductions to *S&S*, *P&P* and *MP* and a 1976 address to the Jane Austen Society, is useful and discerning.

Feminism, language, the arts. Studies of Jane Austen in the early 1970s began to benefit from a social, legal and cultural movement which has not yet resulted in equality of the sexes but has, at least, reached into every aspect of art and language. Rozsika Parker's *Subversive Stitch* (London, 1984), on embroidery, has implications for Jane Austen studies. Penelope Byrde's brief, succint *A Frivolous Distinction* (Bath, 1979) on needlework and fashion is most useful. Margaret Kirkham's *Jane Austen, Feminism and Fiction* (Brighton and Totowa, 1983) is a major, delving work on this writer's artistic sources and her novels in light of women's writing of her day. Jane Spencer's *The Rise of the Woman Novelist: from Aphra Behn to Jane Austen* (Oxford and New York, 1986) gives fair, accurate descriptions of antecedent fiction, to supplement F. Bradbrook (1966). Julia P. Brown's *Jane Austen's Novels* (Cambridge, Mass., 1979) brings social history freshly to bear. L. W. Smith's *Jane Austen and the Drama of Woman* (London, 1983) is especially useful in surveying feminist approaches of the 1970s such as those of Patricia Beer, P. M. Spacks, Sandra Gilbert and Susan Gubar, and Nina Auerbach.

Juliet McMaster on 'Continuity of Jane Austen's Novels' (*Studies in English Literature*, 1970) and 'Surface and Subsurface' (*Ariel*, 1974), and in essays by other critics that she collects in *Jane Austen's Achievement* (London, 1976), offers some of the best work of the 1970s. Laurence Lerner's *Love and Marriage* (London and New York, 1979) may be suggestive in its very uncertainty with Jane Austen. *New Perspectives*, ed. Janet Todd (New York, 1983), is one of the best of recent collections with essays by Joan Austen-Leigh, Angela Leighton, Zelda Boyd, Katrin Burlin, Marylea Meyersohn and David Spring among others; J. Harris uses Chaucer's Wife of Bath (or the story of the Loathly Lady) surprisingly as a good point of departure for an essay on *Persuasion*.

As feminism ceases to be an 'ism' and informs our way of understanding the novels, so linguistics has begun to enrich Austen criticism. Jane Austen's diction, imagistic motifs and style are illuminated by D.Lodge's *Language of Fiction* (London and New York, 1966), Norman Page's *Language of Jane Austen* (Oxford, 1972) and Stuart M.Tave's elegant, less specialized *Some Words* (London and Chicago, 1973). Statistics and the computer are brought to bear on areas of the novelist's diction that had so far eluded analysis in J.F.Burrows's *Computation into Criticism: a study of Jane Austen's novels and an experiment in method* (Oxford, 1987) – a work which may perhaps seem in the future Austen anniversary years of 2017 or 2075 to have predicted a new field of literary study. Her interest in music is valuably treated with exactitude in Patrick Piggott's *The Innocent Diversion* (London, 1979), and L.Bertelsen on 'Miniatures' in *Modern Language Quarterly* (1984) at least touches problems in Jane Austen and painting. R.K.Wallace's *Jane Austen and Mozart* (Athens, Ga., 1983) is adventurous. Criticism of televised productions of the novels includes Alistair Cooke's *Masterpieces* (London and New York, 1981) about Fay Weldon's adaptation of *P&P* in 1980, and Monica Lauritzen's *Emma on Television* (Göteborg, 1981).

Individual novels. The classic 'introductions', three or four pages long, are by Mary Lascelles in Dent's Everyman editions of Jane Austen's novels of the early 1960s. She says in a paragraph what others had not said in fifty pages. Among the good, useful introductions in the Penguin series, Margaret Drabble's for *Lady Susan*, *The Watsons*, *Sanditon*, and D.W.Harding's for *Persuasion* are especially helpful. More factual introductions are in Oxford's World's Classics series. Close studies of the novels include A.Fleishman's *A Reading of Mansfield Park* (Minneapolis, 1967) and J.F.Burrows (Sydney, 1968) and then D.Jefferson (London, 1977) on *Jane Austen's Emma*. Lionel Trilling's influential *Mansfield Park* and *Emma* essays stress the heroines' inwardness, the troublesomeness of themes, and the relevance of these books to modern culture; the first is included in *Critical Essays*, ed. I.Watt (Englewood Cliffs, NJ, 1963), and in *Casebook*, ed. B.C.Southam (London, 1976), and the second in *Casebook*, ed. D.Lodge (London, 1968). Trilling's 'Why We Read Jane Austen' (*Times Literary Supplement*, 5 March 1976), unfinished, on his seminar at Columbia University, is among the most insightful essays on Jane Austen so far written.

Adena Rosmarin's affective approach to *Emma*, in *ELH* (summer 1984), has implications for the other novels. Marian E.Fowler's 'Courtesy-book heroine of *Mansfield Park*' in *UTQ* (1974) gives important data found in no other essay on this novel; her conclusions may be questionable but her research is splendid. Though it is almost invidious to select other essays on individual novels, both R.B.Heilman and Karl Kroeber on *Pride and Prejudice*, Katrin Burlin on *Northanger Abbey* and R.F.Brissenden on 'freedom and the family' in *Mansfield Park* in *Bicentenary Essays* (1975) and the essays by Joel Weinsheimer and others in *Jane Austen Today* (Athens, Ga., 1975) are of special interest. R.F.Hilliard on 'space' in *Emma*, in *Probability*, ed. P.R.Backscheider (New York, 1979) is provocative. Reuben A.Brower's

'Light and Bright and Sparkling' on *Pride and Prejudice* is delightful and shrewd, in *Essays*, ed. I.Watt (1963), which also contains important pieces such as C.S.Lewis's 'A Note on Jane Austen' and Donald Greene's 'Jane Austen and the Peerage'. B.C.Southam's *Casebooks* on the early novels and on *Persuasion* (London, 1976) include memorable essays by Kingsley Amis, Malcolm Bradbury, Brigid Brophy and Q.D.Leavis among others.

Interesting essays by Ruth apRoberts (on *Sense and Sensibility*), Valerie Shaw, Mark Kinkead-Weekes and others are in a special issue of *Nineteenth-century Fiction* (Dec. 1975). Notes on the novels (and novelist) in the journal of the Jane Austen Society of North America, *Persuasions*, are lively, amusing and often useful. Margaret Lenta's feminist approaches to Jane Fairfax in *Ariel* (1981) and to *Emma* in *Critical Quarterly* (1981), concise as they are, carry implications beyond the borders of the topics addressed. Julian Moynahan on 'Pastoralism', Christina Gillis on the garden motif and symbol, and Elaine Jordan on Jane Austen and Mrs Inchbald are among the best of the pertinent essays in *Novel: A Forum on Fiction*. Attempts to trace Jane Austen's early development include essays in the *Sterne* and *Richardson* volumes (London and Totowa, 1984, 1986) edited by V.G.Myer, and 'Jane Austen and the American Revolution' in *University of Leeds Review* (1985–6).

Though its pieces vary in quality (and unaccountably in length) *The Jane Austen Handbook* or *Companion*, ed. J.D.Grey (1986), to which I contributed, seems to me to have several useful aspects. It includes a 'Dictionary of Jane Austen's Life and Works' by H.Abigail Bok with succinct, accurate entries on characters, locales and literary allusions in the novels as well as entries on Jane Austen's family, the places she visited and literary allusions in her letters. Secondly, the *Handbook* includes pieces on features of the novels seldom explored elsewhere, such as Janet Todd's valuable short essay on 'Servants'; there are also essays on characterization (John Bayley), architecture and the picturesque (John Dixon Hunt), contemporary feminism (Margaret Kirkham), music (Patrick Piggott), improvements (A.M.Duckworth), travel (Lorraine Hanaway), post (Jo Modert), Jane Austen's verses (David Gilson), and pieces on other topics relevant to the minor works and each of the major novels.

The selection of studies above is meant to be representative, and this list will only begin to suggest continuities in our biographical and critical study of Jane Austen; other works of value will of course be found listed in the bibliographies. Some of the best insights over the years have been in reviews of books about her. Do we have too much in print about Jane Austen? Year by year new biographical information comes to light, and time changes our perception of her texts. If *Emma* and *Persuasion* are no more defined or settled for us than *Macbeth* or *King Lear* have ever been, we need to write about them to find out what they may mean to us: Jane Austen's novels have new things to tell us about themselves and ourselves. We can harm them in only one way – by not talking or writing about them – and it does seem heartening that so much in recent criticism has been not only provocative but close and intelligent.

Notes

a) Manuscript sources and transcripts:

MS Austen	unpublished holograph letters by James Austen, F.W. Austen, Anna Lefroy and others; holographs of Mrs George Austen, James Edward Austen-Leigh and Caroline Austen; verses by Austens, notes and transcripts; Hampshire.
MS Caroline	Caroline Austen, 'Family Memorials 1804–1874'.
MS Chawton	holograph letters and verses owned by the Jane Austen Memorial Trust.
MS Eliza	holograph letters by Eliza de Feuillide of the 1780s and 1790s in France and England; Hampshire.
MS Family History	Fanny C. Lefroy's 'M.S. Family History' including transcripts of unpublished Austen family letters; Hampshire.
MS India Office	Court Minutes and other unpublished records of the East India Company, India Office, Southwark.
MS Lefroy (or) Lefroy papers	letters, diaries, and other material by and about the Austens' friends, the Lefroys of Ashe.
MS Nat. Mar. Mus.	ships logs, diaries and letters at the National Maritime Museum, Greenwich.
MS Pierpont Morgan	holographs by Cassandra and Jane Austen, Pierpont Morgan Library, New York.
MS Ray	unpublished letters by James and Henry Austen, Frances Austen née Palmer, Jane's Kentish niece Elizabeth and others, in G.N. Ray's collection until 1986, bequeathed to the Pierpont Morgan Library.

(I have also drawn on individual MS items in the Berg Collection, New York Public Library or 'NYPL' and the Winchester College archives.)

b) Other sources:

Austen Papers	*Austen Papers, 1704–1856*, ed. R. A. Austen-Leigh, privately printed, Spottiswoode, Ballantyne, 1942.
Brabourne	*Letters of Jane Austen*, ed. Edward, Lord Brabourne, Bentley, 2 vols., 1884.
Five Letters	*Five Letters from Jane Austen to her Sister . . . 1813*, introd. D. Gilson; Locks', Brisbane, 1981.
Gilson	David Gilson, *A Bibliography of Jane Austen*, Oxford, 1982.
Hill	Constance Hill, *Jane Austen: her homes & her friends*, John Lane, 1902.
Hubback	J. H. and Edith C. Hubback, *Jane Austen's Sailor Brothers*, John Lane and Bodley Head, 1906.
L	*Jane Austen's Letters*, ed. R. W. Chapman, 2nd edn, Oxford, 1979.
Life	The second author's 'Annotated Copy' with notes and corrections in ink and pencil of: W. and R. A. Austen-Leigh, *Jane Austen: Her Life and Letters: A Family Record*, 2nd edn, Smith, Elder, 1913.
Memoir	J. E. Austen-Leigh, *A Memoir of Jane Austen*, 2nd edn, Bentley, 1871.
My Aunt	Caroline Austen, *My Aunt Jane Austen: A Memoir*, Spottiswoode, Ballantyne, 1952.

I have tried to cite other texts briefly. J.A. = Jane Austen; C.E.A. = her sister. *Works* = *The Novels of Jane Austen*, I–V, ed. R. W. Chapman, and *Minor Works*, VI, ed. R. W. Chapman and B. C. Southam, Oxford, 6 vols (citations of *Emma*, *MP*, *NA*, *P*, *P&P* and *S&S* are normally to this edition). *R* = an annual report of the Jane Austen Society at Chawton.

PRELUDE: FRANK AUSTEN'S RIDE

1 Hubback, 19.
2 Vide *Mariner's Mirror*, 1977, 317, 324. The reputation of the Academy was not at its nadir in the 1780s, and life at sea varied from ship to ship. Death sentences were rare, and capital offences were few; vide N. A. M. Rodger, *The Wooden World* (1986).
3 MS Nat. Mar. Mus., F. W. Austen.
4 MS Nat. Mar. Mus., Henry Martin to Philip Stephens, 18 Dec. 1788.
5 Edmund Burke to William Baker, 12 Oct. 1777.
6 Cf. *MP*, 473.
7 Hubback, 192.
8 Vide J. Masefield, *Sea Life in Nelson's Time* (1905), 181–2.
9 A young gentleman could take a three-week leave at Christmas or Whitsun.
10 Hubback, 121.
11 C. W. Chalklin, *Provincial Towns* (1974), 42.
12 *Rural Rides*, ed. A. Briggs (1957), I, 191–2.

CHAPTER 1: A FATHER'S PROGRESS

1 R. W. Chapman, *Facts and Problems* (1948), 38.
2 MS Family History.
3 *Austen Papers*, 13.
4 I am indebted here to research letters by G. P. Hoole, Kent.
5 MS Family History.
6 *Memoir*, 8.
7 *Austen Papers*, 24–9.
8 MS Austen.
9 Ibid.

10 *Austen Papers*, 31.

CHAPTER 2: PLAYTHING

1 For the Antiguan plantation vide *R* 1969 and F. Gibbon in *Camb. Qtly*, 1982–3, 298–305.
2 Quoted in MS Austen, Dec. 1864.
3 *Austen Papers*, 33.
4 Holograph, Dec. 1864.
5 *Hants. Chron.*, 6 Jan. 1777.
6 MS Caroline; *L*, 242.
7 William Austen Leigh and M. G. Knight, *Chawton Manor* (1911), 158.
8 *Emma*, 96.
9 *L*, 265.
10 *Memoir*, 19–20.
11 *Life*, 23.
12 *Lisle Letters*, ed. M. St. Clare Byrne (1961), III, 5.
13 Vide lot 268 in Sotheby's cat. of 13 Dec. 1977.
14 Lefroy papers, transcript.

CHAPTER 3: SOCIAL CLASS, SCHOOL CLASS

1 *Works*, V 152, VI 253.
2 *R* 1966, 9–13.
3 Sir Richard Luce, 'Romney Abbey Registers', *Proc. Hants. Field Club*, 1947, 16.
4 C. Coates, *History and Antiquities of Reading* (1802), 315.
5 *Gentleman's Mag.*, 1797, 983a.
6 Vide *Notes & Queries*, 1985, 333, and *R* 1954, 10–13.
7 *Life and Times of Mrs. Sherwood*, ed. F. J. Harvey Darton (1910), 124.

8 W. Dugdale, *Monasticon Anglicanum*, new edn (1846), v. 4.
9 *Mrs. Sherwood* (1910), 127.
10 J. A. signed over an engraving of Goody and possibly gave her copy to Anna Austen, to whom she gave copies of *Elegant Extracts* and *Mentoria* in 1801.
11 *L*, 8.
12 Cf. M. Butler, *Maria Edgeworth* (1972), 52–4.
13 MS Austen, 'Prologue to The Rivals'.
14 Hill, 82.
15 *Austen Papers*, 249; *L*, 209.
16 *Memoir*, 15.
17 Vide R. W. Chapman, *Facts and Problems* (1948), 17.
18 *Memoir*, 12.
19 *Austen Papers*, 265.
20 She may not have had her pianoforte until after her Abbey School days, since her family had to borrow one in Dec. 1786.
21 'Cassandra', written by F. Nightingale in 1852.
22 Mrs Trench, *Remains* (1862), 334.
23 (1972), II, 230; Gilson K17.
24 Cf. Margaret Lenta in *Ariel*, 12 (1981), 27–41.
25 Lefroy papers.
26 *Memoir*, 54.
27 MS Family History.

CHAPTER 4: LADY FROM FRANCE

1 MS Chawton, 31 Dec. 1786; *Notes & Queries*, 1985, 333–4.
2 On Eliza Hancock's parentage, we have gossip tinged with acrimony: Lord Clive told his wife in 1765 it was 'beyond a doubt' that Mrs Hancock in India 'abandoned herself to Mr Hastings' but Clive's informant seems to have been Jenny Strachey, whom Dr Hancock accused of 'basest ingratitude'. The Austens may have suspected Eliza's illegitimate birth: vide *L*, 324.
3 Calcutta, 7 Sept. 1770. In England an 'attorney' for a man in India might receive and disburse monies for him, and e.g. send him statements of debts.
4 *Austen Papers*, 143–4.
5 MSS Eliza: 'Paris le 16 May [*sic*] 1780', 'Comblaville, le 27 Juin 1780'.
6 'Paris le 16 May 1780'.
7 22 Aug. 1788.
8 MS Chawton, July 1785; MS Eliza, 3 May 1797.
9 *Austen Papers*, 126.
10 MS Eliza, 16 Nov. 1787.
11 Orchard Street, 23 Nov. 1787.
12 *Mrs. Sherwood*, ed. F. J. H. Darton (1910), 43.
13 Vide L. S. Sutherland, *East India Company in 18th-c. Politics* (1952).
14 *La Force de l'Age*, trans. P. Green (1965), 365.
15 MS Austen, 'Prologue to The Wonder. Acted at Steventon Dec:r 28:th & 29th 1787'.
16 S. Centlivre, *The Wonder! A Woman Keeps a Secret* (1714), I, i.
17 MS Austen, 'Epilogue to . . . The Wonder . . . Spoken by a Lady in the Character of Violante'.
18 *Austen Papers*, 125.
19 MS Eliza, 1 Aug. 1791.
20 Cf. B. C. Southam in *Library*, 17 (1962), 235. We believe (but cannot be certain) that J. A.'s earliest surviving *jeux d'esprit*

were composed in 1787–88, or close to the time of Eliza's acting and of rather much theatrical activity at the rectory. One series of MSS indicates that *The Wonder* was acted at the Austens on 28 and 29 Dec. 1787, Garrick's *The Chances* in 'Jan^y: 1788', *The Tragedy of Tom Thumb* (possibly written by James Austen) on 22 March 1788, and that a separate 'private Theatrical Exhibition' also dates from '1788'; Eliza may have been absent when the last two or three of these were put on. The Austens also performed plays such as Isaac Bickerstaff's farce, *The Sultan: or a peep into the seraglio* (with Henry Austen as Sultan and Jane Cooper as Roxalana, in 1790) and James Townley's *High life below stairs* (a comedy by the Headmaster of Merchant Taylors').

21 *Works*, VI, 56.
22 Ibid., 47.
23 *Austen Papers*, 131–2.

CHAPTER 5: SEXUAL POLITICS: *THE LOITERER*

1 MSS Eliza, 1791–6.
2 MS Eliza, 22 Aug. 1788.
3 N. Amhurst, *Terrae-Filius*, 3rd edn (1754).
4 Vide W. C. Costin, *The History of St. John's College 1598–1860* (1958), 219.
5 Cf. Henry Austen's and B. Portal's paper on novel slang in *The Loiterer*, No. 59, 13 March 1790.
6 The text is in possession of Austen descendants.

7 *The Loiterer*, No. 4, 21 Feb. 1789. The journal's motto is: 'Speak of us as we are'.
8 No. 41, 7 Nov. 1789.
9 Nos. 52–3, 23 and 30 Jan. 1790.
10 Vide *R* 1966, 9–13.
11 *Memoir*, 48.
12 Cf. W. Litz in *RES*, 12 (1961), 251–61.
13 [H. T. Austen] Biographical Notice in *NA: and P* (1818), I, vii.
14 *L*, 178–9 (1807). The girl was Catherine Foote.
15 No. 32, 5 Sept. 1789. Henry Austen took his epigraph from Otway, 'What mighty ills have not been done by Woman?'

CHAPTER 6: 'I COULD DIE OF LAUGHTER'

1 *Austen Papers*, 125, 140, and MS Eliza, 26 Oct. 1792.
2 [J. E. Austen-Leigh] *Recollections of the Early Days of the Vine Hunt* (1865), 2.
3 MS Eliza, 26 Oct. 1792.
4 G. P. Hoole.
5 MSS India Office, B128: 5 Dec. 1798; B132: 10 Feb. and 4 March 1801.
6 MS India Office, B151: 1 Aug. 1810.
7 Vide Capt. F. W. Austen in the East India Company's Court Books and Minutes for 1808, 1810.
8 Hubback, 16–20.
9 MS Family History.
10 *Loiterer*, No. 4, 21 Feb. 1789.
11 *Lady's Mag.*, Feb. 1786, 91.
12 In pencil in the Austens' copy of Goldsmith's *History of England*; other citations of juvenilia here are to *Works*, VI.

13 C.E.A.'s medallions for J.A.'s 'History' funnily illustrate this. Elizabeth I has an ugly bulging forehead, long pointed chin and nose, narrow sneering eyes, tight mouth and a violent red outfit with aggressive hat feathers. Mary Queen of Scots is pretty in blue and has a sweet open look.

14 *Works*, VI, 71.

15 Vide *R* 1984, 14–21. George Sawtell on the Lloyds, 'Ibthorp' for Ibthorpe as then accepted spelling.

16 MS Caroline.

CHAPTER 7: AFTER MIDNIGHT

1 *Austen Papers*, 142, 144.

2 Ibid., 150.

3 'Biographical Notice' (1818), and *L*, 44.

4 *Gentleman's Mag.*, 1792, 1151b–1152a.

5 *L*, 476.

6 Mrs Harriett Mozley's letter of 2 Nov. 1838, giving Fulwar William Fowle's description of J.A.; *TLS*, 17 Sept. 1954, 591 (K. Tillotson).

7 *MP*, 257.

8 Comically given to young Miss Lutterell, in 'Lesley Castle', in 1792.

9 Cf. *Opinion de Thomas Payne* (Paris, 1792), 6. Even Paine, a fairly moderate deputy, suggests the revolution can be exported – and British papers did not fail to note the idea.

10 MS Family History.

11 Ibid.

12 Two letters by James Austen survive at Lichfield (27 July 1804, 29 Jan. 1808). He hopes to be excused from residing at Cubbington.

13 MS Family History; *Notes & Queries*, 1983, 173.

14 Cf. the accounts in T. J. Baigent and J. E. Millard's *Basingstoke* (1889), 162–70, and the circumstantial one in MS Family History.

James Austen's marriage helped the Austens to secure patronage with the Admiralty's evangelical faction. On 27 Mar. 1792 he married Anne Mathew at Laverstoke; her father, Edward Mathew (1728–1805), was a son of William Mathew (d. at Antigua, 1753), by William's second wife Anne Smith; by his first wife Ann Hill, William had a son, Daniel Mathew of Felix Hall in Essex, whose daughter Jane married Samuel Gambier (1752–1813), a brother of James Gambier (1756–1833), who became Admiral of the Fleet and was able to help J.A.'s brothers Frank and Charles. Cf. J.A.'s merry comment, 'My father will write to Admiral Gambier. – He must already have received so much satisfaction from his acquaintance & Patronage of Frank, that he will be delighted I dare say to have another of the family introduced to him' (*L*, 1798, 38).

CHAPTER 8: LOVE

1 Cf. D. Williams, 'The Fate of French Feminism', in *Eighteenth-C. Studies*, 14 (1980).

2 Charlotte Smith, *Desmond* (1792), III, 271.

3 Washington, Durham, 19 Sept. 1794.
4 MS Family History.
5 L, 10.
6 P. Piggott, *The Innocent Diversion* (1979), 95–6.
7 R. K. Wallace in *R* 1979, 7–12.
8 Piggott (pl. x) reproduces J. A.'s score; she transcribed seven of Dibdin's songs.
9 MS Eliza, 7 Nov. [1796].
10 MSS Eliza, 7 Nov. and 30 Dec. [1796]; 3 May [1797].
11 *Works*, VI, 293–4.
12 Ibid., VI, 274.
13 L, 14.
14 This is about as well founded as most tittle-tattle – but Mrs Mitford at Alresford was not far from Overton and Ashe, the two livings of which her father (Dr Russell) had held for more than half a century.
15 Lefroy papers.
16 MS Family History.
17 M. K. Woodworth, *Brydges* (1935), and L, 32.
18 Lt-Col. J. A. P. Lefroy, 'J. A.'s Irish Friend', *Proc. Huguenot Soc. of London*, 23 (1979), 148–65, and Col. Lefroy's MS 'Addenda' sent to the biographer. Pertinent (in v. 20 and 23) are J. A. P. Lefroy's 'A Walloon Family' and 'Anthony Lefroy'. Cf. M. Usborne in *Spectator*, 29 Feb. 1952.
19 *P*, 232.
20 L, 1–3.
21 Ibid., 5–6.
22 J. A. P. Lefroy, 'J. A.'s Irish Friend', 151–3.
23 L, 27.

CHAPTER 9: DANCING IN KENT

1 L, 39.
2 *Life*, 73–4.
3 Cf. *R* 1960, 19–22, and N. Pevsner, 'Architectural Setting . . .', *Journ. Warburg and Courtauld Insts.*, 31 (1968), 404–22.
4 J. T. Pryme and Alicia Bayne, *Thackeray Family* (privately printed, 1879), 163–4.
5 L, 27–8.
6 James Fordyce, *Character and Conduct of the Female Sex* (Dublin, 1776); vide *Fordyce Delineated, a Satire* (several edns).
7 J. R. Western, *English Militia* (1965), 382; and *Passages from the Diaries of Mrs. Philip Lybbe Powys*, ed. E. J. Climenson (1899).
8 MS Austen, Edward Knight to Mrs James Austen, 18 May 1826.
9 MS Family History.
10 Vide the text in *Cornhill*, 163 (1947/8), 72–3.
11 MS Austen, Reading, Dec. 1864.
12 L, 45–6.
13 Ibid., 332.
14 Ibid., 10, 15.
15 *Camilla* (1st edn, 1796), 1972, 501.
16 Ibid., 688.
17 Some of the handwriting was lost when J. A.'s copy was rebound.
18 L, 9–14, 205–17.
19 MS Pierpont Morgan, 18 Sept. 1796; L, 12–18.
20 MS Austen, Dec. 1864.
21 MS at St John's.
22 MS Eliza, 3 May [1797], and Mrs James Austen's affidavit given

to H. Godwin, Master in Chancery, concerning C.E.A.'s 'most poignant grief' (Sawtell MS).

23 *Works*, VI, 454–5, and *L*, 24.
24 *Austen Papers*, 168.
25 Vide cancellandum or suppressed p. 638 in Bodleian A.16.15.
26 C. Hussey in *Country Life*, 16 Feb. 1945, 289.
27 Enid G. Hildebrand's 'J.A. and the Law', in *Persuasions*, 16 Dec. 1982; G. H. Treitel in *Law Quarterly Rev.*, 1984, and in *R* 1986.
28 F. Gibbon in *Notes & Queries*, 1983, 217.
29 *Emma*, 172.
30 Cf. R. Williams, *Country and the City* (1975), 143.
31 *L*, 35–52 (1798–9).
32 Ibid., 51.
33 F. Lathom, *The Midnight Bell* (2nd edn, 1825), I, 21; II, 35.
34 *L*, 38.
35 Ibid., 47.

CHAPTER 10: *NORTHANGER ABBEY* AND THE PROSPECT OF BATH

1 MS Eliza.
2 *L*, 18.
3 *Gentleman's Mag.* (1797), 1130.
4 MSS Eliza, Cheltenham, 4 Aug. [1797]; Ipswich, 16 Feb. [1798].
5 *Austen Papers*, 170–1.
6 MS Eliza, 7 Nov. [1796].
7 Ibid.
8 MS Family History.
9 MS Pierpont Morgan MA 3611, and *L*, 407.
10 *NA*, 21–2, 31.
11 Cf. M. Weedon in *TLS*, 26 Nov. 1982.

12 *NA*, 33, 36.
13 Ibid., 241.
14 Ibid., 20.
15 Ibid., 111.
16 Ibid., 108–9.
17 MS Pierpont Morgan, and 'Advertisement' in *NA: and P* (1818), xxiii.
18 *NA*, 38.
19 Cf. A. Walton Litz, *J.A.: A Study* . . . (1965), ch. 1.
20 *L*, 59–60.
21 *Austen Papers*, 280.
22 Ibid., 274.
23 MS Family History.
24 Ibid.
25 *L*, 26, 67.
26 Ibid., 66–7, 61.
27 *L*, 21 May 1801, n.
28 F. D. MacKinnon, *Grand Larceny being the trial of Jane Leigh Perrot* (1937), 81–2.
29 *Austen Papers*, 185.
30 MS Austen, note by R.A.A.-L.; and *Notes & Queries*, 1947, quoting Jekyll to Lady Gertrude Sloane Stanley, 29 Nov. 1832.
31 *Austen Papers*, 205–6.
32 MacKinnon, 82–7; G. H. Tucker (1983), 89.
33 *L*, 127; *Life*, 139.
34 *Austen Papers*, 209–11.
35 MacKinnon, 63; I have drawn on data from E. Duncan-Jones.
36 Vide *P*.
37 MS Pierpont Morgan, 20 Nov. 1800. (*L* omits what J.A. first wrote.)
38 *L*, 75–103.
39 *L*, 98; *Life*, 155.
40 Caroline to her brother, 1 Apr. [1869].
41 Quoted by D. and D. Hopkinson, 'Niece of Miss Austen' typescr.
42 *L*, 101.

CHAPTER 11; NELSON RELAXES

1 *L*, 78–112.
2 MS Nat. Mar. Mus., log of *London* 27 Aug. 1798.
3 *MP*, 60. (Her 'home at my uncle's' is one of adultery, whether or not a smart, urban coarseness is explicit in the 'pun'.)
4 MSS Nat. Mar. Mus., Capt. F.W. Austen from 'Canopus at Sea', 1805.
5 *L*, 256, 410, 467.
6 Nelson to Moira, 30 Mar. 1805 (R.R. Hastings papers: Hist. MSS Com., 3, 240–1).
7 C. Oman, *Nelson* (1947), 395.
8 Ibid., 394, 295.
9 In Austen-Leigh copy of *Remains of the Late Mrs. Richard Trench*; as the widow of Col. St George she had seen the Nelson party at Dresden, 2–10 Oct. 1800. Her granddaughter Melesina Mary married Cholmeley (1829–99), J.E. A.-L.'s eldest son. J.A.'s nephew itty Dordy or George Thomas Austen *later* Knight (1795–1867), on 7 Feb. 1837 married Hilare, Countess Nelson, widow of the Revd Wm Nelson, second Baron and first Earl Nelson of Trafalgar and Merton, brother of Horatio Nelson.
10 *Remains of Mrs. Trench* (1862), 105–8.
11 *L*, 323.
12 Ibid., 99.
13 Ibid., 345–6.
14 Ibid., 101–3.
15 Ibid., 107, 123.
16 J.S. Neale, *Bath* (1981), 121.
17 C.H.C. Baker and M. Baker, *James Brydges* (1949), 299.
18 Nash's prestige at Bath had waned before he died in 1761; his influence on etiquette persisted.
19 Cf. P. Rogers in *TLS*, 7 Aug. 1981.
20 Cf. R.L. Brett, 'The Bishop in Petticoats', *THES*, 2 Dec. 1983.
21 *L*, 122–4, 371–91.
22 Ibid., 124–7.
23 Ibid., 127.
24 Ibid., 127–8.
25 Ibid., 136–7.
26 Ibid., 129–35.
27 Ibid., 126.
28 Ibid., 132–3.
29 Ibid., 120, 137–8.

CHAPTER 12: HARRIS WITHER'S PROPOSAL

1 *L*, 124–36.
2 Ibid., 136.
3 N. Pevsner in *Jour. Warburg and Courtauld Insts.*, 31 (1968), 404–22.
4 *Bath Chron.*, 21 May 1801.
5 *Life*, 173; in l.1 'and' should be 'or'.
6 Cf. Peggy Hickman in *Country Life* (1961), 1522–3, and *L*, 183.
7 *Journals and Letters of Fanny Burney*, ed. J. Hemlow *et al.* (1973), III, 2–3.
8 Ibid., III, 7n.
9 *L*, 85, 107.
10 MS Family History: 'Edridge' in this text, not 'Eldridge'.
11 Cf. R.W. Chapman, *Facts and Problems* (1948), 67–8.
12 MS Family History.
13 MS Lefroy.
14 MS Austen, Anna Lefroy, Monk Sherborne, 8 Aug. [1862].

15 Cf. John H. Hubback in *Cornhill*, 65 (1928), 28.
16 *L*, 56.
17 In *Fair Virtue the Mistress of Philarete* (1622).
18 Reginald F. Bigg-Wither, *Materials for a History of the Wither Family* (Winchester, 1907), 53.
19 *L*, 475, 121.
20 Ibid., 304–5, 157.
21 MS Austen.
22 R. F. Bigg-Wither, *Materials* (1907), 59.
23 MS Austen.
24 *L*, 304.
25 Caroline Austen, Frog Firle, 17 June [1870].
26 *Materials* (1907), 57.
27 Vide *Facts and Problems* (1948), 62.
28 *Works*, VI, 356.
29 *L*, 207.
30 Ibid., 339, 351.
31 Ibid., 142.
32 Ibid., 216.
33 MS Pierpont Morgan, Lyme, 14 Sept. [1804].
34 Ibid.
35 *History and Antiquities of Lyme Regis* (1834), 234.
36 Cf. John Vaughan in *Monthly Packet* (1893), 271–9.
37 Hill, 135–6.
38 *Works*, VI, 314.
39 Ibid., VI, 317.
40 *Memoir*, 364.
41 Benjamin Cole and family: *L*, 141.

3 Hubback, 121.
4 O. Warner, *Vice-Admiral Lord Collingwood* (1968), 121.
5 Dungeness, 23 June 1804.
6 Vide *Yale Review*, 15 (1925–6), 319–35.
7 MS Austen, Ashe, 25 Nov. 1804.
8 Reading, Monday, 24 Dec. 1804.
9 Cf. *Book Collector*, 33 (1984), 26.
10 *Works*, VI, 440–2.
11 *L*, 133.
12 Ibid., 144–7.
13 Bath, 'Sunday Even^g' and 'Monday Night' [1805].
14 Steventon, 30 Jan. 1805.
15 D. Hopkinson in *The Watsons* (1978), postscript, 236.
16 *L*, 148–99.
17 *The Task*, II, 'The Timepiece'.
18 *Austen Papers*, 236.
19 *L*, 149–62; *MP*, 378–80.
20 *The Times*, 27 Dec. 1805.
21 Hubback, 144.
22 Ibid., 147.
23 *DNB*, 'Thomas Louis'; Hubback, 150.
24 MS Nat. Mar. Mus., F. W. Austen.
25 *Journal* (1834), I, pt 2, 262–3.
26 C. W. Pasley, *Essay on the Military Policy* (1810), I, 1–2.
27 *Works*, VI, 380.
28 *P*, 252.
29 Cf. *Hants. Chron.*, Dec. 1805.
30 *Stoneleigh Abbey Pictures* (privately printed, 1921), 30.
31 MS Austen, Anna Lefroy.
32 MS Austen, 13 Aug. 1806.

CHAPTER 13: TRAFALGAR

1 *Autobiography of Miss Cornelia Knight* (1861), I, 15–16.
2 Memoir of Admiral Sir Francis Austen.

CHAPTER 14: A HOUSE WITH MARTHA AND FRANK

1 *Discipline* (1832), 261.
2 *L*, 278, 344, and A. Brunton's memoir (1832).

3 *L*, 368, 24, 499, 58.
4 MS Family History.
5 *Works*, VI, 432.
6 MS Family History.
7 Ibid.
8 *Memoir*, 11.
9 MS Austen, 'To Edward', 30 Jan. 1811.
10 MSS Austen: 'Morning – to Edward', 1814, and 'Lines written at Kintbury – May 1812'.
11 MS Caroline.
12 MSS Austen, 3 Dec. 1817, and 'Steventon Thursday Evening'.
13 *L*, 181 and 3.
14 Ibid., 184.
15 Brabourne, I, 37; G.H.Tucker (1983), 178–9.
16 *MP*, 235.
17 *L*, 486–7.
18 Ibid., 173.
19 Cf. D.Le Faye, 'Two Austenian Dialogues', *Book Collector*, 1984, 296–314.
20 *L*, 174–8.
21 R.A.Austen-Leigh, *J.A. and Southampton* (1949), 16.
22 *Memoir*, 78–9; *L*, 178–248.
23 MSS India Office, Court Minutes, B146: 25 Mar. 1808; B148: 22 Mar. 1809; B151: 1 and 8 Aug. 1810; B152: 12 and 24 Oct. 1810.
24 *L*, 261–2.
25 MS Pierpont Morgan MA 2911; and P.Piggott in *R* 1980.
26 *L*, 118–90.
27 Ibid., 193–200.
28 Ibid., 195–269, 361.
29 Ibid., 208–9.
30 MS Chawton.
31 *L*, 220–34.
32 *R* 1983, 10.
33 *Emma*, 24.
34 *L*, 235, and vide Chapter 12 above.
35 Cf. Peggy Hickman, *A J.A. Household Book* (1977), 25–6.
36 *L*, 15, 235–42.
37 Cf. *Univ. of Leeds Review*, 1985/6, 192–3.
38 *L*, 263–6.
39 *Works*, VI, 455–6.

CHAPTER 15: TWO NIECES AND
SENSE AND SENSIBILITY

1 C.Vancouver, *Agriculture of Hants.* (1813), 400; cf. P.Horn, *The Rural World* (1980).
2 *Memoir*, 80.
3 *My Aunt*, 4.
4 *Life*, 242; *L*, 475; and Sotheby's cat. 18 July 1967.
5 *Five Letters*, 3–4.
6 Hill, 177.
7 *My Aunt*, 7–8; and R.Parker in *Subversive Stitch* (1984), 14–15.
8 Misinformation about J.A.'s Chawton is plentiful. Apart from *L* and the family memoirs, the most useful source is V.G.Hunt's Portsmouth Poly. diss. 'Chawton 1841–1881' (1986); it makes use of the 1838 Chawton Tithe Apportionment, 1841 Census Schedules and school logs to give a retrospective view with accurate maps. Mrs Austen's house (never called 'Chawton Cottage') had a large field on its western side extending north; almost due north is Prowtings, which Austens reached from the garden and field behind their house. North and on the opposite, eastern side of the Alton Road is Denmead where Ann Clement lived; south of it Catherine Prowting came to own a house called Chawton

Cottage. North-east of Mrs Austen's is the house sometimes called Clinkers. 'Ed. Knight Esq.' owned most of the smaller 'cottages' as well as Prowtings (by 1838) and of course the dwelling that we call Jane Austen's House.

9 *L*, 154, 233–508.
10 *Five Letters*, 3–4.
11 *Works*, VI, 448–9.
12 Bodleian MSS; cf. *TLS*, 3 May 1985.
13 *My Aunt*, 5–6.
14 MS Family History.
15 *L*, 275–82; *Works*, VI, 443.
16 Brabourne, II, 120; *L*, 217–74.
17 *L*, 312, 478–86.
18 Cf. *Quarterly Rev.*, 1821, 352–76.
19 A. M. Duckworth, *Improvement of the Estate* (1971), 102–7.
20 Cf. K. L. Moler in *Review of English Studies*, 1966, 413–19.
21 *Rejected Addresses: or The New Theatrum Poetarum* (9th edn, 1813), 123–4.
22 *S&S*, 9–12.
23 Ibid., 235–6.
24 Ibid., 97.
25 *L*, 452–3.
26 *S&S*, 159–60.
27 *Ibid.*, 262–3.
28 Ibid., 362.
29 *L*, 272–3.
30 1st (1811) and 2nd (1813) edns, ch. 1.
31 'Biog. Notice' (1818).
32 *The Double Life* (1972), 120.
33 *Critical Rev.*, 1812, 149–57; *British Critic*, 1812, 527.
34 *Letters of the Princess Charlotte*, ed. A. Aspinall (1949), 26. She was born 7 Jan. 1796.
35 *Works*, VI, 433.
36 In the *Monthly Rev.*, 1790; cf. R. A. Draffen in *History Today*, 1970, 190–7.
37 *L*, 317.
38 MS Family History.

CHAPTER 16 : THE REGENCY AND *PRIDE AND PREJUDICE*

1 [Louis Simond], *Journal of a Tour ... during the years 1810 and 1811* (Edinburgh, 1815), I, 26.
2 Ibid., I and II.
3 Ibid., I, 18, 21.
4 *L*, 268–78.
5 *British Critic*, 1813, 189–90; *Critical Rev.*, 1813, 318–24.
6 *L*, 508.
7 Simond, II, 140 (1 May 1811).
8 In Gilpin's *Art of Sketching Landscape*.
9 *L*, 378.
10 Ibid., 322.
11 Cf. D. Watkin on Regency *Buildings* (1982), 37.
12 Vide Atkinson on his patent, in *New Monthly Magazine*, Aug. 1816, 62.
13 Simond, I, 124–5, 143.
14 *L*, 268–300.
15 Ibid., 314.
16 MS Austen, June 1811; *London Chron.*, 25–6 Dec. 1810.
17 Chawton, June 1811.
18 *L*, 246.
19 Cf. J. Ashton, *Dawn of the XIXth Century* (1906), 150.
20 J. Brooke, *King George III* (1972); E. P. Thompson, 'Patrician Society, Plebeian Culture', *Jour. Social History*, 1974, 382–405.
21 Cf. Brooke, 381.
22 J. H. Jesse, *Memoirs* (1867), III, 548–9.
23 Cf. I. Macalpine and R. Hunter, *George III* (1969), 160–1.

24 Quoted by Brooke, 306.
25 MS parish register, Newtown, Hants., 23 Oct. 1757.
26 Cf. R. Gathorne-Hardy in *TLS*, 26 Jan. 1962.
27 *Five Letters*, 7–9.
28 *R* 1965, and P. S. A. Rossdale on entail in *Notes & Queries*, 1980, 503–4.
29 *P&P*, 135.
30 Ibid., 157.
31 Ibid., 161.
32 Cf. A. Hertz, *Notes & Queries*, 1982, 206–8.
33 Rules for special licences from 1759 to 1822 (T. A. Shippey).
34 *Memoir*, ch. x.
35 MS Austen, 'To Caroline . . . June 18th 1811'.
36 *Five Letters*, 6–7.
37 The three *P&P* reviews are repr. in Southam (1968) and *NCF*, 1974, 336–8.
38 *L*, 311–40.
39 Cf. Gilson, 25–7.
40 *L*, 300. (Although the text of Mr Collins's thank-you is not given, a sentence conjures it up in *P&P* ch. 23.)
41 *L*, 309–10. Lance Bertelsen (*Mod. Lang. Quarterly*, 1984) and others have pursued the search. What is known in 1987 may be summed up: the Society's catalogue (*The Ninth*, 1813, 1–16) lists titles of oils and watercolours on exhibit at Spring Gardens in May, and suggests that J. A. may have found 'Mrs. Bingley' in a white gown with green ornaments in a portrait by Hüet Villiers, C. J. Robertson, James Stephanoff or James Hewlett. Examples of their works found so far favour demure, fresh faces (not character) and Stephanoff's remind one of C. E. A.'s medallion of Mary.
42 *L*, 500, 317.
43 *Works*, VI, 145; *L*, 311–15.

CHAPTER 17 : GODMERSHAM REVISITED

1 *L*, 314.
2 MS Pierpont Morgan, 7.5 × 3.7 cm; unsigned but in C. E. A.'s hand.
3 MS Pierpont Morgan, 11.5 × 9.5 cm, signed 'C. E. A.'.
4 Hill, 200.
5 *L*, 313–15, and *Works*, 432–7.
6 *L*, 319–23, 415, and *R* 1983.
7 *L*, 319–86, and M. Kirkham in *Notes & Queries*, 1975, 388–90.
8 *L*, 392, and *Works*, VI, 434.
9 *L*, 336, and Hill, 202.
10 P. A. Garside on *Wareham Priory*.
11 Gilson, 446.
12 MS Austen, MS Caroline, *L*, 365, and *Austen Papers*, 252.
13 Cf. *L*, 331–54.
14 MSS. Ray: Frances Austen, 1 June 1810, 16 Feb. 1814, and 'Namur Tuesday Morning' [Nov. 1813]. Vide *L*, 339–52, and Burke, *Works*, VIII, 172.
15 MS. Austen, and *L*, 353–7.
16 *L*, 349–67.
17 Ibid., 160–205, 362.
18 *Morning Chron.*, 10 Feb. 1813.
19 *L*, 504.
20 Gilson M720; *MP*, 37.
21 *L*, 298.
22 MS Chawton; *Five Letters*, 6–8.
23 *L*, 317–40, 504.
24 Cf. *Laurence Sterne*, ed. V. G. Myer (1984), 163; R. D. Pepper in *TLS*, 1 Mar. 1985.

25 Cf. K.L.Moler, *J.A.'s Art of Allusion* (1968), 113–15, and M.E.Fowler in *UTQ*, 1974, 31–46.
26 L1. 133–4, 136.
27 Vide M.Kirkham, *Notes & Queries*, 1975, 388–90.
28 *The British Theatre*, with remarks by Mrs Inchbald (1808), 7 (courtesy of Elaine Jordan).
29 *R* 1980, 26; *L*, 485.
30 *Works*, vi, 142–3.
31 *MP*, 473.
32 ms Ray: to Charles Austen, Farnham, 24 Nov. 1822.
33 *Works*, vi, 431.
34 Cf. Maggs' cat. 920 (1969), and *L*, 377–83.
35 *L*, 389–91; Gilson, 49–50.

CHAPTER 18: A PROGRESS TO CARLTON HOUSE

1 ms Family History.
2 ms Caroline; *L*, 329 and M.A.Austen-Leigh, *J.E.A.-L.*, 5.
3 ms Family History.
4 Lefroy papers, B.Lefroy, 'Compton Oct 5th 1819'.
5 *R* 1980, 26.
6 *My Aunt*; *Memoir*, 96.
7 *J.E.A.-L.*, 7.
8 *L*, 468–9.
9 *Memoir*, ch. 10.
10 *Life*, 300–1 ('single blessedness' of course from *A Midsummer Night's Dream*, i.i.78).
11 ms Austen, Anna Lefroy, Dec. 1864.
12 D.Gilson ms.
13 *L*, 387–96.
14 Cf. M.Loveridge, *Notes & Queries*, June 1983.
15 ms, unsigned, formerly owned by R.W.Chapman. The print on the verso, showing a dark-gowned figure 'Futurity' at a masked ball, is captioned 'An interesting scene from the Novel of LOVE, MYSTERY and MISERY'; A.F.Holstein's novel of that title appeared in 1810. Such word-play poems relate to the marital celebration poem, a genre favoured by Austens. Vide the verses, now fully printed in *TLS* (20 Feb. 1987), which J.A. sent to her niece Fanny, as if written by her, about Capt. Francis Austen's arrival with his bride (Mary Gibson) at Godmersham Park for their honeymoon after their marriage at Ramsgate on 24 July 1806. These begin, 'See they come, post haste from Thanet,/ Lovely couple, side by side' and conclude:

To the house the chaise advances;
  Now it stops – They're here; they're here!
How d'ye do, my Uncle Francis?
  How does do your Lady dear?

16 *Book Collector*, 1985, 34; Brabourne, ii, 341–4; *NCF*, 1975, 30.
17 *L*, 396–421.
18 *Memoir*, 148.
19 Cf. M.Kirkham, *J.A., Feminism and Fiction* (1983), 121–9.
20 *Memoir*, 148–9.
21 *L*, 425.
22 *Several Discourses . . . at the Temple Church* (1755), ii, 292.
23 C.T.Haden quoted in *R* 1961.

24 *L*, 426–40, 363.
25 *My Aunt*, 12.
26 *L*, 429–51; *Works*, VI, 430.
27 *L*, 443; *Life*, 310–11.
28 Gilson, 69–70. (The number is dated Oct. 1815, but was not issued until March.)
29 MS Austen, 24 Dec. 1814.
30 *L*, 404; Scott's texts are in Southam (1968).
31 But she pooh-poohed *Emma* to Theresa Villiers in 1816.
32 *L*, 49.

CHAPTER 19: HENRY'S FATE AND *PERSUASION* AND *SANDITON*

1 *L*, 289.
2 *Rept. of Sel. Com. on Land & Assessed Taxes*, 1821.
3 MS Caroline; *L*, 453.
4 MS Ray: 24 Nov. 1822.
5 *L*, 468–76.
6 MS Ray: Admiral Broke.
7 Cf. *Austen Papers*, 303.
8 MS Chawton: Capt. F. W. Austen, 18 Apr. 1812.
9 MS Diary of Mary Lloyd; *My Aunt*, 14.
10 I use remarks by D. Hopkinson.
11 Vide *Diaries of Mrs. Philip Lybbe Powys* (1899).
12 MS 'Chap. 10' of *P*, from photo-facsimile.
13 Cf. Philip Drew, 'J.A. and Bishop Butler', *NCF*, 1980, 127–49.
14 *Flowers of Literature*, 1801/2 (1803) and 1804 (1805), pub. by B. Crosby & Co.
15 *L*, 484: Gilson, 85.
16 *My Aunt*, 13. The neighbour was Mrs Eliza Andrews.
17 *L*, 456–66.
18 MS Austen, 8 Aug. 1862.

19 Vide Margaret Weedon on Wm Enfield, essay to appear in *Brit. Jour. for Eighteenth-Century Studies*. The date at the head of *Sanditon*'s (untitled) MS is 'Jan. 27.-1817'.
20 8 Aug. 1862.
21 Vide D. Le Faye, Occ. Pap. No. 2 of *Persuasions*, 1986.
22 *L*, 465–79; Las Cases, *Conversations* (1824), I, pt 2.
23 IV, sc. 5.
24 Vide Gilson, M1125, and Sir Zachary Cope's tentative conclusions in *BMJ*, 1964, 2, 182–3. Later specialists who have examined the contemporary evidence usually agree that Addison's disease is likely, but they point to a differential diagnosis; use is made here of a summary by the pathologist Dr P. N. Cowen.
25 *L*, 473–512.
26 MS Pierpont Morgan.
27 MS Austen.
28 Public Record Office.
29 *My Aunt*; *L*, 493–5.

CHAPTER 20: WINCHESTER

1 *L*, 497–8.
2 Cf. Ellen Jordan, *TLS*, 23 June 1972.
3 MS Family History.
4 *L*, 496; *My Aunt*, 10.
5 'Monk Sherborne', 8 Aug. 1862.
6 MS Austen, 23 Nov. 1821.
7 MS Ray, 3 Dec. 1819.
8 Cf. M. A. Austen-Leigh, *J.E. A.-L.*, 10.
9 *Hants Chron.*, 14 July 1817.
10 On 17 July Charles at Eastbourne noted, in his journal, the letter 'raising hopes'; the post took about 48

hours to reach him. Two MSS of J.A.'s last poem exist: MS NYPL is very irregular, and MS Chawton is a fair copy.

11 *L*, 513–14.
12 *My Aunt*, 11.
13 Cf. esp. *L*, 300, 358, and *Works*, v, 7.
14 Cf. *J.E.A.-L.*, 164, and D. and D. Hopkinson, 'Niece'.
15 MS Family History.
16 MS 128/C, by courtesy of Warden and Fellows of Winchester College.
17 *R* 1957, 7–8.
18 MS Pierpont Morgan.

Index

Cassandra, 27; absorbs Christian and Stoic views and *noblesse oblige*, 28; condones discipline and a 'thump or two', 28; sensitivity to social class, 29–30; sent to Mrs Cawley at Oxford, 30; contracts typhus at Southampton, 31; attends Abbey School, 31–2; lessons and early reading, 33; her shyness and pride in family, 34–5; would have her 'head cut off' with Cassandra's, 36: benefits from privacy and conceives of space as intrinsic to elegance, 37; admires Richardson's *Grandison*, 38–9; delight in 'Madam' Lefroy, 40; affected by cousin Eliza and theatricals, 49–52; writes early burlesques, 52–3; disliked by cousin Phila, 'whimsical and affected', 54; has 'strong political opinions' in her Tory family, 58; her brothers' *Loiterer* and 'Sophia Sentiment', 58–61; shyness and observation, 62–3; gains insight and reads Henry's comic works, 63–5; reacts to family pressures, 68–70; writes smarter burlesques, 70–2; replies to Henry in *Love and Freindship*, 73; mixes jokes and romantic Toryism in her 'History of England', 74–5; wavers between farce and realism, 76; befriends the Lloyds, 77–9; dancing, 83–7; intrigued by money-and-love, 88; writes as an amused aunt, 91; disillusioned by hardness of people outside her family and by mean social competition, 93; risks her equanimity and well-being as author, 93–4; responds to climate of ideas of 1790s in wartime, 97; her notion of 'taste', 98; music and writing, 98–9;

draws on Eliza's exploits for *Lady Susan*, 101–2; on love, and a woman's scope in society, 102; scorns Mrs Lefroy's brother and his works, 104–5; flirts with Tom Lefroy, flouts conventions, 106–9; miscalculates, 110–11; pride and creativity, 112; flirts and observes, 112–14; to London and Kent, 115–16; reacts to well-bred snobbery, 118; prizes Fanny Burney's fiction, 121–3; dancing and writing, 124; her tactics with Cassandra, 124; comic ferocity, dark humour, 124–5; deep paradoxes in her maturing social attitudes, 126–7; to Godmersham Park, 128–9; the 'estate' and the inheritor's impulses and choices, 130; gains social perspective in Kent, 131–2; family sources for *Northanger Abbey*, 132, 137–8; her experimental narrative voice and themes, 139–44; visits Leigh Perrots, learns from her aunt, 148–9; reporting and inventing, 154; desolate, at first, over plan to live at Bath, 155–6; follows news of brother Frank, 159; responds to naval talk, 160; on Evangelicals, 161–2; reacts to adultery, hero-worship, clothes fetish, and the new gentility, 162–5; protective of her choices, 166; settles at uncle's house in Bath, 171–2; observes her relative the 'Adultress', 173; walks with Mrs Chamberlayne, 174–5; 'stupid' parties and unearned leisure, 175–6; topaz crosses from her brother Charles, 177; studies Bath to match characters with neighbourhoods, 179–81; with her family, settles at Sydney Place, 182; avoids other writers, abets Austen family